Geography Alive!®
Regions and People

Chief Executive Officer: Bert Bower

Chief Operating Officer: Amy Larson

Director of Product Development: Liz Russell

Managing Editor: Laura Alavosus

Content Editors: John Bergez, John Burner

Project Editor: Mali Apple

Production Editors: Tara Joffe, Beverly Cory

Editorial Assistants: Anna Embree, Sarah Sudano

Art Director: John F. Kelly

Production Manager: Lynn Sanchez

Senior Graphic Designer: Christy Uyeno

Graphic Designers: Paul Rebello, James Whitehead, Katy Haun, Don Taka

Photo Edit Manager: Margee Robinson

Art Editor: Eric Houts

Audio Director: Katy Haun

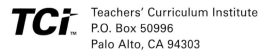 Teachers' Curriculum Institute
P.O. Box 50996
Palo Alto, CA 94303

ISBN13: 978-1-58371-452-2
1 2 3 4 5 6 7 8 9 10 -WC- 16 15 14 13 12 11 10

Manufactured by Webcrafters, Inc., Madison, WI
United States of America, January 2010, Job# 80715

Program Director

Bert Bower

Program Advisors

National Council
    for Geographic Education

Program Author

Diane Hart is a nationally recognized social studies textbook author and assessment consultant. She has authored several basal social studies textbooks for students at all levels. She has also written texts for students with special needs that are used in school, adult literacy, and citizenship classes. In addition to her writing, she consults with state departments of education on the development of standards-based social studies assessments. A former teacher and Woodrow Wilson Fellow, with a master's degree in history from Stanford University, Ms. Hart is deeply involved in social studies education. She is active in California Council for the Social Studies and serves on the Board of Directors of the National Council for the Social Studies. In both her professional and volunteer activities, she is guided by two passions. The first is to engage students in the social studies curriculum by creating compelling, accessible textbooks. The second is to ensure that all students have opportunities to develop the knowledge, skills, and habits of the heart that they will need to be effective citizens in a complex world.

Curriculum Developers

Julie Cremin
Erin Fry
Amy George
Colleen Guccione
Steve Seely
Kelly Shafsky
Lisa Sutterer

Contributing Writers

Wendy Frey
Erin Fry
Brent Goff
Holly Melton
Hilarie Staton
Ellen Todras
Julie Weiss

Teacher and Content Consultants

Melissa Aubuchon
    Indian Trail Middle School
    Plainfield Community Consolidated
        School District 202
    Plainfield, Illinois

Jim Bredin
    Office of the Great Lakes
    Lansing, Michigan

Srinivasan Damodharan
    New Horizon High School
    Bangalore, India

Sarah Giese
    Kenmore Middle School
    Arlington Public Schools
    Arlington, Virginia

Jim Gindling
    Willink Middle School
    Webster Central School District
    Webster, New York

Diana Jordan
    Kenmore Middle School
    Arlington Public Schools
    Arlington, Virginia

Marianne Kenney (NCGE)
    Geography Education Consultant
    Denver, Colorado

Contents

Unit

1

The Geographer's World

Unit

2

Canada and the United States

Unit

3

Latin America

Unit

4

Europe and Russia

Unit

5

Africa

Unit

6

Southwest and Central Asia

Unit

7

Monsoon Asia

Unit

8

Oceania and Antarctica

Maps

Diagrams, Graphs, and Tables

Aerial Photographs and Satellite Imagery

Aerial Photography

Aerial photography is the taking of photographs from above the surface of Earth. A photographer in an airplane or helicopter may hold the camera used to take an aerial photograph. Or the camera may be mounted on an aircraft, a balloon, a rocket, or even a kite. Aerial photographs help geographers see the world in new ways. They show land use patterns and features that may not be visible to a person standing on the ground.

At the beginning of each unit in this book, you will see aerial photographs that may puzzle you. They were taken by a French photographer named Yann Arthus-Bertrand. For more information about these photographs, see pages 514 and 515.

Some of the aerial photographs that appear in this book are listed below.

Satellite Imagery

Satellite imagery is the taking of photographs of Earth or other planets from satellites. A satellite is any object that revolves around a planet. The moon is Earth's largest natural satellite. It revolves around Earth every $27\frac{1}{3}$ days. Today thousands of much smaller artificial satellites circle Earth each day. These satellites are made on Earth and then launched into space on rockets.

The first satellite photographs of Earth were taken in 1960 by a weather satellite. In 1972, the United States started the Landsat program. This program has sent several satellites into space to take photographs of Earth. These pictures are used for many purposes including mapping geographic features, locating mineral deposits, studying environmental problems, finding crop problems, and locating fish at sea.

The satellite images that appear in this book are listed below.

Geography Alive!
Regions and People

The Geographer's World

Introduction

Chapter 1
The Tools of Geography

Chapter 2
A Spatial Way of Thinking

What patterns do you see in this photograph?
See page 514 for details.

▼

Welcome to *Geography Alive! Regions and People.* You have just begun an active, hands-on journey into the world around you. That journey started with the dramatic photograph you saw on the previous page.

Before going back to look at that photo again, picture yourself in a tiny airplane. You are sitting next to a famous landscape photographer named Yann Arthus-Bertrand. You can't talk to him because he is hanging out of his window snapping pictures with his camera. To see what he sees, turn back to the previous page.

What a strange landscape, you think to yourself. As you look more, your mind is flooded with questions. Where are we? Who lives down there? What are they doing? Why does the land look this way? With such questions tickling your brain, you have just entered the geographer's world.

The Field of Geography

Geography is the study of Earth and its people. It helps us understand how people, places, and environments came to be and how they affect each other.

When geographers look at something on Earth, they ask questions. Where is it? Why is it there? How did it get there? How does it affect the people who are living there? How does it affect the natural environment in this area? That "something" could be as ordinary as a nearby factory. Or it could be as extraordinary as a distant, fire-belching volcano.

To answer such questions, geographers look at the world in **spatial** terms. This means they look at how things are arranged in space relative to each other. Look at the photograph of the camels below. The first question to pop into a geographer's mind about this photograph would be a spatial one. Of all the places on Earth, where were these camels when this picture was taken? Why were they there?

Physical Geography

Geographers divide their field into two broad branches: physical and human. The word *physical* means relating to things that can be seen, tasted, or felt. **Physical geography** is the study of natural features on the surface of Earth. These are things that can be seen (and sometimes tasted), such as mountains, plants, and animals. They also include things that can be felt more than seen, such as temperature, wind, and weather.

Physical geographers looking at the camel photograph below would be interested in its desert landscape. They would wonder how this place got to be so very dry and what might live in this sea of sand.

Human Geography

Human geography is the study of people as they have spread across Earth. Human geographers seek to understand who lives where, how, and why. They are also interested in human-made features such as towns, farms, dams, and roads.

Viewing the same camel picture, a human geographer would wonder who is driving those camels. Where did the people come from? Where are they going? And why are they traveling through such a harsh, dry land?

The Geographic Inquiry Process

Geography is a very old field of study. Around 450 B.C.E., a Greek scholar named Herodotus created the first map of the known world. You can see a modern version of it at the bottom of this page. Looking at his map, you may notice two things. First, how much of the world it shows. Second, how much of the world is missing. What you cannot see is how Herodotus created his map. He followed a series of steps known as the *geographic inquiry process.*

Asking Geographic Questions

Herodotus began by asking geographic questions. What is the world like? What lands and seas cover Earth? What peoples does the world contain? Where do they live?

Acquiring Geographic Information

To answer his questions, Herodotus needed geographic information. He traveled widely to see the world. He interviewed other travelers and traders. They told him many tales, some true and some tall, about distant lands. In this way, Herodotus learned about peoples and places he would never see.

Geographers today still travel in search of geographic information. Those travels may take them to nearby places or to distant lands. Like Herodotus, they also look for information gathered by others. This information can often be found in books and on the Internet.

Organizing Geographic Information

Once Herodotus had collected his information, he needed to organize it in some way.

There are many ways to organize geographic information. The most common, however, is the one he chose to organize information about all of the places he had learned about: a map.

A map is a way of showing how things are arranged in space. On his map, Herodotus showed what he had learned about the locations of lands, seas, and peoples.

Analyzing Geographic Information

To analyze means to examine something in detail in order to discover more about it. Analyzing geographic information involves seeing patterns and making connections.

As Herodotus analyzed his information, he compared different ways of life. He noticed that Egyptians, for example, did many things "backward" from a Greek point of view. They wrote from right to left, instead of from left to right. They ate outdoors but washed indoors, while the Greeks did just the opposite.

Answering Geographic Questions

At the end of his inquiry, Herodotus tried to answer the questions he had started with. He wrote down all that he had learned. He also recorded conclusions about peoples based on his analysis. People still read his books today.

Throughout this course, you will be engaged in the geographic inquiry process. You will ask questions and gather information. You will organize and analyze that information. Finally, you will try to answer your questions. You may find, however, that each answer leads to new questions. When that happens, you are thinking like a geographer.

Program Overview

The goal of *Geography Alive! Regions and People* is to help you see the world through a geographer's eyes. With those eyes, you will be able to make better sense of the world around you. Each element of this program has been designed to help you not only to reach this goal, but to have fun doing it.

Mastering the Basics

In this first unit, you will master the basic concepts, skills, and tools that you will be using all year. Chapter 1 introduces the most important tools of geography: maps and globes. In Chapter 2, you will explore different kinds of maps. You will also learn map-reading skills that you will use throughout this program.

Regions and Mapping Labs

After Unit 1, the program is divided into seven world regions. The study of each region begins with a Mapping Lab. In these labs, you will be challenged to use maps to answer questions about a region. Sometimes you will have to organize and analyze information from several maps to find your answer.

While completing your Mapping Lab, take time to read the unit introduction. It will give you a broad overview of the region that you will be studying for the next few weeks.

Chapter Case Studies

You will explore each region through a series of case studies. Each case study takes you to a new place while focusing on a key topic in geography. In one, you will learn how oil has affected countries in Southwest Asia. In another, you will experience what it is like to climb the world's tallest mountain. In still another, you will "step into" an image of a hurricane to learn how such storms form.

A Standards-Based Program

Geography Alive! Regions and People is closely based on the National Geography Standards. These standards set out what every young person should know and be able to do in geography. You can read more about those standards on the next three pages.

Our Trusted Advisors

To ensure that this program meets the National Geography Standards, we asked several geographers from the National Council for Geographic Education to serve as our advisors. We are deeply grateful to them for helping everyone involved in this program's creation see the world through the eyes of a geographer.

The World in Spatial Terms

Geographers look at the world in spatial terms. (Remember that *spatial* means relating to or happening in space.) They are interested in where things are located on Earth and why. They use a number of tools to help show these spatial relationships. Standards 1–3 say that a person educated in geography should know and understand these things:

Standard 1 How to use maps and other geographic representations, tools, and technologies to acquire, process, and report information from a spatial perspective

Standard 2 How to use mental maps to organize information about people, places, and environments in a spatial context

Standard 3 How to analyze the spatial organization of people, places, and environments on Earth's surface

Sample Case Study: Chapter 6
National Parks: Saving the Natural Heritage of the U.S. and Canada

In this case study, you will use topographic maps to plan adventure tours of three national parks. Geographers use this type of map to show the surface features of an area. Topographic maps of national parks show many of the special features that make these places worth preserving.

Places and Regions

You live in a particular place. That place may be in a city, small town, or rural area. It has a name and an address. You also live in a region. A region is not a specific place. Rather, it is a way of thinking about a group of places that have something in common. The Sunbelt, for example, is a region of the United States made up of warm-weather states. Standards 4–6 say that a person educated in geography should know and understand these things:

Standard 4 The physical and human characteristics of places

Standard 5 That people create regions to interpret Earth's complexity

Standard 6 How culture and experience influence people's perceptions of places and regions

Sample Case Study: Chapter 22
Nigeria: A Country of Many Cultures

This case study will introduce you to the more than 250 different ethnic groups that live in the country of Nigeria. You will see how dividing Nigeria into cultural regions helps geographers make sense of this complex country. You will also design an educational Web page about the regions of Nigeria.

Physical Systems

Physical geography focuses on processes that shape and change Earth's surface. The wearing away of coastlines by ocean waves is a physical process. Most physical processes work very slowly over time. But they create the **ecosystems,** or natural environments, in which we live. Standards 7 and 8 say that a person educated in geography should know and understand these things:

Standard 7 The physical processes that shape the patterns of Earth's surface

Standard 8 The characteristics and spatial distribution of ecosystems on Earth's surface

Sample Case Study: Chapter 17
Russia's Varied Landscape: Physical Processes at Work

In this case study, you will learn about four physical processes: volcanic activity, glaciation, erosion, and tectonic movement. You will act out each of these processes to show how they shape Earth's surface. You will also do research on physical processes close to home.

Lava: liquid rock that erupts from a volcano

Crater: the hole at the top of a volcano where land around the opening has collapsed

Main vent: the place where magma bursts through Earth's crust

Magma chamber: the place deep underground where magma collects

Human Systems

People are central in the study of geography. Human activities—such as trade, migration, settlement, and warfare—affect where and how people live. Standards 9–13 say that a person educated in geography should know and understand these things:

Standard 9 The characteristics, distribution, and migration of human populations on Earth's surface

Standard 10 The characteristics, distribution, and complexity of Earth's cultural mosaics

Standard 11 The patterns and networks of economic interdependence on Earth's surface

Standard 12 The processes, patterns, and functions of human settlement

Standard 13 How the forces of cooperation and conflict among people influence the division and control of Earth's surface

Sample Case Study: Chapter 32
The Global Sneaker: From Asia to Everywhere

In this case study, you will learn how economic interdependence brings you sneakers. You will see how making sneakers has become a global business. You will also find and map other "global" products in your home.

Stages in the Making of a Sneaker

Designing — Manufacturing
Locating materials — Distributing

Environment and Society

People constantly interact with their physical, or natural, environment. Human geographers look at how physical environments shape the way people live. They also study how human activities change physical environments. Standards 14–16 say that a person educated in geography should know and understand these things:

Standard 14 How human actions modify the physical environment

Standard 15 How physical systems affect human systems

Standard 16 The changes that occur in the meaning, use, distribution, and importance of resources

Sample Case Study: Chapter 26
The Aral Sea: Central Asia's Shrinking Water Source

This case study takes you to what was once a large freshwater lake in Central Asia. You will learn how human activities have turned this lake into a shrinking, saltwater sea. You will also create documentaries that explore how the shrinking of the Aral Sea has affected people living in this region.

The Uses of Geography

Geography opens up a window on the world we live in today. It helps us to understand the past and to plan for the future. Standards 17 and 18 say that a person educated in geography should know and understand these things:

Standard 17 How to apply geography to interpret the past

Standard 18 How to apply geography to interpret the present and plan for the future

Sample Case Study: Chapter 35
Antarctica: Researching Climate Change at the Coldest Place on Earth

You will travel to Antarctica in this case study to do research on global warming. You will visit research stations to gather data on air temperatures, ice shelves, and penguins. After analyzing your data, you will write a dialogue that explores different views about global warming and how it may affect our future.

The Tools of Geography

1.1 Introduction

In the early 1800s, the United States was just starting to expand across North America. No European Americans had ever crossed the land that lay west of the Mississippi River. This vast area was mostly a huge blank space on their maps.

To find out about this land, Meriwether Lewis and William Clark led a team of explorers on a journey to the Pacific Ocean. Lewis and Clark mapped mountains and rivers as they crossed them. They collected samples of wildlife and plants. They also learned about the Native Americans of the West and how they lived.

In many ways, today's geographers are explorers like Lewis and Clark. They study the natural features of the land, the sea, and even the sky. They try to understand the way people interact with the world around them. For example, they look at where people choose to live and why. They study the way people use Earth's resources, such as forests, water, and minerals. They explore the advantages that come with living in cities or in the country. Often they use maps as a basic tool for recording information and making new discoveries.

In this chapter, you will learn how to use different kinds of maps. You will see how maps can show information about people and places on Earth. You will use these tools throughout your own study of geography.

Essential Question

How do geographers show information on maps?

A geographer made this map to show information about the world. The words, lines, and symbols are clues from the geographer to help you make sense of the map. Keep this map and its clues in mind as you try to answer the Essential Question.

Graphic Organizer

Physical Features of the World

Elevation

Feet	Meters
Over 10,000	Over 3,050
5,001–10,000	1,526–3,050
2,001–5,000	611–1,525
1,001–2,000	306–610
0–1,000	0–305

0   1,500 3,000 miles

0   3,000 kilometers

Goode's Homolosine projection

◀ Antique map and sundial compass

1.2 The Geographic Setting

In September 1805, Lewis and Clark crossed the Rocky Mountains on their way to the Pacific Ocean. They wanted to find the Columbia River, which could take them to the ocean. But they didn't know how to find it. A Native American chief named Twisted Hair came to the rescue. He drew a map on a white elk skin that showed how to reach the Columbia. The river, said Twisted Hair, was "five sleeps" away.

Today we still use maps to find the locations of places and how far apart they are. Like Twisted Hair's drawing, the most basic map is a diagram that shows what is where.

Locating Things on Earth: The Main Purpose of Maps For geographers, maps are tools that show where things are on Earth. With these tools, we can find the **absolute location** of any place in the world. Every feature is located at a precise, or absolute, point on Earth. There are many ways to describe this precise point. Your street address, for example, indicates the absolute location of your home. Later in this chapter, you'll learn how a grid, or system of lines, can be used to show the absolute location of places on a map.

Maps also show the **relative location** of places on Earth. This is the location of one place compared to another. For instance, one place might be located east or west of another one. You probably use relative location when you give directions. Suppose you want to tell a friend how to find the street where you live. You might tell her to go down a main street and turn right one block past the park. You would be telling her your street's location relative to a place she knows well.

Distortion: The Big Problem with Maps Maps are great tools, but they're not perfect pictures of Earth's surface. Maps are two-dimensional, or flat. Earth is three-dimensional and shaped like a sphere, much like an orange. The only way to show a round Earth on a flat map is by stretching some parts of it. This changes the shape, size, and position of its features. These changes are called **distortion**. The picture at the right shows how severe this distortion can be.

One way geographers deal with the problem of distortion is to use globes. Because they are spheres, globes are better models of the whole Earth than maps. They show the size, shape, distance, and direction of places on Earth very accurately. Unfortunately, globes cannot show a lot of detail without becoming huge. Maps can show smaller areas of Earth and include much more detail. In addition, maps are much easier than globes to carry around.

A second way to deal with distortion is to use **map projections**. A map projection is a particular way of showing Earth on a flat surface. All map projections have some kind of distortion. For example, a projection that accurately shows the sizes of places will distort their shapes. One that shows accurate shapes will distort sizes and distances. Geographers choose the projection that best suits the kind of information they want the map to show.

▶ Geoterms

absolute location the precise point where a place is located on Earth

distortion a change in the shape, size, or position of a place when it is shown on a map

map projection a way of representing the spherical Earth on a flat surface

relative location where a place is located in relation to another place

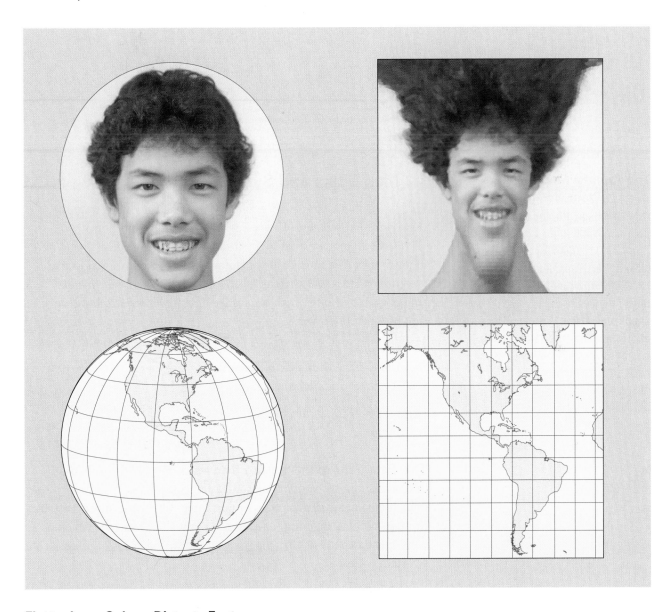

Flattening a Sphere Distorts Features

A person's head is shaped almost like a sphere. If you try to flatten a head, its features stretch and change shape. As a result, the person becomes almost unrecognizable. In a similar way, flat maps can distort information about Earth's features.

Political Boundaries of the World

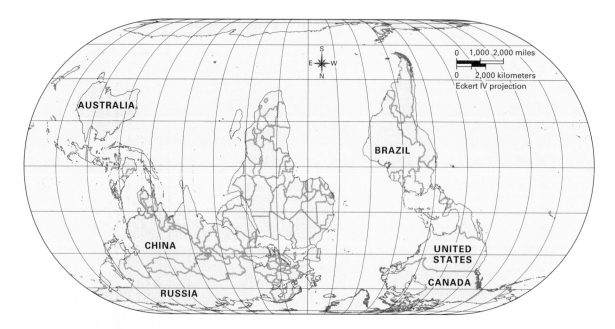

The Top of a Map Doesn't Always Point North

On most maps, the top of the map points north, but not all maps work this way. This map turns our usual view of Earth upside down. The map isn't right or wrong. After all, Earth does not have a "right" side up as seen from space. When you look at any map, be sure to check the compass rose so you know which direction is which.

1.3 Map Titles and Symbols

Like Lewis and Clark, early explorers often had no maps to guide them on their journeys. Lewis Carroll, the English author of *Alice in Wonderland,* made fun of their situation in a poem called *The Hunting of the Snark.* The poem tells of sailors in search of an imaginary creature called a *snark.* To assist them, the ship's captain unrolls a large map of the sea without a trace of land. The snark-hunting sailors, Carroll wrote,

> *were much pleased when they found it to be*
> *A map they could all understand . . .*
> *"A perfect and absolute blank!"*

Luckily for us, maps are not blank. Instead, they are filled with information.

The Title Tells What a Map Shows A map's title gives us our first clue about its content. It usually describes the area shown on the map. It also identifies the map's main topic. The topic might be gold mining, politics, farming, or even the night sky. Often the title lists a date. The date tells us that the map shows the locations of places at a certain time.

A Compass Rose Shows Directions on a Map Have you ever used a magnetic compass to find your way in a strange place? If so, you know that the needle of a compass always points north, or toward the North Pole. Knowing where north is can help you decide which way to go.

Mapmakers use a diagram called a **compass rose** to show directions on a map. On early maps, these diagrams often looked like a flower. For this reason, sailors called this direction-finding tool a compass rose.

A simple compass rose has two short lines that cross at right angles. The points at the ends of the lines are labeled north, south, east, and west. These four directions are called **cardinal directions**. A more complicated compass rose has lines between the cardinal points. These lines show the **intermediate directions**. They are northeast, southeast, southwest, and northwest.

A Legend Identifies Symbols on a Map

A compass rose is one of many symbols used to show information on a map. Some symbols use color to show features. Blue lines, for example, are symbols showing rivers. Lakes and oceans are often colored blue as well. Other symbols use shapes to show information. A bold star is a common symbol for the capital of a state or country. Tiny airplanes are often used to show the location of airports.

The symbols used on a map are usually identified in a box known as the **map legend,** or sometimes the **map key**. The map legend lists each symbol and explains what it shows on the map.

Marshall Gold Discovery State Historic Park

A Grid Organizes Space on a Map

Mapmakers often use a system of imaginary lines to divide up space on their maps. This system of lines is called a **map grid**. You can see an example of a grid on the map above. To form this grid, the mapmaker drew horizontal lines and vertical lines that meet at 90-degree angles. (Remember that horizontal lines go straight across. Vertical lines go up and down.)

Geographers make map grids useful by giving each line a label. For instance, on some maps horizontal lines have letters, and vertical lines have numbers. Once the grid is labeled, any location on the map can be indicated by a letter and number combination, such as C3 or H7. The letter and number indicate where a horizontal and vertical line meet. Find this point, and you will have found the place you are looking for close by.

One very useful type of grid is the system of latitude and longitude. This **global grid** allows you to locate any place on Earth with a simple number code. You'll learn more about the global grid in the next section.

Using a Map's Title, Compass Rose, Legend, and Grid

You can use this map to tour a historic site. The map title tells which site you will be exploring. The compass rose shows which way north is on the map. The map legend tells you what the symbols on the map mean. Once you know what you want to visit, the map grid will help you locate it on the map.

1.4 The Global Grid: Longitude and Latitude

In early November of 2003, a hiker set up camp high in the Adirondack Mountains of New York. Heavy snow trapped him there with no way to hike out. Luckily, he had a Personal Locator Beacon. He pressed a button to call for help. A helicopter soon flew him to safety.

How did the rescuers find the stranded hiker? His locator beacon showed his location on the global grid. Geographers use this same global grid to show the absolute location of every place on Earth.

Lines of Latitude Parallel the Equator The global grid system is made up of two sets of imaginary lines. The first are called **parallels of latitude**. These lines run east and west around the globe.

The **equator** is the most important parallel of latitude. It circles Earth exactly midway between the North and South poles. All other lines of latitude are parallel to the equator. Parallels of latitude are measured in degrees (°). The equator is 0° latitude. It is a reference for measuring other parallels of latitude.

Latitude Lines Run East to West

Latitude Is Measured from the Equator

Lines of Longitude Run from Pole to Pole The other lines in the global grid are half-circles that run from the North Pole to the South Pole. These lines are called **meridians of longitude**. They are not parallel to each other, so the distance between them varies.

The most important of these north-south lines is the **prime meridian**. It runs through Greenwich, England. Like parallels of latitude, meridians are measured in degrees. The prime meridian is 0° longitude. It is a reference for measuring other meridians of longitude.

The next most important meridian is the **International Date Line**. This line runs though the Pacific Ocean halfway around the world from the prime meridian. When travelers cross this line, they cross over to a different day. Travelers moving west across the line go forward a day. Travelers moving east across it go back a day.

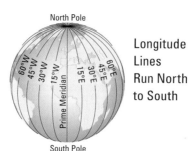

Longitude Lines Run North to South

Longitude Is Measured from the Prime Meridian

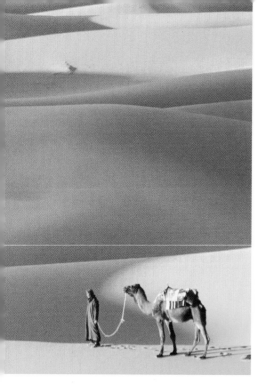

32° North, 4° West

Any place on Earth, no matter how lonely, has an exact address on the global grid. This lonely spot lies 32° north of the equator and 4° west of the prime meridian.

Cities Around the World

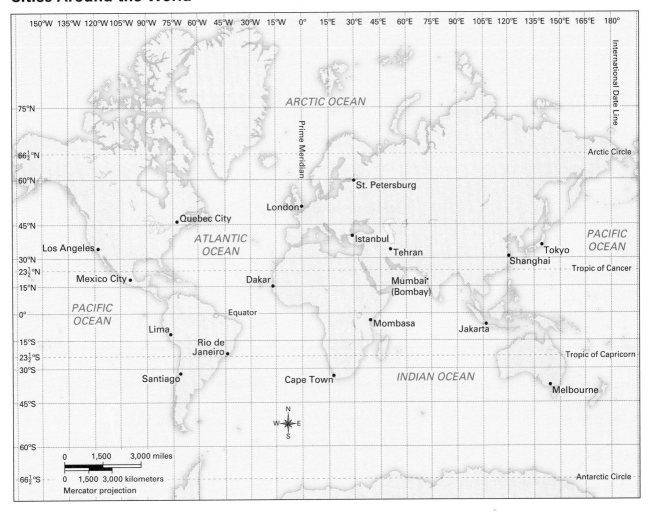

Latitude and Longitude Mark Absolute Location The numbering system of this global grid makes it easy to locate any place on Earth.

Moving north from the equator, the parallels of latitude increase in number from 0° up to 90°N (north) at the North Pole. The same thing happens moving south of the equator. There the numbers of the parallels increase from 0° to 90°S (south) at the South Pole. One degree of latitude covers about 69 miles, or 111 kilometers.

Meridians of longitude start from 0° at the prime meridian. Going east from there, the numbers on lines of longitude increase until they reach 180° at the International Date Line. These numbers are labeled E (east). The same thing occurs going west from the prime meridian. The numbers increase until they reach 180° at the date line and are labeled W (west).

The absolute location of any place on Earth can be described as the meeting point of a parallel of latitude and a meridian of longitude. The numbers of these lines are the geographic **coordinates** of a place. These coordinates are like a street address for your house. They tell exactly where that place is located.

The Absolute Location of Cities

Latitude and longitude mark the absolute location of cities. The coordinates of Rio de Janeiro are 23°S, 43°W. To find this location, look for the parallel of latitude that is 23 degrees south of the equator. Move your finger along it until you come to the prime meridian. Now move west along the same line until you reach 43 degrees. You should be pointing to Rio de Janeiro.

1.5 Dealing with Distances: Map Scale

In Ithaca, New York, there is a winding path called the Sagan Planet Walk. The path takes people past models of the sun and the planets. In less than a mile, walkers pass through a model of the entire solar system. The model shrinks the vast distances of space to make them easier to understand. For instance, people can see that the planet Mars is about one and a half times Earth's distance from the sun.

A map does a similar thing for the area it shows. The scale on a map tells you how the distances on the map compare to the actual distances on Earth.

How Scale Affects Details A map can be large scale or small scale. A large-scale map gives a close-up view of a small area. It shows lots of detail. You could use a large-scale map to find a store in a mall or on a neighborhood street. A small-scale map shows a larger area, but with fewer details. Small-scale maps are best for finding your way between cities, states, and larger areas.

Estimating Distance with a Map Scale A **map scale** appears on most maps. The scale tells you how to read the distances on the map. For instance, an inch on a map might equal 10 miles on Earth.

The map scale is usually made up of two short lines with notches on them. One line measures distance in miles, the other in kilometers. The easiest way to use a map scale is to make a scale strip. Take a strip of paper and place it under the map scale. Mark the scale's notches on the paper, and label the marks with the numbers of miles or kilometers. Then place your strip with the "0" mark at one point on the map. Line up the strip with a second point. Now read the closest number on your strip to this second point. You've just figured out the distance between the two points.

Maps with Different Scales

The map on the left is a small-scale map. It shows where Washington, D.C., is located in relation to nearby cities. The map does not show details like city streets. But it does show larger features, such as major highways. The map on the right is a large-scale map. It focuses on Washington, D.C. You could use it to find your way through the city's streets to the White House or other monuments.

Washington, D.C., and Surrounding Areas

Downtown Washington, D.C.

1.6 Hemispheres, Continents, and Oceans

"One of my favorite things to do when I have time off is to just watch the world go by," said astronaut Ed Lu about his time in space. In 2003, Lu watched Earth go by from the International Space Station. "It isn't exactly seeing the Earth like a big blue marble," he explained. "It's more like having your face up against a big blue beach ball." On the "beach ball," he saw Earth's wide continents and blue oceans.

Few of us will ever see Earth from an astronaut's point of view. But we can use maps and globes to get a view of our planet's natural wonders. Geographers make these features easier to understand by dividing Earth into different areas.

A Hemisphere Is Half a World Geographers divide Earth into halves. These halves are called **hemispheres**. The equator divides Earth into two hemispheres. The northern half is the Northern Hemisphere. The southern half is the Southern Hemisphere.

Geographers also divide Earth in half by longitude. The Western Hemisphere lies west of the prime meridian. The Eastern Hemisphere is east of it. The two hemispheres divide again at the International Date Line.

Continents and Oceans Cover Earth Geographers also divide Earth's lands and seas into areas. Ocean water covers more than 70 percent of Earth. This ocean is really just one big body of water. But geographers usually divide it into four oceans. They are the Atlantic, Pacific, Indian, and Arctic oceans.

These oceans lap the shores of **continents,** the largest areas of land on our planet. Geographers identify seven continents. From largest to smallest, they are Asia, Africa, North America, South America, Antarctica, Europe, and Australia. Europe and Asia are actually parts of one huge **landmass**. But geographers usually think of them as two continents because they have different cultures and histories.

Hemispheres

The equator splits the globe into Northern and Southern hemispheres. The prime meridian and International Date Line split the globe into Eastern and Western hemispheres.

The World

Earth's Continents and Oceans

You can see from this map that oceans cover most of Earth. The four major oceans are actually a single body of water that surrounds the seven continents.

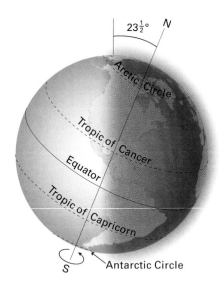

The Tilted Earth

The tilt of Earth on its axis means that some areas receive more sunshine than others each day. This difference creates Earth's seasons.

1.7 Earth and the Sun

For centuries, most people believed that Earth stood still in space. Today we know that our planet is in constant motion. That motion creates our years, months, and days. It also helps to create our seasons.

The Moving Earth Earth moves around the sun in a nearly circular path called an *orbit.* One round trip, called a **revolution,** takes about $365\frac{1}{4}$ days. This is an Earth year.

As Earth revolves around the sun, it spins like a giant top on its **axis**. The axis is an imaginary line that runs from the North Pole to the South Pole through the center of Earth. The spinning motion of Earth is called **rotation**.

Earth makes one full rotation about every 24 hours. As Earth spins, it is daytime on the side facing the sun. On the side facing away from the sun, it is night.

Earth's Tilt Creates the Seasons Earth's axis is tilted at an angle relative to the sun. Because of this tilt, the Northern and Southern hemispheres receive different amounts of sunlight as Earth moves around the sun. These differences create Earth's seasons.

Look at the diagram on the next page to see the changing seasons in the Northern Hemisphere. During the north's summer, this half of Earth is tilted toward the sun. At this time the Northern Hemisphere receives more sunlight for more hours, and most places enjoy hot days. Winter comes when this hemisphere tilts away from the sun. Then the days are short and cool.

Of course, during these same months the Southern Hemisphere tilts toward the sun, so in the south it is summer. Similarly, when it is summer in the Northern Hemisphere, it is winter in Earth's southern half.

Tropics, Circles, and Zones Because of Earth's tilt, the sun never beats straight down on places in the far north and south. Two lines of latitude mark the northernmost and southernmost points where the sun's rays ever beat straight down. The northern line is called the **Tropic of Cancer**. The southern line is called the **Tropic of Capricorn**. The areas between these two lines and the equator are known as **tropical zones**. Tropical zones receive a lot of sunshine. They are hot all year round.

Two other lines of latitude mark the points farthest north and south where the sun doesn't shine at all on one day each year. On that day, night lasts a full 24 hours. These lines are the **Arctic Circle** and the **Antarctic Circle**. The areas between these circles and the North and South poles are known as **polar zones**. These zones receive little direct sunlight and are cold most of the year.

Between the tropical and polar zones lie the **temperate zones**. Generally, in these zones summers are warm and winters are cool.

The Revolution of Earth Around the Sun

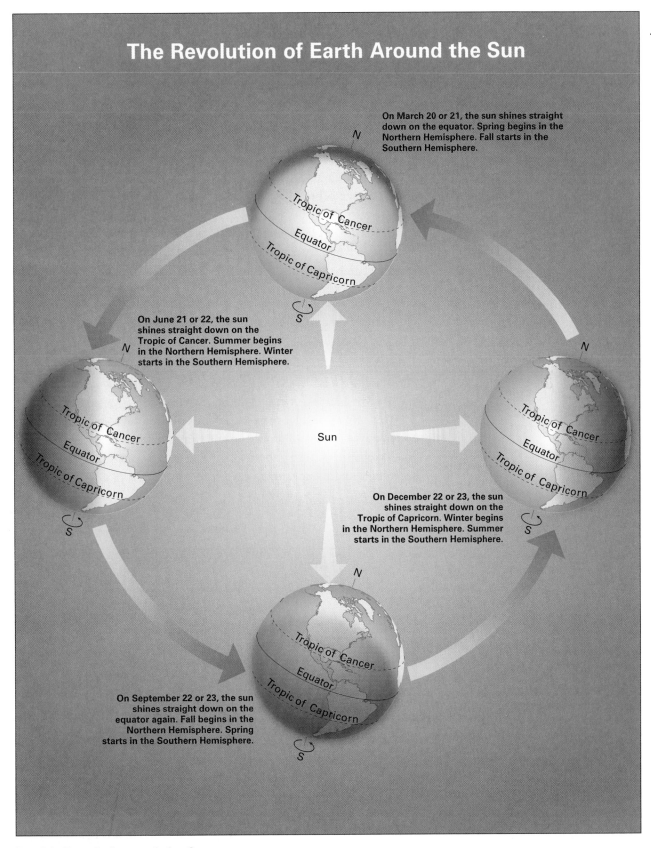

On March 20 or 21, the sun shines straight down on the equator. Spring begins in the Northern Hemisphere. Fall starts in the Southern Hemisphere.

On June 21 or 22, the sun shines straight down on the Tropic of Cancer. Summer begins in the Northern Hemisphere. Winter starts in the Southern Hemisphere.

On December 22 or 23, the sun shines straight down on the Tropic of Capricorn. Winter begins in the Northern Hemisphere. Summer starts in the Southern Hemisphere.

On September 22 or 23, the sun shines straight down on the equator again. Fall begins in the Northern Hemisphere. Spring starts in the Southern Hemisphere.

Sun

Earth's Revolution and the Seasons

This diagram shows how Earth's tilt creates the seasons during our planet's year-long trip around the sun. Notice that the seasons are reversed in the Northern and Southern hemispheres.

The World

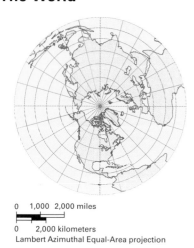

```
0    1,000  2,000 miles
0       2,000 kilometers
Lambert Azimuthal Equal-Area projection
```

Lambert Projections Show Polar Areas that Other Maps Distort

A Lambert projection is a circular map. It shows size accurately at its center, but not distance or shape. It is good for showing the areas around the North or South pole. Most other map projections distort the shape and size of the Arctic and Antarctica.

1.8 Showing a Round World on a Flat Map

In this chapter, you have learned how geographers show information on maps. A map's title, legend, and symbols can help you understand what a map shows.

You learned how geographers describe where a place is in terms of its absolute location. The global grid allows mapmakers to indicate the exact location of any place on Earth using lines of latitude and longitude. Map scales are useful for describing the relative location of two places. Using a scale, you can estimate about how far two places are from each other.

All Flat Maps Have Distortion Geographers use maps to show features of Earth, such as oceans and continents. But every flat map involves some distortion. The size or shape of landmasses may be distorted. The distances between places may not be accurately shown.

To deal with distortions, mapmakers use different map projections. Many projections are named after the mapmakers who designed them. For example, Arthur Robinson designed the Robinson projection. The world map on page 19 is a Robinson projection. It is a popular projection because it balances the distortions of size and shape. In this way it gives a fairly accurate picture of the world.

You can see several map projections on this page and the next. Note how each projection does some things better than others. As you look at them, think about what type of information each map projection might show best.

The World

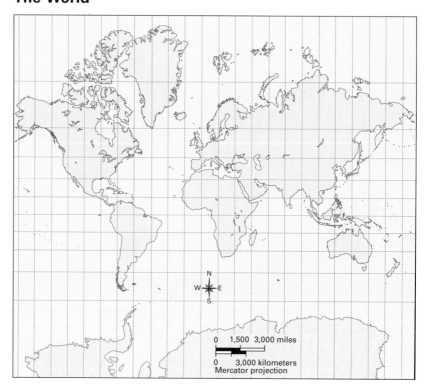

```
0    1,500  3,000 miles
0       3,000 kilometers
Mercator projection
```

Mercator Projections Show Direction but Distort Size

Gerardus Mercator designed his map projection in 1569. It shows directions between places accurately near the equator. But it distorts the size of continents, especially near the North and South poles. This is called *area distortion*.

The World

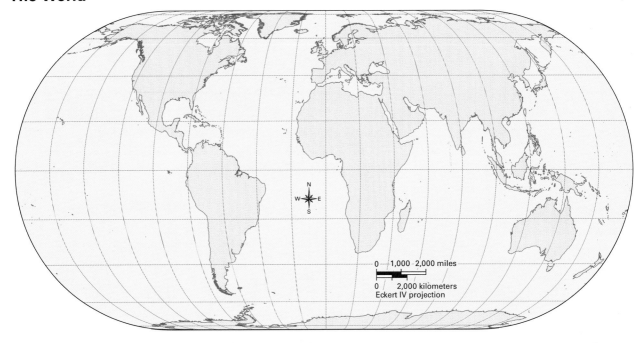

Eckert IV Projections Show Size but Distort Shape

The Eckert IV projection is an equal-area map. Equal-area maps show
the sizes of places accurately. However, they distort shape near the poles.
This is called *shape distortion*. Geographers often use Eckert IV projections
to show the number of people in different areas.

The World

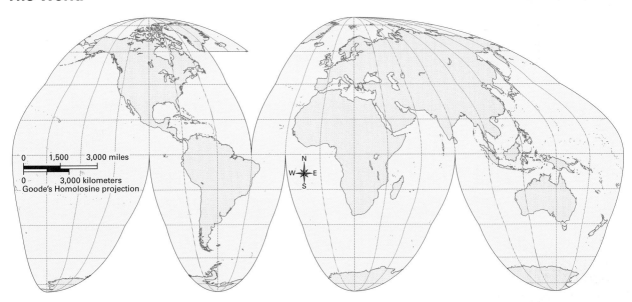

Goode's Homolosine Projections Show Continents but Distort Oceans

Goode's Homolosine projection uses a trick to help us see how the
continents compare in size. It snips bits out of the oceans. This trick
allows the continents to stretch without distorting their shapes. But it
distorts the shape and size of the oceans.

A Spatial Way of Thinking

2

2.1 Introduction

In the late summer of 1854, a dreaded disease called *cholera* struck a neighborhood in London, England. People suddenly began suffering cramps, vomiting, and terrible thirst. Many died within hours. In just 10 days, the disease killed about 500 people. Wagons carried away corpses for mass burials.

No one knew how cholera spread or how to stop it. But one doctor, John Snow, had an idea. Snow convinced officials to remove the handle from a water pump on Broad Street so that no one could use the pump. Soon the cholera stopped spreading. Snow had guessed correctly that the disease was spread through polluted drinking water.

Snow had, in effect, solved the mystery by using the skills of the geographic inquiry process. First he asked a question: How was cholera spread? Next he gathered information by going door to door to find out where people were dying. He then organized his information on a neighborhood map, marking the house of each cholera death. His next step was to analyze his map. He was able to answer his question: The Broad Street pump must be spreading the disease, because most of the deaths were clustered around it.

John Snow's map is an example of a **thematic map**. A thematic map presents information related to only one theme or topic. In this chapter, you will learn how to identify and read different types of thematic maps. You will see how geographers use these tools to make sense of Earth's physical and human features.

<table>
<tr><td>

Essential Question

Why do geographers use a variety of maps to represent the world?

Geographers use maps for many purposes. A map legend tells you what kind of information the map shows. Colors, for example, can show different climates. Symbols can show physical features like rivers. Or they can identify human features such as roads and cities. Keep this fictitious map and its legend in mind as you try to answer the Essential Question.

</td><td>

Graphic Organizer

</td></tr>
</table>

◀ Thematic maps of South America

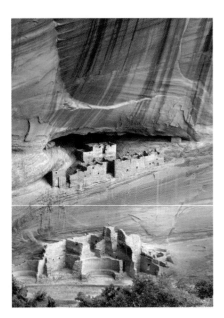

The Steep Rock Walls of Canyon de Chelly

A canyon is a landform found mostly in the southwestern United States. Canyon de Chelly was once home to Anasazi Indians. They built their villages in the steep canyon walls. You can find Canyon de Chelly on a physical features map of Arizona.

2.2 The Geographic Setting

Thematic maps are all around us. Tune in to a news program and you're likely to see a weather map showing high and low temperatures. To find your way on the local bus system, you might use a map of bus routes. These maps focus on a specific topic, or theme. They show information about some aspect of physical or human geography.

Thematic Maps Can Show Physical Geography Some thematic maps focus on **physical features**. Physical features are natural parts of Earth's surface. They include **landforms** like mountains, plains, and **plateaus**. They also include bodies of water. A physical features map of Earth will show oceans, seas, bays, rivers, and lakes.

Thematic maps can show other aspects of the physical environment. For example, some maps focus on **climate,** or long-term patterns of weather. Climate maps show how much rainfall various areas receive. They also show how hot or cold places tend to be in winter and summer.

Climate has a big effect on the types of **vegetation,** or trees and other plants, that will grow in an area. You can see this by comparing a climate map of Earth with a vegetation map. A vegetation map shows the kinds of trees and other plants that grow in various places. In many ways it looks like a climate map, although other factors also affect what will grow where.

Thematic Maps Can Show Human Geography Thematic maps can also focus on human geography. John Snow's map of the cholera deaths near the Broad Street pump is a good example. Another example is a political map. The map on the next page shows the borders of the 50 U.S. states. It also shows the borders between countries. In addition to borders, political maps also show important cities, such as the capitals of states and countries.

Another type of thematic map shows **population density**. This is the number of people per unit of area, such as a square mile. The higher the number, the more crowded an area is. A population density map reveals where large numbers of people cluster.

Besides showing where people live, a thematic map can show what they do. A map of **economic activity** focuses on the ways people produce, buy, and sell goods and services. This kind of map might show the main types of business and industry in an area. It might also show the **natural resources** that fuel the area's economy. Natural resources are useful items found in nature, such as wood, coal, and oil.

A Map's Title and Legend State Its Theme To read a thematic map, first look at its title. The title states the topic of the map. Then look at the map legend. It tells you how to read the map's symbols. On the U.S. political map, the legend shows the symbols for the national and state capitals. A map legend may also explain how the map uses colors. For instance, a thematic map might use colors to show differences in elevation or population density.

▶ Geoterms

climate the pattern of weather over a long period of time

economic activity any action that relates to the making, buying, and selling of goods and services

landform any natural feature of Earth's surface that has a distinct shape. Landforms include major features such as continents, plains, plateaus, and mountain ranges. They also include minor features such as hills, valleys, canyons, and dunes.

physical feature any natural characteristic of Earth's surface, such as landforms and bodies of water

population density the average number of people who live in a unit of area, such as a square mile. Population density measures how crowded an area is.

region an area defined by one or more natural or cultural characteristics that set it apart from other areas

thematic map a map that shows a particular theme, or topic

vegetation all the plants and trees in an area

Political Maps

Political maps help us see where countries, states, and important cities are located. On this map of the United States, you can see the borders of your state. A star marks the state's capital. A star with a circle around it shows the nation's capital.

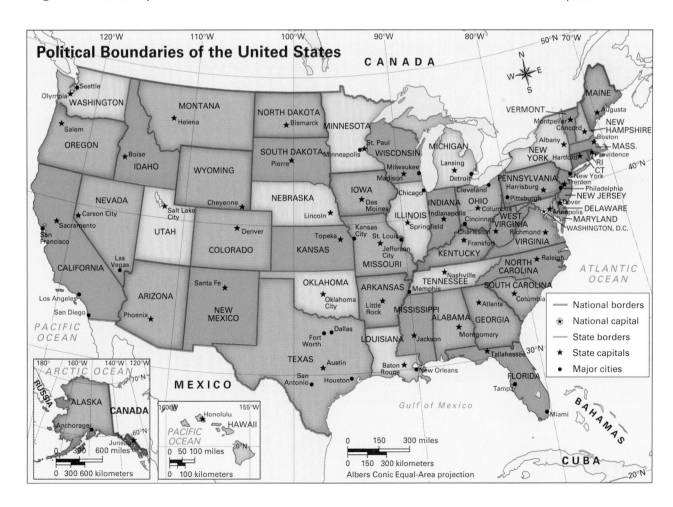

Political Boundaries of the United States

2.3 Mapping Earth's Physical Features

In the winter, snowboarders look for a snowy mountain to practice their sport on. In the summer, vacationers often cool off by a lake or river. These are just three of the landforms and bodies of water that you might see on a physical features map.

Common Landforms Geographers have given names to the many landforms found on Earth. Some landforms have distinctive shapes when viewed from above. A long, narrow peninsula, for example, juts out from a continent into water. Other landforms, like mountains, have distinct shapes when viewed from the ground.

Physical features maps show the shapes of features as seen from above. They also show the **elevation,** or height above sea level, of various features. Usually physical features maps use colors and shading to show changes in elevation.

Bodies of Water Geographers also label bodies of water on physical features maps. Many kinds of water bodies appear on the continents. For example, rivers flow down from mountains and make their way to the sea. Lakes are entirely surrounded by land. Other water bodies are created where oceans and seas meet the continents. A bay is partly enclosed by a wide, curving stretch of land. A strait is a narrow channel that connects two larger bodies of water.

Landforms and Water Bodies

You will see both landforms and bodies of water labeled on maps. This diagram shows many of these physical features.

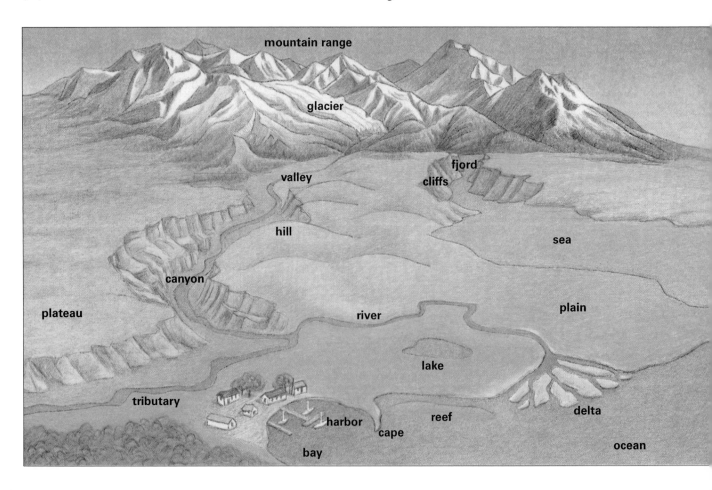

Physical Features of India

Physical Features Maps

This map shows major physical features in India. The Himalayas are India's highest physical feature. Two long rivers, the Ganges and the Brahmaputra, flow out of the Himalayas. They form one of the world's largest river deltas where they meet the Bay of Bengal.

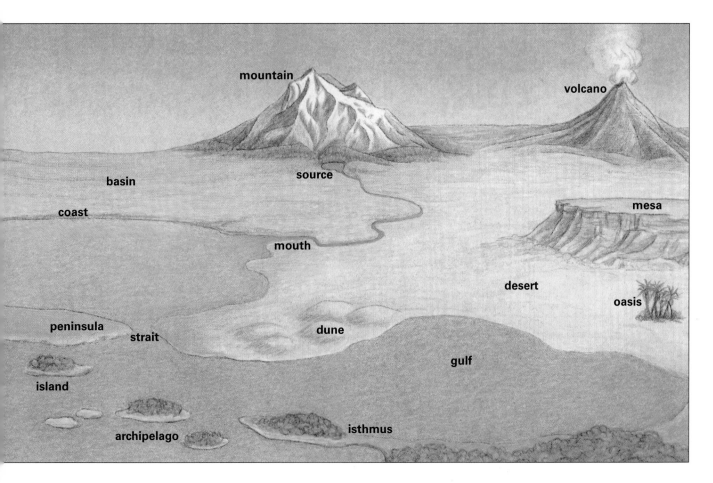

2.4 Hot, Cold, Wet, Dry: Earth's Climates

Do you check a weather report each morning to see what the day will be like? Are most days sunny? Or does it rain a lot where you live? Such long-term patterns in weather are called *climate*.

Climate Zones To study climates, geographers divide Earth into **climate zones**. Each zone has a particular pattern of temperature and **precipitation**—rain, snow, or other moisture. This pattern is often shown on a **climagraph,** like those you see below.

A climagraph shows the average temperature and precipitation in a place over a year. The letters along the bottom of the graph stand for the months of the year. The curved line indicates the average monthly temperatures. The bars show the average monthly precipitation.

Location Affects Climate Many factors affect a place's climate. One of the most important is latitude. Places in tropical latitudes, close to the equator, get the most direct rays from the sun all year. Most of these places have hot weather year-round. Places at high latitudes, close to the North and South poles, receive much less sunlight. As a result, they are very cold.

Another factor affecting climate is elevation, or altitude. Places at high elevations have colder climates than those lower down. You'll learn more about the factors that affect climate throughout this book.

World Climate Zones

Climagraphs for the 12 climate zones found around the world are shown below.

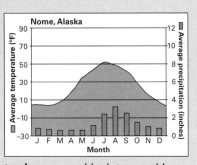

tundra very cold winters, cold summers, and little rain or snow

ice cap very cold all year with permanent ice and snow

subarctic cold, snowy winters and cool, rainy summers

highlands temperature and precipitation vary with latitude and elevation

marine west coast warm summers, cool winters, and rainfall all year

humid continental warm, rainy summers and cool, snowy winters

Climate Zones of Australia

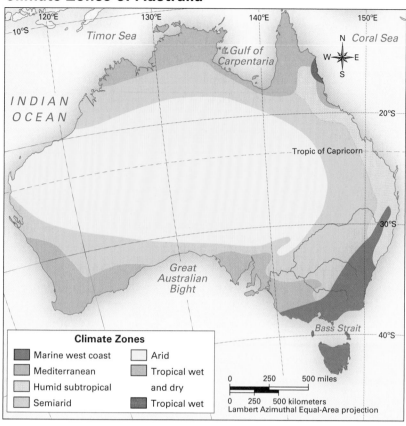

Climate Zones

- Marine west coast
- Mediterranean
- Humid subtropical
- Semiarid
- Arid
- Tropical wet and dry
- Tropical wet

0   250   500 miles
0   250   500 kilometers
Lambert Azimuthal Equal-Area projection

Climate Maps

Australia has seven climate zones. This climate map shows each zone in a different color.

Mediterranean warm all year with dry summers and short, rainy winters

semiarid hot, dry summers and cool, dry winters

tropical wet and dry hot all year with rainy and dry seasons

humid subtropical hot, rainy summers and mild winters with some rain

arid hot and dry all year with very little rain

tropical wet hot and rainy all year

2.5 Trees and Other Plants: Earth's Vegetation

Think about the climate where you live. Now think about the kinds of plants that grow nearby. In an **arid** climate, like a **desert,** you might see hardy cacti. In a **humid continental** climate, you might see lofty trees that stay green all year. Climate has a major effect on the kind of vegetation that grows in a place.

Vegetation Is Adapted to Its Environment Plants of some kind grow nearly everywhere on Earth. But in order to survive, plants must adapt to their environment.

Plants can adapt to even extreme environments. A tundra climate zone is very cold and dry. Yet small plants and bushes grow there. In arid climates, cacti can go for long periods without water. Other kinds of vegetation need lots of rainfall to survive.

Other factors besides climate affect what plants grow where. Among them are elevation, amount of sunlight, and richness of the soil.

Global Vegetation Zones Geographers study where different plants grow by dividing the world into **vegetation zones**. In each zone, a certain mix of plants has adapted to similar conditions.

Like climate zones, vegetation zones are affected by their location on Earth. They range from the barren ice cap zones at the poles to the dense broadleaf evergreen forest zones near the equator.

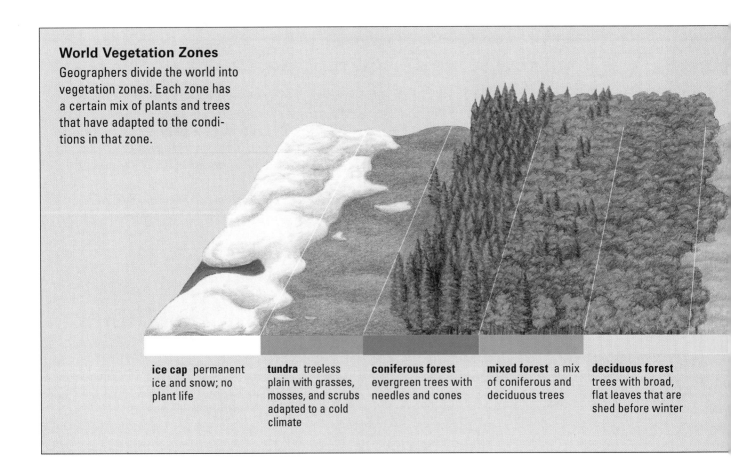

World Vegetation Zones
Geographers divide the world into vegetation zones. Each zone has a certain mix of plants and trees that have adapted to the conditions in that zone.

ice cap permanent ice and snow; no plant life

tundra treeless plain with grasses, mosses, and scrubs adapted to a cold climate

coniferous forest evergreen trees with needles and cones

mixed forest a mix of coniferous and deciduous trees

deciduous forest trees with broad, flat leaves that are shed before winter

Vegetation Zones of North Africa

Vegetation Zones
- Highlands
- Desert
- Desert scrub
- Temperate grassland
- Tropical grassland
- Chaparral
- Broadleaf evergreen forest

Mediterranean Sea

Red Sea

Tropic of Cancer

0   250   500 miles

0   250   500 kilometers
Sinusoidal projection

Vegetation Maps

This map shows the vegetation zones found in North Africa. Chaparral thrives beside the Mediterranean Sea. Desert and desert scrub are found in the dry Sahara. A narrow band of broadleaf evergreen forest appears in the northeast corner of North Africa. What do you think allows tropical trees to survive in such an arid region?

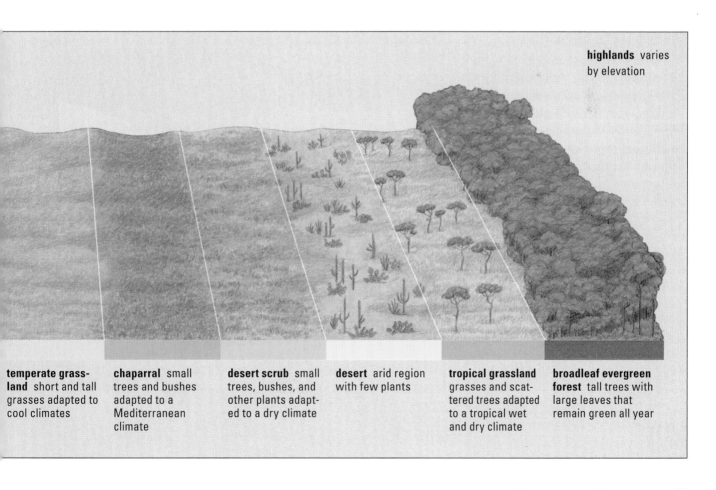

highlands varies by elevation

temperate grassland short and tall grasses adapted to cool climates

chaparral small trees and bushes adapted to a Mediterranean climate

desert scrub small trees, bushes, and other plants adapted to a dry climate

desert arid region with few plants

tropical grassland grasses and scattered trees adapted to a tropical wet and dry climate

broadleaf evergreen forest tall trees with large leaves that remain green all year

2.6 Where People Live: Population Density

In 2007, about 8 million people lived in New York City. They were jammed into an area of about 300 square miles. Compare this with the town of Skwentna, Alaska, where approximately 150 people were spread out over about 450 square miles. When it comes to crowding, these two places are about as different as they can be. Geographers show these kinds of differences using population density maps.

Population Density Measures Crowding Population density tells us how crowded a place is. To calculate the density of a place, divide the number of people there by its land area. The higher the result, the more crowded the place is. In 2007, New York City had a population density of about 26,000 people per square mile. In contrast, Skwentna had less than 1 person per square mile.

Population density affects how people live. In Skwentna, houses are spread out. There are no roads. People use airplanes, boats, or snowmobiles to get to the local store and the post office. Skwentna's version of rush hour comes in February, when dogsled racers speed through town.

In New York City, people live packed in high-rise apartments. They may have hundreds of neighbors just in their own building. Every day millions of "straphangers" hold on tight as they jostle one another in the city's crowded subways.

Population Density from High to Low

Population density is a measure of crowding. Some countries are very densely populated. Others are not. These photographs show places with different population densities.

More Than 250 People per Square Mile

Dhaka, Bangladesh, is one of the most crowded places on Earth. On average, many more than 250 people live in a square mile of this busy city.

125 to 250 People per Square Mile

Austria is a fairly crowded country. On average, between 125 and 250 people live in every square mile of this mountainous land.

Population Density of China, 2009

Urban Population

Number of People
- Over 8,000,000
- 4,000,000–8,000,000
- 1,000,000–4,000,000

Population Density

Per sq. mi.	Per sq. km
Over 250	Over 100
125–250	50–100
25–125	10–50
2–25	1–10
Under 2	Under 1

0 250 500 miles

0 250 500 kilometers

Lambert Azimuthal Equal-Area projection

Population Density Maps

Population density maps show patterns of where people live. On this map, much of the North China Plain is colored purple. So are many coastal areas. These are the most crowded parts of China.

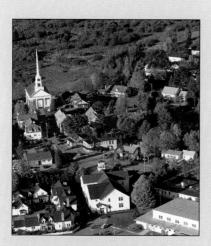

25 to 125 People per Square Mile

This uncrowded New England village has a lot of space for living. On average, between 25 and 125 people live in every square mile of the town.

2 to 25 People per Square Mile

This photograph of Ireland's countryside shows a thinly populated country. Ireland has some big cities. But in most of Ireland, there is an average of 2 to 25 people per square mile.

Fewer Than 2 People per Square Mile

These herders in Mongolia live in an almost empty country. Fewer than 2 people live in every square mile of areas like this one.

2.7 Economic Activity: Land and Resources

Do you like chocolate? This sweet treat comes from cocoa beans, the fruit of the cacao tree. The cacao tree grows only in hot, tropical areas near the equator. But factories that use cocoa beans to make chocolate candy are found in Europe and the United States. The locations of cocoa **plantations** and candy factories are examples of the kind of information you might see on an economic activity map.

Land Use Shows How People Make a Living Economic activity maps often show patterns of **land use**. Land use is the way people use the land they live on to meet their needs. In some areas, people use land for farming. In others, they may use it for mining.

Natural Resources Affect Economic Activities Economic activity also depends on a country's natural resources. **Forestry,** or the harvesting of trees to produce wood products, is important in forested areas. Near oceans, fishing is an important industry.

Many resources lie hidden beneath the ground. This is true of both minerals and **fossil fuels** such as oil, coal, and natural gas. Uranium is another underground energy resource. It provides fuel for nuclear power plants. In contrast, moving water is an easy-to-find energy resource. Dams can be built on rivers to harness the moving water's energy and convert it to **hydroelectric power**.

Land Use and Resources

How people use land depends on the natural resources in their area. Some still get their food by hunting and gathering. Some grow crops and raise animals to sell. Others make and sell goods created from natural resources. Natural resources are not evenly distributed around the world.

Hunting and Gathering in Greenland

Many people still hunt animals and gather plants for food. Most live in small groups that move from place to place. This hunter in Greenland tracks polar bears and seals across ice and snow.

Subsistence Farming in Africa

Some farmers grow only enough crops to feed their own families. This is called *subsistence farming*. More than half of the land in Africa is used for subsistence farming. Most of the subsistence farmers in Africa are women.

Commercial Farming in Colombia

Commercial farmers raise crops or livestock to sell. Commercial farms are often very large. Many grow a variety of crops. Others, like this coffee farm in Colombia, specialize in just one crop.

Nomadic Herding in China

Millions of people around the world are nomadic herders. They move around often to find food and water for their animals. This herder in China uses the animals' milk, hides, and other products.

Economic Activity of Europe

Land Use
- Hunting and gathering
- Subsistence farming
- Commercial farming
- Nomadic herding
- Commercial fishing
- Forestry
- Trade and manufacturing
- Little or no activity

Resources
- ⚒ Coal
- ⚡ Hydroelectric power
- Iron
- ⬤ Natural gas
- Petroleum (oil)
- Precious metals (gold, silver, copper)
- ❋ Uranium

0 250 500 miles
0 250 500 kilometers
Lambert Azimuthal Equal-Area projection

ATLANTIC OCEAN

Arctic Circle

Black Sea

Mediterranean Sea

Economic Activity Maps

The colors on this map show land use patterns in Europe. The most widespread land use is commercial farming. The symbols show the locations of important resources in Europe. Where is petroleum, or oil, found in Europe?

Livestock Raising in Australia

Cattle, sheep, and goats are raised on huge ranches. More than half of the farmland in Australia is used for raising sheep and cows. Australian livestock raisers lead the world in production of wool for clothing and carpets.

Commercial Fishing in Asia

Many people make their living by fishing the world's oceans, lakes, and rivers. The Pacific Ocean yields more than half the world supply of fish. In 2004, 41 million people worked in the fishing industry. More than 30 percent were in Asia.

Forestry in the United States

Forestry uses trees as a resource for making homes, furniture, and paper. In 2005, the United States was the leading supplier of wood in the world. The United States also used up more forest resources than any other country.

Trade and Manufacturing in Ireland

Manufacturing turns resources into goods to sell. In this Irish factory, workers assemble computers for shipment around the world.

2.8 Organizing Earth's Surface: Regions

As you have learned, geographers use many kinds of maps to make sense of the world. Some of these maps focus on physical geography. Others focus on human geography. All of them reveal interesting patterns to explore.

Geographers use these patterns to organize the Earth's surface into **regions**. A region is an area with one or more features that set it apart from other areas. As you'll see, the concept of region allows geographers to divide the world in useful ways.

Unique Features Define a Region Think about the community you live in. Does it have a business district? A shopping mall? An industrial park? A civic center? A residential neighborhood? Each of these areas has features that set it apart from other areas. You might think of one as a business region, another as a shopping region, and still another as a housing region. Each region looks different. Each has a different purpose. Each has different needs.

Transportation Region Maps
A region is an area with one or more features that set it apart from other areas. A feature might be something physical like climate. Or it might be a human feature such as roads and train lines. The network of routes on this map defines a transportation region in the San Francisco Bay Area.

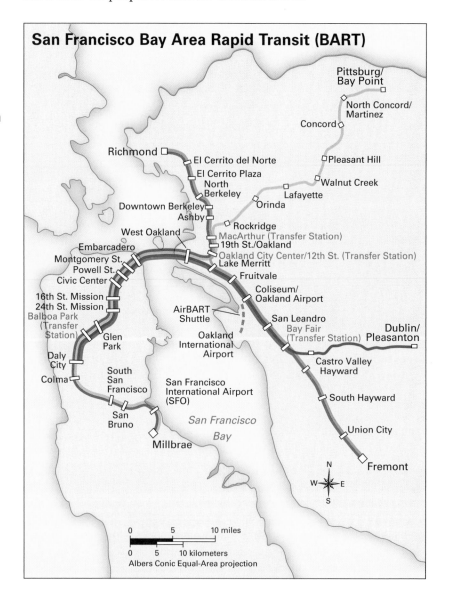

San Francisco Bay Area Rapid Transit (BART)

Geographers define regions in several ways. The Sunbelt is a region defined by physical features. It is a region made up of states in the southern part of the United States. What sets the Sunbelt apart from other regions is its warm, sunny climate. The Corn Belt is a region defined by human features. It is made up of states in the center of the country where raising corn is an important economic activity.

Dividing the World into Seven Major Regions The world is a very large place to make sense of. For this reason, geographers usually divide it into regions to study. These world regions are still very large. But each has its own special features.

This book divides the world into seven major regions. Each region is shown in a different color on the world regions map below. These colors are your guide to finding each region in this book. Your study of a region will begin with an introduction to its most important physical and human features. In that introduction, you will begin to see what makes each of these regions unique.

World Regions Maps

This book divides the world into seven large regions. Each region has certain distinct physical features. Each also has unique human features.

Regions of the World

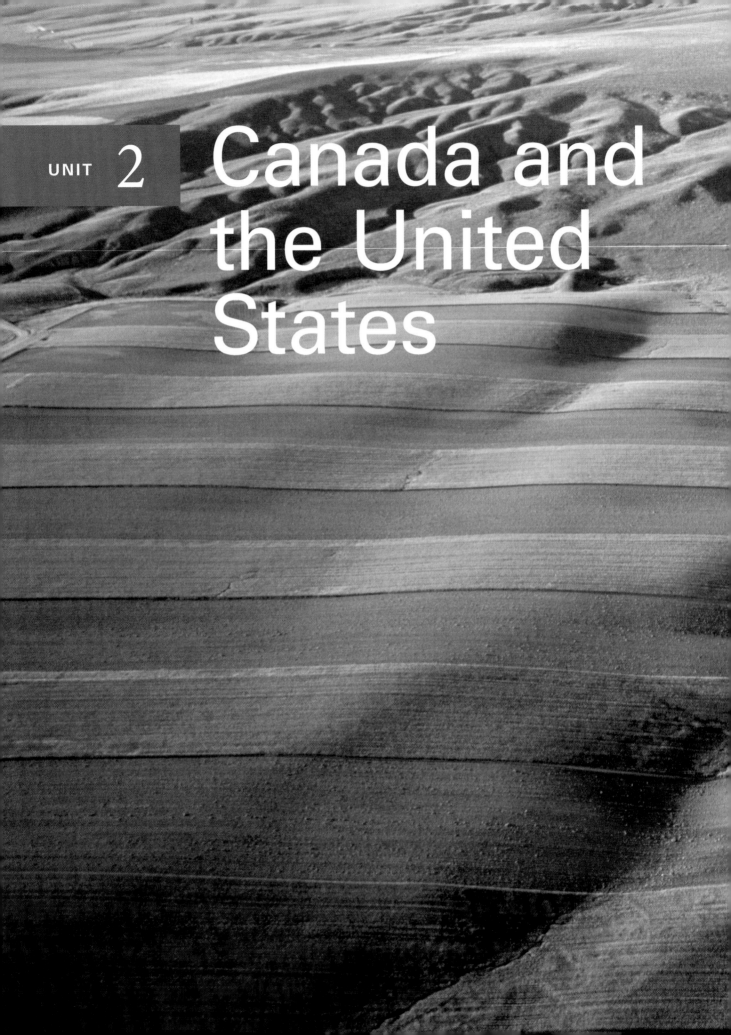

UNIT 2 Canada and the United States

Introducing the Region:
Physical and Human Geography

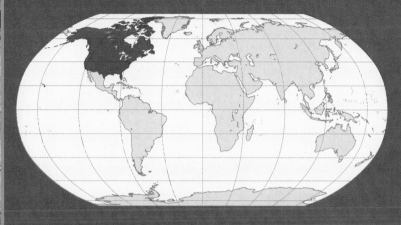

What patterns do you see in this photograph?
See page 514 for details.

▼

Canada and the United States make up the **region** that covers most of North America. This region is bounded by the Atlantic Ocean on the east and the Pacific Ocean on the west. The Arctic Ocean lies to the north of this region. The Gulf of Mexico lies to the south. North America is the third largest continent in the world.

This large region contains two subregions. Canada and Alaska make up the northern part. The 48 continental United States make up the southern part. West of the Great Lakes, the two subregions are separated by the 49th parallel of latitude. East of the Great Lakes, the St. Lawrence River separates the two subregions.

Physical Features of Canada and the United States

Physical Features

If you look at a physical map of this region, you see mountains running along both sides, with a large, flat area in the center. This flat area runs from the Arctic Ocean to the Gulf of Mexico. It is made up of **shield** and plains.

The term *shield* refers to the large core of very old rock that lies at the base of each continent. In North America, this rock core was exposed thousands of years ago. During the ice ages, **glaciers** scraped across the land, taking the soil with them. They left just a thin layer of soil in eastern and central Canada.

Plains are flat or gently rolling areas of land. Much of the soil that glaciers scraped from the Canadian Shield ended up on the plains of Canada and the United States.

Canada and Alaska

The Canadian Shield covers almost half of Canada. The rest of this subregion contains islands, lakes, plains, and mountains.

The glaciers that scraped the shield also dug the huge holes that became the Great Lakes. These lakes lie between Canada and the United States. They are the world's largest group of **freshwater** lakes. The St. Lawrence River connects the Great Lakes to the ocean.

To the far north are many smaller lakes and Hudson Bay. The region extends past the Arctic Circle and ends with a scattering of islands. The largest is named Baffin Island.

In the Atlantic Ocean, off the southeast coast of Newfoundland, lie the Grand Banks. The ocean is very shallow here.

The Rocky Mountains stretch more than 3,000 miles through North America.

Far to the west, in the Alaska Range, is the highest peak in North America. Mount McKinley rises 20,320 feet above sea level.

Continental United States

Two major mountain ranges run through the continental United States. In the east, the Appalachians are a gentle range of rounded peaks and deep valleys. In the west, the Rocky Mountains jut up into jagged, snow-capped peaks. The Rockies reach all the way from Alaska to New Mexico.

Between these two ranges, wide plains stretch across the middle of the continent. This vast, mostly flat region extends about 2,500 miles north and south. From the Rockies, the dry and treeless Great Plains slope down to the central lowlands.

A large system of rivers drains most of the plains between the Rocky Mountains and the Appalachians. These rivers all flow into the muddy Mississippi River. The Mississippi empties into the Gulf of Mexico.

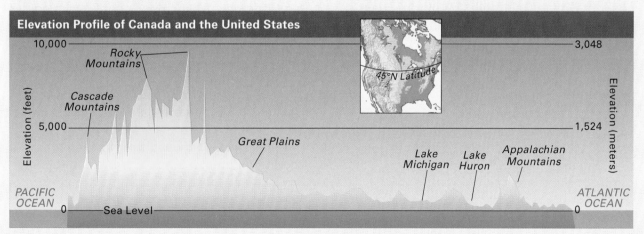

Elevation Profile of Canada and the United States

Elevation (feet)

10,000

5,000

0 Sea Level

Elevation (meters)

3,048

1,524

0

Rocky Mountains

Cascade Mountains

Great Plains

45°N Latitude

Lake Michigan

Lake Huron

Appalachian Mountains

PACIFIC OCEAN

ATLANTIC OCEAN

Climate

Climate varies widely across this large region, which reaches from the chilly Arctic to the warm waters of the Gulf of Mexico.

The northern parts of this landmass fall in **tundra** and **subarctic** climate zones. In subarctic climates, winters are very long, cold, and snowy. Summers are very short. They may be cool and rainy.

The tundra climate zone is even more severe. Here it is cold all year, even in summer. Winter temperatures are usually well below 0°F. In summer, the high temperatures may not be far above freezing (32°F). Areas with tundra climate get very little rain or snow. Beneath the surface, the ground is always frozen.

These colder climates occur in places that don't get a lot of direct sunlight. The sun's rays are most direct at the equator. In general, the farther a region is from the equator, the colder the climate will be. Since the northern part of this region is very far from the equator, it is very cold.

Mount Washington in New Hampshire has been called "Home of the World's Worst Weather." The fastest recorded wind speed ever, 231 mph, was recorded there in 1934. The research station is open year-round. In what month do you think this picture was taken?

Canada and Alaska

Most of Canada and Alaska have either a tundra or a subarctic climate. But the climate warms up as you move farther south. The area closest to the continental United States enjoys a mostly **humid continental** climate. Winters are still freezing cold, but summers can be hot and steamy.

Nearly all of Canada and Alaska have heavy snows in the winter. But on the west coast of British Columbia, the **marine west coast** climate brings more rain than snow. There, and in the southern part of Canada, summers are warmer and drier.

Continental United States

No part of the continental United States has a tundra or subarctic climate. The climate here can vary greatly, depending on where you are. One state, California, has as many as five different climate zones.

The southern part of the United States is generally warm year-round. The Southeast has a **humid subtropical** climate, influenced by the Gulf of Mexico. Hot, rainy summers follow mild winters that see some rain. The climate of Florida's southern tip is **tropical wet and dry**. There, it is hot all year, with both rainy and dry seasons.

Arid and **semiarid** climates are common in the Southwest. This area is hot and dry in the summer and pleasant in the winter, with very little rain. Many older people from colder climates choose to retire in the Southwest.

The rest of the western United States has a variety of climates. The Sierra Nevada and Rocky mountains have a **highlands** climate. Along the northern Pacific Coast, a marine west coast climate brings mild winters and lots of rain.

Most of the Midwest and Northeast have a humid continental climate. People here enjoy four distinct seasons. Summers are quite warm and winters are cold, often with snow and ice storms.

Vegetation

Just as the climate varies across Canada and the United States, so does the vegetation.

One widespread **vegetation zone** in this region is **temperate grassland**. Mainly short and tall grasses grow in temperate grasslands. Few trees grow in this zone because there is not enough rain. The Great Plains area of the United States and Canada is one of the world's largest temperate grasslands. This area combines a long growing season with fertile soil. As a result, the Great Plains provide very productive farmland.

Another special vegetation zone in this region is **tundra**. This vegetation zone shares a name with the tundra climate zone, where it is cold year-round. The tundra vegetation zone is like a very cold **desert**. Few large plants can grow here.

Like temperate grasslands, the tundra is treeless. Because the ground is frozen, trees cannot send their roots down into the soil. Only very low grasses, mosses, and scrub cover the ground during the short summer. They provide food for the grazing animals that live on the tundra.

Canada and Alaska

The tundra spreads across the far northern islands and coasts of Canada. Much of Alaska's land is tundra as well. In the **ice cap** on Alaska's highest peaks and glaciers, no plant life grows at all. Most of Canada and the rest of Alaska are covered in **coniferous forests,** filled with trees such as cedar, fir, pine, and spruce. The needle-like leaves of these trees stay green all year.

The warmer climate in southeastern Canada supports **mixed forest**. Here you find a mix of both coniferous and deciduous trees. Deciduous trees, such as oak, elm, and birch, have broad leaves that they shed each fall. The south-central part of Canada is temperate grassland.

Continental United States

The vegetation of the continental United States ranges from tropical palms to desert sagebrush. There are thick pine forests in the West, grasses on the central plains, and forested swamps in the South.

Spreading up and down the East Coast are forests of all types—coniferous, deciduous, and mixed. The extreme Southeast—along the Gulf Coast and in Florida's Everglades—is home to **tropical grasslands**. The tough saw-grass and scattered trees in the Everglades are adapted to the tropical wet and dry climate.

Across the central part of the United States is a wide band of temperate grassland. This area was once thick with prairie grasses. However, much of the land has been plowed for farming. It is now covered with fields of corn, wheat, and other crops.

In the West, coniferous forests blanket the mountains. **Desert scrub** grows throughout the deserts and canyons of the Southwest and Great Basin. Along the California coast, **chaparral** dots the Coast Ranges.

Mangrove trees grow in the swamps of Everglades National Park in Florida.

Introducing the Region: Human Geography

All of the other regions of the world are made up of many countries. However, this region is made up of just two large countries: Canada and the United States. In land area, Canada is the second largest country in the world. Yet its population is quite small for its size. The United States is almost as large as Canada in land area. But the U.S. population is nine times the size of Canada's.

The two countries share a common cultural background. Most of the people are English-speaking, although Canada officially uses French as well. Both countries have native populations. Both countries were colonized by settlers from Europe about 500 years ago. In later years, immigration from all parts of the world has enriched the two countries with a wide variety of cultures.

Political Boundaries of Canada and the United States

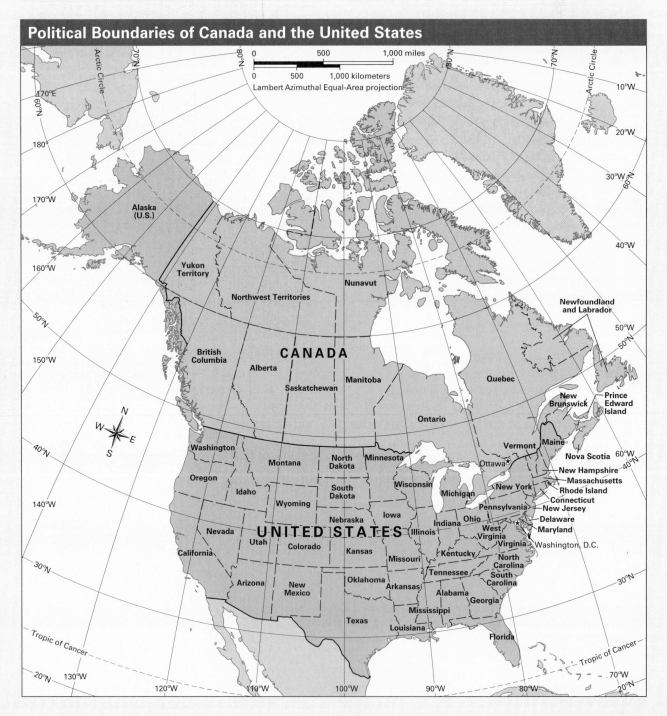

History

The histories of Canada and the United States reveal why these countries are so similar.

Early Times

Scholars believe that North American history began when bands of hunters migrated to Alaska from Asia. This happened more than 10,000 years ago. Over time, these first bands settled throughout the region. As they adapted to their environment, each group developed its own culture.

The Inuit, or Eskimo, people stayed in the far north. They hunted Arctic animals for food and clothing. Other groups settled along the west coast of the continent. Fish and trees were plentiful there and provided food, clothing, and shelter. Many groups settled in the central and eastern parts of the region. A group called the Anasazi built cliff houses in the southwestern United States.

The Colonial Period

Europeans began coming to North America in the 1500s. The French and British set up colonies along the eastern coast. The Spanish colonized Florida, Texas, and California.

The American colonies revolted against Britain in 1775. A successful war for independence followed. In 1783, the United States became an independent country.

Yet there was not freedom for everyone. Millions of slaves lived in the United States.

The country split over the question of slavery. It fought a **civil war** between 1861 and 1865. In 1865, slavery ended in the United States.

Canada was first colonized by the French. After a war, France turned Canada over to Great Britain in 1763. French culture still remains strong in Canada. Many Canadians speak French as their first language.

In 1867, Canadians won the right to govern themselves. Yet Canada still was part of the British Empire.

The Modern Era

In the twentieth century, Canada and the United States formed a strong bond. Canada gained its independence from Great Britain in 1931. People on both sides of the U.S.–Canadian border welcomed this event.

In 1939, war broke out in Europe. War was also raging in Asia. This global conflict is known as World War II. The United States and Canada worked closely together to end this war. Since then, they have continued to work together for world peace.

Today Canada and the United States are closely linked by trade. Canadians buy many products that are made or grown in the United States. Americans also buy many Canadian products. In 1994, the North American Free Trade Agreement (NAFTA) took effect. NAFTA made trade between the two countries easier. This trade pact allows most goods to move freely among Canada, the United States, and Mexico.

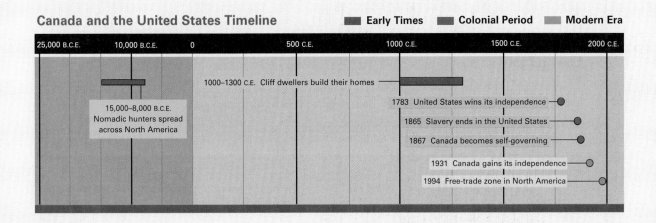

Canada and the United States Timeline — Early Times — Colonial Period — Modern Era

| 25,000 B.C.E. | 10,000 B.C.E. | 0 | 500 C.E. | 1000 C.E. | 1500 C.E. | 2000 C.E. |

1000–1300 C.E. Cliff dwellers build their homes

15,000–8,000 B.C.E. Nomadic hunters spread across North America

1783 United States wins its independence

1865 Slavery ends in the United States

1867 Canada becomes self-governing

1931 Canada gains its independence

1994 Free-trade zone in North America

Population

More than 337 million people altogether live in Canada and the United States. This is about 6 percent of the world's population. The population of this region is growing very slowly compared with other parts of the world.

Some parts of this region are almost empty. The western deserts are too dry, and the far north is too cold for settlement. Very few people live in these places. Northern Canada is thinly settled, with a **population density** as low as one person per 43 square miles.

Most Canadians live close to the U.S. border. Toronto is the largest **urban** area in Canada. Throughout the region people tend to cluster in or near cities, where more jobs can be found.

Most people in Canada and the United States are Christian. Almost one fourth of these are Roman Catholics. Islam is the fastest growing religion here. Other faiths include Judaism, Buddhism, and Hinduism. One out of 10 people have no religion.

Canada and the United States: Major Religions

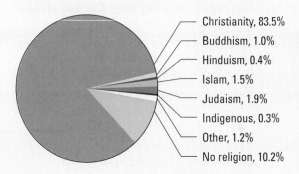

- Christianity, 83.5%
- Buddhism, 1.0%
- Hinduism, 0.4%
- Islam, 1.5%
- Judaism, 1.9%
- Indigenous, 0.3%
- Other, 1.2%
- No religion, 10.2%

Canada and the United States: Urban and Rural Population, 2007

Urban, 81.3%

Rural, 18.7%

10% of = the total population

Canada and the United States: Population Growth, 1950–2050

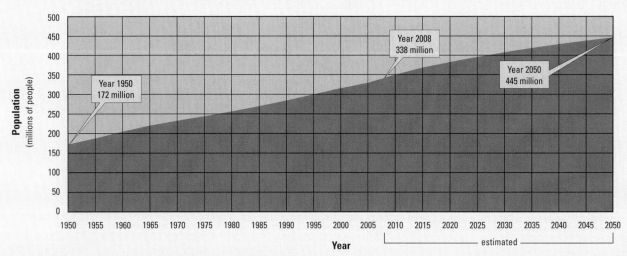

Year 1950
172 million

Year 2008
338 million

Year 2050
445 million

Population (millions of people)

Year

estimated

Sources: United Nations Department of Economic and Social Affairs, Population Division. Encyclopædia Britannica.

Economic Activity

Canada and the United States are rich in many kinds of resources. One of these is good farmland. As a result, **commercial farming** is an important **economic activity** in this region.

Commercial farming is the growing of farm products for sale to others. Wheat, for example, is a commercial crop. It is grown widely in the U.S. Midwest and in the prairie provinces of Canada—Alberta, Manitoba, and Saskatchewan. The farmers of this region sell their crops around the world. They produce about half of the world's grain exports. From California and Florida, farmers ship fruits and vegetables. They help make this region the world's leading food exporter.

Forestry is also important to this region. Forestry is the planting, growing, and harvesting of trees. North America was once covered with thick forests. Over time, many trees were cut down for fuel and lumber. In southern Canada and in several corners of the United States, logging is still a big industry.

Resources

Canada and the United States also have a wealth of mineral resources. Oil and coal, used for energy, are the most important. Texas, Alaska, and Alberta have thriving oil industries. Coal is plentiful in the Appalachian

Cold winters have little impact on oil fields in Alberta, Canada. Oil is pumped all year, regardless of the season.

and Rocky mountains. It is also mined in the river valleys of the central United States.

Mines in Quebec, Ontario, and British Columbia produce gold, nickel, and copper. In the western United States, New Mexico has large reserves of uranium. Arizona is rich in copper deposits.

Land Use

Much of this region is used for raising livestock. Cattle graze widely across the western range. Sheep ranches are also common.

Trade and manufacturing are strong in the urban centers of this region. In the United States, manufacturing plays an especially big role in the Midwest and Northeast. Factories there produce cars, steel, plastics, glass, and textiles.

Orange groves need lots of sunshine and frost-free winters. Oranges are an important crop in Florida and California.

Settlement Patterns and Ways of Life in Canada

3

3.1 Introduction

James is a sixth grade student in Pond Inlet, a town in Nunavut. Nunavut is in the far north of Canada. When James goes to school in January, the sun never comes up. If he looks out his classroom window in the dark winter months, all he sees are streetlights and the lights of cars. Some of his classes are taught in English. Others are in Inuktitut, the language of the Inuit. James and most of the other sixth graders also speak Inuktitut at home. In their language, the town's name is Mittimatalik.

Compare James with Marie, a sixth grader in Quebec City. Marie is French Canadian. All of her classes are taught in French. It is always light outside when she is in school. Marie can see many people on the streets outside her school. James and Marie live in the same country. But their experiences are very different.

Canada is a large, very diverse country. It is often called a **plural society**. This term reflects the fact that its people have come from many countries and cultures. While most people share a Canadian identity, many also keep the traditions of their parents and grandparents.

Canadians often divide their country into five **regions**. In this chapter you will learn about these regions. You will look at how differently people live in each one. You will also find out how location influences the way people live.

Essential Question

How does where you live influence how you live?

This illustration shows the five regions of Canada. Each region has a different climate. Each region's history and economy are different too. These differences affect how people live in Canada. Keep this illustration in mind as you try to answer the Essential Question.

Graphic Organizer

NORTHERN

ATLANTIC

PACIFIC

PRAIRIE

CORE

◄ Satellite image of Canada and the United States in winter

3.2 The Geographic Setting

In area, Canada is the world's second largest country. It covers most of the northern part of North America. The United States is its neighbor to the south. The two countries share a 5,000-mile-long border. This is the longest unguarded border in the world.

Canada's Three "Founding Peoples" The first people to settle in Canada probably came from Asia tens of thousands of years ago. They crossed over a land bridge between Siberia and Alaska. In time, they became the Inuit and other Native American groups. These native peoples still live in Canada. Today they are known as Canada's first "founding peoples."

Canada's second and third founding peoples came from Europe. Colonists from France settled Quebec in the 1600s. Later, English colonists settled on the Atlantic coast. In the 1700s, France and England fought a war for control of North America. When the war ended in 1763, France agreed to give up Canada to England.

During the 1800s, large numbers of English settlers came to Canada. But the French-speaking people held on to their language and way of life. Meanwhile, Canada also attracted settlers from Ireland, Scotland, Sweden, Norway, and Germany. By the early 1900s, Italians, Ukrainians, and Jews were arriving from southern and eastern Europe. Some settled in the big eastern cities. Others began farms on the flat land in Canada's center. Chinese, Japanese, and Filipino people came from Asia as well. Many of them settled along Canada's Pacific coast.

All of these groups have helped shape Canada's plural society. Its founding peoples have kept their languages and traditions. Newer settlers have also held on to traditional ways from other cultures. Yet all are Canadians.

A Thinly Settled Country Canada is large in area but small in population. In 2008, more than 33 million people lived there. That is fewer people than lived in the state of California.

Approximately 8 out of every 10 Canadians live in an **urban** area. These are areas in or around cities. The rest of the population make their homes in **rural** areas. These are parts of the country that are not near cities.

Most of Canada's people live within 100 miles of the United States. This strip of land lies within Canada's **ecumene**. An ecumene is any region that is well suited for people to live there permanently.

Many Americans think that Canadians' lives are just like theirs. This is not the case. It is true that many Canadians live close to the United States. It is also true that Canada and the United States are each other's most important trading partner. And it is true that they are good allies. But there are many differences between the two countries. Some of these are political. Others are economic, and some are cultural.

Canada's Population, 2007

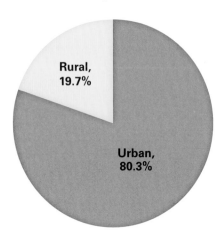

- Rural, 19.7%
- Urban, 80.3%

Most Canadians Live in Cities

Eight out of 10 Canadians live in urban areas. Only one fifth live in rural areas. Most Canadians live in the ecumene as well. This is found in the southern part of the country, mainly the southeast.

▶ Geoterms

ecumene a geographic region that is well suited for permanent settlement by people. Areas not included in the ecumene are generally too dry, too cold, or too rugged for permanent human settlement.

plural society a society in which different cultural groups keep their own identity, beliefs, and traditions

rural found in or living in areas that are not close to cities

urban found in or living in a city

Canadians Cling to the Border
Canada has only about one tenth as many people as the United States. Much of the Canadian north lies outside the ecumene. It is so cold that few people choose to live there. Most of Canada's people live within 100 miles of the U.S. border.

Population Density of Canada

People per Square Mile
- Over 250
- 125–250
- 25–125
- 2–25
- Under 2

3.3 Canada's Five Regions

Canada is divided into provinces and territories. There are 10 provinces. Each has its own government. In this way, provinces are much like states in the United States. Territories are areas that have too few people to be provinces.

Geographers often divide Canada into five large regions. They are outlined in black on the map you see here. As you will learn, each region has its own geography. Each also has its own history and way of life.

Atlantic Region This region lines the Atlantic coast of Canada. It includes the provinces of Newfoundland and Labrador, Prince Edward Island, Nova Scotia, and New Brunswick. Some of these provinces are islands in the Atlantic Ocean.

Core Region This region stretches north of the Great Lakes. It includes the two large provinces of Ontario and Quebec.

Prairie Region This region covers Canada's central plains. It includes the provinces of Manitoba, Saskatchewan, and Alberta.

Pacific Region This region is on Canada's Pacific coast. It is made up of the province of British Columbia.

Northern Region This region lies to the north of the provinces. It reaches far into the Arctic Ocean. It includes Canada's three territories. These are the Yukon Territory, the Northwest Territories, and Nunavut.

The Five Regions of Canada

Resources

⚒ Coal
⚡ Hydroelectric power
⚗ Iron
🜂 Natural gas
🛢 Petroleum (oil)
⬗ Precious metals (gold, silver, copper)
☢ Uranium

Elevation

Feet	Meters
Over 10,000	Over 3,050
5,001–10,000	1,526–3,050
2,001–5,000	611–1,525
1,001–2,000	306–610
0–1,000	0–305

REGION

NUNAVUT

Baffin
Bay

Iqaluit

Labrador
Sea

Kuujjuaq

NEWFOUNDLAND &
LABRADOR

Churchill

MANITOBA

REGION

Hudson
Bay

Goose Bay

QUEBEC

ATLANTIC
REGION

Lake
Winnipeg

PRINCE EDWARD ISLAND

ONTARIO

CORE REGION

ATLANTIC

NEW
BRUNSWICK

OCEAN

Quebec

NOVA
SCOTIA

Halifax

Lake Superior

Montreal

St. Lawrence River

Ottawa

N

W   E

S

Lake
Huron

Lake Michigan

Toronto

Lake
Ontario

0   250   500 miles

Niagara Falls

0   250   500 kilometers

Lake Erie

Lambert Azimuthal Equal-Area projection

3.4 Settlement Patterns: Who Lives Where?

Imagine that you could spread Canada's people out evenly. About eight people would live in every square mile. But Canada's people do not live like this. Outside of the large cities, an average of only two people live in every square mile.

The Atlantic Region This was the first area where Europeans settled in Canada. They came because fishing was so good in the North Atlantic. Until recent years, most people here made a living by fishing. But the ocean has been overfished. The government now limits fishing to make sure there will be fish in the future. As a result, many people have moved away.

The Core Region Most Canadians live in Canada's core region. This region has three of Canada's largest cities. They are Toronto, Montreal, and the **capital city** of Ottawa. In the past, people came to Ontario to work in its many factories. More recently they have come for jobs in banks, computer companies, and other businesses.

The Prairie Region More than 5 million people live in the three prairie provinces. Farming was once the main activity here. Today the oil and gas business is booming in Alberta. As a result, Alberta is the fastest-growing province in Canada. Its biggest cities are Edmonton and Calgary. Both are popular urban areas.

A Population on the Move

Parts of Canada lost people between 2001 and 2006. Other parts gained people. The numbers show the percent of the loss (−) or gain (+) compared with the 2001 population. Although Nunavut shows a large population growth, its total population in 2006 was only about 29,000 people.

Population Change in Canada, 2001–2006

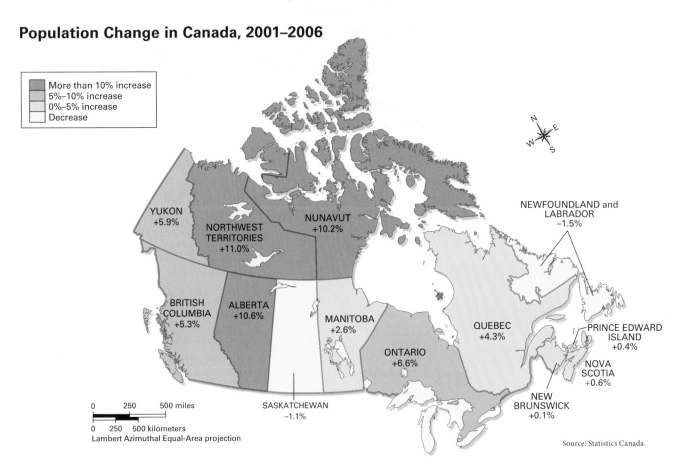

- More than 10% increase
- 5%–10% increase
- 0%–5% increase
- Decrease

YUKON +5.9%
NORTHWEST TERRITORIES +11.0%
NUNAVUT +10.2%
NEWFOUNDLAND and LABRADOR −1.5%
BRITISH COLUMBIA +5.3%
ALBERTA +10.6%
MANITOBA +2.6%
ONTARIO +6.6%
QUEBEC +4.3%
PRINCE EDWARD ISLAND +0.4%
NOVA SCOTIA +0.6%
NEW BRUNSWICK +0.1%
SASKATCHEWAN −1.1%

0   250   500 miles
0   250   500 kilometers
Lambert Azimuthal Equal-Area projection

Source: Statistics Canada.

The Pacific Region British Columbia is home to more than 4 million people. Most live in or near Vancouver and Victoria. People also live on the western slopes of the Rocky Mountains. Many people from Asia have moved to this region, because of its location on the Pacific Ocean.

The Northern Region This is the largest region in land area. But it has the fewest people. Only about 100,000 people live in all three territories. The region is costly to live in because it is so far from other places. There are so few roads that goods are often flown in by plane.

3.5 A Plural Society: Who Speaks What?

If you walked around Toronto, you would hear people speaking many different languages. Of course, you would hear English and French. But many other cultural groups live there as well. Toronto has one of the most multicultural school districts in the world. More than half the students in the city speak a language other than English at home.

The Atlantic Region Most people in this region speak English as their first language. Their families came from Great Britain to farm or fish many years ago. Some French speakers settled here as well. French remains their first language.

The Core Region In Ontario, most people speak English. But in Quebec, most people speak French. Chinese, Italian, and Portuguese are other languages spoken here. For years, Canadians argued about which language their government should use. Now both French and English are its official languages. Some people in Quebec think their province should be a separate country. In 1995, the people of Quebec voted on this question. They decided to stay part of Canada, but it was a close vote. Since then, enthusiasm for independence has declined. In fact, support for independence has dropped well below 40 percent in public opinion polls.

The Prairie Region European settlers first came to this region to farm. Now, oil in Alberta attracts newcomers. English is the first language for more than four out of five people in this region. But people who speak French, German, and Ukrainian have moved here too.

The Pacific Region Here, English is the first language. But many people from Asia also live in this region. Chinese is the second most common language. People from India speak Punjabi. People from the Philippines speak Tagalog.

The Northern Region Almost two thirds of the people in the north speak English as their first language. Many are English-speaking Canadians who moved here to work for the government. Most of the founding peoples, such as the Inuit, have kept their cultures. The Inuit continue to speak Inuktitut.

Canada's Official Languages
Canada has two official languages. Signs all over the country are in both English and French. The 2007 census showed that about 21 percent of Canadians speak French most often at home. Almost 67 percent speak English most often at home. The third most spoken language is Chinese.

Surf's Up in the Winter

In the winter, storms slam into Vancouver Island, often creating 15-foot waves. Winter surfing is attempted by only the most dedicated surfers. To survive the cold, they wear rubber suits with hoods, gloves, and booties.

Winterlude: A Festival of Winter

Winterlude celebrations take place in Ottawa in February. Here, people play on an ice slide in a park. In the background is a snow sculpture of one of the Parliament Buildings. These buildings are the center of the national government.

3.6 Having Fun in the Cold

Winters are long and summers are short in this northern country. Canadians have adjusted by finding ways to have fun in all seasons. In summer, for example, people use the Rideau Canal in Ottawa for boating. But in the winter the canal freezes. For a few months it becomes the longest skating rink in the world.

The Atlantic Region This area has a fairly mild **humid continental** climate. Winters can be very wet. Halifax, for example, gets five inches of **precipitation** in January alone.

Nova Scotia is said to be the birthplace of ice hockey. The story goes that Canadians were unhappy spending the long winter months indoors. They knew of a game that is like field hockey. Someone thought to put on skates, and ice hockey was born. Today ice hockey is popular in the United States too.

The Core Region The southern part of this area has a humid continental climate. Toronto's average temperature in July is a pleasant 63°F.

Every February, Canadians celebrate Winterlude in Ottawa. People ice skate and ride sleighs along the Rideau Canal. There are races and figure-skating contests. You can learn how to make ice carvings. Or you can eat at a cafe carved from ice!

The Prairie Region The southern part of this region has a **semiarid** to humid continental climate. The northern part has a **subarctic** climate. In Churchill, the average January temperature is a frosty –16°F.

Churchill is called the "Polar Bear Capital of the World." Once a year, more than 1,000 migrating polar bears pass through this town. People travel each year to Churchill to see this event.

The Pacific Region The coast of British Columbia has a **marine west coast** climate. In Vancouver, January temperatures average 37°F. This is much warmer than most parts of Canada.

Winter surfing is a popular sport off the Pacific coast. Large waves from winter storms challenge surfers there. Farther inland lie the Coast Mountains and the Rockies. The high altitudes here mean long, cold winters. You will find some of Canada's best ski resorts in this region.

The Northern Region Much of this area is treeless **tundra**. The most northern part has very few plants. The southern part has a subarctic climate. The temperature in the town of Whitehorse in July averages 57°F.

The all-terrain vehicle has replaced the dog sled in the north. But people still love to compete in dog sled races. A long-distance race can cover 1,000 miles and take up to two weeks.

3.7 Different Traditions and Needs: What's Built Where?

Let's say you are visiting the Museum of Civilization, a short trip from Ottawa. You see houses of Canada's native peoples. Later you look at a lumber camp. Then you walk past an oil derrick or a fishing village. You soon see how people's needs and traditions, as well as their locations, have led them to build different kinds of structures.

The Atlantic Region Lighthouses dot the coast in this region. This is because of the importance of fishing. Lighthouses help sailors figure out their position on the ocean. They let ships know that land is near and warn of dangerous rocks. Canada still has several hundred lighthouses in operation.

The Core Region Many buildings here combine British and French influences. The Parliament Buildings in Ottawa were built in the Gothic revival style. British and French settlers brought this style from Europe. These large stone buildings have tall, pointed windows and carved ornaments. Another example of this style is the Château Frontenac. This is a famous hotel in Quebec City.

The Prairie Region Farms cover the southern part of this region. The typical farm sits on hundreds of acres. Beside the barn is a silo. This is a tall structure for storing grain. Farmers in this rural region usually grow spring wheat. This crop is planted in the spring and harvested in late summer. It grows well in climates with harsh winters.

The Pacific Region British influence is strong here. Victoria was the first city in British Columbia. It is known as the most British of Canadian cities. Some buildings there look almost like castles.

The Northern Region This region has long, cold winters. In the past, some Inuit made winter igloos from snow blocks. The word *igloo* means "house." Igloos can also be made of other materials, such as sod, stone, or wood. Today, most Inuit have houses made from kits. Such a house is put together from sections made in factories. Inuit live in widely scattered villages along the Arctic Ocean or Hudson Bay.

A Variety of Building Styles
Each region of Canada has its own styles of buildings. Sometimes these styles grow out of the needs of the people living there. Sometimes they reflect ideas that settlers brought with them from Europe about what buildings should look like.

3.8 How People Make a Living

Canada is rich in **natural resources**. Furs and lumber were early exports. Today oil and minerals are important as well. Even so, most Canadians today work in service industries. These industries produce a service for people rather than goods. Examples include restaurants, dry cleaners, and banks.

The Atlantic Region In the 1800s, this region had a strong economy. Good fishing in the Atlantic Ocean made it easy to make a living. But, as you read earlier, overfishing has led to limits on fishing. That, in turn, has put many people out of work.

Coal mining and farming are also economic activities here. But poor soil limits farming to small patches of good land. **Forestry** is a growing industry. Forestry companies produce lumber and pulp for paper.

The Core Region Most of Canada's factories are located here. This region is also a strong farming center. More than a third of Canada's farm products are grown here. Recently, the region has become a large producer of **hydroelectric power**. This is electricity generated from flowing rivers. Some power plants are located on rivers in northern Quebec. Others are found near Niagara Falls or along the St. Lawrence River.

Canada's Plentiful Resources

This map shows the natural resources found in Canada. The location of natural resources tells much about a region's economy. It also shapes land use in a region.

Economic Activity in Canada

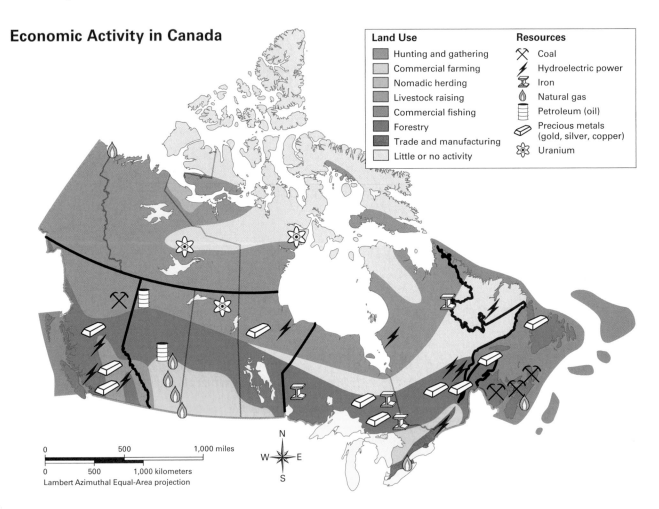

Land Use
- Hunting and gathering
- Commercial farming
- Nomadic herding
- Livestock raising
- Commercial fishing
- Forestry
- Trade and manufacturing
- Little or no activity

Resources
- Coal
- Hydroelectric power
- Iron
- Natural gas
- Petroleum (oil)
- Precious metals (gold, silver, copper)
- Uranium

0   500   1,000 miles

0   500   1,000 kilometers
Lambert Azimuthal Equal-Area projection

N   S   E   W

The Prairie Region This region produces half of the country's farm products. Its southern plains are good for raising grains. Mining is also important. More than half of Canada's minerals are mined here. They include coal, nickel, copper, zinc, and uranium.

Much oil is trapped in the oil sands of northern Alberta. This area is thought to contain more oil than the entire Middle East. It is expensive to separate oil from the sand. But because demand for oil is high, Alberta's oil business is booming. The same is true in Edmonton, one of the fastest-growing cities in Canada.

The Pacific Region Forestry and fishing are important in British Columbia. But now newer industries have passed these by. Both metals and coal are mined in this region. The shipping industry is growing as well. Shippers on the coast carry Canadian products to all parts of the world. Many rivers have been dammed to produce hydroelectric power. Much of the electricity generated in the region is sold to the United States.

The Northern Region Some native peoples still follow the nomadic, or wandering, life of herders and hunters. But most are settled in small villages. Because there is little business in most villages, jobs are few. Canadians from the south sometimes come here to work for short periods. They find jobs with the government, churches, or mining companies. Many people in the territories believe that there are undiscovered precious minerals still to be found here.

Living Outside the Ecumene
People who live outside the ecumene have adapted to harsh conditions. This Inuit hunter is warmly dressed even on a summer day.

3.9 Beginning to Think Globally

In this chapter, you have learned about settlement patterns and ways of life in Canada. You have read about the different groups that make up Canada's plural society. You have learned about urban and rural areas in Canada.

For the most part, people have settled in Canada's ecumene. But not all Canadians live in the ecumene. Some people live in the subarctic region of Canada. A few even live in the far northern tundra zone.

This variety of settlement is found in many places around the world. Consider Australia, for example. Many **aborigines,** the native people of Australia, choose to live in remote **deserts**. There they are able to keep their way of life. But they face other problems, such as lack of work and the challenge of keeping their culture alive. Think about these relationships between location and ways of life as you explore settlement patterns around the world in the next section.

3.10 Global Connections

This map shows where people live around the world. The areas in purple are the most densely populated regions. These are population hot spots in the global ecumene. The gray areas are very thinly populated. They lie outside the global ecumene. Notice that different parts of the ecumene have different population densities. Why do you think this might be so?

What climate zones are likely to be found in the global ecumene? The climates found in the ecumene are neither too hot nor too cold. People can live there comfortably. Areas outside of the ecumene often have extreme temperatures. Few crops can be grown in such climate regions. That helps explain why they are not part of the ecumene.

Which physical features are likely to lie outside the global ecumene? Some of Earth's physical features are not well suited for human settlement. Very few people live in major deserts. These areas are too dry to support life. Most mountainous regions are thinly settled. They are too rugged for most people. Many large swamps also lie outside the ecumene.

What might life be like for people who live outside the ecumene? Most of the world's people live within the global ecumene. However, some people live in less populated areas. They survive by finding ways to stay warm, keep cool, find water, or keep dry—even in the harshest conditions. In later chapters, you will look at different ways people adapt to living in extreme environments outside the ecumene.

Ecumene Around the World

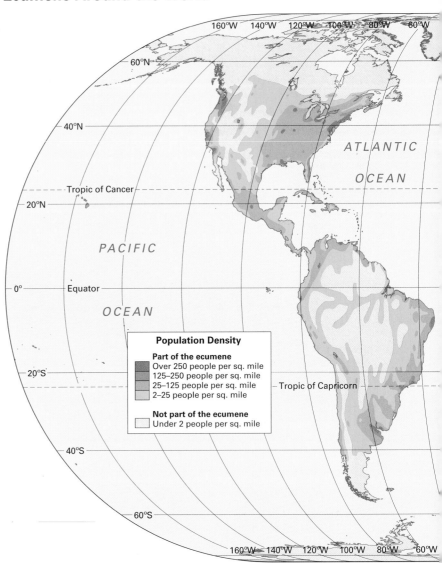

Population Density

Part of the ecumene
- Over 250 people per sq. mile
- 125–250 people per sq. mile
- 25–125 people per sq. mile
- 2–25 people per sq. mile

Not part of the ecumene
- Under 2 people per sq. mile

The Great Lakes: The U.S. and Canada's Freshwater Treasures

4

4.1 Introduction

A massive sheet of ice, the last of the Ice Age **glaciers,** crept across the North American continent. It inched south, across the vast region that is now Canada. It glided heavily over what is today the northern United States. Finally, it slid to an icy stop near the present-day city of Chicago. All the while, the sheer weight of the huge glacier flattened mountains and reshaped the landscape.

After thousands of years, Earth began to warm. The vast blanket of ice began to retreat. It left behind high ridges and huge holes that the ice sheet had gouged into the land. As the ice melted, clear, fresh water filled the huge holes. In this way, the Great Lakes were born.

Over time, a rich **ecosystem** developed on the land left bare when the glaciers retreated. An ecosystem is a community of all the living things in an area. It includes plants, animals, and the physical environment in which they live. Ecosystems can be as small as a lawn or as large as Earth. The Great Lakes make up the world's largest **freshwater** ecosystem.

It took many thousands of years for the movement of glaciers to create the Great Lakes. In just decades, however, human activity has greatly changed this region. In this chapter, you will learn how people can upset an ecosystem. And you will find out what can be done to solve some of the problems that human activity has created in the Great Lakes ecosystem.

Essential Question

How can people best use and protect Earth's freshwater ecosystems?

The diagram shows some of the main ways that people use the Great Lakes. All of these uses affect the lakes' ecosystem in some way, large or small. Keep this diagram in mind as you try to answer the Essential Question.

Graphic Organizer

Agriculture

Recreation

Industry

Shipping and Transportation

Homes and Business

◀ Satellite photograph of the Great Lakes looking eastward toward the Atlantic Ocean

Herring gull eggs: 124 ppm

Lake trout: 4.83 ppm

Smelt: 1.04 ppm

Phytoplankton: 0.025 ppm

Source: U.S. Environmental Protection Agency.

The Food Web and Toxic Waste

When poisons enter a waterway, they may also enter the food web. Some toxic chemicals are stored in living things. When a larger animal eats smaller animals, the poison becomes concentrated in the larger animal. In this diagram, notice how chemicals called PCBs build up within a food chain. PCBs are measured in parts per million, or ppm.

4.2 The Geographic Setting

Five lakes—Superior, Michigan, Huron, Erie, and Ontario—make up the Great Lakes. All of the Great Lakes, except Michigan, are shared by Canada and the United States. Together they form the world's largest group of freshwater lakes.

More than one tenth of the U.S. population and one quarter of the Canadian population live in the Great Lakes region. People in both countries use the lakes in many ways. They depend on them for drinking water. They use water from the lakes in factories. They use the lakes for shipping, fishing, and recreation. And they build cities on their shores.

One of North America's Largest Watersheds Think of standing on a hill and pouring water from a large container onto the ground. The water would flow downhill. While running downhill, some of the water would soak into the ground. If there were a hole along the way, water would fill it to form a tiny lake. You would have created your own tiny **watershed**.

A watershed is a geographic area that includes all of the land and waterways that drain into a body of water. Watersheds come in many shapes and sizes. They can include hills and valleys and cities and towns. Smaller watersheds can drain into larger watersheds. The Great Lakes region is one of the largest watersheds in North America.

The Great Lakes are so big that they look and act like oceans. In fact, people have called them "the fourth seacoast" of the United States. But unlike the oceans, the lakes are filled with fresh water that has little or no salt. That is why they are also called "the sweetwater seas."

A Vast and Varied Ecosystem The Great Lakes region is a vast ecosystem. One way to understand how the living things in the Great Lakes ecosystem are related to each other is to look at who eats what. These relationships make up what scientists call a **food web**. Food webs include both plants and animals that feed on each other.

Every ecosystem has its own food web. A food web is made up of many **food chains**. A food chain is a series of plants and animals, each of which depends on the next for food. In the Great Lakes ecosystem, for example, one food chain might begin with plants that grow in lakes and rivers. The next link in the chain might be insects that feed on those plants. These insects are eaten by tiny fish. The tiny fish are then eaten by larger fish. The larger fish, in turn, may be eaten by an eagle sitting at the top of the food chain. Another food chain might begin with tiny organisms known as algae and end with a river otter.

The food web is an important part of any ecosystem. If one part of the food web is harmed, it affects all of the living things in the ecosystem. For example, if a fish is poisoned by **pollution**, any animal that eats that fish will be poisoned as well. Or, if a type of plant or fish is lost from an ecosystem, all animals that feed on that plant or fish will lose part of their food supply. In this way, all living things in a food web depend on each other for their survival.

▶ Geoterms

ecosystem a community of all the living things in an area and the environment in which they live

food chain a series of plants and animals, each of which depends on the one below it for food. A food chain usually forms part of a much larger food web.

food web all of the feeding relationships within an ecosystem. Each living thing in a food web provides food energy to other living things within that ecosystem.

freshwater made up of water that is fresh, not salty. This term is also used to describe creatures that live in fresh water, such as freshwater fish.

watershed a geographic area that includes all of the land and waterways that drain into a body of water. Sometimes a watershed is also called a *drainage basin*.

An Enormous Ecosystem

The Great Lakes region includes eight U.S. states and one Canadian province. The lakes and waterways contain almost one fifth of the world's supply of fresh water.

The Great Lakes Region

4.3 The Great Lakes in 1969

For many years, people didn't worry about the Great Lakes ecosystem. The Great Lakes and its rivers were so large that most people didn't think human activity could affect them much. By the late 1960s, though, it was clear that there were problems. News articles similar to the one below made people aware that the Great Lakes were heavily polluted.

The Sad State of Our Once-Great Lakes

July 28, 1969

The Cuyahoga River in Cleveland, Ohio, looks like a melted chocolate mess. It is mud-brown, with a layer of oil on top. Gases bubble strangely on its surface. So it was not surprising when the filthy river, part of the Lake Erie watershed, burst into flames last month.

A Burning River and Dead Ducks

No one knows exactly what started the Cuyahoga River fire on June 22. It might have been a spark from a passing train. Whatever the source, the spark ignited picnic benches, piles of logs, and other garbage in the river. The burning debris set fire to oil floating on the river's surface. The flames blazed across the river and up in the air. They reached about five stories in height.

While the Cuyahoga River burned in Cleveland, another event was taking place on the Detroit River. A Detroit official was showing news reporters around the waterfront. As he assured them that the water was not as polluted as it looked, two ducks flew in for a landing. They paddled around the polluted river for a brief moment. Suddenly, they began choking, keeled over, and died.

These events show the terrible condition of the rivers that flow into the Great Lakes. But what of the Great Lakes themselves? Local residents have described the lakes as "cesspools" and "industrial wastebaskets." They claim that the lakes are used

A River in Flames

It's hard to believe that a river could catch on fire. But as this 1952 photograph shows, the Cuyahoga River did. And it burned again this year. Cleveland mayor Carl Stokes said that the river's polluted state is "a longstanding condition that must be brought to an end."

as dumping grounds for every kind of pollutant, from sewage to toxic chemicals.

Out-of-Control Algae

Television ads boast about the long-lasting suds of laundry detergents. Those suds may not cost a lot at the supermarket. But detergents are taking a toll on the Great Lakes.

Visitors to Lake Erie today see large mats of algae near the shore. This algae explosion is caused by phosphorus, a chemical in detergents. Algae need phosphorus to grow, but too much of it causes algae to grow out of control. Lake Erie is covered with algae mats that are up to two feet thick.

Algae mats create many problems. They choke fish. They clog filters in water treatment plants. They cover beaches in slime. And they make lake water taste like rotting vegetation.

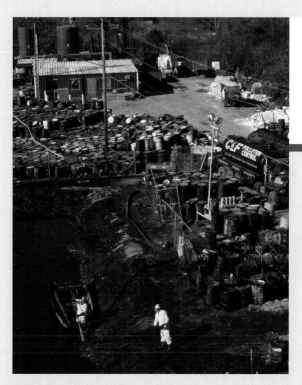

DDT Kills More Than Mosquitoes

For years, the pesticide DDT has been used in the Great Lakes region to control insects. It is sprayed on crops and on waterways to kill mosquitoes and other pests. But when DDT enters rivers and streams, it also enters the Great Lakes food web.

Today, America's national bird, the bald eagle, has almost disappeared from the Great Lakes because of DDT poisoning. The eagles feed on fish that live in water polluted with the pesticide. Over time, a toxic amount of DDT builds up in their bodies.

The DDT doesn't kill the adult birds. Instead, it weakens the eagles' eggshells. The shells of eggs laid by female eagles are so thin that most break before the young are ready to hatch. The few eaglets that do hatch may already have DDT in their blood.

Invading Lampreys and Alewives

Bald eagles are not the only disappearing species. For the past century, people have fished the lakes for fun and profit. Fishing boats once harvested millions of pounds of fish every year. Now, due partly to overfishing, whole populations of fish have almost disappeared.

While some fish are disappearing, species that are not native to this area are overrunning the lakes. The invasion of nonnative species began in 1829 when the Welland Canal connected the Great Lakes to the Atlantic Ocean. The canal allowed species from the Atlantic Ocean to swim or be carried by boats to the Great Lakes.

One deadly invader is an eel-like animal known as the sea lamprey. Lampreys act like vampires. They suck the blood out of fish. Over time, sea lampreys have killed most of the whitefish, lake trout, and other fish native to the Great Lakes.

Another invader is the alewife, a type of herring. Alewives are small but have huge appetites. They have devoured entire species of fish. They also compete with other fish for food. The first alewife wasn't discovered in Lake Michigan until 1949. Yet by the mid-1960s, alewives made up 9 pounds of every 10 pounds of fish swimming in the lake.

Alewives die off in the spring. Every year, tons of dead alewives wash up on lake beaches. Clouds of flies lay eggs on the rotting fish. Soon, the smelly fish are riddled with maggots. As a result, most beaches are unbearable during the die-off season.

Can the Lakes Be Saved?

Scientists today have begun to talk about the death of the Great Lakes. They warn that unless the lakes are cleaned up soon, they may become lifeless ponds. The question is, will people do what is needed to save them?

A week ago, two American astronauts became the first humans to walk on the moon. If the United States can accomplish such an incredible feat, then surely Americans can meet the challenge of restoring the Great Lakes.

4.4 The Great Lakes Today: Pollution

During the 1960s and 1970s, the state of the Great Lakes worried many people. Dr. Seuss, the famous children's author, wrote about Lake Erie in his book *The Lorax*. In this 1971 book, fish living in a polluted lake decide to look for a new home. Dr. Seuss wrote,

> *They'll walk on their fins and get woefully weary,*
> *In search of some water that isn't so smeary.*
> *I hear things are just as bad up in Lake Erie.*

By 1991, however, Lake Erie had improved so much that this last line was removed from *The Lorax*. This amazing change was due to cleanup work done on both sides of the U.S.-Canada border.

Making Laws to Reduce Pollution In 1972, the United States and Canada created the first Great Lakes Water Quality Agreement. They pledged to clean up and protect the Great Lakes ecosystem. The first cleanup efforts involved **point-source pollution**. This is water pollution from a single place, such as a discharge pipe at a sewage treatment plant or a factory.

New laws put strict limits on the amount of phosphorus and other chemicals that industries and sewage treatment plants could release into the waters. Soap makers stopped putting phosphorus into detergents. Industries stopped dumping oil and other pollutants into rivers. Other laws banned the use of a number of toxic chemicals, like PCBs and DDT.

The new laws worked. The Cuyahoga River was no longer flammable, or easy to catch on fire. Algae growth was greatly reduced. The lakes turned from green back to blue. PCBs and DDT in the food chain declined. And, as the amount of DDT in fish dropped, the bald eagle made a comeback.

The Chicago Waterfront

The city of Chicago lies on the shores of Lake Michigan. For years, the city dumped untreated sewage and factory wastes into the lake. At the same time, it depended on the lake for its water supply. In 2009, the city was drawing 1 billion gallons of water a day from the lake. This water met the needs of Chicago and 124 neighboring towns. Today, Chicago treats its wastewater. The result is a cleaner lake and safer drinking water for millions of people.

Continuing Pollution Challenges One great challenge in the Great Lakes today is **non-point-source pollution**. This is pollution that does not come from a single location. When rainfall, snowmelt, and irrigation water run across the land, the water picks up **pollutants** from the soil. **Runoff** from storms also picks up waste from industrial and construction sites.

Old toxic waste dumps also pollute. Many contain poisons that leak into waterways. There are as many as 250 dumps on the shores of the Niagara River alone.

Pollution from the air damages watersheds as well. Mercury, among other things, is released into the air when coal is burned. This highly toxic metal falls back to Earth mixed with rain or as dust. It then enters waterways and the food web.

Canada and the United States are working to clean up non-point-source pollution. They have made new laws to limit harmful chemicals that go into the air, water, and soil. They are also cleaning up toxic **sediment** in waterways. Toxic sediment is polluted soil that has settled to the bottom of lakes and rivers. Removing such sediment is both difficult and costly.

The best way to deal with pollution is to prevent it. Today, education programs encourage prevention. People in industry and farming are using fewer harmful chemicals. Consumers are also choosing products that are safer for the environment.

The Toronto Skyline
Toronto lies on the shores of Lake Ontario. The Great Lakes provide drinking water for three fourths of Ontario's people.

Sources of Pollution in the Great Lakes
This diagram shows several sources of pollution in the Great Lakes region. The United States and Canada have both passed laws to reduce pollution of the air, water, and soil.

Invasive Zebra Mussels

Zebra mussels are native to Eastern Europe. They are a threat to the food supplies of native fish in the Great Lakes. One problem they cause for humans is clogging water pipes.

Invading Asian Carp

Asian carp invaded the Mississippi, Missouri, and Ohio rivers in the 1980s. They pose a danger to boaters and water skiers. They jump into the air and slam into boats and people.

4.5 The Great Lakes Today: Invasive Species

Scientists estimate that there are more than 185 **invasive species** in the Great Lakes today. These are nonnative plants and animals that invade a new ecosystem. The sea lamprey described earlier is one such invader.

Most Invaders Arrive by Sea Most invasive species travel to the Great Lakes by water. Some come in the ballast water of ships. Ballast water is water pumped into the bottom of a ship to keep it stable. When the ship arrives at a port, it releases the water. It also releases any creatures in the water.

Other invaders, like the zebra mussel, hitch rides on the bottom of ships. Once zebra mussels reach a suitable place, they multiply quickly. Up to 70,000 mussels can thrive in a single square meter of water.

Invasive Species Upset the Ecosystem Invaders like the zebra mussel, sea lamprey, and alewife have all damaged the Great Lakes ecosystem. Zebra mussels, for example, steal food from native species. They clog water pipes. They attach to docks and make swimming dangerous because of their sharp shells.

The Asian carp is another big threat to the Great Lakes. Catfish farmers in the American South brought this large fish from Asia to clean their ponds. Some carp have escaped into rivers and are migrating toward Lake Michigan. Many people fear that the Great Lakes will someday become giant carp ponds.

Canada and the United States are working to prevent more nonnatives from entering the lakes. Shippers are being asked to treat their ballast water more carefully. A barrier has been built to keep nonnative fish in the Mississippi River from entering the Great Lakes. Several states have also banned the sale of live Asian carp for fear they will have disastrous effects on the Great Lakes food web.

Another approach has been to stock the lakes with species that will eat the invaders. Pacific salmon have been introduced to the Great Lakes to control alewives. Alewife numbers have dropped greatly as a result. And native fish have begun to recover.

4.6 The Great Lakes Today: Habitat Loss

A century ago, loggers in the Great Lakes region told folktales of a giant lumberjack named Paul Bunyan. Bunyan was a giant who could cut down a forest in minutes. One tale tells how he scooped out ponds to provide drinking water for his big blue ox, Babe. Today, those ponds are the Great Lakes.

In the time of the Paul Bunyan stories, dense forests covered the Great Lakes region. Nobody worried about **habitat** loss. A habitat is the natural environment in which a plant or an animal lives. But habitat loss is a big worry in the region today.

Restoring Forest Habitat When settlers moved into the Great Lakes region in the 1800s, they cleared patches of forest for farms. Later, loggers cut down more trees. Still later more land was cleared for factories and cities. In time, almost half of the region's original forest was lost to development. When habitats are lost, the plants and animals that live there are often lost as well.

Today people are working to reverse forest loss in the Great Lakes watershed. Timber companies are cutting trees in ways that are less harmful to forests. They also replant trees in areas that have been logged. The result is that forests around the Great Lakes are now expanding instead of shrinking.

Protecting Precious Wetlands Like forests, **wetlands** were also lost during the settlement of the Great Lakes region. A wetland is an area where the soil is usually wet all year. Examples are marshes, bogs, and swamps. Wetlands provide habitats for a wide variety of wildlife. They also help to control flooding during storms.

In the past, wetlands were viewed as worthless bogs. Over time, more than half of the wetlands in the region disappeared. Only in recent years did people begin to see the value of wetlands habitat.

Today, public and private groups are working to protect wetland habitats. One way is by creating nature preserves on existing wetlands. Another is by teaching landowners how to protect wetland areas. In some places, developers must create more than one acre of new wetland for every acre they destroy.

Population Pressures

The Great Lakes region has become densely populated. Each yellow dot below represents 2,500 people. The areas that are almost solid yellow have the most people. As the population has grown, forests and wetlands have disappeared. More habitats will be lost unless they are protected from development.

Population Density of the Great Lakes Region

• One dot represents 2,500 people.

Getting Water from a Well

This well in India draws large crowds every day. In many rural areas, the task of finding water falls to women. They often walk many miles each day to get water for their families.

4.7 Beginning to Think Globally

In this chapter, you read that the Great Lakes are the world's largest freshwater ecosystem. You saw how plants and animals in this ecosystem form a complex food web. You learned how pollution and invasive species are threatening the health of the Great Lakes. And you found out how people are working to clean up and preserve this large watershed.

Water Is Essential to Life Managing freshwater ecosystems is important around the world. All living things need water. About 70 percent of Earth's surface is covered by water. But nearly 98 percent of that water is too salty for human use. Of the remaining 2 percent that is fresh water, three fourths is frozen in ice caps. That leaves less than 1 percent of Earth's water to meet human needs.

People get fresh water from many sources. Some draw water from rivers, lakes, and streams. Others depend on wells that tap into underground water supplies. In still other places, people collect and store rainwater to meet their needs.

Not all fresh water is safe for human use. Of the more than 6 billion people in the world, at least 1 billion don't have a steady supply of clean, safe drinking water. Unsafe water creates huge health problems. Every day, 4,000 children die from diseases that could have been prevented by having clean water to drink. Every year, more than 2.2 million people die from diseases related to unsafe drinking water.

Water Shortages Are Increasing Every year, the number of people on Earth grows. But the supply of fresh water is not increasing. As a result, more than 1.6 billion people live in areas facing water shortages.

China is one of those countries. To meet the water needs of its large population, China is pumping large amounts of water out of underground supplies. However, these supplies are slowly shrinking. This is happening because more water is being pumped out than is replaced by rainfall each year. Also, some rivers in China are so polluted that their water can't be used to irrigate crops.

Competition for limited water supplies can cause conflict. Some rivers flow through many countries. When one country dams a river for irrigation water, it may reduce the amount of water flowing to countries downstream.

Egypt, for example, has a population of more than 81 million people. However, it receives almost no rainfall. Instead, Egyptians depend on the Nile River to meet all of their water needs. Before reaching Egypt, the Nile travels through several countries. If any of those countries reduced the flow of the Nile, Egypt could be starved for water. This result could be a water war.

Climate Change May Shrink Water Supplies In the last 25 years, Earth's climate has warmed slightly. Many scientists believe that this warming trend will continue. This change in climate may affect water supplies. Some areas might get less rainfall than they do today. Others might see more frequent floods.

If these changes occur, managing water supplies will become more important than ever. Countries with shortages will need to improve their water collection and storage methods. Those with too much water will need to improve their flood defenses. Think about these possible problems as you look at maps showing changes in the world's freshwater supplies in the next section.

A Thirsty World

Asia uses more water than any other continent, in part because it has such a large population. However, North Americans and Europeans use more water *per person* than people in other continents.

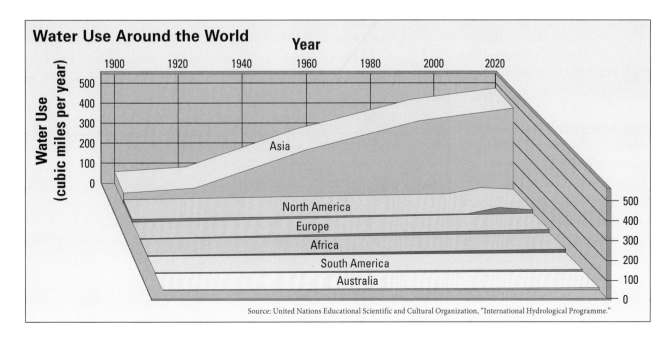

Water Use Around the World

Source: United Nations Educational Scientific and Cultural Organization, "International Hydrological Programme."

4.8 Global Connections

The maps show the world's average freshwater supplies for three different years. Each map shows the availability of water per person on six continents. The maps do not show the total amounts of water available in each year. The map for 2025 is based on population estimates for that year.

What factors might cause the changes in freshwater availability you see in the maps? Population is growing rapidly in places like India and Africa. But the amount of fresh water is not growing. So the same amount of water must be shared by far more people. Climate changes in the future may also reduce the amount of clean, fresh water available. In addition, some sources of fresh water, such as wells, have been polluted. These sources of water are no longer safe.

What concerns for the future can be drawn from the maps? The maps show that water shortages are likely to increase over time. This could lead to rising water costs. It could lead to less food production, since many crops require irrigation. Public health problems could also arise as people turn to less safe water supplies to survive.

How can people best use and manage the world's freshwater resources? People can do many things to better manage sources of fresh water. One is to reduce water pollution. Another is to find better ways to store and distribute existing water supplies. Using less water in homes and on farms can stretch limited supplies. So can recycling water so that it is used again and again.

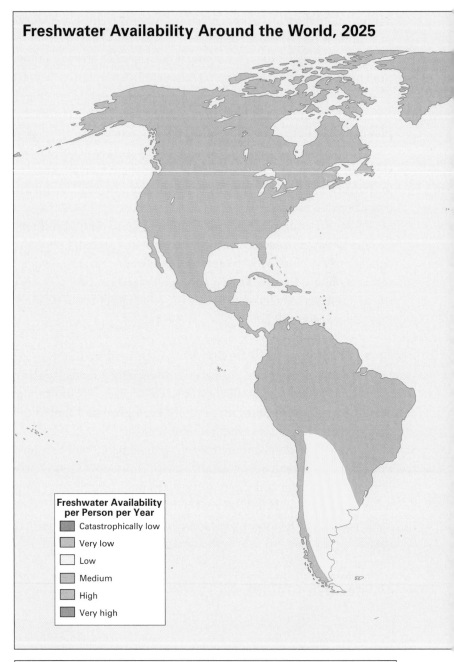

Freshwater Availability Around the World, 2025

Freshwater Availability per Person per Year
- Catastrophically low
- Very low
- Low
- Medium
- High
- Very high

1950

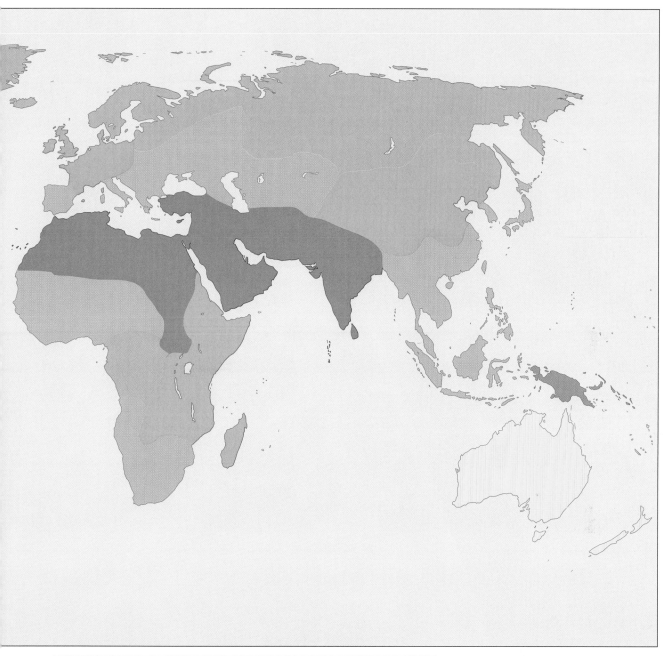

Source: Sustainable Development Networking Programme, "International Year of Freshwater."

1995

Urban Sprawl in North America: Where Will It End?

5.1 Introduction

Would you be surprised if you brought a picnic to a place called Hickory Woods, and there were no woods? Or if you took a drive to Partridge Farms, and there were no farms? What if you went for a walk through the Meadowlands and discovered that there were no meadows?

You might be confused at first. Then you would see what these places had in common: houses—lots and lots of houses. Hickory Woods, Partridge Farms, and the Meadowlands are all housing developments. Across North America, housing developments have been named after the types of land that were cleared in order to build new homes.

For many decades, urban development in the United States and Canada has been moving out from cities into **suburbs**. A suburb is an area of housing built at the edge of a city. Developers create suburbs by buying up land outside a city. They replace this open space with mile upon mile of housing tracts, shopping centers, and office parks. Often the only way to get from place to place in a suburban area is by car on traffic-clogged roads.

The rapid and often poorly planned spread of cities and suburbs is known as **urban sprawl**. In this chapter, you will learn why urban sprawl happens. You will see how it affects people and the environment. And you will find out how people in three North American cities have dealt with it.

Essential Question

How does urban sprawl affect people and the planet?

Most cities begin as a small, compact urban core, as shown in the center ring of this diagram. As more people move to the city, development pushes outward to form an urban fringe. Beyond this is an area of rural, or open, land. This is called the rural fringe. Keep this diagram in mind as you try to answer the Essential Question.

Graphic Organizer

Urban core

Urban fringe

Rural fringe

◀ Housing development in Las Vegas, Nevada

Stages of Urban Growth

This diagram shows how a city becomes a sprawling metropolitan area. The old "walking city" lies at the center. Over time, this urban core expands along rail lines and highways. The result is an urban fringe. Later growth pushes development out into the rural fringe.

5.2 The Geographic Setting

"Welcome to LA!" say signs in the Los Angeles International Airport. Most people seeing these signs are visitors. They have come to Los Angeles for business or to see the sights. But some are people who have come to stay. While growth has dwindled in recent years, the LA **metropolitan area** is still growing by more than 70,000 new residents a year. A metropolitan area is a major city and its surrounding suburbs.

Today 8 out of 10 people in the United States and Canada live in a metropolitan area. In the United States, New York City ranks first with more than 18 million people. In Canada, Toronto leads the way with more than 5 million residents. These two metropolitan areas have followed a similar pattern of growth.

The Old Walking City: The Urban Core The oldest Canadian and American cities were founded during colonial times. At that time, cities had to be small enough for people to get around on foot or by horse. Homes and workplaces were in one small area. Today that old "walking city" is a city's **urban core**. People often think of this urban core as their city's "downtown" or business district.

By the 1890s, many cities were bursting at their seams with people. Around that time, electric streetcars and commuter rail lines were developed. People began to build homes near these rail lines. They took trains or streetcars into the city center to work and shop. As a result, the urban core began to bulge outward along rail lines.

Suburbs Around the City: The Urban Fringe By the 1920s, cars were becoming part of American life. No longer did city dwellers have to live near a rail line to get to their jobs. They could buy a car and commute.

As cars became common, people began to build new housing areas farther away from the old urban core. In time, suburbs ringed most cities. These suburbs formed a new **urban fringe**.

As people moved out of the urban core, some businesses moved out, too. The loss of people and businesses led to decay in older city neighborhoods. Meanwhile, people in the suburbs built their own town centers. These new communities were complete with shops, businesses, theaters, and parks.

Where City Meets Country: The Rural Fringe Beyond the urban fringe lies an area with fewer people. Here, small towns mix with farms and open space. These less-developed areas form a **rural fringe** around a metropolitan area. This rural fringe is connected to the city by roads and highways.

As populations grow, more and more of the rural fringe is developed. New homes, schools, shopping centers, and business parks seem to spring up almost overnight. Some people see this growth as a sign of progress. Others see it as harmful urban sprawl. In this chapter, you will explore both points of view.

► Geoterms

metropolitan area a major population center made up of a large city and the smaller suburbs and towns that surround it

rural fringe the small towns, farms, and open spaces that lie just beyond a city's suburbs

suburb a developed area at the edge of a city that is mainly homes. Many suburbs also have stores and businesses.

urban core the older part of a big city. Often the urban core serves as the downtown or central business district of a city.

urban fringe the ring of small towns and suburbs that surround a big city

urban sprawl the rapid, often poorly planned spread of development from an urban area outward into rural areas

Urban Sprawl in Two Countries
Metropolitan areas are found across the United States and Canada. Most people in both countries now live in cities and suburbs. As urban areas grow, they tend to sprawl outward.

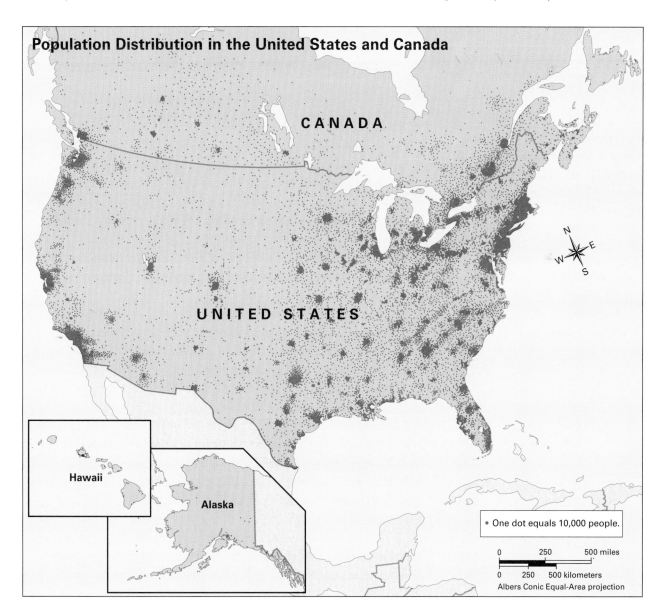

Population Distribution in the United States and Canada

CANADA

UNITED STATES

Hawaii

Alaska

• One dot equals 10,000 people.

0   250   500 miles

0   250   500 kilometers
Albers Conic Equal-Area projection

U.S. Farmland Converted to Developed Land, 1982–1997

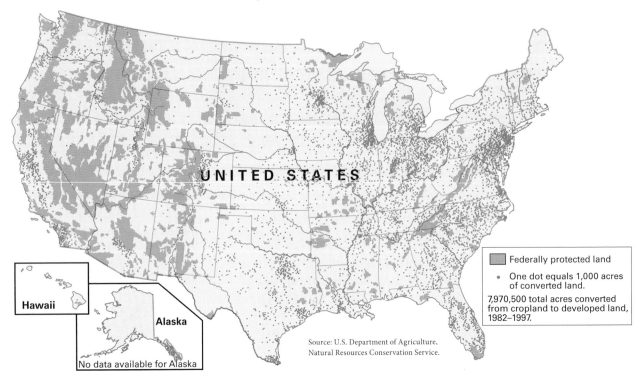

UNITED STATES

Hawaii

Alaska

No data available for Alaska

Federally protected land

• One dot equals 1,000 acres of converted land.

7,970,500 total acres converted from cropland to developed land, 1982–1997.

Source: U.S. Department of Agriculture, Natural Resources Conservation Service.

Urban Sprawl and Farmland

Between 1982 and 1997, the United States lost almost 7 million acres of farmland to urban sprawl. This is an area about the size of Maryland. Only about a tenth of Earth's land is suitable for farming. If sprawl continues, will there be enough land left to feed Earth's growing population?

5.3 The Case for and Against Urban Growth

Suppose a developer wants to build a housing development at the edge of a city. In many cities, a planning commission would need to approve the project. This body is made up of citizens chosen to guide a city's growth. The commissioners listen to people who support and oppose a project. Here are some of the arguments they might hear.

Urban Growth Creates Needed Homes Everyone knows that when populations grow, new homes are needed. The question is where and at what cost to families.

Those who favor growth argue that the best way to meet the need for housing is to develop empty land outside a city. Generally, land in rural areas is cheaper than city land. Building costs in the country are lower than in the city. This keeps new homes affordable. In addition, many people want homes outside of cities. They believe that suburbs are better places than cities to raise a family.

Pro-growth people say that urban growth has other benefits as well. New housing projects create jobs for construction workers. As people move into new homes, they spend money on things like furniture and garden supplies. All of this spending is good for local stores. The new homeowners also pay taxes. These taxes help fund roads, schools, and other city services.

Urban Sprawl Damages the Environment Everyone agrees that people need housing, say those who oppose urban sprawl. The question is where and at what cost to the environment.

These people argue that the worst way to meet the need for housing is to develop open spaces outside a city. Open spaces are not empty land. They are **habitats** for plants and animals. When land is developed, that habitat is lost and with it the wildlife that lived there. The National Wildlife Foundation warns that more than a thousand animal and plant species are in danger of dying out because of habitat loss to urban sprawl.

Anti-sprawl people say that urban sprawl creates other problems as well. When housing is spread out, people rely on cars for transportation. This creates traffic jams and air **pollution**. Urban sprawl can also hurt people living in small towns. They often see their taxes go up when nearby land is developed. The extra tax money is needed to pay for roads, schools, and other services required when a small town suddenly grows.

5.4 Portland, Oregon, 1973

The Willamette Valley in Oregon is 120 miles long and 25 to 40 miles wide. The valley has Oregon's richest farmland. More than 170 crops are grown there. Orchards produce pears, plums, apples, and nuts. Fields of sweet corn and green beans mix with colorful flowerbeds and vineyards. The Willamette Valley is not all farmland, though. Oregon's largest city, Portland, is located at its northern edge.

Growth Threatens the Willamette Valley Portland is known as the "City of Roses." Fragrant rose bushes fill its parks and gardens. Still, Portland is very much a big city. It has a downtown and many businesses. Its attractions include colleges, museums, and shopping areas. And, like all big cities, Portland has a lot of people.

It was Portland's growing population that first began to worry people in the 1960s and 1970s. They feared that urban sprawl would soon gobble up the farms and forests of the Willamette Valley.

A Difficult Decision: How Best to Grow? In 1973, Governor Tom McCall called on the state legislature to deal with this issue. "We are in dire need of a state land-use policy," McCall said. Oregon lawmakers agreed. But they weren't sure how best to control urban growth.

There were many options the lawmakers might have considered. One might have been to allow growth to continue, but with a condition. For each acre of land that was developed, they would require that another acre be set aside to be preserved as open space.

A second option might have been to create firm boundaries around cities. Once this was done, no new development would be allowed outside these boundaries.

A third option was to ban all development in some rural areas, such as the Willamette Valley. Growth could be allowed in other areas that did not seem so valuable.

Whatever lawmakers decided, one thing was clear. Their actions would affect the future of Oregon's people and its environment.

Portland's Natural Setting
The city of Portland lies at the north end of the Willamette Valley. In the distance you can see Mt. Hood. As Portland grew in the 1960s and 1970s, its urban fringe gave way to housing. People began to fear that the rest of the valley would soon be paved with homes and shopping malls.

5.5 Portland Plans for Smart Growth

In 1973, Oregon became the first state to create a set of **land use** planning laws. These laws promote an approach to land use planning known as *smart growth*. The basic idea of smart growth is to control sprawl by making better use of land that has already been developed.

Urban Growth Boundaries Limit Sprawl Smart growth in Oregon began with a law creating **urban growth boundaries**. An urban growth boundary is a legal border. It separates urban land from rural land. New development is allowed inside the growth boundary. But it is not allowed on rural land outside the boundary.

An urban growth boundary was drawn around the Portland metropolitan area. It included not only the city of Portland, but also several suburbs. To control growth inside this boundary, voters created a new regional government called Metro. Its main job is to plan growth inside the growth boundary.

Smart Growth in Portland
Portland is known for its smart growth policies. One of these policies calls for mixed-use developments like those shown here overlooking South Waterfront Park. Mixed use combines housing and business in one area.

Mixed Use Helps Portland to Grow Up, Not Out Oregon's land use planning laws have worked well. Today, Portland is a compact city with controlled growth. Its downtown area is friendly to pedestrians. It has hundreds of beautiful parks and open spaces. It also has a well-planned **public transit system**. Its buses and streetcars make it easy to get around without a car.

These improvements have attracted many new residents to Portland. To provide housing for more people, the city is developing up, not out. Older, run-down neighborhoods have been revived with new **mixed-use developments**. This is development that combines housing and businesses in one area. For example, a building might have shops and offices on the ground floor and apartments above.

Supporters of mixed-use development argue that it encourages people to live, work, and shop in one neighborhood. People can walk to jobs or shops instead of driving. This reduces traffic and air pollution. Opponents, however, argue that mixed-use development limits the kind of new homes that can be built. For people who want a big house on a large lot, a city apartment over a business is not their dream home.

Getting Around on MAX
Portland's light rail system is called the Metropolitan Area Express, or MAX. In 1986, MAX had 15 miles of track. By 2009, it had 38 miles of track. MAX connects downtown Portland to three suburbs and Portland's airport.

5.6 Toronto, Ontario, 1999

Toronto, Ontario, is Canada's largest metropolitan area. It is also its main business center. Toronto leads Canadian cities in printing and publishing. Television and movie production are important as well. With more than 5 million people, the city has been growing for decades. For a time, it managed this growth by stretching up. But Toronto soon began to sprawl out.

Building Up and Filling In Limits Sprawl Toronto has a long history. It began as a fur-trading post. In the 1800s, it became a factory town. Later still it developed into a banking center. But by the 1960s, its urban core was run down. Something had to be done to keep the downtown alive.

In 1965, Toronto announced a plan to renew its urban core. The plan encouraged **infill** over sprawl. Infill involves filling in empty or run-down parts of a city with new development. Building an apartment high-rise on an empty lot is an example of infill. So is building a shopping mall on the site of an old amusement park.

During the 1960s and 1970s, Toronto rebuilt its urban core. The new buildings included some of the world's tallest skyscrapers. These towers had offices, shops, museums, parking, and housing.

Rapid Growth on Toronto's Rural Fringe Toronto kept growing in the 1980s and 1990s. But instead of building up, it began to spread out. Urban sprawl took over farmland, forests, and wetlands. Traffic clogged suburban highways. Air pollution increased. Traffic and air quality both got worse as the years went by.

By 1999, officials in Toronto knew they had to do something to control sprawl. There were many ideas they considered. One was to reduce sprawl by encouraging smart growth ideas like mixed-use development. Another idea was to ban all growth in rural areas. A third was to allow a lot of growth in part of the city while limiting it in the rest. Whatever was decided would shape Toronto's future.

Urban Sprawl in Toronto
Toronto has been growing at a rapid pace for many years. By 2009, urban sprawl stretched for miles and miles beyond the city limits.

5.7 Toronto Plans for 30 Years of Growth

On May 27, 2002, the mayor of Toronto gave a speech about urban growth. "Toronto is a great city, and we want it to stay that way," he said. "Where we go from here depends on all of us." He then introduced a document known as the Official Plan. It contained a plan for controlling Toronto's growth for the next 30 years.

Future Land Use in Toronto

Toronto's Official Plan includes a map showing how land is to be used in the city. This part of the map shows the downtown area bordering Lake Ontario. Development will be limited in neighborhoods marked in yellow and orange. Mixed use is encouraged in red areas. Parks and open space are shown in green. The brown areas near the waterfront are marked for redevelopment.

Planning for Future Growth The Official Plan took three years to complete. The effort was led by Toronto's city council. The council heard ideas from people across the city. It also got advice from land use experts. The result was a plan that allows some growth in some places.

The Official Plan allows growth to continue in 25 percent of the city. Most areas targeted for growth are in the urban core. They include the old downtown area and the waterfront area on Lake Ontario. Growth is also allowed in four "centers" in outlying parts of the city. Public transportation is to be expanded to link these growth areas together.

In the remaining 75 percent of the city, development is to be limited. This area includes the city's residential neighborhoods. It also includes waterways, parks, and open space.

The Official Plan also lays out what kind of growth Toronto should encourage. New developments are to be mainly infill and mixed-use projects. Such projects will bring new homes, shops, and businesses into the urban core.

Concerns About Infill Supporters of the Official Plan believe it offers a sensible approach to controlling sprawl. But while infill sounds like a good idea, not everyone supports it. Developers raise concerns about its hidden costs. Such costs include the extra time and money needed to clean up abandoned sites. This work must be done before new development can begin. If a site is polluted with toxic chemicals, these costs can rise very quickly.

People living in neighborhoods marked for growth raise a different concern about infill. They worry that building new developments on empty lots will make the urban core more crowded.

5.8 Atlanta, Georgia, 1998

In 1996, Atlanta, Georgia, hosted the summer Olympic Games. People came from around the world to watch the events. They filled hotels and restaurants. They cheered the athletes in new stadiums and arenas. Few visitors, however, traveled outside the city. Only those who did could see why Atlanta has been called "the fastest-spreading human settlement in history."

Rapid Growth Leads to Traffic Jams During the 1990s, the Atlanta metropolitan area boomed. Atlanta led the nation in new jobs, homes, and highways. It also led the nation in urban sprawl. Hundreds of acres of forest were cleared each week to make room for new residents. Without controls on development, housing tracts pushed deep into the rural fringe.

The people who bought these new homes relied on cars to get around. Atlanta's commuters drove more miles every day than drivers anywhere else in the world. If you added up all the miles that Atlanta commuters drove in just one day, they would stretch all the way to the sun. There were traffic jams night and day.

Air Pollution Threatens Highway Funds All those cars on Atlanta's roads also led to air pollution. The air became so polluted that it caused asthma attacks and other health problems.

Atlanta's dirty air also violated the Clean Air Act. This is a federal, or national, law that sets limits on air pollution. In 1998, the federal government ordered Atlanta to meet the law's clean air standards. If it did not, Atlanta would lose federal highway funds. These are funds the federal government gives to cities to improve roads.

Atlanta had to make a decision. One option was to do nothing to control growth. This would mean giving up federal highway funds. Another was to continue growing but to create a regional transportation system. Such a system could cut pollution by getting people out of their cars. A third option was to limit sprawl in some areas while requiring mixed-use development in others. Over time, this option could also reduce car trips and air pollution.

Atlanta's Crowded Roads
Traffic jams are a daily event in the Atlanta area. All of this driving creates major air pollution problems. In 1998, 13 counties in the Atlanta region failed to meet the Clean Air Act. A plan was needed to cut pollution in the entire metropolitan area.

5.9 Atlanta Fights Pollution with Public Transit

In 1998, Roy Barnes was elected governor of Georgia. In his campaign, he promised to do something about the problems caused by sprawl. He made it clear, though, that he was not an enemy of development. "I'm no tree hugger," he said. "I'm a businessman who thinks you can't let your prosperity slip through your fingers."

A Regional Transportation Authority Is Born Governor Barnes wanted Atlanta to continue to grow. At the same time, he wanted to meet Clean Air Act standards. And so he focused on **public transit**.

Under Barnes' leadership, the state created the Georgia Regional Transportation Authority. This agency had three goals. First, reduce traffic jams. Second, reduce air pollution caused by cars. Third, reduce poorly planned development.

The Georgia Regional Transportation Authority works with other government agencies to get people out of their cars. One approach has been to promote mixed-use development. As you read, in mixed-use neighborhoods, people can walk to shops and jobs. Another has been to encourage people to walk or bike instead of drive. New bike trails and walking paths have been built.

In addition, the region's public transit system had been expanded. The Metropolitan Atlanta Rapid Transit Authority (MARTA) is a system of trains and bus lines. It serves the entire Atlanta region. New rail lines have been built. A regional subway system has been expanded. New buses and bus routes have been added. The new buses don't pollute the air as much as older ones.

Atlanta Continues to Grow

The growth of public transit has helped Atlanta meet federal air-quality standards. But it has not slowed growth.

Urban sprawl remains a hot issue. Many people think the region should do more to control sprawl. Others say that Atlanta is doing just fine. They point out that there is new mixed-use development for those who want it. But they also think that people who want to buy new houses on the rural fringe should be allowed to do so.

Rails and Trails in Atlanta

Rather than slowing growth, Atlanta is trying to reduce air pollution with a better transit system. This map shows major rail lines. It also shows existing and future hiking and biking trails. As more people use rails and trails, traffic jams should decrease.

5.10 Beginning to Think Globally

In this chapter, you learned about urban sprawl. You learned that cities grow outward. They expand from the urban core to the urban fringe to the rural fringe. You visited three metropolitan areas in the United States and Canada. And you saw how those areas are trying to deal with growth.

Cities Continue to Sprawl The United States and Canada are still growing. As their populations increase, so does their need for housing. Even though sprawl isn't good for the environment, development continues to push into the rural fringe.

As you have seen, there are many reasons why sprawl continues. Land and building costs are cheaper in the rural fringe than in the urban core. Some people prefer suburban homes to city apartments. Others don't like laws that limit where people could choose to live.

Sprawl Is a Worldwide Problem Cities around the world are struggling with urban sprawl. The Indian city of Mumbai (formerly known as Bombay) is a good example. In 1950, Mumbai had barely 3 million people. By 2007, the city's population had grown to more than 20 million. All those people could no longer fit into the old urban core. By 2025, Mumbai's population is expected to rise to 26 million. The only way it will be able to house so many people is by sprawling outward.

Mumbai is not alone. Over the last century, the percentage of people living in urban areas has risen rapidly. In 1900, about 14 percent of people worldwide lived in cities. By the end of 2008, roughly half of the world's population was living in urban areas. Think about this as you look at the map of urban areas around the world in the next section.

Urban Sprawl in India
Urban sprawl looks different in different parts of the world. In the urban fringe of Mumbai, India, new high rises have sprung up to house the wealthy. Nearby are shantytowns where poor people live.

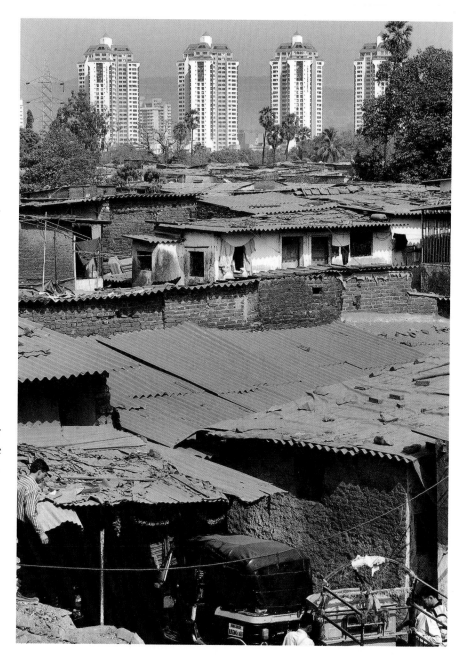

5.11 Global Connections

This map shows metropolitan areas around the world. Cities with more than 5 million people are marked with large black dots. The bar graph shows how the populations of six cities have grown over time.

Why might some regions have more metropolitan areas than others? Wealthy regions tend to have more large cities than poor ones. That's because most jobs in wealthy countries are found in cities. Climate, landforms, and vegetation zones also play a role. There aren't many big cities in extremely cold or arid regions. Nor are there many urban areas in mountains or rainforests.

Why are there so many cities with more than 5 million people in Asia? The simple answer is this: Asia has more people than any other continent. More than 3 billion people live in Asia. Together, China and India are home to 4 out of 10 of the world's people. Also, the economies of many Asian countries are changing. They are shifting from farming to manufacturing and trade. Such economic activity generally takes place in urban settings. As a result, metropolitan areas are growing rapidly in Asia.

What special problems might urban sprawl create for poor countries? Poor countries often have little control over how their cities grow. People moving to a city simply build homes wherever they find space. The governments of such countries lack money to provide growing cities with basic services. These services include clean water, paved roads, electricity, sewers, medical care, and schools.

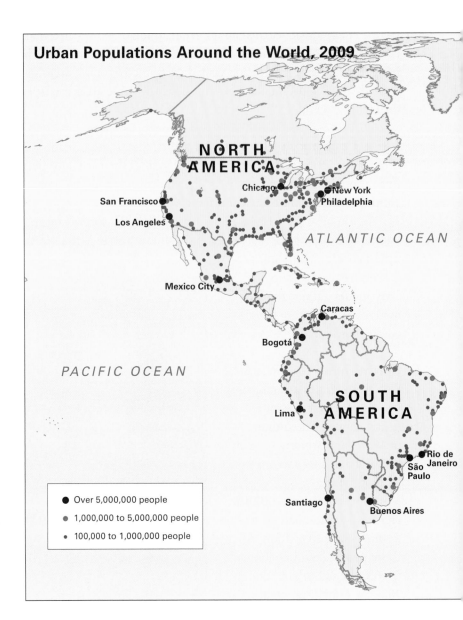

Urban Populations Around the World, 2009

- ● Over 5,000,000 people
- ● 1,000,000 to 5,000,000 people
- ● 100,000 to 1,000,000 people

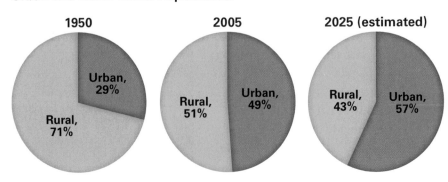

Urban and Rural World Populations

1950 — Urban, 29%; Rural, 71%
2005 — Rural, 51%; Urban, 49%
2025 (estimated) — Rural, 43%; Urban, 57%

Populations in Six World Cities

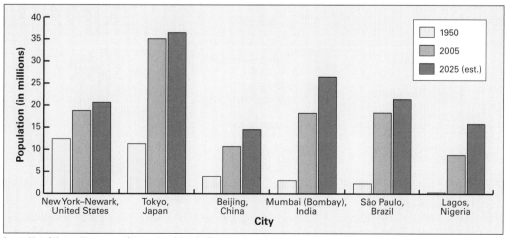

Source: United Nations Department of Economic and Social Affairs, Population Division.

Topography of Grand Canyon National Park (detail)

	River		Roads		Index contour
	Intermittent stream		Buildings	**BM 4844**	Elevation above sea level
	Trail		Campground	★	Tour stop
	Picnic area		Contour lines	Ⓐ←●→Ⓑ	Elevation profile locator

0 _____ 1 _____ 2 miles

0 _____ 1 _____ 2 kilometers

Distance between contour lines = 80 feet
Distance between index contours = 400 feet

Grand Canyon National Park

Arizona

National Parks: Saving the Natural Heritage of the U.S. and Canada

6.1 Introduction

Imagine standing on the rim of the Grand Canyon. You are looking out at one of the world's most spectacular sights. The canyon is enormous—18 miles across at its widest point. Its colorful walls look like an artist painted them in shades of red, orange, yellow, and green. A mile below, the Colorado River winds like a ribbon along the bottom of the canyon. You feel lucky that this special place is open to anyone who wants to visit it.

The Grand Canyon is available to visit because it is a **national park**. National parks are large areas of land that governments have set aside in order to preserve them in their natural state. Today there are 58 national parks in the United States and 42 in Canada. Most of them were created to protect land and wildlife because of their rarity, beauty, or other qualities. Some parks preserve bits of history as well. Often a single park serves many purposes. Grand Canyon National Park is a good example. Besides the majestic canyon, the park boasts abundant wildlife and plants. It also has ruins of ancient Native American pueblos, or villages.

In this chapter, you will explore some of North America's national parks. To do so, you will use **topographic maps**. These are large-scale maps that show the landforms and other surface features of an area, both physical and human. Their curved lines, called contour lines, show different elevations. The maps will help you understand the special features of each park.

Essential Question

What features make national parks special and worth preserving?

This map legend is from a topographic map of a national park. This type of map uses symbols and contour lines to show a region's physical and human features. Keep the symbols on this legend in mind as you try to answer the Essential Question.

Graphic Organizer

Symbol	Feature	Symbol	Feature
	River	Campground	Campground
	Intermittent stream		Contour lines
	Trail		Index contour
Picnic Area	Picnic area	BM 4844	Elevation
	Roads	★	Tour stop
	Buildings	A B	Elevation profile locator

Grand Canyon National Park

Arizona

0   1   2 miles
0   1   2 kilometers

Distance between contour lines = 80 feet
Distance between index contours = 400 feet

◀ Topographic map of a section of Grand Canyon National Park

Flora in Yellowstone National Park

Fauna in Yellowstone National Park

6.2 The Geographic Setting

When fur trappers explored the Rocky Mountains in the 1800s, they came across a remarkable place. They saw pools of water so hot that they were covered with clouds of steam. They found puddles of boiling mud that sputtered and spattered day and night. They saw springs called **geysers** that threw jets of hot water into the air. Some of the geysers erupted on regular schedules. Others would suddenly blow sky high with no warning. The trappers called this strange landscape "the place where hell bubbles up." Today we know it as Yellowstone National Park.

At first, people thought the trappers' stories of boiling springs were just "tall tales." In 1870, the government sent an expedition to explore the area. It turned out that the tales were all true.

Yellowstone is a unique place. It has about 300 geysers. This is two thirds of all the geysers in the world. It also has more than 10,000 hot springs, mud pots, and steam vents.

Yellowstone Becomes the First National Park In the 1800s, more and more people moved west. As Americans turned wilderness into farms and ranches, some people began to talk about protecting Yellowstone as a public park.

The idea of a national park for the public was new. European cities had public gardens. But no country had ever set aside a large area of wilderness for its citizens to visit and enjoy.

In 1872, Congress passed a law creating Yellowstone National Park. It was the first national park in the world. Over time, Americans created more national parks. The national park movement eventually spread to Canada and other countries.

Parks Protect Special Places for Future Generations National parks have been created to protect many different places. Some parks preserve unique landforms and bodies of water. Others protect unusual **flora,** or plant life. Some provide homes for rare **fauna,** or animal life. And some preserve historic reminders of the past.

The movement to set aside special places as parks was led by people called **conservationists**. Probably the best-known American conservationist is John Muir. Muir was born in Scotland, and his family moved to the United States when he was 11. As a young man, he suffered an injury that left him temporarily blind. When his sight returned, he vowed to turn his eyes to nature. He walked across much of the American West. On that journey, he fell in love with the West's plains, mountains, and forests.

Muir spent most of his life trying to preserve beautiful wild places as parks. "Everybody needs beauty as well as bread," he wrote, "places to play in and pray in, where nature may heal and give strength to body and soul alike." Today many people remember him as "The Father of the National Parks." In this chapter, you will learn more about the special features of several national parks.

► Geoterms

conservationist someone who works to protect the beauty and natural resources of the environment from destruction or pollution

fauna all the animal life in a particular region

flora all the plant life in a particular region

topographic map a map that uses contour lines and symbols to show a region's physical and human features. These features may include hills, valleys, rivers, lakes, roads, trails, and buildings.

Three Views of the Grand Canyon

This photograph looks out over the Grand Canyon from near Maricopa Point on the West Rim. The ship-shaped rock formation at its center is known as the Battleship. The section of topographic map below the photo shows this same feature. It also shows Bright Angel Trail, which leads down Garden Creek to the canyon floor. The elevation profile below the map shows this same area from a different point of view. It traces changes in elevation from Maricopa Point to a ridge near Pipe Spring.

6.3 Waterton-Glacier International Peace Park

About 10,000 years ago, huge **glaciers** covered the tops of the Rocky Mountains and slid down their slopes. A glacier is a large, slow-moving mass of ice. Because of their enormous size and weight, glaciers act like bulldozers. They scrape and reshape the land as they move. Almost everywhere you look in Waterton-Glacier International Peace Park, you can see strange and wonderful shapes carved by glaciers.

Two Parks into One Waterton-Glacier International Peace Park unites two parks, one on each side of the border that divides the United States and Canada. This area was once home to Kootenai and Blackfoot Indians. Both tribes fished the mountain rivers and hunted herds of buffalo. During the 1800s, European settlers arrived. The newcomers began clearing land for farms and ranches. In 1895, the Blackfoot sold their homeland to the United States.

By that time, many people in both the United States and Canada wanted to protect some wilderness areas as parks. In 1895, Canada set aside the Waterton Lakes area as a park. In 1910, the U.S. Congress created Glacier National Park. The two countries joined the parks in 1932 to create the world's first international park. It was called a peace park in honor of the long friendship between the two countries.

Natural Attractions and History Waterton-Glacier park is notable for a number of physical and human features. To begin with, the park straddles the **Continental Divide**. The Continental Divide is a ridgeline along a chain of mountains stretching from Mexico to Canada and Alaska. Rivers on the west side of the divide run toward the Pacific Ocean. Rivers on the east side flow toward the Atlantic Ocean and the Gulf of Mexico.

One of the most popular things to do in Glacier is to drive along Going-to-the-Sun Road. This highway links a valley on the east side of the divide and a valley on the west side. Along the drive, the road climbs through a spectacular mountain pass.

Driving the highway is a good way to experience the different **climates** on each side of the divide. On the west side, the weather is mild, with a lot of rainfall. Here you see cedar and hemlock forests, like those along the Pacific coast. On the east side, the climate is colder and drier. Forests of spruce, fir, and pine are common.

As you might expect, glaciers are one of the park's main features. In fact, Waterton-Glacier park is home to 26 glaciers. It is unusual to find glaciers so far south in the Rocky Mountains.

Waterton Lakes park is famous for its rich diversity of fauna and flora. Here you might see bighorn sheep, moose, black bears, and wolves. The park protects prairie grasslands, mountain forests, and more than 900 types of wildflowers.

The park is also rich in history. Waterton Lakes has two national historic sites. One site is the first oil well in western Canada. The other is the Prince of Wales Hotel, which opened on July 25, 1927.

Sperry Glacier

Mountain goat

Lake Ellen Wilson

Topography of Waterton-Glacier International Peace Park (detail)

Lake

River

Intermittent stream

Cascades/ falls

Glacier/ snowfield

Continental Divide

Trail

Roads

Buildings

Campground

Picnic area

Contour lines

Index contour

Elevation

★ Tour stop

Distance between contour lines = 80 feet
Distance between index contours = 400 feet

0   1   2 miles
0   1   2 kilometers

Glacier National Park

Montana

Sand dunes

Green Gables house

Red sandstone cliffs

6.4 Prince Edward Island National Park

It was broad daylight when Anne awoke and sat up in bed....
For a moment she could not remember where she was. First
came a delightful thrill, as something very pleasant; then a
horrible remembrance. This was Green Gables and they didn't
want her because she wasn't a boy!

Maybe you recognize this scene. It is from *Anne of Green Gables*, a novel about an orphan named Anne Shirley. At about the age of 11, Anne came to live with an elderly couple in Green Gables, a house on Prince Edward Island in Canada.

The book's author, Lucy Maud Montgomery, knew the island well because she had grown up there. A local farm gave her the inspiration for the house she called Green Gables. Today, Green Gables house is just one of the attractions that brings visitors from all over the world to Prince Edward Island National Park.

A Fragile Island Environment Prince Edward Island has a fragile environment. Along part of its shore, ocean waves have carved steep cliffs into the red sandstone. Forests of beech, sugar maple, yellow birch, and red oak were once found on the island. Today there are **evergreens** such as fir, spruce, and tamarack.

More than a thousand years before Europeans reached North America, the Micmac Indians lived on Prince Edward Island. They called the island Epekwitk, which means "resting on the waves."

Between about 1720 and 1911, French and then English settlers made Prince Edward Island their home. In their eagerness to build homes and make a living, the settlers cleared the forest from more than half the island. They cut down trees for farming, exporting timber, and shipbuilding. In 1937, the Canadian government created Prince Edward Island National Park to protect and preserve the delicate environment of a portion of the island.

Old Settlements and Moving Dunes Visitors come to Prince Edward Island National Park to explore its natural and historical heritage. At Green Gables they can see how people lived on the island in the late 1800s. They can wander through old homes of early settlers.

Visitors to the park can also spot many types of birds and rare plants. There are marshes, woods, and sandy beaches to explore. Migrating sand dunes draw visitors to the park's north shore. A dune is a hill of sand that has been piled up by the wind. A migrating sand dune is one that moves. On Prince Edward Island, the winds are slowly driving the dunes from the edge of the beach inland.

Seeing the dunes move, over a period of months and years, is like watching nature playing a game of leapfrog. The island's migrating dunes have covered up parts of forests, killing the trees. As they move on, they reveal a "skeleton forest" of trees that were previously buried.

Topography of Prince Edward Island National Park

Legend:

- 〰 River
- 〰 Trail
- ▤ Roads
- ■ Building
- ⋀ Campground
- ⊤ Navigational beacon
- ▦ Park
- 〰 Contour lines
- *100* Index contour
- ★ Tour stop

Prince Edward Island National Park

0 — 3 — 6 miles
0 — 3 — 6 kilometers

Distance between contour lines = 100 feet
Distance between index contours = 100 feet

Gulf of St. Lawrence

Cavendish Sandspit
Cavendish Beach
New London Bay
Cavendish
Green Gables
Orby Head
North Rustico
North Rustico Harbour
Rustico Island
Rustico Bay
Brackley Beach
Brackley Bay
Covehead Bay
Cape Stanhope
Ross Lane Beach
Stanhope Beach
Dalvay
Stanhope
Tracadie Bay

Trout River
Hunter River
Wheatley River
Black River
Winter River

Hunter River
Winslow

West River
Clyde River
North River
Hillsborough River

DeSable River

Charlottetown
Cornwall
Stratford

Bonshaw

West River

Hillsborough Bay

Northumberland Strait

N W E S

Half Dome

El Capitan

Yosemite Falls

6.5 Yosemite National Park

High in the Sierra Mountains of California is a valley called Yosemite. It was a favorite camping site of the conservationist John Muir. One night in the late 1800s, a fierce thunderstorm hit the valley. Legend has it that Muir climbed to the top of a tall Douglas fir tree to watch as lightning forked across the dark sky. Muir could easily have been killed as he swayed in the howling winds. Luckily, he survived to see his beloved camping ground become Yosemite National Park.

A Gold Rush, Miners, and Tourists The first people in Yosemite were Miwok Indians. They roamed the valley for thousands of years before Europeans arrived. The park was named after a Miwok tribe.

In 1849, Europeans discovered gold in the foothills of the Sierra Nevada. Thousands of miners rushed in, hoping to get rich. In their eagerness to find gold, they cleared forests. They polluted streams and rivers. They hunted animals for food until many were in danger of disappearing. The miners also killed Miwok who did not flee the area.

Meanwhile, word spread about the beauty of Yosemite Valley. Tourist began to visit. They came on foot, on horseback, and by stagecoach. People built hotels. They planted orchards.

Led by John Muir, conservationists appealed to Congress to protect the valley and the land around it. In 1890, Congress agreed to create Yosemite National Park. It was the nation's third national park.

Granite Domes and Giant Trees Rounded mountains and tall, pointy rock towers circle Yosemite Valley. Millions of years of glacial activity created these amazing rock walls.

One of the most famous features rising above the valley floor is called Half Dome. Once it was a huge granite mountain with a rounded top. Long, long ago, a moving glacier sliced the mountain in two. The ice left just half of the dome behind, with a sheer 2,200-foot cliff.

El Capitan is a favorite wall for experienced rock climbers. This 3,600-foot-high block of granite forms the north wall of the valley. Climbers from all over the world come to Yosemite to climb "The Captain." A few climb the incredibly steep cliff in less than 24 hours. Others take a week or two to make their way to the top.

Yosemite Falls is one of the most photographed attractions in the park. It is really three connected waterfalls. Together, they drop almost 2,500 feet from the valley's rim to its floor. Yosemite Falls is the highest waterfall in North America and among the tallest in the world.

The park's fauna includes California bighorn sheep, coyotes, golden eagles, and black bears. Among its flora is the mariposa lily, a white flower that resembles a butterfly. The park also boasts groves of sequoia trees. Giant sequoias can be up to 30 feet around and more than 300 feet tall. They are the largest of all trees on Earth. They are also among the oldest living things. A tree known as Grizzly Giant in Yosemite's Mariposa Grove is believed to be at least 2,700 years old.

Topography of Yosemite National Park (detail)

Legend:

River	Campground
Intermittent stream	Contour lines
Trail	Index contour
Picnic area	Elevation
Roads	★ Tour stop
Building	

Yosemite National Park

California

0   0.5   1 mile

0   0.5   1 kilometer

Distance between contour lines = 40 feet
Distance between index contours = 200 feet

Mt. McKinley

Polar bears at Wapusk Park

Alligator in Everglades Park

6.6 Peaks, Bears, and a Water Wilderness

You have read about two national parks and one international park in North America. There are many other parks to explore in the United States and Canada. Each has its own special attractions. Here is a sampling of three very different national parks.

Denali National Park Alaska's Denali National Park is home to Mt. McKinley. More than 20,000 feet tall, Mt. McKinley is the highest mountain in North America. The mountain was originally called Denali, an Indian word meaning "The Great One" or "The High One." It was renamed for President William McKinley in 1896.

Mt. McKinley is not the only mountain in Denali. The park includes other impressive mountains in the Alaska Range. Glaciers cover many of the tallest peaks.

Cars are not allowed in most of the park. Instead, visitors tour Denali in big green park buses. The bus drivers are very good at spotting wildlife. On a good summer day, visitors might see grizzly bears, moose, caribou, beaver, and bald eagles.

Wapusk National Park Wapusk National Park is Canada's 37th national park. The name Wapusk is a Cree Indian word that means "white bear." It's a good name for this park. Wapusk National Park was created to protect one of the world's largest known polar bear denning areas. A denning area is a place where mother bears give birth to their cubs each spring.

Wapusk is not an easy park to visit. It is located in northern Manitoba, far from any road. Much of the park is **tundra**. The ground freezes hard in winter. In summer, it becomes a swamp.

The park is home to beluga whales, hundreds of thousands of birds, and a wide variety of wildflowers. But its most important animals are bears. Every year, around 100 pregnant polar bears come to the park to dig dens in the damp earth. Here they give birth to their cubs.

Everglades National Park A tall, long-necked bird called a great egret stands with one leg drawn up in the shallow water of a river. On the bank, an alligator is sunning itself. Nothing moves. Suddenly, with a flip of its tail, the alligator slides into the water. The egret flies off in a rush. Then everything is still again in Everglades National Park.

Everglades National Park spans the southern tip of the Florida peninsula. It is the only North American preserve with a **humid subtropical** climate. A preserve is an area where animals are protected from hunting. Summers here are hot and rainy, while winters are mild.

Everglades Park contains many different environments. It has ponds, rivers, and swamps. It also has sawgrass prairies and pineland forests. These environments support a great variety of birds and animals. The park is known for its large wading birds, like the spoonbill, the wood stork, the great blue heron, and the egret. It is also the only place in the world where alligators and crocodiles live near one another.

6.7 Beginning to Think Globally

As you have read, the United States was the first country in the world to set aside wilderness areas as national parks. The idea of protecting land in parks soon spread to Canada. People from all over the world come to both countries to visit national parks. Some of these parks are known for their scenic beauty. Others are visited for their flora and fauna.

Threats to National Parks The United States has led the movement to preserve wilderness areas. However, putting land in a park does not guarantee that it will be preserved from harm.

Many parks face threats from outside their boundaries. Air pollution, for example, drifts into parks from other areas. Great Smoky Mountains National Park spans Tennessee and North Carolina. Air pollution from nearby power plants is harming plants and wildlife there.

Local development can also hurt parks. Water levels are dropping in the Everglades because people are taking too much water away from the rivers that feed the park. The water that does reach the park is often polluted with **sewage** and **toxic waste**.

Loving Parks to Death Popular parks are also in danger of being loved to death. Large numbers of visitors are hard on parks. Their cars cause pollution. Their feet wear away fragile soil. Careless campers sometimes litter areas with trash or start fires.

Parks rich in natural resources face other threats. People eager to use those resources may pressure governments to open parks to farming, logging, mining, or oil drilling.

Around the world, lands set aside for parks or wildlife face similar threats. Think about these threats as you look at preserved land around the world in the next section.

Air Quality in the Great Smokies

Air pollution is a major problem in many national parks. These images are of Great Smoky Mountains National Park on a clear and a polluted day. Factories and cars outside parks create pollution that is carried by wind over the parks. The resulting haze and smog can destroy the beautiful views that people come to see. Air pollution can also harm a park's flora and fauna.

6.8 Global Connections

The map shows amounts of land preserved for parks and wildlife around the world. Some of these areas are preserved as national parks. Some are protected as national forests or wilderness areas. Some are set aside as special preserves for rare or unique flora and fauna.

What problems make it hard for countries to set land aside for parks? In many countries, the cost of creating parks may be a problem. Poor countries may decide they are better off spending their money on things their citizens need more than parks. If a country lacks schools, parks may look like a luxury it cannot afford.

What challenges do countries face in managing lands already set aside? Often the biggest challenge is finding the right balance between preserving and using land. Some people argue that preserved land should be closed to all uses. They believe this is the best way to protect special places. Others feel just as strongly that people should be able to use and enjoy protected lands. They believe that this is the best way to build public support for parks. Balancing these two views is not easy.

Has the world done a good job of setting aside unique lands for preservation? Thousands of special areas have been preserved around the world. Still, many people think we can and must do better. The world is getting more crowded year by year, they argue. Unless we act now to protect more land, many other special places may be lost forever.

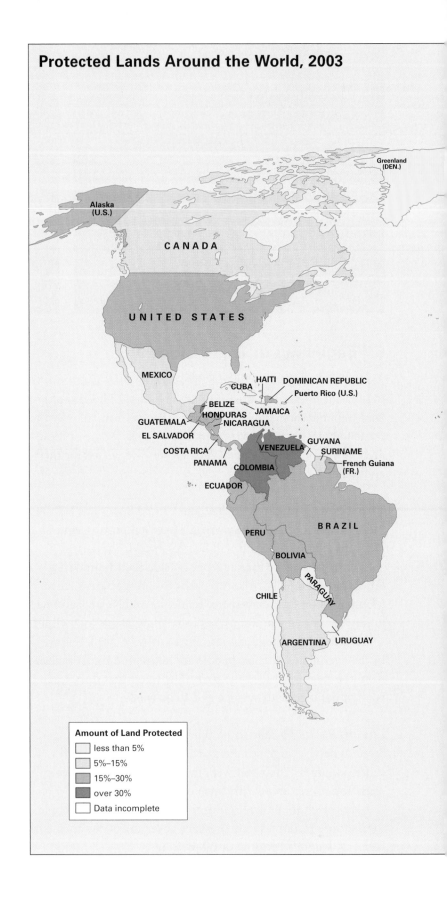

Protected Lands Around the World, 2003

Amount of Land Protected
- less than 5%
- 5%–15%
- 15%–30%
- over 30%
- Data incomplete

Source: World Resources Institute, EarthTrends: The Environmental Information Portal.

Consumption Patterns in the United States: The Impact of Living Well

7.1 Introduction

Americans are eager consumers. They buy and use a lot of goods and services. Shopping centers in the United States offer consumers a huge variety of products. Supermarkets are filled with foods for every taste. Car dealers tempt buyers with row upon row of shiny cars. Meanwhile, the Internet has turned home computers into a virtual shopping mall.

Americans have made **consumption** a way of life. Consumption means the using up of goods or services. Some goods, like food, can be consumed only once. Others, like clothing, can be used again and again until they are worn out.

The average American spends thousands of dollars each year on personal consumption. This includes spending on everything from food and clothes to gas and rent. This amount is typical for people living in **developed countries**. These are wealthy countries like the United States and Canada. But it is more than most people in **developing countries** earn in a year. These are poor countries like Mexico and India.

In this chapter, you will read about consumption patterns in the United States. You will discover how they compare with those of other countries. And you will read about the impact of American consumption on the planet.

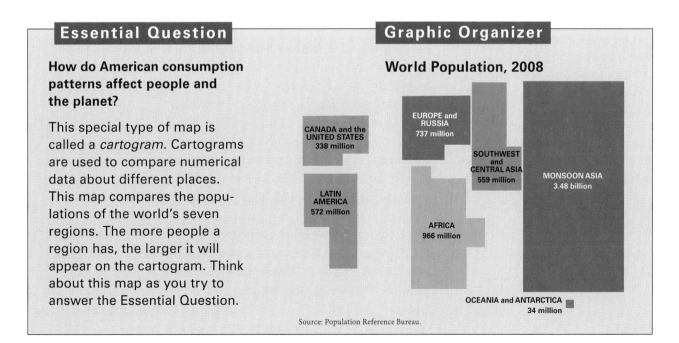

Essential Question

How do American consumption patterns affect people and the planet?

This special type of map is called a *cartogram*. Cartograms are used to compare numerical data about different places. This map compares the populations of the world's seven regions. The more people a region has, the larger it will appear on the cartogram. Think about this map as you try to answer the Essential Question.

Graphic Organizer

World Population, 2008

CANADA and the UNITED STATES
338 million

LATIN AMERICA
572 million

EUROPE and RUSSIA
737 million

SOUTHWEST and CENTRAL ASIA
559 million

MONSOON ASIA
3.48 billion

AFRICA
966 million

OCEANIA and ANTARCTICA
34 million

Source: Population Reference Bureau.

◀ A crowded shopping mall in Syracuse, New York

7.2 The Geographic Setting

In 2009, the United States had a population of more than 300 million people. This made it the third most populated country in the world. But it was still much smaller than the two largest countries, China and India. They each had a population of more than 1 billion people. Even so, the United States consumed far more than either China or India. This difference was the result of many factors. The most important, however, was the countries' different levels of development.

Consumption Depends on Levels of Development The United States is one of the world's developed, or wealthy, countries. Today there are more than 30 developed countries around the world. Most countries in Western Europe belong to this group. So do Japan, Canada, Australia, and New Zealand.

People in developed countries live well compared to most of the world. Most live in urban areas and work in factories or offices. Their governments provide them with many benefits. These include public schools, fire protection, and safe drinking water. Most workers in developed countries earn good wages. They can afford to consume a lot of things.

In contrast, there are more than 150 developing countries in the world today. These are countries that are still building their economies. This group includes most of the countries in Asia, Africa, and Latin America. Most of these countries have too few industries to provide good jobs for their people. Many also lack a strong and stable government.

People in developing countries are more likely to live in rural areas and work on farms. Their governments provide them with only limited benefits. They may not have access to good schools or safe drinking water. Most of these people earn low wages. As a result, their consumption may be quite limited.

Per Capita GDP Is One Measure of Development There are many ways to measure a country's level of development. One is to look at how many years of schooling people in the country have. Another is to look at how long its people live.

The most common measure of development is based on a country's **gross domestic product,** or **GDP.** This is the total value of goods and services that a country produces in a year. Goods are things that are produced for sale or use. Food, clothing, and cars are all goods. Services are tasks done by some people for other people. Teaching is a service. So is repairing a car or a computer.

A country's level of development depends on its **per capita** GDP. Per capita means "per person." Per capita GDP is calculated by dividing a country's total GDP by its population. The result is a rough measure of how rich or poor a country is. The United States has a high per capita GDP. This means that it is a wealthy country. This fact shapes how much Americans consume year by year.

Gross Domestic Product in Six Countries, 2008

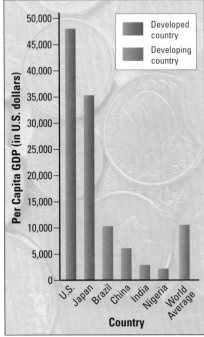

Source: Central Intelligence Agency.

Levels of Development

This bar graph compares per capita GDP in six countries. Per capita GDP is the value of goods and services produced per person in a country in a year. Developed countries have a high per capita GDP. People in those countries have more money to spend on consumer goods. As a result, they consume more.

▶ Geoterms

consumption the using up of goods and services. This term is also used to describe the purchase and use of goods and services by consumers.

developed country a wealthy country with an advanced economy. Developed countries have many industries and provide a comfortable way of life for most of their people.

developing country a poorer country with a less advanced economy. In general, developing countries are trying to increase their industries and improve life for their people.

gross domestic product (GDP) the total value of goods and services produced in a country in a year

per capita by or for each person. A per capita figure is calculated by dividing the total amount of something by the number of people in a place.

Resources Help Development

As this map shows, the United States has many natural resources. It has fertile farmland and vast forests. It is rich in minerals and fossil fuels. Over time, Americans have used these resources to develop the United States into one of the world's richest countries.

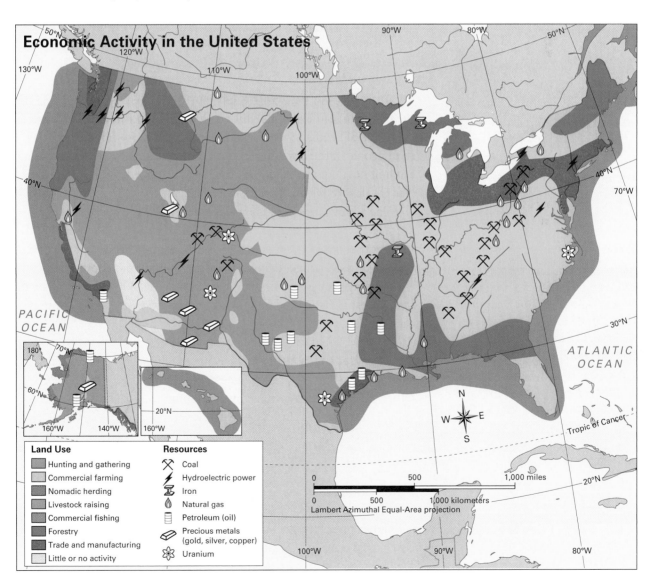

Economic Activity in the United States

Land Use
- ▨ Hunting and gathering
- ▨ Commercial farming
- ▨ Nomadic herding
- ▨ Livestock raising
- ▨ Commercial fishing
- ▨ Forestry
- ▨ Trade and manufacturing
- ▨ Little or no activity

Resources
- ✗ Coal
- ⚡ Hydroelectric power
- ⚖ Iron
- ◊ Natural gas
- ⬛ Petroleum (oil)
- ⬗ Precious metals (gold, silver, copper)
- ✿ Uranium

Lambert Azimuthal Equal-Area projection

More Than Enough Food

Food is plentiful in the United States. Supermarkets offer a wide range of foods from around the world.

7.3 Food Consumption Patterns

Imagine a wealthy diner sitting down to eat in a fancy restaurant. The table is set with fresh flowers and fine china. The food looks as good as it smells and tastes. Outside, however, another person stands in the cold, dressed in rags, and has not eaten all day. These two people represent the world's rich and poor countries. As your mental image suggests, such countries are likely to have different food consumption patterns.

Enough for All, But Some Go Hungry There is enough food on the planet to feed everyone. But much of that food stays in the developed world. People in rich countries consume more **calories** per day than people in the developing world. Calories are a measure of the amount of energy in food. On average, adults need about 2,700 calories per day to live healthy lives.

The average person in many developed countries consumes an average of about 3,300 calories a day. This is more than enough food to meet their nutritional needs. Meanwhile, many people in the developing world do not get enough to eat. In some of the poorer countries, average consumption per person is about 2,400 calories a day. In the poorest parts of Africa, half of the population goes to bed hungry each night.

Poverty Leads to Hunger As you read, hunger is not caused by a worldwide shortage of food. The developed world produces more food than it can consume. Many developing countries also produce enough food to feed their people. However, poor people in both rich and poor countries may not earn enough money to buy that food.

India, for example, has the largest number of people living in poverty in the world. It also has the largest number of hungry people. Farmers in India produce enough food to feed the entire population. But many of them export their crops to other countries. There they get higher prices for their crops than they would at home. Higher crop prices are good for Indian farmers. However, they may mean that poor Indians have less to eat.

7.4 Oil Consumption Patterns

Picture morning rush hour in any city in the developed world. The streets are filled with gas-guzzling cars, motorcycles, and buses. Now picture that same scene in a city in the developing world. You will still see lots of cars, buses, and motorcycles. But most people are riding bicycles or walking to work.

As these mental images suggest, oil consumption follows a pattern similar to food. Oil is a **fossil fuel** that has many uses. It is refined into gasoline. It is used to make asphalt to cover roads. Oil is also used to make plastics, nylon, and other products.

Oil Fuels the Developed World Developed countries depend on oil to meet most of their energy needs. Their cars, trains, and planes burn fuels made from oil. Their power plants burn oil to generate electricity. They use oil to heat buildings in the winter.

The United States leads the world in oil consumption. Americans make up just 5 percent of the world population. But they consume 24 percent of the oil pumped out of the ground each year. Most of the oil Americans consume is burned as gasoline.

Oil Use in the Developing World Is Growing As poor countries develop their economies, more of their people are able to afford luxuries like cars. Oil consumption is increasing in many developing countries as a result.

China is a good example. In 1990, there were just over 5 million cars in China. Ten years later, China had more than 16 million cars. By 2025, that number could rise to more than 130 million. To keep all those cars running, China will need far more oil than it uses today.

At present, there is enough oil to meet world demand. But oil will run out someday. Some experts expect oil production to peak around 2020. Then it will begin to decline. If they are right, the world may face an oil shortage in the not-too-distant future.

U.S. Fuel Oil Uses, 2007

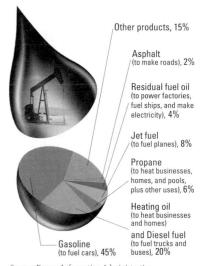

Other products, 15%

Asphalt (to make roads), 2%

Residual fuel oil (to power factories, fuel ships, and make electricity), 4%

Jet fuel (to fuel planes), 8%

Propane (to heat businesses, homes, and pools, plus other uses), 6%

Heating oil (to heat businesses and homes) and Diesel fuel (to fuel trucks and buses), 20%

Gasoline (to fuel cars), 45%

Source: Energy Information Administration.

How Americans Use Oil

This circle graph shows the major ways that oil is consumed in the United States. Notice how much oil is used to fuel motor vehicles and airplanes. A smaller share is used for heating. Think about how we might meet these various needs if the world ran out of oil.

Goods Made from Oil

Oil is the main ingredient in most goods made of plastic, nylon, or vinyl. This family in Ohio is shown with everything they own that was made from oil.

Computers Making Cars
Computers control the machines at work in this automobile assembly plant. Only the more developed countries have the technology to make cars this way.

7.5 Computer and Internet Use Patterns

Walk into almost any school in the United States today, and you will see students and teachers using computers. Walk into a school in a poor village in India, and you may not see a single computer. In fact, you may not even see a light bulb. Many Indian villages do not yet have electricity.

Developed and developing countries differ in their access to **technology**. Technology is the creation and use of tools to meet practical needs. Most people in poor countries are limited to cheap and simple technologies. People in wealthy countries have access to advanced technologies such as computers and the Internet.

Computers Are Everywhere in the Developed World It is hard to imagine life in developed countries without computers and the Internet. Governments and businesses use computers to store and manage information. Businesses also use the Internet to reach customers. Families use computer e-mail to stay in touch with relatives.

Computers and the Internet were invented in the United States. Americans also lead the world in their use of this technology. By 2008, about 75 percent of American adults reported using a computer and the Internet. The majority of U.S. households also owned a computer.

Developing Countries Face a Digital Divide Access to computers is more limited in the developing world. By 2008, only 16 out of every 100 Chinese used the Internet. In India, the number was 18 out of every 100. This number is much less in other developing countries around the world. This gap between people with access to computers and the Internet and those without is called the **digital divide**.

Many poor countries are working to reduce this divide. India is an example. Today, more than 1,150 colleges and universities in India offer computer classes to students. India is also bringing Internet access to thousands of schools across the country.

7.6 The World's Greatest Producers

You have read that the United States consumes more than many other countries. But it also produces more. The GDP of the United States is greater than that of China and India combined. Several factors contribute to this high GDP. They include abundant natural resources and advanced technologies. However, the greatest source of wealth for any country is its people.

An Educated Workforce The United States has a highly skilled workforce. It was one of the first countries to create a public education system. Today most young people in the United States complete high school. About half go on to some form of higher education after graduation. Many adults return to school during their lifetime to learn new skills. All of this schooling makes American workers among the most productive in the world.

A Strong Work Ethic Education is not the only reason Americans are so productive. Another factor is the American work ethic. This is a belief in the moral value, or goodness, of hard work. Most Americans believe that working is good for people. They believe that work gives purpose to life. It also benefits families and communities.

This strong work ethic is tied to another belief. Most Americans grow up believing that they can be successful in life. Many view success as making a lot of money. Others see success as having work they love to do.

Both the work ethic and the drive for success encourage Americans to work hard. On average, Americans work longer hours than workers in most developed countries. They also take less vacation. All of this hard work helps Americans to produce more than workers elsewhere. And because Americans produce more, they have the money to consume more.

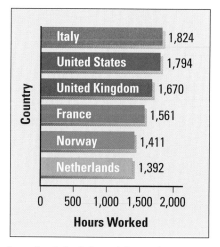

Average Hours Worked per Person per Year, 2007

Country	Hours Worked
Italy	1,824
United States	1,794
United Kingdom	1,670
France	1,561
Norway	1,411
Netherlands	1,392

Source: Organization for Economic Co-operation and Development.

Hardworking Americans

This graph compares hours worked per year in six developed countries. Notice that Americans work more hours than most. One reason may be Americans' strong work ethic and drive for success.

Educated Americans

In 1900, only about 1 in 10 Americans completed high school. Today more than four fifths of all students graduate from high school. One in 4 goes on to graduate from college. These students graduated from New York City's Baruch College in 2004. So many students graduated that year that Baruch held its ceremony in New York's famous sports and entertainment stadium, Madison Square Garden.

The Consumer Class, 2003

Source: Matthew Bentley, "Sustainable Consumption: Ethics, National Indices and International Relations" (Ph.D. dissertation, American Graduate School of International Relations and Diplomacy, Paris, 2003).

Growing Consumption

This graph compares the number of people in the consumer class in developed and developing countries. This growing class is made up of people who earn $7,000 or more a year. In 2003, the global consumer class was 1.7 billion people strong.

7.7 Beginning to Think Globally

In this chapter, you have read about patterns of consumption. You saw that consumption of food, oil, and computers varies in different parts of the world. Generally, developed countries consume more than developing countries. Developed countries like the United States can afford to consume more goods and services because they are more productive. Consumption, however, creates new challenges.

The Growing Global Consumer Class Consumption is growing worldwide. One reason is population growth in developing countries. More people means more consumers.

Another reason is the growth of the global consumer class. This class of consumers is made up of people who earn at least $7,000 a year. About 75 percent of people in developed countries belong to this group. Only about 16 percent of people in developing countries are members of the consumer class. Still, nearly half of the global consumer class lives in developing countries.

Income levels in the consumer class vary widely. A few people are very rich. Most people have more modest incomes. But even in developing countries, most members of the consumer class can afford televisions and telephones. Those with more money own cars, have computers, and use the Internet to shop.

Pressure on Resources and the Environment Wherever they live, most members of the consumer class would like to consume the way people in wealthy countries do. This might create two kinds of problems. One is pressure on resources. The other is harm to the environment.

Most resources in the world are limited. There is only so much fertile land, fresh water, and oil available to meet human needs. If current consumption patterns continue, there may not be enough of these resources to go around. The result could be shortages of food, water, or fuel.

Increased consumption may also do great harm to the environment. China, for example, already has dirty air from burning coal in power plants. As China's consumption of gasoline increases, air pollution is likely to get worse.

Increased consumption creates another problem for the environment. The more people consume, the more trash they produce. Most of what people buy is eventually thrown away. This is true for everything from milk cartons to cars.

Much of what consumers throw out ends up in landfills or dumps. Many landfills are already overflowing with garbage. Worse yet, some of the trash in them is toxic, or poisonous. Old computers and cell phones, for example, are filled with toxic materials. Over time, these poisons can leak into water supplies.

Living Well While Protecting the Planet Consumption is a part of life. People need food, clothing, and shelter to survive. Goods like cars and computers improve people's quality of life. Unlimited consumption, however, may be bad for the planet. Fortunately, there are ways to live well while consuming less.

One way is to cut back on waste. Most people buy more food than they can eat. They leave lights on in unused rooms. They drive cars when they could walk. Reducing such waste is a way to live well while using less.

A second approach is to find ways to do more with less. The first computers, for example, were large machines that filled an entire room. Over time, engineers found ways to make computers smaller. Today, a thin laptop can do far more computing than the old giants could. But a laptop uses far less material and energy to do the job.

A third way is to use cleaner resources. Most of the electricity we use today is generated by burning fossil fuels. This creates air pollution. But new technologies are making it possible to use sun and wind power to generate electricity. Neither of these alternative energy sources pollutes the environment. And the world is not about to run out of sunshine or wind.

Still another way to help the planet is by **recycling**. Recycling turns used goods into materials that can be used to make new ones. Many people already recycle glass, plastic, paper, and metals. Other materials, from lumber scraps to computer parts, can also be recycled. Recycling saves resources. It also reduces trash. You will learn more about trash and recycling in the next section.

China's New Consumer Class
China has a huge population. And it is quickly becoming a country of consumers. Every year, the Chinese are buying more televisions, computers, and cars. If all Chinese owned cars, however, there wouldn't be enough oil in the world to keep them running.

7.8 Global Connections

The map shows how much municipal waste various countries produce. Municipal waste is the garbage and trash collected from homes and businesses. The circle graph shows the makeup of municipal waste in the United States. The bar graph shows how much was being recycled in 2007.

Which countries appear to produce the most waste? Developed countries appear to produce the most waste per person. People there may throw more stuff away because they consume more. Comparisons between rich and poor countries are difficult, however. Most developing countries don't have data on their waste production. Their governments may not provide trash-collection services. Or trash may be collected but not measured.

How effective is recycling as a way to reduce trash? Recycling can reduce trash in landfills. Between 1990 and 2000, the amount of waste per person in the United States dropped by about a third because of recycling. Government recycling programs are less common in poor countries. But that does not mean that their people don't recycle. Poverty forces people in poor countries to reuse everything they can rather than throw it away.

How can recycling help people and the planet? Recycling creates jobs and saves resources. This is good for people who need work. It also reduces pressure on the planet to provide resources. By 2007, the U.S. steel industry was recycling 95 percent of the nation's leftover automobile scrap steel. More than a third of the paper produced in this country came from recycled paper.

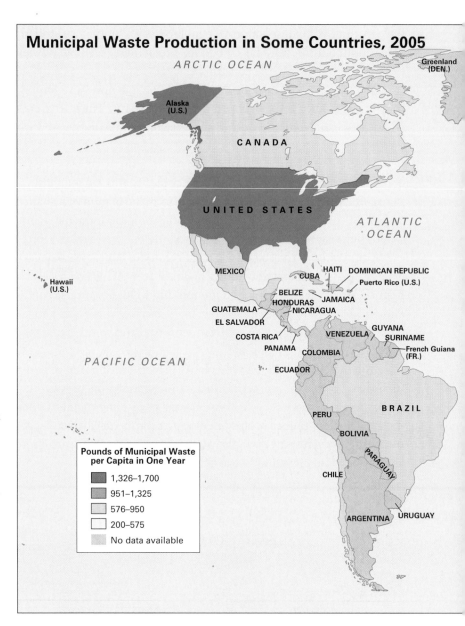

Municipal Waste Production in Some Countries, 2005

Pounds of Municipal Waste per Capita in One Year

- 1,326–1,700
- 951–1,325
- 576–950
- 200–575
- No data available

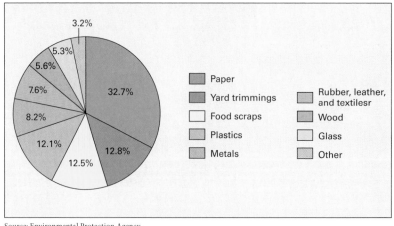

U.S. Municipal Waste, 2007

- 32.7%
- 12.8%
- 12.5%
- 12.1%
- 8.2%
- 7.6%
- 5.6%
- 5.3%
- 3.2%

- Paper
- Yard trimmings
- Food scraps
- Plastics
- Metals
- Rubber, leather, and textilesr
- Wood
- Glass
- Other

Source: Environmental Protection Agency.

Source: Organization for Economic Co-operation and Development.

Recycling Rates in the United States, 2007

Source: Environmental Protection Agency.

Migration to the United States: The Impact on People and Places

8.1 Introduction

Has your family moved recently? If so, was the move a big change or a small change? Many families change their neighborhood when they move to a new place. Others change their city or state. Some families change the country in which they live.

Making the decision to **emigrate,** or move away from one's home country, is never easy. It means leaving behind family and friends. And yet millions of people around the world make this decision every year. Many come to the United States.

When people **immigrate,** or move to a new country, they experience many changes. They leave familiar things behind and come to a place where most things are new to them. Often they need to learn a new language. They also need to learn how to make a living in a strange place. These changes can be very hard to adjust to at first. People also bring their culture and traditions with them. Their different ways can sometimes be hard for their new neighbors to adjust to.

In this chapter, you will learn why people decide to emigrate from their home countries. You will find out why people immigrate to the United States. You will also learn about the impact that different **migration streams,** or flows of immigrants, have had on this country. And you will see how migration affects the countries that people leave behind.

Essential Question

How does migration affect the lives of people and the character of places?

This map shows the migration of people from around the world to the United States in 2007. Each arrow represents a migration stream. Each arrow's thickness reflects the number of people in that migration stream. Keep this map in mind as you try to answer the Essential Question.

Graphic Organizer

◀ Street signs in an immigrant neighborhood in New York City

Top Ten Countries of Origin of U.S. Immigrants, 2007		
Country	Number of Immigrants	Percentage of All U.S. Immigrants
Mexico	148,640	14.1%
China	76,655	7.3%
Philippines	72,596	6.9%
India	65,353	6.2%
Colombia	33,187	3.2%
Haiti	30,405	2.9%
Cuba	29,104	2.8%
Vietnam	28,691	2.7%
Dominican Republic	28,024	2.7%
Korea	22,405	2.1%

Source: Department of Homeland Security.

Immigrants to the United States

The table shows where many migrants to the United States came from in 2007. Note that the largest numbers of people came from countries in Latin America and Asia.

A World of Immigrants

The map shows which countries attract the most immigrants. The United States leads the world, with more than 30 million immigrants.

8.2 The Geographic Setting

Both **push factors** and **pull factors** drive people to move to a new country. Push factors encourage people to emigrate from where they are to a new place. Such factors include war and poverty. Pull factors attract people to a new place and encourage them to immigrate there. These factors include freedom and opportunities for a better life.

Push and pull factors have helped to drive one of the most dramatic migrations in history. Since 1820, more than 65 million people have come to the United States. This enormous migration came in three great waves.

Three Waves of Immigrants The first great wave of immigration began with the founding of the United States. These early immigrants came mostly from northern Europe. Many were escaping from poverty or hunger. Some settled in cities, but most found land to farm.

In the late 1800s, a second wave of immigrants began to arrive from eastern and southern Europe. Many were **refugees** fleeing war or **persecution** because of their religious beliefs. Most found work in the growing cities of the United States.

A third great wave of immigration began in the late 1960s and is still going on today. Between 1970 and 2005, more than 28 million people moved to the United States. A high percentage of those people came from Latin America and Asia.

Many Asians found new homes on the West Coast. Most of the Mexican immigrants settled in the Southwest. Cubans flocked to Florida. New York City attracted people from other Caribbean islands. Like earlier immigrants, these newcomers are both adjusting to and changing life in the United States.

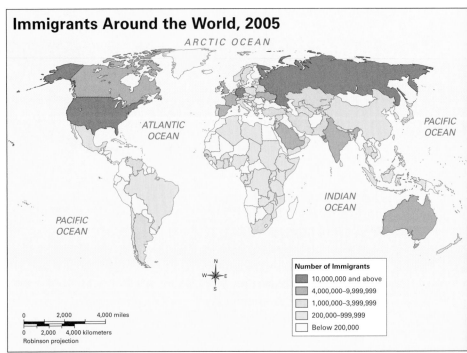

Immigrants Around the World, 2005

Number of Immigrants
10,000,000 and above
4,000,000–9,999,999
1,000,000–3,999,999
200,000–999,999
Below 200,000

Source: United Nations Department of Economic and Social Affairs, Population Division.

▶ Geoterms

emigrate to move from a country. People who leave a country are called *emigrants*.

immigrate to move to a country. People who move to another country are called *immigrants*.

migration stream the constant flow of migrants from one country into another country. The largest migration stream into the United States today is from Mexico.

pull factor something that encourages people to move to a new place

push factor something that encourages people to leave a place behind

refugee someone who seeks safety by going to another country. Refugees may be escaping political unrest or war. Or they may fear being attacked because of their beliefs.

Origins of Immigrants

Since 1820, the United States census, or official count of the population, has tracked immigration to this country. The early waves came from Europe. More recently, most immigrants have come from Asia and Latin America. By the early 2000s, the United States was taking in about 1.5 million immigrants each year.

U.S. Immigration, 1820–2000

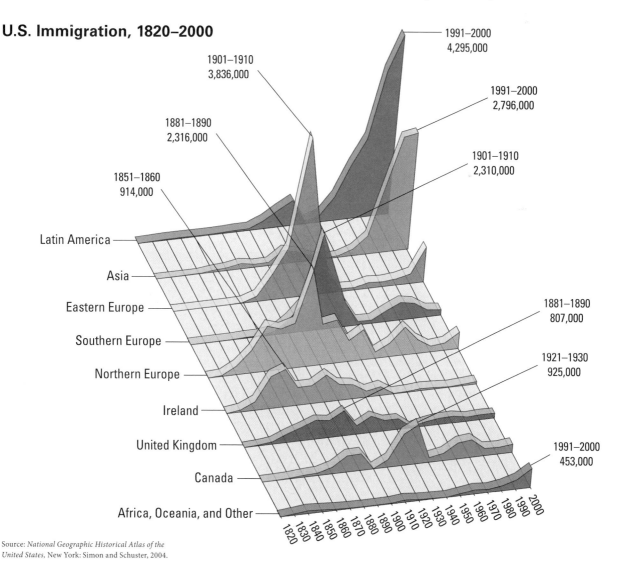

1991–2000
4,295,000

1901–1910
3,836,000

1991–2000
2,796,000

1881–1890
2,316,000

1901–1910
2,310,000

1851–1860
914,000

1881–1890
807,000

1921–1930
925,000

1991–2000
453,000

Latin America

Asia

Eastern Europe

Southern Europe

Northern Europe

Ireland

United Kingdom

Canada

Africa, Oceania, and Other

1820 1830 1840 1850 1860 1870 1880 1890 1900 1910 1920 1930 1940 1950 1960 1970 1980 1990 2000

Source: *National Geographic Historical Atlas of the United States,* New York: Simon and Schuster, 2004.

The Push Factor of War

These refugees are fleeing a war in the country of Bosnia in 1996. Recent wars have caused millions of people to leave their homelands. Sometimes the refugees return home when the conflict ends. But often they stay in their new country.

8.3 What Push Factors Drive Emigration?

One night in the late 1980s, John Deng James awoke to the sound of gunfire. The terrified child ran barefoot into the nearby woods. There he found other frightened children. They were too young to know why their homeland, the African country of Sudan, was at war. But they did know that they had to escape the horror. And so they began to walk.

John Deng James is part of a group of political refugees known as the "Lost Boys of Sudan." The Lost Boys, and other children who lost parents in the war, walked for hundreds of miles in search of safety. Many died along the way of hunger and thirst. Those who survived finally reached a camp for refugees in the country of Kenya. The survivors were among countless people around the world who have been pushed to emigrate by war, violence, or **genocide**. Genocide is the organized elimination of a national, political, racial, or ethnic group.

Political Push Factors War is one political factor that can create refugees. Political refugees may flee a country because they fear its leaders. Or they may fear **persecution**. Persecution is unfair treatment of people because of who they are or what they believe. These push factors all involve how a government treats its people. People are not likely to flee a government that treats citizens fairly. But a government that rules through fear may create many political refugees.

Many Cuban immigrants have come to the United States as political refugees. Cuba is an island in the Caribbean Sea, south of Florida. In 1959, a leader named Fidel Castro took over Cuba's government. Castro quickly made himself a dictator. If Cubans spoke out against Castro or the way he ran Cuba, they risked being jailed. Faced with that threat, thousands of Cubans have fled to the United States.

Environmental Push Factors Changes in the environment, such as a long-term **drought,** can push people to emigrate. In the 1840s, a devastating plant disease struck Ireland. A fungus destroyed Ireland's most important crop, the potato. Faced with starvation, 1.5 million people left Ireland. A great many of these Irish emigrants came to the United States.

Other changes in the environment are the result of human activity. In 1986, an explosion rocked the Chernobyl nuclear power plant in what is now Ukraine. This accident left a large area of poisoned soil, air, and water around the power plant. Tens of thousands of people were forced to leave their homes and move to safer areas. You will read more about the Chernobyl accident in Chapter 16.

Economic Push Factors The most common push factors are economic. Most of the early immigrants to the United States were poor farmers or working people. They saw no way to improve their lives in Europe, so they chose to try their luck in a new country.

These same economic push factors are still at work today. Many people around the world want a better future than they can see in their homeland. Some of them will seek that future in another country. Often, that country is the United States.

8.4 What Pull Factors Draw Immigration?

In 2001, some of the "Lost Boys of Sudan" began another long journey. This one took them from a refugee camp in Africa to a new life in the United States. They arrived in the city of Boston in winter. "I was wearing very light clothes, and we'd never seen snow before," recalled John Deng James. "When we went outside, we couldn't feel our hands and our ears."

Like many refugees, the Sudanese teenagers looked forward to feeling safe, going to school, and getting jobs. These are just some of the "pull factors" that attract immigrants to the United States.

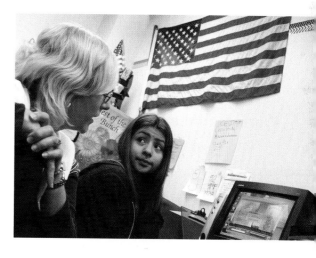

The Pull of Education
Free public schools are a strong pull factor for many immigrant families. This student from Mexico is taking a computer class in her middle school in Texas. Few Mexican schools are well equipped with computers.

Family Pull Factors Another powerful pull factor is the desire to unite divided families. Often young men are the first members of a family to immigrate to another country. Once they find jobs and a place to live, they send for their wives, children, and parents. Between 1965 and 1975, more than 142,000 Greeks came to the United States. Almost all of them were joining relatives who were already living here.

Education Pull Factors Education is a strong pull factor in immigration. Many families migrate so that their children can attend good schools. One of every 15 students in this country's schools was born in another country. Older students come to attend colleges and universities. In the 2007–2008 school year, there were more than 623,000 foreign college students in the United States.

A Refugee Finds Work
Peter "Nyarol" Dut, one of the "Lost Boys of Sudan," is seen here working at a new job in the United States. Like other U.S. workers, he pays taxes out of his earnings.

Workers in the U.S., 2007

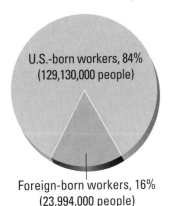

U.S.-born workers, 84% (129,130,000 people)

Foreign-born workers, 16% (23,994,000 people)

Source: U.S. Census Bureau, Bureau of Labor Statistics.

Immigrants in the Workforce
Today, about 16 percent of all U.S. workers are immigrants. Some hold low-paying jobs as farmworkers or household help. But others hold well-paid jobs as doctors, nurses, and engineers.

Quality-of-Life Pull Factors Most people, however, move hoping to improve the quality of their lives. In the United States, this hope is called the "American Dream." This is the belief that people here can create better lives for themselves and their children.

For many refugees, a better life begins with a sense of safety. For much of their history, Jews have been persecuted for their religious beliefs. In the United States, Jewish immigrants found freedom to worship without fear.

For other immigrants, a better life usually starts with a better job. Even low-wage jobs in the United States usually pay more than most immigrants could earn back home. With more money, immigrant families can afford better food, housing, and health care.

8.5 How Does Immigration Affect the U.S.?

For John Deng James and other "Lost Boys," adjusting to life in a new land was hard. At first they were terribly homesick. They were also hungry. They did not know how to shop for food in supermarkets. Nor did they know how to cook. They had never seen a stove or a microwave before. They had never even used a telephone.

Like millions of other immigrants, the Sudanese refugees found their way. Within six months, James had two jobs and was studying for college. These changes affected how James thought about life. "In the United States, you determine who you are," he told a reporter. "Now I have a vision of my future. I can go to school, I can work, and I can do what I want." At the same time, he and the other "Lost Boys" were starting to have an impact on their adopted country.

Economic Impacts: Jobs The United States has long depended on immigrants for labor. Early immigrants cleared large tracts of forests for farms. Later immigrants built roads and railroads across the continent. They filled jobs in mines and factories. And they helped fight this country's wars.

Some of the immigrants entering the United States today arrive with few skills. As a result, they are often limited to low-paying jobs. Some work as farm laborers. They plant and harvest crops on large farms. Others find jobs as cab drivers, house cleaners, restaurant workers, or nannies.

Not all immigrants take low-paying jobs. Some newcomers are highly educated and skilled. They contribute to the economy in many ways. They work as doctors, professors, and computer programmers. Some become famous athletes, musicians, or artists. Still others start new businesses. Those who succeed create jobs for immigrants and native-born workers alike.

Some native-born Americans resent having to compete with immigrants for work. They complain that the immigrants are "taking our jobs." Often, however, the jobs immigrants find are ones that native-born workers are not eager to fill.

Economic Impacts: Taxes Like native-born workers, immigrants who work pay taxes. Their taxes help support public schools, libraries, and health clinics. These public services are important to immigrants and native-born Americans alike.

At the same time, many immigrants also need services that are paid for out of tax money. For example, immigrants who don't speak English may need language classes. Those who can't work may need public assistance or free health care.

In states with many immigrants, such as California and Texas, the cost of providing such welfare services is high. Some taxpayers resent these costs. Others believe the benefits immigrants bring to their state outweigh the cost to taxpayers.

Cultural Impacts: Neighborhoods, Foods, and Holidays

Immigrants create cultural as well as economic change. They introduce Americans to different ways of life from all over the world. This process of spreading cultural features from one place to another is called **diffusion**. Mixing cultures sometimes leads to conflict. But it also makes life more interesting.

Newcomers to the United States often live close to other people from their homeland. These immigrant neighborhoods sometimes have names like Chinatown or Little Italy. Here immigrants can speak their native language. They can find familiar foods and eat in restaurants that cook dishes they grew up eating. And they can hear news from their homeland. Such immigrant neighborhoods have made American cities more exciting places.

Immigrants bring new foods to the United States. Some of these foods, such as potstickers, bagels, and tacos, have become very popular. They now seem almost as American as apple pie.

Immigrants have introduced new holidays to American life. People from many backgrounds enjoy celebrating St. Patrick's Day, Chinese New Year, and Cinco de Mayo. Newcomers bring their music, art, and stories with them as well. The result is a rich mix of ideas, sights, and sounds.

Chinese New Year Celebration
The dragon dance is a colorful part of Chinese New Year celebrations. Once such events were limited to immigrant communities. Today they are enjoyed by Americans from many backgrounds.

Finally, immigrants help their new neighbors to learn about the world. Many Americans knew very little about Sudan before seeing news stories about John Deng James and his fellow Sudanese refugees. But once people read about the "Lost Boys," they could no longer ignore Sudan and its problems.

Top Countries with Brain Drain to the U.S., 2007

Country	Number of Immigrants
India	157,613
Canada	26,209
United Kingdom	25,507
Mexico	18,165
China	16,628
Japan	14,435
France	14,109
Germany	12,714
Korea	11,479
Venezuela	10,596

Source: Department of Homeland Security.

Skilled Immigrants

A brain drain occurs when a country loses its most talented people to emigration. The table shows the number of highly skilled people coming to the United States from 10 countries in 2007. These people came to work for American companies that wanted their skills.

A Money Office in Mexico

The sign in this money office says "We send and receive money orders to and from the USA." Payments sent home by immigrants help support families left behind. By 2009, one of every 10 people in the world was either sending or receiving such payments.

8.6 How Does Emigration Affect the Homelands People Leave Behind?

When the "Lost Boys of Sudan" left their homeland, Sudan lost their talents and energy. Still, it may not have lost them forever. "I have a vision that I may be going back to Sudan," John Deng James told a reporter. "I want to make the economy stronger."

Economic Impacts: Brain Drain and Gain When people emigrate, they take with them whatever they might have contributed to life in their homeland. When doctors or engineers leave, the homeland loses their skills and training as well. Experts call the loss of such well-educated people a **brain drain**. A country suffers from brain drain when its most talented people leave for better jobs in other countries.

As painful as these losses are, they may benefit the home country in some ways. The first is by bringing in needed money. Many immigrants send money back to their families. These payments are called **remittances**. In many countries, money sent by emigrants to their families is a very important source of income. Mexico, for example, receives more money from remittances than from anything else except tourism and the sale of its oil.

Brain drain can also turn into "brain gain." Not all emigrants stay forever in their new countries. Sometimes, people leave to go to school or to work and then return. The result is a gain in skills and experience for the home country.

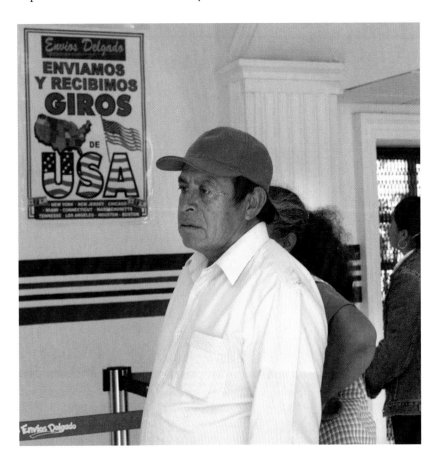

Social Impacts: Divided Families and Community Improvements

Emigration can have mixed social impacts as well. On the minus side, when young people leave to find jobs in another country, families are splintered. Family members may remain separated for years. Emigrants sometimes never return to their homelands.

On the plus side, the money that emigrants send home can have positive effects. Families may use remittances to care for aging parents or to send children to school. Some emigrants have sent enough money to help their home village build a well or a school. These improvements can make life better for the entire community.

Political Impacts: Working for Better Government

Emigration can also have political impacts on the home country. Many refugees have come to the United States to flee political unrest. Once here, some refugees work hard to bring democracy to their homeland.

Valdas Adamkus is a good example. He was born in Lithuania, a small country in northeastern Europe. He came to the United States after the Soviet Union took over Lithuania in the 1940s. Adamkus went to college in Illinois. Later he led efforts to clean up the Great Lakes. He also led an organization that worked to free Lithuania from Soviet rule.

Adamkus saw his dream of a free Lithuania come true in 1991. He then returned to his homeland to help shape its new government. In 1998, Adamkus was elected president of Lithuania. "Growing up in a western democracy you have a different outlook," he said on taking office. Lithuanians liked that outlook—so much so that they elected Adamkus to a second term in 2004.

From Refugee to President
Here you see U.S. immigrant Valdas Adamkus voting in Lithuania. Adamkus left this small European country in the 1940s. He came to the United States as a political refugee. Adamkus returned in the 1990s to become president of Lithuania.

8.7 Beginning to Think Globally

In this chapter, you have learned about migration. You have explored some of the push factors that encourage people to emigrate from their home countries. You have also looked at some of the pull factors that lead people to immigrate to the United States.

Since its founding, the United States has attracted migration streams from around the world. Some immigrants have come as refugees. Others have come in search of jobs and schooling. Of course, the United States is not the only country with many immigrants. As you read in Chapter 3, Canada has attracted large numbers of people from other countries.

Today countries in other **regions** are also attracting immigrants. Two examples are Spain in Europe and Australia in Oceania. Think about why people might be moving to these places as you look at migration streams around the world in the next section.

8.8 Global Connections

The map shows migration streams around the world. The color of each country reflects its wealth in terms of average income per person. The starbursts show areas of armed conflict, or warfare, from 1990 through 2008.

Why might some regions "push" more migrants than they "pull"?
Two big push factors drive migration streams today: poverty and conflict. Both factors come together in Africa. In most of the world, poverty has decreased since 1990. In parts of Africa, it has grown worse. Africa has also seen a large number of wars in that time. These conditions have forced many Africans to flee their homelands. Some stay in nearby refugee camps, and others emigrate.

Why might other regions "pull" more migrants than they "push"?
Migrants generally are attracted to developed regions. Often emigrants move to the developed region nearest their homeland. For North Africans, this is Europe. For Latin Americans, it is the United States or Canada.

How does migration change the places people leave and those they come to? The effects of migration are complicated. Some nations depend on immigrant labor, but native-born workers may feel that immigrants take jobs. Immigrants pay taxes but put pressure on services. When workers migrate, they may create a brain drain. They leave their families when they migrate, but the money they send home will improve their families' lives. Also immigrants may return home to bring new skills and work for increased democracy.

Migration Streams Around the World

Income per Person, 2007
- ▨ $10,000 and over
- ▨ $5,000–$9,999
- ☐ $4,999 and under
- ▨ No data

Areas of conflict
- ✳ Armed conflicts, 1990–2008

Annual Net Migration Streams

◀ 500,000 people

◄ 10,000 people

Net migration equals the flow of people into a region minus the flow out of the region.

Sources: World Bank. *The State of the World Atlas* by Dan Smith, London: Penguin Group, 1999.

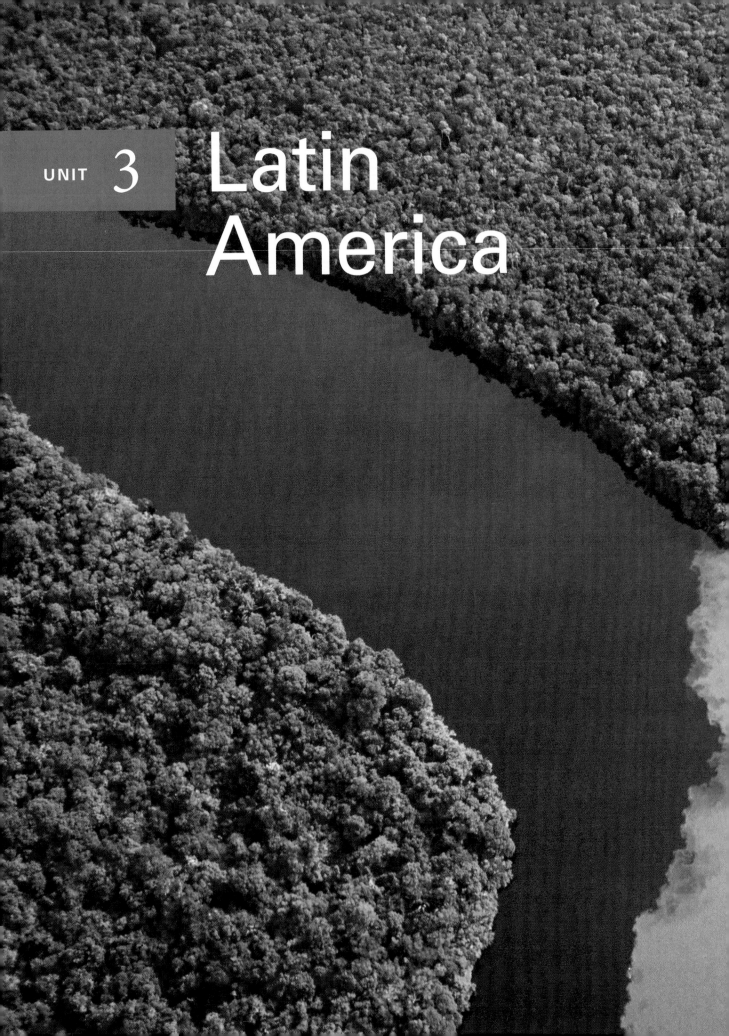

Latin America

Introducing the Region:
Physical and Human Geography

What patterns do you see in this photograph?
See page 514 for details.

▼

Introducing the Region: Physical Geography

Latin America includes all the countries in the Western Hemisphere, except the United States and Canada. It has three sub-regions: Mexico and Central America, the Caribbean islands, and South America.

To the north lies Mexico, which shares a border with the United States. Mexico is connected to South America by a 1,200-mile-long land bridge. This land bridge is known as Central America. East of Central America lie the many islands of the Caribbean Sea. South America is a long continent. Its hot northern lands span the equator. Its cool southern tip reaches toward the Antarctic Circle.

Physical Features of Latin America

Physical Features

Smoking **volcanoes,** dripping **rainforests,** and bone-dry **deserts**—Latin America has them all. Almost every physical feature on Earth is found in this vast **region**. But one feature runs from the north of Mexico to the tip of South America: mountains. For centuries, these mountains have kept the peoples of Latin America isolated from one another.

Mexico and Central America

On a map, Mexico and Central America look like a kite with a long tail. Baja California dangles off the top of the kite. The Yucatán Peninsula juts out from the bottom into the Gulf of Mexico.

Two great mountain ranges run north and south through Mexico. The Sierra Madre Occidental lines the west coast. The Sierra Madre Oriental lines the east coast. A high plain called the Mexican Plateau lies between the two ranges.

Mountains also run through Central America. Many of these mountains are active volcanoes. From Panama's highest peak, you can look down on two different oceans.

The Isthmus of Panama connects Central America to South America. An **isthmus** is a narrow strip of land that links two larger **landmasses**. The Panama Canal was built across this isthmus in the early 1900s. It allows ships to travel between the Atlantic and Pacific oceans without going around all of South America.

The Caribbean Islands

The Caribbean islands curve in an arc from the tip of Florida to the north coast of South America. There are at least 7,000 dots of land in this island group. A few of these islands support large populations. Others are too small to put on most maps.

Many of these islands are the tops of submerged mountains. **Volcanic islands** rise steeply from warm beaches to rugged peaks. Tiny sea creatures known as coral formed other islands. Coral islands are flat and sandy.

South America

South America is shaped like a giant triangle. The Andes Mountains line the western side of the triangle. Plains and **plateaus** cover the rest. The vast Amazon **basin** covers much of the center of the continent. Further south lie grassy plains called the *Pampas*.

South America has many amazing physical features. They include these:

- the Amazon River—the world's second longest river. The Amazon carries more water than any other river in the world.
- Lake Titicaca—the highest lake in the world that can be used for boat travel. This large lake has more than 40 islands.
- the Atacama Desert—one of the driest places on Earth. Average rainfall in the Atacama is only half an inch a year.
- Angel Falls—the world's highest waterfall. The water drops down a rocky cliff for nearly two thirds of a mile.

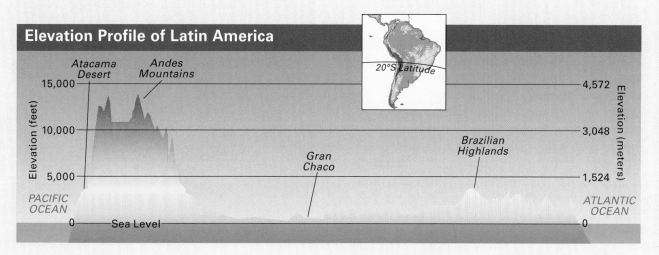

Elevation Profile of Latin America

Climate

Latin America is a region of many **climates.** One reason is that it spans a huge range of latitudes. As you read in Chapter 2, climate generally varies with latitude. Low latitudes, close to the equator, have a year-round tropical climate. High latitudes, near the poles, have short summers and long, cold winters. Between those two extremes lie the middle latitudes, which have more **temperate,** or mild, climates.

Another reason Latin America has such diverse climates is its wide range of altitudes. Altitude has much the same effect on climate as latitude. The higher the altitude, the colder the climate. At lower elevations, mountain climates may be tropical. At higher elevations, the climate can be very cold.

Mexico and Central America

Mexico's climate ranges from **arid** in the north to tropical in the south. The Mexican Plateau is more temperate, with a **semiarid** climate. Closer to the coast, the climate becomes **tropical wet and dry.** Mexicans call this tropical area the "Tierra Caliente," or hot land.

The climate of Central America is tropical near the coast. The air becomes cooler in the mountains. The mountains of Costa Rica are home to a rare **ecosystem** known as a **cloud forest.** Low clouds hang over this forest all year round. Mist from the clouds collects on leaves and drips off the trees like rain. The result is a high-elevation rainforest.

The Caribbean Islands

Most of the Caribbean islands also have a tropical wet and dry climate. People from North America and Europe enjoy winter vacations on these tropical islands.

Huge storms called **hurricanes** are common during summer months. These huge swirling storms form over warm seas near the equator. Then they move toward the poles in a wide, destructive path. Hurricane winds can reach more than 150 miles per hour. At that speed, they can easily knock over trees and tear the roofs off houses.

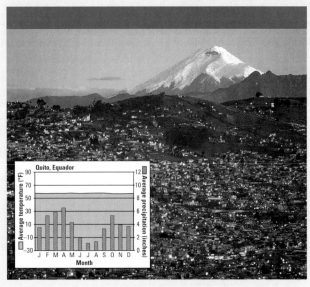

Quito, Ecuador, lies high in the Andes Mountains. Based on the climagraph, what would be the best month for a Quito family to go on a mountain hike?

South America

In South America, climate varies with both latitude and altitude. The northern half of the continent nearest the equator is mostly **tropical wet.** Further south, the climate becomes subtropical and even arid. The Andes Mountains have a **highlands** climate. This means that the climate varies by elevation, getting colder the higher one goes.

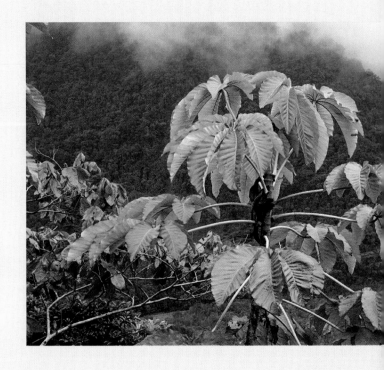

Vegetation

With so many climates, it is no surprise that Latin America is home to an incredible variety of plants. The most widespread type of vegetation is **broadleaf evergreen forest**. It occurs in both tropical wet and tropical wet and dry climate zones.

In a broadleaf evergreen forest, most or all of the trees have leaves rather than needles. But unlike broadleaf trees in cooler climates, these trees do not lose their leaves in winter. Instead they are green all year round. Rainforests and jungles are examples of broadleaf evergreen forests. So are the cloud forests of Central America.

Mexico and Central America

In Mexico, what plants grow where depends mainly on rainfall. **Desert scrub** covers the arid north. Cactus plants survive here with little water. Forest once covered the Mexican Plateau. Over time, most of the trees were cleared to make way for farms.

Southern Mexico and Central America are covered with broadleaf evergreen forest. Pine and oak trees are found in the high cloud forests. Along the coasts, palms, figs, vines, and Spanish moss create a dense rainforest.

Huge cactus plants grow with little rain in the deserts of northern Mexico.

The Caribbean Islands

The Caribbean islands have a mix of **tropical grasslands** and broadleaf evergreen forests. Black and red mangrove trees and coconut palms are typical trees. Underwater coral reefs circle many of the islands. These reefs are home to broad-leafed turtle grass, feathery green algae, and red algae that can make the coral look rusty.

South America

The largest **vegetation zone** in South America is the Amazon rainforest. This broadleaf evergreen forest is home to more kinds of plants than any other place on Earth. There are hardwood trees, such as mahogany and rosewood, which people use to make furniture. There are also Brazil nut and rubber trees. The **forest floor** is a tangle of plants, vines, and colorful orchids.

Tropical grasslands and **temperate grasslands** cover most of the rest of South America. Cacti and flowering plants bloom in desert scrub regions. The Atacama Desert is so dry that almost no plants survive there.

A unique ecosystem known as a cloud forest is found in the mountains of Central America.

atin America is home to 33 countries and more than 570 million people. Brazil is the largest country in both area and population. About 195 million people lived in Brazil in 2008. This means that one Latin American out of three was a Brazilian. Brazil is the largest country in the world where Portuguese is the first language.

This region is called *Latin* America because most of its people speak Spanish or Portuguese. Both are modern languages based on Latin. This was a language spoken in the Roman Empire about 2,000 years ago. Languages based on Latin are called Romance languages because of their Roman roots.

Political Boundaries of Latin America

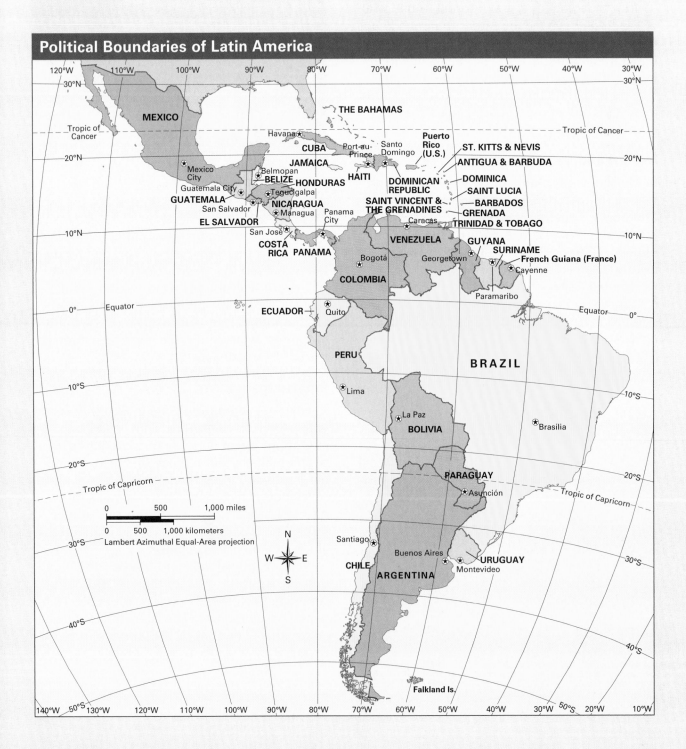

History

Over time, many peoples have come to Latin America. Each group has left its mark on the history of this region.

Early Times

The first Americans were probably hunter-gatherers from Asia. They may have followed animals they hunted across a land bridge that once connected Asia to Alaska. Their descendents spread to the tip of South America.

Over time, some native peoples learned how to farm. Their most important crops were maize (corn) and the potato. Farming allowed native peoples to settle down in one place. It also led to the growth of civilizations.

The Maya created civilizations in Mexico and Central America. Four hundred years later, the Aztecs built their **empire** in Mexico. The Incas built a large empire that spread down the western coast of South America.

The Colonial Period

In 1492, a European explorer named Christopher Columbus landed in the Caribbean. His discovery brought more Europeans to the Americas. They brought European animals, plants, and diseases. They took back to Europe plants, animals and diseases that had not been seen before. This swapping of items is called the Columbian Exchange. It changed how people in Europe and the Americas lived.

In the early 1500s, Spain conquered the Aztec and Inca empires. This began a long period of European colonization. Many native peoples died fighting the colonists. But European diseases were even deadlier than war. As the native peoples died, Europeans brought Africans over to work as slaves.

Spain and Portugal took over most of Latin America. Spanish and Portuguese replaced many native languages. Many native peoples became Christians.

In time, Latin Americans began to rebel against the European rulers. Wars for independence began in 1791 with a slave uprising in Haiti. By 1825, most of Latin America had thrown off colonial rule. One of the first acts of the newly independent countries was to outlaw slavery. The exception was Brazil, which did not free its slaves until 1888.

The Modern Era

Independence did not bring democracy to Latin America as it had to the United States. From Mexico to Argentina, military leaders seized power and ruled as **dictators**. Most dictators were only interested in holding onto power. They cared little about the rights or welfare of their people.

By the 1980s, Latin Americans were weary of dictators. In one country after another, the people demanded the right to choose their leaders. Today, elected governments run most Latin American countries. Democracy has not solved all of Latin America's problems. Poverty is widespread. Schools are poor. Governments are unstable. Living standards remain low. But for many Latin Americans, the right to vote has brought with it hope for a better future.

Latin America Timeline

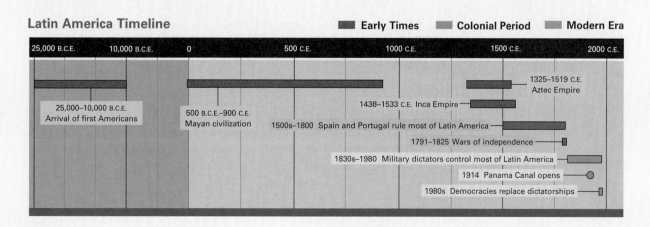

Early Times · Colonial Period · Modern Era

25,000 B.C.E. | 10,000 B.C.E. | 0 | 500 C.E. | 1000 C.E. | 1500 C.E. | 2000 C.E.

25,000–10,000 B.C.E. Arrival of first Americans

500 B.C.E.–900 C.E. Mayan civilization

1325–1519 C.E. Aztec Empire

1438–1533 C.E. Inca Empire

1500s–1800 Spain and Portugal rule most of Latin America

1791–1825 Wars of independence

1830s–1980 Military dictators control most of Latin America

1914 Panama Canal opens

1980s Democracies replace dictatorships

Population

Latin America includes more than 15 percent of the world's land area. But it is home to less than 12 percent of the world's people. Still, its population is growing fast. From 1950 to 2008, the number of Latin Americans more than tripled. Only Africa has a higher growth rate.

As the population grows, it is becoming more **urban**. In 1950, more than half of Latin Americans lived on farms. Today, three fourths live in urban areas. Most large cities are located on the coasts.

Most Latin Americans are Christian. This region is home to nearly half of the world's one billion Roman Catholics. However, other Christian churches are gaining members.

Some Latin Americans still follow indigenous religions. These are traditional beliefs held by native peoples. The "Other" category in the circle graph below includes several religious traditions. Some of these traditions were brought to the Americas long ago by Africans. Others were brought by more recent immigrants from Asia.

Latin America: Major Religions

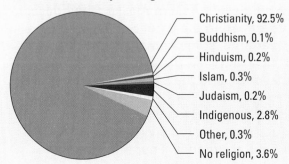

- Christianity, 92.5%
- Buddhism, 0.1%
- Hinduism, 0.2%
- Islam, 0.3%
- Judaism, 0.2%
- Indigenous, 2.8%
- Other, 0.3%
- No religion, 3.6%

Latin America: Urban and Rural Population, 2007

Urban, 78.1%

Rural, 21.9%

= 10% of the total population

Latin America: Population Growth, 1950–2050

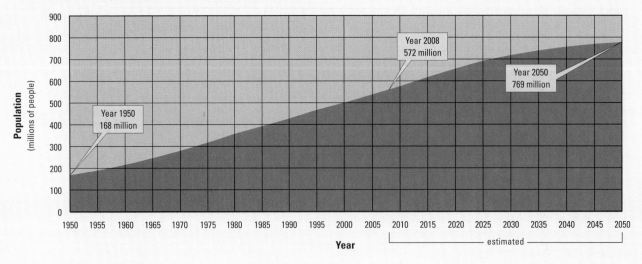

Year 1950 — 168 million

Year 2008 — 572 million

Year 2050 — 769 million

Population (millions of people)

Year

estimated

Sources: United Nations Department of Economic and Social Affairs, Population Division. Encyclopædia Britannica.

Economic Activity

Latin America has a wealth of **natural resources**. Those resources support a broad range of **economic activities**. The most widespread economic activities are **livestock raising** and **subsistence farming**.

Subsistence farmers usually grow only enough food to feed their families. Good weather may sometimes allow them to produce a crop surplus. They can then sell or **barter** their extra food for other things they need. But surpluses are rare. As a result, subsistence farmers are generally poor. The most important crops grown by subsistence farmers are corn, potatoes, and beans.

Resources

The Europeans who first came to Latin America wanted its mineral wealth. They were interested mainly in mining silver and gold. Later, people mined copper, uranium, and other minerals as well. Most of these metals are found in the Andes Mountains.

Today Latin America is better known for its energy resources. This region has about 9 percent of the world's petroleum, or oil supply. Large oil deposits have been found in Mexico and Venezuela.

Latin American rivers are another source of energy. Dams on rivers in Brazil and Paraguay produce large amounts of **hydroelectric power**.

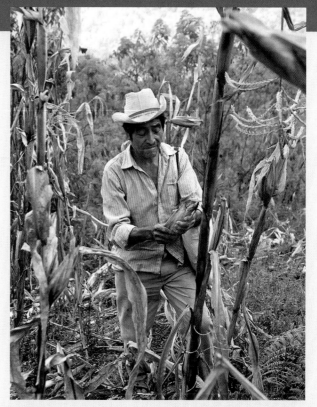

A subsistence farmer in Mexico harvests corn. Subsistence farming is widespread in Latin America.

Land Use

Farming and ranching are important across Latin America. One of the most important **commercial farming** crops is coffee. Coffee beans are grown on large **plantations** in Brazil, Colombia, and Central America. Ranchers raise mostly cattle and sheep. The largest cattle ranches are found on the Pampas of Argentina.

Forestry is another major industry. Many types of trees are harvested from Latin American forests. This wood is used for building materials and fuel. It is also used to make products such as furniture and musical instruments.

Some areas in Latin America specialize in a particular activity. The most important industry in the Caribbean islands, for example, is **tourism**. Mexico, in contrast, is strong in manufacturing. Many of the cars you see on American roads were made in Mexico.

This dam supplies electricity to industries in northern Brazil.

Spatial Inequality in Mexico City: From Cardboard to Castles

9.1 Introduction

Anna Romero lives in a poor part of Mexico City. She and her family share a simple two-room house. The house is made of concrete bricks and scraps of wood and cardboard taken from the dump. There is no glass in the windows, and there is no running water.

Six days a week, Anna travels by bus to her job on the other side of the city. She works as a maid in the Alba household. The Albas live in a beautiful 15-room house with a large garden and swimming pool. To Anna, it seems like a castle. Anna earns $6 for working a 12-hour day. At 7:00 P.M., as the Albas sit down to a big meal of chicken, meat, or fish, Anna heads home to cook rice and beans for her family.

The Albas and Romeros live just 15 miles apart. But they live in very different worlds. The contrast in their lives is an example of **spatial inequality**. This is an unequal distribution of wealth or resources over a geographic area. It means that some places within that area are richer or poorer than others. Mexico City offers many examples of spatial inequality.

In this chapter, you will learn about the growth of Mexico City as an urban area. You will read about the causes and effects of the city's rapid growth. You will also learn about the spatial inequality that has resulted from the city's expansion.

Essential Question

Why does spatial inequality exist in urban areas?

This map shows the Federal District of Mexico. This district is the capital of Mexico. Most of Mexico City is located here. The district is divided into areas called *delegaciones* (shown here in different colors). Some neighborhoods are wealthy. Others are very poor. Keep this spatial inequality in mind as you try to answer the Essential Question.

Graphic Organizer

◀ An aerial view of Mexico City, Mexico

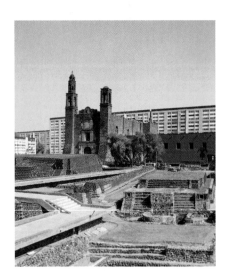

A Blend of Old and New
The Plaza of Three Cultures shows the mix of cultures that makes up Mexico City today. The stone platforms in this photograph are Aztec ruins. The church was built by the Spanish. The office buildings represent modern Mexico.

9.2 The Geographic Setting

Mexico City is one of the world's largest cities in population. It sits in a highland **basin** at about 7,000 feet above sea level. This basin is called the Valley of Mexico. The valley is surrounded by mountains. It has a mild climate and rich soil. The Valley of Mexico has been an important place of settlement since ancient times.

A City of Wonders: The Aztec Capital of Tenochtitlán The first settlers in the Valley of Mexico arrived thousands of years ago. At the time, several large, shallow lakes covered the valley floor. Small cities later grew up around these lakes.

In 1325, a group known as the Aztecs settled on an island in Lake Texcoco. There they founded a city called Tenochtitlán. The Aztecs were great warriors. They soon built a mighty empire. Their city grew, too. By the time the Spanish arrived in 1519, Tenochtitlán was one of the greatest cities in the world. Around 200,000 people lived in the Aztec capital. Up to a million lived in the Valley of Mexico.

Tenochtitlán was a marvelous place. One Spaniard said it was like an "enchanted vision" from a fairy tale. Great pyramids and temples towered above the city. Fine palaces and homes lined its streets and **plazas**. Many canals crossed the island. Three causeways, or raised roads, connected it to the shore. A huge market sold exotic goods from around the empire.

The people of Tenochtitlán enjoyed a high **standard of living**. This term refers to people's overall level of comfort and well-being. City residents had plenty of food from farming, fishing, and trade. An **aqueduct** brought in fresh water from the surrounding hills. The houses were well built. People lived in clean, orderly neighborhoods.

A Bustling National Capital: Mexico City In 1521, Spain conquered the Aztec Empire. The Spanish destroyed the Aztec capital. They built a new city in its place. Over time, Mexico City became one of the most beautiful cities in the Americas.

In 1821, Mexico won its independence from Spain. Mexico City became the capital of the new country. It continued to grow slowly. By the 1950s, the city was a blend of modern and historic buildings. Broad avenues and tree-filled parks made it a pleasant place to live.

Today, Mexico City remains the center of Mexican life. But it is no longer the graceful city of old. In the past 50 years, **urbanization,** or city growth, has increased at a rapid rate. In 1970, the city had over 8 million people. Ten years later, it had almost doubled in population. There are now at least 19 million people in Mexico City's **metropolitan area**. This area includes the city and its **suburbs**.

A key factor in Mexico City's growth is migration from **rural** parts of the country. Many people have moved to the capital because of **rural decline,** or increasing poverty in the countryside. Life in rural areas is hard. But for many people, the city has become a difficult place to live, too, as you will see.

▶ Geoterms

rural decline worsening economic conditions in the country-side, including rising unemployment and growing poverty. Rural decline drives migration to cities.

spatial inequality the unequal distribution of wealth or resources in a geographic area, so that some places are richer than others

standard of living the overall level of comfort and well-being of a group or a country. People in developed countries generally have a higher standard of living than people in developing countries.

urbanization the movement of people from rural to urban areas, resulting in the growth of urban areas

District, City, State

The Federal District is the capital of Mexico. Like the District of Columbia, where the U.S. national capital is located, it is not part of any state. You can see below how the urban area has spread from the Federal District into the state of Mexico.

Mexico City and the Federal District

STATE OF MEXICO

STATE OF MEXICO

Lake Texcoco

FEDERAL DISTRICT

- - - Lake Texcoco, 1519
—— Lake Texcoco and surrounding salt marshes, today
⬛ Urban areas

N
W E
S

0   1   2 miles
0   1   2 kilometers
Albers Conic Equal-Area projection

STATE OF MORELOS

9.3 Rural Decline Causes Urban Migration

Juan Ortiz and his family live in a small village in central Mexico. Like his father and grandfather before him, Juan is a farmer. He grows corn, beans, and other vegetables on a few acres of land. But conditions have declined in the countryside. Juan can no longer support his family by farming. He has to find other work. Like many farmers, Juan plans to leave his village and move to the city. He is part of the large urban migration caused by rural decline in Mexico.

Farmers Struggle in the Countryside Life for most Mexican farmers is tough. Only about 15 percent of the land in Mexico is suitable for farming. The rest is too dry, rocky, or mountainous. Most of the best land is held by a small number of wealthy owners.

There are several types of farms in Mexico. Some are small private farms. Others are larger farms held in common by groups of farmers. These **communal lands** are called *ejidos*. A third type of farm is a large commercial farm that grows food for export.

At one time, small farmers were the backbone of Mexican society. Now they are finding it hard to survive. To compete with large farms, they have to increase their production. But they don't have the money to buy seeds, fertilizer, and farm machinery. Many of them end up selling their land. Sometimes they go to work for wages on the large farms. But such jobs are few, and wages are low. As a result, poverty and **unemployment** have increased in rural Mexico.

Migration to the City Brings Renewed Hope Faced with rural decline, many farmers choose to migrate to the city. There they hope to find jobs that will pay them a decent wage and give their families a higher standard of living. They also hope their children will have an opportunity to get a good education in city schools.

For years, most rural migrants headed to Mexico City. During the 1970s and 1980s, around 1,000 people a day moved to the capital. That rate has declined as life in Mexico City has become more difficult. Many migrants now choose to move to other cities in Mexico. Others try to cross the border into the United States.

The Urbanization of Mexico

This graph shows the percentage of urban and rural residents in Mexico over time. In 1950, more Mexicans lived in rural areas than in cities. But that had changed by 1960. Today, more than 75 percent of all Mexicans live in cities. The graph also shows estimates for the future.

Mexico's Urban and Rural Population

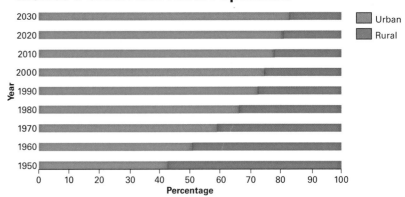

Source: United Nations Department of Economic and Social Affairs, Population Division.

Polluted City Air

Mexico City has some of the worst air pollution in the world. About 70 percent of this pollution comes from vehicles. The government tries to limit the number of vehicles on city streets. But there are still about 7 million cars in the city.

9.4 Urbanization Creates New Problems

Julio Cu is a professional diver. But he doesn't go diving in the ocean. Instead, he dives under the streets of Mexico City. On workdays, Julio puts on a special diving suit and swims into the city's giant sewer system. He clears trash and other objects from sewer pipes. Once he even found half a car! It's a nasty job, but someone has to do it. Mexico City's sewers are overloaded. This is just one of the problems caused by rapid urbanization.

Too Many People, Too Little Land You have read that rural migration is a key factor in Mexico City's growth. Large families have also played a part. In recent years, however, both migration from rural areas and the number of children in the average family have gone down. As a result, the city is not growing as fast as it once did.

Still, Mexico City is continuing to expand. Its suburbs are spreading up the sides of the Valley of Mexico. Newcomers are also filling in areas that were once covered by the valley's lakes. Most of the lake water was drained out long ago to allow for expansion. But there is still not enough land or housing for the city's growing population.

Urbanization has caused other problems, too. Clean water is in short supply. Roads are clogged with traffic. Buses and subways are packed. Mexico City is bursting at the seams.

Pollution, Poverty, and Crime Rapid growth has had an impact on Mexico City's environment. One of the city's worst problems is air **pollution**. Years ago, residents had a clear view of two great, snow-capped **volcanoes** that lie just east of the city. But now the mountains are rarely visible. A thick blanket of **smog** often hangs over the city. Sometimes it's hard just to see across the street.

Because of poor **air quality,** many city residents suffer from asthma and other illnesses. On some days the air is so bad that schools are closed and people are warned to stay inside. Recent laws to limit pollution have helped, but the problem persists.

Social problems have also grown with urbanization. There are not enough jobs in the city to keep everyone employed. Poverty has increased. So has crime. Mexico City was once a relatively safe place to live. Now many residents fear for their safety.

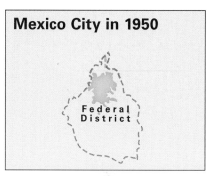

Mexico City in 1950

Federal District

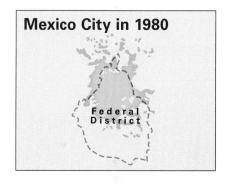

Mexico City in 1980

Federal District

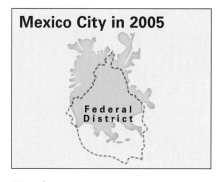

Mexico City in 2005

Federal District

The Growing City

These maps show the growth of Mexico City from 1950 to 2005. About one out of every five Mexicans lives in Mexico City. The urban area once lay entirely within the Federal District. It has since spread well beyond those boundaries. Much of this growth consists of poor neighborhoods.

9.5 A City of "Haves" and "Have Nots"

Sylvia Martinez lives in one of Mexico City's huge garbage dumps. She sorts through piles of trash to find bits of glass, metal, and other materials that she can recycle for cash. She is one of the millions of "have nots" in Mexico City.

The "have nots" are poor people who have little money and few possessions. They make up the majority of the city's population. In contrast, the "haves" are people with money and more comfortable lives. The differences between these two groups are reflected in the spatial inequalities of Mexico City.

The "Have Nots" Struggle to Survive The poorest of the "have nots" are typically recent migrants to the city. They often live in slums on the edge of the city. Most houses in these **slums** are one-room shacks made of cardboard and other junk. Many of these houses lack electricity. They also lack running water. The streets are seldom paved and are often littered with trash. Many of the people who live in these slum areas have little or no work.

Migrants who have been in the city for a while may live in somewhat better conditions. Most have some kind of work. Many hold more than one job. They may work as maids, dishwashers, cooks, construction workers, street vendors, or bus drivers. Most of them work long hours for little pay. They may have to travel for hours by public transportation to get to their jobs.

It's not just recent arrivals who are poor. Many of Mexico City's people are "working poor." They have jobs that are too low-paying to lift them out of poverty. Most live in working-class neighborhoods that are usually closer to the center of the city than the slums. Some of the working poor live in cinder-block homes with metal or tar-covered roofs. Others live in large **tenements,** or rundown apartment buildings. Houses in these neighborhoods generally have electricity, though some may lack water. The streets are usually paved. Even so, life for the working poor of Mexico City is a struggle.

Cardboard Housing for "Have Nots"

Shacks like this one are located in slums on the outskirts of Mexico City. Houses are made of scrap materials like cardboard boxes and bits of wood and metal. The people who live in these slums are often recent migrants to the city. Many end up selling cheap goods on the street or begging for a living.

The "Haves" Live Well The "haves" are members of Mexico City's middle and upper classes. They make up around one fourth of the city's residents.

A very small number of "haves" belong to the upper class. These very wealthy people are large landowners or leaders in business or government. They enjoy a luxurious standard of living. Many live on large castle-like **estates** with high walls and security systems. They often hire the working poor to serve as their maids, gardeners, and drivers.

Members of the middle class live in houses or apartment buildings near the center of the city. Or they live in modern suburbs farther away. Many work in business, education, or government. They can usually afford some luxuries, such as a telephone at home.

Life has become harder in recent years for many middle-class Mexicans. The Mexican economy has suffered from hard times. Some middle-class families can no longer save money or send their children to good private schools. They are struggling just to maintain their middle-class standard of living.

9.6 Beginning to Think Globally

In this chapter, you have learned about spatial inequality in Mexico City. You read how rural decline has increased migration to the city. You learned about problems that have come with rapid urbanization. You have also seen how rich and poor have very different standards of living. These differences can be seen in their housing and transportation, and in many other aspects of city life.

Spatial inequality doesn't exist only in large cities. It can be found in any area where differences in wealth affect how people live. Such differences can be found in small towns as well as in suburbs and cities.

Spatial inequality also exists on a global scale. Think about this as you look at the map on the next two pages. It compares the standard of living in countries around the world.

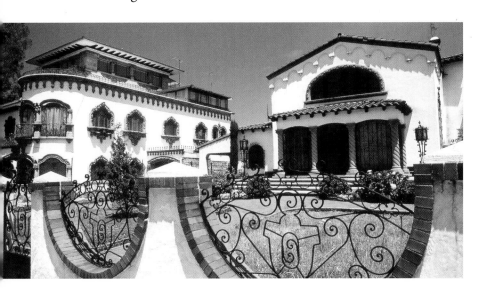

The Good Life

This home is located in a wealthy area of Mexico City. Homes like this often have large gardens and many rooms. They may also have security systems to guard against crime. Only a tiny portion of the city's population can afford to live like this.

9.7 Global Connections

This map compares how well people live around the world. The rankings are based on a measure of living standards called the Human Development Index. The HDI looks at how well countries do in their economies, societies, and basic living standards. The HDI includes information on life expectancy, education levels, and per capita GDP, among other things.

Why do some countries have a higher HDI rank than might be expected? The blue circles on the map show countries that rank higher in the HDI than their GDP might lead you to think. In such countries, the differences between rich and poor are not great. Also, many of these countries provide education and health care to all of their citizens.

Why do some countries have a lower HDI rank than might be expected? The countries marked by a red square rank lower in the HDI than you might expect from their GDP. In such countries, there is likely to be a large gap between rich and poor. The rich live well. The poor have limited access to schools and health care.

How do patterns of spatial inequality change over time? Each year, the HDI ranks of some countries rise. Living standards in these countries are improving. Other nations drop in rank. Often such changes reflect government policies. In Zimbabwe, for example, decisions by the government have hurt the economy. Living standards have declined as a result. In Malaysia, government policies have helped raise living standards.

Standard of Living Around the World, 2006

ARCTIC OCEAN

Greenland (DEN.)

ICELAND

NORWAY SWEDEN FINLAND

UNITED KINGDOM
IRELAND
DEN.
NETH.
BEL.
FRANCE
SWITZ.
LUX. CZ. REP.
GER.
POLAND BELARUS
SLOV.
AUS. HUNG.
ROMANIA
UKRAINE
MOLDOVA

PORTUGAL SPAIN
ITALY
MONT.
CRO.
B.H.
SERB.
KOS.
MAC.
GREECE
ALB.

RUSSIAN FEDERATION

KAZAKHSTAN

MONGOLIA

N. KOREA
S. KOREA
JAPAN

PACIFIC OCEAN

MOROCCO
TUNISIA
ALGERIA
LIBYA

Western Sahara
MAURITANIA
MALI
NIGER
CHAD
SUDAN

SENEGAL
GAMBIA
GUINEA BISSAU
GUINEA
SIERRA LEONE
LIBERIA
CÔTE D'IVOIRE
GHANA
TOGO
BENIN
NIGERIA
BURKINA FASO
CAMEROON
CENTRAL AFRICAN REPUBLIC
EQ. GUINEA
SÃO TOMÉ & PRINCIPE
GABON
CONGO
DEM REP. OF THE CONGO
UGANDA
RWANDA
BURUNDI
KENYA
TANZANIA
MALAWI

CYPRUS
ISRAEL
GEORGIA
ARM.
AZER.
LEB.
SYRIA
IRAQ
Gaza Strip
West Bank
JORDAN
EGYPT
BAHRAIN
QATAR
U.A.E.
OMAN
YEMEN
ERITREA
DJIBOUTI
ETHIOPIA
SOMALIA

TURKEY
IRAN

UZBEKISTAN
TURKMENISTAN
KYRGYZSTAN
TAJIKISTAN
AFGHANISTAN
PAKISTAN

KUWAIT
SAUDI ARABIA

CHINA
BHUTAN
NEPAL
INDIA
BANGLADESH
MYANMAR (BURMA)
LAOS
THAILAND
VIETNAM
CAMBODIA

Taiwan

SRI LANKA

PHILIPPINES

BRUNEI
MALAYSIA
SINGAPORE

INDONESIA

EAST TIMOR

PAPUA NEW GUINEA

SOLOMON ISLANDS

FIJI

INDIAN OCEAN

ANGOLA
ZAMBIA
ZIMBABWE
NAMIBIA
BOTSWANA
MOZAMBIQUE
MADAGASCAR
SWAZILAND
SOUTH AFRICA
LESOTHO

ATLANTIC OCEAN

AUSTRALIA

NEW ZEALAND

0   1,500   3,000 miles

0   1,500   3,000 kilometers
Robinson projection

ANTARCTICA

Source: United Nations Development Programme.

Indigenous Cultures: The Survival of the Maya of Mesoamerica

10.1 Introduction

You are traveling by bus through the **highlands** of Guatemala. The road winds through steep, misty mountains. It passes small mud-brick houses set in fields of corn. The bus is piled high with bags, bundles, and even a crate of live chickens.

Most of the passengers are Mayan Indians. The woman next to you is wearing a colorful headdress and a beautiful woven blouse called a *huipil*. She feeds her children corn tortillas and talks to them in a strange language. You feel like you're in another world. Suddenly, you hear a ringing sound. The woman reaches into her bag, pulls out a cell phone, and begins speaking in Spanish.

You have just witnessed an example of how old and new are blending in the Mayan world. The Maya are one of the largest groups of **indigenous peoples** in the Americas. Indigenous peoples are natives of an area who have been conquered or dominated by others who came later. Indigenous peoples often try to preserve their **traditional culture,** or the customs and ways of life handed down from their ancestors.

The Maya still maintain much of their traditional culture. But they have also changed along with the world around them. In this chapter, you will learn how the Maya have both preserved their traditions and adapted to, or changed with, modern life.

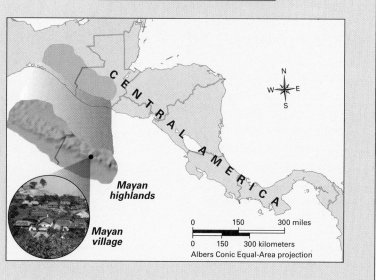

Essential Question

How do indigenous peoples preserve their traditional culture while adapting to modern life?

This illustration shows where the highland Maya live. The Mayan highlands stretch from southern Mexico through Guatemala. Notice the photograph of a highland village. You will learn about key features of Mayan life in a village like this one. Keep this illustration in mind as you try to answer the Essential Question.

Graphic Organizer

CENTRAL AMERICA

Mayan highlands

Mayan village

0   150   300 miles
0 150 300 kilometers
Albers Conic Equal-Area projection

◀ A Mayan family at home

10.2 The Geographic Setting

The Maya live in an ancient cultural region known as Mesoamerica. A cultural region is an area with a distinct culture or set of similar cultures. Mesoamerica stretches from central Mexico to the Isthmus of Panama. This **region** includes hot jungle **lowlands,** dry **plateaus,** and cool mountain highlands.

The Maya Created an Advanced Civilization About 2,000 years ago, the Maya created a remarkable civilization in Mesoamerica. They built great stone cities with towering pyramids. They created a writing system. They also developed an accurate calendar system.

Around 900 C.E., the Mayan civilization collapsed. **Drought,** warfare, and other problems led the Maya to abandon their cities. In the 1500s, Spanish soldiers arrived and conquered the Mayan region. Later the Mayan cultural region was divided among several countries.

Geography Isolates the Maya from Modern Life Today there are around 6 million Maya. Some still live in the lowlands, especially Mexico's Yucatan Peninsula. But most live in the highlands of Guatemala and the Mexican state of Chiapas.

The Mayan highlands are a rugged **landscape** of steep mountains and deep valleys. Heavy clouds often hang over the mountains. Moisture from the clouds helps produce dense **cloud forests**. A line of great **volcanoes** rises up along the southern edge of the highlands. These volcanoes have erupted many times in the past, covering the land with **lava** and ash. Several of these volcanoes are still active.

Volcanic ash has enriched the soil in much of the highland region. As a result, the land is generally fertile and good for farming. Most Maya practice **subsistence farming**. That is, they farm mainly to provide food for themselves and their families. In general, they sell very little of the food they grow.

The mountain geography of the highlands has helped isolate the Maya. Few roads cross the highlands. Many Maya live in remote areas miles from the nearest town. This isolation has limited contact between the Maya and the rest of the world. But it has also helped the Maya survive as a people and preserve their culture.

One People Speaking Many Languages Mountains are not the only factor separating one Mayan group from another. Over time, the Maya in different areas developed their own customs and languages. More than two dozen Mayan groups now live scattered across Mesoamerica. Each group speaks its own language. Each also has its own special form of dress.

Despite these differences, the Maya are still a single **ethnic group**. They share common physical features and a cultural identity. They also share the challenge of making **adaptations** to modern life. An adaptation is a change in a way of life to suit new conditions.

Mayan Languages

A Mixture of Languages

There are as many as 31 Mayan languages. Each is spoken in a particular part of the Mayan region. Among the most widely spoken highland languages are Quiché, Cakchiquel, Tzotzil, and Tzeltal. Many Maya also speak Spanish.

▶ Geoterms

adaptation a change in a way of life to suit new conditions

indigenous peoples natives of an area who have been conquered or dominated by others who came later. Native American tribes, such as the Cherokee and Navajo, are indigenous peoples.

subsistence farming farming carried out mainly to provide food for farm families, with little surplus for sale to others

traditional culture customs and ways of life handed down from ancestors

Elevation
Feet
- Over 9,000
- 6,000–9,000
- 3,000–6,000
- 0–3,000

The Highlands of Guatemala and Southern Mexico

The Mayan highlands isolate groups of Maya from one another and from the outside world. High peaks and deep valleys separate one mountain range from another. Some Mayan villages are perched on high mountain ridges. Many can be reached only on narrow paths.

10.3 A Strong Sense of Community

Several Mayan judges are seated at a table. Two men are standing before them. One man claims that the other killed and ate one of his chickens. The other says the chicken entered his yard and ate his chicken feed. Finally, one of the judges speaks up. In the Quiché language, he says, "You will pay the man for his chicken by working for three days in his fields."

This is an example of Mayan community justice. The Maya are deeply attached to their local villages. They try to preserve their community's way of life while adapting to the modern world.

Local Government The highland Maya are citizens of either Mexico or Guatemala. Over time, their communities have adapted to the demands of national life. For example, most highland towns have a mayor. He governs the community according to national laws.

The Maya also have their own traditional forms of government. Many towns have a municipal council that follows Mayan customs. The council members are respected members of the community. They make decisions based on traditional values.

Mayan towns also have religious brotherhoods. In Guatemala, the brotherhoods are called *cofradias*. In Chiapas, they are called *cargos*. They guard the images of Catholic saints. They organize ceremonies and festivals. The heads of these brotherhoods are also important community leaders.

A Mayan Community

Mayan villages are a mix of old and new. The ancestral shrine (on the left) and sacred tree in this illustration are traditional. The tree connects heaven and earth in the ancient Mayan religion. The plaza, with its Spanish colonial buildings, is an adaptation to the outside world.

Meeting Community Challenges The Maya work hard to keep their communities together. One way they do this is through their justice system. Mayan judges rarely send offenders to jail. This would take them away from their families and hurt the community. Instead, offenders usually pay for crimes through labor or community service. This traditional form of punishment is called *restitution*. But the Maya have also adapted to national laws. For serious crimes, such as murder, they turn offenders over to the national courts.

Mayan communities face other challenges. Most lack jobs, schools, and good health care. Some Maya adapt by leaving their villages. They move to cities to find work or to get an education.

10.4 The Traditional Home and Family

Home and family are the foundation of Mayan life. Most Mayan families live in simple one-room dwellings made of wood or mud brick called **adobe**. But the Maya don't see a house as just an arrangement of building materials. They see it as a living thing, with a soul like a person. In fact, they believe that everything on Earth is alive. Before they build a house, they hold a ceremony to ask the Earth's permission.

The Old and New at Home A traditional Mayan house is simple on the inside. The floors are made of packed earth. There is little furniture. A family might own hammocks for sleeping. They also might have a small wooden table and chairs. A cook fire typically sits in the middle of the floor, with a few clay pots by the side. Or there might be a small cookhouse next door. There is also a family altar for religious worship.

The traditional Mayan home is also changing. Some houses in larger towns have electricity and running water. Some have a radio or a television. Metal and plastic cooking utensils are now common. Some homes even have gas stoves, blenders, and other appliances.

Men's and Women's Roles There is still a very clear division of labor in most Mayan communities. The men work in the fields and sometimes hunt. They plant, weed, and harvest the crops. The women work at home. They care for the children and weave clothes for the family.

Women also cook the meals, which consist mainly of beans and tortillas. Most women make tortillas the old way. They pat the corn dough out by hand and fry it on a griddle. Some women, however, use a tortilla press made of metal.

Most children go to school, though many quit at an early age to help out at home. They learn traditional skills such as farming and weaving from their parents. They also learn the old customs that they are expected to pass on to their children. Many young Maya also adopt new ways. They may listen to popular music and wear jeans, T-shirts, and sneakers instead of traditional Mayan clothing.

Weaving on a Belt Loom
This woman is weaving on a traditional belt loom. The loom is made of two wooden rods linked together with threads. One end is attached to a post or a tree. The other is attached to the weaver's belt. In the past, each village had its own designs. Today, villages borrow designs from each other.

10.5 Changing Ways of Work

Two farmers are heading off to work in a highland Maya village. Farming is important to the Maya. It connects them to the land they depend on to survive. But the work of these two farmers is very different. One is walking to his field on the slopes above town. The other is catching a bus for the lowlands. The first farmer will work to provide food for his family, as the Maya have done for hundreds of years. The second will work for cash on a large, modern **plantation**.

Traditional Farming Most Maya are subsistence farmers. They grow corn, beans, squash, and other vegetables on small plots called *milpas*. Corn is their most important crop. In fact, corn is sacred to the Maya. It is the "giver of life." With luck, at harvest time Mayan farmers gather enough food to feed their families for the year.

Traditionally, Mayan farmers cleared their land using the **slash-and-burn method**. They cut down the forest and burned the plants after the trees and brush dried out. Then, using simple wooden tools, they dug the ash into the ground to fertilize the soil. Some also mixed in manure and other natural fertilizers to help their crops grow.

Some Maya still follow traditional farming methods. But in many parts of the highlands, much of the land has already been cleared. As a result, slash-and-burn agriculture is no longer as common as it once was among Mayan farmers. Many farmers have adapted by using more modern farm tools, such as axes with steel blades, as well as chemical fertilizers to enrich the soil.

Working for Wages Mayan farmers have adapted in other ways. Many spend part of the year working for wages on commercial farms. When the Spanish colonized Guatemala, they took over most of the best land. Little has changed since then. About 2 percent of the population still owns 70 percent of the land. Most of these landowners raise sugarcane, coffee, cotton, and other crops for export.

Mayan farmers travel to the lowlands to work on these plantations. These **migrant workers** spend weeks or even months away from their families. When they return, they usually have some money saved. But plantation wages are low. Many farm families still struggle to make a living.

Land Use in Guatemala

This map shows a mix of old and new in farming. Subsistence farming takes place mainly in the highlands, where most Maya live. Commercial farming takes place at lower elevations. Many Maya work on lowland plantations as migrant workers.

Farming and Major Crops in Guatemala

GUATEMALA

Commerical farming
Subsistence farming

Crops
- Maize and other food crops
- Coffee
- Bananas
- Sugarcane
- Cotton

N
W E
S

0   50   100 miles
0   50   100 kilometers
Albers Conic Equal-Area projection

10.6 Making the Most of Market Day

It's market day in Chichicastenango, Guatemala. At 7:00 A.M. a chilly mist still hangs over the town, but already the plaza is jammed with people. Most are Maya from the surrounding countryside. They have come to buy and sell food, tools, and other goods. There are also many tourists from around the world. They have come to see one of the most famous markets in the Mayan world.

Market day is an important tradition in the Mayan highlands. Markets still offer a strong flavor of Mayan culture. They also reflect many changes taking place in the Mayan world.

Trading Goods and Services Mayan markets are held one or two days a week. Sunday is a popular choice for market day.

A Mayan market typically spreads out from the central plaza into surrounding streets. Stalls selling the same type of goods are usually grouped together. Fruits and vegetables are found in one area, household goods in another. Markets also have food stalls to feed hungry shoppers. They may offer other services too, such as shoe repair, portrait photography, and money lending.

The Growing Tourist Trade Highland markets have changed as tourists have come to the highlands to see historic Mayan sites. In Chichicastenango, a large part of the market is devoted to tourist items. Some are traditional Mayan products, like weavings and wood carvings. Other items, such as purses and baseball caps, are designed and made just for tourists.

Other changes in the market also show adaptations to the modern world. Many years ago, **barter,** or trade, was a common way to obtain goods in Mayan markets. For example, a Maya might exchange a basket of vegetables for a certain amount of salt or sugar. Now most trading is done with money.

There are other changes as well. For instance, once most market trading was done in Mayan languages. Now Spanish is the common tongue. In addition, many goods in highland markets, from radios to plastic toys, show adaptations to modern life.

Mayan Markets and Tourism
Mayan markets are colorful affairs. While many tourists come to Guatemala to see Mayan ruins, they also visit highland markets. Here they find traditional crafts, some of which are made especially for tourists.

10.7 Keeping Mayan Traditions Alive

On a hillside above Chichicastenango sits the Mayan shrine of Pascual Abaj. The Quiché Maya come here to worship their ancient gods. They kneel before a small, carved altar and burn candles and incense. They ask the gods to bring a good harvest and cure the sick. Five hundred years after the Spanish conquest, the Maya still practice their traditional beliefs.

Religion and Celebrations The ancient Maya worshiped many gods. These gods represented elements of the natural world, such as the sun, rain, and lightning. For the Maya, everything in the world, even rocks and water, had a spirit.

When the Spanish arrived in the 1500s, they began to convert the Maya to Christianity. Spain was a Catholic country, and over time most Maya became Catholics. But they also kept their ancient beliefs. In fact, they blended their old beliefs with Catholicism to form a new kind of religion.

The Maya saw little conflict between their old and new beliefs. They could worship Catholic saints and still remain faithful to their own gods. Many saints even took on features of the Mayan gods.

Today this blended religion is seen in religious festivals throughout the Mayan highlands. Easter week and Christmas are major holidays. The Maya attend Catholic mass and carry images of the saints through the streets. They also celebrate these occasions in Mayan fashion. They listen to traditional music played on Mayan instruments. They watch traditional dances performed by masked dancers in Mayan costumes. And they pray to Mayan gods in **rituals** that date back thousands of years.

At festivals, the Maya dress in their finest traditional clothes. Women wear beautiful woven blouses, or *huipiles*. They also wear colorful skirts, belts, and headdresses. Even men, who usually wear modern clothing, may dress in Mayan style. The designs in traditional clothing reflect the history and myths of the Mayan people. They provide a living link to the Mayan past.

Marimba Players

Music plays a key role in Mayan celebrations. Musicians play traditional instruments such as drums, flutes, and the marimba. A marimba is a type of xylophone.

Mayan Healer
Mayan healers are experts in herbal medicine. They know how to use plants and other natural remedies to cure disease. They preserve other traditions, too, such as sacred rituals and the ancient calendar. But they are also familiar with modern medicine. They will send patients to modern doctors when necessary.

Traditional Medicine The Maya have also preserved their traditional medicine. They may go to modern doctors for major problems. But many still prefer to visit traditional healers.

Mayan healers have great knowledge of their natural environment. They use medicinal plants to cure disease. They know how to fix broken bones and heal snakebites. But they don't treat only physical illness. The Maya believe that illness has both physical and spiritual causes. For this reason, healers also use rituals to treat the soul and mend the spirit.

The most skilled Mayan healers are also the wise men of their community. They may also become "daykeepers." These are men who preserve knowledge of the ancient Mayan calendar. They perform rituals on key days to maintain harmony among people, the gods, and the natural world.

10.8 Beginning to Think Globally

In this chapter, you read about Mayan culture in the highlands of Guatemala and southern Mexico. You learned that the Maya have kept many of their traditional customs and beliefs. Yet they have also adapted to the modern world.

Other indigenous groups have also tried to preserve their culture while adapting to modern life. The Navajo people of the American Southwest are one example. The Navajo still practice their traditional crafts and their old religion. But they also drive cars, go to college, and leave home to find work.

Indigenous peoples live all around the globe. In the next section, you will find out more about how they preserve their culture and yet adapt to the modern world.

10.9 Global Connections

The map shows indigenous groups around the world. There are at least 250 million indigenous peoples spread across 70 countries. Note that some groups live in areas that span national borders. Why might this be?

What do indigenous peoples gain by adapting to modern life? The graphs below the map show that indigenous peoples are generally poorer than other people in their countries. They may benefit from adopting the language and customs of the majority population. They may also gain access to better jobs, health care, and schools.

What is most often lost when indigenous peoples adapt to modern life? Indigenous peoples often lose their language, history, and customs when they join modern society. They forget the things that make their culture special. As a result, they may lose their sense of identity. At the same time, the world loses some of its cultural diversity. Notice the number of languages in the chart below the map. As indigenous people adapt, many of those languages will disappear.

Can indigenous peoples preserve their traditional culture while adapting to modern life? Many are trying to do so. The Maori of New Zealand, for example, turned to modern courts to regain their traditional lands and fishing areas. The Inuit of Canada are using rifles and snowmobiles for their traditional hunting activities. Like other indigenous peoples around the world, they are using new tools to preserve ancient ways.

Indigenous Populations Around the World

Arctic
1. **Arctic:** Inuit (Eskimo) in Alaska, Canada, Greenland, and Russia

North America
2. **Central Canada:** Innu, Cree
3. **Plains:** Crow, Cheyenne, Arapaho, Pawnee, Comanche, Oglala Sioux, Shoshone

Central America
4. **Mexico Mayan descendants:** Lacandon, Yucatec
   Aztec descendants: Huichol, Tarahumara, Nahua, Zapotec

South America
5. **Amazon Basin—Brazil:** Tukano, Xavante, Kayapo, Yanomami
   Amazon Basin—Ecuador, Bolivia, Peru, Colombia, Venezuela: Amarakaeri, Amuesha, Tukano, Panare, Quichua
6. **Argentina, Chile:** Mapuche

0   1,000   2,000 miles
0 1,000 2,000 kilometers
Robinson projection

Source: *The Gaia Atlas of First Peoples,* by Julian Burger, London: Gaia Books, 1990.

Languages in Active Use

Country	Number of Languages
Papua New Guinea	820
Indonesia	742
Nigeria	516
India	427
United States	311
Mexico	297
Australia	275
China	241
Brazil	200
Russia	129

Source: Gordon, Raymond G., Jr. (ed.), 2005. *Ethnologue: Languages of the World, 15th ed.* Dallas, TX: SIL International.

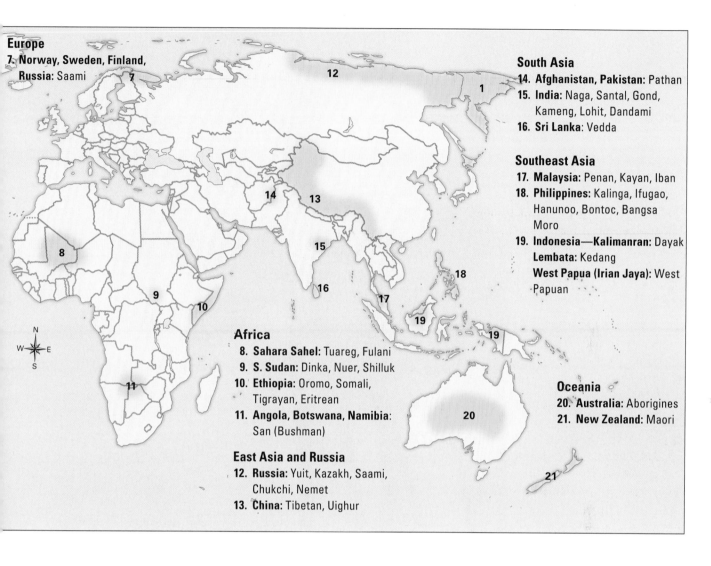

Europe
7. **Norway, Sweden, Finland, Russia:** Saami

South Asia
14. **Afghanistan, Pakistan:** Pathan
15. **India:** Naga, Santal, Gond, Kameng, Lohit, Dandami
16. **Sri Lanka:** Vedda

Southeast Asia
17. **Malaysia:** Penan, Kayan, Iban
18. **Philippines:** Kalinga, Ifugao, Hanunoo, Bontoc, Bangsa Moro
19. **Indonesia—Kalimanran:** Dayak **Lembata:** Kedang **West Papua (Irian Jaya):** West Papuan

Africa
8. **Sahara Sahel:** Tuareg, Fulani
9. **S. Sudan:** Dinka, Nuer, Shilluk
10. **Ethiopia:** Oromo, Somali, Tigrayan, Eritrean
11. **Angola, Botswana, Namibia:** San (Bushman)

East Asia and Russia
12. **Russia:** Yuit, Kazakh, Saami, Chukchi, Nemet
13. **China:** Tibetan, Uighur

Oceania
20. **Australia:** Aborigines
21. **New Zealand:** Maori

Poverty Among Indigenous and Non-indigenous Populations in Latin America

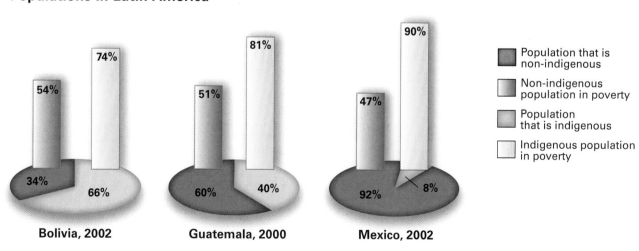

Bolivia, 2002: 54%, 74%, 34%, 66%
Guatemala, 2000: 51%, 81%, 60%, 40%
Mexico, 2002: 47%, 90%, 92%, 8%

Legend:
- Population that is non-indigenous
- Non-indigenous population in poverty
- Population that is indigenous
- Indigenous population in poverty

Source: *Indigenous People and Poverty in Latin America,* by George Psacharopoulos and Harry A. Patrinos, World Bank Group.

Dealing with Extreme Weather: Hurricanes in the Caribbean

11.1 Introduction

On September 7, 2004, Hurricane Ivan slammed into the Caribbean island of Grenada. "It was absolutely terrifying," one resident said. "The winds were gusting over 145 miles per hour and just tearing off roofs." Ivan damaged just about every home on the island and destroyed almost half of them. More than 30 people lost their lives in the storm. One woman whose roof was torn off spent the storm huddled under a mattress with her family. "I stared death in the face," she said. "What could be more scary than that?"

Hurricanes like Ivan are an example of **extreme weather**. This term refers to severe or unusual weather conditions. Along with hurricanes, extreme weather includes **tornadoes,** blizzards, and even severe heat waves or cold spells. Extreme weather is often destructive. People may try to prepare for these natural events, but it isn't always possible. Extreme weather can be hard to predict or guard against. When great damage or loss of life occurs, an extreme weather event is called a **natural disaster**. Hurricanes often produce natural disasters.

In this chapter, you will learn about hurricanes in the Caribbean **region**. You will look at their causes and effects. You will also find out how people in the region deal with this form of extreme weather.

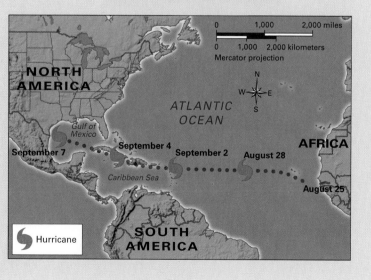

Essential Question

What causes extreme weather, and how do people deal with it?

This map shows the course of a hurricane from the coast of Africa to the Caribbean Sea. Notice that the storm passes through several locations on its journey. At each location, people must deal with the hurricane as a dangerous form of extreme weather. Keep this map in mind as you try to answer the Essential Question.

Graphic Organizer

◀ Hurricane Georges hit Puerto Rico in September 1998 with winds of 110 miles per hour.

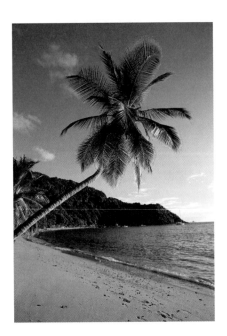

**A Sun-Drenched Beach
on the Island of Trinidad**

Tourism is a key industry in the Caribbean. Tourists are attracted to the region by sunny beaches like this one in Trinidad. Tourist areas have sprung up to meet their needs. These areas have fine hotels, restaurants, and shops. Outside these areas, however, many people still live in poverty.

11.2 The Geographic Setting

The Caribbean islands stretch in a gentle arc from the tip of Florida to the northern coast of South America. They are also known as the West Indies. They divide the Atlantic Ocean from the Caribbean Sea and the Gulf of Mexico. Thousands of islands make up this chain. Many of them are tiny, with only a few people living on them. But some, like Cuba and Hispaniola, are big islands with millions of people.

Islands in the Sun The Caribbean islands lie within one of Earth's **tropical zones**. They have a warm to hot climate year-round. Regular sea breezes cool the islands and make days pleasant.

These islands were first settled by small groups of Native Americans. The word *hurricane* comes from one of these groups, the Taino. The Taino believed that a storm god called Huracan controlled extreme weather events.

During the 1600s, European countries claimed the islands as colonies. The colonists set up **plantations,** or large farms. There they planted warm-weather crops like tobacco and sugar. The planters tried to make native peoples work on their land. But in a short time, the native peoples died out. Most were killed off by diseases brought by Europeans to the Caribbean. After that, the colonists brought large numbers of Africans to the islands to work on their farms as slaves.

During the 1800s, almost all the Caribbean islands gained their independence. Slavery was also ended. But independence brought new challenges. One was creating stable governments. Another was dealing with widespread poverty.

Today many Caribbean islands still base their economies on agriculture. Sugar remains a major **cash crop**. Bananas, coffee, and spices are also important. In recent years, **tourism** has become a key industry on many islands. Tourists flock to the Caribbean to enjoy the region's warm weather, beautiful beaches, and clear blue waters.

Extreme Weather Is a Part of Island Life Despite its pleasant climate, the Caribbean does get hit by extreme weather. Severe thunderstorms sometimes strike the islands. Heat waves and dry spells also occur.

The most extreme form of weather in the region is the **tropical cyclone**. In the Caribbean, tropical cyclones are called *hurricanes*. This is a powerful storm with winds of 74 miles per hour or more. From above, the storm looks like a giant pinwheel. It forms over warm water. As it grows, it produces heavy rain and high waves.

Our knowledge of tropical cyclones comes from **meteorology**. This is the scientific study of climate and weather. Meteorologists study weather patterns and the forces that cause them. The size and power of tropical cyclones make these storms especially challenging for meteorologists. But they have made progress in understanding these severe storms. Through their work, they hope to limit the damage and loss of life caused by these extreme weather events.

▶ Geoterms

El Niño a warm ocean current that flows off the west coast of South America every few years. An El Niño event changes weather patterns around the world. It may also cause extreme weather in some regions.

extreme weather severe or unusual weather conditions, such as hurricanes, tornadoes, and blizzards

meteorology the scientific study of climate and weather patterns

natural disaster great destruction or loss of life caused by natural forces rather than by human actions

tropical cyclone a severe storm with high winds that spiral around a calm center. Depending on where they form, tropical cyclones are called *hurricanes, typhoons,* or *cyclones.*

One Day's Weather

This map shows weather conditions in the Caribbean and surrounding areas on a specific day. Weather maps are important tools in meteorology. Scientists use them to analyze weather patterns. With this information, they can predict the weather for the next few hours or days.

Sample Weather Map

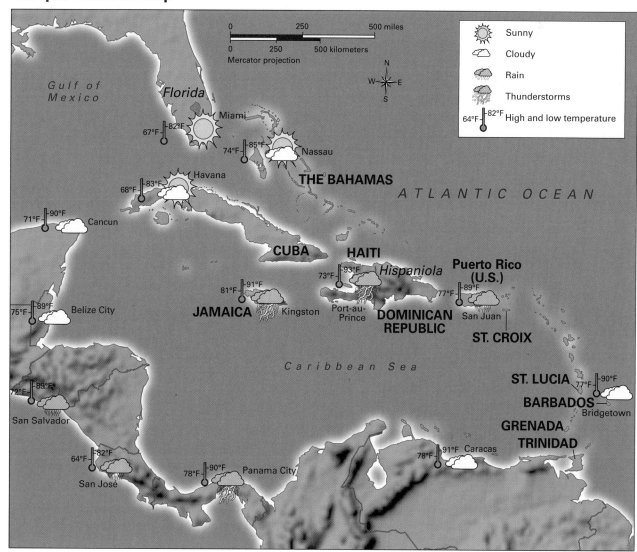

11.3 Understanding the Weather Machine

Weather doesn't just happen by itself. It is the product of natural forces working together like a machine. This "weather machine" takes energy from the sun, Earth, and the **atmosphere** and turns it into rain, wind, and other forms of weather.

Weather affects us every day, in big and small ways. Extreme weather, such as hurricanes, can have extreme effects. Storms with powerful winds can pick things up and drop them miles away. In 1997, toads rained down on the town of Villa Angel Flores in Mexico. A whirlwind had picked up the toads from a nearby body of water and then dropped them over the town!

The Sun Starts It All Weather is caused by interactions among heat, air, and water. The sun is the "engine" that drives the weather machine. As you read in Chapters 1 and 2, the sun warms Earth's surface unevenly. Its rays fall most directly between the Tropic of Cancer and the Tropic of Capricorn. Higher latitudes receive less direct sunlight. That's why temperatures are generally warmer near the equator and cooler near the poles.

The sun's heat is distributed around Earth through a process called **convection,** or heat transfer. This transfer occurs in both gases and liquids, like air and water. Warm air and warm water are less dense than cooler air and water. As a result, warm air tends to rise in the atmosphere. And warm water rises in the oceans.

When warm air or water rises out of an area, cool air or water flows in to take its place. The steady movement of air or water due to convection is called a **current**.

Winds and Trade

This map shows the main prevailing winds around the globe. Notice the winds blowing toward the equator from higher latitudes to the north and south. They are known as *trade winds*. These winds were named for their ability to move sail-powered ships carrying trade goods across the seas.

Prevailing Winds Around the World

Prevailing winds
Lower latitudes
Middle latitudes
Higher latitudes

Air and Water Move in Predictable Patterns

The movement of air and water around the globe occurs in regular patterns. In general, warm air and water currents flow from the equator toward the poles. At the same time, cool air and water currents flow from the poles toward the equator.

This predictable pattern creates **prevailing winds**. These are winds that usually blow in one direction. If Earth didn't rotate, the prevailing winds would move in straight lines between the equator and the poles. But Earth's rotation causes the wind currents to move in a curving pattern. This pattern is called the **Coriolis effect**. You can see how prevailing winds curve on the map above.

Cyclones Around the World

Small Changes Can Cause Extreme Weather Wind and ocean currents have an important influence on weather. That's because they distribute heat and cold around the world. Even minor changes in prevailing winds or ocean currents can cause major changes in weather.

A good example of this effect is the impact of an **El Niño**. An El Niño is a warm ocean current that sometimes flows along the west coast of South America. This warm current doesn't appear every year. But when it does, it usually shows up during the Christmas season. That's why it's called El Niño, which is a nickname for "the Christ child" in Spanish.

In an El Niño year, the weather on the Pacific coast of North and South America gets warmer. Rainfall increases, and flooding is common. At the same time, weather on the other side of the Pacific gets drier. Severe forest fires sometimes occur in Southeast Asia and Australia during these dry spells. The effects of an El Niño's appearance can be felt as far away as India and Africa.

Tropical Cyclones: The Most Violent Weather Events In the tropics, the weather machine can be very powerful. That's because there is more energy from the sun to warm the air and water. This energy produces tropical cyclones, the most violent storms on Earth.

Tropical cyclones occur only where ocean temperatures reach at least 80°F. Lots of warm, moist air is needed to start these storms. That's why they usually occur in the warmer months of the year.

Tropical cyclones form in three oceans. In the Atlantic Ocean and the eastern Pacific, they are called *hurricanes*. In the western Pacific, they are usually called *typhoons*. In the Indian Ocean, these storms are called *cyclones*.

Tropical Cyclones

The word *cyclone* comes from a Greek word that means "moving in a circle." Tropical cyclones form over three oceans at different times of the year. In the Atlantic Ocean and the eastern Pacific, the season runs from June through November. In the western Pacific, the season lasts from April to December. In the Indian Ocean, the season is from December to April.

Tropical Disturbance

rising warm, moist air

developing thunderclouds

rain

warm ocean waters

incoming warm, moist air

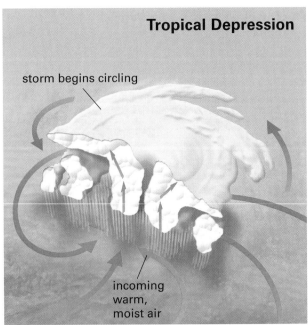

Tropical Depression

storm begins circling

incoming warm, moist air

Birth of a Hurricane

A hurricane develops in four main stages. First, various storms come together to form a tropical disturbance. Second, the disturbance grows into a tropical depression. Third, the depression becomes a tropical storm. Finally, the storm becomes a tropical cyclone, or hurricane. In each stage, wind speeds increase as the storm sucks in more air and moisture.

11.4 Extreme Weather: A Hurricane Is Born

Have you ever seen a thunderstorm approaching? The wind picks up and the temperature drops. Clouds roll in and the sky grows dark. A bolt of lightning pierces the sky, followed by a crack of thunder. Suddenly it's pouring rain. In some parts of the world, such a storm might be the first stage of a hurricane.

Tropical Thunderstorms Begin the Process Hurricanes in the Atlantic Ocean usually start out off the coast of Africa. In the summer, water temperatures in that part of the ocean rise to 80°F or more. The ocean releases warm, moist air into the atmosphere. As the warm air rises, the moisture **condenses** to form clouds and rain. The result is a tropical thunderstorm.

Sometimes several thunderstorms come together to create a **tropical disturbance**. This is a cluster of thunderstorms that move together with the prevailing winds.

From a Tropical Disturbance to a Hurricane As a tropical disturbance grows, more warm, moist air rises from the ocean. In the Northern Hemisphere, this rising air begins to circle in a counter-clockwise direction. This is due to the Coriolis effect, which you read about earlier. When wind starts circling inside a tropical disturbance, the storm becomes a **tropical depression**.

When conditions are right, a tropical depression will suck up still more warm air and moisture. Once wind speeds inside the storm reach 39 miles per hour, a tropical depression is called a **tropical storm**.

Most tropical storms die out in time. But a few continue to grow in size and wind speed. When wind speeds reach 74 miles per hour, the storm becomes a tropical cyclone. A hurricane is born!

Tropical Storm

Winds are greater than 39 mph but less than 74 mph.

descending cool air

incoming warm, moist air

Tropical Cyclone

Winds are 74 mph or greater.

eye

eye wall

rainbands

11.5 Inside a Monster Storm

A hurricane is a huge, whirling storm. And it packs a powerful punch. In just one day, a hurricane releases more energy than 500,000 atomic bombs. If you could turn that energy into electricity, it would be enough to satisfy the electrical needs of the United States for six months!

The Parts of a Hurricane A hurricane is made up of three key parts. The first part is the **eye**. This is a calm spot at the center of the storm. The eye of a hurricane might be 20 to 40 miles across. The winds of a hurricane swirl around the calm eye.

The second part is the **eye wall**. The eye wall is made up of thunderstorms that surround the eye. From the center of the storm, the eye wall looks like a great curtain of clouds. This wall of storms can be anywhere from 5 to 30 miles thick.

Rainbands are the third key part. These are bands of dense clouds that swirl around the eye wall. The rainbands spiral toward the center of the hurricane as it moves across the ocean. They drop large amounts of rain as the storm travels.

The Path of Hurricanes As you read, Atlantic hurricanes are born off the coast of Africa. Once a monster storm develops, trade winds blow it from east to west across the Atlantic. The hurricane spins rapidly as it moves, like a giant top.

The exact track, or path, of a hurricane is unpredictable. A hurricane may change course with a shift in wind direction. It also may speed up, slow down, or even stop for a while and build up strength. As long as a hurricane stays over warm water, it can continue to grow in both size and power. Severe storms can swell to 1,000 miles across in size and pack wind speeds of up to 200 miles per hour.

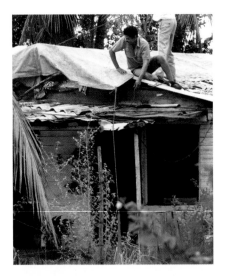

Getting Ready for a Hurricane

This Cuban is tying a tarp over his roof in preparation for a hurricane. People in this region know how to prepare for big storms. Hurricane survival kits typically include these things:

- Water: 1 gallon a day per person for 3 to 7 days
- Food: enough to feed people and pets for 3 to 7 days
- First aid kit and medicines
- Blankets and clothes
- Flashlight and batteries
- Battery-powered radio
- Tools for repairing storm damage

11.6 Tracking and Preparing for a Hurricane

"Hold on," the pilot says to his crew. "We're going in!" The plane shakes violently as it enters the storm's eye wall. But then the shaking stops. The plane has reached the calm eye of the hurricane.

This plane and its crew are part of a special Air Force unit called the Hurricane Hunters. The Hurricane Hunters fly into tropical storms to record weather data. The work is dangerous, but the crews believe that what they learn is worth the risks. "The bottom line for all of us," says a pilot, "is that we do save lives."

Meteorologists Track and Name Hurricanes The Hurricane Hunters work with meteorologists to track the paths of tropical storms. The meteorologists use satellite images and data from the flight crews to decide when a storm has become a hurricane. At that point, they give the hurricane a name.

Meteorologists have alphabetical lists of male and female names to use in naming hurricanes. The name of the year's first hurricane always begins with the letter A. When a very destructive hurricane hits land, its name is retired and never used again. Since 1954, at least 70 hurricane names have been retired.

Preparing for a Hurricane Once meteorologists know the track of a storm, they warn people in its path. When a storm might hit land within 24 to 36 hours, they issue a *hurricane watch*. When the storm is less than 24 hours away, they issue a *hurricane warning*. These predictions are not always perfect, but they do give people a chance to prepare for the storm.

Meteorologists use the **Saffir-Simpson scale** to rate a hurricane's strength. This scale rates hurricanes from 1 to 5. The higher the number, the more damage the storm can cause. This information helps people decide whether to board up their windows and stay home or to seek a safer shelter away from the coast. Storms often change ratings as they travel. In 2003, Hurricane Isabel stayed at level 5 for over 30 hours. This made it one of the longest-lasting Category 5 storms on record.

The Saffir-Simpson Scale

Scientists rate hurricanes using the Saffir-Simpson scale. Category 5 storms are the most dangerous. But less powerful storms can also be deadly.

Category 1 hurricane   Category 2 hurricane

11.7 Landfall: A Natural Disaster Begins

When a hurricane hits land, its power is truly awesome. "The wind is at a ferocious roar and coming in powerful bursts," wrote a reporter who witnessed Hurricane Ivan's landfall in Jamaica in 2004. "Even stepping outside for a minute would mean serious injury or worse. Hurricane Ivan has arrived in all its fury and it's terrible indeed."

The Power of Wind and Rain When a hurricane strikes, it lashes everything in its path with wind and rain. The most powerful hurricanes carry winds of up to 200 miles per hour. Such fierce winds can uproot trees or snap them in half. They can shatter windows, blow off roofs, flip over cars, and hurl boats through the air.

Heavy hurricane rains often cause terrible flooding. They can also loosen rocks and soil on hillsides. The result may be deadly mudslides that crush everything in their path. In 1998, a Category 5 hurricane called Mitch dropped more than 75 inches of rain on Honduras, a small Central American country bordering the Caribbean Sea. The rain caused floods and mudslides that killed about 11,000 people.

Storm Surge: The Most Dangerous Force of All The most destructive feature of a hurricane is the **storm surge**. A storm surge is a wall of water pushed ashore by a storm. A storm surge can rise as much as 33 feet above sea level. That's as high as a three-story building. When this wall of water hits land, it can destroy everything in its path. Storm surges cause about 9 out of every 10 deaths from hurricanes.

The more powerful the hurricane, the higher the storm surge is likely to be. In 1999, a Category 4 storm named Lenny hit several Caribbean islands. In St. Croix, Lenny's 15-foot storm surge knocked over power poles, threw boats up on shore, and destroyed a ballpark. In St. Lucia, dozens of people were left homeless when their homes were washed away. A Category 5 storm named Katrina tore through the region in 2005. Katrina's storm surge flattened levees that protected the U.S. city of New Orleans from flooding. When the storm ended, much of New Orleans was under water. Damage was so widespread that Katrina became the costliest Atlantic hurricane of all time.

Storm Surge from Hurricane Ivan
A storm surge is a hurricane's most deadly feature. When this wall of water hits land, it causes massive floods. In 2004, a storm surge from Hurricane Ivan flooded this beach home in Cuba. This monster storm killed about 70 people across the Caribbean.

Category 3 hurricane

Category 4 hurricane

Category 5 hurricane

Rescuing Survivors of Jeanne

These people are being rescued from a flooded house in Puerto Rico after Hurricane Jeanne in 2004. The worst damage from this storm occurred in Haiti. About 3,000 Haitians died as a result of flooding and mudslides. Many Haitians may never fully recover from this disaster.

11.8 Cleaning Up After a Natural Disaster

A hurricane can have a very powerful impact. But the problems don't end when the storm moves on. Although the hurricane may be over, the effects of the natural disaster continue.

Hurricanes Lose Strength over Land Luckily, hurricanes don't last forever. Hurricane John, the world's longest-running storm, lasted nearly a month and crossed 5,000 miles of ocean. But most hurricanes die out sooner than that. The main reason is that they hit land.

Hurricanes die when they lose their main source of energy. Remember that these storms need warm ocean water to keep them going. Once they hit land or cross cool water, they begin to weaken. In the Caribbean, storms can cross an island and then pick up force on the other side. But they lose steam when they hit a large **landmass** like the United States or Mexico. At that point, they usually die out in a few days.

Rebuilding After a Natural Disaster Once a hurricane has passed, people in its path face the task of rebuilding. This is often a huge challenge. A hurricane may destroy many of the homes on a hard-hit island. It may damage schools, hospitals, roads, bridges, and power lines. Many people may be left homeless. Hunger and disease may be serious problems.

The first task after a storm passes is to rescue people caught in the wreckage. Relief agencies are set up to find and treat the injured. Relief workers also work to supply food, water, shelter, and clothing to those in need.

The next task is cleaning up. Floodwaters have to be drained from low-lying areas. Water and **sewage** lines have to be repaired to provide clean water and **sanitation**. Roads need to be cleared. Electrical power has to be restored. Damaged buildings must be knocked down. This work requires time and money. It can take months or even years for a Caribbean island to fully recover from a severe hurricane.

11.9 Beginning to Think Globally

In this chapter, you have learned about extreme weather in the Caribbean. You learned how tropical cyclones get started and how they develop into deadly storms. You read about the methods that meteorologists use to analyze and track these storms. You also learned how natural disasters caused by these storms affect people and communities in the Caribbean.

Few Places Escape Extreme Weather Tropical cyclones are tremendously destructive. But they are not the only example of extreme weather. Tornadoes, blizzards, and heavy rains can all do great harm as well.

Most parts of the world experience some form of extreme weather. In the United States, tornadoes rip through towns and destroy property every spring. In the winter months, blizzards block roads, knock out power lines, and stop air travel. The story is much the same on other continents. In South Asia, heavy rains often cause flooding. In parts of Africa, sandstorms destroy crops.

El Niño's Impact on Weather El Niño plays a key role in extreme weather. As you have learned, El Niño is a warm ocean current that flows from time to time along the Pacific coast of South America. When an El Niño occurs, it can trigger extreme weather in the Pacific region and in other parts of the world.

A major El Niño appeared off the coast of South America in 1997 and 1998. This warming of the ocean caused heavy rains and flooding in South America. It also produced tornadoes in Florida. At the same time, it caused dry spells that led to wildfires in Southeast Asia, Australia, and Central America.

Scientists are still trying to understand the role El Niño plays in extreme weather. But the effects are clear. You will look at El Niño's impact around the world in the next section.

Counting the Costs

This table shows effects of five recent hurricanes in the Caribbean. These estimates are rough. It is difficult to gather accurate information about the loss of lives and property caused by extreme weather events.

Five Destructive Hurricanes in the Caribbean, 1998–2008

Hurricane	Year	Major Areas Affected	Estimated Deaths	Estimated Damage
Ike	2008	Turks and Caicos, Bahamas, Haiti, Dominican Republic, Cuba, Florida Keys, Mississippi, Louisiana, Texas, Mississippi Valley, Ohio Valley, Great Lakes region	195	$28 billion
Katrina	2005	Bahamas, South Florida, Cuba, Mississippi, Alabama, Louisiana (especially Greater New Orleans), Florida	1,836	$81 billion
Jeanne	2004	U.S. Virgin Islands, Puerto Rico, Dominican Republic, Haiti, Bahamas, Florida	3,005	$7 billion
Ivan	2004	Grenada, Jamaica, Grand Cayman, Cuba, Alabama, Florida, Texas, Louisiana	92	$18 billion
Mitch	1998	Honduras, Nicaragua, El Salvador, Guatemala	11,000	$5 billion

Source: National Hurricane Center.

11.10 Global Connections

The small map shows warmer than usual ocean currents during an El Niño year. Notice that the warmest ocean area is off the west coast of South America. The large map shows how different areas of the world are affected during a major El Niño year. The table shows some extreme weather events that occurred in the United States between 1997 and 2007.

What parts of the world are most affected by an El Niño? As you might expect, lands bordering the Pacific Ocean show the greatest effects from an El Niño. The west coasts of North and South America experience weather that is wetter than usual. Areas on the other side of the Pacific suffer from very dry weather.

What relationship do you see between an El Niño and extreme weather? An El Niño can affect weather in ways you might not expect. The years 1997, 2002, 2003, 2004, 2005, 2006, and 2007 were all considered to be El Niño years. As the table shows, there were fewer hurricanes in the Atlantic in those years. There were also fewer extreme temperature events in the United States than in an average year.

How can understanding an El Niño's effects help meteorologists to predict extreme weather? Just how an El Niño shapes climate is not yet fully understood. But the more meteorologists learn about the factors that shape our climate, the better they will be at predicting extreme weather. This, in turn, could help people prepare for natural disasters caused by weather.

El Niño's Effects Around the World

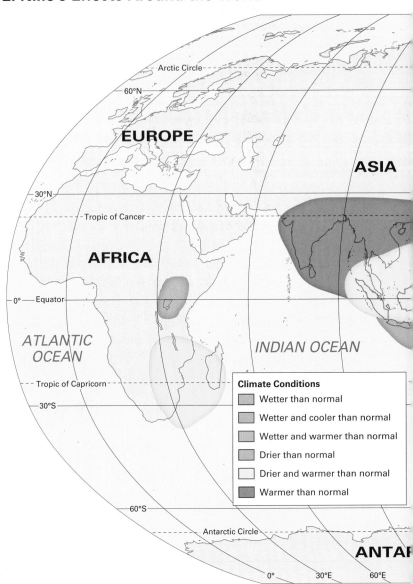

Climate Conditions

- Wetter than normal
- Wetter and cooler than normal
- Wetter and warmer than normal
- Drier than normal
- Drier and warmer than normal
- Warmer than normal

Sea Surface Temperatures in an El Niño Year

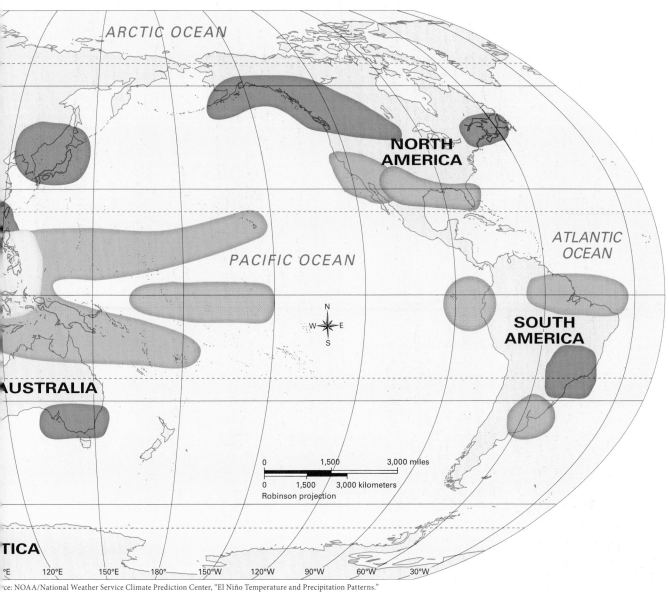

ce: NOAA/National Weather Service Climate Prediction Center, "El Niño Temperature and Precipitation Patterns."

Extreme Weather Events in the United States, 1997–2007

El Niño Year	1997	1998	1999	2000	2001	2002	2003	2004	2005	2006	2007
Atlantic Hurricanes	3	10	8	8	9	4	7	9	15	5	6
Violent Tornadoes	10	14	18	3	8	6	13	8	1	2	5
Extreme Hail Events	65	100	73	71	69	75	95	99	72	116	67
Extreme Temperature Events	238	344	395	418	285	251	126	165	153	214	360

Sources: National Oceanic and Atmospheric Administration. Jan Null, "El Niño and La Niña Years: A Consensus List," Oct. 2004, *Golden Gate Weather Services.*
Weather Underground, "Hurricane Archive," www.wunderground.com.

Dealing with Extreme Weather: Hurricanes in the Caribbean   **175**

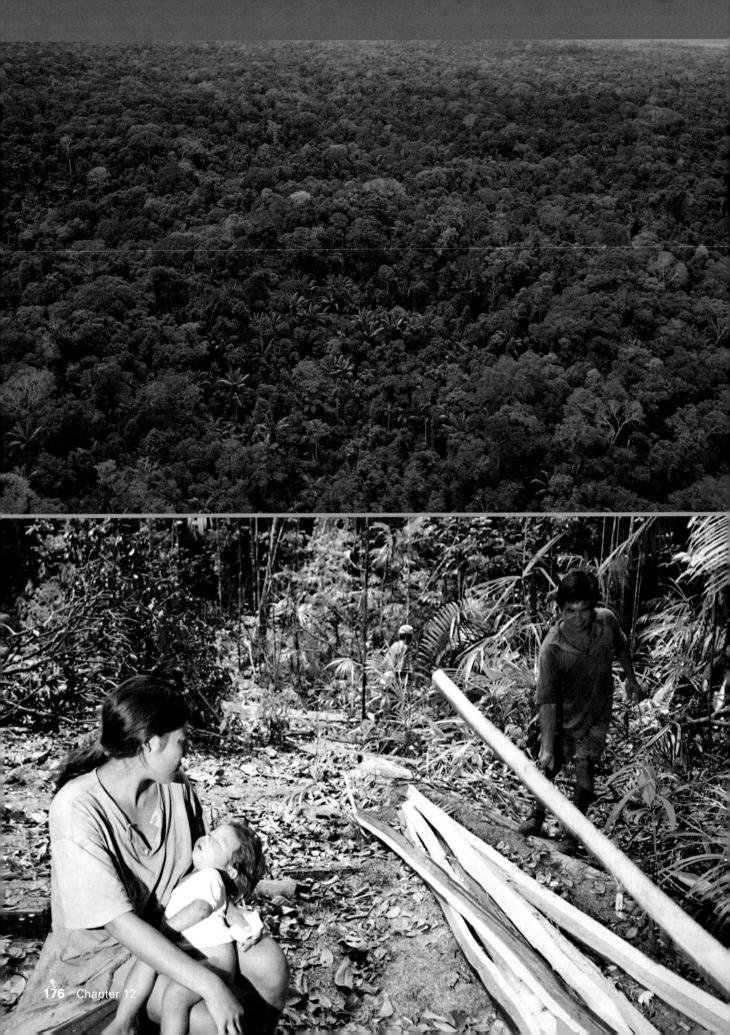

Land Use Conflict in the Amazon Rainforest

12

12.1 Introduction

Picture yourself in a hot, steamy forest. It has just stopped raining. Everything around you is green and moist. Green vines wind around the slender trunks of trees that reach more than 100 feet into the air. High overhead, a tangle of vines, branches, and leaves nearly blocks out the sun. Except for the buzzing of insects, the forest is nearly silent. Then you hear a strange barking sound coming from the treetops. You look up and get your first glimpse of a red howler monkey.

Welcome to the Amazon rainforest, a huge **tropical rainforest** in South America. The rainforest seems timeless, yet it is changing rapidly. For thousands of years, small groups of **indigenous peoples** have made their home here. These native Amazonians live by hunting and gathering. In more recent times, other groups have come to the rainforest. They include rubber tappers, farmers, cattle ranchers, and loggers. In addition, the rainforest is of great interest to environmental groups. These are organizations that work to protect the natural world.

Each of these groups has its own ideas about the Amazon rainforest. Some want to use the rainforest to make a living. Others want to preserve it in its natural state. These differences have led to **land use conflict,** or arguments about the best ways to use the land. In this chapter, you will learn what the different groups want. You will also learn about possible solutions to land use conflict in the Amazon rainforest.

Essential Question

How should the resources of rainforests be used and preserved?

This illustration shows six groups that are interested in the Amazon rainforest. Some want to use the resources of the rainforest to make a living. Others want to preserve the rainforest in its natural state. Keep the possible conflicts among these groups in mind as you try to answer the Essential Question.

Graphic Organizer

Native Amazonians | Rubber Tappers | Loggers | Settlers | Cattle Ranchers | Environmentalists

◀ The Amazon rainforest (top), Brazilian family cutting wood (bottom)

The Amazon Basin

The World's Largest Rainforest

The Amazon basin covers much of northern Brazil and several other countries in South America. It contains the world's largest rainforest. It receives 80 to 115 inches of rain a year. The Amazon rainforest is home to more types of plants and animals than any other place on Earth.

12.2 The Geographic Setting

Tropical rainforests are a type of **broadleaf evergreen forest**. They are found near the equator, where the **climate** is warm and wet all year. The Amazon rainforest is the largest tropical rainforest in the world. It covers more than 2 million square miles. That is more than half the size of the United States! Most of this vast rainforest lies in Brazil. It also covers parts of Colombia, Ecuador, Peru, Bolivia, and Venezuela.

A Many-Layered Ecosystem A rainforest is a complex **ecosystem** with many layers. The bottom, or ground, layer is the **forest floor**. The thick layer of overlapping tree branches at the very top of the forest is called the **canopy**. Between the forest floor and the canopy is a layer of shrubs and smaller trees. This layer is called the **lower story**.

An amazing variety of plants and animals live in the various layers of the rainforest. Rainforests cover about 6 percent of the Earth's surface. But they are home to about 50 percent of the world's living things.

Scientists use the term **biodiversity** to describe the variety of plants and animals living in one area. The great biodiversity of rainforests attracts scientists who study flora and fauna.

Other groups have different reasons for coming to the rainforest. Some people come to clear land for farming or ranching. The result is **deforestation,** or the removal of trees from large areas. Other people are more interested in **sustainable development**. This means finding ways to use the resources of the rainforest without destroying it.

The Lungs of the Earth Many people around the world worry about the fate of the Amazon rainforest. A major reason for their concern is that tropical rainforests affect life far beyond their borders. The trees and plants that grow in these dense forests have been called the "lungs of the Earth."

This nickname comes from the key role that rainforests play in Earth's **carbon-oxygen cycle**. This series of events turns a gas called carbon dioxide, or CO_2, into oxygen. Then it turns the oxygen back into CO_2. In this way, carbon and oxygen are "cycled" among the living things that need them to survive.

Here is how the cycle works. When people and other animals breathe, their bodies take in oxygen and breathe out CO_2. Cars and factories also produce CO_2 as a waste product when burning fuel. Trees and other plants absorb CO_2 from the air. The plants use the carbon for their growth. They release the oxygen back into the air as a waste product. When people and other animals breathe in this oxygen, the cycle begins again.

Because they are rich in plant life, rainforests are a major part of the carbon-oxygen cycle. Scientists believe that the Amazon rainforest alone creates a quarter of Earth's oxygen. The oxygen you are breathing right now may have come from a rainforest tree.

▶ Geoterms

biodiversity the variety of plants and animals living in one area. The term can also mean the great variety of all living things on Earth.

carbon-oxygen cycle the process by which carbon and oxygen cycle among plants, people and animals, and the environment

deforestation removing or clearing away the trees from a forest. Deforestation is often done to clear land for farming or ranching.

sustainable development using resources in ways that meet the needs of people today without hurting the ability of future generations to meet their own needs. This means finding ways to use resources without using them up.

tropical rainforest a broadleaf evergreen forest found in wet and hot regions near the equator

Canopy:
100–165 feet

Lower story:
3–100 feet

Forest floor:
0–3 feet

The Three Layers of a Rainforest

A tropical rainforest grows in three layers. Shade-loving mosses and ferns thrive on the dark forest floor. Small trees and vines fill in the lower story, or middle layer. Trees reaching for sunlight form a canopy of branches at the top of the forest. Some very tall trees even poke their heads above the canopy.

A Native Amazonian Hunter
Native peoples have lived in the rainforest for about 12,000 years. This man is using a traditional bow and arrow to hunt for game. In recent years, native Amazonians have lost much of their land to loggers, farmers, and ranchers.

12.3 What Native Amazonians Want

Once there were as many as 10 million native people living in the Amazon rainforest. Today the number of native Amazonians is much smaller. Those who remain want one thing above all: to continue their traditional way of life.

A Sustainable Way of Life Native people have lived in the rainforest for about 12,000 years. Many live as they always have. They hunt and fish, and they grow crops on small plots of land they have cleared in the forest. When a field is no longer fertile, they clear a new one somewhere else. Over time, new forest covers the old field. This is a sustainable way of life. It uses the resources of the Amazon rainforest without causing long-term damage.

In the 1960s, the government of Brazil decided to open the Amazon basin to development. It began by building a highway into the rainforest. Farmers, ranchers, and loggers followed the road into the Amazon region.

The arrival of so many newcomers has hurt native Amazonians. Many native people have been driven from their homelands to make room for farms and ranches. Some have died from diseases brought by newcomers. Others have been killed or injured in land use conflicts.

Save the Forest to Save Us Today native Amazonians are fighting to save parts of the rainforest from development. They say they have a right to preserve themselves and their way of life. As native leader Davi Kopenawa has said, "I want to live where I really belong, on my own land."

In their struggle to survive, native Amazonians have had to learn new skills. One is how to speak Portuguese, the official language of Brazil. Another is how to work with Brazil's government and legal system. Native groups have called on the Brazilian government to make them the legal owners of their homelands. Only then will they be able to keep others from destroying their rainforest home.

12.4 What Rubber Tappers Want

Rubber tappers have lived in the Amazon basin for many generations. Rubber tappers "tap," or collect, the sap from rubber trees that grow in the rainforest. The sap is then dried to make rubber products such as erasers or tires for cars and bikes.

Rubber Tapping Does Not Hurt the Forest Rubber tappers first came to the Amazon in the 1870s. They were hired to work on rubber tree plantations in the rainforest. When the price of rubber dropped, most of the plantations were abandoned. But some rubber tappers stayed and continued to make their living in the rainforest.

Rubber tappers remove sap from a rubber tree by making diagonal cuts in the bark. They collect the sap in cups. Removing the sap in this way does not harm the tree. This makes rubber tapping a sustainable activity. It is one way to use the resources of the rainforest without harming the environment.

In the 1960s, the government of Brazil decided that there were better ways to use the rainforest. It encouraged people to clear the forest for farms and ranches. In the deforestation that followed, many rubber trees disappeared. This led to land use conflict between rubber tappers and newcomers.

Let Us Continue Our Sustainable Way of Life Rubber tappers want to go on making a living from the rainforest. To do this, they need to stop the widespread clearing of trees. They have asked the government to create protected **reserves** in the rainforest. These areas would be set aside for sustainable activities like rubber tapping.

Rubber tappers believe that their right to the rainforest comes from having worked there for so long. They also argue that their way of life does not harm the rainforest. For this reason, they believe, the government should protect their activities.

Scoring a Rubber Tree

Rubber tappers collect sap from rubber trees without hurting them. One tapper, Chico Mendes, became a leader in the fight to preserve the rainforest. Eventually, because of his activities, he was murdered. His death brought world attention to the rubber tappers' cause.

12.5 What Loggers Want

Logging companies began moving into the Amazon basin in the 1960s. Loggers harvest trees from forests for use in wood products. These products range from paper to fine furniture.

The Rainforest Is a Source of Valuable Hardwoods A great variety of trees grows in the Amazon rainforest. The most valuable are hardwood trees such as mahogany and rosewood. Furniture makers all over the world use the beautiful wood from these trees.

Unfortunately, these valuable trees are scattered throughout the rainforest. This makes it hard to find and cut just the hardwoods. Instead, loggers **clear-cut** whole patches of rainforest. This means that they cut down all of the trees in an area. Once all the trees are removed, the loggers move on to another patch.

Logging companies argue that clear-cutting is the only way they can make money. But clear-cutting is also a major cause of deforestation. The larger the area that is stripped of its trees, the longer it takes for the rainforest to grow back.

Logging also leads to other types of development. Logging companies build roads deep into the rainforest so that they can move logs by truck. Settlers looking for land follow these logging roads into the forest. Once there, they claim land for farming and ranching.

We Need Trees to Help Brazil's Economy Many groups oppose clear-cutting of the rainforest. Loggers reply that they are helping Brazil's economy grow. Logging, they say, creates jobs for people in the **forestry** industry. It also provides wood for Brazil's furniture factories and paper mills.

Lumber companies also argue that they have made forestry a valuable **economic activity** for Brazil. In 2005, Brazil exported more than $5 billion worth of wood. The money earned from these sales is helping Brazil to pay off its debts. It is also making life better for many people.

Loggers Lead the Way in Developing the Rainforest

In the 1960s, loggers began building dirt roads into the rainforest. Other groups began to develop land near these roads. In time, some logging roads became paved highways.

Clearing Rainforest for Farming
Settlers who come to the rainforest clear the trees off their land to create farm fields. Farming in this environment is not easy. The constant rain washes away the soil's nutrients. Tropical insects also kill many crops.

12.6 What Settlers Want

Brazil has the eleventh largest economy in the world. Yet about one quarter of Brazilians are poor. In **rural** areas, even more of the population is poor.

In the 1960s, the Brazilian government began encouraging poor people to move to the Amazon rainforest. The settlers came in large numbers, looking for land to farm.

A Lot of Land, but Not for the Poor Brazil is a vast country but has limited areas of farmland. And this land is not shared equally. A few wealthy families have long owned most of the best farmland. Millions of poor Brazilians own no land at all. For many families, the idea of owning a farm in the Amazon basin once seemed like a distant dream.

The Brazilian government did what it could to make this dream come true. Poor families were brought to the rainforest by the government. They were given free land and money to plant their first crops.

We Need Land to Feed Our Families Over time, the settlers' dream has become a nightmare for many farm families. As native Amazonians learned long ago, farming in a rainforest is difficult. The thin soil is surprisingly poor in **nutrients,** the substances that make a field fertile. Constant rainfall soon washes away whatever nutrients the soil once contained. As the soil loses its fertility, the amount of food it can produce shrinks. Native Amazonians solved this problem by clearing new fields every few years. Over time, their abandoned fields regained some fertility.

Brazilian settlers cannot move so easily. As more settlers have cleared land for farming, opposition to them has grown. Native Amazonians, rubber tappers, and ranchers all want settlers to leave the rainforest. Settlers argue that there is no land for them in other parts of Brazil. They say they must look to the rainforest for land to feed their families.

A Cattle Drive in the Rainforest

Cattle like these are a common sight in the Amazon basin. Cattle ranching is now one of the main causes of deforestation in the rainforest. Ranchers say they are raising food for the world. And many countries are happy to buy Brazilian beef.

12.7 What Cattle Ranchers Want

A rainforest may not seem like cattle country. But since the 1960s, parts of the Amazon basin have become just that. Although Amazon cattle ranchers are a small group, they own large areas of rainforest land.

Cattle Need Grasslands to Graze Rainforest cattle graze mainly on grass. They eat the grass in an area all the way down to the dirt. Then they are moved to a new area with fresh grass to eat. Moving cattle from place to place gives grazed areas a chance to grow new grass. It also uses up a lot of land.

Today cattle can be found grazing on vast areas of grassland in the Amazon basin. Loggers cleared some of this land. Farmers and ranchers cleared the rest. Once large areas of rainforest are cleared, the trees seldom grow back. Instead, the cleared areas become grasslands. This permanent deforestation upsets many people. But it is a great benefit to ranchers.

We Need Land to Feed the World Many people argue that cattle don't belong in a rainforest. Cattle ranchers strongly disagree. They say they are making good use of rainforest land by raising food for the world and earning money for Brazil.

Many countries import beef from Brazil. In fact, the United States is one of the biggest buyers of Brazilian beef. Some environmental groups are not happy with this trade. They estimate that 55 square feet of rainforest have to be cleared for every hamburger sold in the United States.

Like logging, cattle ranching has become an important economic activity in Brazil. In 2008, the value of beef exported to other countries was more than $3 billion. Brazil can use the money earned from beef sales to help pay its debts and take care of its citizens.

12.8 What Environmental Groups Want

Not all Brazilians want to see the Amazon basin developed. Environmental groups have worked for years to slow the clearing of the rainforest. Their ideas have led to conflict with many other groups.

Protecting the Biodiversity of the Rainforest Scientists and **environmentalists** began coming to the rainforest in the 1970s. Some came to study rainforest plants. They hoped to find plants that could cure diseases. Others came to study rainforest animals. Still others came to work with native peoples.

All these groups are united in wanting to protect the rainforest and its biodiversity. Scientists estimate that a 2.5-acre patch of rainforest contains 750 kinds of trees. The same patch supports 1,500 kinds of flowering plants. It is home to 125 species of mammals and 400 kinds of birds. And these numbers include only the plants and animals that scientists already know about. Countless unknown species also live in the rainforest.

We Want Slower, Smarter Rainforest Development

Environmental groups argue that all rainforest species have a right to exist. This means saving their rainforest home. Environmentalists therefore want to slow down development of the rainforest. This would give scientists time to study the effects of new activities. With that information, better decisions can be made for the future.

In 2000, environmental groups won a major victory against ranchers. They were able to block a law that would have let ranchers clear rainforest land without restrictions. Another victory came in 2004. In that year, Brazil's government created two large rainforest reserves. Only sustainable activities like rubber tapping are allowed in these places. In 2008, Brazil's leaders set up a $21 billion fund. It will pay for conservation and sustainable development in the Amazon. Norway has already promised to give a billion dollars to this fund.

Number of species: 1,500 · 1,400 · 1,300 · 1,200 · 1,100 · 1,000 · 900 · 800 · 700 · 600 · 500 · 400 · 300 · 200 · 100

amphibian · reptile · mammal · butterfly · bird · tree · flowering plant

Source: The Nature Conservancy.

The Rainforest Is Home to Earth's Greatest Biodiversity

Experts estimate that we are losing over 100 plant, animal, and insect species every day to rainforest deforestation. Some of these species haven't even been discovered yet! Look closely at this illustration. Why are these plants and animals drawn in unusual sizes relative to one another?

Ecotourism in the Rainforest

Ecotourism attracts people who like being close to nature. Visitors to the rainforest learn about its great variety of plants and animals. Meanwhile, the money they spend creates jobs.

12.9 Ideas for Reducing Land Use Conflict

Each of the groups you have read about has its own ideas for how best to use or preserve the Amazon rainforest. Often this has led to land use conflict. A few groups, however, are looking at ways to balance preservation and development. In this way, they hope to meet the needs of people while reducing harm to the rainforest. Here are some of their ideas.

Promote Ecotourism Most countries encourage **tourism**. This is the business of organizing travel for pleasure. Attracting tourists helps a country's economy. Tourists spend money on hotels, meals, services, and souvenirs.

Some tour companies are promoting a new type of tourism called **ecotourism**. This kind of travel attracts people who want to visit unique ecosystems, such as a rainforest. Boat tours of the Amazon rainforest attract ecotourists from all over the world.

Ecotourism offers many benefits. It creates jobs for people in the tourist industry. It helps the economy by bringing in money. Most important, it gives people a reason to preserve the places that ecotourists come to see. The great danger of ecotourism is overuse. If too many tourists visit a fragile area, they may help to destroy what they have come to see.

Encourage Sustainable Development Another way to balance development and preservation is to encourage sustainable development. In Brazil, this means finding ways to use the rainforest without destroying it. One way is by growing crops that don't require large areas to be cleared.

An example of such a crop is shade-grown coffee. This method of growing coffee makes good use of rainforest trees. The coffee bushes are planted under a canopy of trees. The trees keep the bushes from getting too much sun. Leaves from the coffee bushes enrich the soil.

Loss of Tropical Rainforest Worldwide

Area of tropical rainforest, 2008

Original area of tropical rainforest

0 1 million 2 million 3 million 4 million 5 million 6 million

Area (square miles)

Coffee bushes also provide **habitat** for birds. The birds, in turn, eat bugs that attack coffee plants. This type of farming uses little or no chemicals. This is good for both coffee planters and coffee drinkers.

Another less harmful way of using the rainforest is strip logging. Instead of clear-cutting large areas, strip loggers clear long, narrow strips of forest. The forest grows back in these strips far more quickly than in large clear-cut areas.

Buy Products that Protect the Rainforest Consumers can help protect the rainforest by buying products that support sustainable development. Examples include ice creams and cereals made with Brazil nuts. The companies that make these products buy the nuts from native Amazonians. This helps native peoples make a living without damage to the rainforest.

Another example is wood products. Not all wood is harvested in the same way. Some wood is logged in ways that destroy a forest. And some is harvested with care and respect for the forest.

Until recently, there was no way for people to know if they were buying "good wood." Then, in the 1990s, logging companies and environmental groups created certification programs to help wood buyers. Under these programs, products from well-managed forests are certified, or labeled. The label tells a buyer that the product comes from "good wood." Consumers today can buy many certified "good wood" products from forests in Brazil. They include lumber, charcoal, pencils, furniture, and musical instruments.

12.10 Beginning to Think Globally

In this chapter, you read about land use conflict in the Amazon rainforest. You learned that the rainforest is an important part of the carbon-oxygen cycle. It is also rich in biodiversity. But since the 1960s, loggers, settlers, and ranchers have cleared large parts of the rainforest. Native Amazonians, rubber tappers, and environmental groups oppose this deforestation. Still, the rainforest is shrinking year by year.

Not all countries are losing forests as rapidly as Brazil. Some are even gaining forests. This is called **reforestation**. In some places, this process is happening naturally. In the eastern United States, forests have taken over abandoned farm fields. In other places, people are planting trees to create new forests. In the next section, you will look at deforestation and reforestation around the world.

Shrinking Rainforests
These satellite images show the same part of the Amazon rainforest in 1992 and 2006. The tan-colored patches are areas of deforestation. Rainforests are shrinking worldwide. A few thousand years ago, they covered 12 percent of Earth's surface. Today only about 5 percent of Earth is covered with rainforests.

12.11 Global Connections

The map shows deforestation and reforestation in countries around the world. Notice that some of the countries show little forest loss over the five-year period. This may be because they are doing a good job of protecting their forests. Or it may be because they have no more forest to lose.

What factors contribute to the loss of forest worldwide? There are many reasons why people cut down forests. One is population growth. As the number of people in the world grows, so does their need for farmland and wood products. Another is poverty. Poor people in many countries depend on wood for cooking fuel, heating, and building materials. To meet those needs, they cut down trees.

Can deforestation be slowed or reversed? Some countries have been able to slow deforestation. Others, like Ireland, have begun reforestation. For thousands of years, the Irish stripped their land of trees to create farmland. By 1900, less than 1 percent of Ireland was forested. Since the 1950s, the Irish government has supported tree planting. It has also educated its people about the importance of forests. Today about 10 percent of Ireland is forested.

What is the best way to use and preserve the world's forests? Each country has to find its own answer to this question. In recent years, deforestation has slowed worldwide. This suggests that some countries are doing more to preserve their forests. Still, both rich and poor countries are continuing to lose forests. Some of these forests may be gone forever.

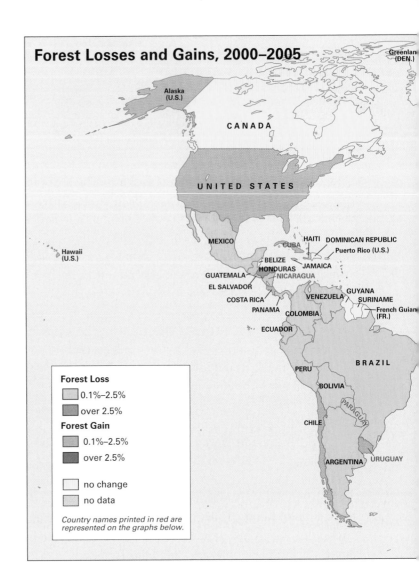

Forest Losses and Gains, 2000–2005

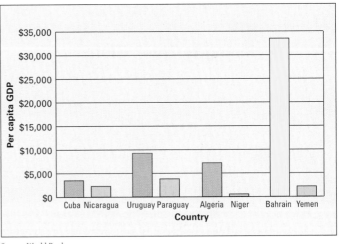

Per Capita GDP of Neighboring Countries, 2005

Source: World Bank.

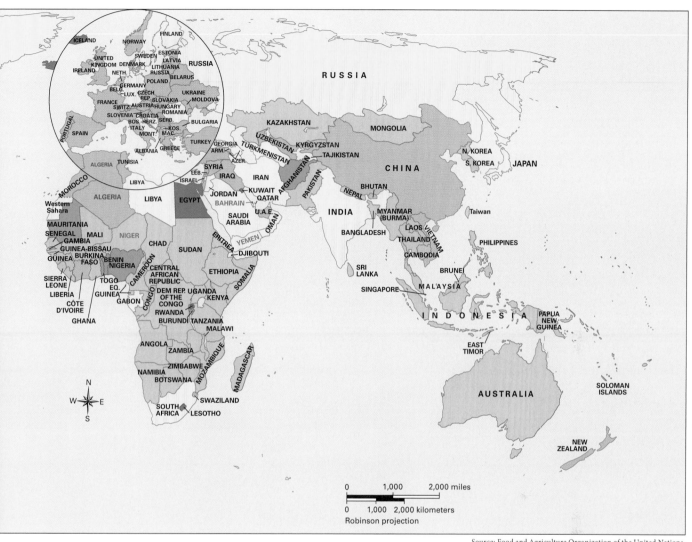

Source: Food and Agriculture Organization of the United Nations.

Population Growth of Neighboring Countries, 2005

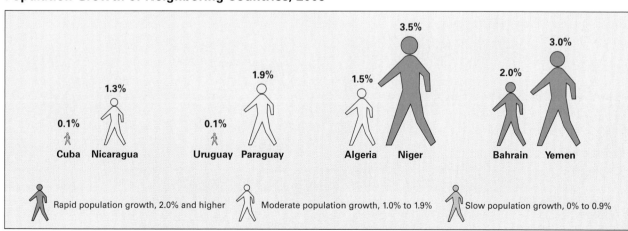

Source: World Bank.

The two graphs show four pairs of neighboring countries with different rates of forest loss or gain. The color of each country on the bar graph matches its color on the map. What connections do you see among deforestation, poverty, and population growth?

Life in the Central Andes: Adapting to a Mountainous Region

13.1 Introduction

La Paz, Bolivia, is the highest big city in the world. It sits at 12,000 feet above sea level in the central Andes Mountains of South America. This high elevation can produce some odd effects. Golfers in La Paz can hit a golf ball much farther than they can at sea level. At a nearby ski resort, a skier may need an oxygen tank to go skiing.

These effects are the result of thin air. The air is thinner at high elevations because the force of gravity pulls air downward. That means there's less oxygen in the air at high elevations. This is why the skier in La Paz needs an oxygen tank. It's also why a golf ball travels farther at 12,000 feet. There is less air to cause friction on the ball and slow it down.

The people of La Paz are used to living at high elevations. Like all peoples of the Andes, they have had to adapt to the effects of elevation. The Andes include some of the highest mountain peaks in the world. Many of these peaks rise much higher than La Paz. The various elevation levels in these mountains influence the way people live.

In this chapter, you will read about life in the central Andes. You will also learn about **altitudinal zonation**. This term refers to the division of mountainous land into zones based on altitudes, or elevations. You will find out about the four main elevation zones in the Andes and how the people living there have adapted to each zone.

Essential Question

How do people adapt to living in a mountainous region?

This diagram represents the Andes Mountains of South America. Notice that the mountain is divided into four zones based on elevation. Each zone has its own range of temperatures. It also has its own distinct plant and animal life. The features of each zone influence how people live. Think about this diagram as you try to answer the Essential Question.

Graphic Organizer

Elevation
- 12,000–15,000 feet
- 6,000–12,000 feet
- 3,000–6,000 feet
- 0–3,000 feet

Tierra Helada
20°F–55°F

Tierra Fría
55°F–65°F

Tierra Templada
65°F–75°F

Tierra Caliente
75°F–80°F

◀ A mountain valley and snow-covered volcano in Ecuador

13.2 The Geographic Setting

South America is the world's fourth largest continent. It includes 12 countries and a wide range of environments. It has deserts, **tropical rainforests,** and several mountain ranges. The greatest mountains of South America are the Andes.

The Andes: Backbone of South America The Andes are made up of several mountain ranges called *cordilleras.* These cordilleras form the longest chain of high mountains on Earth. The Andes stretch for 4,500 miles down the west coast of South America. They are sometimes called the backbone of South America.

The Andes pass through seven countries. Along the way they feature many different landscapes. Some parts of the Andes are covered with dense forest. Others are rocky and bare. More than 50 peaks in the Andes reach elevations of more than 20,000 feet. These lofty peaks are always covered with snow and ice.

The Andes can be grouped in three sections. The northern Andes cross Venezuela and Colombia. The southern Andes run through Chile and Argentina. The central Andes cover Ecuador, Peru, and Bolivia. This chapter focuses on the central Andes.

The Four Elevation Zones of the Andes In the introduction, you read about altitudinal zonation. You learned that there are four main elevation zones in the Andes. These zones are also called **climate zones** because elevation helps determine **climate**. The four elevation zones are shown in the diagram on the facing page.

The elevation zones in the Andes are known by their Spanish names. The lowest zone is called *tierra caliente,* or hot country. Above that is *tierra templada,* or cool country. Next comes *tierra fría,* or cold country. The highest zone is known as *tierra helada,* or frost country.

The link between climate and elevation is based on two factors. The first is **solar energy,** or heat and light given off by the sun. This energy warms Earth's surface. Some solar energy is also reflected by Earth back into the air. The air closest to the surface absorbs most of this reflected heat.

The second factor is gravity. Gravity pulls air in the **atmosphere** down toward Earth. This makes the air denser at lower elevations. The denser the air, the more heat it can absorb. As you move higher, the air thins and holds less heat. For every 1,000-foot rise in elevation, the temperature of the air drops by around 3.5°F.

The higher you go in the Andes, the cooler it gets. This is true even near the equator. For example, both of Ecuador's two largest cities, Guayaquil and Quito, lie near the equator. Guayaquil has an annual average temperature of 77°F. Quito's average temperature is much cooler, just 55°F. The reason for the difference is elevation. Guayaquil is located at sea level, while Quito sits at an elevation of 9,350 feet. One city lies in tierra caliente, the other in tierra fría.

A Mountain City

La Paz, Bolivia, is the highest big city in the world. It is located at 12,000 feet in the heart of the Andes Mountains. The Andes run the length of South America. The only higher mountains in the world are the Himalayas of Asia. The people of the Andes have had to adapt to life at high elevations.

▶ Geoterms

altitudinal zonation the division of land into zones based on elevation, which in turn helps determine climate and vegetation

snow line the lowest elevation on mountains where snow remains year-round

terracing the creation of flat areas on mountain slopes for the purpose of farming

tree line the highest elevation where trees grow on a mountain

vertical trade the trading of crops between lowland and highland areas

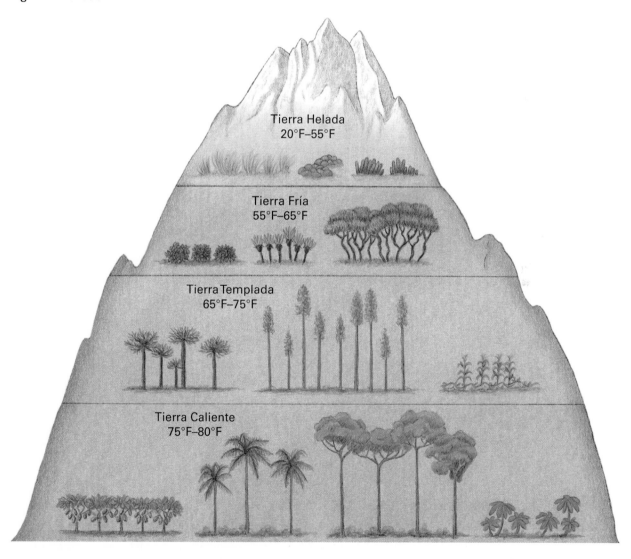

Tierra Helada
20°F–55°F

Tierra Fría
55°F–65°F

Tierra Templada
65°F–75°F

Tierra Caliente
75°F–80°F

Altitudinal Zonation in the Andes

This diagram shows the four elevation zones of the Andes. Notice how the climate cools the higher you go. That's because the air gets thinner and holds less heat.

13.3 The Tropical Lowlands: Tierra Caliente

A worker is picking bananas on a plantation in Ecuador. It's hot, and he has to stop often to wipe the sweat from his brow. He also has to watch out for spiders. Tarantulas like to hide in the banana stalks. Their bite may not be deadly, but it is painful.

This banana plantation is located in the tierra caliente. Most of this zone is tropical lowlands. It lies at the foot of the Andes on both the eastern and western sides. People here must adapt to a hot year-round climate.

Physical Characteristics The tierra caliente is the lowest of the Andes' four elevation zones. It goes from sea level to approximately 3,000 feet. The climate is generally hot and humid. The average temperature range is 75°F to 80°F.

Broadleaf evergreen forests cover the eastern slopes of the Andes heading into the Amazon River basin. On the western slopes, natural vegetation ranges from lush rainforests to **tropical grasslands**.

The Pacific coast of Peru is different. It also lies in the tropics, but gets little rainfall. Here the land is desert. Great sand dunes rise up in some places. Other parts are flat and rocky. Where there is water from rivers or streams, however, the vegetation is tropical.

**Tierra Caliente
75°F–80°F**

The Tierra Caliente

The tierra caliente is the lowest elevation zone in the central Andes. Conditions here are tropical. People dress in light clothing and live in houses open to the air. They also have to cope with tropical diseases like malaria.

Banana Plantation

Bananas thrive in the tierra caliente. They are grown on large plantations like this one. Many plantation workers are descended from Africans brought to South America as slaves.

Human Adaptations The tropical heat of the tierra caliente can make it a difficult place to live. As a result, it is less populated than cooler, higher zones. Some inhabitants are descended from Africans who were brought by the Spanish to work on large plantations as slaves. **Indigenous peoples** also live in some parts of the tropical rainforest.

People in this zone have adapted to life in the tropics. Farmers plant crops that do well in the heat. Among the most common crops are bananas, rice, and sugarcane. People dress in light clothing. They live in houses that are open to cooling breezes. Their houses are often made of bamboo or wood, with palm-thatch roofs. Some are raised on stilts to protect against flooding.

13.4 The Pleasant Uplands: Tierra Templada

In the rolling hills of Ecuador's tierra templada, gardeners are raising flowers. They tend rows of carnations, daisies, and roses. The flowers they grow will be shipped to buyers thousands of miles away. In fact, many of the roses enjoyed by Americans on Valentine's Day come from Ecuador. The mild weather of Ecuador provides the perfect climate for growing flowers.

Physical Characteristics The tierra templada is the second elevation zone of the Andes. It lies between approximately 3,000 and 6,000 feet above sea level. At these elevations, the climate is **temperate**. Temperatures range from 65°F to 75°F, and there is rarely any frost. This pleasant weather lasts all year. People often call the tierra templada "the Land of Eternal Spring."

In this zone, the vegetation changes with the elevation. At lower elevations, tropical plants like palms, bamboo, and jungle vines are common. At higher elevations, broadleaf evergreen forest is typical.

Human Adaptations The mild climate of the tierra templada makes it a good place to live. As a result, this zone is more populated than the tierra caliente. Many of the people here are *mestizos*. Mestizos are a mixture of indigenous and European peoples. European cultural influences are strong here.

Farmers in this zone choose their crops based on elevation. At lower levels, they grow heat-loving crops, like bananas and oranges. Higher up, they grow corn, beans, and other vegetables. They also grow flowers for export. But the main commercial crop of the tierra templada is coffee. The conditions here are ideal for growing high-quality coffee beans. Most of the coffee is grown on small farms. But there are also large coffee plantations.

People who live in this zone have adapted their housing and dress to the comfortable climate. They live in solid homes made of concrete brick or plaster and covered with tile roofs. Richer residents may live on large estates called *haciendas*. During the heat of the day, people wear light clothing. They switch to warmer clothing for the cool mornings and evenings.

The Tierra Templada

The tierra templada is the second elevation zone in the Andes. It has a pleasant, springlike climate year-round. This mild weather appealed to European settlers. Some of the largest cities in Latin America are found here.

Flower Growing

Flowers like these roses are an important crop in the tierra templada. Most flowers are shipped to Europe and the United States. Flower prices rise and fall depending on events in those distant markets. Flowers are one of the first things people stop buying in hard times.

Tierra Fría
55°F–65°F

The Tierra Fría

The tierra fría reaches elevations of 12,000 feet. Many native peoples live in this zone. They have developed larger lungs to take in more oxygen from the thin air at these heights. Five hundred years ago, the centers of the Inca Empire were located here.

Market Day in Peru

The people at this market are wearing the dress of highland Indians. Highland markets are centers of vertical trade. Potatoes and wheat from the highlands are traded here for bananas and oranges from the lowlands.

13.5 The Cool Highlands: Tierra Fría

A woman rises early in the highland city of Cuzco, Peru. This is tierra fría, and the morning air is cold. The woman puts on a warm sweater and shawl and heads off to the market to buy food. She walks down old stone streets built by her ancestors, the Incas. A light frost on the stones makes them slippery, so she steps carefully. She is used to life in the highlands.

Physical Characteristics The tierra fría covers much of the central Andes. This zone lies between 6,000 and 12,000 feet. Average temperatures vary from 55°F to 65°F. But the nights are colder. At high elevations, temperatures often dip below freezing.

Mountains and valleys are the main physical feature in this zone. The mountains are steep and rugged. But flat **basins** and **plateaus** can be found among the peaks.

A high plateau called the Altiplano lies at an average of over 11,000 feet between Peru and Bolivia. It contains Lake Titicaca, the world's highest **navigable lake**. A navigable lake is one that is large and deep enough for big boats. Lake Titicaca is rumored to hold hidden treasure. Legends say the Incas threw a huge amount of gold into the lake to keep it away from Spanish invaders.

Vegetation in this zone depends partly on rainfall. In some places, enough rain falls to support dense forests. Pines and other **conifers** are found there. In other places the land is so dry that only shrubs and grasses will grow.

Elevation also affects what grows where. The **tree line** in the central Andes lies between 10,000 and 12,000 feet. The tree line is the highest elevation at which trees will grow.

Human Adaptations Around half the population of the central Andes are indigenous peoples. Most live in the tierra fría. The two main indigenous groups are the Quechua and the Aymara. Both groups were once part of the mighty Inca Empire.

Over the centuries, the native peoples of the Andes have adapted to life at high elevations. They wear warm woolen clothes to protect them from the cold. They also build thick-walled houses out of stone or **adobe** brick. Even their bodies have adapted. They have developed larger lungs to get more oxygen from the thin mountain air.

Farmers have adapted their practices to the highland environment. They grow crops that do well at high elevations. These include potatoes, wheat, barley, corn, apples, and pears.

Farmers also use **terracing** to carve fields out of steep hillsides. They build walls on the slopes and fill them in with soil to create flat land for planting. They irrigate the terraces with mountain streams. This method of farming goes back to ancient times. The Incas used terracing to build a great civilization.

Inca Terraces
In the 1400s, the Incas created an advanced civilization in the Andes. These are the ruins of Machu Picchu, an Inca city in Peru. Notice the terraced fields at the edge of the city.

Another sign of adaptation is **vertical trade**. This is the trade of farm products between higher and lower zones of the Andes. Highland farmers can't grow crops from lower zones, such as bananas, oranges, and tomatoes. So traders bring those products up to highland markets. They also take highland crops, like potatoes and wheat, down to lowland markets. Through vertical trade, people who live in one zone can have access to foods grown in other zones. In this way, they can get a more balanced and varied diet.

Making Freeze-Dried Potatoes
Long ago, Indians in the high Andes learned how to make *chuño,* or freeze-dried potatoes. They leave the potatoes out in the cold night air to freeze. The next day, they squeeze the water out of the thawing potatoes. They rinse them in the riverbed and then leave them out to dry. Chuño can be stored for years without spoiling.

The Tierra Helada

The tierra helada is the highest zone of the central Andes. Conditions here can be harsh. The climate is cold, and vegetation is sparse. People grow hardy crops like quinoa, a grain that is rich in protein. They also work in mines. The mines of Bolivia were once among the richest in the world.

13.6 The Icy High Elevations: Tierra Helada

Every year, many Quechua Indians hike to a shrine in the mountains high above the city of Cuzco. They go to worship the *apus,* or mountain gods. "We make offerings to the mountains," says one pilgrim, "asking them to send water for our crops and livestock."

The shrine above Cuzco is set in the tierra helada, the highest elevation zone of the Andes. The pilgrims who make this journey have to walk slowly. The air is very thin. If people move too fast, they can get altitude sickness from a lack of oxygen. Altitude sickness can cause headaches, fatigue, shortness of breath, and nausea.

Physical Characteristics The tierra helada lies between 12,000 and 15,000 feet. Average temperatures vary from 20°F to 55°F. This is an extreme environment. The climate is cold and windy. It often freezes at night, and snow falls at the higher elevations. The **snow line** lies at the upper edge of this zone. The snow line is the elevation where permanent snow and ice begin. Above this level, snow stays on the ground year-round.

Most of the tierra helada lies above the tree line. That means that trees are very rare in this zone. The most common forms of plant life are low-lying shrubs and hardy grasses. These are found in **alpine** meadows, called *paramos* or *punas.*

Human Adaptations The tierra helada is a tough environment for humans. Relatively few people live at these heights. Most are indigenous peoples like the Quechua and the Aymara.

Spinning Wool

These highland women are spinning wool from an alpaca into yarn. The yarn will then be woven into cloth. Alpaca wool is finer and straighter than sheep wool. It is one of the best fibers for making soft, warm garments.

People have adapted to life in the tierra helada in various ways. As in the tierra fría, they dress in warm clothing. They plant the few crops that will grow at high elevations. These include a native grain called *quinoa,* along with certain types of potatoes. They also raise llamas and alpacas. Both of these animals are related to the camel. They produce thick wool for blankets, bags, and clothing. Llamas also make good pack animals for carrying heavy loads across the mountains.

Some people in this zone work in mines. The high Andes have many mineral deposits, including tin, lead, copper, and silver. Working conditions in the mines are difficult. Many miners get lung disease or are injured on the job. But mining provides one of the few sources of cash income in this harsh environment.

Above the Snow Line The highest part of the Andes lies just above the tierra helada. This area extends from the snow line to the tops of the tallest peaks. It is cold and rocky here. Snow and ice cover much of the land.

This part of the Andes is generally not inhabited. But it plays a key role in Andean life. The reason is **glaciers**. These large ice fields cover the highest peaks in the Andes. Large amounts of water are stored here above the snow line. During the summer, water from melting glaciers flows down to people living at lower elevations. Streams fed by glaciers form a crucial part of the water supply.

Glaciers are very sensitive to changes in climate. They grow or shrink depending on changes in temperature and precipitation over time. If they melt too fast, the result can be disastrous for the people living below. "Glaciers don't always behave nicely," said a scientist who studies them. "Some glaciers have a nasty habit of storing up large amounts of water and then releasing it suddenly in a massive melt…which may involve floods, landslides, or avalanches."

Shrinking Andes Glaciers

This satellite image shows a shrinking glacier in the Andes. There is still enough ice in this glacier to feed mountain streams year round. But if the glacier disappears, some of those streams may run dry part of the year.

13.7 Beginning to Think Globally

In this chapter, you have read about the four elevation zones in the central Andes. Each zone has its own climate and vegetation. You have seen how people have adapted to the conditions in each zone.

In other parts of the world, people have made different adaptations to mountain living. In general, however, relatively few people in the world live at high elevations. The conditions of life there are just too difficult.

In the future, mountains may become more attractive to people. There are signs that the world's climate is getting warmer. If this trend continues, life will change at high elevations. For example, tree lines and snow lines are likely to rise. As mountains become warmer, more people may choose to live at higher elevations. At the same time, a warmer climate is likely to have a negative effect on mountain glaciers. Keep this in mind as you look at glaciers in the next section.

13.8 Global Connections

The map on this page shows glaciers around the world. There are about 160,000 glaciers worldwide today. Some are found in lowland cold areas such as Antarctica. Others have formed on high mountain peaks. Can you find examples of both lowland and mountain glaciers on the map?

What is happening to mountain glaciers around the world? Many mountain glaciers are retreating, or shrinking. Look at the image of the Gangotri Glacier. This mountain glacier is located in the Himalayas. The lines on the photograph show how it has retreated over time. Not all glaciers are shrinking, however. Some are staying the same or growing.

Why are some mountain glaciers retreating? Most scientists blame climate change for shrinking glaciers. They say that Earth's climate is slowly warming. Rising temperatures are causing glaciers to melt more than they used to. As their ice turns to water, the glaciers retreat.

What impact do retreating glaciers have on people living in mountainous regions? Around 75 percent of the world's fresh water is frozen in glaciers. When glaciers melt, they provide water for people to use. For example, glaciers near Quito, Ecuador, supply 80 percent of the city's water. If Quito's glaciers continue to shrink, they will provide less and less water to the city. "It's kind of like a bank account," said one scientist. "When you've withdrawn all the water, there isn't any more."

Glaciers Around the World, 2007

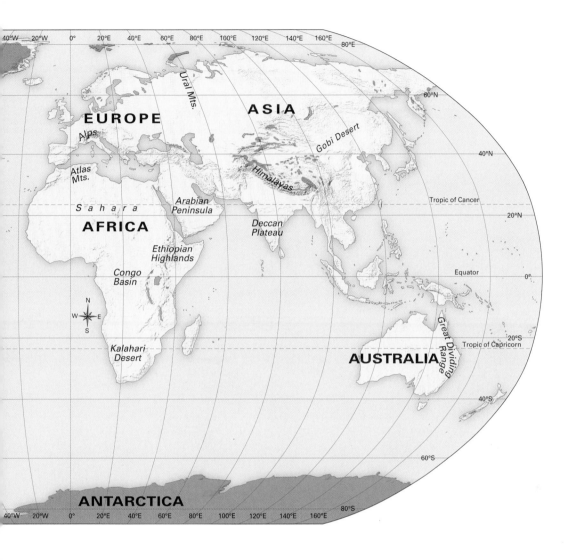

Lake Raphstreng Tsho ◀

This diagram shows changes in Raphstreng Tsho, a glacial lake in the Himalaya mountain range of Asia. As the glaciers that feed the lake melt, its water level rises. Between 1986 and 1996, the lake's water level rose by 89 feet.

Gangotri Glacier ▶

This satellite image shows the Gangotri Glacier in 2001. It is one of the largest glaciers in the Himalayas. The lines added to the image show how this glacier has shrunk since 1780.

UNIT **4**

Europe and Russia

Introducing the Region:
Physical and Human Geography

What patterns do you see in this photograph?
See page 514 for details.

▼

Europe and Russia occupy part of the huge **landmass** called Eurasia. Eurasia reaches from the Atlantic to the Pacific Ocean. It is so large that geographers divide it into two continents, Europe and Asia.

Europe is the world's second smallest continent. Oceans and seas border Europe to the north, south, and west. Asia borders Europe on the east.

Russia is the world's largest country. It spreads over two continents. Western Russia lies on the continent of Europe. Eastern Russia stretches across Asia to the Pacific Ocean. The Ural Mountains, at 60°E longitude, mark the dividing line between Europe and Asia, and between western Russia and eastern Russia.

Physical Features of Europe

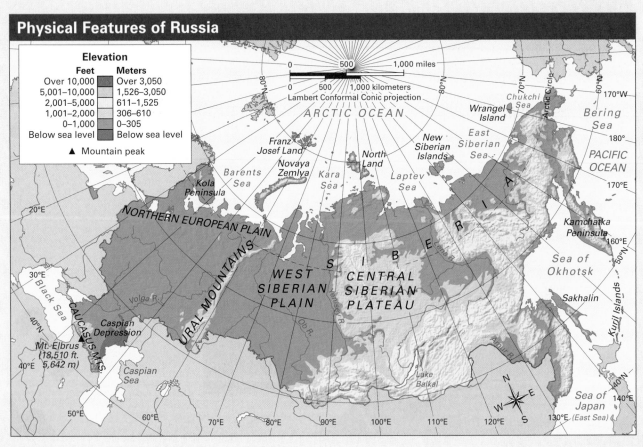

Physical Features of Russia

Physical Features

Europe and Russia share a **landscape** of sweeping plains and rugged mountains. Large rivers wander across the broad plains. These rivers drain into three of the world's four oceans—the Atlantic, the Pacific, and the Arctic oceans.

Europe

On a map, the European landmass looks like a giant **peninsula** attached to Eurasia. Smaller peninsulas jut out from all sides of Europe. They include the Balkan Peninsula, the Iberian Peninsula, Italy, and Scandinavia. Various seas, bays, and gulfs are tucked in between. Several big islands are also part of Europe.

Much of Europe lies on the Northern European Plain, which is one of the largest expanses of flat land on Earth. It extends almost 2,500 miles from east to west. Several mountain ranges cross Europe. The Alps form a major barrier between central and southern Europe. The Pyrenees separate France and Spain. The Apennines run through Italy.

Europe's rivers serve as water highways. They also provide drinking water and power for electricity. The Danube River flows through six countries, more than any other major river in the world. The Rhine river valley is one of the most productive industrial and farming areas in the world.

Russia

Much of Russia also lies on broad plains. The western, or European, part of Russia shares

The Alps cut through France, Italy, Switzerland, Liechtenstein, Austria, and Slovenia.

the Northern European Plain. Western Russia extends to the Ural Mountains in the east and to the Caucasus Mountains in the south.

From the Ural Mountains, eastern Russia spreads across the full width of Asia. This area is called Siberia. The West Siberian Plain is a large area of flat land with many lakes and swamps. To the east lies the Central Siberian Plateau. Rivers have carved narrow canyons through this high, flat plateau.

Russia has thousands of lakes. The largest is Lake Baikal, the oldest and deepest lake in the world. It holds one fifth of Earth's fresh water. In winter, the lake freezes with ice up to three feet deep.

The Kamchatka Peninsula at the eastern edge of Russia reaches into the Pacific Ocean. More than 100 **volcanoes** rise from this finger of land. No roads or railroads connect the peninsula to Siberia. Everything must arrive by airplane or boat.

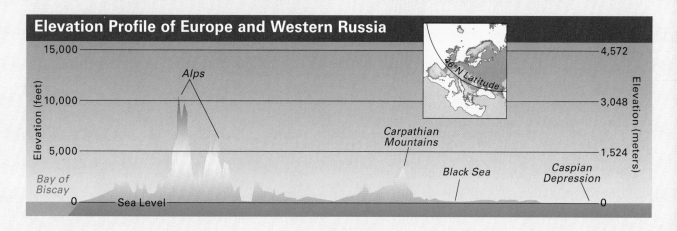

Elevation Profile of Europe and Western Russia

(Elevation in feet): 15,000 — 10,000 — 5,000 — 0 Sea Level

(Elevation in meters): 4,572 — 3,048 — 1,524 — 0

Bay of Biscay — Alps — Carpathian Mountains — Black Sea — Caspian Depression

46°N Latitude

Climate

Three factors shape Europe's climates. The first is latitude. Areas south of the Alps have more **temperate** climates than areas to the north.

The second factor is **relative location**. Areas near the ocean have a **marine climate**. *Marine* means "found in or close to the sea." Ocean winds and warm ocean currents help keep temperatures about the same all year. Inland areas far from the sea have a **continental climate**. *Continental* means "influenced by a large landmass." Ocean winds and currents do not affect places with a continental climate. As a result, summers are usually hotter than near the sea, while winters are colder.

Mountain ranges are the third factor. The Alps and Carpathians block the cold air from the north that influences the climate of southern and eastern Europe.

Europe

Every year, crowds of tourists head to the Mediterranean Sea for vacation. Southern Europe has a **Mediterranean** climate. Its summers are longer, hotter, and drier than in northern Europe. Mediterranean winters are short and mild.

Most of northern Europe has a **marine west coast** climate. A warm current that flows across the Atlantic from the Gulf of Mexico keeps winters from being too cold. Cool ocean breezes keep summers from being too hot and bring year-round rain to northern Europe.

Russia

Russia is known for its long, harsh winters. The Arctic Ocean on Russia's northern border is frozen most of the year. As a result, it does not have a marine influence on Russia's climate. In some areas, snow covers the ground for eight or nine months of the year.

The most northern part of Russia has a **tundra** climate. The weather is so cold all year that the land is always frozen. Winter temperatures can drop as low as –90°F.

Much of Siberia has a **subarctic** climate. Winters are still long and very cold. Summers are too cool and short for farming.

Moscow, the capital of Russia, has a humid continental climate. When are people living in Moscow likely to have very high heating bills?

Areas to the south and west have milder climates. Much of western Russia has a **humid continental** climate. Winters here are still freezing cold, but summers can be hot and steamy. The most southern parts of Russia have a **semiarid** climate. Here the hot summers and cool winters are both fairly dry. Most of Russia's crops are grown in these areas with longer growing seasons.

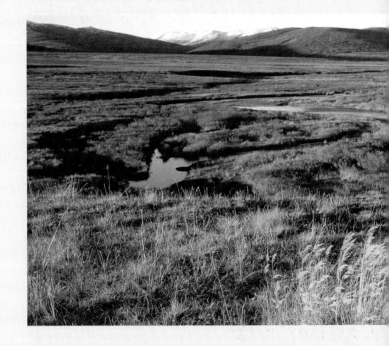

Vegetation

Europe and Russia have a mix of **vegetation zones,** but forests are the most common. The largest forest on Earth, the Russian **taiga,** stretches across most of the Eurasian landmass.

Three types of forests are found in this region—**deciduous, coniferous,** and **mixed forests**. All three are named for the types of trees that are found in them. Deciduous trees have broad, flat leaves that drop each fall. Coniferous trees have needle-like leaves that stay green all year. Mixed forests have both deciduous and coniferous trees.

Europe

All three types of forests once thrived in Europe. But over time, people cleared the forested areas to use the land for farming. Pockets of deciduous and mixed forests can still be found. Large coniferous forests survive in the far northern parts of the continent.

The coastal parts of Europe bordering the Mediterranean Sea are covered with **chaparral**. Here the small trees and bushes are well adapted to long, rainless summers. They send their roots deep into the soil to search for hidden water sources. Most have thick bark and small leaves that keep them

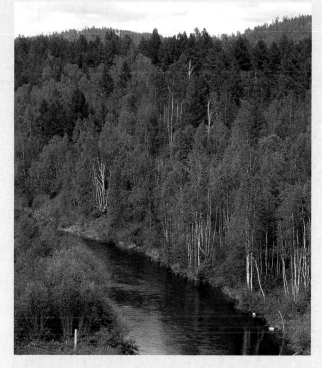

The Russian taiga accounts for about one fifth of Earth's total forested area.

from losing water during the dry season. Olive trees and cork trees are common in this vegetation zone.

Russia

In northern Russia, the **tundra** is treeless. Because the ground is always frozen under the surface, trees cannot send their roots down into the soil. During the short summer, the top layer of soil thaws. Then, for about two months, mosses, grasses, and scrubs cover the ground.

South of the tundra lies the taiga, a vast region of thick, dark forests. The taiga consists mainly of coniferous trees such as cedar, fir, pine, and spruce. Further south, the taiga becomes more mixed forest with the addition of aspen, birch, and other deciduous trees.

Far to the south lie the **steppes,** or grassy plains, of Russia. This region of **temperate grasslands** is too dry to support trees. The steppes have mostly been plowed for farms.

Summer sun thaws the surface of Siberia's tundra. With the return of winter, this boggy area will freeze solid.

The region of Europe and Russia is home to 44 countries. You've learned that Russia is the world's largest country. It covers about 6.6 million square miles. At the other extreme, Vatican City is the world's smallest country. It covers only 109 acres. It lies in the center of the city of Rome, Italy.

The people of Europe and Russia are linked together by language and culture. At least 50 languages are spoken here. Yet most of them belong to just three language families: Latin, Germanic, and Slavic. Europeans and Russians also share many elements of culture. These include art, music, and religion.

Political Boundaries of Russia

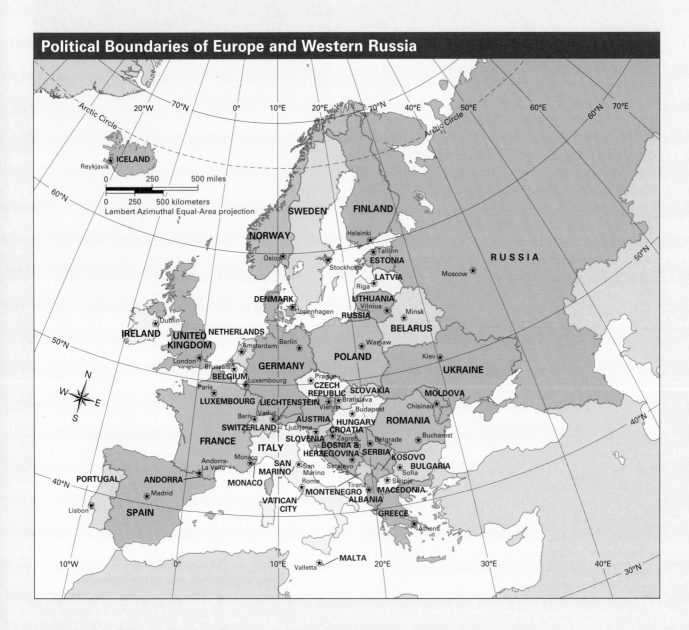

Political Boundaries of Europe and Western Russia

History

Europeans and Russians are linked by history. For thousands of years, peoples and armies have moved back and forth across this region. Ideas and ways of life have moved with them.

Early Times

Two great civilizations appeared in Europe in ancient times. The first arose on the Greek peninsula in the 700s B.C.E. The Greeks created distinct styles of art and literature. They also invented the idea of democracy.

The second great civilization arose on the Italian peninsula. Around 500 B.C.E., the city of Rome began to grow. It would become a mighty **empire**. At its peak, the Roman Empire included most of Europe.

Roman rule collapsed in the late 400s. But the Romans left behind their language and ideas about law and government.

The Rise of Nations

After Rome fell, many small kingdoms arose in Europe and Russia. The times seemed dangerous and uncertain to many. People focused on faith and their relationship to God.

In the 1300s, some began looking back to the ideas of ancient Rome and Greece. This began the Renaissance, which means "rebirth." Thinking focused more on science than on faith. The Renaissance began in the Italian city-states. By the late 1500s, it had spread throughout Northern Europe.

In the meantime, rulers increased their power. They formed modern **nations**. In 1469, for example, Ferdinand of Aragon married Isabella of Castile. Together, they created the nation of Spain. In 1533, Ivan the Terrible, the Grand Prince of Moscow, began to conquer vast lands. By 1547, he was czar, or ruler, of all Russia.

Soon rulers looked for new lands to conquer. The Russian czars expanded their control east across Asia. European rulers created colonies in the Americas, Africa, and Asia.

The Modern Era

More recently, two kinds of revolutions shaped Europe and Russia. The first was economic. The **Industrial Revolution** began in the 1700s. It moved the production of goods out of homes and into factories. Machines began to take over work that had been done by hand. European nations led this revolution. They became the world's first **developed countries**.

The second kind of revolution was political. Political revolutions led to changes in how countries were ruled. In some cases, they led to the rise of democratic governments. The Glorious Revolution of 1688–89 is an example. It limited the power of England's monarchs. This was a step toward democracy.

In other cases, political revolutions led to the rise of **dictators**. A dictator is a leader who rules a country with absolute power, and often with brutal force. In 1917, the Russian Revolution drove the last czar from power. A series of dictators then ruled for more than 70 years.

Today, elected governments rule most countries in this region.

Europe and Russia Timeline   ■ Early Times   □ Rise of Nations   ■ Modern Era

500 B.C.E. | 0 | 500 C.E. | 1000 C.E. | 1500 C.E. | 2000 C.E.

700s–300s B.C.E. Greek civilization

500 B.C.E.–500 C.E. Roman civilization

1469–1492 Ferdinand and Isabel unite Spain

1300 Renaissance begins

1547 Ivan the Terrible crowned czar of Russia

1688 England's Glorious Revolution

1917 Russian Revolution

Population

Europe and Russia are home to one seventh of the world's people. In 2008, about 735 million people lived in this region. Most of them live west of the Urals.

Europe has long been very **urban**. Rome was the first city to reach 1 million people. That was 2,000 years ago. In 1810, London became the first modern city to reach a million people. Today, most Europeans and Russians live in towns and cities. **Rural** eastern Russia is thinly settled.

Most parts of the world have growing populations. But in parts of Europe and Russia, populations have stopped growing. Some are even shrinking. The main reason is a drop in the **birth rate,** or the number of births per 1,000 people.

Christianity is the most common religion in Europe and Russia. More than half of all Europeans belong to the Roman Catholic Church. Most Christians in Russia follow the Russian Orthodox faith. Islam is the second largest faith in this region.

Europe and Russia: Major Religions

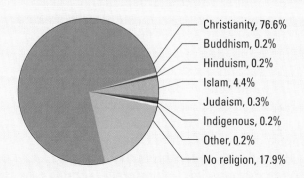

- Christianity, 76.6%
- Buddhism, 0.2%
- Hinduism, 0.2%
- Islam, 4.4%
- Judaism, 0.3%
- Indigenous, 0.2%
- Other, 0.2%
- No religion, 17.9%

Europe and Russia: Urban and Rural Population, 2007

- Urban, 72.1%
- Rural, 27.9%
- ☺ = 10% of the total population

Europe and Russia: Population Growth, 1950–2050

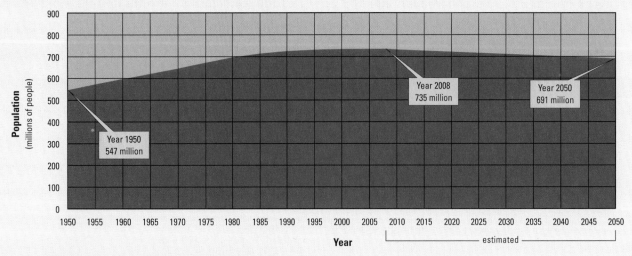

Year 1950
547 million

Year 2008
735 million

Year 2050
691 million

Population (millions of people)

Year

estimated

Sources: United Nations Department of Economic and Social Affairs, Population Division. Encyclopaedia Britannica.

In Poland, much of the land is used for commercial farming.

Economic Activity

Europe and Russia are both important industrial areas. Russian factories produce heavy machinery, such as electric motors and tractors. Factories in Denmark turn out stereos, furniture, dishes, and silverware. German factories produce steel, automobiles, and electronics. Swiss factories turn out watches, chocolate, and medicines. Global trade has made Europe and Russia one of the world's richest regions.

Resources

Europe and Russia are rich in **natural resources**. These include **fossil fuels** and minerals. About a third of the world's coal reserves are found in Siberia. In addition, Siberia has mines for gold, copper, lead, and diamonds.

In the North Sea and Russia, people drill for petroleum and **natural gas**. Russia is also a major producer of **hydroelectric power**. Most of this power comes from dams located along Russia's rivers.

Land Use

Outside of its cities, Europe is largely a land of farms. Commercial farms are spread out along river valleys and across the vast Northern European Plain. In Western Europe, farmers use machines to produce large **cash crops**. In poorer parts of Eastern Europe, however, some families are limited to **subsistence farming** on small plots of land.

In Scandinavia, **forestry** and fishing are both big industries. Even though Norway is very far north, a warm ocean current keeps some of its ports free of ice. As a result, fishing can continue all year. Fishing is also the main industry of Iceland.

Manufacturing has become important to Russia over the last 75 years. But many Russians still use their land in more traditional ways. In southern Russia, farmers grow a wide variety of crops, from wheat to apples. Across the taiga, forestry is a major industry. On the northern tundra, people herd reindeer. Reindeer are a source of meat and hides.

Supranational Cooperation in the European Union

14.1 Introduction

Have you ever traveled from the United States to another country? If so, you know that crossing international borders isn't like going from one state to another back home. You probably had to stop and show identification. You might have had to trade your U.S. dollars for a different kind of money.

Now imagine that you're in Europe. You're crossing the border from France to Germany. You don't have to stop to show your passport. You use the same money in both places. The main difference you notice is that people are speaking German instead of French.

People today travel easily among many European countries because of the **European Union,** or EU. The EU is a *supranational* organization. In 2009, it had 27 member countries. *Supra* means "over" or "on top of." The government of the European Union stands above the governments of its members. As a result, the EU has been able to remove many barriers that once made travel among its members difficult. Members of the EU have "open" borders with each other. Many also use the same form of money.

EU countries use **supranational cooperation** to work toward shared goals. At the same time, they remain separate countries. While they are united in some ways, they are divided in others. In this chapter, you will learn about the forces that work for and against supranational cooperation in the EU.

Essential Question

What forces work for and against supranational cooperation among nations?

These two maps show Europe. The highlighted countries are members of the European Union. The map on the left represents things that unite EU countries. The map on the right represents things that pull EU countries apart. Keep these maps in mind as you try to answer the Essential Question.

Graphic Organizer

◀ European Union flag flying over a city in the Czech Republic

World War II Destruction
On May 14, 1940, German planes bombed the city of Rotterdam in the Netherlands. Much of the city was destroyed. Many other cities in Europe were also bombed during World War II. The EU was formed to make sure such horrors never happened again.

14.2 The Geographic Setting

Europe is a region made up of many peoples and countries. Throughout its history, different forces have brought its peoples together and pulled them apart. The forces that bring things together, or unite them, are called **centripetal forces**. The forces that divide things, or move them away from one another, are called **centrifugal forces**. The European Union was formed to unite countries that had been torn apart by years of war.

A History of Bloody Conflict For much of its history, Europe has been a battleground. This was true of the first half of the 20th century. In this time, two great wars began in Europe. Both were so widespread that they are remembered as "world wars."

The First World War began in 1914. This bloody conflict lasted four years and killed over 21 million people. The Second World War broke out in 1939. On one side were Germany, Italy, Japan, and their allies. Great Britain, the Soviet Union, the United States, and other countries opposed them.

World War II was even more terrible than World War I. It lasted six long years and left some 50 million people dead worldwide. Many European cities and farms were left in ruins. When the guns finally fell silent, Europeans wanted to make sure that such horrors never happened again.

Creating a Future of Peaceful Cooperation On May 9, 1950, a French leader named Robert Schuman made a famous speech. In his talk, he put forward ideas for bringing a lasting peace to Europe. These ideas led to what is now the European Union.

Schuman suggested that France, Germany, and other European countries work together to manage their coal and steel production. If these countries learned to work together, he said, they would not be so likely to make war on each other.

Six countries agreed with Schuman. By 1952, they had all ratified the treaty creating the European Coal and Steel Community. This group created a **common market** for steel and coal products. In a common market, nations reduce or remove trade barriers, such as **tariffs**. Tariffs are taxes on goods that cross country borders.

By 1958, the same six countries created the European Economic Community (EEC). This group removed trade barriers for all kinds of goods. The EEC came to be known as the Common Market. Over the years, more European countries joined the Common Market.

In 1993, twelve Common Market countries formed the European Union. The EU works to create jobs, protect citizens' rights, and preserve the environment. It also promotes freedom, security, and justice. Its main goals, however, are to encourage peace and prosperity, or economic well-being. In 2009, the EU had 27 member countries spread across Europe. Several other countries also hope to join.

▶ Geoterms

centrifugal force a force that divides people and countries

centripetal force a force that unites people and countries

common market a group of countries that acts as a single market, without trade barriers between member countries

supranational cooperation a form of international cooperation in which countries give up some control of their affairs as they work together to achieve shared goals

The European Union, 2009

The Growth of the European Union

Before 2004, all of the European Union countries were in Western Europe. In 2004, ten new member countries put Central and Eastern Europe on the EU map. Two more countries joined in 2007. The European Union promotes cooperation among member countries.

14.3 Economic Cooperation in the EU

In the United States, people move freely across state borders. Some work in one state and live in another. Europe is slightly larger than the United States. Yet before the European Union was formed, national laws made it hard for citizens of one country to live or work in another.

Each country had its own rules about who could live or find work there. Each had its own **currency,** or type of money. Each country charged tariffs, or taxes, on imports from its neighbors. These taxes raised the price of imported goods.

Today members of the EU work together toward shared economic goals. Many centripetal forces promote such economic cooperation. But other centrifugal forces work against it.

Economic Forces That Unite the EU The creation of a common market has been an important economic force uniting the EU. This single market benefits EU consumers in several ways. With goods moving freely across borders, people have more choices in what to buy. With no tariffs on EU goods, prices are lower. The single market benefits workers as well. They are able to travel freely to other EU countries to find work.

The adoption of a common currency in 2002 also helped to unite the EU. The common currency is called the **euro**. In many EU countries, the euro has replaced the national currency. No longer do Europeans change money when they cross most borders. The euro makes it easier to travel and trade across the EU.

By joining their economies, EU members have also created a powerful **trade bloc**. Hundreds of millions of consumers live in the EU trade bloc. As a result, outside nations are eager to do business in the EU. The size of its market has made the EU trade bloc an important force in the global economy.

The EU has other shared economic goals. It works to create jobs, develop resources, and make improvements that encourage trade. For example, the EU has spent large sums to upgrade highways. It has also helped farmers modernize their operations.

The EU Trade Bloc

This graph compares the GDP of the EU to other large countries. GDP is the total value of goods and services produced in a place. By joining together, members of the EU trade bloc have far more economic power than they would have acting alone.

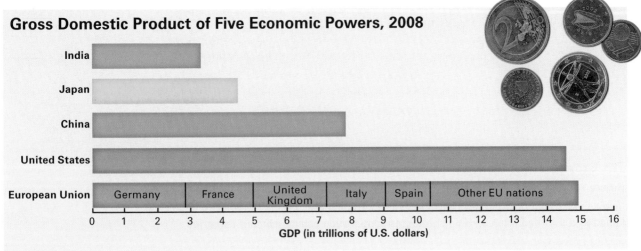

Gross Domestic Product of Five Economic Powers, 2008

GDP (in trillions of U.S. dollars)

Source: Central Intelligence Agency.

Clay Bennett ©2002 Christian Science Monitor

Erasing EU Borders

In January 2002, the euro became the currency in 12 EU countries. About 291 million people traded in their old money for euros. To prepare for this change, banks were stocked with 12.5 billion new bills and 76 billion coins. According to this cartoon, what effect has the euro had on Europe?

Economic Forces That Divide the EU Other forces work against economic cooperation. EU members don't always agree on the many issues they face. Nor do they always agree on how EU money should be spent.

In general, the Western European members of the EU are wealthier than those in Central and Eastern Europe. In an effort to bring all of its members up to the same level, the EU spends large sums on projects in its poorer nations. Some Western Europeans object to so much EU money being spent outside their own area.

Economic differences between EU members create other strains. In general, workers in Western Europe are paid higher wages than those in Central and Eastern Europe. Living costs are higher in Western Europe as well. This has led some Western European businesses to move their factories to poorer EU countries. Costs are lower there, and they can pay workers less. As a result, workers in Western Europe worry about losing jobs to poorer EU countries.

Wage differences also encourage workers in poorer EU countries to move to richer ones in search of jobs. Workers in the wealthier countries often resent these immigrants. They also fear that too many newcomers from poor countries will drive down wages for everyone.

There are centrifugal forces at work in the use of the euro as well. Not all EU countries adopted the common currency in 2002. Three members decided to keep their own currency and make their own decisions about money. Other countries have not been allowed to adopt the euro. Before joining the euro zone, they must show that they have developed stable economies. (See the map in Section 14.2, which shows which countries use the euro.)

As you can see, both centripetal and centrifugal economic forces are at work in the EU. But overall, member nations have decided that the economic benefits of supranational cooperation far outweigh the costs.

The EU Headquarters

The EU government works on issues shared by member countries. Its headquarters is in Brussels, Belgium. By 2009, this was the center of government for more than 494 million people in 27 countries. Because of this, some might call Brussels the "capital of Europe."

14.4 Political Cooperation in the EU

Before the EU was formed, there were many political divisions among European countries. Each nation was independent. Each nation set its own policies. Nations could choose to work together, but they did not have to. As you have read, political conflict was often more common than cooperation.

The EU encourages political cooperation among its members. They all take part in a common EU government. The EU government does not replace the governments of its member nations. Instead, it is a supranational government. That is, it works above the governments of the EU countries.

How the EU Government Unites Europe The EU government works in two ways to unite Europe. First, it brings its members together to work on issues they all share. For example, it tries to take a common approach to environmental problems.

Second, the EU encourages Europeans to think of themselves as citizens of Europe. This is on top of their citizenship in their home countries. With European citizenship, citizens of member nations can live and work anywhere in the EU. They can also vote in EU elections. They have this right no matter where they live in the EU.

The EU government has several important bodies. The Council of the European Union is the main decision-making body. It is made up of national leaders from each member country. The council sets overall goals for the EU.

The European Commission is the executive body. It is made up of commissioners who are appointed by member governments. The commission's main duty is to see that EU decisions are carried out.

The European Parliament is the largest EU body. Citizens of the EU countries directly elect its 700 members. The parliament's role is to watch over the work of the European Union. It can approve or block the EU budget. This budget says how money should be spent on EU projects.

The EU government helps to unite Europe by speaking with one voice for all of its members. Within Europe, the EU focuses on shared issues, such as transportation and the environment. Outside of Europe, the EU works to strengthen Europe's role in the world. By working together, EU members have more power in world affairs than any one European country would have by itself. In these ways, the EU government acts as a centripetal force in Europe.

How the EU Government Divides Europe There are centrifugal forces at work as well in the EU government. When a country joins the European Union, it is expected to give up some power to the EU government. This may mean carrying out decisions made by the EU that it does not agree with.

Giving up power has been a problem for many EU members. Some countries still want to make independent decisions in areas like defense and foreign affairs. This is more often true when they don't agree with EU decisions.

The growing size of the EU is also a centrifugal force. By 2009, the EU included more than 494 million people in 27 countries. As the size of the EU has increased, so have the differences among the EU's nations and peoples. With more countries and cultures, cooperation has become more difficult.

Finally, the idea of European citizenship has been hard for some Europeans to adjust to. A recent poll of Europeans found that almost half would not mind if the EU simply disappeared. People who feel this way may fear that their national identity will get lost in the push for a more united Europe. For them, the advantages of political cooperation may never be worth the costs.

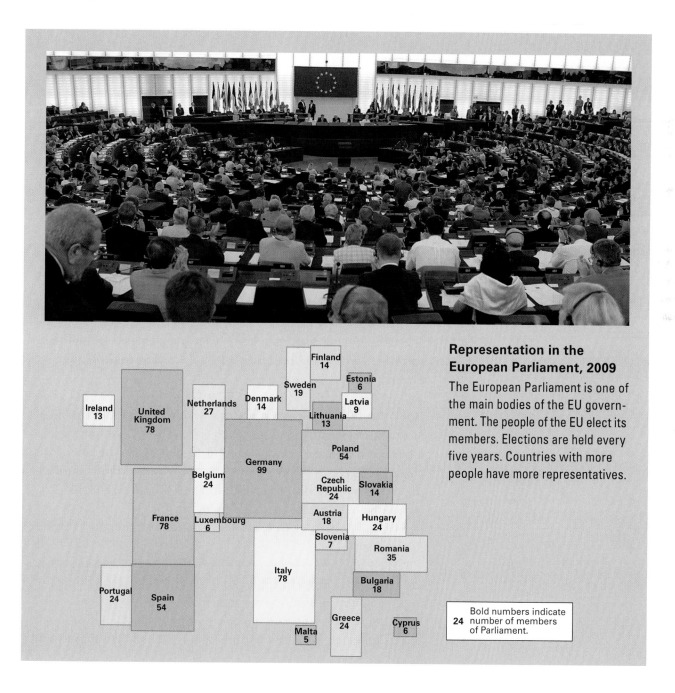

Representation in the European Parliament, 2009

The European Parliament is one of the main bodies of the EU government. The people of the EU elect its members. Elections are held every five years. Countries with more people have more representatives.

Ireland 13
United Kingdom 78
Netherlands 27
Denmark 14
Finland 14
Sweden 19
Estonia 6
Latvia 9
Lithuania 13
Belgium 24
Germany 99
Poland 54
Czech Republic 24
Slovakia 14
France 78
Luxembourg 6
Austria 18
Hungary 24
Slovenia 7
Romania 35
Portugal 24
Spain 54
Italy 78
Bulgaria 18
Malta 5
Greece 24
Cyprus 6

Bold numbers indicate **24** number of members of Parliament.

Europe Day in the EU

Celebrations and symbols help create a cultural identity. Every year on May 9, people celebrate Europe Day. The day honors Europe's "birthday." It was on this day in 1950 that Robert Schuman proposed creating a more united Europe. Symbols like the EU flag add to the feeling of a shared culture.

14.5 Cultural Cooperation in the EU

In the year 2000, students across the European Union took part in a contest. The contest was to create a motto for the EU. Students from many countries sent in more than 2,000 ideas. After considering the students' suggestions, the EU announced its choice in 2003. The official motto is "United in Diversity."

The words in this motto are important. The goal of the EU is to unite Europeans into an "ever closer union." Since the EU was formed, it has promoted a common European **cultural identity**. At the same time, the EU recognizes the **diversity** of its members. The word *diversity* refers to all the ways in which people are different from one another. They may include language, religion, beliefs, traditions, and values. These are the things that make each member nation of the EU unique.

How the EU Promotes a European Cultural Identity A common cultural identity is a centripetal force. The EU has worked in many ways to create a European cultural identity. For instance, it has created common cultural symbols. The EU has its own flag, which shows 12 stars on a blue background. The EU has also adopted its own anthem. Its choice was "Ode to Joy" by the German composer Ludwig van Beethoven. And every year on May 9, Europeans celebrate Europe Day.

The EU supports many cultural programs across Europe. One example is the European Union Youth Wind Orchestra. It brings together young musicians from across Europe. Also, each year the EU chooses one or two cities to be a European Capital of Culture. The EU pays for special shows and events that highlight the city and its culture.

The euro and EU passports make travel within the EU easy. As more Europeans visit other EU countries, they begin to view Europe as a united region. The EU also encourages people, especially youth, to learn other European languages.

Forces Working Against a European Cultural Identity Despite EU efforts at cultural unity, Europe remains diverse. Many languages are spoken in the EU. When people speak different languages, it's hard for them to communicate. The diversity of languages creates extra work for the EU government as well. Every EU speech and document must be translated into 20 languages. In 2008 alone, the EU had to translate almost 2 million pages.

Other centrifugal forces work against a shared cultural identity. National pride is one of them. So are competition and rivalry between countries.

Even cultural traditions can get in the way of cooperation. For example, traditional Czech foods are often cooked slowly. They taste even better the next day. Yet EU rules state that cooked food can't be served if it is more than two hours old. One Czech citizen complained, "This will make many of our best dishes illegal."

Cultural Clashes in the EU
Cultural traditions can divide EU members. For example, bullfighting is a cultural tradition in Spain. Every year, matadors kill thousands of bulls in bullfights. In other EU countries, bullfighting is seen as cruel. Many Europeans think that bullfights should be banned.

14.6 Beginning to Think Globally

In this chapter, you have learned about the European Union. The EU is built on supranational cooperation. You have read about centripetal forces that work for such cooperation. You have also read about centrifugal forces that work against this kind of cooperation.

The EU is the best example of supranational cooperation in the world today. It works because its member nations have been willing to give up some power. Just how much power remains an issue. Some Europeans want the EU to become a "United States of Europe." Others fear giving up any more power to the EU.

Cooperation among nations is not limited to Europe. Other countries also work together on problems they share. In the next section, you'll look at several examples of international cooperation around the world.

14.7 Global Connections

The map shows international organizations in the world today. The countries in these organizations work together on common issues. The most truly international organization is the United Nations (UN). Its members include almost every country in the world.

What kinds of international organizations do countries join?

Countries form many kinds of organizations. Some work to promote the economic well-being of their members. The Free Trade Area of the Americas (FTAA) is a good example. Others bring nations together to defend themselves. The North Atlantic Treaty Organization (NATO) is a defense organization.

Are all international organizations like the EU?

The EU is the best example of a true supranational organization. Other organizations have more limited goals and powers. For example, NATO commits its members to defend one another. They promise to view an attack on one member as an attack on all. But NATO countries don't give up as much control in other areas as EU nations do.

What forces might work against supranational cooperation in the United Nations?

The United Nations (UN) is the world's largest international organization. Its 192 member countries range in size from a few thousand to more than a billion people. Each has its own interests. For such diverse countries to cooperate, they must agree to put the world's interests above their own. This is often difficult or impossible for UN members to do.

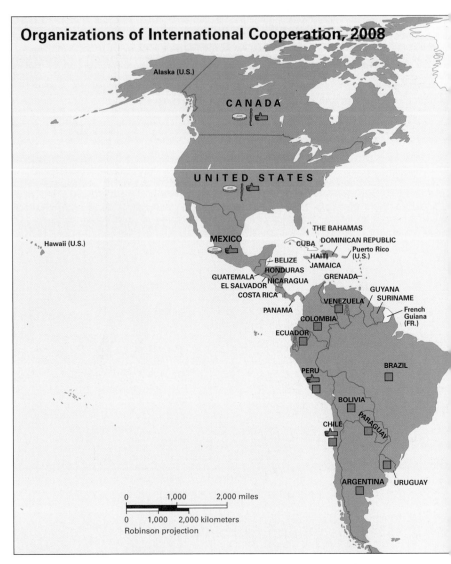

Organizations of International Cooperation, 2008

The UN Headquarters

The United Nations was founded in 1945. Its goal is to promote peace and cooperation among the countries of the world. Member countries meet at the UN headquarters in New York City to discuss world issues.

Economic Cooperation

The United Nations Flag

The UN flag shows a world map centered on the
North Pole. Two olive branches frame the map.
The world map represents all the people of the
world, while the olive branch is a symbol for peace.

Economic Cooperation

- Asia-Pacific Economic Cooperation (APEC)
- Association of Southeast Asian Nations (ASEAN)
- Commonwealth of Independent States (CIS)
- Organization of American States (OAS)
- Organization of Economic Cooperaton and Development (OECD)
- Organization of the Petroleum Exporting Countries (OPEC)
- Southern Cone Common Market (Mercosur)

Economic and Political Cooperation

- African Union

Political Cooperation

- North Atlantic Treaty Organization (NATO)

Political and Cultural Cooperation

- League of Arab States

Economic, Political, and Cultural Cooperation

- European Union (EU)

Population Dilemmas in Europe

15.1 Introduction

You are driving in the south of Italy on a hot summer day. As you wind your way through dry, brown hills, you decide to stop for a cold drink. You park your car in the tiny village of Cersosimo. As you begin to walk through the old narrow streets, you notice something strange. Cersosimo is filled with elderly people! In fact, for every three faces you see, two of them are over 65 years old. Looking in at the village school, you see that children of all ages are studying together in just one small class.

Finally you find a shop where you can buy your cold drink. You ask the shopkeeper why there are so many old people and so few children in Cersosimo. He replies that families here just aren't having babies these days. A few years ago, the village tried to change this. They offered to pay mothers a "birth bonus" for every baby born in Cersosimo. But this did not seem to change anything.

The story of Cersosimo is the story of Italy. Scientists who do research in **demography** say that it is also the story of Europe. Demography is the study of human populations. Demographers look at **birth rates** and **death rates** and migration of people. They study how populations change over time. They also track population trends, or movements. In Europe, for example, they are tracking a trend toward smaller families.

In this chapter, you will learn about population trends in Europe. You will see some of the problems created by shrinking family sizes. And you will see how European countries are trying to address those problems.

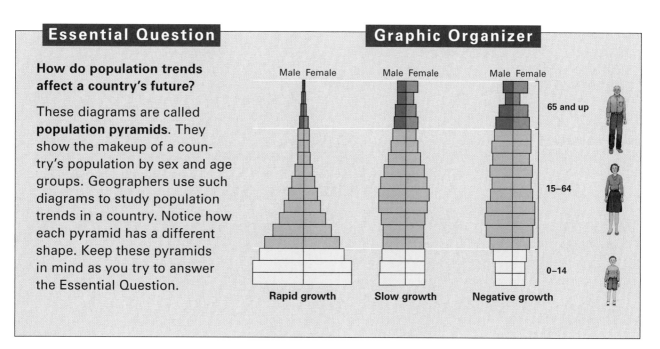

Essential Question

How do population trends affect a country's future?

These diagrams are called **population pyramids**. They show the makeup of a country's population by sex and age groups. Geographers use such diagrams to study population trends in a country. Notice how each pyramid has a different shape. Keep these pyramids in mind as you try to answer the Essential Question.

Graphic Organizer

Male Female   Male Female   Male Female

65 and up

15–64

0–14

Rapid growth   Slow growth   Negative growth

◀ Dolceacqua, a small town in Italy

Europe, 2000

Europe, 2030 (Estimated)

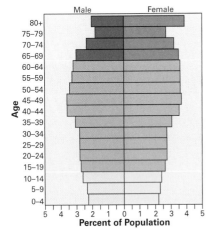

Source for all population pyramid data:
United Nations Population Division.

Population Trends in Europe

A population pyramid is made up of two back-to-back bar graphs. One shows the number of males in different age groups. The other shows the number of females. The first of these pyramids graphs Europe's population in 2000. The second reveals how that makeup is likely to change by 2030.

15.2 The Geographic Setting

Europe is one of the smallest continents in area. But about an eighth of the world's people live there. This may not be true much longer for two reasons. First, Europe has the oldest population of any continent. Second, it has the lowest birth rate, or number of births per 1,000 people. As a result, its population is shrinking.

Population Change: Births, Deaths, and Migration The study of population trends focuses on births, deaths, and migration. Whether a population grows or shrinks depends on these three factors.

Children are born every day in Europe. But the average number of babies born to each woman is low. This average number of births is called the **total fertility rate,** or TFR. In 2008, for example, the TFR in Italy was just under one and a half babies per woman.

If the TFR remains this low, Italy's population will continue to shrink. To stop this trend, the total fertility rate will need to rise to the **replacement rate**. This will happen when enough babies are born to replace the people who die each year. In Italy, the replacement rate is just over two babies per woman.

People also die every day in Europe. But they don't die as young as they used to. Over the past century, **life expectancy** has increased there. Life expectancy is the number of years a person can expect to live. In 2008, the average person in France could expect to live about 81 years. A century earlier, life expectancy in France was only 50 years.

People move into and out of Europe every day as well. In the past, most of the movement was out of Europe. Today more people are moving into Europe than are leaving it. But not enough are coming in to keep the population stable.

Population Pyramids Show Growth Trends Geographers use graphs shaped like pyramids to study population. These graphs show the ages and sexes in a population. The youngest ages are at the bottom. The oldest are at the top.

The shape of a population pyramid shows how a country's population is growing. A pyramid that is wide at the bottom shows rapid population growth. More babies are being born each year than the number of people who die. A pyramid with straight sides shows slow population growth. Births and deaths are nearly equal in that country. A pyramid that is narrow at the bottom shows negative population growth. More people are dying each year than are being born.

Population growth affects a country's **dependency ratio**. This ratio compares the number of people too young or old to work with a country's working-age population. Most young people under the age of 16 in Europe don't work. And most people over the age of 64 are retired. Both groups depend on other people to support them. A low dependency ratio means that workers have few dependents to support. A high dependency ratio means just the opposite. There are a lot of young or old people for workers to support.

▶ Geoterms

demography the study of human populations, including how they change due to births, deaths, aging, and migration

dependency ratio the number of old and young dependents who don't work compared with the working-age population. The higher the ratio, the more young and old people the workers have to support.

life expectancy the average age that a person in a given population can expect to live to. Life expectancy varies from one country to another.

replacement rate the total fertility rate needed for a population to replace itself. This number varies by country, but is about 2.1 in most developed countries.

total fertility rate (TFR) the average number of children a woman in a given population will have in her lifetime. This number is different in different countries.

Factors That Cause Population Change

This equation shows the factors that cause the size of a population to change from one year to the next. Births and immigration cause a population to grow. Deaths and emigration cause a population to shrink.

Population in one year + **Births − Deaths** + **Immigration − Emigration** = **Population in the next year**

A Large Royal Family

In the 1800s, Queen Victoria and Prince Albert had nine children. A century later, Prince Charles and Princess Diana had two children.

15.3 Population Change in Europe

In 1840, Queen Victoria of Britain married a German prince, Albert of Saxe-Coburg and Gotha. The couple had nine children. Victoria's family was the model for other English families. In those days, large families were common in Europe. Such large families are rare today. In fact, Europe's growing population is now stable or shrinking.

From Slow to Fast to No Growth Before the 1750s, the population of Europe rose and fell over time. In bad years, plagues, famines, and wars killed huge numbers of people. In good years, there was enough food to support large families. Overall, there were slightly more births than deaths. This kept population growth low.

In the 1750s, Europe entered a long period of rapid population growth. Sanitation and health care improved. Food supplies increased. As a result, death rates dropped.

After 1900, most Europeans moved from farms to cities. They no longer needed large families to plant and harvest crops. Birth rates began falling. By 2000, Europe had entered a period of no, or even negative, population growth.

A Model of Population Change Demographers have identified several stages of population growth. The four major stages are shown below in the **demographic transition model**. A model is a simple version of something complex that can be used to make predictions. According to this model, populations go through transitions, or changes, as a country develops its economy.

Stage 1: Low population growth. In this stage, high birth rates and high death rates result in little population change. All populations begin at this stage.

Stage 2: Rapid population growth. Birth rates remain high as economic development begins. But death rates fall as food supplies increase and health care improves. The result is rapid growth.

Populations in Transition

The demographic transition model shows population change over time. The word *transition* means change. There is no fixed time for each stage. Some countries may pass through all four stages as they develop. Others may not.

The Demographic Transition Model

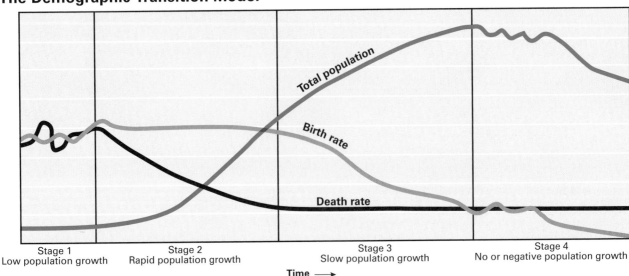

Total population

Birth rate

Death rate

| Stage 1 | Stage 2 | Stage 3 | Stage 4 |
| Low population growth | Rapid population growth | Slow population growth | No or negative population growth |

Time ⟶

Stage 3: Slow population growth. As the economy improves, birth rates drop. Death rates stay low. Population growth begins to slow down.

Stage 4: No or negative population growth. In **developed countries,** both birth rates and death rates drop to low levels. As a result, there is little or no population growth. Over time, birth rates may fall behind death rates. The result is a shrinking population.

15.4 Dilemma One: A Shrinking Population

Between 2005 and 2050, Italy's population is expected to shrink from 58 million to 54 million people. Looking ahead, there may be empty schools, vacant apartments, and miles of lonely countryside.

Causes of Negative Population Growth A country's total fertility rate is an important factor in determining its future population. By 2004, Italy's TFR had fallen well below the replacement rate of 2.1 children per woman. But Italy was not alone. Across Europe, total fertility rates were on the decline.

There are many reasons for Europe's low birth rates. Family finances play a part in how many children people have. Housing costs and living expenses are high in much of Europe. Young couples often need two incomes to buy a home. Young women often put off having children in order to work.

Working couples who want children face different problems. In the past, mothers cared for their children at home. When both parents work, they need help to care for their children during the day. But good childcare is often hard to find. This discourages couples from having large families.

Other factors also contribute to negative population growth. Family-planning methods allow couples to control the number of children they have. In addition, many young women put off having babies while they focus on education or a career. Women who make this choice tend to have smaller families.

Problems Caused by Negative Growth Many problems arise when populations shrink. Fewer children need fewer schools and teachers. Over time, this means that schools may have to close. Teachers may lose their jobs. Other people who work with children may also find themselves out of work. And toy stores and children's clothing stores may go out of business.

Babies grow up to be workers. So low birth rates are likely to lead to labor shortages. As populations shrink, businesses may not be able to find enough workers. Some may move to countries where there are more workers. This could hurt Europe's economy.

Negative growth also means fewer people to serve in military forces. As a result, European countries may lose some of their power and importance in the world.

Italy, 2008

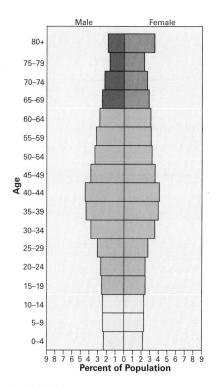

A Shrinking Population in Italy
This pyramid shows the population of Italy in 2008. Notice how narrow the graph is at the base. This is a sign of a shrinking population.

Childcare in France

These young children attend a childcare center in France. Good, affordable childcare is a must in nations that want to encourage higher birth rates.

15.5 Responses to Negative Growth

In the past, the Italian government promoted large families as part of Italy's culture. However, many couples did not have more babies. In 2003, the government tried something new. If families with at least one child had another baby, it would pay them a "birth bonus." The amount was 1,000 euros, or about $1,000.

Cash and Benefits for Having Babies It may seem strange to pay families for having babies. Yet Italy is not the only country in Europe to do so. France, for example, gives a birth bonus for every child born in the country. A family with three or more children receives additional benefits, such as reduced rents and lower taxes. But it's not clear whether paying cash for having babies works well over time. Sometimes birth rates rise for a few years. But then they drop again.

Other countries don't believe in paying families to have babies. Instead, some try to lower the costs of having children. Sweden helps parents pay for daycare for small children.

Family-Friendly Policies for Parents The cost of raising children isn't the only reason people are having so few babies. Another is the difficulty of balancing work and family life. Working parents often want to take time off work to care for their children. But they fear that if they do so, they may lose their jobs.

Many European governments now have family-friendly policies to help working parents. One policy allows a new parent to stay home with a baby without losing his or her job. This time away from the job is called a *leave*. During the leave, the parent is still paid. When the leave ends, the parent goes back to work. Other policies include flexible work hours and the right to work part-time. Governments hope that policies like these will make being parents more appealing to couples.

15.6 Dilemma Two: An Aging Population

Europe is sometimes called "the old continent" because of its aging population. By 2050, the average age of a person in Spain will be 50 years. This will make the population of Spain the oldest in the world. It will also mean more old people for Spain to care for.

In the past, most old people in Spain lived in their own homes or with relatives. With people living longer today, new living arrangements are needed. To help meet that need, a home for the elderly was built near Madrid, the capital of Spain. The home is large, with space for 600 people. Not only is it filled, but also there are 20,000 people on a waiting list who would like to move in! That list will get longer as Spain's elderly population grows.

Causes of an Aging Population A population ages for two reasons. The first is a rise in life expectancy. The second is a drop in the birth rate. Both are happening across Europe today. The result is that there are more old people. At the same time, there are fewer young people.

Europe will age even more rapidly in the years ahead because of an earlier **baby boom**. A baby boom is a sudden increase in the birth rate. Europe's baby boom began not long after World War II ended in 1945. During the 1950s and 1960s, women had a lot of babies. In the 1970s, birth rates began to fall.

By the year 2000, the first people born during Europe's baby boom were entering their 50s. Soon many of them will retire. As the baby boomers age, Europe's population will age with them.

Problems Caused by an Aging Population Most people would agree that having longer, healthier lives is a good thing. Yet an aging population creates problems for a society. The two biggest concerns are **pensions** and health care.

A pension is a fixed amount of money paid to a retired person by a government or former employer. Pensions are usually paid from the time people retire until they die.

As people age, their need for health care increases. Older people are more likely to suffer from such diseases as cancer, diabetes, or arthritis. They are more likely to need expensive surgeries and costly medicines. Some may need special care available only in nursing homes. All of this costs money.

Most European countries provide pensions and health care for the elderly. The money to pay for both comes from taxes paid by working people. This system works as long as the dependency ratio is low. But with fewer young people joining the workforce, the dependency ratio is rising. An ever-smaller workforce is supporting an ever-larger elderly population.

The simplest solution to rising costs is to budget more money for pensions and health care. Most governments have done this. But there are limits to how much workers are willing to be taxed.

Spain's Elderly Population

Population Aging in Spain

This line graph shows how the percentage of people aged 65 and over has increased in Spain since 1950. It also predicts how that population will grow in the future. One reason for the change since 1950 is a steady rise in life expectancy.

15.7 Responses to an Aging Population

In 2002, Spain hosted the United Nations Second World Assembly on Ageing. Kofi Annan, the UN's secretary-general, opened the meeting. For the first time in history, he reported, older people will soon outnumber the young. Borrowing a line from a song by the English band the Beatles, Annan asked the assembly, "Will you still need me, will you still feed me, when I'm 64?" Then he added, "I trust the answer is yes."

Dealing with Pension Costs One of the issues discussed at the assembly was how to deal with rising pension costs. There are more retired people in Europe than ever before. Also, they are living longer than in the past.

One way to reduce pension costs is to cut the amount of money each worker receives. But cutting pensions too much seems unfair to people who depend on this income to live.

Another approach is to raise the retirement age. This keeps people in the workforce longer. It also shortens the time during which they will need government pensions. Germany, Italy, and the United Kingdom have all increased the age at which pensions begin. Other countries give bonuses to people who delay retirement. Spanish workers get a higher pension if they put off retirement until after age 66.

Providing Health Care Governments are also looking at smarter ways to care for the elderly. In Germany, two principles guide this effort. The first is that preventing health problems is better than treating them. The second is that home care is better than care in a nursing home.

Many countries are looking at ways to encourage family members to care for older relatives at home. Home care costs less. Also, older people prefer it. Italy provides special health services to families who care for relatives. Austria pays pensions to people who give up jobs to care for family members.

Spain, 2030 (Estimated)

Spain's Baby Boom "Bulge"

Note the "bulge" in this population pyramid. It represents Spain's baby boomers. Over time, the bulge will move up the pyramid. At this happens, the number of pensioners in Spain will increase.

Lining Up for Pension Checks

These Italians are waiting for their pension checks. Like most older Europeans, they live on monthly payments from their government.

Changes in Germany's Population and Labor Supply

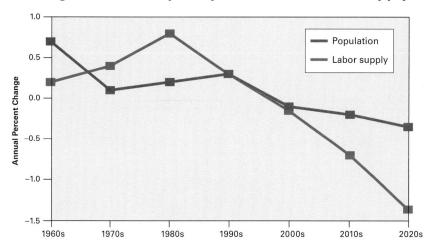

Fewer Workers in Germany's Future

Germany's shrinking population creates problems for business. One problem is fewer customers. Another is a shortage of skilled workers. This will get worse as baby boomers retire. Look at the percentage of change for each decade. Note the major change predicted to occur by the 2020s.

15.8 Dilemma Three: A Declining Workforce

In 2004, a German museum opened an exhibit called "Shrinking Cities." It showed what happens when a city like Leipzig, Germany, loses most of its workforce. Leipzig's problems began with a drop in the birth rate. Fewer babies meant fewer young people in the city's workforce. Faced with worker shortages, businesses left the city. Workers left as well in search of better jobs. Now Leipzig is mainly a city of the old and the unemployed.

Causes of Workforce Decline The main cause of workforce decline across Europe is simple. More workers retire each year than join the workforce. The decline will grow worse when baby boomers start to retire. The number of workers in Germany, for example, will likely fall from 55 million to 30 million over the next 50 years.

Workforce decline leads to changes in the dependency ratio. As you recall, this is the ratio of dependents to workers. Dependents are people too young or too old to work. In 2000, 100 workers in Germany supported 87 dependents. By 2030, 100 workers will be supporting 121 dependents. That's a rise of 39 percent.

Problems Caused by Workforce Decline In many European countries, young people have trouble finding jobs. To them, a shrinking workforce looks like a good thing. As older workers retire, there will be more jobs for young workers.

For a business, however, workforce decline can be a problem. By 2050, the number of highly skilled German workers will decline by about 2 million people. Faced with this shortage, some businesses may leave Germany. Others may shrink or close their doors altogether. The German economy may start to shrink as well.

Workforce decline is also a big problem for a government. Workers pay most of the taxes that support government programs. Fewer workers will mean less tax money just at a time when the dependency ratio is rising.

Germany, 2008

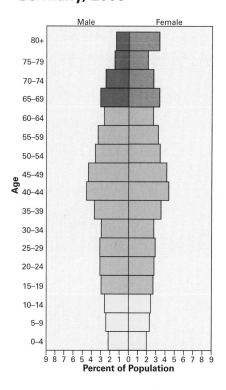

Germany's Working-Age Population in 2008

Germany's working-age population is shown in medium colors in the middle part of this graph. People too young to work are shown in light colors at the bottom. People too old to work are in dark colors at the top. In 2008, working-age people outnumbered these dependents. By 2030, just the opposite will be true.

Making Cars in Germany
These workers are assembling a car in a German factory. As the workforce shrinks, this factory may be moved to another country.

15.9 Responses to a Declining Workforce

In 2007, about 1.5 million jobs in Germany went unfilled. Employers could not find enough skilled German workers to fill them. Then a new immigration law was passed. The new law made it easier for companies to hire skilled workers from other countries. With this change, Germany hoped to slow its workforce decline.

Finding More Workers in Europe Many countries in Europe are trying to slow workforce decline. One approach is to keep older workers working longer. Germany, for example, retrains older workers. It also gives aid to companies that hire older workers. Other countries encourage older people to work part-time or at home.

Another approach is to encourage more women to join the workforce. In the past, women left the workforce after having their first child. Mothers who tried to work found it hard to balance work and family life. They also made less money than men.

Governments hope that family-friendly work policies will encourage more women to enter the workforce. You read earlier about giving parents paid time off work when they have a baby. Flexible schedules can also help women work while meeting family needs.

Looking for Workers Outside of Europe Another way to deal with workforce decline is to look for workers outside of Europe. This can be done in two ways. This first is to move jobs once done in Europe to other parts of the world. For example, the German company Volkswagen no longer makes all of its cars in Germany. Workers in Brazil, Mexico, South Africa, and other countries now make cars for Volkswagen.

A second way is to encourage workers from other regions to immigrate to Europe. Not all Europeans, however, welcome this idea. They worry that immigration may cause more problems than it solves.

15.10 Beginning to Think Globally

In this chapter, you have learned about demography, the study of human populations. You learned how population pyramids show the population makeup of a country. These graphs show whether a population is likely to grow, stay the same, or decline.

Negative Growth in Europe You also learned that most countries in Europe face negative population growth. This happens because the total fertility rate has dropped below the replacement rate. In other words, women are not having enough babies to replace the people who die each year. At the same time, Europe's population is aging. This is because life expectancy is rising.

The growing population of old people is pushing up dependency ratios. Most retired Europeans depend on their government for pensions and health care. Governments depend on taxes paid by working people to pay for these benefits. But every year, there are fewer workers to pay those taxes. And there are more old people depending on those taxes for support.

Global Population Trends Europe is not the only place with an aging population. Developed countries in other regions are seeing the same trend. Japan, for example, is aging as rapidly as Europe.

A different trend is found in many developing countries. Total fertility rates are dropping more slowly. Life expectancy is rising slowly as well. For example, in Nigeria, the total fertility rate in 2008 was just over five children per woman. Life expectancy for a child born that year was about 50 years. As a result, Nigeria's population is young. It is also still growing.

Think about these trends as you look at developed and developing countries around the world in the next section.

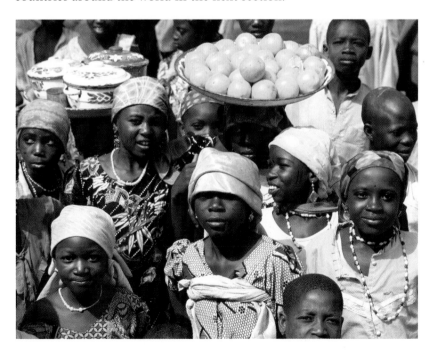

A Young Population in Nigeria
Nigeria has a much higher birth rate than Italy. As a result, 42 percent of its population is under the age of 15. Only 14 percent of all Italians are under the age of 15.

15.11 Global Connections

This map divides the world into developed (rich) and developing (poor) countries. Most rich countries have industrial economies and a high per capita GDP. Most poor countries have an agricultural economy and a low per capita GDP. The pyramids compare the populations of rich and poor countries in 2000 and in 2025.

Why do developed countries have lower birth rates than developing ones? People in all countries want children. But in developed countries, children usually aren't needed to support a family or aging parents. Instead, the cost of raising children is seen as an expense. Also, family-planning methods are more available to help couples to limit their families to what they want and can afford.

Why do developing countries have higher birth rates than developed ones? In poorer countries, poverty plays a role in family size. Children are expected to help support their families. They support their parents in old age, since the government often doesn't. As a result, a large family is seen as a benefit, not an expense. Many poor countries also have a high infant mortality rate. Couples choose to have many children, fearing that some may die early in life.

How might high birth rates affect a country's future? Countries with high birth rates have more young than old people. They may not have enough schools to educate their children. They may not have enough jobs to employ their young adults. Anger over the lack of schools and jobs may lead to widespread frustration and unrest.

The Developed and Developing World, 2008

0   1,000   2,000 miles
0 1,000 2,000 kilometers
Robinson projection

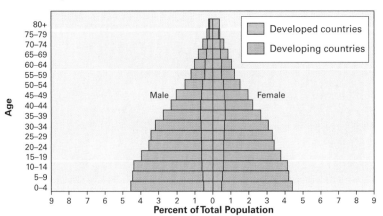

World Population, 2000

Developed countries
Developing countries

Male   Female

Age

Percent of Total Population

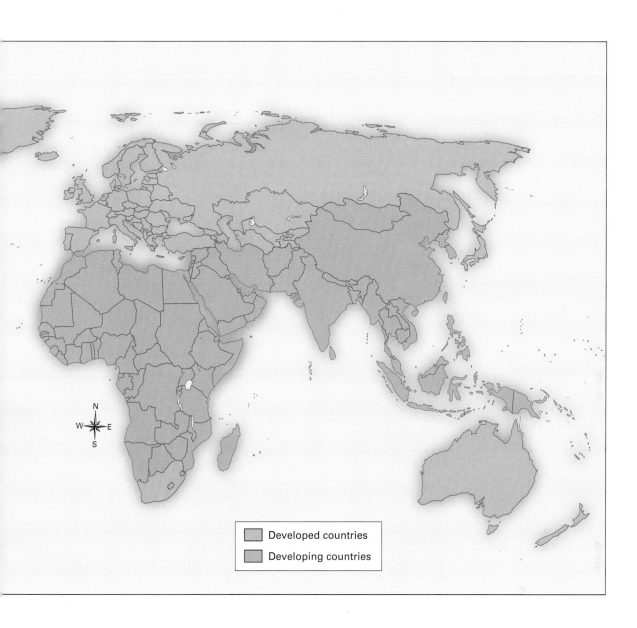

Developed countries

Developing countries

World Population, 2025 (Estimated)

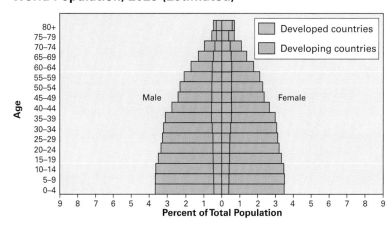

Developed countries

Developing countries

Male

Female

Age: 80+, 75–79, 70–74, 65–69, 60–64, 55–59, 50–54, 45–49, 40–44, 35–39, 30–34, 25–29, 20–24, 15–19, 10–14, 5–9, 0–4

Percent of Total Population: 9 8 7 6 5 4 3 2 1 0 1 2 3 4 5 6 7 8 9

Invisible Borders: Transboundary Pollution in Europe

16

16.1 Introduction

On April 28, 1986, scientists at a nuclear power plant in Sweden listened in horror as their computers began to beep. The beeps meant that there were high levels of **nuclear radiation** in the air. This is a form of energy produced by nuclear power plants. In large amounts, it is deadly to living things. A radiation leak is a sign that something has gone very wrong in a power plant.

The scientists searched the plant for a leak. But the radiation was not from their plant. It was not even from anywhere in Sweden. Winds had carried it to Sweden from the Soviet Union. Eventually, the world learned why. There had been an accident at a Soviet nuclear power plant called Chernobyl.

The Chernobyl accident is an example of **transboundary pollution**. As you know, **pollution** is damage to the environment that is caused by harmful substances. The word *transboundary* means "across country boundaries." Transboundary pollution starts in one country. Then it spreads to other countries.

In this chapter, you will learn about several cases of transboundary pollution in Europe. You will find out how different kinds of pollution begin. You'll see how pollution can easily cross borders between countries. You'll also learn about efforts to reduce transboundary pollution.

Essential Question

How can one country's pollution become another country's problem?

This illustration shows parts of Europe and Russia. It also shows one source of transboundary pollution in this region. Notice how this pollution spreads across borders. Keep this illustration in mind as you try to answer the Essential Question.

Graphic Organizer

◀ Destruction after an explosion at the Chernobyl nuclear power plant in 1986

16.2 The Geographic Setting

Beginning in the 1700s, Europe went through a great change known as the **Industrial Revolution**. More and more goods were produced by machines instead of by hand. As a result, work moved from homes into factories. This shift created great benefits for many people. It also created big problems for the environment.

From Handmade to Machine-Made Goods Before the Industrial Revolution, people made almost everything they needed using simple hand tools. Most work was done at home or in small workshops. Goods were costly because they took so long to make.

All this changed with the Industrial Revolution. The change began with the invention of machines to make cloth. These machines spun cotton into thread. Other machines then wove the thread into cloth. The new machines produced cloth much faster than people could with hand looms. Over time, machines were invented to produce everything in the modern home, from clocks to computers.

The Industrial Revolution has made life better in many ways. Machine-made goods are usually cheaper than those made by hand. As a result, many people today can afford to buy goods that only the rich could buy in the past. However, this revolution has also created big environmental problems. The factories that churn out these goods produce pollution.

Water Pollution Then

This 1858 illustration shows the River Thames in England during the Industrial Revolution. The figure in the rowboat is a symbol of death. The artist used it to represent the poisoning of the Thames by pollution.

The Granger Collection

How Pollution Occurs and Spreads

Pollution occurs when dangerous substances, such as certain chemicals, are added to the air, water, or soil. Pollution sometimes has a natural cause. A volcano, for example, may pollute the air with poisonous gases. More often, however, it is the result of human activity.

People create two kinds of pollution. One is **accidental pollution**. This is pollution that occurs as the result of an accident, such as an oil tanker spilling oil into the sea. An oil spill may kill fish and seabirds.

The other kind is **general pollution**. This is pollution caused by everyday activities such as burning coal to make electricity. Smoke from coal-burning power plants pollutes the air. It also contributes to **acid rain**. This is rain that has been turned slightly acid, like vinegar, by pollution in the air. Acid rain can harm plants, animals, and buildings.

Pollution is an even bigger problem when it spreads. Wind currents can quickly spread pollution into the atmosphere. Water currents can spread it almost as rapidly through a **river system**. A river system includes a river and all the streams that flow into it. Pollution in one country can quickly become another country's problem.

acid rain rain that can damage the environment because it contains acid from factory smoke and car exhaust. Acid rain can damage plants, fish, animals, and even buildings.

nuclear radiation a form of energy that comes from nuclear reactions. Radiation has no smell or taste, but it can be very harmful to living things. Materials polluted with nuclear radiation are said to be radioactive.

river system a river and all the streams that flow into it. The streams that flow into a river are called *tributaries*.

transboundary pollution pollution that starts in one country and crosses boundaries into other countries. Generally, transboundary pollution is carried by wind or water.

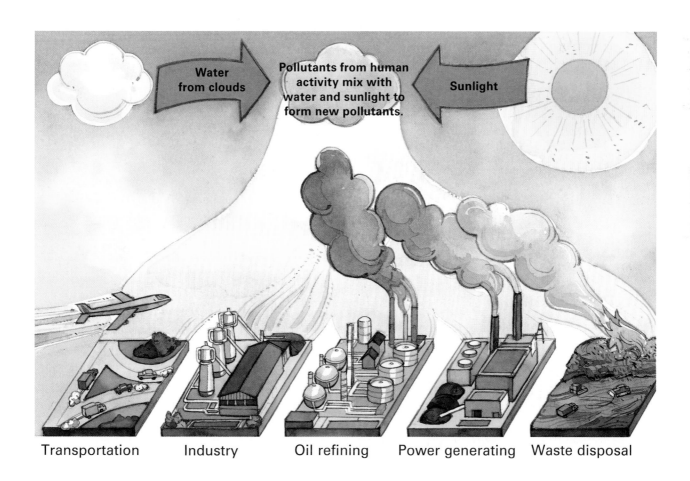

Transportation   Industry   Oil refining   Power generating   Waste disposal

Air Pollution Has Many Causes

There are many sources of air pollution. Most air pollution is caused by the burning of fossil fuels. Fossil fuels include coal, oil, and natural gas. Burning fossil fuels releases energy for heating, running motors, and making electricity. It also releases harmful chemicals into the air.

16.3 The Chernobyl Radiation Accident

At 1:24 A.M. on April 25, 1986, an explosion rocked the Chernobyl nuclear power plant. A fireball of radioactive dust rose three miles into the air. Soon the radioactive cloud rode the winds to places thousands of miles away. A terrible accident at a single power plant became a matter of concern for the entire world.

Human Error Creates a Deadly Radiation Leak The Chernobyl nuclear plant lies near the city of Kiev in Ukraine. At that time, Ukraine was part of the Soviet Union. Ukraine later became independent, after the breakup of the Soviet Union into 15 separate countries.

Chernobyl was one of hundreds of nuclear power plants operating in about 30 countries. These plants use uranium for fuel. The uranium is mined from the ground, like coal or copper. Then it is put in a special container called a *nuclear reactor*. Inside the reactor, the uranium gives off energy in the form of heat. This heat is used to boil water to create steam. The steam powers a turbine to produce electricity.

During the Chernobyl accident, one of the reactors got too hot to control. This accident did not just "happen." It occurred when workers doing a routine check failed to follow their own safety rules. As a result, an explosion blasted through the reactor.

The explosion started a fire that quickly raged out of control. But the biggest problem was not the fire. It was the huge cloud that formed over Chernobyl after the explosion. This cloud was made up of deadly radioactive dust.

The Radioactive Cloud Spreads Across Europe The radioactive cloud did not remain over Chernobyl for long. Winds sent it north toward Sweden and then south toward Central Europe. Radiation also moved east across Asia. It eventually crossed the Pacific Ocean to reach the United States.

A Deadly Explosion at Chernobyl

The explosion at the Chernobyl nuclear power plant left a pile of rubble on the ground. It also spread radioactive pollution over a wide area. Children who were exposed to this radiation have a higher than normal risk of getting cancer.

The Chernobyl Nuclear Power Plant

Countries close to the disaster suffered the most. The hardest hit was Belarus, which borders Ukraine to the north. About 70 percent of the radioactive dust from Chernobyl fell on Belarus. The dust contaminated soil and water. As a result, the people of Belarus eat, drink, and breathe radiation every day. This has led to higher rates of cancer among Belarusians.

The people of Lapland also suffered. Lapland is an area in the far north of Europe, including part of Sweden. Many people here fish for a living. Others raise herds of reindeer. After the Chernobyl accident, radiation polluted their fishing grounds and reindeer herds. Many animals died. Those that survived were not safe to eat.

Radiation Spread from Chernobyl

April 26, 1986

• Radioactive cloud spread

Chernobyl

April 30, 1986

Chernobyl

May 4, 1986

Chernobyl

Efforts to Reduce Radioactive Pollution At first, the Soviet government denied that there had been an accident. But Swedish scientists raised alarms about rising radiation levels. Finally, an announcement was made on Soviet television.

> *An accident has taken place at the Chernobyl power station, and one of the reactors was damaged. Measures are being taken to eliminate the consequences of the accident. Those affected by it are being given assistance.*

The government sent an army of engineers into Chernobyl. Over the next few weeks, they built a huge concrete box around the damaged reactor. This giant tomb will have to remain in place until the reactor is no longer dangerously radioactive. That will not be for hundreds of years.

The Soviet government moved people living closest to the plant to safer areas. About 135,000 people had to leave their homes. Often they had no warning. Rescue workers suddenly appeared, looking like spacemen in their protective clothes. The workers hurried residents onto buses. Workers also destroyed contaminated crops, food, and animals. Despite these efforts, thousands of people will eventually die in Ukraine from health problems caused by radiation.

Chernobyl was the world's worst nuclear accident. Since then, great attention has been paid to improving safety at nuclear power plants. Reactors have been changed to make them less likely to overheat. Other improvements make it easier to shut reactors down in emergencies. These efforts reduce the chances that accidents at power plants will cause major radiation pollution.

A Deadly Cloud
These maps show how quickly winds spread radiation released by the Chernobyl explosion.

Checking for Radiation
This inspector is checking a train in Germany for radiation after the Chernobyl accident. He is using a Geiger counter. This device clicks when it measures radiation nearby. The more radiation there is, the faster a Geiger counter clicks.

The Black Triangle Region

GERMANY   POLAND
Black
Triangle
CZECH REP.

NORWAY
SWEDEN

A Region of Dying Trees

A "black triangle" of factories and power plants spreads across Central Europe. Air pollution in this region is killing forests and fish.

16.4 The "Black Triangle" and Acid Rain

Tourists flock to Europe each year to visit its famous stone monuments. Some of these monuments, such as ancient Greek temples and Roman bridges, are more than 2000 years old. They have survived wars, floods, and fires. But they may not survive modern pollution. Acid rain is slowly eating away at these precious relics.

Soot from Factories Creates Acid Rain As you read earlier, acid rain is caused by pollution of the air. People cause most air pollution by burning things. A century ago, when many people burned coal to heat their homes, thick clouds of soot hung over many cities. Today, exhaust from factories and cars are the main sources of air pollution.

Air pollution is a problem in many places, but some areas create more pollution than others. One major source of air pollution, and acid rain, is the "triangle" where Germany, Poland, and the Czech Republic meet. Many factories and power plants are located in this area. Most of them burn lignite, a soft brown coal, as their main fuel. Because soot from the burning coal blackens the air, this area is often called the "Black Triangle."

When lignite burns, it gives off two chemicals. One is sulfur dioxide. The other is nitrogen oxides. When these two chemicals react with water, they form acids. Acids have a sour taste. You can taste acid in vinegar. Acids are also corrosive. This means that they will slowly eat away at something until it is destroyed.

Acid rain results from sulfur dioxide and nitrogen oxides mixing with water in the air. When acid rain falls on lakes, it can make the water acidic. In some lakes, high acid levels have killed fish. Acid rain can also harm forests. It weakens trees by eating away at their leaves or needles.

The Sudety Mountains are on the border between Poland and the Czech Republic. They are just east of the Black Triangle. That means that they are **downwind,** or in the direction the wind is blowing, of some of the worst pollution in Europe. If you go there, you will see many, many sick trees without leaves.

Air Pollution Brings Acid Rain to Other Countries Ever since people began burning coal as a fuel, acid rain has been a problem. Since most factories were located in cities, however, acid rain was mainly an **urban** problem.

In the 1950s, coal-burning factories and power plants began building very high chimneys. The smoke coming out of these chimneys was carried away by high winds. This change improved the air in industrial cities. But it led to the spread of air pollution over much wider areas.

Today air pollution from the Black Triangle brings acid rain to many countries. In Sweden and Finland, a great majority of the pollution that causes acid rain comes from other countries, especially Germany and Poland.

Efforts to Reduce Acid Rain The countries of Europe are trying to reduce acid rain in many ways. One approach is to reward companies that reduce pollution. Some governments propose to do this by letting companies that pollute less pay lower taxes.

Another approach is to promote new technologies that result in less pollution. Many factories and power plants that burn coal now use smokestack scrubbers. These scrubbers take harmful substances out of the smoke as it goes up the chimney. As a result, far less pollution enters the air.

A third approach is to reduce the use of coal as a fuel for power plants and factories. Scientists today are looking for new ways to harness the power of the wind, water, and the sun. Using wind, water, and sun to generate electricity does not pollute the air or cause acid rain. You will learn more about these alternative energy sources in Chapter 24.

The Impact of Acid Rain

Acid rain is rain that pollution has turned acidic. When acid rain falls on forests, leaves and needles turn brown. Acid rain also dissolves nutrients in the soil. The nutrients then wash away before plants can use them.

| Factories, power plants, and vehicles release sulfur dioxide and nitrogen oxides into the air. | Some pollutants fall to the ground. Other pollutants mix with water in clouds to form sulfuric acid and nitric acid. | Acid rain falls from the clouds. Acid in soil and water damages plants and wildlife. Acid rain also harms buildings and cars. |

16.5 The Tisza-Danube Cyanide Spill

On January 30, 2000, a large amount of cyanide spilled into a river in Central Europe. Cyanide is a **toxic chemical** that is used in mining and other industries. This accidental spill triggered the worst environmental disaster in Europe since Chernobyl. In fact, many people called the spill the "water Chernobyl."

The Tisza-Danube River System

Location of cyanide spill
Major cities along affected rivers
Poisoned rivers

0   25   50 miles
0 25 50 kilometers
Albers Conic Equal-Area projection

A Burst Dam Releases Deadly Chemicals The accident took place at a mining operation in Romania. At the time, Romania was one of 13 Central European countries in the Danube river system. The mining company used cyanide to separate gold from less valuable rock. The cyanide was then stored in a pond formed behind a small dam.

On the night of the spill, it was raining hard. Water from the storm raised the level of the pond to the danger point. Suddenly, the dam burst. About 100,000 cubic meters of water laced with cyanide spilled out of the pond. This is enough **toxic waste** to fill about 30 Olympic-size swimming pools.

Poisoned from Source to Sea

The Tisza-Danube river system was poisoned in 2000. The source of the poison was a cyanide spill in Romania. Rivers carried the poison all the way to Black Sea.

Cyanide Flows into the Danube River System

The cyanide spilled first into the Szamos River in Romania. As the Szamos flowed across Hungary, it entered the Tisza River. The Tisza then emptied into the Danube River. The Danube carried the toxic spill across Serbia and Montenegro and Bulgaria. Finally, the toxic waste emptied into the Black Sea.

The first sign of this transboundary pollution was dead fish. The cyanide killed approximately 200 tons of fish as it washed down the Tisza River. Otters died by the hundreds after they ate the poisoned fish.

Fearing pollution, towns along the Tisza and Danube shut down their water systems. People near the rivers flew black banners and posted warning signs for people to stay away from the water. Many tourists canceled their trips to the area.

Sources of Water Pollution

Water pollution comes from both urban and rural areas. Factories and farms create waste that pollutes water. Garbage and sewage from towns and cities add to the problem. Acid rain pollutes water as well.

Sewage from towns and cities may be dumped into river systems.

Pollutants from garbage seep into the groundwater.

Efforts to Reduce Water Pollution As deadly as the cyanide was, its effects did not last long. Cyanide breaks down in sunlight. By the time the spill reached the Danube, it was no longer toxic to fish. Even so, scientists do not know how long it will take for the river to recover completely. Most agree that it could take many years.

The spill did have one good outcome. It focused people's attention on pollution in the waterways that make up the Danube river system. Mining accidents are only one source of pollution. Many towns dump untreated **sewage** into these waterways. Farms and factories also pollute rivers with fertilizers and chemicals.

In 1998, the International Commission for the Protection of the Danube River was established. The members of the commission represent the 13 countries that share the Danube river system. They are working together to find ways to reduce transboundary pollution in this region.

On June 29, 2004, the commission held its first "Danube Day." On that day, millions of people gathered along the banks of the Danube. They came together to celebrate the river's past and to think about its future. Different events were held in each country. But they all began with this simple truth: "Everybody lives downstream."

16.6 Beginning to Think Globally

In this chapter, you have read about transboundary pollution in Europe. Pollution has many causes. Sometimes it occurs naturally. But more often, people cause pollution. Radioactive pollution, like that released from the Chernobyl power plant, is usually the result of an accident. Acid rain is the result of more general air pollution.

You also saw how easily pollution can be spread by wind and water. The Tisza-Danube cyanide spill showed how an accident in one country can affect an entire river system.

Transboundary pollution is not only a problem in Europe. Wind currents can carry pollution across oceans and continents. Because of this, one country's pollution can create problems in countries halfway around the world. Think about this as you look at global wind patterns in the next section.

Acid rain runs off into lakes and rivers.

Fertilizers and pesticides run off into waterways.

Chemicals are released into rivers.

16.7 Global Connections

The map at the bottom of this page shows levels of acid rain around the world. They range from "acid rain detected" to "acid rain potential." *Detected* means already found. These are places where acid rain is already a serious problem. *Potential* means possible. These are places where acid rain is not yet a problem but may be in the future. Also notice the diagram of wind currents. It shows how winds can carry the chemicals that cause acid rain over vast distances.

Why do North America and Europe have the highest acid rain levels? North America and Europe were the leaders of the Industrial Revolution. They have more cars and factories than other parts of the world. As you have learned, pollution from factories and cars are the two main causes of acid rain.

What changes in Asia are raising the acid rain potential there? China, India, and other countries in Asia are developing at a rapid rate. More and more factories and power plants are being built. The number of cars in these countries is rising rapidly as well. The result is likely to be an equally rapid increase in air pollution.

Why must acid rain be tackled as a global problem? As you have seen, pollution is not always a local issue. Wind and water can carry toxic waste long distances. For this reason, a country that creates pollution may not have to live with all of its effects. Only by working together will countries be able to tackle problems that may begin halfway around the world.

Pollution Patrol Plane
This airplane is used to study air pollution. The pods on the end of its wings contain scientific instruments. These devices detect chemicals in the air.

Acid Rain Around the World

Source: National Institute of Public Health and the Environment, as reported in *Nystrom Desk Atlas*, Chicago: Nystrom Herff Jones, 2007.

Most pollution falls close to the industrial areas where it is created.

Farther away, rain and snow wash pollution from the sky.

Upper-level winds carry small amounts of pollution far distances, even across oceans.

Surface winds

Upper-level winds

The Spread of Pollution from North America

Most air pollution falls close to where it is produced. But winds high above Earth, or upper-level winds, can also carry pollution over great distances.

Russia's Varied Landscape: Physical Processes at Work

17

17.1 Introduction

In 1687, an English scientist named Isaac Newton proposed an amazing idea. He suggested that humans could launch a craft into space. This artificial satellite would orbit Earth, just as the moon does. Newton's idea finally came to pass in 1957. That year Russian scientists launched a satellite known as Sputnik into space. Since then, a number of countries have launched more than 5,000 satellites. Cameras and other instruments on satellites have given humans a new view of Earth.

Geographers use **satellite images** to study Earth. These views of Earth from space show how landscapes develop and change. It may seem like mountains and valleys have always been where they are and always will be. Actually, Earth's surface is forever changing. **Physical processes,** or natural forces, are always at work on the landscape. Some physical processes build up land into mountains. Others wear down land into valleys and plains.

In this chapter, you will learn about four physical processes that shape our Earth. You will also learn how those processes have changed Russia's landscape. Russia is the largest country in the world. It covers almost one eighth of the world's land surface. Because of its great size, Russia has a large variety of landscapes to explore.

Essential Question

Graphic Organizer

How do physical processes shape Earth's landscape?

The map at the center shows the physical landscape of Russia. The four drawings around the map represent physical processes that have shaped the Russian landscape. Two have built up the landscape. Two have worn it down. Keep this illustration in mind as you try to answer the Essential Question.

Tectonic movement

Erosion

Volcanic activity

Glaciation

◄ Satellite image of Lake Baikal in southeastern Russia

17.2 The Geographic Setting

Russia is a giant country that covers almost 7 million square miles. It includes a large part of Europe and Asia. It is so big that it has 11 **time zones**. By contrast, the continental United States has only 4 time zones.

The western part of Russia is one large plain. At the eastern edge of this plain are the Ural Mountains. East of the Urals lies Siberia, another vast plain. High plateaus, icy mountains, and deep valleys surround Siberia. Physical processes have shaped this varied landscape. These processes begin deep inside our planet.

Inside Planet Earth Earth was once a liquid fireball. It has been cooling for more than 4 billion years. Inside Earth, though, temperatures are still so high that in some places rock and metals are a fiery liquid.

At the center of Earth lies the **core**. The core has two parts. The inner core is solid iron. The outer core is liquid iron. The core is the hottest part of Earth. Temperatures in the core may reach over 10,000 degrees Fahrenheit.

The next layer out from the core is called the **mantle**. It is made up of molten, or liquid, rock called **magma**. The mantle makes up about two thirds of Earth's mass.

The outermost part of Earth is called the **lithosphere**. The lithosphere includes a layer of solid rock and, above that, the **crust**. The crust is the only cool layer of Earth. It is where we live.

Forces Below the Crust Build Up Land Two physical processes build and shape land from below. They are **tectonic movement** and **volcanic activity**.

Tectonic is a Greek word that means "builder." Tectonic movement is movement inside Earth that results in changes on the surface. Over millions of years, tectonic movement builds mountains. It also triggers earthquakes.

Volcanic activity includes the formation and eruption of **volcanoes**. Volcanic activity also begins below the surface of Earth. When volcanoes erupt, they can change the landscape suddenly and dramatically.

Forces Above the Crust Wear Down Land Two physical processes work above the crust to reshape landscapes. They are **erosion** and **glaciation**. Erosion is the wearing away of Earth's surface. The most common sources of erosion are wind and running water. Glaciation is the formation of large sheets of ice called **glaciers**. Glaciers can erode, or wear down, Earth's surface as they move across the land. Erosion and glaciation create change very slowly.

These four physical processes have been changing Russia's landscape for millions of years. These processes have worn down plains and mountains and have carved out canyons and valleys. In this chapter, you will find out more about how these four physical processes have shaped not only Russia, but also the rest of our planet.

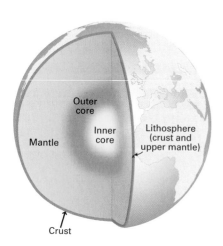

A Cutaway View of Earth

Earth may seem cool on the surface, but deep inside lies a hot liquid core. Earth's crust "floats" on this molten core. Cracks in the crust may result in volcanic activity or tectonic movement.

▶ Geoterms

erosion the gradual wearing away of Earth's surface by the action of wind, water, ice, and gravity

glaciation the creation and movement of glaciers

physical processes natural forces that change Earth's physical features, including forces that build up and wear down Earth's surface

tectonic movement the movement of plates below Earth's surface

volcanic activity the formation and eruption of volcanoes

Physical Features of Russia

The World's Largest Country

Russia stretches from Europe across Asia to the Pacific Ocean. Tectonic activity and volcanoes have created its mountains. Erosion and glaciation have shaped its vast plains and plateaus.

Earth's Tectonic Plates

A Crust of Moving Plates

Earth's solid crust is made up of tectonic plates. These plates float on the liquid rock that makes up the middle layer of Earth. There are at least 14 plates, some very large in area, some smaller.

17.3 How Tectonic Movement Shapes Earth

In 1906, a terrifying earthquake shook San Francisco, California. "Trolley lines snapped like threads" and buildings "crumbled like card houses," wrote one eyewitness. "The cobblestones danced like corn in a popper." No one at that time understood how or why earthquakes happen. Today we know that they are caused by tectonic movement.

The Continents and Oceans Rest on Plates Scientists solved the mystery of earthquakes in the 1960s. They discovered that the lithosphere is broken into huge pieces called **tectonic plates**. Earth's lands and seas rest on these plates, which lie below the surface of our planet. The plates float like rafts on Earth's liquid mantle.

Tectonic plates move in three ways. They can move away from each other. They can move toward each other. Or they can scrape sideways past each other. When two plates collide, one usually slides under the other.

Tectonic plates are incredibly heavy. When they meet, friction can lock them into place for long periods. During this time, enormous pressure builds up below Earth's crust. When the pressure gets too great, the plates come unstuck and move with tremendous energy. We feel this sudden movement as an earthquake.

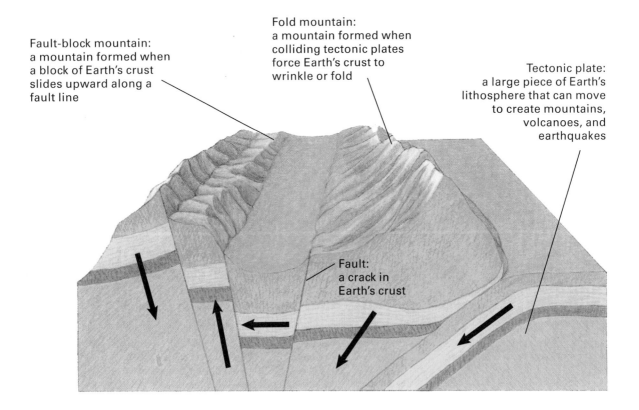

Fault-block mountain: a mountain formed when a block of Earth's crust slides upward along a fault line

Fold mountain: a mountain formed when colliding tectonic plates force Earth's crust to wrinkle or fold

Tectonic plate: a large piece of Earth's lithosphere that can move to create mountains, volcanoes, and earthquakes

Fault: a crack in Earth's crust

Mountain Building

Over millions of years, the slow movement of tectonic plates has created mountains. When plates collide, they push rock upward to form mountains.

The Movement of the Plates Creates Mountains The movement of tectonic plates forms mountains. When plates collide head-on, they can build mountains in two ways.

Sometimes the pressure of colliding plates forces Earth's crust to fold, or wrinkle, without breaking. The resulting folds form mountains. The Appalachian Mountains and the Urals are examples of **fold mountains**.

At other times, the collision of plates causes the crust to crack into huge blocks. The cracks between the blocks are called **faults**. As pressure builds up, the blocks of crust tilt and tip. Some tilted blocks slide upward along **fault lines** to form mountains. The Sierra Nevada range in California is made up of **fault-block mountains**. So is the West Sayan range in Russia.

17.4 Signs of Tectonic Movement in Russia

Russia covers a large part of both Europe and Asia. Its mountain ranges show how tectonic movement can shape a landscape.

The Ural Mountains in western Russia are considered the dividing line between Europe and Asia. Even though Europe and Asia form one **landmass,** this division makes good geographic sense. The Urals mark the place where two tectonic plates meet beneath Earth's crust. Over millions of years, pressure from these colliding plates pushed the crust upward to create the Urals.

Ural Mountains The Urals slice through Russia from north to south. This long chain of mountains separates the Northern European Plain to the west from the West Siberian Plain to the east.

The Urals are fold mountains. In some places, erosion has worn these mountains down into rolling hills. Other areas still have rugged peaks. Mount Manaraga in the northern Ural Mountains is sometimes called Bear's Paw because of its jagged ridge.

Caucasus Mountains The Caucasus Mountains are in southwestern Russia. They run west to east on a narrow strip of land between the Black Sea and the Caspian Sea.

Like the Urals, the Caucasus Mountains are fold mountains. Snow brushes their high peaks with dabs of white.

West Sayan Mountains The West Sayan Mountains are in southern Siberia, just west of Lake Baikal. Around Lake Baikal, major faults separate high mountains and plateaus from deep valleys and basins.

The West Sayan Mountains are fault-block mountains. In this range, erosion has worn away loose soil and rocks from the peaks. This process has left behind steep ridges and exposed layers of rock on the upper slopes of the mountains.

Snowy Caucasus Ridges
The Caucasus Mountains mark the southeastern edge of Europe. This mountain range was formed by moving plates around 25 million years ago.

Volcanic Activity

Inside Earth is a layer of liquid rock called *magma*. When magma reaches the surface, it creates a volcano. Volcanic eruptions can be quite violent. Lava flows and falling ash can change the surrounding landscape. Eruptions can also build up and reshape mountains.

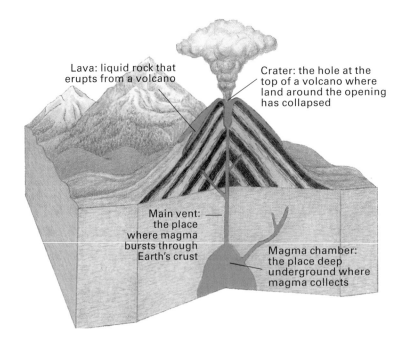

Lava: liquid rock that erupts from a volcano

Crater: the hole at the top of a volcano where land around the opening has collapsed

Main vent: the place where magma bursts through Earth's crust

Magma chamber: the place deep underground where magma collects

17.5 How Volcanic Activity Shapes Earth

Like earthquakes, volcanoes can reshape the landscape with awesome force. In 1883, an erupting volcano destroyed most of Krakatau, an island in Indonesia. People heard the explosion more than 2,000 miles away. Clouds of ash flew 20 miles or more into the air. Dust from the eruption created colorful sunsets around the world. Two thirds of Krakatau disappeared into a hole under the sea.

Volcanoes Form Below Earth's Surface As you read earlier, hot liquid rock called *magma* lies beneath Earth's crust. This molten rock is always moving. Sometimes magma pushes its way to the surface through cracks in the crust. Scientists call the place where magma reaches the surface a *volcano*. When magma erupts from a volcano, scientists call the liquid rock **lava**.

Volcanoes often occur along the edges of tectonic plates. The hot magma rises through cracks between two plates. Magma can also rise at "hot spots," or weak points, in Earth's crust. Either way, the result might be a single volcano. Or it could be a chain of volcanoes. The Hawaiian Islands are an example of a chain of volcanoes.

Volcanic Explosions Alter the Landscape Some volcanic eruptions are relatively quiet. Lava oozes out or sprays like a fountain. At other times, volcanoes can explode with enormous force. They literally blow their tops off. In 1980, a huge eruption shook Mount St. Helens in the state of Washington. Afterward, the mountain was at least 1,300 feet shorter than it was before the eruption.

Violent eruptions hurl tiny bits of rock, or ash, into the air in an enormous cloud. Eventually, the hot ash falls to Earth. If thick enough, the ash can bury people and buildings. Sometimes ash mixes with steam to create a fast-moving mudslide. Such a slide can bury everything in its path. After a violent eruption, the land around a volcano may collapse, creating a large **crater,** or hole.

17.6 Signs of Volcanic Activity in Russia

Two huge tectonic plates meet under the easternmost edge of Russia. As a result, this area is one of the world's most active earthquake zones. It is also the location of most of Russia's volcanoes. Most of them are on the Kamchatka Peninsula.

Some of the volcanoes in this region are dormant, or inactive. They have not erupted for a very long time. Others remain active. When they erupt, they can change the landscape through lava flows, mudslides, and deposits of ash. Some eruptions also change the shape of the volcanoes themselves.

The Kliuchevskoi Volcano The Kliuchevskoi Volcano rises out of the northern part of the Kamchatka Peninsula. It is the most active volcano in the country. It is also the highest. Snow covers its upper slopes all year.

In 1994, Kliuchevskoi erupted with great force. Rivers of lava flowed down the sides of the volcano. A cloud of gray ash rose almost 12 miles into the air. Still more ash combined with melting snow to trigger major mudflows.

The Maly Semyachik Volcano The Maly Semyachik Volcano rises out of the center of the Kamchatka Peninsula. It has a large crater at the top called Troitsky Crater. The crater is filled with warm, bright blue water.

The Krenitsyn Volcano The Krenitsyn Volcano is on Onekotan Island, which is part of the Kuril Island chain. During one of its eruptions, part of the volcano collapsed. The collapse left a large hole at the base of the volcano. Once the mountain cooled, the hole filled with water. Today the hole is called Ring Lake.

Russia's Karymsky Volcano
The Karymsky Volcano is one of 160 volcanoes located on Russia's Kamchatka Peninsula. Of these, 29 are still active. Karymsky has erupted 29 times since 1771.

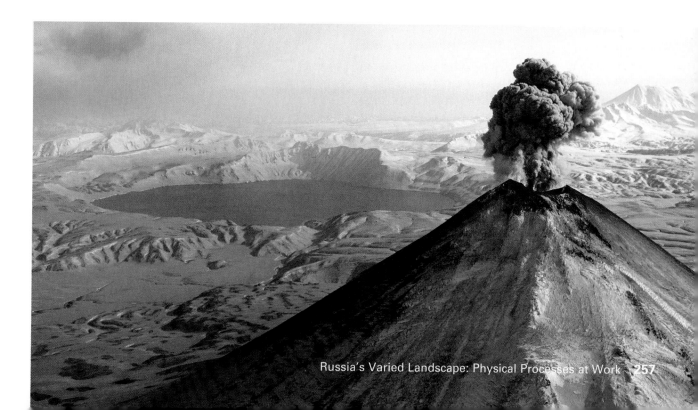

17.7 How Erosion Shapes the Landscape

Landslide! A hill starts to move, sending dirt, rocks, and trees tumbling down its slope. If you lived in the house at the bottom of the hill, you would probably see this event as a terrible disaster. As a geographer, you would also see it as an example of how erosion can reshape the surface of Earth.

Wind, Water, Ice, and Gravity Cause Erosion Erosion takes place everywhere on Earth. Wind, moving water and ice, and gravity all can wear down the land around us.

Wind erodes land by picking up tiny grains of dirt and carrying them to distant places. This process wears away the layer of soil that covers Earth's crust. Wind can also grind away rocks and hills by blasting them with gritty sand and dirt.

Moving water also shapes the land. Rivers can erode the land to create deep **V-shaped valleys**. The faster a river flows, the more soil it can wash away and carry downstream. Along coastlines, ocean waves can wear away the shoreline to create steep banks and cliffs. Waves can also erode soil at the base of cliffs, causing the land to collapse. When this happens, homes built on the cliffs may slide down into the sea.

Glaciers can reshape the land as well. These sheets of ice move slowly. They can carve out valleys or create new landforms by depositing rock and soil. Over time, they can push huge quantities of rocks and soil over great distances.

Sources of Erosion

Wind, water, ice, and gravity all cause erosion. Wind moves soil from one place to another. Moving water and ice create cliffs and valleys. Gravity pulls land downhill in landslides and mudslides. Erosion caused by wind and water created the Grand Canyon.

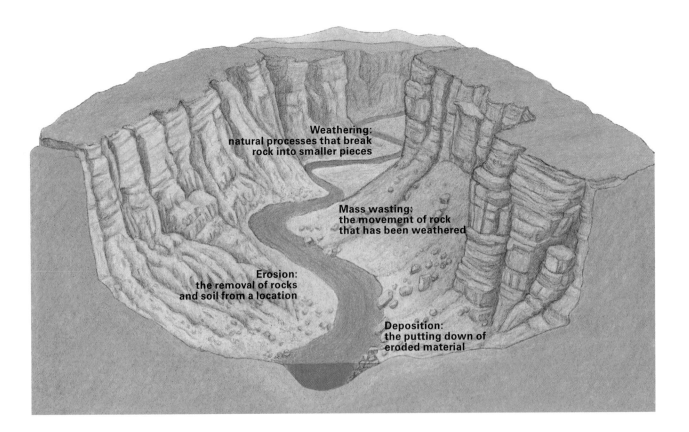

Weathering: natural processes that break rock into smaller pieces

Mass wasting: the movement of rock that has been weathered

Erosion: the removal of rocks and soil from a location

Deposition: the putting down of eroded material

Gravity is a constant force on the landscape. Anything that is not well rooted, or attached, to the ground will eventually move downhill. This movement can occur so slowly we may not be aware of it. Or it can occur quickly, as in a landslide or mudslide.

Floods Build Up Land On flat plains, water can build up as well as wear away land. After heavy rains, rivers overflow their banks and flood the surrounding plain. When the river returns to its banks, soil carried by the floodwater is left behind on the **floodplain**. This fresh layer of soil makes floodplains good places to farm. But the floods that create floodplains also make them dangerous places to live.

17.8 Signs of Erosion in Russia

Much of Russia is covered with plains. On the west side of the Ural Mountains is the Northern European Plain. On the east side are the West and Central Siberian plains. Over millions of years, wind, water, ice, and gravity have worn away any high ground on these plains. The flat or gently rolling land of the plains today is the result of this erosion.

The Volga River Many major rivers crisscross Russia's plains. One of them, the Volga, is Europe's longest river.

The Volga wanders south across the Northern European Plain. It carries along many tons of **sediment,** or soil and sand, as it travels. During floods, the river leaves some of the sediment on the surrounding land. This process is called *sedimentation*. Eventually, the Volga deposits its remaining sediment into the Caspian Sea. The sediment turns the sea a cloudy green.

The Volga flows through the agricultural and industrial heartland of Russia. Almost half of the Russian population live in the Volga River basin. No wonder Russians call the Volga "Matushka," or "Mother."

The Amur River The Amur River flows from the mountains of northeast China and through eastern Siberia to empty into the Sea of Okhotsk. This sea is a large arm of the Pacific Ocean on the eastern boundary of Russia. Frequent springtime floods have created flat and fertile floodplains along the river's banks. For 1,000 miles, it forms a natural boundary between Russia and China. Large boats travel most of the length of the Amur River from April to November.

The Lena River The Lena River flows northward through Siberia into the Arctic Ocean. Seen from above, this river looks like a black snake winding its way across the plains. In late spring, ice blocks the flow of water at the mouth of the Lena. Water backed up behind this ice dam floods the land.

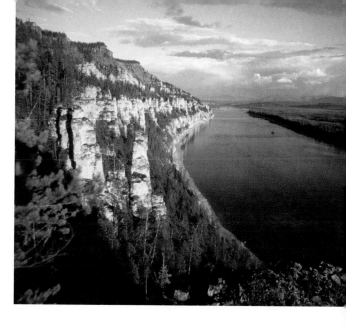

The Lena River Delta
This land along the Lena River shows signs of both flooding and erosion. Flooding built up the land that forms the Lena's banks. Erosion has worn it away.

U-shaped valley: a valley shaped like a U and formed by a moving glacier

Horn: the pointed peak of a mountaintop shaped by a glacier

Moraine: a mound of dirt and rocks left by a glacier

Glacier: a large, moving mass of ice on Earth's surface

A Landscape Carved by Glaciers

Continental glaciers are large ice sheets that form over land with extremely cold weather. Their weight forces them to spread outward. Alpine glaciers form at the top of some mountains. Gravity pulls them downhill. Glaciers act like bulldozers, grinding and pushing land as they move. Glaciers can move between two inches and two feet a day.

17.9 How Glaciation Shapes the Landscape

In the coldest places on Earth, large fields of winter snow turn into ice that stays frozen all year. These sheets of ice are called *glaciers.*

About 20,000 years ago, during the last ice age, glaciers covered one third of the world. Most of North America was covered by ice. Gradually, the glaciers retreated, changing the landscape as they moved. Today glaciers cover only one tenth of Earth's surface. But they can still shape the landscape in dramatic ways.

Two Kinds of Glaciers Geographers have identified two kinds of glaciers. **Continental glaciers** form in huge, thick sheets in low areas near the poles with extremely cold climates. Much of Antarctica, for instance, is buried under continental glaciers. The weight of the ice sheet eventually forces the edges of the glacier to push outward. Scientists call this movement *creeping.*

Alpine glaciers form in high mountain valleys where snowfall is plentiful and temperatures are low. Instead of creeping outward, these rivers of ice slide downhill as they are pulled by gravity.

Glaciers Reshape the Land as They Move Glaciers move very slowly, but they have enormous power. They can grind the hardest rock into fine soil. They can also push great loads of rock and dirt over long distances.

Continental glaciers erode land as they spread outward. They pick up rocks and soil as they creep. They can pile up dirt and rock into mounds called **moraines**. Sometimes they leave behind finger-shaped holes in the land. When the glaciers melt, these holes become lakes. The movement of continental glaciers during the last ice age formed the Great Lakes of North America.

Alpine glaciers reshape the land as they travel downhill. Sometimes they scrape away whole hillsides, turning rounded mountaintops into pointed peaks called **horns**. As they move down canyons, they carve narrow V-shaped river valleys into broad **U-shaped valleys**. California's famous Yosemite Valley was reshaped in this way by an alpine glacier.

17.10 Signs of Glaciation in Russia

Earth has seen several long cold periods when glaciers covered vast regions. During the last of these ice ages, continental glaciers covered parts of Russia. As the climate warmed, those glaciers melted. But alpine glaciers can still be found in high mountains. Both types of glaciers have left their mark on Russia's landscape.

The Kolka Glacier The Kolka Glacier is in the Caucasus Mountains. It is located on Mount Kazbek, one of the highest peaks in the Caucasus range. In 2002, an **avalanche** occurred on the mountain. Rocks and chunks of ice from the avalanche are still scattered on top of the Kolka Glacier.

The Amanauzsky Glacier The Amanauzsky Glacier is located in the western Caucasus Mountains. As this glacier slides downward, it creates a large valley between two jagged mountain ridges.

The Glaciated Yamal Peninsula The Yamal Peninsula juts into the Arctic Ocean in northwestern Siberia. Continental glaciers once scraped across this peninsula. Today summers are just warm enough to melt each winter's snowfall. The melted water then fills the holes left behind by glaciers.

Glaciers in the Caucasus
Glaciers have covered the Caucasus Mountains since the last ice age. But over the last century, many have been melting. Curiously, as glaciers shrink, their numbers increase. This happens when big glaciers break up into smaller ones.

17.11 Beginning to Think Globally

In this chapter, you learned how four physical processes shape our planet. They are tectonic movement, volcanic activity, erosion, and glaciation. You have also seen these processes at work in Russia.

Tectonic movement is the slowest of these processes. Over time, however, it has reshaped Earth's surface. Scientists believe that about 200 million years ago, all of Earth's land formed one enormous continent. Over time, this supercontinent broke apart into tectonic plates. The movement of these plates formed the continents that we know today.

Tectonic movement is still a powerful force. We see that every time an earthquake rattles windows or a volcano starts to smoke. Keep this in mind as you look at tectonic plates around the world.

17.12 Global Connections

The map shows the boundaries of the world's tectonic plates. It also shows active volcanic and earthquake zones. Notice how many volcanoes are located around the rim, or edge, of the Pacific Ocean. Scientists call this zone of volcanic activity the Ring of Fire.

Why is the Ring of Fire located around the Pacific Rim? A vast tectonic plate lies under the Pacific Ocean. This Pacific Plate stretches from Asia to North America. When it moves against plates around the Pacific Rim, one plate is forced under the other. As the plate sinks, friction and Earth's heat cause part of it to melt. This melted part rises to the surface to form a volcano.

Why isn't there a Ring of Fire around the edge of the Atlantic Ocean? Look closely at edges of the Atlantic Ocean in North America and Europe. Notice that there are no plate boundaries there. The North American Plate and the Eurasian Plate meet in the middle of the Atlantic Ocean. As a result, there are no colliding plates around the edge of the Atlantic—and no Ring of Fire.

How has tectonic movement shaped human life on Earth? Imagine our world without tectonic movement. All humankind might be living together on one flat super-continent. Tectonic movement not only broke up the supercontinent, but it also built most of Earth's mountains. In the past, mountains kept people isolated from each other. As a result, many human cultures have developed over time in different landscapes.

Volcanoes and Earthquakes Around the World

Largest Earthquakes, 1900–2008

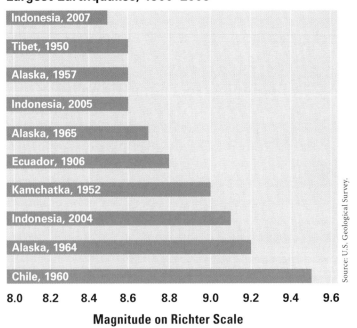

Magnitude on Richter Scale

Source: U.S. Geological Survey.

North American Plate

Eurasian Plate

African Plate

Nazca Plate

South American Plate

Antarctic Plate

Lava flow in Hawaii Volcanoes National Park

New Nation-States from the Old Soviet Empire: Will They Succeed?

18.1 Introduction

"Iron Felix" Dzerzhinsky was a brutal man. Under his direction, hundreds of thousands of people were killed in the Russian Revolution of 1917. The revolution destroyed the old **empire** of Russia. In its place rose a new empire called the Soviet Union.

The new government chose Iron Felix to set up a secret police force. Its job was to destroy all opposition. The secret police arrested millions of people who were suspected of being disloyal. A statue of Dzerzhinsky in a Moscow square reminded people that the police were always watching.

By 1991, people had had enough. An angry crowd attacked the statue of Iron Felix. They cheered wildly as the symbol of fear came down. By year's end, the government had fallen as well. The Soviet Union was no more.

Fifteen new **nation-states** were formed out of the ruins of the Soviet empire. The term *nation-state* combines two ideas. The first, **nation,** refers to a group of people who share a common history and culture. Another term for people with such a shared identity is **ethnic group**. The second, **state,** refers to a political unit that controls a fixed territory. A nation-state is a country whose people mostly share a common identity.

In this chapter, you will read about the Soviet Union and five of the new nation-states that replaced it. And you will find out what makes a new nation-state likely to succeed or fail.

Essential Question

What factors contribute to the success or failure of new nation-states?

This illustration names 5 of the 15 new nation-states that came out of the old Soviet Union. Their success will depend on both economic and political factors. Keep this illustration in mind as you try to answer the Essential Question.

Graphic Organizer

LITHUANIA

BELARUS

RUSSIA

KAZAKHSTAN

AZERBAIJAN

◀ Statue of "Iron Felix" Dzerzhinsky in Moscow (top), Russian protesters toppling the statue in 1991 (bottom)

Voting in a New Nation-State

Every year an organization called Freedom House rates countries on how free they are. Freedom House looks at how well a country protects two kinds of rights. The first is political rights, such as the right to vote or run for office. The second is civil rights, including the right to speak and worship freely. Freedom House rates a country as free, partly free, or not free.

18.2 The Geographic Setting

The Soviet Union was a vast country. It covered more than half of Europe and nearly two fifths of Asia. In area it was almost two and a half times the size of the United States. It had the third largest population in the world. Only China and India had more people.

From Superpower to Failed State From 1945 to 1990, the Soviet Union was one of the world's two great **superpowers**. (The United States was the other.) Its armed forces were the largest in the world. For much of this time, it led the world in exploring space.

In 1991, this superpower collapsed. That year, the Soviet Union became the world's largest **failed state**. The question is why. One way to answer this question is to compare the Soviet Union with a successful nation-state.

Features of Successful Nation-States Many factors affect the success of a nation-state. But five are very important. They are security, political freedom, economic growth, quality of life, and national unity.

The most important job of a nation-state is to keep its people safe. A successful state can protect its people from foreign enemies. Its police work to keep people safe from crime. As you read, in the Soviet Union, the secret police made people feel less, not more, secure.

A successful nation-state protects the rights and freedoms of its citizens. In a free country, the people choose their leaders. Elections are honest and fair. People vote freely without fear of arrest. Elected leaders usually have strong public support. By contrast, the Soviet Union was ruled by **dictators**. These are leaders who govern by force without the people's consent.

A successful nation-state uses its resources and location to promote economic growth. Its **gross domestic product** (GDP) rises over time. GDP is the total value of goods and services produced in a country. As GDP rises, incomes rise. As incomes rise, poverty declines. In the Soviet Union, GDP rose slowly or not at all.

A successful nation-state also tries to improve its people's quality of life. It works to provide its people with safe food, clean water, and good medical care. As people live healthier lives, **life expectancy** increases. Also, fewer babies die in their first year. In the Soviet Union, however, quality of life was not improving for many people.

Successful nation-states inspire patriotism, or love of country. People who love their country work to make it succeed. Successful nation-states also inspire **nationalism,** or feelings of pride and loyalty toward one's nation. In countries like the Soviet Union that have many ethnic groups, nationalism can create a sense of unity.

However, ethnic group nationalism can sometimes work against national unity. By 1991, ethnic loyalty in the Soviet Union had more support than loyalty to country. At this point, many ethnic groups had decided that they would be better off as independent nation-states than as part of a failing Soviet Union.

▶ Geoterms

ethnic group a group of people in a country who share a unique culture and identity

nation a large group of people who share a common history and culture. Not all nations have their own government or control a territory. But in common use, the word *nation* often means a country or nation-state.

nationalism feelings of loyalty and pride toward one's nation or ethnic group. Nationalism sometimes includes the belief that one's nation or group is better than all others.

nation-state an independent state, or country, whose people mostly share a common identity

state a political unit that controls a particular territory

A Diverse Region

More than 100 ethnic groups lived in the Soviet Union at the time of its collapse. This map shows the major ethnic groups that were in various areas. Conflicts among ethnic groups helped bring about the collapse of this state.

Major Ethnic Groups in the Soviet Union

Kazakh Herders

For centuries, the Kazakhs were mainly nomads, people who move from place to place. They raised sheep, goats, cattle, and horses for meat, wool, and hides. They traveled hundreds of miles each year in search of pasture for their herds. A few Kazakhs still follow this ancient way of life.

18.3 Kazakhstan: A Central Asian Giant

Kazakhstan is a Central Asian giant surrounded by other giants. To the southeast lies China. To the north lies Russia. To the west lies the Caspian Sea.

An Arid Land with Many Resources Much of Kazakhstan is too **arid** for agriculture. But many crops are grown in the northern region and some irrigated areas in the south. Its people also raise cattle, goats, poultry, pigs, and sheep.

Kazakhstan is rich in minerals. It has large deposits of coal, lead, copper, iron, and zinc. Some of the world's largest oil reserves lie under the Caspian Sea. Oil production is a major part of the country's economy.

In the future, oil will become even more important. This is due to Kazakhstan's location between China and the Caspian Sea. Once pipelines are built across the country, oil will flow from the Caspian Sea to oil-thirsty cities of China.

Ethnic Conflicts Create a Split The Kazakhs are the main ethnic group in Kazakhstan. They make up about half of the nation's population. Russians make up about a third of the population. Most Kazakhs are Muslim. Most Russians are Christian. Religious and cultural differences divide the groups.

Most Russians live in northern Kazakhstan. Under Soviet rule, heavy industry developed in the north. Many Russians still work in these industries. Most Kazakhs live in the south. This settlement pattern has created a serious north-south split in the country.

Meanwhile, Kazakhstan faces serious environmental problems. Under Soviet rule, poor irrigation methods damaged farmland. **Pesticides** seeped into the water supply. Factories released **toxic waste**. The Soviets also carried out secret nuclear weapons testing. As a result, many people still suffer serious health problems.

Looking ahead, Kazakhstan's survival will depend on several factors. One is using its resources wisely to raise incomes. Another is solving its environmental problems and improving the quality of life. A third is calming the ethnic unrest, or conflict among ethnic groups, that divides the country. If it can succeed at all three, its future may be bright.

18.4 Azerbaijan: Where Europe Meets Asia

Together, the new nation-states of Armenia, Georgia, and Azerbaijan are known as the Caucasus. That's because the steep Caucasus Mountains tower over them. This region is one of the world's great crossroads, where Europe meets Asia. Azerbaijan's location and resources hold the key to its future.

A Country Rich in Oil Azerbaijan has huge deposits of oil. Oil is its greatest source of wealth and its number one export. The capital city of Baku, on the shore of the Caspian Sea, is the center of its oil industry.

Azerbaijan lies between Iran and Russia. During Soviet rule, oil pipelines were built to send all of Azerbaijan's oil to Russia. When the Soviet Union collapsed, so did its hold on Azerbaijan. The new country was then free to sell its oil anywhere.

Since 1991, Azerbaijan has signed agreements with many foreign oil companies. Pipelines are being built to move its oil to customers outside of Russia. Working with foreign oil companies is not easy. But if Azerbaijan succeeds in opening new markets for its oil, its future looks bright.

Ethnic Warfare Clouds the Future One obstacle to progress is conflict between ethnic groups in Azerbaijan and neighboring Armenia. The Azeris are the main ethnic group in Azerbaijan. They make up over 90 percent of the population. Most Azeris are Muslim. About 2 percent of the population in Azerbaijan is Armenian. Most Armenians are Christians. The Azeris and the Armenians have a long history of conflict.

Nagorno-Karabakh is a region within Azerbaijan. Most of the people there are Armenians. They want to be independent from Azerbaijan. In 1992, war broke out over the issue. Thousands of people were killed. Almost a million people fled from the fighting. A cease-fire was called in 1994, but the problem was not solved. The violence continues to this day.

A Wealth of Oil

Oil is Azerbaijan's most important resource. It has enough oil to fill 7 billion barrels. One barrel of oil produces about 19 gallons of gasoline.

BELARUS

RUSSIA

18.5 Belarus: Between Europe and Russia

The word Belarus means "white Russia." No one knows for sure why the color is part of the country's name. It might refer to the snow that often covers the land. It might describe the white bark of the birch trees in its forests. The "rus" part of Belarus reflects its location next to Russia on the east. On the west, it borders Europe.

A Landlocked Country of Many Lakes This nation of rolling plains and dense forests is **landlocked**. In other words, it is surrounded entirely by land. Long ago, glaciers scraped across its plains. The ice sheets created the 11,000 lakes that dot the Belarus landscape.

In the past, the country's economy was based on farming and logging. Both are still important today. But about a fifth of its farmland and forestland can no longer be used. This land was poisoned when the nearby Chernobyl nuclear power plant exploded in 1986. Much of this large area will never be safe for farming or logging again.

Belarus Looks East to Russia Almost 8 out of 10 people in Belarus are Belarusians. Russians make up about 11 percent of the population. During Soviet rule, Russian workers and government officials did much to develop Belarus. They cleared and drained its land to create farms run by the government. They brought manufacturing and industry to its cities. They shaped its political system and influenced its culture.

Today, Belarus still has close ties to Russia. Most of its foreign trade is with Russia. Belarus depends on gas and oil from Russia to run its industries. The two countries have signed agreements to work together closely in the future.

However, relations between Belarus and Russia are not always smooth. The two countries disagree about labor and trade issues. They have different ideas about how much power the government should have over its citizens and industries. Although the economy of Belarus is growing, there are many challenges ahead.

A Belarus Tractor Factory

Making farm machines is a large industry in Belarus. These tractors were built in Minsk, the capital of Belarus.

18.6 Lithuania: One of Three Baltic States

Three former parts of the Soviet Union—Lithuania, Latvia, and Estonia—are known as the Baltic States. They line the eastern shore of the Baltic Sea. Lithuania can look either east or west for political ties. More and more, it looks west.

An Economy Based on Soil and the Sea The fertile soil of Lithuania produces good crops. Farmers grow potatoes, sugar beets, and flax for cloth. Fields of grain cross the central plains. There are dairies everywhere. Cattle, sheep, pigs, and poultry provide meat, eggs, and milk. The Baltic Sea provides food, too, with its fishing grounds and fish farms.

Lithuania has limited mineral resources. Limestone, gravel, sand, and clay are mined to make cement, glass, and ceramics. But fossil fuels and metals are in short supply.

Lithuania Looks West to Europe Nationalism is a strong force in Lithuania. Lithuanians united as a nation around 1200. Their nation was the first part of the Soviet Union to declare its independence in 1990.

Since then, Lithuanians have reformed their political system. Today the nation has a democratic government. Its leaders are chosen in free and fair elections.

In 2004, Lithuania became a member of the **European Union,** or EU. Chapter 14 explores the EU in detail. Lithuania receives money from the EU to develop its economy.

Lithuania has also joined the North Atlantic Treaty Organization, or NATO. Members of NATO promise to defend each other if attacked by another country. By joining NATO and the EU, Lithuanians hope to create a future of peace and prosperity.

18.7 Russia: The Largest Nation on Earth

Imagine watching from space as your country breaks apart and then ceases to exist. That's what Soviet astronaut Sergei Krikalev did in 1991. He flew up to the Mir space station as a citizen of the Soviet Union. While he circled the Earth 16 times a day, the Soviet Union collapsed. When he finally set foot on land, he was still a citizen of the largest nation on Earth. But that nation was now Russia.

Rich Resources in a Vast Land Although Russia is not as large as the Soviet Union was, it's still huge. It has vast forests and large deposits of coal and minerals. Its most important resources are oil and natural gas. Because of its cold **climate,** however, less than 8 percent of its land is suitable for farming.

During Soviet rule, the government owned and ran this vast country's farms, factories, and businesses. With the end of Soviet rule, the government sold its factories and businesses. But these sales did not help the Russian people. Powerful political leaders grabbed the best businesses for themselves.

Today, most Russian businesses are privately run. But they are not always run well. Many factories sold by the government were old and in need of repair. But often the new owners had no money to make the needed repairs. Other businesses made goods of such poor quality that no one wanted to buy them. As a result, many businesses failed.

Still, with all its challenges, Russia's economy has been growing every year. Oil exports are a big reason for this growth.

St. Basil's Cathedral

Ivan the Terrible, the first czar of all Russia, built St. Basil's Cathedral. Legend says that when the church was finished, Ivan ordered its architect to be blinded. This, the czar hoped, would prevent him from ever creating anything so beautiful again. However, the architect did go on to design another cathedral.

The Challenges Facing Russians Today Life is not easy in Russia. The crime rate is high. Housing is very costly. Negative population growth is a major challenge. Alcohol abuse and pollution are also big concerns.

Ethnic nationalism has caused problems as well. Russia's 142 million people come from dozens of ethnic groups. Not all of these groups are pleased to still be a part of Russia. In addition, most Russians belong to the Russian Orthodox Church. However, Russia also has Islam, Judaism, Buddhism, and other Christian groups. The activities of some religious groups are limited by law. For example, some are prevented from printing religious literature or operating religious schools.

In an area known as Chechnya, opposition to Russian rule has led to rebellion. During the Soviet Union's collapse in 1991, a group of Chechen leaders declared their independence from Russia. In 1994, Russian tanks rolled into Chechnya to crush the movement. More than 100,000 Chechens died in the war. A cease-fire brought an official peace to Chechnya in 1996, but the conflict continues. Battles, bombings, and terrorist attacks have killed thousands on both sides.

18.8 Beginning to Think Globally

In this chapter, you have learned about five factors that affect whether a new nation-state will succeed or fail. These factors are security, political freedom, economic growth, quality of life, and national unity. You have seen the power of nationalism to unite a country. You have also seen how conflict among ethnic groups can tear a country apart.

Each nation-state that arose from the former Soviet Union has its own story. Only time will tell whether they will succeed. The same could have been said about the United States in its first years. It won its war of independence only with outside help. Its people felt more loyal to their states than to any country. They distrusted the first government under the Articles of Confederation, which could not hold the new nation together. And the country's economy was weak.

The world is always changing. Empires rise and collapse. New nations are born and die. Think about this as you look at the map showing the rise of new nations in the next section. Which nations will succeed? And which are likely to fail?

Air Pollution in Russia

During Soviet rule, new factories were built across Russia. But little attention was paid to pollution. In 84 of Russia's largest cities, air pollution is still 10 times the level that is considered safe.

18.9 Global Connections

The map shows new nations that have arisen since 1945. The table below gives data about three nations that have gained their independence since 2002. Think about what the information in the table might reveal about each nation's chance of success.

What were these new nations before they gained their independence? Most of the new nations formed since 1945 were once colonies ruled by other nations. Other new nations were part of dying empires or failed states. Serbia and Montenegro, for example, were once part of the failed state of Yugoslavia. Still other new nations were once parts of nations that still exist. For example, East Timor was a part of Indonesia from 1976 until 2002, when it won its independence.

How did these new nations gain their independence? Most new nations gain their independence through violent struggle. Serbia, Montenegro, and East Timor all had to fight to become independent nations. Some new nations, however, have a peaceful start. When the Soviet Union collapsed in 1991, its 15 republics peacefully gained their independence.

Which of these new nations are most likely to succeed? The answer, as you have learned, depends on many factors. For example, Namibia, a country that gained its independence in 1990, is rich in mineral resources. However, its black majority is divided among many ethnic groups. Serbia, Montenegro, and East Timor are not so divided as Nigeria, but all three are struggling to rebuild economies devastated by years of war.

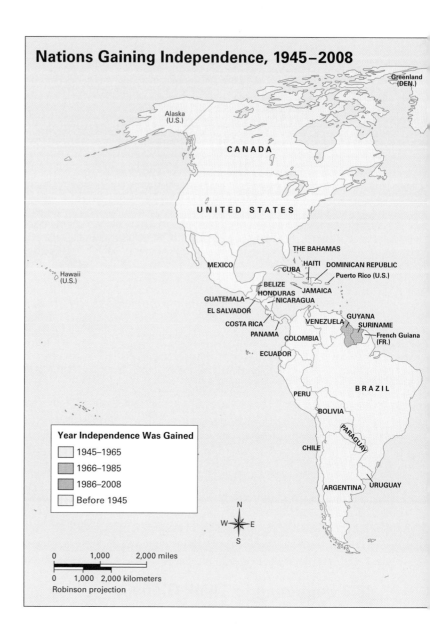

Nations Gaining Independence, 1945–2008

Year Independence Was Gained
- 1945–1965
- 1966–1985
- 1986–2008
- Before 1945

0   1,000   2,000 miles
0   1,000 2,000 kilometers
Robinson projection

Information About Three New Nations

Nation	Life Expectancy (years)	GDP per Capita	Population Below Poverty Line
Serbia	75	$8,200	7%
Montenegro	(no information available)	$10,600	7%
East Timor	67	$2,500	4%

Sources: CIA World Factbook. Freedom House.

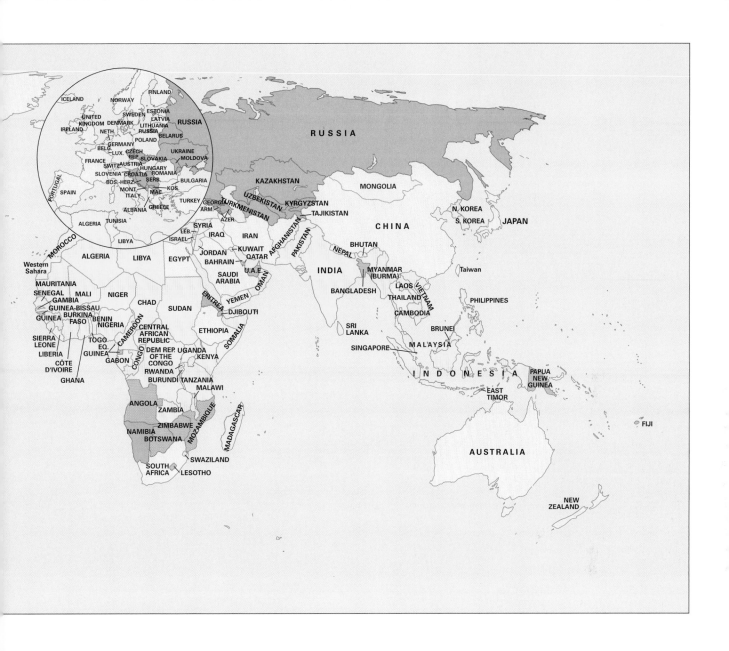

Infant Mortality (deaths per 1,000 births)	Ethnic Diversity	Freedom Index Ranking*	Year of Independence
(no information available)	Serb 83%, Hungarian 4%, Bosniak 2%, Roma 1%, Montenegrin 1%, other 8%	political rights, 3 civil liberties, 2	2006
(no information available)	Montenegrin 43%, Serbian 32%, Bosniak 8%, Albanian 5%, other 12%	political rights, 3 civil liberties, 3	2006
42	Austronesian, Papuan, small Chinese minority	political rights, 3 civil liberties, 4	2002

*On this scale, 1 represents the highest degree of freedom, and 7 the lowest.

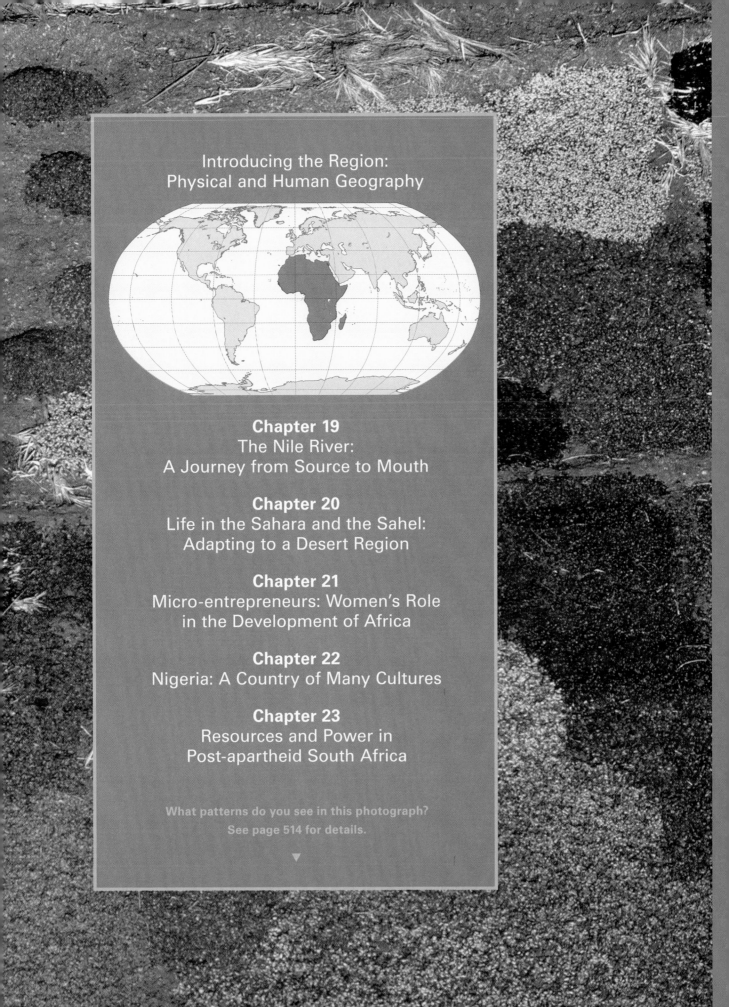

Introducing the Region:
Physical and Human Geography

What patterns do you see in this photograph?
See page 514 for details.

▼

Africa is the second largest continent. The Atlantic Ocean lies to the west. The Indian Ocean lies to the east. The Mediterranean Sea and Red Sea lie to the north. A small piece of land in the northeast corner connects Africa to Asia. There are 47 countries on the continent of Africa. Six island **nations** are also part of the **region**. The largest of these islands is Madagascar.

Africa is made up of four subregions. The subregions of North Africa, East Africa, and West Africa occupy the northern half of the continent. The southern half is one large subregion called Central and Southern Africa.

Physical Features of Africa

Physical Features

Africa is often called the "plateau continent." The land is shaped like an upside-down pie plate. Much of the center of Africa is a high, dry **plateau**. At the edges of the continent, this plateau sometimes slopes to a coastal plain. In other places, it drops sharply into the sea.

There are huge, low-lying areas called **basins** in several places on this plateau. Four mighty rivers flow from these basins to the sea. Sometimes the land falls steeply as the rivers flow downstream. As a result, ships are not able to sail very far up these rivers into Africa's interior.

North Africa

The Sahara is the main **physical feature** in North Africa. It is the world's largest **desert**. The Sahara has sand dunes, bare rock, gravel plains, and mountains. The Nile, Africa's longest river, runs through this desert and empties into the Mediterranean Sea. The Atlas Mountains stretch across the northwestern part of this region.

West Africa

South of the Sahara lies the Sahel region. The plains of the Sahel are mostly dry grassland. The Niger River runs through the western Sahel. This is the third longest river in Africa. Also in the Sahel is a large lake called Lake Chad. This lake shrinks and grows depending on the season. In general, it has been getting smaller for many years.

Mount Kilimanjaro towers over the grasslands in East Africa.

East Africa

Three large lakes lie in or near the Great Rift Valley. Lake Tanganyika is the longest **freshwater** lake in the world. Lake Victoria is the world's second largest freshwater lake, and Lake Malawi is the ninth largest.

To the east of Lake Victoria, Mount Kilimanjaro rises from the plains. At 19,340 feet, this peak is the highest point in Africa.

The Ethiopian Highlands lie to the north of the lake. This rugged area covers two thirds of the country of Ethiopia.

Central and Southern Africa

The Congo basin is a major physical feature of Central and Southern Africa. This large, low-lying area sits at the center of the continent. The Congo River loops through this basin and empties into the Atlantic Ocean. Farther south lies the Zambezi River. This river has many waterfalls. The largest of these is the beautiful Victoria Falls. Two deserts, the Namib and Kalahari, make up much of the southern part of this region.

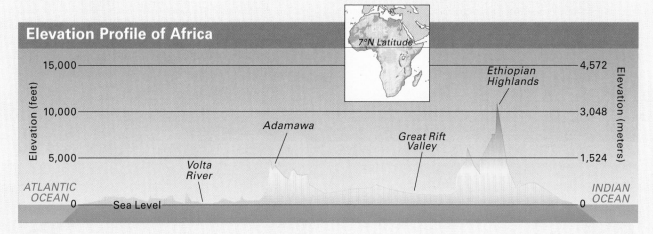

Elevation Profile of Africa

7°N Latitude

Elevation (feet): 15,000 — 10,000 — 5,000 — 0 Sea Level

Elevation (meters): 4,572 — 3,048 — 1,524 — 0

ATLANTIC OCEAN

INDIAN OCEAN

Volta River

Adamawa

Great Rift Valley

Ethiopian Highlands

Climate

The equator divides Africa nearly in half. As a result, the **climate** in most of Africa is warm all year. However, some regions are very wet and others very dry.

As you read in Chapter 2, places near the equator are warm because the sun is almost directly overhead all year. As the air over the equator warms, it expands and rises. Once it rises, the air begins to cool. If the air is wet, it drops moisture in the form of rain as it cools. In Africa, this rain falls in a wide band north and south of the equator.

After rising, this air begins to move toward the North or South poles. But by this time, it is quite dry. As a result, little or no rain falls on parts of Africa farther away from the equator. This lack of rainfall has created vast deserts in northern and southern Africa.

North Africa

Most of North Africa is very dry. Some places in the Sahara can go for six or seven years without rain. Areas of North Africa near the Mediterranean Sea enjoy a **Mediterranean** climate. Here it is warm all year with dry summers and short, rainy winters.

West Africa

The climate of West Africa varies widely from north to south. The northern part is **arid** and **semiarid**. Moving south, the climate changes to **tropical wet and dry**. This area is hot all year with rainy and dry seasons. Closer to the equator, coastal areas have a **tropical wet** climate. This means it is hot and rainy all year. Some coastal areas get an average of more than 120 inches of rain a year.

East Africa

The parts of East Africa that lie in or close to the Sahara have an arid or semiarid climate. But the Ethiopian Highlands and Mount Kilimanjaro have a **highlands** climate. In these areas, the higher land is cooler and wetter. The lower land is warmer and drier. The southern part of East Africa has a tropical wet and dry climate.

Boats sail on the Nile River near the city of Aswan, Egypt. Would you ever need an umbrella in Aswan?

Central and Southern Africa

In this large subregion, the land nearest the equator has a tropical wet climate. Farther south, the climate shifts to tropical wet and dry, and finally to arid or semiarid.

The climate shifts again in the southern-most part of this subregion. Some coastal areas along the Indian Ocean have a **marine west coast** climate. People there enjoy warm summers, cool winters, and rainfall year-round. Other coastal areas have a **humid subtropical** climate. Summers are hot with heavy rains. Winters are mild with some rain.

The large island of Madagascar has three **climate zones**. The eastern half has a tropical wet climate. The northwestern and central areas have a tropical wet and dry climate. The southwestern part has a semiarid climate.

Vegetation

About two fifths of Africa's land is **tropical grassland**. Another name for this vegetation zone is **savanna**. In addition to short and tall grasses, shrubs and trees are scattered over this rolling grassland. Both the grasses and trees are adapted to a tropical wet and dry climate. Many trees drop their leaves in the long dry season. Some have trunks that can store water. The grasses have long roots that reach for water deep in the earth.

Heavy rain makes travel difficult in the tropical rainforests of the Congo basin.

North Africa

Desert and **desert scrub** cover most of North Africa. Few plants grow in the desert. Small trees, bushes, and other plants adapted to a dry climate make up desert scrub.

The land along the Mediterranean Sea is covered with **chaparral** plants. The small trees and bushes of this area are adapted to long, dry summers. A narrow strip of **broadleaf evergreen forest** runs along the Nile River through Egypt. Tropical grasslands cover the southern edge of the Sahara.

West Africa

Tropical grassland blankets much of West Africa. But over the years, some of this grassland has become desert. This has happened partly because of long dry periods with very little rain.

The southern part of West Africa is a broadleaf evergreen forest. This is also called **rainforest**. Many trees grow to 100 feet or taller. The shady floor of this forest zone gets little direct sunlight. As a result, few bushes or grasses grow there.

East Africa

Tropical grassland also covers most of East Africa. Some coastal lands are broadleaf evergreen forests. Much of Ethiopia lies in a **highlands** vegetation zone. There, the kinds of plants change with the altitude. Bamboo, cedar trees, and tree ferns grow in lower areas. On the higher slopes are meadows covered in grasses and flowers. Mosses and lichen grow near the mountaintops.

Central and Southern Africa

Broadleaf evergreen forest covers the Congo basin, which lies on the equator. Hundreds of kinds of trees live in this forest. South of this basin, most of the land is tropical grassland.

The Namib and most of the Kalahari have desert and desert scrub vegetation. The eastern Kalahari has tropical grassland. Mountain ranges in Southern Africa have highlands vegetation. The southern tip of this region is blanketed in chaparral.

Zebras thrive on the tropical grasslands in East Africa.

Africa is home to 53 countries. The largest one is Sudan. It covers almost 1 million square miles. The smallest African country is Seychelles. This is a group of about 115 small islands scattered over the Indian Ocean, north of Madagascar. Together these islands have a land area of only about 176 square miles.

Africa is a region of many cultural and language groups. By some estimates, Africans speak at least 2,000 languages. Some of these, such as Arabic and Swahili, are widely used. Others are spoken only by small groups. Despite their differences, all Africans share a long history.

Political Boundaries of Africa

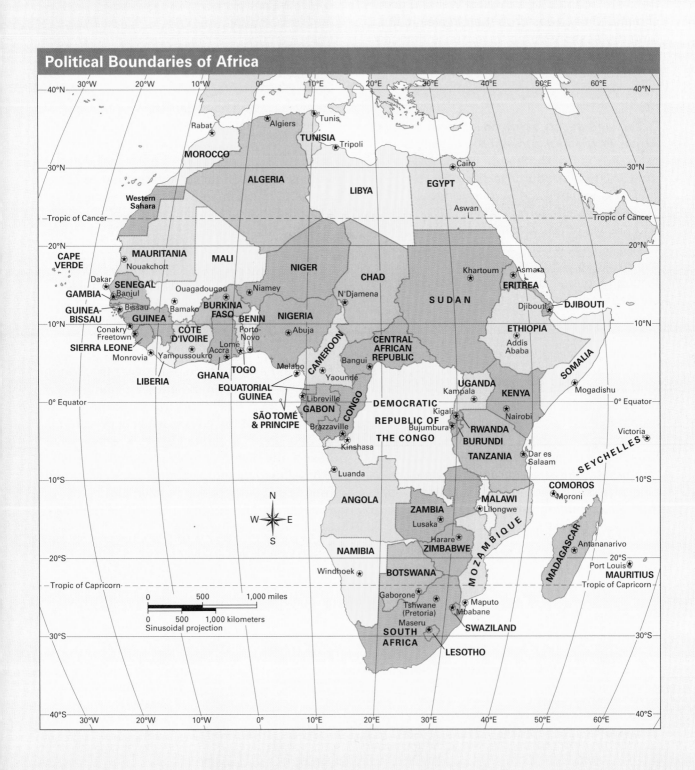

History

Scientists have found the bones of a human-like species that lived in eastern Africa millions of years ago. For this reason, people call Africa the birthplace of the human race.

Early Times

Early African people were hunters and gatherers. Learning to farm changed the way people lived. By 5000 B.C.E., Africans were raising animals and growing crops.

The Nile River valley was home to one of the world's earliest civilizations. The Egyptian civilization lasted for more than 3,000 years. The ancient Egyptians invented a kind of paper and a form of picture writing. They learned how to preserve the bodies of the dead as mummies. They also built the Egyptian pyramids, which still stand today.

Kingdoms and Colonies

Beginning around 300 C.E., three great kingdoms arose in West Africa. The first one, Ghana, ruled until the mid–11th century. After the fall of Ghana, the kingdom of Mali rose to power. The last of the three, the Songhai **empire**, rose and fell between 1400 and 1600.

The wealth of these kingdoms came from their control of trade across the Sahara. Arab traders from North Africa brought salt and copper from mines in the Sahara to West African markets. They traded these goods for gold, ivory, and slaves. The traders carried their faith with them. They spread the religion of Islam across much of Africa.

Europeans began to explore Africa in the 1400s. The Portuguese set up trading posts along the west coast of Africa. At first they were interested in gold. But they soon began to ship Africans to Europe as slaves.

The slave trade expanded after Europeans set up colonies in the Americas. The European colonists needed workers to help them raise crops like sugar and tobacco. To meet that need, millions of Africans were captured and shipped across the Atlantic Ocean as slaves. The Atlantic slave trade did not end until around 1850.

In the 1700s and 1800s, Europeans began setting up colonies in Africa. The Belgians took control of the Congo basin. France gained control of Algeria and Tunisia. Great Britain took over Egypt. By 1914, European countries had divided up most of Africa.

The Modern Era

In 1957, Ghana became the first black African colony to gain its independence. Over the next 10 years, most of Africa threw off colonial rule.

Few of the new countries were prepared for self-rule. Since gaining their independence, they have struggled to create stable governments. Tensions between **ethnic groups** have led to unrest in many countries.

In 2002, most African countries came together to form the African Union. The African Union helps its members work together for the benefit of all Africans. It promotes peace and human rights. It also works to improve public health.

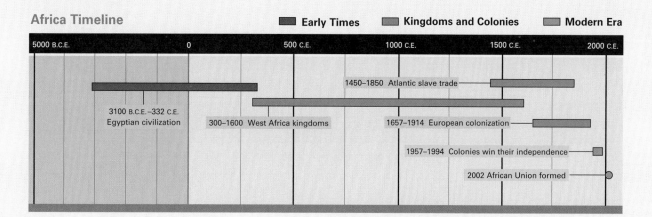

Africa Timeline ■ Early Times ■ Kingdoms and Colonies ■ Modern Era

5000 B.C.E. — 0 — 500 C.E. — 1000 C.E. — 1500 C.E. — 2000 C.E.

3100 B.C.E.–332 C.E. Egyptian civilization

300–1600 West Africa kingdoms

1450–1850 Atlantic slave trade

1657–1914 European colonization

1957–1994 Colonies win their independence

2002 African Union formed

Population

As of 2008, about 967 million people lived in Africa. This is one seventh of the world's people. Only Asia has more people. Africa has the fastest growing population in the world.

About three fifths of Africans live in **rural** areas. Most of them live in small villages, much as their ancestors did. In recent years, however, a growing number of Africans have been moving to cities.

People in Africa follow many different religions. About 4 out of 10 Africans are Muslims. Most Muslims live in North and West Africa. Christians just slightly outnumber Muslims. The majority of Christians live in West, East, and Central and Southern Africa.

More than 100 million people practice indigenous religions. There are hundreds of these local faiths. But they have many features in common. Like most other religions, they explain how the universe was created. They also teach what is right and wrong.

Africa: Major Religions

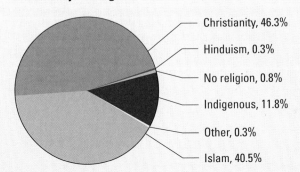

- Christianity, 46.3%
- Hinduism, 0.3%
- No religion, 0.8%
- Indigenous, 11.8%
- Other, 0.3%
- Islam, 40.5%

Africa: Urban and Rural Population, 2007

Urban, 38.6%

Rural, 61.4%

= 10% of the total population

Africa: Population Growth, 1950–2050

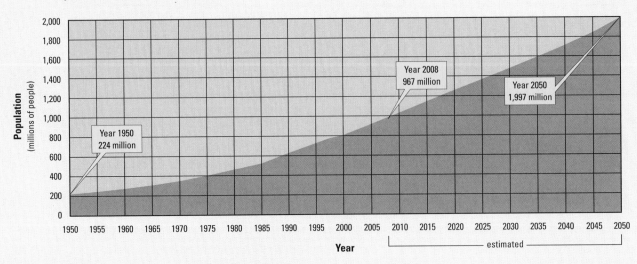

Year 1950
224 million

Year 2008
967 million

Year 2050
1,997 million

Population (millions of people)

Year — estimated

Sources: United Nations Department of Economic and Social Affairs, Population Division. Encyclopaedia Britannica.

Economic Activity

Mining is an important **economic activity** in Africa. Mining is the process of digging minerals and coal out of the ground. Mining most likely began in Africa thousands of years ago. Today half of the value of Africa's exports is from mining.

There are many methods of mining. Each method depends on where a mineral deposit is located. When the deposit is near the surface, mining can be done in large, open pits. When the deposit is deep underground, miners must dig tunnels to reach it. Both open pit and underground mines are used in Africa to get at its mineral wealth.

Resources

Oil is a key resource in parts of North and West Africa. Most of the oil imported into Europe comes from this region.

Central and Southern Africa are centers for diamond mines. In fact, Africa produces almost three fourths of the world's diamonds.

Gold is another important resource. More gold is mined in Central and Southern Africa than in any other region of the world.

Land Use

The grasslands of North and East Africa are used for **nomadic herding**. Herders move from place to place to find food and water for their animals.

A herder in Senegal gives his goats water from a well. Senegal lies in the arid western Sahel.

More than half of Africa's farmland is used for **subsistence farming**. This means that the farmers are raising just enough food to feed their families.

In recent years, many Africans have turned to **commercial farming**. Egyptian farmers raise cotton along the Nile River and in the Nile Delta. Large groves of date palms grow around **oases** in the Sahara. The rainforests of West Africa produce cocoa beans. These are used to make chocolate.

Most trade and manufacturing takes place in South Africa. This country produces about two fifths of Africa's manufactured goods, including cars, clothing, steel, and electronics. Many other nations across Africa are working to promote the growth of industry.

As African countries continue to develop, the importance of trade and manufacturing will increase. There will be more jobs for highly skilled workers like this lab scientist in Nairobi, Kenya.

The Nile River: A Journey from Source to Mouth

19

19.1 Introduction

Thousands of years ago, the Nile River gave rise to one of the world's first civilizations. The ancient Egyptians built great cities, temples, and pyramids along the river. They grew crops on the river's banks. They sailed boats on its waters. They wrote songs and poems in praise of the river. The Nile gave life to ancient Egypt. Today, it is still a key part of Egyptian life.

The Nile is not just an Egyptian river. The river begins its journey in the **highlands** of East Africa far from Egypt. Along its way to the Mediterranean Sea, it crosses mountains, **plateaus,** plains, and **deserts**. The **river basin** of this great waterway covers more than 1 million square miles, or about one tenth of the African continent. A river basin is the area drained by a river and the smaller streams that flow into it. The Nile River basin includes parts of 10 African countries. Forty percent of all Africans live in these 10 countries.

In this chapter, you will follow the course of the Nile River. You will discover how the river changes during its long journey from the highlands to the sea. You will read about the origins of the river and the explorers who traced it to its sources. You will also learn about the impact of the river on the people and environment of the Nile River basin.

Essential Question

How do rivers change as they flow across Earth's surface?

This map shows the course of the Nile River on its journey from its sources to the sea. The Nile flows through several countries. It also crosses several parallels of latitude, including the equator and the Tropic of Cancer. During its long journey, the Nile changes in many ways. Keep this map in mind as you try to answer the Essential Question.

Graphic Organizer

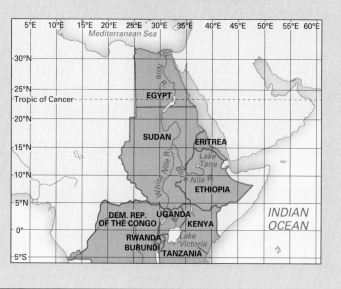

◀ Ancient mosaic of life on the Nile River

19.2 The Geographic Setting

Most of Egypt is a barren, sandy desert. The ancient Egyptians could not have survived without the Nile's life-giving waters. For that reason, the Greek scholar Herodotus called Egypt the "gift of the Nile." But despite the river's importance, the ancient Egyptians never knew just where it came from. In fact, the sources of the Nile remained a mystery for thousands of years.

The World's Longest River The Nile River has two main branches: the White Nile and the Blue Nile. The White Nile is the longest branch. From the White Nile's most distant **tributary** in the highlands of Burundi, the Nile runs north for about 4,160 miles. This is more than twice the distance from Chicago to Los Angeles. At this length, the Nile is the world's longest river.

Every year, the waters of the Nile rise and fall with the seasons. These changes in river level are tied to the water cycle that brings rain to the highlands of Africa. The **water cycle** is the constant movement of water from Earth's surface to the **atmosphere** and back again. After the rainy season, rising water often floods the land along the Nile's banks.

The Gifts of Water, Transportation, and Power The Nile has long been essential to the people who live along its banks. They use its water for drinking, washing, and cooking. They also use it for farming. In ancient times, the flooding of the Nile left deposits of rich **silt** on farmlands near the river. Farmers planted their crops in this fine, dark soil. They also used the floodwaters to irrigate their fields. Later on, they developed **perennial irrigation**. This is a system that distributes water to farm fields year round.

The Nile is also useful for transportation and energy. People along the Nile have long used the river as a water highway. Boats carry goods and people from place to place. The Nile also has great **hydroelectric potential**. That means that the river can be used to generate electrical power. Cities along the Nile depend on **hydroelectric power** to meet their energy needs.

Two Views of the Nile

This satellite image shows the Nile River valley. What patterns of vegetation and landforms do you see? The diagram below shows the change in the Nile's elevation along its entire length. From its source to the Mediterranean Sea, the river drops more than a mile in elevation.

Elevation Profile of the Nile

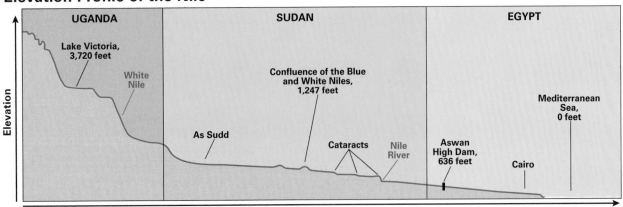

▶ Geoterms

hydroelectric potential the electrical power that can be generated from flowing water

perennial irrigation a system that allows for the year-round watering of crops

river basin the area drained by a river and its tributaries. These tributaries are the smaller streams that flow into the main river. Rain falling anywhere in a river basin will eventually flow into the main river.

water cycle the movement of water from the surface of Earth to the atmosphere and back again. During this cycle, water evaporates from rivers, lakes, and oceans, rises and condenses into clouds, and then falls back to Earth as rain, hail, sleet, or snow. This process is also known as the *hydrologic cycle*.

Two Branches, Ten Countries

The Nile River basin is outlined in dark blue on this map. It covers around one tenth of the African continent. The Nile, with its two main branches and many tributaries, travels through ten countries: Congo, Tanzania, Burundi, Rwanda, Uganda, Kenya, Ethiopia, Sudan, Eritrea, and Egypt.

The Nile River Basin

The Nile River: A Journey from Source to Mouth **289**

19.3 The Beginnings of the Nile

The ancient Egyptians believed that the Nile sprang forth from an underground lake in southern Egypt. The ancient Romans later tried but failed to find the Nile's source. It was only in more recent times that explorers finally discovered the origins of the Nile. Like all rivers, however, the Nile really begins with the water cycle.

From Rainwater to Rivers: The Water Cycle You have read that the water cycle recycles water from Earth's surface to the atmosphere and back again. This never-ending process moves water through the environment. Some water ends up in rivers like the Nile.

The water cycle begins with the **evaporation** of water from oceans, lakes, and rivers. This occurs when the sun heats the water. When water evaporates, it becomes **water vapor**. Steam is a form of water vapor that you can see.

As water vapor rises into the air, it cools down. The cooling causes the vapor to **condense** into tiny water droplets. The droplets then come together to form clouds. Under certain conditions, the droplets become too large and heavy to stay in the air. At that point, they fall to Earth as **precipitation**. Precipitation can take several forms, including rain, snow, sleet, and hail.

Several things can happen to precipitation after it hits the ground. Some gets stored as snow and ice in glaciers. Some soaks into the ground in a process called **infiltration**. And some runs off the ground to form streams. In areas with lots of **runoff,** streams come together to form rivers. Most rivers eventually flow into the sea. At that point, the water cycle begins again.

The Water Cycle

This diagram shows how nature recycles water. The water cycle is a "closed system." No water is ever lost. However, some water may collect unseen under the ground. This water can be tapped for human use.

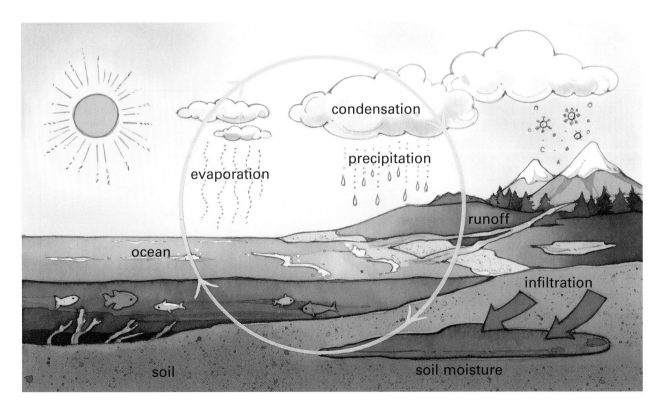

Lake Tana: Source of the Blue Nile Both main branches of the Nile, the Blue and the White, are fed by rainfall and runoff in the East African highlands. In the lush, forested hills of Ethiopia, this runoff flows into Lake Tana. This lake is considered the main source of the Blue Nile. The **headwaters** of the Blue Nile, however, are found above Lake Tana. Headwaters are the stream or streams that make up the beginnings of a river.

The Blue Nile is a fast and powerful river. Fed by heavy summer rains, it roars down from Lake Tana through deep canyons to the plains below. Along the way, it picks up lots of dark soil. Most of the silt that ends up on flooded farmlands downstream comes from the Blue Nile.

The source of the Blue Nile remained a mystery to outsiders until the 1600s. Around 1615, a Spanish priest named Pedro Páez made his way to Lake Tana. There he found the outlet where the river leaves the lake. In the late 1700s, the Scottish explorer James Bruce also reached the source. He later published a book about his travels and took credit for the discovery.

Lake Victoria: Source of the White Nile The other main branch of the Nile starts farther to the south. As you may recall, the White Nile's headwaters consist of a stream flowing out of the mountains of Burundi. But the river's main source is Lake Victoria, which is a large, shallow lake in Uganda.

For years, however, the origins of the White Nile remained as mysterious as those of the Blue Nile. Various explorers tried to follow the river from Egypt to its source. But they lost their way in swamps or were turned back by river rapids.

Then, in the 1850s, the English explorer John Hanning Speke reached Lake Victoria. Convinced that this was the White Nile's source, he returned a few years later. In 1862, he found a river flowing out of the north side of the lake. He followed the river for a distance. Then he returned to England to announce that he had discovered the source of the White Nile.

At first, many scholars doubted Speke's claim. They thought he hadn't explored the area well enough. But later expeditions confirmed that Lake Victoria was the main source of the White Nile. In 1937, a German explorer named Bruckhart Waldekker traced the river's headwaters farther south into Burundi.

Like the Blue Nile, the White Nile flows out of Lake Victoria as a rushing torrent. It passes through two more lakes and over a large waterfall before reaching the flat plains of Sudan. There it slows down. Along the way, the river takes on a muddy gray color. This gray color gives the White Nile its name.

Murchison Falls

North of Lake Victoria, the White Nile thunders over Murchison Falls. This is one of the most dramatic spots on the Nile's long journey to the sea. Today, these falls are part of a national park in Uganda. Park wildlife includes elephants and giraffes. Hippos and crocodiles are often found in these waters.

Watered by Two Niles

Al Jazirah, a state in Sudan, lies between the White and Blue Niles. Irrigation canals begun in the 1920s turned this state into a cotton-growing center. Today wheat is Al Jazirah's most important crop.

19.4 Two Niles Meet: Confluence and Cataracts

After leaving the highlands, the White Nile crosses the plains of Sudan. Along the way, it passes through a huge swamp called the As Sudd. Here the river spreads out into many small channels. These channels are clogged with **vegetation** and are hard to navigate. In the first century C.E., a Roman expedition sent out to find the source of the Nile got lost in this swamp.

The White and Blue Niles Meet at Khartoum Beyond the As Sudd, the White Nile continues its sluggish journey north. Just to the east, the Blue Nile also flows northward from the Ethiopian highlands. In north-central Sudan, the two branches of the Nile finally meet. This **confluence,** or coming together, takes place at the city of Khartoum, the capital of Sudan.

At this point, the Nile becomes a much larger river. This is especially true during the summer rainy season. Although the flow of the White Nile remains much the same throughout the year, the Blue Nile grows much larger as a result of summer rains. It is this rise of the Blue Nile that causes most of the flooding downstream.

At first, the waters of the two rivers don't mix. The gray flow of the White Nile runs alongside the darker waters of the Blue Nile. After a few miles, though, the rivers blend. Finally, the Nile truly becomes one river.

Rough Waters Slow River Travel North of Khartoum, the Nile rolls on for another 800 miles before reaching the southern border of Egypt. The river makes a wide turn to the south and west during this stage of the journey. This turn is called the "great bend." The Nile also passes over six **cataracts**. These are rapids or low waterfalls where the river drops over rock outcroppings.

The Nile cataracts have been famous throughout history as a barrier to river travel and trade. Boats can sail on stretches of water between the cataracts. But the rapids are far too dangerous for river travel. In ancient times, river traders had to unload their boats and move their goods by land around these rough waters.

19.5 Through the Desert: Wadis and Dams

North of Khartoum, the Nile flows through one of the harshest landscapes in the world. Rain rarely falls here. But when it does, it can cause a flash flood. During a storm, rainwater suddenly fills normally dry riverbeds, called **wadis**. If you're in a wadi when a storm hits, you'd better move fast. Otherwise you might be swept away by a wall of water.

An Arid Landscape In northern Sudan, the Nile enters a vast desert that continues northward through Egypt. Here, the land on both sides of the river is sunbaked and desolate. To the west lies the Sahara, the world's largest desert. It stretches for thousands of miles across northern Africa. To the east, between the Nile and the Red Sea, lies the Nubian Desert. This is a land of rocky hills, sand dunes, and wadis. Few people live here.

The Nile provides relief from this **arid** landscape. Here and there, trees grow up along its banks. In some places, people have settled down and irrigated small plots of land for farming. Farther north, in Egypt, farming and settlement increase along the Nile. Here, the land along the river looks like a ribbon of green stretched across the red-brown sands of the desert.

Controlling the Nile: The Aswan High Dam After winding for hundreds of miles through Sudan, the Nile finally reaches Lake Nasser. This lake straddles the border between Sudan and Egypt. It is not a natural lake, however, but a **reservoir**. In fact, it is one of the largest reservoirs in the world. It was formed in 1970 by the construction of the Aswan High Dam, in Egypt.

The dam was built for two main reasons. One was to develop the Nile's hydroelectric potential. The power plant at the dam generates an enormous amount of electricity. This power has helped Egypt and Sudan develop their cities and new industry.

The second reason was to control the river's flow. As you know, in the past the Nile flooded nearly every year. Those floods brought benefits to Egypt, but they also destroyed villages along the river. Some years, rainfall in the mountains was light and the floods didn't occur. In those years, Egypt lacked water.

The Aswan High Dam holds back the floodwaters that used to cause problems. Instead, water is released in a more steady flow from Lake Nasser. In this way, the dam provides a reliable, year-round supply of water for Egyptian farms and cities.

Along with its benefits, the Aswan High Dam has also had some negative effects. When Lake Nasser was formed, thousands of people had to move because their homes were covered by water. Also, the dam traps most of the rich silt that used to flow down to Egyptian farmlands. That silt now sits at the bottom of the lake. As a result, farmlands downstream are less fertile. Farmers must now buy artificial fertilizers to enrich the soil.

The Aswan High Dam

This photograph, taken from the space shuttle, shows the Aswan High Dam and its reservoir, Lake Nasser. The dam is enormous. Enough rock was used in its construction to build 17 pyramids the size of the Great Pyramid at Giza, Egypt. The lake is huge, too. It stretches for 300 miles from Egypt into Sudan.

Aswan High Dam

19.6 Across Egypt: Floodplains and Delta

For most of its journey through Egypt, the Nile flows through a narrow valley. In this Nile River valley, **floodplains** lie between the banks of the river and low cliffs on either side. Near the river's end, the Nile fans out to form a large **delta**. Together, the floodplains and delta make up just 3 percent of Egypt's land area. But they are home to most of its people. Approximately 95 percent of all Egyptians live along the Nile. The delta contains 60 percent of all the nation's farmland.

A Narrow Strip of Farmland Lines the River The floodplains of the Nile River valley have served as farmland for thousands of years. In most places, the floodplains are just a few miles wide. But the ancient Egyptians used them to produce bountiful harvests of wheat, barley, and other crops. These harvests made it possible for Egyptians to create one of the greatest early civilizations.

Until recent times, farmers along the Nile depended on annual floods to water and add fertile soil to their fields. They also used traditional irrigation techniques to bring water from the river. They built canals and moved water with simple machines like the *shaduf*. This is a pole with a bucket at one end and a weight at the other. The pole is attached to a brace so it can move up and down. The farmer dips the bucket into the water and lets the weight pull it out again.

The construction of the Aswan High Dam brought major changes to farming along the Nile. Lake Nasser now supplies water for a large system of perennial irrigation. With this water, farmers have been able to increase the amount of land under cultivation. As a result, Egyptian harvests have grown. Cotton, in particular, is a major export crop.

Water for Rapidly Growing Cairo About 600 miles from the Aswan High Dam, the Nile reaches Cairo, the capital of Egypt. The river flows through the center of the city. Broad, tree-lined avenues and modern skyscrapers line its banks. In the evening, people stroll along the Nile or sit in cafes overlooking the water.

With more than 11 million people, Cairo is one of the largest cities in the world. Like the rest of Egypt, Cairo gets most of its water from the Nile. This has worked well in the past. But the city is growing rapidly. Therefore, water needs are growing as well. At the same time, Cairo is pouring **sewage** and industrial waste into the river. These two factors—population growth and pollution—are putting pressure on the water supply. Cairo will have to plan carefully to avoid water problems in the future.

Old and New Irrigation

As in ancient times, some Egyptian farmers still rely on oxen to draw water from the Nile for their crops. Today, many farmers use electric pumps to irrigate their fields. With a steady water supply, Egypt has increased its farmland by almost 50 percent.

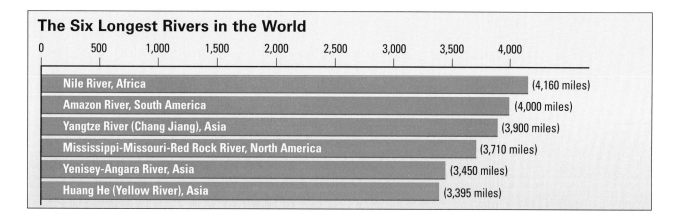

The Six Longest Rivers in the World

Nile River, Africa	(4,160 miles)
Amazon River, South America	(4,000 miles)
Yangtze River (Chang Jiang), Asia	(3,900 miles)
Mississippi-Missouri-Red Rock River, North America	(3,710 miles)
Yenisey-Angara River, Asia	(3,450 miles)
Huang He (Yellow River), Asia	(3,395 miles)

The River's Final Gift: The Nile Delta North of Cairo, the Nile travels another 100 miles before emptying into the sea. Here the floodplains of the Nile spread out in a broad, triangular delta. At its widest point, on the coast, this fan-shaped delta measures 155 miles across. This fertile area produces much of Egypt's food.

The Nile Delta began forming many thousands of years ago. When the river reached the coastal plain, it slowed down and divided into several branches. As the Nile slowed, it dropped the remainder of the load of silt it brought down from the highlands. Over time, this silt built up into a thick layer of soil. The Nile Delta became the richest farmland in Africa, and some of the richest in the world.

In ancient times, the Nile split into seven channels while crossing the delta. Over time, silt has filled some of those channels. Today, only two remain. At the end of its long journey, the Nile pours from two mouths into the Mediterranean Sea.

19.7 Beginning to Think Globally

In this chapter, you have read about the journey of the Nile River from its sources to the sea. You read about the water cycle and how it gives rise to rivers like the Nile. You learned where the Nile River basin is located and how the river changes as it flows downstream. You also learned about some of the benefits the Nile brings to people who live along its banks. These include hydroelectric potential and water for perennial irrigation.

The Nile is one of many great rivers in the world. The Amazon River is another. It drains a larger area than even the Nile. The Amazon starts in the snowy Andes Mountains of South America. It flows east through the world's largest **tropical rainforest** to the Atlantic Ocean. The Ohio, Missouri, and Mississippi rivers also form a mighty river system. This system stretches from the Appalachians west to the Rocky Mountains. It drains a large part of the North American continent into the Gulf of Mexico.

All rivers change as they flow across the surface of Earth. Some changes are natural. Others are the result of human activity. Think about this as you look at how hydroelectric dams affect rivers around the world.

From Tributary to Mouth

The length of each of these six rivers is measured from its most distant tributary. It's hard to measure rivers, though, and experts sometimes disagree. For example, some geographers believe that the Amazon is longer than the Nile.

19.8 Global Connections

This map shows major rivers and hydroelectric dams around the world. The graph shows the energy produced by the largest dams. A megawatt (MW) equals 1 million watts. This is enough electricity to serve the needs of about 1,000 people. A large dam can produce 1,000 MW of energy. The diagram shows how a hydroelectric dam works to produce all of this power.

What are the main benefits of building hydroelectric dams?

Hydroelectric dams produce clean energy. They don't pollute the air the way power plants that burn fossil fuels do. They don't produce radioactive waste products the way nuclear power plants do. They control flooding and provide water for farms and cities. Dams also create lakes that are used for recreation.

What are the main costs of building hydroelectric dams?

Giant dams cost billions of dollars to build. They have environmental costs as well. The lakes that form behind dams flood large areas. Towns, farms, and forests may be submerged by rising water. Many people may be forced to move. Wildlife may suffer as well from loss of habitat.

Do the benefits of damming rivers outweigh the costs?

Hydroelectric dams have clear benefits. But these benefits must be weighed against the costs. All rivers change as they flow across the surface of Earth. But large dams change rivers in ways that can have a major impact on people and the environment.

Major River Systems Around the World

The Power of Water

A hydroelectric dam turns waterpower into electric power. Water flowing through the dam turns the blades of a turbine. The spinning turbine creates an electric current inside a generator. This current travels over power lines to distant towns and cities.

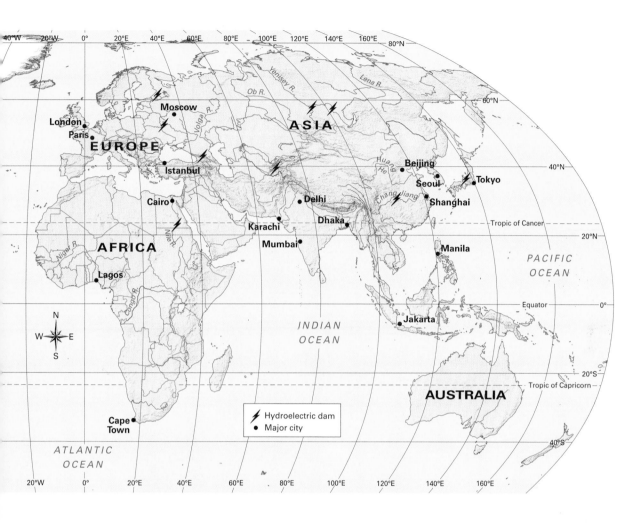

Major Power-Generating Hydroelectric Dams

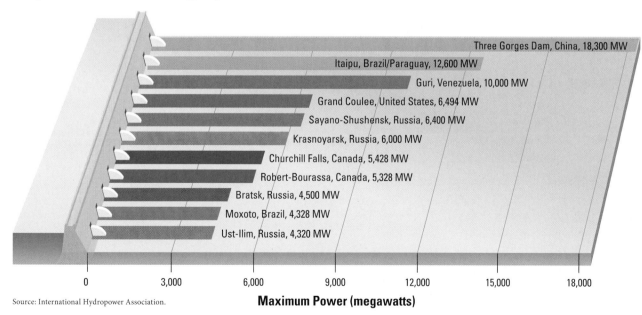

Three Gorges Dam, China, 18,300 MW
Itaipu, Brazil/Paraguay, 12,600 MW
Guri, Venezuela, 10,000 MW
Grand Coulee, United States, 6,494 MW
Sayano-Shushensk, Russia, 6,400 MW
Krasnoyarsk, Russia, 6,000 MW
Churchill Falls, Canada, 5,428 MW
Robert-Bourassa, Canada, 5,328 MW
Bratsk, Russia, 4,500 MW
Moxoto, Brazil, 4,328 MW
Ust-Ilim, Russia, 4,320 MW

0   3,000   6,000   9,000   12,000   15,000   18,000

Source: International Hydropower Association.

Maximum Power (megawatts)

Life in the Sahara and the Sahel: Adapting to a Desert Region

20.1 Introduction

The Saharan **region** is filled with the unexpected. Just ask someone who has survived the Dakar Rally. In this rally, cars, trucks, and motorcycles race against each other. They also race against the wind, sand, and heat of this **desert**. With few roads, drivers speed over shifting dunes, rocky plains, and dry grasslands. They cross dry riverbeds that have not seen water in years. They struggle through sandstorms and scorching heat. If driving across the Sahara is this hard, think how much harder it must be to live there.

The Sahara is one of the harshest environments on Earth. Through the years, however, people have adapted to living in this hot, **arid** region. Most people live near a desert **oasis**. An oasis is an isolated spot where water is found in a desert.

The Sahel is a semiarid grassland along the Sahara's southern edge. Its environment is not quite as harsh as the Sahara. But the Sahel often suffers from **drought,** or long periods with very little or no rain. This decrease in rainfall has made life there even more challenging.

In this chapter, you will read about the **physical features** of the Sahara and the Sahel. You will find out how the environments of these regions have been shaped by changes in **climate**. You will also learn how people in the past have adapted—and still are adapting—to these arid lands.

Essential Question	Graphic Organizer
How do people adapt to living in a desert region? This map shows the vast Saharan region, which includes the Sahara and the Sahel. The Sahara is the world's largest desert. The Sahel is a wide belt of semiarid lands to the south of the desert. Over many centuries, people have found ways to survive in both of these dry landscapes. Keep this map in mind as you try to answer the Essential Question.	**The Sahara and the Sahel** Mediterranean Sea Nile R. Niger R. Desert Oases Sahel

◀ A camel caravan carries trade goods across the Sahara.

Shrinking Lake Chad

Lake Chad is a large, shallow lake in the Sahel. The lake shrinks or grows depending on the amount of rainfall. But its overall size is slowly shrinking.

20.2 The Geographic Setting

The Sahara stretches across most of North Africa. It covers about 3.5 million square miles. This is an area roughly equal to that of the continental United States. This huge desert is bordered on the east by the Red Sea and on the west by the Atlantic Ocean. To the north, it begins at the Atlas Mountains. From there it sweeps south for more than 1,000 miles. Then the Sahara merges with the semiarid Sahel. Together the Sahara and Sahel cover all or parts of 15 African countries.

The World's Largest Desert The Sahara is the largest desert in the world. Its name comes from the Arabic word *sahra,* which means "desert." Its climate is very hot and very dry. The world's highest known daytime temperature, 136°F, was recorded there in 1922. Average rainfall is less than five inches a year.

The Sahara has not always been so dry. Many thousands of years ago, the region had a much wetter climate. Rivers and lakes were filled with fish. Elephants and other animals roamed through grasslands and forests. People settled in the region and lived by hunting and fishing.

About 6,000 years ago, the climate of North Africa changed. Year by year, less rain fell. In time, the Saharan region began to turn into a desert. Ever since then, the desert has slowly been expanding.

Trade winds blowing across North Africa help to keep the region dry. These winds begin in northern latitudes and blow south toward the equator. As trade winds pass over the Sahara, they pick up any moisture on the ground below. So little moisture is left that few clouds ever form over the Sahara. With no clouds to provide shade, the sun beats down on the land, making it even drier.

Parts of the Sahara are so dry that nothing lives there. In other areas, an oasis makes life possible. Most of the plants and animals that live in the Sahara are found at its oases.

The Sahel: On the Sahara's Edge The Sahel lies on the southern border of the Sahara. Its name comes from the Arabic word *sahel,* which means "border" or "shore." This region receives more rain than the Sahara, but it often suffers from long periods of drought.

Most of the Sahel is **marginal land**. This is land that is not well suited for farming. People who farm marginal land may harvest barely enough food to survive.

For thousands of years, **pastoral nomads** have adapted to life on the Sahel's marginal lands. Pastoral nomads are herders. They wander endlessly in search of water and grazing land for their animals. Once their herds have grazed an area, the nomads move on. This gives marginal grazing land a chance to recover.

In recent years, the Sahel has been undergoing **desertification**. This is a process in which an area becomes increasingly dry. In this chapter, you will find out why parts of the Sahel are turning into desert and what that means for the people who live there.

▶ Geoterms

desertification the process by which land becomes more and more dry until it turns into desert. This may be caused by climate change, human activities, or both.

drought an unusually long period in which little or no rain falls

marginal land land that is not well suited for growing crops

pastoral nomads groups of herders who move with their animals from place to place in search of pasture and water

The Sahara and the Sahel

A Vast Desert Region

The Sahara and Sahel stretch across most of North Africa. You can see how large this region is by looking at the inset map, which compares it to the size of the continental United States. The mountainous parts of this region receive the most rainfall. The water seeps into underground streams that flow down to the desert. In low areas, it may bubble up to the surface and create oases.

The Sahara's Sea of Sand

Ergs, or vast expanses of sand, cover about 13 percent of the Sahara's land area. Sand dunes move like slow-breaking waves through these "seas of sand." Little grows on the dunes, and in some places the sand is so soft that camels sink halfway to their knees in it.

20.3 The Desert Environment

A line of 500 camels stretches for a mile across the desert. This camel caravan is going to pick up blocks of salt from a distant mine. Its 400-mile round trip will take 30 days. Along the way, the caravan will pass camel bones and abandoned trucks. Travel is not easy in the Sahara.

The Desert Landscape: More Than Just Sand Many people picture the Sahara as a sea of burning sand. But its **landscape** is far more diverse. In just one afternoon, a traveler in the Sahara saw "pink and yellow dunes, blue craggy cliffs, black volcanic rubble... an eroded gulch, two dry rivers, a cone, a canyon, [and] many badlands [barren hills]."

The Sahara has three main types of **landforms:** ergs, regs, and hammadas. **Ergs** are great seas of sand with tall sand dunes. These dunes can rise over 400 feet. Most dunes are slowly blown across the desert by the wind. **Regs** are gravel-covered plains. **Hammadas** are high, rock-covered flatlands. Some hammadas are so tall that maps show them as mountains.

Only two rivers flow through the Sahara: the Nile and the Niger. The water in both rivers comes from mountains outside the desert. There are also dry riverbeds called **wadis** that can turn into raging rivers after a rain. Then they quickly dry up again.

The Harsh Desert Climate Temperatures vary greatly between day and night. Daytime temperatures often soar above 100°F. At night, temperatures may drop to below freezing. According to an old saying, "Nighttime is the winter of the desert."

Sandstorms can begin when strong winds pick up dark clouds of dust and sand from the desert floor. A severe sandstorm can reduce visibility to almost nothing. It also gets sand into everything.

Rain is unpredictable in the desert. During a desert storm, it may rain three inches in one spot, while nearby no rain falls. When rain does come, it may quickly fill the wadis. These flash floods can carry away rocks, people, and even trucks.

Plants adapt to these conditions in several ways. Some sprout quickly after a rain and then set seed and die. The seeds then lie in wait—sometimes for years—for the next rain. Other plants send roots deep into the ground to find water. Deep roots also hold these plants in place during sandstorms and flash floods. Most desert trees and shrubs have small, waxy leaves that lose little moisture. During long periods of drought, they may shed their leaves.

20.4 Adaptations to Life in the Desert

Many desert nomads belong to a group known as the Tuareg. The Tuareg live in six countries in the southern Sahara and Sahel.

The Wandering Tuareg The nomadic Tuareg raise camels, goats, cattle, or sheep. When the pasture in one area is used up, they move their animals to a fresh grazing area.

The Tuareg are known as the "Blue Men of the Desert" because of their flowing blue robes. Their long, loose clothing protects them from the burning sun. Men also wear blue cloth wrapped around their heads and across their faces. Some Tuareg men never remove this face cover, even in front of close family members.

Tuareg nomads live in family groups of fewer than 100 people. These groups are always ready to move. It takes a Tuareg family only two hours to take down the tents that are their homes and pack up their belongings. Everything a family owns fits on one camel or two donkeys. When they reach an oasis, the nomads trade meat, cheese, or milk for grain, vegetables, fruit, and water.

Tuareg traders lead camel caravans across the desert. Camels are well suited for desert travel. A camel can walk long distances over sandy ground with little food or water. It is easy to get lost in the Sahara, but the Tuareg know the local landmarks. They also know how to use the stars to find their way. This allows them to travel at night, when the air is cooler.

Technology Makes Life Easier Modern **technology** has improved life for many desert dwellers. Pastoral nomads have found many uses for lightweight plastic and metal containers. Some desert traders can afford satellite phones to keep in touch with their customers.

Technology has created new oases. Drilling machines cut through rock to find underground water. Electric pumps then draw this water to the surface.

Trucks and planes have improved desert transportation. Trucks are replacing camels for hauling heavy loads. Small planes are also used to fly people and goods between oases.

Nomads Tend Their Herds
Tuareg nomads move their herds to find water or better pasture. The Tuareg depend upon their animals for milk. They trade milk, cheese, and some meat for the goods they cannot make or grow themselves.

Trucks Replace Camels
Trucks are gradually replacing camels in the Sahara. There are not many roads, though, so trucks are built to deal with the rough and sandy desert. The owner of this truck has to clear away the sand that has piled up overnight before beginning the day's work.

20.5 The Oasis Environment

The Sahara holds many surprises. In a hidden canyon oasis, crocodiles feed on fish and on animals that come to drink. At a larger oasis, thousands of date palms shade fruit trees. Wild gazelles graze nearby. In this arid land, where there is water there is life.

Islands of Water Surrounded by Desert For travelers crossing the Sahara, no sight is more welcome than a distant palm tree. The palm is a sign that an oasis is nearby. Each oasis is an island of fresh water in a sea of dry sand and rock.

Some oases are natural. Many are created by springs that bubble up to the surface from streams beneath the ground. Other oases appear in low spots. Here the land dips down to meet an underground stream.

Humans create some oases. In the past, people made oases by digging wells by hand. As you read, drilling machines are now being used to dig deep into the ground to locate hidden water.

Large and Small Centers of Life The Sahara has about 90 large oases. Here there is enough water to support a village and small farms. There are many small oases as well. Some may support only one or two families.

Many kinds of plants and animals are found at a desert oasis. Acacia and baobab trees mix with smaller shrubs. Gazelles and other animals drink in the pools. Butterflies, crickets, and other insects flit through oasis gardens.

Date palms are by far the most important and common oasis plant. Every part of this tree is useful. Its fruit, the date, is eaten fresh or dried. Its trunk and leaves are used as building materials. Fiber from its bark is made into rope. Date pits, or seeds, are burned as fuel or fed to animals. A visitor to the Sahara once wrote,

Those magnificent palm groves are the blood and bone of the desert; life in the Sahara would be unthinkable without them.... The size of an oasis is reckoned by the number of trees it contains, not by the number of square miles it covers.

Desert Oases

An oasis is a place in the desert where water is found. Some oases are natural. Others have been created by people. However they came to be, all oases are precious. They allow life to exist in one of the world's harshest environments.

Rock layers

Oasis formed by a spring bubbling up to the surface

Oasis formed at a low spot

Groundwater

Artificial oases created by humans

20.6 Adaptations to Life in the Oases

Most oasis settlements are small, with fewer than 2,000 people. The largest ones may have thousands of date palms. But in an oasis with little water, several families may share a single date palm.

The Traditional Ways of Oasis Settlers

Trading and farming are the major **economic activities** at an oasis. While most people are subsistence farmers, others grow **cash crops** like dates, wheat, barley, and vegetables. Farmers trade their produce for goods brought in by camel, truck, and plane. Visiting nomads trade their meat, milk, and cheese for water and food. Caravans and trucks stop to trade and to fill their containers with water.

Most homes in an oasis town are made of mud bricks. They have few windows in order to keep out the heat. Little work is done during the hottest part of the day. In the cool of the evening, people gather to discuss the day's news.

An oasis farmer is always fighting the desert. Blowing sand and creeping dunes will quickly cover crops unless they are protected by **windbreaks**. A windbreak is a wall or hedge that breaks the force of the wind. It can also stop sand from piling up on a farm field.

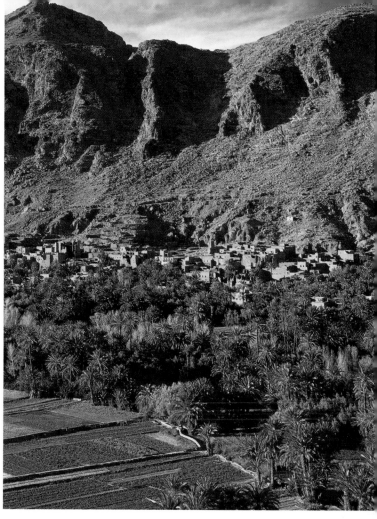

Palms Produce a Cash Crop
Date palms produce the desert's most valuable cash crop. Other fruit trees are often planted in the shade of date palms.

Water Problems Limit the Growth of Oasis Towns

Oasis settlements come in many sizes. Most are small villages. A few are growing into towns and cities. As an oasis settlement grows, its water problems grow as well.

People move to an oasis for many reasons. Some may be looking for jobs on date farms or in date-processing plants. These factories get dates ready for export. Nomads sometimes settle at an oasis when they can no longer find pasture for their animals. Refugees from drought or war may move to an oasis in search of water, food, and safety.

Growing oasis towns face two kinds of water problems. The first problem is how to get water to people as the town expands. New housing areas and camps set up to shelter refugees often lack wells or piped water. If people cannot walk to water sources, water may have to be brought to them by truck.

The second problem is water shortages. In some oases, palm groves have been expanded into the surrounding desert. The new trees are kept alive with water pumped out of the ground. If too much water is pumped out, the underground streams that create an oasis could run dry.

Cattle in the Sahel

Overgrazing by cattle is a major cause of desertification in the Sahel. When too many cattle graze in an area, they destroy its cover of plants. Without this protective cover, the soil is eroded by wind or water.

20.7 The Sahel Environment

A television ad in southern Niger begins by panning across a desert landscape. The next scene follows camels, donkeys, and trucks carrying firewood into towns. A quick cut shows a coal-mining operation. The ad ends by showing a woman cooking with coal in her smoke-free kitchen. The ad is intended to persuade people in Niger to switch from wood to coal for cooking. Such a switch could help to preserve Niger's trees. It might also prevent desertification.

The southern area of Niger is part of the Sahel. Other areas include Gambia and parts of Senegal, Mauritania, Mali, Burkina Faso, Nigeria, Chad, and Sudan. In good years, just enough rain falls in the Sahel to grow crops. During years of drought, life in the region becomes very difficult.

A Landscape Threatened by Drought and Desertification

The Sahel begins at the Sahara's edge. The land here is marginal for farming. The soil is not fertile, and water is scarce most of the year. The natural **vegetation** is a mix of grasslands, acacia trees, baobab trees, and small bushes. Farther south, where rain is more plentiful, vegetation is more varied.

Drought is a fact of life in the Sahel. One severe drought began in 1968. Little rain fell for the next six years. Since then, there has been some rain, but not enough for the land to recover fully.

As the drought continued, desertification began. In areas with little rain, few plants grew. Without plants to hold the dry soil in place, desert winds picked it up and carried it away. When this happened, marginal lands turned into desert. Experts aren't sure whether this desertification is a short-term problem or whether these marginal lands are lost forever to an expanding Sahara.

20.8 Adaptations to Life in the Sahel

Most people in the Sahel are farmers or herders. In the past, they adapted to the challenge of farming and herding on marginal land in many ways.

One **adaptation** was to plant crops like millet and sorghum. These are grains that will grow in dry places. Another was to use a farming system known as **shifting agriculture**. A farmer cleared a field and planted it with crops for a year or two. Then the farmer moved on to a new field. Herders used a similar system to feed their animals. They moved their herds from one grazing area to another throughout the year. Both systems gave worn-out fields a chance to rest.

Human Causes of Desertification Changing ways of life in the Sahel may be contributing to desertification. Some farmers, for example, have begun to raise cash crops, like peanuts. These cash crops often wear out the soil faster than traditional crops. Once the soil is worn out, it may blow away before it can recover its fertility.

Similarly, some nomads have increased the size of their herds so that they have animals to sell for cash. The result is too many animals on limited grazing land. Loss of vegetation from overgrazing may also contribute to desertification.

Yet another problem is **deforestation**. Most people in the Sahel use wood as their fuel for cooking. In their search for firewood, they cut down trees. With the trees gone, soil **erosion** increases. That is why the government of Niger is promoting coal as a cooking fuel. "I think that with coal, our sparse forests could be saved," says a forestry expert in Niger.

Cooking with coal is only one change people are making to fight desertification. Farmers are testing new farming methods that save water and slow soil erosion. Many are working to keep desert sand from burying their fields by building windbreaks of trees and brush.

No one can say how successful this war against the desert will be. But for the people of the Sahel, it is a fight they cannot afford to lose.

20.9 Beginning to Think Globally

In this chapter, you learned how people have adapted to living in the Sahara and the Sahel. Pastoral nomads survive by staying on the move. Farmers adapt by settling around oases that serve as farming and trading centers in this arid land. You found out how people have learned to raise crops and animals on the marginal lands of the Sahel. And you have seen how drought and desertification have affected this region.

The Sahel is not the only area in the world threatened by desertification. About a third of Earth's land is arid or semiarid. And some of these desert regions are expanding. In China, the capital city of Beijing is sometimes blasted by sandstorms. The blowing sand comes from parts of China that are undergoing desertification. Think about this as you look at the world map of arid regions in the next section.

Sahel Sandstorm
Sandstorms like this one in Mali are made worse by desertification. Winds pick up loose soil from worn-out land and blow it away. Dust from the Sahel is sometimes carried across the Atlantic Ocean. When this dust reaches Florida, it creates reddish sunsets.

20.10 Global Connections

This map shows the world's deserts and areas threatened by desertification. The diagram illustrates one set of human activities that may lead to desertification. Other factors, such as years of drought, may also play a part.

Are the world's deserts growing or shrinking? Many areas of marginal land are being threatened by desertification. These places could, in time, become new deserts. Climate change is a factor in this process. In some areas, droughts may speed desertification. In other areas, unusually wet weather may help to slow it down.

What human activities contribute to desertification? The ways people use marginal lands may lead to desertification. Poor farming methods can wear out thin soil. Overgrazing can strip areas of their protective plant cover. Nonnative plants can crowd out native ones better suited to a dry climate. Deforestation can leave marginal lands open to erosion. All of these factors can contribute to the spread of deserts in arid regions.

How might people adapt to living in areas threatened by desertification? People deal with desertification in many ways. Villagers in China are learning new methods of farming. Their goal is to reduce soil erosion. Australia has developed new programs to prevent wildfires. These programs are designed to keep fire from destroying forests and grasslands. Many developing countries, however, cannot afford such projects. They look to other countries and the United Nations for help in keeping their deserts from spreading.

Desert Regions Around the World

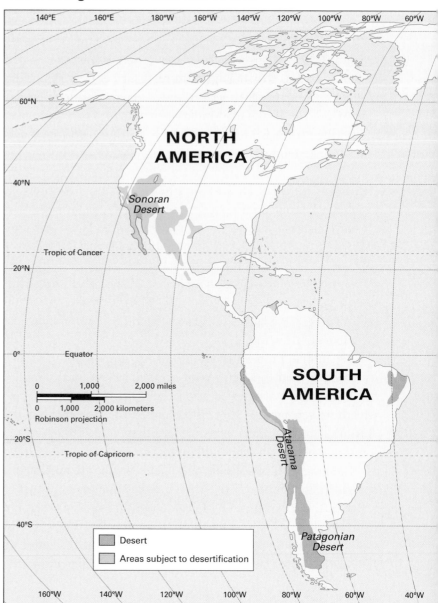

A Problem with Many Causes ▶

As this diagram shows, desertification is a problem with many causes. Long periods of drought can kill off the vegetation that holds soil in place. Farming and grazing on marginal lands can also leave soil without a protective cover of plants. Without such a cover, soil is easily eroded by wind and rain. The result is an arid wasteland of sand and rock in which little will grow.

EUROPE

ASIA

Garagum
Desert

Gobi
Desert

Syrian
Desert

Taklamakan
Desert

Arabian
Desert

Thar
Desert

S a h a r a

AFRICA

Tropic of Cancer

Equator

Namib Desert

Kalahari
Desert

AUSTRALIA

Great Victoria
Desert

Tropic of Capricorn

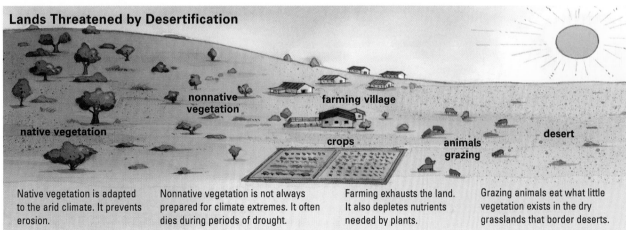

Lands Threatened by Desertification

native vegetation

nonnative
vegetation

farming village

crops

animals
grazing

desert

Native vegetation is adapted to the arid climate. It prevents erosion.

Nonnative vegetation is not always prepared for climate extremes. It often dies during periods of drought.

Farming exhausts the land. It also depletes nutrients needed by plants.

Grazing animals eat what little vegetation exists in the dry grasslands that border deserts.

Micro-entrepreneurs: Women's Role in the Development of Africa

21.1 Introduction

Hassana lived in a small village in West Africa. She was a widow with five children. With so many mouths to feed, she often lacked money to buy clothes and school supplies for her children. She had no money saved in case someone got sick. Sometimes even buying food was difficult.

But Hassana had an idea for a small business, or **micro-enterprise**. She wanted to bake bread and sell it in the local street market. Hassana borrowed money from an organization set up to help women start businesses. She used the money to buy an oven. With her earnings from selling bread, Hassana was able to repay the loan. She was also able to slowly grow her business and take better care of her family.

Small business owners like Hassana are called **micro-entrepreneurs**. Entrepreneurs are people who start businesses. *Micro* means tiny. Micro-entrepreneurs are people who start very small businesses. Hassana's business may be tiny, but the effect that micro-entrepreneurs are having in developing countries is not so small. Hassana's story is one of many about women in Africa who are making life better by starting new businesses.

In this chapter, you will learn about some of the challenges faced by poor women in Africa. You will read how some women are pulling themselves out of poverty by becoming micro-entrepreneurs. And you will find out how these women, by helping themselves, are changing their communities.

Essential Question

How are women micro-entrepreneurs in developing countries changing their communities?

Pictured in this outline of the continent of Africa is a micro-entrepreneur. She is one of many African women who have started their own businesses. These women are playing a growing role in the development of Africa. Keep this image in mind as you try to answer the Essential Question.

Graphic Organizer

◀ Selling bread in an African street market

21.2 The Geographic Setting

In this chapter, you will visit three countries in Africa. All three are located south of the Sahara. Mali is in West Africa. Uganda is in East Africa. Botswana lies in the center of Southern Africa.

A Developing Country Most of Africa is made up of **developing countries**. Twenty-one of the world's 30 poorest countries are in Africa. Nearly half of the Africans in these countries live on less than $1 a day.

Poverty makes survival a daily challenge. In 2007, an estimated 236 million Africans were **undernourished**. This means they did not get enough food to lead healthy lives. Lack of food has stunted, or slowed, the growth of about a third of all African children.

Disease is a serious challenge. Malaria, for example, affects people in many parts of Africa. Mosquitoes spread the parasite that causes this illness. Malaria can be deadly, especially to children. Health experts estimate that every 30 seconds, a child in Africa dies from malaria.

Natural disasters create other challenges. In recent years, **drought** has struck many African countries. The lack of rain has led to crop failures for farmers. For **pastoral nomads,** it has led to the death of their animal herds. The result has been severe food shortages.

War is another serious challenge. Many countries, like Rwanda, Liberia, and Angola, have been torn apart by **civil war**. A civil war is a war between groups living in the same country. Each of these conflicts has left hundreds of thousands of people dead.

Women Face Added Challenges These challenges affect most Africans. But they often weigh heaviest on women. One reason for this is Africa's traditional **gender-based division of labor**. This is the division of work in a society based on a person's sex, or gender.

Traditionally, men in Africa are the money earners. They earn money by raising cash crops or working for wages. Women are responsible for the care of the family. This often includes growing food on small plots of land to feed their families. As important as this work is, it does not earn money.

Poor women who need to earn money face added challenges. One is a lack of education. In many parts of Africa in 2007, more than 30 percent of women ages 15 to 24 could not read. Few jobs are open to them.

Often the only place poor women can find to make money is in the **informal economy**. People in the informal economy exchange goods and services without much government control. They might, for instance, sell food in a street market or trade childcare for firewood. They do not have a license for their business. And they do not pay taxes on any money they might make.

For many African women, the informal economy has become an area of opportunity. In the informal economy, women can start a new business without a lot of money. In this chapter, you will meet some of these women micro-entrepreneurs.

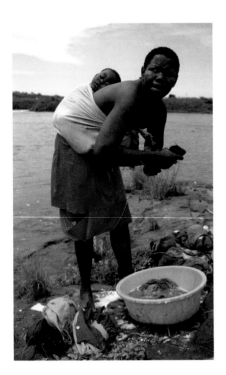

Women Carry a Heavy Load
There is a traditional division of labor in Africa between men and women. Men hunt, herd, or work for wages. Women take care of the family. This often involves hauling firewood and water over long distances.

▶ Geoterms

gender-based division of labor the division of work into two categories based on sex, or gender. The result is that men and women do different kinds of work.

informal economy the part of the economy in which goods and services are exchanged outside of government control. People who work in the informal economy often sell goods on the street or in a street market.

micro-enterprise a very small business with few or no employees

micro-entrepreneur a person who starts and runs a very small business

Gender Differences in Africa

This map compares the relative condition of men and women in Africa. It is based on a ranking system called the Gender Development Index (GDI). This index rates countries by comparing men and women in three areas: education, income, and life expectancy. In all three areas, women fare worse than men in Africa. As a result, the GDI rankings of African countries are low.

Gender Equality in Africa, 2006

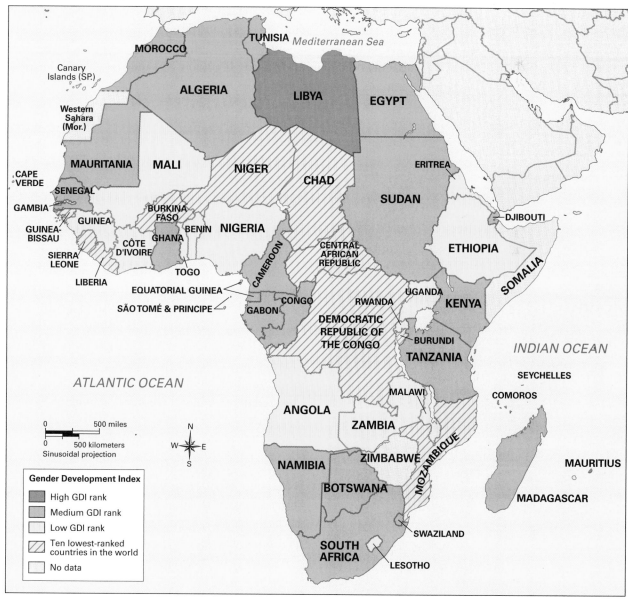

Source: United Nations Development Programme and World Health Organization.

21.3 Grinding Peanuts in Rural Mali

The sound of wood hitting wood is common in many villages in Mali. It is the sound of women preparing two of Mali's most common foods for cooking: grains and peanuts. It takes a lot of energy to grind these crops to the point that they can be made into meals.

Mali is one of the poorest countries in the world. Much of its population lives in rural villages. Women work especially hard. But things are changing in some villages in Mali. And women micro-entrepreneurs are leading the way.

A Machine Changes the Way Women Work In the village of Sanankoroni in Mali, a machine grinds peanuts so the village women do not have to pound them by hand. The machine grinds the peanuts much faster. It also does a better job.

Grinding peanuts is just one of the things that this machine, called a *multifunctional platform,* can do. The multifunctional platform is a simple, sturdy machine that can be used in many ways. Its heart is a small engine that runs on diesel fuel or on oil from plants. Rubber belts connect the engine to different tools. The people of Sanankoroni connect their engine to a grinding tool. This tool grinds their peanuts into peanut butter.

The multifunctional platform was the brainchild of a Swiss inventor. He believed that it would make women's lives easier and change entire villages. He was right. His invention has changed how women like Biutou Doumbia spend their time. Doumbia used to spend three days grinding 100 pounds of peanuts by hand. Now the machine grinds that amount in a little more than an hour. Doumbia uses some of the time she has gained to grind extra peanuts. She then sells this peanut butter in the local market.

The women of Sanankoroni bought the machine with the help of the United Nations Development Programme. The UNDP is an international organization that works to reduce poverty in developing countries. The women formed a group called the Sanankoroni Women's Association. This group raised $2,000, or half the cost of the machine. The UNDP provided the rest of the money.

A Machine with Many Functions

The multifunctional platform is built around a simple engine. But the things it can do are anything but simple. This machine can be attached to different tools. Depending on the tool, it can grind grains, pump water, generate electricity for lights, charge batteries, and much more.

The Country of Mali

Mali is a large country in West Africa. The Sahara covers the northern half of Mali. Grasslands spread across most of the southern half.

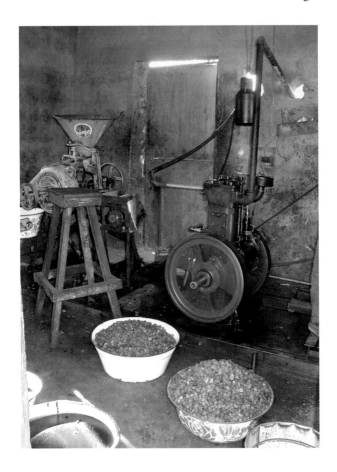

Earning While Learning New Skills The Sanankoroni Women's Association has started a peanut-grinding business with their multi-functional platform. Customers from Sanankoroni and nearby villages pay a fee to use the machine to grind peanuts. The women earn money by running the machine for their customers.

The new business owners have learned many new skills. They have learned how to run the machine and keep it in good repair. They have learned how to set up schedules for their workers and customers. And they have learned how to handle the money they earn so that they have enough to buy fuel and to pay their workers.

Improving the Quality of Life In Mali, 350 villages now have a multifunctional platform. The quality of life in these communities has improved as a result. For example, families in Sanankoroni have more time together now that women do not spend all day grinding peanuts by hand.

Attitudes toward education have changed. Before the machine came, only 9 women in this village of 460 people could read and write. A year after the machine arrived, more than 40 women were attending classes to learn how to read. Girls who used to stay home to help with chores are now going to school.

The machine has improved the lives of men as well. The Sanankoroni Women's Association hired several men to work as mechanics. Their job is to maintain and repair the machine. "It's better than farming," says one mechanic.

In the village of Mountougoula, women bought an electrical generator to connect to their machine. A generator is used to produce electricity. They also set up a lighting system in their village to use electricity produced by their generator. The lights have made the village safer at night. Storeowners are making more money now that people can shop after dark.

One man in the village is teaching his daughters to read at night. He has seen for himself that women can change the world. All they need is education and encouragement.

Grinding Peanuts
This woman is grinding peanuts using a multifunctional platform. Despite their name, peanuts are not true nuts. They grow in the ground rather than on a tree. For this reason, they are often called *groundnuts*. Peanuts are raised both to eat and to press for their oil.

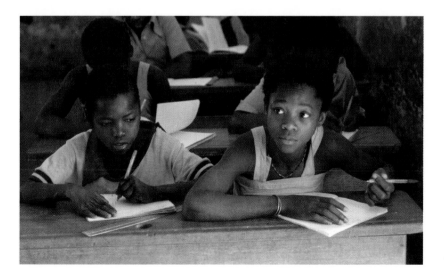

A Machine Brings Change
The multifunctional platform has changed the lives of many people in Mali. More girls are attending school because they no longer need to stay home and help with chores like grinding. Women are hiring men to repair and run the machines. Families have more time to be together.

The Country of Uganda

Uganda is a densely populated country in East Africa. Its capital, Kampala, lies on the shores of Lake Victoria. This is Africa's largest freshwater lake.

Open-Air Markets Are Popular

Much of the buying and selling in Uganda goes on in outdoor markets like this one. Some micro-entrepreneurs build stalls. Others sell their goods and services in the open. Such markets are part of Africa's informal economy.

21.4 Selling in Uganda's "Poor Man's Market"

Kalerwe market in Uganda is an amazing place to visit. From the center of the market, stalls stretch as far as the eye can see. Buyers roam the muddy, crowded lanes between the stalls. Sellers shout information about the food, goods, and services they have to sell. Kalerwe is known as the "poor man's market." But it attracts all kinds of people from nearby Kampala, the capital of Uganda. They are drawn to the market by its bargain prices.

Markets like this are common in Uganda and most other African countries. They are part of the informal economy. People can sell goods and services in these markets without having to get a business license. Often they can pocket the money they make without having to pay taxes. Many successful women micro-entrepreneurs got their start in such markets. Margaret Saajjabi is one of them.

Soap and Drinks Fund a Micro-enterprise Margaret Saajjabi runs profitable micro-enterprises in Uganda. She owns a quarter acre of land in Kalerwe market. She rents 27 market spaces to other people. Some of her tenants have built stalls in the space. Others sell their goods and services in the open air. Her tenants include hairdressers, electricians, vegetable sellers, and cooks.

Saajjabi was born into a very large family. She was in high school when her father told her there was not enough money for her to continue her education. She left school and worked for the police and then as a telephone operator. But Saajjabi wanted her own business.

She got her start by selling laundry soap and bottled soft drinks. Because she had no money to buy goods, she talked sellers into letting her sell their products. She got a small percentage of the money she took in from customers. Slowly she saved the money she earned. Eventually she had enough to buy land in Kalerwe market.

An Outdoor Beauty Shop
Some of Africa's most successful micro-enterprises can be found in local markets. Many are owned by women. With the money they earn, women can send their children to school or build homes for their families.

Saajjabi has found many ways to use this land. In addition to renting out market spaces, she has set up a water-selling business there. She sells water in large cans to local people. She also created a parking lot that holds 50 cars. People who come to Kalerwe pay to park there.

Saajjabi found that women face special challenges in business. One challenge is getting the money needed to start or expand a business. Men in Uganda are able to borrow start-up money from other men. But few men will loan money to women. To get around this problem, Saajjabi created a savings club with several other women. The women in the club help one another save their money. And when they need a loan, they borrow from other women in the club.

Supporting an Extended Family Margaret Saajjabi is a good example of how one woman's success can benefit many others. In her case, the people who benefit the most are members of her large family. She supports 6 children of her own. She is also helping to raise 19 nieces and nephews.

Most of these children are in school. Saajjabi believes that both girls and boys need a good education. She also believes that all children should learn the value of work. Her children, nieces, and nephews all come to Kalerwe market to work during their school holidays.

Creating New Economic Opportunities Saajjabi's success has rippled outward and helped others in her community. She has hired six guards for her parking business. She has plans to build more shops and to hire young women to work for her. In addition, the people who rent space from her now have a way to make money for their families.

Saajjabi encourages other women to start their own businesses. "You have to be confident," she says when asked for advice. "Develop the skills of your trade. Don't beg off and say, 'I'm just a woman.'" If Saajjabi had thought that way, she would still be selling someone else's soap and soft drinks.

A Micro-entrepreneur at Work
Margaret Saajjabi has built a successful business from very small beginnings. She once sold soap and soda. Now she rents out space to other micro-entrepreneurs.

The Country of Botswana

Botswana is a sparsely populated country in the center of Southern Africa. Gabarone is its capital and largest city. The city is located on the border between Botswana and South Africa.

21.5 Cooking Up Comfort Food in Botswana

Kgosi lives and works in Gabarone. This busy city is the capital of Botswana, a country in southern Africa. But Kgosi grew up in a rural village. At lunchtime, he used to long for a hot dish of *stampa* (shredded beef) or *papa* (mixed corn and beans). These are "comfort foods" that he grew up with. But the only restaurants near his workplace in Gabarone were fast-food chains.

One day Kgosi looked down the street and saw a colorfully painted caravan, or trailer. The sign above it read "Mama's Fast Food." Wonderful smells were drifting out of the caravan. Kgosi knew at once that the foods of his childhood were cooking inside.

A Used Trailer Becomes a Street-Side Restaurant Kgosi is typical of many people in Gabarone. They grew up in the country and then moved to the capital to find work. Most eat breakfast and lunch near their workplaces. This has created an opportunity for many women in the city. These micro-entrepreneurs have opened restaurants in caravans. The caravans are similar to vacation trailers that families in the United States might use to go camping.

A woman must do several things to open such a restaurant. First she needs to buy a caravan. Most are purchased in neighboring South Africa. Because of the cost of the caravans, women often have to borrow money from parents or family members. Others have to save money for years before they can buy one.

The caravan must then be converted into a restaurant. Most come with a small stove and a cooler already installed. The women hire someone to build shelves for dishes and racks to hold the gas tanks needed to fuel the stove.

Caravans Dish Up Popular Food

Most street-side restaurants seat people outside. Some caravans are big enough to seat people inside. Here, diners can enjoy a tasty meal of "comfort food."

Finally, a woman must find a place to park her caravan. Any place where many people work and shop is a good location. After choosing a good spot, the owner removes the caravan's wheels. The result is an instant street-side restaurant. At most caravans, people eat outside under a canvas canopy. They sit on plastic chairs at plastic patio tables to enjoy a meal that reminds them of home.

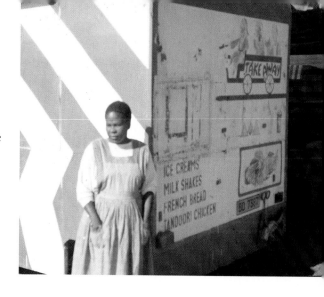

Creating Jobs Along with Food Successful caravan owners make enough money to repay their loans and expand their business. Some save up enough money to buy a small truck. This makes it easier to buy supplies in South Africa, where prices are usually lower.

As their businesses grow, some women are able to hire workers. Most are family members who help cook, clean, and transport supplies. Some micro-entrepreneurs also create opportunities for other women who want to start their own businesses. For example, a restaurant owner might prepare "box lunches" for another woman to sell in a different part of the city. The arrangement benefits both women.

The families of micro-entrepreneurs receive many benefits. Some relatives get jobs. Many women use the money they make to send their children to school. Some have even been able to buy land and build homes.

Micro-entrepreneurs are not only changing their communities. They are improving their nations, too. The people of Botswana and other African nations benefit from the new jobs that are created. New jobs help strengthen the economy and increase the nations' GDP.

Open for Business

Many women in Botswana have set up restaurants like this one. Often these restaurants are parked illegally on public streets.

21.6 Beginning to Think Globally

In this chapter, you learned that women in Africa face many challenges. Poverty is widespread. However, gender-based division of labor makes it hard for women to earn money. You have met micro-entrepreneurs who have started small businesses in the informal economy. Through their micro-enterprises, these women are helping to pull their families and communities out of poverty.

Women micro-entrepreneurs can be found in every country. Most face similar problems. One problem is finding the money needed to start a business. Often the amounts are small. Still, banks are generally unwilling to make loans to the poor.

Many groups have been formed to make small business loans to poor people. The average loan is usually less than $100. Because the amounts are so small, these groups are called *micro-credit organizations*.

Micro-credit organizations often make loans to groups of women. No one in the group can take out the next loan until everyone's first loan is repaid. The group makes sure each woman repays her loan. As you look at the map of micro-credit organizations in the next section, think about how these loans can change lives.

21.7 Global Connections

The map shows where micro-credit organizations make the most loans worldwide. You can learn about these loans in the table under the map.

In what parts of the world are micro-credit organizations most active? Why might this be so?
Micro-credit organizations are most active in Africa, Asia, and Latin America. Most banks in these regions do not make loans to poor people. Micro-credit organizations have stepped in to help poor people get start-up loans. More than 500 million people in developing countries own small businesses. Many of these micro-entrepreneurs got their start with small business loans.

Which gender gets the most micro-loans? Why might this be so? More than 70 percent of small business loans are made to women. In part, this is because women need the most help. The majority of people living in poverty are women and their children. Micro-credit organizations have also learned that women are a good risk. Ninety-five percent of women who get small loans pay the money back. Also, women are more likely than men to invest their earnings in their families and communities.

How do micro-credit organizations help women change their communities? Micro-credit organizations help people help themselves. When women begin to earn money, they can send their children to school. They create jobs and opportunities for other people in the community. In some countries, more than half the people who get micro-credit loans are able to rise out of poverty within 10 years.

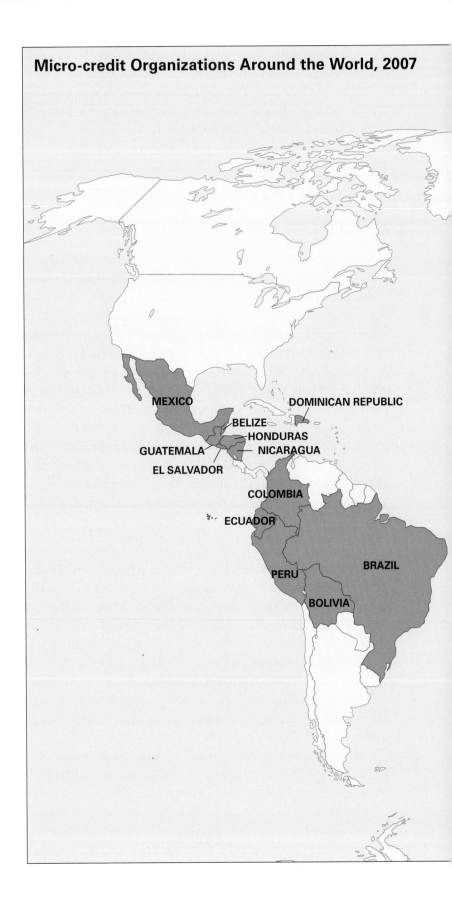

Micro-credit Organizations Around the World, 2007

MEXICO
DOMINICAN REPUBLIC
BELIZE
HONDURAS
GUATEMALA
NICARAGUA
EL SALVADOR
COLOMBIA
ECUADOR
BRAZIL
PERU
BOLIVIA

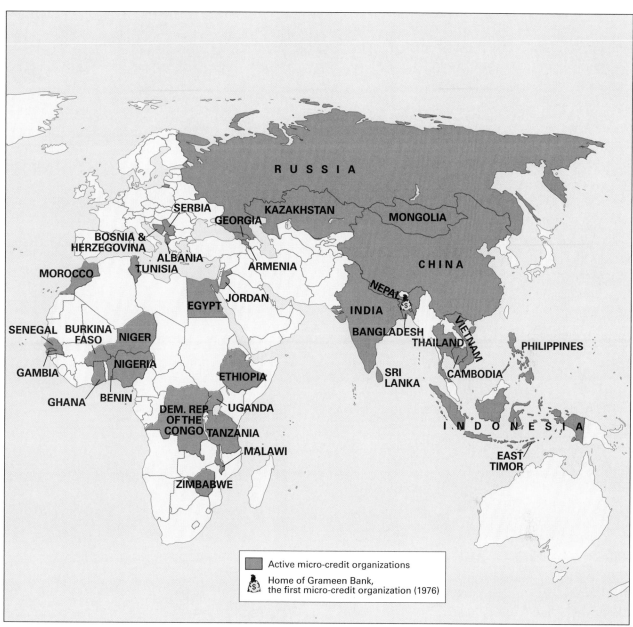

Source: Forbes.com.

Fast Facts About Micro-credit

More than 500 million people in developing countries run micro-enterprises.

Less than 3% of micro-entrepreneurs obtain loans from banks.

More than 3,500 micro-credit organizations served more than 150 million clients in 2007.

More than 95% of micro-entrepreneurs who get loans pay them back.

More than 70% of micro-loans are made to women.

More than 90% of the income earned by women from micro-loans is used to support their families.

About 40% of the income earned by men from micro-loans is used to support their families.

In some countries, more than 50% of micro-credit clients rise out of poverty within 10 years.

Nigeria: A Country of Many Cultures

22.1 Introduction

Long ago, people from many parts of Africa met to trade in the land now known as Nigeria. Nomads from the **desert** came to trade with forest people. They exchanged salt, cloth, and weapons for slaves, ivory, and kola nuts. Over time, many **ethnic groups** settled in this area. An ethnic group is a group of people who share a common culture. Each of these different groups kept its own identity and way of life.

Nigeria today has more than 250 ethnic groups living within its borders. Each group has its own name. Each speaks its own language. Together these groups create great **ethnic diversity** in Nigeria. No other country in Africa is home to such a wide variety of people, each with its own culture.

With such ethnic diversity, Nigeria can be a confusing place to study. To help examine a diverse area, geographers often divide it into **regions**. In Chapter 2, you learned that a region is an area defined by one or more characteristics that set it apart from other areas. One way to understand Nigeria is to divide it into **cultural regions**. Each region is set apart by the way of life of the people who live there.

In this chapter, you will explore the three main cultural regions of Nigeria. You will learn about the **physical features** of each region. You will meet the largest ethnic group living there. And you will learn about the region's culture and economy.

Essential Question	Graphic Organizer
How can dividing a diverse country into regions make it easier to understand? This map shows the African country of Nigeria. Notice that it is divided into three regions: northern, western, and eastern. Each region is home to one of Nigeria's three largest ethnic groups. Keep the map in mind as you try to answer the Essential Question.	Northern region Western region Eastern region

◀ A street market in Lagos, the largest city in Nigeria

Abuja: A New Capital City

The city of Lagos in western Nigeria was the country's first capital. In 1991, the capital moved to Abuja. The new capital is in the center of the country. Many people hoped the move would help to unite this diverse country.

Ethnic Groups of Nigeria

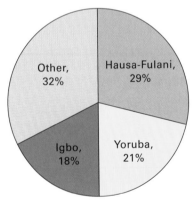

Source: Central Intelligence Agency.

Nigeria's Diversity

Nigeria has hundreds of ethnic groups, some large and some small. Within an ethnic group, more than one language may be spoken. As a result, there are more than 450 linguistic groups in this country.

22.2 The Geographic Setting

To find Nigeria on a map of Africa, follow its Atlantic coastline to the Gulf of Guinea. The country lies beside this large inlet of the sea. Two rivers form a Y inside Nigeria. Together they divide the country into three regions. The Benue River forms the right arm of the Y. It flows from east to west across the country. The Niger River forms the left arm and the stem of the Y. It flows from west to east to meet the Benue. After the two rivers meet, the Niger turns south to the sea.

From Many Ethnic Groups to One Country For most of its history, the area around the Niger River has been home to many peoples. Its hundreds of ethnic groups are further divided into **linguistic groups**. These are groups of people who share a distinct language.

In the mid-1800s, **colonialism** came to West Africa. Colonialism is a system in which one country rules other places as colonies. The ruling country controls trade with its colonies for its own benefit.

During this time, Great Britain took over areas of West Africa. In 1914, it joined parts of these areas to form the colony of Nigeria. As the ruling country, Britain gained control of Nigeria's **natural resources**. The most valuable of these were oil, tin, and gold. At the same time, Nigeria became a new market for many goods that were made in British factories.

Under British rule, some groups of people were treated better than others. These groups were more willing to cooperate with their colonial rulers. They got more education and the best jobs. Other groups resented the favored groups. They resented their British rulers as well.

Resentment finally led to demands for self-rule. Protestors marched in the streets and refused to work. As the protests grew, Britain found it harder to control Nigeria. On October 1, 1960, Nigeria became an independent country.

Ethnic and Religious Tensions Divide Nigeria After independence, Nigerians adopted a federal system of government. But conflict between ethnic groups made governing the country very difficult. A more stable government was finally elected in 1999. Today Nigeria is divided into 36 states. Each state has its own local laws. An elected president heads Nigeria's national government.

Cultural differences still divide Nigeria's many ethnic groups. Language is just one of these differences. The country has made English its official language. English is taught in schools across the country. However, each group still speaks its own language at home.

The people are also divided by their religious beliefs. Almost half follow the religion of Islam. Around two fifths are Christians. Many Nigerians also follow traditional beliefs. One of these beliefs is that all natural objects, such as trees and clouds, have spirits. Another belief is that the dead live on as spirits to guide and help the living in their journey through life.

▶ Geoterms

colonialism a system in which one country rules another area as a colony. The ruling country controls trade with its colony for its own benefit.

cultural region an area that is set apart from other places by the way of life of the people who live there

ethnic diversity a variety of people from different ethnic groups

linguistic group a group of people who share a common language

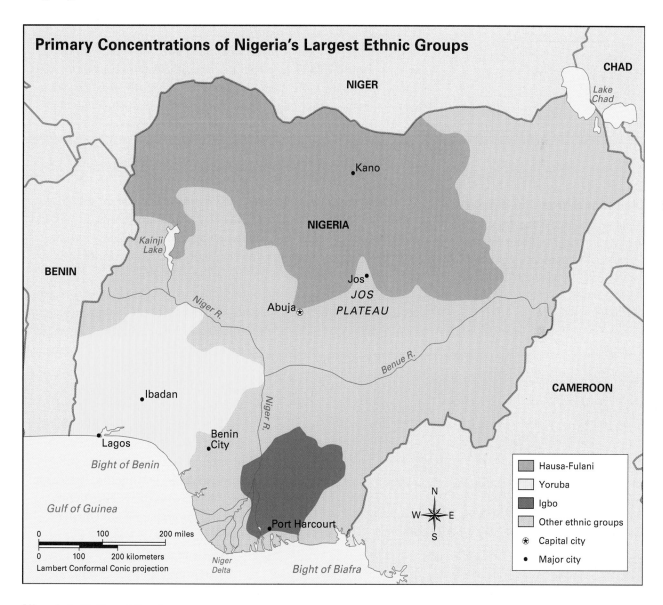

Primary Concentrations of Nigeria's Largest Ethnic Groups

Legend:
- Hausa-Fulani
- Yoruba
- Igbo
- Other ethnic groups
- ⊛ Capital city
- • Major city

Nigeria's Cultural Regions

This map shows the primary cultural regions of Nigeria's three largest ethnic groups. Members of each group also live in other parts of the country. About 32 percent of Nigerians belong to hundreds of smaller ethnic groups.

22.3 Life in Northern Nigeria

One of the first things a geographer notices about northern Nigeria is how dry it is. In many places, women walk for miles each day to get water. During the six-month dry season, little rain falls. Some rivers dry up completely. Lakes shrink so much that a 5-mile walk for water in the wet season can become a 10-mile walk in the dry season.

Physical Environment: A Land of Little Water Much of northern Nigeria is high, flat plains. Grasses and thorn trees covered the plains before people cleared the land to farm. The Jos Plateau rises up out of the plains. The weather there is cooler and wetter than on the plains below. Many people live and farm on this high ground.

Lake Chad is an important source of water for many people in the region. Over the last 40 years, however, the lake has been shrinking. In the 1960s, Lake Chad covered as much as 4,000 square miles in its driest season. By 2000, as a result of **drought** and increased use of its water for irrigation, the lake was less than one tenth that size. Some geographers fear that Lake Chad could dry up completely.

A powerful wind, called the *harmattan,* also affects life in the north. The harmattan blows south from the Sahara between October and March. It coats everything with fine, gritty sand.

Dust Clouds from the Harmattan
October to March is the dry season in northern Nigeria. Winds from the Sahara blow hot across the land. People call this wind the *harmattan.* It brings huge dust storms to the northern region.

Ethnic Groups: The Hausa and Fulani The two largest ethnic groups in northern Nigeria are the Hausa and the Fulani. The Hausa came to this region about 1,000 years ago. Their villages grew into important trading centers and, eventually, kingdoms. In the 1200s, the Fulani also began to settle in northern Nigeria.

Over time, people from both groups married and created a connected culture. As a result, some people refer to the two groups as the Hausa-Fulani. But there are differences between them. One is language. About a third of Nigerians speak Hausa. Traditional Fulani speak Fulfulde, a less common language.

The two groups also differ in where they live. The Hausa tend to be more **urban**. Most Fulani still live in **rural** areas. During the dry season, they travel with their cattle herds, looking for grazing land. During the rainy season, the Fulani live in villages and plant crops.

The Hausa and the Fulani are united by their faith. Both groups are Muslim. In contrast, many other groups in Nigeria are Christian. Tension between Muslims and Christians has grown in recent years.

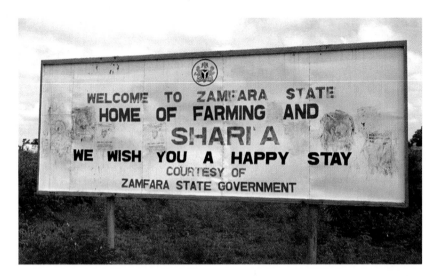

Religious Conflict
Muslims are a majority in northern Nigeria. Some states there base their legal system on shari'a, or Islamic laws. This has caused conflict between Muslims and Christians. From the mid-1990s to 2008, it is estimated that around 50,000 people were killed in religious clashes.

One reason is that some states have chosen to make **shari'a,** or traditional Islamic laws, the basis of their legal system. These laws cover many aspects of daily life, like marriage and divorce. Non-Muslims often resent having to live under laws that do not agree with their religious beliefs.

Culture: Thatched Roofs and Kalangu Drums Northern Nigeria's hot **climate** affects the kinds of homes people build. In the city, most houses have flat roofs. People may sleep on their roofs on hot nights. In the country, people build round homes out of mud and cover them with roofs woven out of reeds or palm leaves. These materials provide good shelter from the sun.

Northern Nigerians favor loose clothes that protect them from the sun. Men wear floor-length robes over baggy cotton pants. The front of the robe is often heavily embroidered. They also wear an Arab-style hat called a *fez*. Women also wear robes that cover the entire body. Some women wear a cloth headdress. Muslim women wear a *hijab*, or headscarf, that covers the hair and neck. Some also wear a veil that hides most of the face.

Tension drums are a popular traditional instrument. They are made from wood, with an animal skin stretched tightly over the drum's top. The Hausa tension drum is called a *kalangu*. It makes sounds like those heard in Hausa speech.

Economy: Farming, Herding, and Trading Many northern Nigerians make their living as farmers and herders. Hausa farmers grow crops such as corn and millet, a kind of grain. They eat some of what they produce and sell the rest in local village markets. Fulani herders make their living by selling milk or products made from milk, like butter, to villagers. They rarely kill cows to sell as meat.

The Hausa have traditionally made beautiful cloth and leather goods. People once came from all over Africa to buy Hausa crafts. Some Hausa also work as traders and merchants. They sell traditional crafts and factory-made goods to local people and tourists.

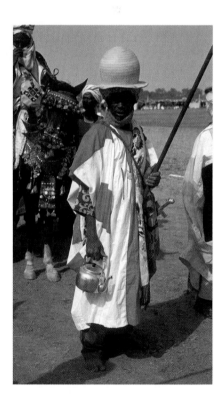

Traditional Hausa Dress
The Hausa people have long been known for their richly embroidered robes. Until recently, the embroidery was done by men. Today, women also do this work. Some Hausa women sell their robes to buyers in the United States.

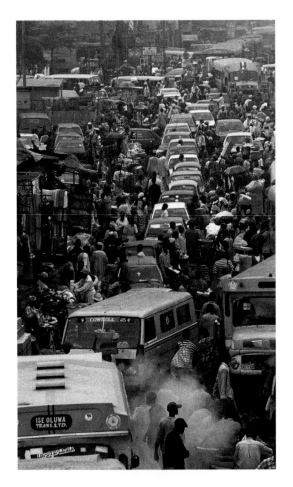

22.4 Life in Western Nigeria

It is rush hour in Lagos, the largest city in Africa. The streets are packed with cars, buses, trucks, and bicycles. The city is famous for its "go-slows," or traffic jams. Young boys crowd around the stopped vehicles. They sell everything from smoked fish to brushes. Girls also sell things while balancing bags of water on their heads. They offer drinks, nuts, candy, and even watches and makeup to the frustrated drivers.

The Physical Environment: Rainforest to Savanna

Western Nigeria sits on the Gulf of Guinea beside a wide bay called the Bight of Benin. The Niger River forms the northern and eastern borders of this part of Nigeria.

Before people settled in this area, a **tropical rainforest** grew along the coastline. Over time, most of the forest was cleared for farming or cut to sell as timber. Much of western Nigeria is a **savanna**. This broad, flat land is covered with tall grasses and scattered trees.

Twenty years ago, almost everyone in this region lived in villages. Since then, many have moved to cities to seek work. By 2008, about half of all Nigerians lived in cities. About a fifth of these city dwellers lived in western Nigeria's two largest cities, Lagos and Ibadan.

A "Go-Slow" in Lagos

Many cities in Nigeria are famous for their traffic jams. Cars, buses, trucks, and bicycles crowd the streets during rush hour. These "go-slows" create a marketplace for thousands of street vendors. They weave through stopped cars and trucks selling drinks, nuts, sweets, and other goods.

Ethnic Groups: The Yoruba The Yoruba make up the largest ethnic group in western Nigeria. Many Yoruba are Christian, although some follow Islam or traditional beliefs.

The Yoruba first came to Nigeria around 100 B.C.E. They lived in villages that grew into kingdoms. Each Yoruba kingdom had its own king. Each also had its own **dialect**. A dialect is a version of a language that is spoken in a specific area. A person from one Yoruba kingdom might not easily understand the dialect spoken in another kingdom. In recent years, Yoruba dialects have become more similar. Today, about one fifth of Nigerians speak forms of Yoruba.

Culture: Tin Roofs, Beadwork, and Royal Statues Many Yoruba have moved from the countryside to one of western Nigeria's cities. Those who are well-off live in one-story houses or in apartments. The poor live in shacks that are clustered on the outskirts of cities. These **shantytowns** lack electricity, running water, and garbage service.

In the countryside, the Yoruba live in houses made of mud bricks. The typical home is topped with a steeply sloped roof of tin or iron. During hot weather, the overhanging roof provides shelter from the sun. During the wet season, people put buckets under the edge of their roofs to collect rainwater.

The Yoruba are known for their colorful cloth and beadwork. The cloth is woven by Yoruba women and sold at markets in the cities. Yoruba kings wear beautiful robes covered with beads. In fact, every object made for a king is beaded, from his shoes to his crown. Yoruba crowns have beaded birds perched on them. The birds look as if they were suddenly going to fly away. Yoruba crowns also have a beaded fringe to hide the identity of the king.

Much of Yoruba art has been made to honor their long line of kings. Yoruba artists create fancy wood masks for their kings. They also make bronze or clay statues to represent kings who have died.

Like the Hausa, the Yoruba are also known for their drums. One tension drum, called a *dundun,* is shaped like an hourglass. It is wide at the top and bottom and skinny in the middle. It imitates some of the sounds of the Yoruba's spoken language.

Economy: Farms, Factories, and Markets Those Yoruba who live in cities hold a variety of jobs. Some work in factories. Others work in offices. Still others are teachers, engineers, or doctors.

Some urban Yoruba commute back to the country to work on small family farms. This is the reverse of what many Nigerians do, which is to commute from the country to the city.

Yoruba women often make money selling goods in street markets. They sell food, like yams, from their farms. They also sell homemade cloth, baskets, and other goods that tourists might want to buy.

Yoruba Beadwork
This Yoruba crown is covered with beadwork. In earlier times, colorful glass beads were very valuable.

Waiting for a Ride
These Yoruba women are waiting for a ride to take them to the market where they will sell their yams. Yams, like potatoes, are a root crop. They are an important part of the Yoruba diet.

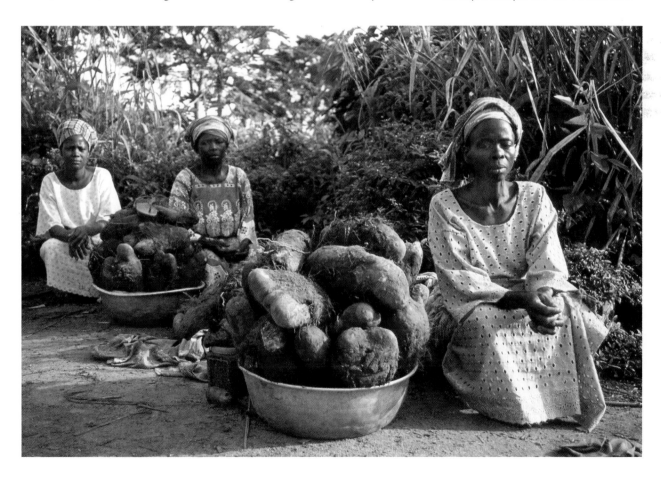

22.5 Life in Eastern Nigeria

For centuries, the Niger River was an important source of fish for the people of eastern Nigeria. Then oil was found in the river's **delta**. Today, **pollution** from oil spills has killed most of the fish in the delta. For all of the wealth oil brings, it has made life hard for eastern Nigerians who used to depend on the river for water and food.

Physical Environment: Rivers and Rich Resources Eastern Nigeria sits on the Gulf of Guinea beside a second bay known as the Bight of Biafra. The Benue River forms the northern edge of the region. The Niger River forms the western edge.

This region receives more rainfall than other parts of Nigeria. Long ago, there were rainforests here. But people have cut down most of the trees to sell as timber. Today, swamps line the coast.

The Niger River has built up a large delta where it enters the Gulf of Guinea. The Niger Delta is one of the world's largest **wetlands**. It also has Nigeria's large oil deposits.

Ethnic Groups: The Igbo The Igbo (pronounced *ee-bo*) are the largest ethnic group in eastern Nigeria. They settled here thousands of years ago. Unlike the Yoruba, they did not develop kingdoms. Instead, they lived in villages, each ruled by a council of elders.

Each village spoke its own dialect of the Igbo language. There are more than 300 of these dialects. Some, however, may soon disappear. Although about 18 percent of Nigerians are Igbo, only about 1 percent speak dialects of Igbo. The rest speak English as their first language.

During colonial times, the Igbo worked with British missionaries and officials. Most became Christian. Many were educated at church schools. The British rewarded them with jobs in business and government throughout the colony.

After Nigeria became independent, things did not go well for the Igbo. Other ethnic groups resented their power. Igbo who had migrated to other regions were killed by the thousands. At least a million more Igbo fled in terror back to their home region. They remained deeply suspicious of their neighbors to the north and west.

In 1967, the Igbo tried to break away from Nigeria. Their goal was to form a country of their own called Biafra. The Nigerian government sent troops to the region to stop the breakaway. Hundreds of thousands died in the war that followed. In 1970, Nigeria was once more united. But memories of the war are still fresh in the minds of many Igbo.

Ethnic Conflict in Nigeria
These people are celebrating the end of Nigeria's civil war. The war began when the Igbo tried to leave Nigeria in 1967 to form their own country. Their rebellion ended 31 months later. More than a million Nigerians died as a result of fighting, hunger, and disease brought about by this conflict.

Culture: Houses on Stilts, Colorful Wraps, and Masked Dancers In the cities, the Igbo build houses using mud bricks. Metal roofs protect the houses from heavy rains. In swampy areas, people build their houses on stilts. During the rainy season, they paddle canoes to their homes and climb ladders to get inside.

Igbo wear colorful cloths. Igbo women wear one cloth wrapped around the lower body and another around the head. Men wrap cloth around the lower body. The traditional hat for men is a small cap.

Across Africa, people create masks for ceremonies. Masked dancing is popular among the Igbo. They make masks of wood or leather and decorate them with teeth, hair, fur, and other materials. The Igbo design their masks in secret and keep them hidden until they wear them. That way, the masks remain mysterious and important.

Economy: Oil and Education
Farming used to be Nigeria's main economic activity. Today it is oil. Most of Nigeria's wealth comes from selling oil to other countries.

But foreign oil companies are in charge of the country's oil industry. They are much like the past colonial powers. They still control areas of the country. They take most of the oil profits. They also have a good deal of political power. In the past, these companies also brought in foreign workers instead of hiring local people.

Nigeria's government has changed some of these practices. Today, many Igbo work in the oil industry. But Nigeria does not benefit as much as it could from its oil.

The Igbo have also used education to make their lives better. During colonial times, many Igbo went to college. Their children and grandchildren now work in Nigeria as doctors, lawyers, and teachers.

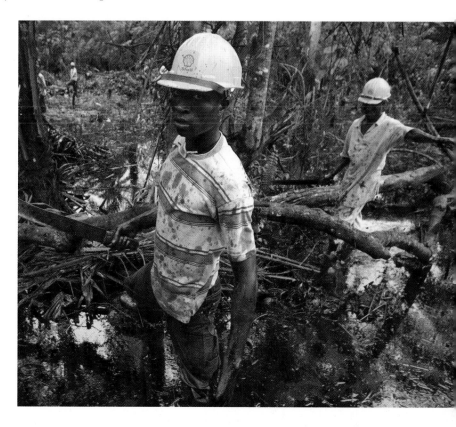

Cleaning Up After an Oil Spill
These workers are cleaning up after an oil spill in the Niger Delta. More than 4,000 spills have occurred in this region since oil production began in the 1950s.

22.6 Beginning to Think Globally

In this chapter, you learned about Nigeria and its ethnic diversity. You explored the country's three main cultural regions. You read about some problems that face a country with so many ethnic and linguistic groups.

Ethnic conflict is a problem in many places. In Africa, ethnic tensions were made worse by colonialism. The colonial powers established most of Africa's present-day national boundaries. But they gave little thought to how groups within a country might get along. Think about this as you look at the map of African ethnic groups in the next section.

22.7 Global Connections

The small map shows how Africa was divided into colonies in 1914. The large map shows Africa today. The red lines indicate where people of various ethnic groups live. The black lines are country borders.

Why do most African countries have so many cultural regions?

In Africa, it is rare for ethnic boundaries and political boundaries to match. Most African countries were created during colonial times. European countries divided Africa into colonies to suit their own needs. They did not think much about tensions between groups living in the same colony.

What problems do countries with many cultural regions face?

Countries with many cultural regions have found it hard to choose a national language. Each group wants its own language to be chosen. To prevent conflict, many former colonies ruled by Britain or France have chosen English or French as their common language. Ethnic conflict is another serious problem. Some groups have a long history of disagreements. Old hatreds have often erupted into war.

What are some ways governments might reduce cultural conflicts?

One way of reducing cultural conflict is to promote a common identity for everyone. In Nigeria, for example, this means persuading people to think of themselves as Nigerians first and as part of an ethnic group second. Another way is to give local governments more power. In this way, each group can shape the laws in its own area to suit its way of life.

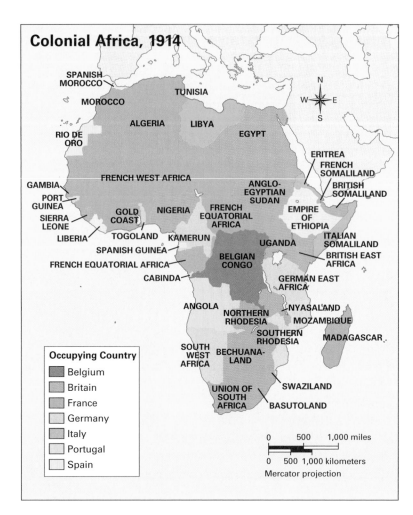

The Colonization of Africa

Around 1500, European countries began setting up trading posts in Africa. By the 1800s, Europeans were competing fiercely for control of Africa and its resources. They divided most of Africa into the colonies shown on this map. Resistance to colonial rule grew over time. Between 1950 and 1980, 47 African colonies gained their independence.

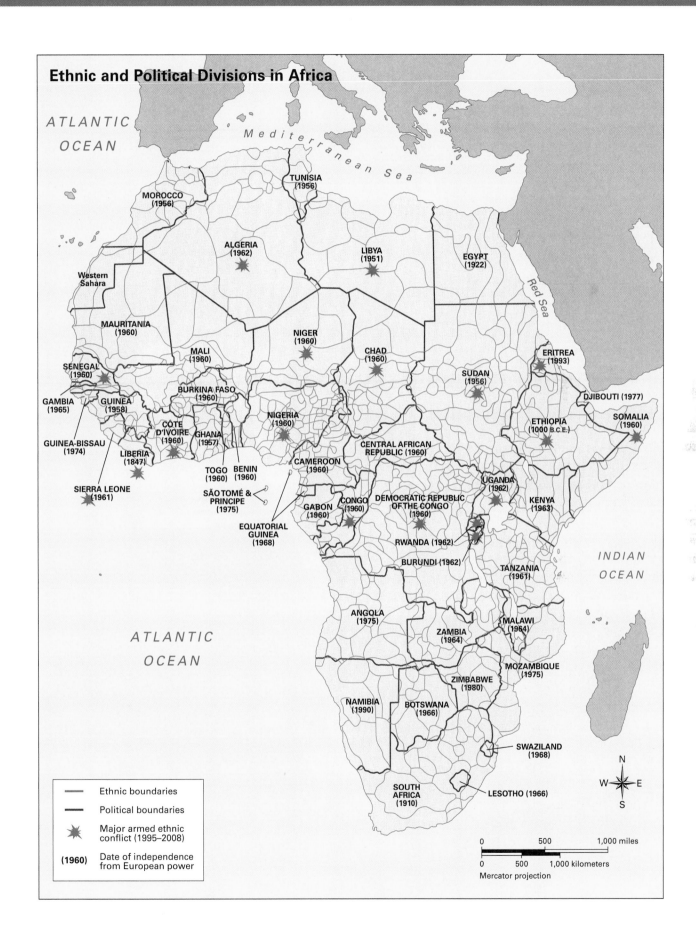

Ethnic and Political Divisions in Africa

ATLANTIC OCEAN

Mediterranean Sea

TUNISIA (1956)

MOROCCO (1956)

ALGERIA (1962)

LIBYA (1951)

EGYPT (1922)

Western Sahara

Red Sea

MAURITANIA (1960)

NIGER (1960)

CHAD (1960)

SUDAN (1956)

ERITREA (1993)

MALI (1960)

DJIBOUTI (1977)

SENEGAL (1960)

GAMBIA (1965)

GUINEA (1958)

BURKINA FASO (1960)

NIGERIA (1960)

SOMALIA (1960)

GUINEA-BISSAU (1974)

CÔTE D'IVOIRE (1960)

GHANA (1957)

CENTRAL AFRICAN REPUBLIC (1960)

ETHIOPIA (1000 B.C.E.)

LIBERIA (1847)

TOGO (1960)

BENIN (1960)

CAMEROON (1960)

UGANDA (1962)

KENYA (1963)

SIERRA LEONE (1961)

SÃO TOMÉ & PRINCIPE (1975)

GABON (1960)

CONGO (1960)

DEMOCRATIC REPUBLIC OF THE CONGO (1960)

EQUATORIAL GUINEA (1968)

RWANDA (1962)

BURUNDI (1962)

TANZANIA (1961)

INDIAN OCEAN

ANGOLA (1975)

MALAWI (1964)

ZAMBIA (1964)

ATLANTIC OCEAN

MOZAMBIQUE (1975)

ZIMBABWE (1980)

NAMIBIA (1990)

BOTSWANA (1966)

SWAZILAND (1968)

SOUTH AFRICA (1910)

LESOTHO (1966)

N W E S

Ethnic boundaries

Political boundaries

Major armed ethnic conflict (1995–2008)

(1960) Date of independence from European power

0   500   1,000 miles

0   500   1,000 kilometers

Mercator projection

Resources and Power in Post-apartheid South Africa

23.1 Introduction

The tall, gray-haired man walked up to the ballot box. At 76 years old, he looked strong, fit, and determined. With a warm smile, he pushed his ballot into the box. Like other blacks in South Africa, he was being allowed to vote in an election for the first time. This elderly man was not just anyone, however. He was Nelson Mandela. And when all the votes were counted, Mandela was the newly elected president of South Africa.

South Africa is a **multiracial** society. This is a society that is made up of many **ethnic groups**. South Africa has four major ethnic groups. South Africans call the four groups blacks, whites, coloreds, and Asians. Before that election day in 1994, black South Africans could not vote or hold office.

For nearly 50 years, whites had ruled South Africa under a policy called **apartheid**. The word *apartheid* means "separateness." Under apartheid, whites and nonwhites lived apart from each other. This policy of racial **segregation** hurt nonwhite ethnic groups. They had fewer economic resources than whites. They also had less political power.

In this chapter, you will learn about life in South Africa under apartheid. You will find out how the **distribution,** or division, of power and resources changed after the end of apartheid. Finally, you will read about some of the challenges facing the people of South Africa today.

Essential Question

How might ethnic group differences affect who controls resources and power in a society?

This circle graph shows four main ethnic groups in South Africa in 2008. Note the size of the white ethnic group. Until 1994, this group controlled most of the nation's wealth and power. Keep this graph in mind as you try to answer the Essential Question.

Graphic Organizer

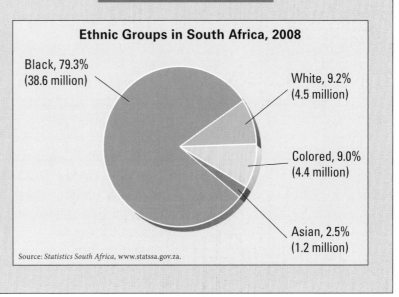

Ethnic Groups in South Africa, 2008

Black, 79.3% (38.6 million)

White, 9.2% (4.5 million)

Colored, 9.0% (4.4 million)

Asian, 2.5% (1.2 million)

Source: *Statistics South Africa*, www.statssa.gov.za.

◀ "Whites Only" signs were common under apartheid.

Farming in South Africa
South Africa has two main types of farming. White farmers raise cash crops on large modern farms. Black farm families produce food mainly for their own needs on small plots of land.

23.2 The Geographic Setting

South Africa is located at the southern tip of Africa. Compared with many African countries, it is small in land area. But it is the most developed African country. Only about 5 percent of Africans live in South Africa. Yet it produces two fifths of Africa's factory goods and about half of its minerals. South Africa also produces about a fifth of the continent's farm products.

A Land Rich in Natural Resources Much of South Africa's wealth is built on mineral resources. It has large deposits of gold, copper, and other valuable minerals. The development of these resources has made South Africa an economic powerhouse.

South Africa's mild **climate** and rich soil are also valuable resources. Many **cash crops** grow well here, including corn, wheat, and sugarcane. Cattle, sheep, and goats graze on vast ranch lands.

South Africa has a great variety of **wildlife**. In the past, these animals were important for groups of people who lived by hunting. In recent years, wildlife has become a tourist attraction. Visitors come from all over the world to see elephants, lions, zebras, and other animals in their natural **habitats**.

The Development of a Multiracial Society People have lived in what is now South Africa for a very long time. The ancestors of most South African blacks came from Central Africa. They probably migrated south about 2,000 years ago. This large ethnic group is made up of many smaller groups, each with its own language and culture.

Europeans began to settle in Southern Africa in 1652. Dutch colonists came first. They were called *Boers,* the Dutch word for "farmers." Their settlement was called Cape Colony. In time, settlers from other parts of Europe joined the Boers. Dutch remained the language of the colonists. But it picked up many words from other settlers and from black Africans. The result was a new language called Afrikaans. The white colonists who spoke this language came to be known as Afrikaners.

Settlers from Great Britain began to arrive in Cape Colony around 1820. Most were farmers. In 1867, a rich diamond field was discovered in the colony. A few years later, gold was found. These discoveries attracted more colonists. Descendents of Afrikaners and British colonists make up South Africa's white ethnic group.

Over time, some blacks and whites in Cape Colony married and had families. The children from these mixed marriages were described as colored. Today their descendents form South Africa's third major ethnic group, the coloreds.

Asians first came to South Africa in the 1860s. Most were from India, which was then a British colony. They came to work for British colonists on their sugarcane plantations. Their descendents in South Africa are still called Asians. They form the last major ethnic group in this multiracial society.

▶ Geoterms

apartheid the former official South African policy of separating people according to race. Apartheid gave most of the political and economic power to whites.

distribution the way people or things are spread out over an area or space. This term can also refer to the way resources, power, or goods are divided among people or groups.

multiracial made up of people from several ethnic groups

segregation the separation of one group of people from another, such as by race. Segregation can involve laws or customs that require different groups to use different facilities and live in separate areas.

Mines, Farms, and Factories

South Africa is Africa's most developed country. Its mines produce more gold than any other country. Its farms grow enough food to feed its people. Its factories produce everything from clothing to cars. This wealth is not, however, evenly distributed among its four main ethnic groups.

Economic Activity of South Africa

Land Use
- Commercial farming
- Nomadic herding
- Livestock raising
- Commercial fishing
- Forestry
- Trade and manufacturing
- Little or no activity

Resources
- Coal
- Diamonds
- Iron
- Precious metals (gold, silver, copper)
- Uranium

BOTSWANA
MOZAMBIQUE
SWAZILAND
NAMIBIA
SOUTH AFRICA
LESOTHO
INDIAN OCEAN
ATLANTIC OCEAN

0   200   400 mi.
0   200   400 km
Conic projection

23.3 South Africa During Apartheid

South Africa's colonial period ended in 1910. That year, the Union of South Africa became an independent country. The new country's constitution gave whites complete power over the government.

Apartheid Makes Segregation an Official Policy Segregation became a way of life in South Africa after independence. Then, in 1948, ruling whites took this practice a step further. They made apartheid an official government policy.

Under the new apartheid laws, South Africans were classified by race. Whites and nonwhites were kept separate from one another. They lived in segregated neighborhoods. They went to different schools, hospitals, movie theaters, and restaurants. They were separated on trains and buses. Signs appeared on public beaches and in parks announcing "For White Persons Only."

Apartheid Treats Each Ethnic Group Differently Under apartheid, whites in South Africa lived well. They had the best schools, the best jobs, the best health care, and the best living conditions. They ran the government and the economy.

Asians and coloreds were treated as second-class citizens. They did not have the same job opportunities as whites. Their schools were inferior to those of whites. Their political rights were limited as well.

No group, however, was treated as poorly as blacks. Many black families were forced to move to poor **rural** areas called *homelands*. There were few jobs or resources in these areas. Homeland schools were very poor. There was little access to health care.

Blacks were not allowed to move freely throughout the country. They could leave their homelands to work in distant cities. But those who did were forced to live in **townships**. These were **slums** just outside the cities. A typical township home was a shack with no water or electricity. During the day, black workers went to their jobs in the "white" cities. At night, they had to return to the townships.

Homelands in South Africa During Apartheid

Segregated Homelands

Beginning in the 1960s, South Africa's government forced more than 4 million blacks to move to segregated homelands. The government claimed that the move was to give blacks self-rule. But for the most part, the lands were barren.

Soweto: A Black Township

Soweto is the largest black township in South Africa. It is located near Johannesburg, the country's most important city. Today, housing in Soweto ranges from shacks to mansions. During apartheid, the township was a center of protest.

23.4 Protests Lead to Political Change

Long before apartheid, blacks had formed groups to protest unfair treatment by whites. The most important, the African National Congress (ANC), was formed in 1912. "The white people of this country have formed what is known as the Union of South Africa," said one of the group's founders, "a union in which we have no voice in the making of the laws." It would take the ANC decades of protest to gain that voice for blacks.

The Fight Against Apartheid The ANC led the struggle against apartheid. In 1952, it began its "Campaign for the Defiance of Unjust Laws." An ANC lawyer named Nelson Mandela took charge of this fight to end apartheid laws. In 1962, Mandela was sent to jail for his protest activities. He remained in prison for the next 27 years.

The struggle continued. At times it also turned deadly. The worst violence began in the township of Soweto in 1976. On a June morning, 10,000 students gathered for a protest march. The police tried to break up the crowd. Some students threw rocks in response. The police opened fire. By the end of the day, 172 protesters lay dead. The protests quickly spread to other townships. Nearly 600 people had died by the time the demonstrations were finally crushed.

Some whites, coloreds, and Asians in South Africa joined the struggle. People around the world protested as well. Many countries refused to trade with South Africa until it ended apartheid. Mandela became the world's most famous prisoner. The United Nations called for his release from jail.

Apartheid Ends and Blacks Gain Political Power In 1989, an Afrikaner named F. W. de Klerk became president of South Africa. In the past, de Klerk had supported segregation. But later he decided that South Africa would never be at peace until apartheid ended. He quickly freed Mandela and other political prisoners. By 1991, South Africa's apartheid laws had been ended.

In 1993, de Klerk and Mandela were awarded the Nobel Peace Prize. This is a prize given each year to those who have done the most to bring peace to the world. The two South Africans were honored for their work to end apartheid.

A year later, all South Africans could both vote and run for office. As a result, the distribution of political power changed. The ANC became South Africa's most powerful political party. Its leader, Nelson Mandela, became the country's first black president.

Under Mandela's leadership, South Africa established the Truth and Reconciliation Commission. *Reconciliation* means the ending of conflict between groups. The commission investigated many unjust acts that took place under apartheid. South Africans saw this as a needed step toward healing the wounds left by those acts. As Bishop Desmond Tutu, the head of the commission, explained, "You cannot forgive what you do not know."

Waiting to Vote

These people are waiting to vote in South Africa's 1994 election. This event was the first time people of all colors could vote for their national leaders. Some new voters walked for miles and stood in line for hours to cast their first ballot.

Voter Turnout in South Africa

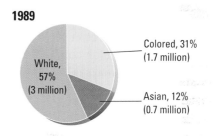

1989

White, 57% (3 million)
Colored, 31% (1.7 million)
Asian, 12% (0.7 million)

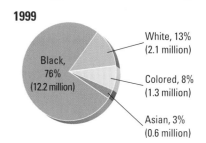

1999

Black, 76% (12.2 million)
White, 13% (2.1 million)
Colored, 8% (1.3 million)
Asian, 3% (0.6 million)

Sources: *Election '99: South Africa from Mandela to Mbeki,* Andrew Reynolds, ed., New York: St. Martin's Press, 1999. *South African Institute of Race Relations,* http://www.sairr.org.za/.

Changes in Voting

These graphs show who voted during and after apartheid. In 1989, whites made up more than half of all voters. This gave them control of the government. By 1999, all South Africans were voting. With this change, political power shifted to black South Africans.

Unemployed South Africans

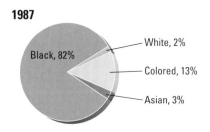

1987

Black, 82%
White, 2%
Colored, 13%
Asian, 3%

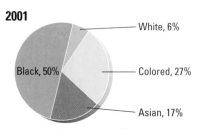

2001

White, 6%
Black, 50%
Colored, 27%
Asian, 17%

Sources: *South Africa, 1989–1990: Official Yearbook of the Republic of South Africa*, 15th ed., Pretoria: Bureau of Information, 1990. PBS, "Wideangle."

Out of Work

South Africa has suffered from years of slow economic growth. This has caused a rise in unemployment, or joblessness. These circle graphs show unemployment by ethnic groups during and after apartheid. What changes do you see?

Poverty Comes in All Colors

This white family is part of South Africa's growing number of people living in poverty. Some South Africans, both white and nonwhite, have done very well since the end of apartheid. But the poor seem worse off than ever.

23.5 South Africa Today: Job Opportunities

In 2001, for the first time ever, blacks took home more than half of all the income earned by South Africans. Before then, whites had always earned the most money. Yet this fact does not tell the whole story. As you know, there are far more blacks than whites in South Africa. This means that blacks still earned far less **per capita** than whites.

Government Programs Open Up Job Opportunities During apartheid, whites got the best jobs. They also earned the most money. When apartheid ended, the ANC-led government took steps to change the distribution of job opportunities. One step was to help blacks start businesses. By 2010, the government wants 25 percent of businesses in the country to be run by blacks.

In 1998, the government also passed the Employment Equity Act. This law opens job opportunities to all South Africans. It identifies groups that have been unfairly denied jobs in the past. These groups include blacks, coloreds, Asians, women, and the disabled. The law requires businesses to hire people from these groups when filling jobs. They must also pay all workers fairly.

The Employment Equity Act has opened to all groups jobs that were once limited to whites. At the same time, it has caused resentment among white job seekers. They argue that it is unfair to deny them jobs just because they are white.

Slow Economic Growth Hurts All Ethnic Groups Despite these changes, many South Africans still lack jobs. One reason for this is the slow growth of the economy. Not enough jobs are created each year to hire everyone who wants to work. In 2005, four out of 10 job seekers could not find work. Some of these job seekers were whites. But blacks, coloreds, and Asians are still more likely to be out of work than white South Africans.

Slow economic growth has also led to an increase in poverty. By 2005, half of all South Africans did not make enough money to take care of their basic needs. Many of the poor were struggling just to survive.

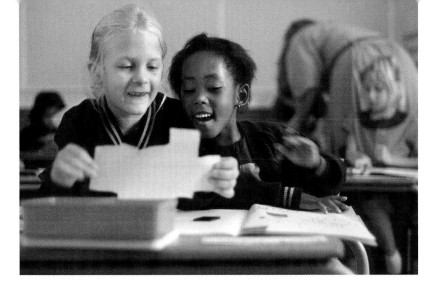

23.6 South Africa Today: Education

Any students attending a public school in South Africa today will learn not only reading and writing but also math and science. This was not always the case. During apartheid, there were separate schools for each ethnic group. Students who attended a black school did not study much science or math. This was not an accident. The government knew that people with math and science skills could get higher-paying jobs. By not teaching those skills to blacks, the government made sure that South Africa had a supply of cheap labor.

The Link Between Education and Opportunity In general, the more years of school a person has completed, the more money he or she makes as an adult. In South Africa, more than half of the adults with no education are poor. But only 5 percent of South Africans who have gone to college are poor.

During apartheid, nonwhites had limited educational opportunities. Their schools were poorly built. Their teachers were undertrained and not well paid. Children were supposed to go to school from the ages of 7 to 16. But this law was not enforced. More than 10 million nonwhite adults never went to high school. Over 4 million received no schooling at all.

Schools Are Now Open to All Ethnic Groups The end of apartheid brought big changes to education. The amount of money the government spends on schools has risen sharply. Also, students of all ethnic groups now attend the same public schools.

Schools in South Africa today are teaching the skills all students will need to get good jobs. There is a strong focus on science and math. Students of all groups are strongly encouraged to stay in school. As a result, the percentage of students who finish high school has risen in every ethnic group.

The number of nonwhites going to college has increased as well. This is true despite the fact that total college enrollment has been hurt by slow economic growth. As more nonwhite children receive college educations, their opportunities for good jobs will improve.

High School Graduates in South Africa

Source: PBS, "Wideangle."

Staying in School
More South Africans than ever are finishing high school. This graph shows the percentage of each ethnic group that graduated from high school in 1991 and 2001. For blacks and coloreds, the percentages more than doubled.

23.7 South Africa Today: Living Conditions

During apartheid, most whites in South Africa lived well. They had nice homes in the city. Their homes had electricity and running water. Many had swimming pools. Today, most whites still have those comforts. But they also have something they didn't have during apartheid: neighbors who are not white. A few nonwhites now live in the nice neighborhoods of South African cities.

Cities Are Becoming Less Segregated During apartheid, many South African cities were "whites only." Blacks could work there during the day. But they had to leave at night. After apartheid, people could live wherever they could afford housing. Some cities have become racially mixed as nonwhites have moved in.

Most nonwhites, however, cannot afford to live in nice city neighborhoods. The poor often settle in slums around the cities. Most homes in these slums are built out of scrap metal or wood. Few have running water or electricity. Often these poor areas become a breeding ground for crime.

Housing Conditions Are Improving South Africa's constitution guarantees decent housing to all citizens. In the first decade after apartheid, the government provided 1.6 million homes to poor South Africans. Efforts to create more housing for the poor are continuing.

The government is also working to improve **urban** slums. Streets have been paved in some poor areas. Water systems have been built to provide safe water. Streetlamps have been installed to combat crime. The government is starting to replace shacks with better housing. It is also starting to build schools, police stations, and health clinics in poor neighborhoods.

Health Care Remains Limited Along with housing, the government is working to improve health care. During apartheid, most doctors and hospitals were located in "white" cities. People in rural areas had a hard time finding health care. Although cities are no longer segregated, 9 out of 10 doctors still work in urban areas.

Today, South Africa is trying hard to bring health care to all. By 2005, the government had built more than 500 health clinics in rural areas. New doctors are asked to work for a year in a rural clinic. This helps to reduce the shortage of doctors outside cities. Pregnant women and children under six get free health care.

The need for health care has risen sharply with the spread of HIV/AIDS in South Africa. The human immunodeficiency virus (HIV) attacks the body's ability to fight disease. Acquired immune deficiency syndrome (AIDS) is the medical condition that results from an HIV infection. Victims of AIDS slowly grow weak and lose weight. Eventually, most die. There is no cure. But treatment can help people infected with the virus live longer.

South African Households with Electricity

Source: *Statistics South Africa*, http://www.statssa.gov.za/.

Power to Homes

As this graph shows, housing conditions are improving in South Africa. By 2001, more than 60 percent of blacks had electricity in their homes. Many blacks, however, still live in shacks on the edges of cities.

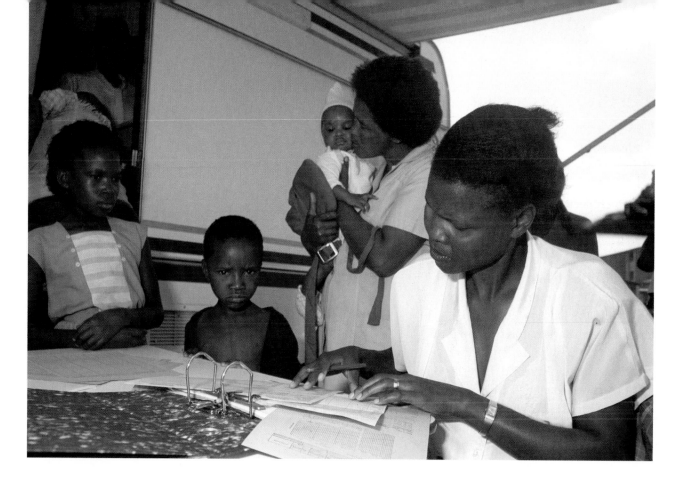

South Africa has the highest number of people living with HIV/AIDS in the world. By 2008, almost 6 million South Africans had become victims of this disease. Almost 1,000 people die from HIV/AIDS in that country every day. The loss of so many people presents a huge challenge to South Africa's hope for a better future.

23.8 Beginning to Think Globally

In this chapter, you learned about life in South Africa before, during, and after apartheid. You saw how segregation divided a multiracial society. You learned how the distribution of power and resources in the society changed over time. And you read about some of the challenges that face South Africa today.

One of those challenges is the continued spread of HIV/AIDS. When this disease first appeared in humans, no one knew how the virus was spread. Today, we know that the virus is found in blood and other body fluids. The virus is passed through the transfer of blood or other body fluids from person to person. It can also be passed from mother to child during pregnancy and birth.

South Africa is not the only country dealing with HIV/AIDS. The disease is a global health threat. In 2007, about 33 million people worldwide were living with HIV/AIDS. About 3 million people were newly infected with the virus that year. And around 2 million people died from the disease. Think about this as you look at the map of HIV/AIDS infection rates around the world in the next section.

Mobile Health Care

This mobile clinic brings health care to people living outside South African cities. Despite government efforts, health care remains poor in many areas. Because of the country's high rate of HIV infection, life expectancy in 2008 was just under 49 years.

23.9 Global Connections

This map shows the percentages of adults infected with the HIV/AIDS virus worldwide. Note the areas with no color. These are places where no one has collected information on the disease.

Why has Africa been more affected by HIV/AIDS than other regions? Scientists think the disease may have begun in Africa in the 1950s. This means the virus has been infecting people in this region for longer than in other parts of the world. Poverty has also contributed to the spread of the disease in Africa. Poor countries lack money for education programs that might slow the spread of the virus.

What factors have contributed to the global spread of HIV/AIDS? Unlike many diseases, AIDS develops slowly. The virus that causes the disease can hide in the body for years without the person knowing it. As a result, victims can transmit the infection without knowing they have it. Improved transportation is also a factor in its spread. Today, people travel easily from country to country. As they do so, they take the disease with them.

How might HIV/AIDS hurt the countries that are most severely affected? Most victims of the disease are working-age adults. The loss of these adults hurts a country in many ways. As people sicken and die, they leave the workforce. This can hurt a country's economy. They also leave children behind. Caring for many orphans is a burden for a poor country. If too many working-age people die, a country may be left with a population of the very old and very young.

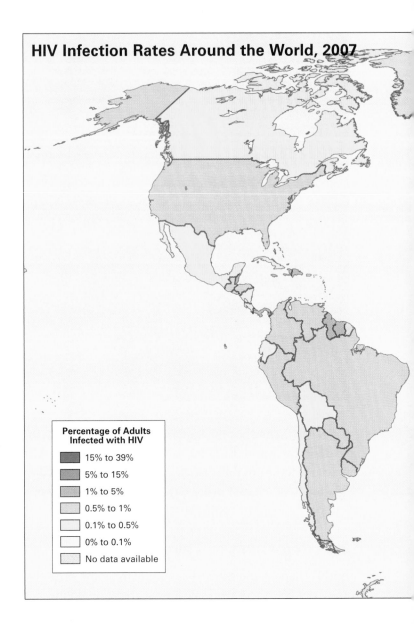

HIV Infection Rates Around the World, 2007

Percentage of Adults Infected with HIV

- 15% to 39%
- 5% to 15%
- 1% to 5%
- 0.5% to 1%
- 0.1% to 0.5%
- 0% to 0.1%
- No data available

An AIDS march in South Africa

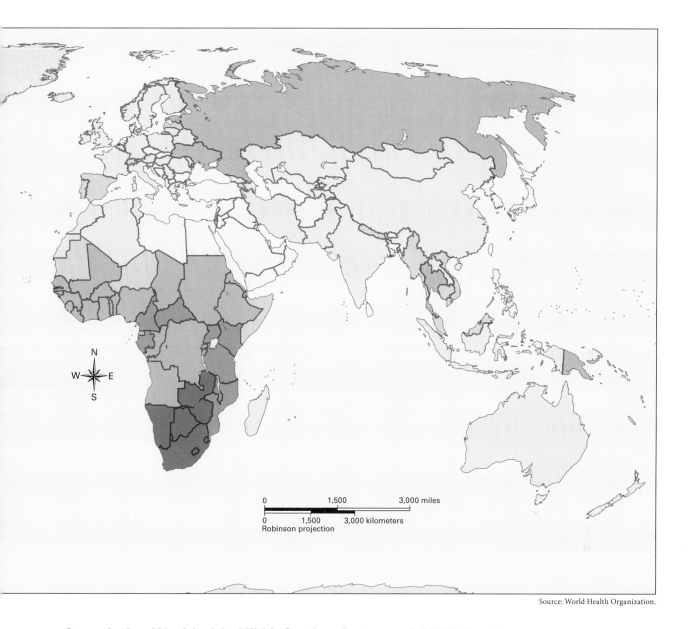

Source: World Health Organization.

Cumulative Worldwide HIV Infection Rates and AIDS Deaths

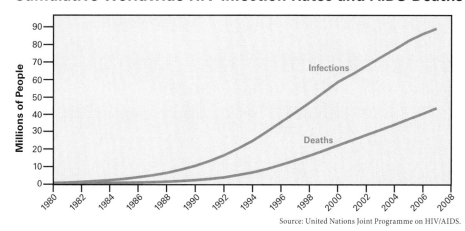

Infections

Deaths

Millions of People

Source: United Nations Joint Programme on HIV/AIDS.

The Impact of HIV/AIDS

This line graph shows the cumulative effect of HIV/AIDS. *Cumulative* means becoming larger with each addition. Since 1980, the cumulative number of people infected with HIV has risen as new cases are added each year. So has the cumulative number of people who have died from AIDS.

Resources and Power in Post-apartheid South Africa **345**

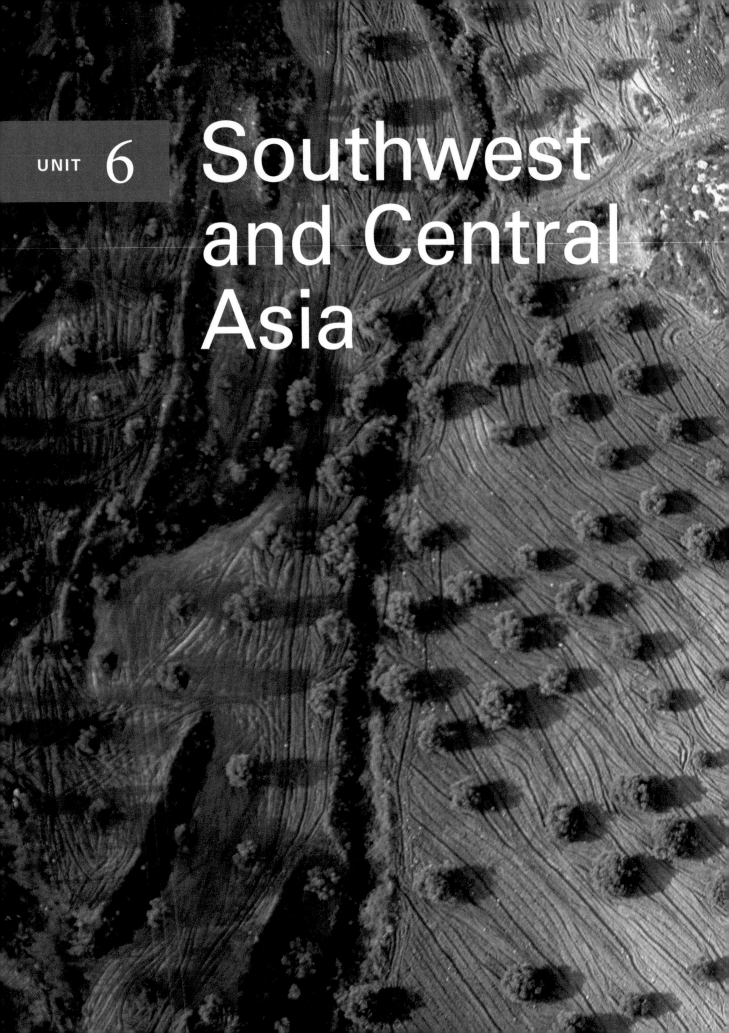

Southwest and Central Asia

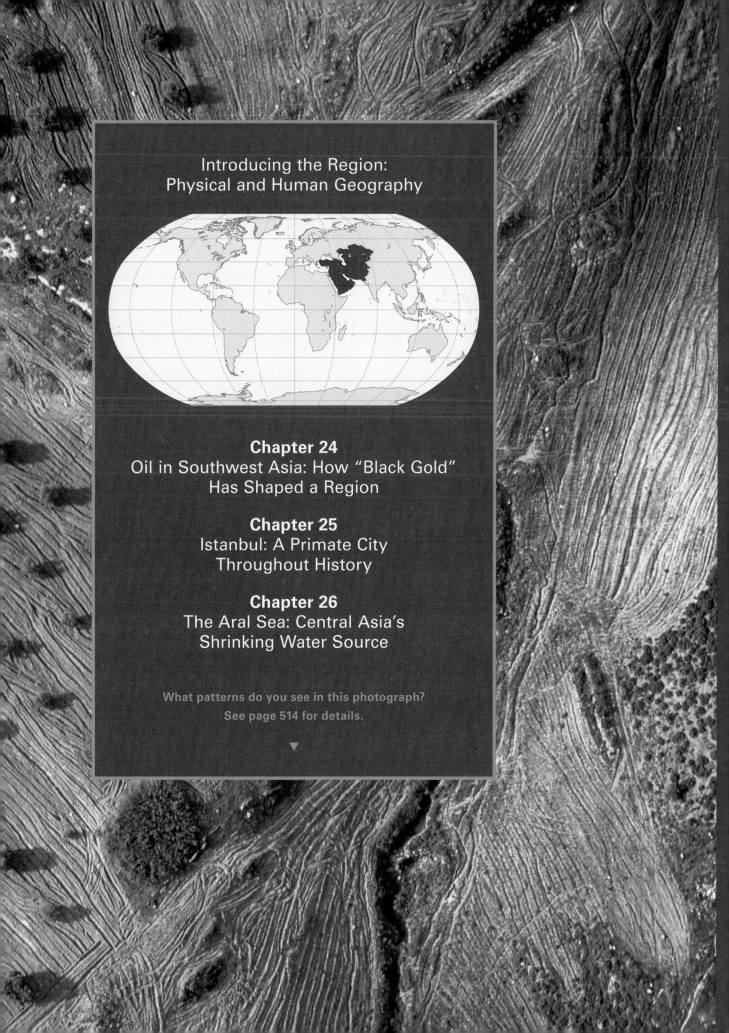

Introducing the Region:
Physical and Human Geography

What patterns do you see in this photograph?
See page 514 for details.

▼

Southwest and Central Asia are spread across one large section of the Eurasian **landmass**. The **region** is surrounded by seas, plains, and mountains.

Southwest Asia lies at the crossroads of Africa, Europe, and Asia. All three continents meet here at the Mediterranean Sea. Central Asia occupies the lonely center of the Eurasian landmass. Central Asia is a region of treeless plains and **deserts**.

Southwest Asia is bordered by several seas. The Mediterranean and Black seas mark the northwestern border. The Red Sea runs along the western side of the region. The Arabian Sea cradles the southern border.

Central Asia's northern border looks over the plains of Siberia. Rugged mountains rise along the southern and eastern borders. These mountains include the Hindu Kush, one of the highest ranges in the world.

Physical Features of Southwest and Central Asia

Physical Features

The physical landscape of Southwest and Central Asia is marked by great contrasts. This region includes both the lowest spot on Earth and some of the highest peaks. Dusty deserts cover much of the region. Yet there are also large bodies of water, such as the Persian Gulf. A **gulf** is an arm of the sea that is partly surrounded by land. The Persian Gulf is about 600 miles long. It averages almost 125 miles in width.

Southwest and Central Asia also have several **inland seas**. These are large bodies of salt water with little or no connection to the ocean. The Caspian Sea is the world's largest inland body of water. Its waters are salty, but not as salty as the ocean. As a result, this inland sea is home to both **freshwater** and saltwater fish.

Southwest Asia

Southwest Asia is a land of **peninsulas** and **plateaus**. The Arabian Peninsula occupies the southern part of the region. Covering more than 1 million square miles, it is the largest peninsula in the world.

Farther north lies the Anatolia Plateau. This rugged region stretches across much of modern Turkey. The center of the plateau has **landscapes** that are often described as "moonscapes." **Erosion** by wind and water has carved the hills in this volcanic region into caves, cones, and strange shapes called "fairy chimneys."

This satellite photograph shows two gulfs in Southwest Asia. You can see the Gulf of Oman at the bottom and the Persian Gulf at the top.

Southwest Asia has other interesting features, including

- the Arabian Sea—a shipping route known as a "hurricane alley" because of the violent storms that develop there.
- the Tigris-Euphrates Valley—one of the most fertile river valleys of the ancient world.
- the Dead Sea—an inland sea between Israel and Jordan. At about 1,349 feet below sea level, it is the lowest place on Earth. The Dead Sea is nine times as salty as the ocean. This is so salty that almost nothing can live in its waters.

Central Asia

Central Asia also varies greatly in elevation. The Caspian Sea lies below sea level. But some Hindu Kush peaks rise over 25,000 feet.

Central Asia boasts some of Earth's largest inland seas. The Black Sea covers an area larger than the state of California. The Aral Sea was another large inland sea, but it is rapidly shrinking in size.

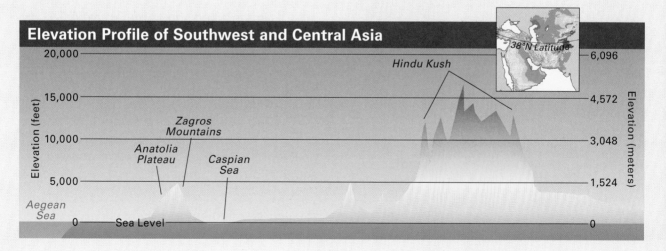

Elevation Profile of Southwest and Central Asia

38°N Latitude

Elevation (feet): 20,000 / 15,000 / 10,000 / 5,000 / 0 Sea Level

Elevation (meters): 6,096 / 4,572 / 3,048 / 1,524 / 0

Hindu Kush

Zagros Mountains

Anatolia Plateau

Caspian Sea

Aegean Sea

Climate

Despite the many seas in this area, Southwest and Central Asia is a region of arid and semi-arid **climate zones**. Areas with an **arid** climate zone receive less than 10 inches of **precipitation** a year. But that is an average. An arid area may receive no rainfall for several years. Then, large amounts of rain might fall in a few hours. Areas with a **semiarid** climate have some rain now and then.

Arid and semiarid climate zones are often the hottest places on Earth. Summer temperatures may reach 100°F or higher during the day. Winters are usually mild. There are, however, cold deserts. Some are cold because they lie at a high altitude. Others are cold because they are far from the equator. Still others are chilled by cold winds.

Southwest Asia

Temperatures inland on the arid Arabian Peninsula can climb to 115°F in the summer. There is little moisture in the air, so the air cools rapidly at night. Temperatures can drop sharply in just a few hours.

Riyadh, the capital of Saudi Arabia, is located near the center of the Arabian Peninsula. When are air conditioners in Riyadh likely to work the hardest?

In coastal areas, the seas create a more moderate climate. For example, coastal Turkey enjoys a **Mediterranean** climate. The same climate zone extends south along the sea-coast into Israel. Summers here are warm and dry. Winters are mild and rainy.

The climate varies more in the mountainous parts of this region. In general, temperatures drop as one goes up in elevation.

Central Asia

The tall mountains that bound Central Asia prevent storms that form over the Indian Ocean from reaching the center of the continent. As a result, little rain falls in this inland region. Thus, most of Central Asia has an arid or semiarid climate.

Two large deserts cover much of the Turan Lowland. North of this arid plain lie the **steppes**. Precipitation on these rolling plains is less than 15 inches a year.

The mountains of Central Asia have varied climates, depending on elevation. The highest peaks of the Hindu Kush are covered with snow throughout the year.

Enough rain falls in the foothills of the Hindu Kush to support farming.

Vegetation

Vegetation in Southwest and Central Asia is limited by the dry climate. **Desert scrub** covers much of the region. Desert scrub is mostly small trees and shrubs that can survive long periods without rain.

Plants adapt to arid conditions in many ways. For example, desert plants rarely grow close together. By being spread out, each plant can pull water from a larger area.

Some plants obtain water from deep beneath the ground. The roots of the acacia tree may reach as much as 100 feet underground in search of water. Other plants store

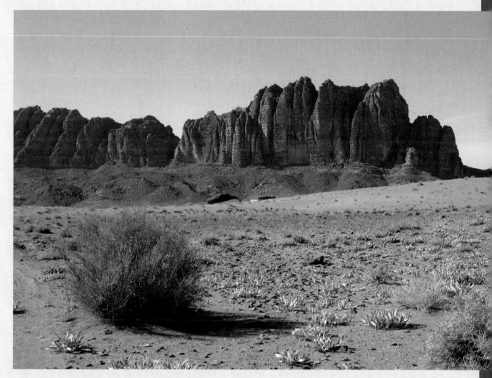

Desert scrub is found in much of the region, as seen here in southwest Jordan.

precious rainwater in their leaves, roots, or stems. For example, the aloe plant stores water in its long, thick leaves. Aloe leaves have a waxy surface that limits water loss.

Many other desert plants also survive by reducing water loss through their leaves. The leaves of desert bushes tend to be small and sparse. During very dry periods, plants may shed their leaves altogether.

Southwest Asia

Southwest Asia has a mixture of **vegetation zones**. The type of plants growing in a particular place depends mostly on the temperature and rainfall.

Patches of **temperate grassland** appear on the central Anatolia Plateau. These grasses are adapted to the cooler climate found in this highland area.

Hills and river valleys are covered with **mixed forests**. Both deciduous and coniferous trees grow in these areas. At higher elevations, only coniferous trees grow.

The Mediterranean coastline supports **chaparral**. The small trees and bushes of this

area are well adapted to a Mediterranean climate.

Desert scrub covers the deserts in southern Israel and much of the Arabian Peninsula. The more arid parts of this peninsula are too dry to support much plant life.

Central Asia

Temperate grasslands cover the steppes that stretch across the northern part of Central Asia. Steppes are broad, treeless plains that are usually covered with grasses.

Farther south, much of the region is covered in desert scrub. In the spring, the desert grasses and shrubs burst into bloom. Later on, the heat of summer dries them out.

Trees grow in areas with adequate water. The saxaul tree grows only in Central Asia. For thousands of years, people have relied on saxaul for firewood. The region is also known for its walnut trees. **Deciduous** and **coniferous forests** grow in highland areas.

In the eastern part of Central Asia, the mountains are very high. This small **ice cap** zone is too cold to support any plant life.

The Southwest and Central Asia region has 25 countries. Pakistan has by far the largest population. More than 162 million people live there. The largest country in area is Kazakhstan. The United Arab Emirates is the wealthiest country on a **per capita** basis. It is also one of the smaller countries in this region.

Southwest and Central Asia have long been linked by trade. Camel caravans carried trade goods from Southwest Asia across Central Asia to China and back as far back as 2,000 years ago. The two parts of this region are also linked to each other by a common faith. Most people in this region follow the religion of Islam.

Political Boundaries of Southwest and Central Asia

History

Southwest Asia is known as the "cradle of civilization." Farming began here. The world's first cities arose here. This region is also the birthplace of three major religions. All three share the belief that there is only one God. Each religion began with a single person. And each has its own sacred writings, or holy book.

Early Times

According to the Torah, or Jewish holy book, Judaism was founded around 1800 B.C.E by a man named Abraham. God told Abraham to leave his home on the Euphrates River. Abraham obeyed and moved his family to the land now known as Israel. God promised Abraham that this land would belong to him and his descendents if they would set the example of how God wants people to live. Abraham's descendents are known as Jews.

Christianity began with a Jew named Jesus about 2,000 years ago. The Gospels, part of the Christian Bible, or holy book, say that Jesus became a preacher in Israel. His words attracted many followers. They also created enemies powerful enough to have him killed. The Gospels say Jesus rose from the dead and appeared to his followers. Those who follow the teachings of Jesus are known as Christians.

Islam was founded on the Arabian Peninsula by a prophet named Muhammad. In 610 C.E., Muhammad told his family that he had seen an angel sent by God. The angel came many times, bringing Muhammad messages from God. These messages were later collected in the Qur'an, the holy book of Islam. Those who follow the teachings of the Qur'an are known as Muslims.

Conquest and Colonies

After his death, Muhammad's followers spread Islam across Southwest Asia, North Africa, and Spain. By the late 800s, Muslim kingdoms were centers of a brilliant culture.

Later, Turks from Central Asia established the Ottoman Empire in this same region. Islam was the empire's official religion. But Ottoman rulers allowed people of other faiths to live in peace in their empire.

The Ottoman Empire collapsed in 1922. Its territory was carved up into a patchwork of countries and colonies. The Soviet Union took over parts of Central Asia. Britain and France created colonies in Southwest Asia.

The Modern Era

In time, most countries in Southwest and Central Asia threw off colonial rule. Iraq became independent in 1932. Israel was founded as a Jewish state in 1948. The countries of Central Asia broke away from the Soviet Union after its collapse in 1991.

Today, deep conflicts divide this region. Many stem from religious differences. In many parts of Southwest Asia, Muslims oppose the existence of the Jewish state of Israel. In some Muslim countries, there is conflict between the two main branches of Islam—Sunnis and Shi'ites. In Central Asia, Christians sometimes clash with Muslims.

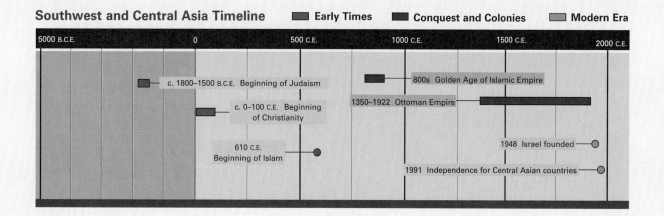

Southwest and Central Asia Timeline ■ Early Times ■ Conquest and Colonies ■ Modern Era

5000 B.C.E.　　　0　　　500 C.E.　　　1000 C.E.　　　1500 C.E.　　　2000 C.E.

c. 1800–1500 B.C.E. Beginning of Judaism

c. 0–100 C.E. Beginning of Christianity

610 C.E. Beginning of Islam

800s Golden Age of Islamic Empire

1350–1922 Ottoman Empire

1948 Israel founded

1991 Independence for Central Asian countries

Population

About 559 million people live in Southwest and Central Asia. They make up only 8 percent of the world's population. People are not spread evenly across the region. A few places have a **population density** of well over 250 people per square mile. Many more places have less than 2 people per square mile.

This region is still mostly **rural**. Yet the population has become more **urban** in recent years. In Saudi Arabia, for example, only one Saudi in four lived in a city in 1970. By 2007, four out of five Saudis lived in urban areas.

The Southwest and Central Asia region has one of the fastest-growing populations in the world. It also has one of the youngest populations. The majority of its people are younger than 25.

Most people in this region are Muslim. About 85 to 90 percent of these are Sunni Muslims. Only about 10 to 15 percent are Shi'ites. The region is also home to smaller numbers of Jews and Christians. Jerusalem, the capital of Israel, has holy sites sacred to each of these three religious groups.

Southwest and Central Asia: Major Religions

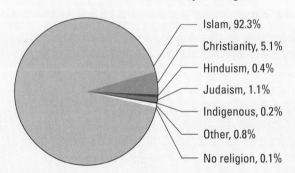

- Islam, 92.3%
- Christianity, 5.1%
- Hinduism, 0.4%
- Judaism, 1.1%
- Indigenous, 0.2%
- Other, 0.8%
- No religion, 0.1%

Southwest and Central Asia: Urban and Rural Population, 2007

Urban, 52.0%

Rural, 48.0%

= 10% of the total population

Southwest and Central Asia: Population Growth, 1950–2050

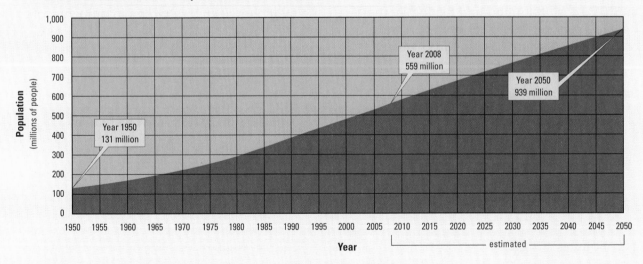

Year 1950
131 million

Year 2008
559 million

Year 2050
939 million

Population (millions of people)

Year

estimated

Sources: United Nations Department of Economic and Social Affairs, Population Division. Encyclopaedia Britannica.

Economic Activity

Two resources shape **economic activity** in Southwest and Central Asia. The first is petroleum, or oil. The second is water. Oil is important because the region is rich in it. Water is important for the opposite reason—because the region has so little of it.

As in other arid places, a lack of water limits commercial farming and livestock raising. In many areas, there is not enough water to grow large crops.

Nomadic herding, however, is still important in this region. Nomadic herders move around to find food and water for their herds. Their camels, sheep, and goats graze on the wild grasses in one area. Then, when the grass is gone, the herders move their animals to a fresh grazing area. Herders depend on their animals to meet most of their needs. They use and sell their animals' milk and meat. They also make tents and clothing from their animals' skin and wool.

Resources

Fossil fuels are key resources in this region. Southwest Asia has the world's largest known oil deposits. Because refined oil is used to fuel cars, trucks, and planes, it is in great demand worldwide. Countries with large oil deposits have grown rich meeting this demand.

Onions grow in the Negev Desert of Israel, watered with salt water and drip irrigation.

In Central Asia, coal is an important fossil fuel. Coal is used for heating and for generating electricity. It is plentiful in Kazakhstan and Afghanistan. Pakistan has large natural gas fields.

Land Use

Commercial farming is an important economic activity in some parts of this region. Olives, wheat, and fruit grow well along the Mediterranean coast. Dates grow in Saudi Arabia, Yemen, and Iran. Cotton is an important crop in Iran and Central Asia.

In some very dry areas, farmers have worked hard to make the most of their scarce water. Israel, for example, is more than half desert, yet it produces 95 percent of the food its people need.

Large cities are centers of trade and manufacturing. In Israel, many companies develop computer software and other advanced products. Israel also has a diamond cutting industry. In Pakistan, factories turn out cotton cloth and clothing for export. Industries in Iran produce building materials, leather goods, and tools.

These desert herders are using a truck to bring water to their flocks.

Oil in Southwest Asia: How "Black Gold" Has Shaped a Region

24.1 Introduction

A lot can change in 50 years. Fifty years ago in the United States, there were no computers, no cell phones, and no Internet. Only a few American homes had color televisions. But some parts of the world, like Southwest Asia, have changed even more dramatically.

Look at the two photographs of the port city of Dubai on the facing page. Dubai is one of seven **states** that make up the United Arab Emirates. Fifty years ago, it was a small town. Electricity had only recently been introduced. Bedouin **nomads** roamed the **desert** nearby. Today, Dubai is a modern city with one of the world's largest human-made harbors.

Dubai, like much of Southwest Asia, has been transformed by oil. Southwest Asia has the world's largest known **oil reserves**. This term refers to underground oil that has been discovered but remains unused. There are also large reserves of **natural gas**. This is gas within Earth's **crust,** or outer layer. Money from the sale of oil and natural gas has been used to pave roads and construct modern buildings in Southwest Asia. It has also provided medical care that helps people live longer.

In this chapter, you will learn how vast oil and natural gas reserves have affected Southwest Asia's economic development. You will also discover how these resources have changed the lives of many people in the **region**.

Essential Question

How might having a valuable natural resource affect a region?

This diagram shows 10 oil-rich countries in Southwest Asia. Together, they export millions of barrels of oil each year. The sale of this valuable natural resource has changed life in these countries. Keep this map in mind as you try to answer the Essential Question.

Graphic Organizer

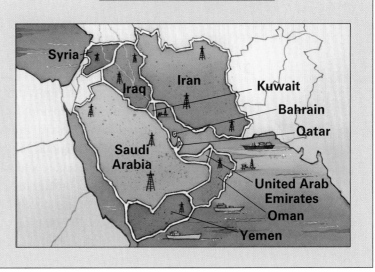

Syria
Iraq
Iran
Kuwait
Bahrain
Qatar
Saudi Arabia
United Arab Emirates
Oman
Yemen

◀ The port city of Dubai in the early 1950s and in 2004

Oil in the Desert

The Arabian Desert covers an area of about a million square miles. Most of this region is too arid to farm. However, beneath the sandy wastes lie vast reserves of oil and natural gas. Oil rigs like this one bring that oil to the surface.

24.2 The Geographic Setting

Southwest Asia lies at the crossroads of three continents. Europe, Africa, and Asia all come together here. In ancient times, this location brought traders from distant lands to this region. Most traveled by land over dusty caravan routes. Traders from all over the world still come to Southwest Asia today. But now, many arrive in huge tanker ships looking for only one product: oil.

Oil: Southwest Asia's Hidden Treasure On the surface, Southwest Asia doesn't look very welcoming. Much of it is hot and dry. The Arabian Desert is so barren that some people call it "the place where no one comes out." But hidden beneath the region's deserts are vast reserves of oil and natural gas.

More than half of the world's proven crude oil reserves lie under Southwest Asia. **Crude oil** is another name for petroleum as it is found in the ground. Proven crude oil reserves are known deposits that can be pumped to the surface at a reasonable cost.

Worldwide demand is high for oil and natural gas. **Developed countries** depend on these fuels to meet most of their energy needs. Modern forms of transportation run mainly on oil. Power plants burn oil and natural gas to generate electricity. Oil is also a raw material for plastics, medicines, and other goods. Some countries in Southwest Asia have grown rich meeting the world's ever-growing demand for oil.

Although Southwest Asia has large oil reserves, it lacks other resources. Fresh water, for example, is in short supply across the region. Moreover, oil is a **nonrenewable resource**. There's only a limited amount of it. Once it is used up, it can't be replaced.

When the oil is gone, the world will have to turn to **renewable resources**. These are resources that will not run out or that can be replaced. Renewable energy resources include sunlight, wind, and **geothermal energy,** or heat from the center of Earth. Waterpower and trees are other renewable resources.

Many Ethnic Groups, One Major Religion Most people in Southwest Asia are Arabs, or people who speak Arabic. Other major **ethnic groups** include Kurds and Persians. Kurds live in parts of Turkey, Syria, Iraq, and Iran. Persians are mostly in Iran.

Islam is the most important religion in Southwest Asia. Only one country in the region, Israel, does not have a Muslim majority. There are, however, several branches of Islam. Conflict among different ethnic and religious groups has led to unrest and violence.

In this chapter, you will look at how oil has shaped the development of 10 countries in Southwest Asia. These countries differ in area and population. But each has large oil reserves. And each has used oil in different ways to meet its people's needs. The countries are Bahrain, Iran, Iraq, Kuwait, Oman, Qatar, Saudi Arabia, Syria, United Arab Emirates, and Yemen.

► Geoterms

crude oil petroleum as it comes out of the ground and before it has been refined or processed into useful products

nonrenewable resource a resource that takes so long to form that it can't be replaced. Oil, which takes millions of years to form, is such a resource.

oil reserves oil that has been discovered but remains unused in the ground

renewable resource a resource that can't be used up or that can be replaced quickly as it is used up. Sunlight is a renewable resource that cannot be used up. Wood is a renewable resource that can be replaced by planting more trees.

Major Oil-Producing Countries

The 10 Southwest Asia oil countries labeled in bold type possess about half of the world's known oil reserves. Notice that many of these countries border the Persian Gulf.

Southwest Asia

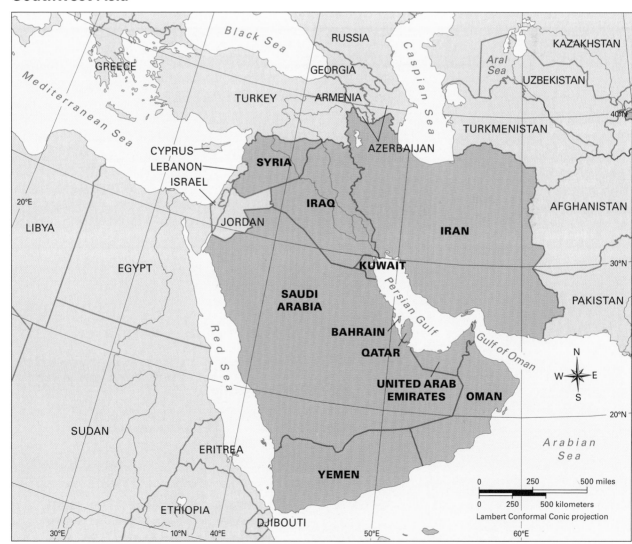

24.3 The Geology and Geography of Oil

For most Americans, oil comes from a gas station. That's where they buy oil to lubricate car engines. They also buy gasoline made from oil to run those engines. In some parts of the country, people heat their homes by burning oil. The oil that Americans burn in their cars and homes took a long time to form. And more often than not, it has traveled a very long way to get to this country.

Oil Was Formed Millions of Years Ago The oil that is pumped out of the ground today was formed a very long time ago. It began as tiny plants and animals that lived and died in the oceans. After they died, these creatures sank to the ocean floor. Over time, most of their remains turned to rock. Layer after layer of rock was formed this way. But some of their remains did not turn to rock. The weight of the water, heat from Earth's core, and chemical changes combined to transform some of the remains into oil and natural gas.

Over time, the oil and natural gas seeped into pores, or tiny holes, in the rock. These pores may be too small to see. But they are big enough to hold oil and gas, much like a sponge holds water.

At times, some of this oil or gas rises to Earth's surface. But most remains trapped under a layer of **impermeable rock**. *Impermeable* means "preventing the passage of liquid or gas." Geologists call this layer a cap rock because it works like the cap on a container. This cap rock keeps most oil and natural gas contained deep inside the earth.

From Sea Creatures to Crude Oil

The oil we use today was formed millions of years ago. It began as tiny creatures that sank to the bottom of the sea. As the creatures decayed, parts of their remains slowly turned into oil. Because oil formation is so slow, oil is a nonrenewable resource.

Oil Is Found in Pockets Deep in the Earth A lot of the world's oil lies buried under Southwest Asia. One reason for this is that millions of years ago, this area was under water. The sea that covered the region contained the tiny plants and animals that began the process of making oil.

Another reason that oil formed under Southwest Asia has to do with the movement of Earth's crust. You read in Chapter 17 that

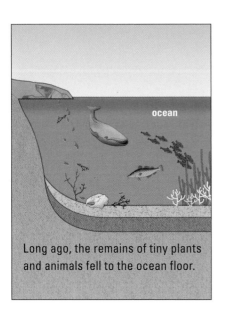

Long ago, the remains of tiny plants and animals fell to the ocean floor.

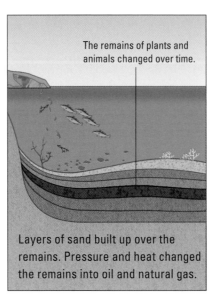

Layers of sand built up over the remains. Pressure and heat changed the remains into oil and natural gas.

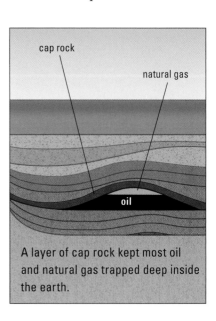

A layer of cap rock kept most oil and natural gas trapped deep inside the earth.

Earth's crust is broken into giant sections called **tectonic plates**. The plates drift very slowly over the surface of Earth. When two plates collide, they may create pockets where oil can form. This is what happened in Southwest Asia very long ago. The Iranian Plate and the Arabian Plate bumped up against each other, creating spaces where oil and gas were formed and trapped.

It takes a lot of work to get oil out of underground pores and pockets. Oil companies drill through the cap rock to get at the oil underneath. Then they pump the oil up to the surface. However, sometimes pumping doesn't work. When that happens, petroleum engineers inject water or gases into the well. The added pressure forces oil out of the rocks.

The oil that reaches Earth's surface doesn't look much like the product people see at their local gas station. Crude oil is usually combined with water and natural gas when it comes out of the ground. Oil companies have to refine this crude oil to make it into gasoline and other useful products. Some petroleum products are asphalt, plastics, and the wax used to make candles.

Oil Is Not Distributed Equally Very specific conditions were necessary for the creation of oil. So it is not surprising that these conditions existed in some places and not in others. Southwest Asia was one of the regions where a great deal of oil formed long ago.

Within Southwest Asia, however, the **distribution** of oil is uneven. Saudi Arabia is the largest country in this region. It also has the most oil. About one quarter of the world's proven oil reserves lie under its desert sand.

Kuwait, in contrast, is a tiny country. Saudi Arabia could hold 125 Kuwaits and still have space left over. But little Kuwait holds almost a tenth of the world's known oil reserves. Other countries in the region, such as Syria and Yemen, have less oil. But they still have more oil than most other countries in the world.

Oil Reserves in Southwest Asia, 2007

Country	Proven Oil Reserves (in millions of barrels)
Saudi Arabia	264,200
Iran	138,400
Iraq	115,000
Kuwait	101,500
United Arab Emirates	97,800
Qatar	27,400
Oman	5,600
Yemen	2,800
Syria	2,500
Bahrain	125

Source: Central Intelligence Agency.

Who Has the Oil?

The table lists the proven oil reserves of 10 Southwest Asian countries. Proven reserves are deposits that oil companies know they can pump to the surface at a reasonable cost.

Today, oil companies drill through the cap rock and pump crude oil to the surface.

Oil refineries heat the crude oil to produce fuels, oils, and chemicals.

Products made from oil include gasoline, plastics, and materials used throughout our homes.

Per Capita GDP of Southwest Asian Oil Countries, 2008

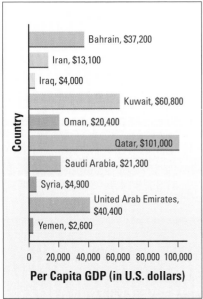

Per Capita GDP (in U.S. dollars)

- Bahrain, $37,200
- Iran, $13,100
- Iraq, $4,000
- Kuwait, $60,800
- Oman, $20,400
- Qatar, $101,000
- Saudi Arabia, $21,300
- Syria, $4,900
- United Arab Emirates, $40,400
- Yemen, $2,600

Source: Central Intelligence Agency.

Wealth from Oil

This bar graph compares the per capita GDP of 10 Southwest Asian countries. Per capita GDP shows how rich one country is compared to another. But it does not show whether a country's wealth is being divided evenly among its people.

Rich and Poor

Oil has brought great wealth to some people in Southwest Asia. But as these images show, that wealth is not distributed evenly. Some people are fabulously rich. Others are desperately poor.

24.4 Oil Wealth and People's Well-Being

Oil has made Saudi Arabia's royal family very rich. Consider their 2002 vacation. King Fahd and 3,000 guests visited the town of Marbella in Spain. The royal family spent $185 million getting the Marbella palace ready for the vacation. After the king arrived, he had flowers delivered daily. Each day's flowers cost about $1,500.

Not many people in Saudi Arabia live like the royal family. Just as some countries have more oil reserves than others, some people living in oil-rich countries have more wealth than others.

Oil Has Made Many People Better Off In general, oil money has improved the lives of many people in Southwest Asia. In 2002, researchers from the United Nations studied changes in the region over the past 30 years. They found that **life expectancy** has increased by 15 years. They also found that the number of infants who die in their first year of life has dropped by two thirds.

Oil has made some countries rich. But just how rich? There are two common ways to measure a country's wealth. The first is to look at a country's **gross domestic product**. As you read in Chapter 8, GDP is a measure of the goods and services produced by a country each year. The second is to look at the **per capita** GDP of a country. Per capita GDP measures the average income of the people in a country. To get this per-person figure, divide the total GDP by the number of people in the country.

Per capita GDP varies from country to country for many reasons. The United Arab Emirates and Kuwait, for example, both have a high GDP from selling oil. Both also have small populations. So each has a per capita GDP that is relatively high. Countries with larger populations, such as Saudi Arabia and Iran, have to divide their GDP among many more people. The result is a lower per capita GDP.

Bahrain, in contrast, has far smaller oil reserves than the other oil-rich countries of Southwest Asia. But its per capita GDP is quite high. This is because Bahrain earns much of its GDP by processing, instead of pumping, crude oil. It has also become an international banking center.

Per Capita GDP Does Not Tell the Whole Story Per capita GDP is an average. It assumes that a country's wealth is divided equally among its citizens. In reality, some people may be very rich and others quite poor. So per capita GDP doesn't always reflect people's well-being.

Another way to measure how well people are living is the United Nations' Human Development Index (HDI). As you read in Chapter 9, the HDI looks at a country's per capita GDP along with other factors that reflect quality of life. One of these factors is life expectancy. Another is education. How many people are literate, or know how to read? How many children receive a high school education? When these numbers are added up, countries are ranked from best to worst, with 1 being best.

Based on the HDI, Bahrain is third in Southwest Asia in terms of living well. This is true even though Bahrain does not have the most oil or the highest per capita GDP. It does, however, use its wealth to educate its population. Almost all of its young people, both boys and girls, attend school. It also invests in health care. The **infant mortality rate** in Bahrain is one of the lowest in Southwest Asia. The infant mortality rate is the number of deaths of babies under age one per 1,000 births in a year.

Oil Has Not Improved Life for All Oil money hasn't ended poverty in Southwest Asia. For example, Yemen remains one of the 60 poorest countries in the world. Its population is about 80 percent of Saudi Arabia's. But its oil reserves are only about 1 percent the size of those in Saudi Arabia. This means the amount of oil produced by Yemen each year has not been enough to pull its people out of poverty.

Other Southwest Asian countries have made a lot of money from oil. But they have not used that money to improve people's lives. Iraq, for example, has the second-largest oil reserves in the region. But from 1979 to 2003, a dictator named Saddam Hussein controlled Iraq's oil income. He spent most of Iraq's oil money building an army, buying weapons, and fighting wars. Very little money went to make life better for ordinary Iraqis.

HDI Ranks in Southwest Asia, 2008

Country	World Rank
Kuwait	29
United Arab Emirates	31
Bahrain	32
Qatar	34
Oman	53
Saudi Arabia	55
Iran	84
Syria	105
Yemen	138

Source: *HDR 2004*, "Human Development Reports."

Measuring Well-Being

The Human Development Index measures the well-being of a country's people. This table shows the ranks of most of the oil-rich countries in Southwest Asia. Note that Bahrain ranks third in this region but 32nd in the world. Iraq is missing from this list because of the lack of data needed to rank it.

Oil Flows from Southwest Asia

OPEC and Oil Flow

This map shows the members of OPEC, the Organization of the Petroleum Exporting Countries. It also shows where the oil-exporting countries of Southwest Asia send their oil. The United States alone uses one quarter of the world's oil. That's an average of three gallons of oil per person every day.

24.5 The Price and Flow of Oil

Thick black smoke filled the sky, darkening what had been a bright, sunny day. Kuwait's oil fields were on fire. The year was 1991. Iraq had invaded Kuwait, hoping to take over its oil reserves. This invasion led to a conflict known as the Persian Gulf War. When the war ended, retreating Iraqi troops torched some of Kuwait's oil wells.

The Persian Gulf War was one of many conflicts over oil in Southwest Asia. These conflicts have involved both oil-exporting countries and oil-importing countries.

Oil-Exporting Countries: Working to Control the Price of Oil

Most oil-exporting countries depend on oil sales to support their economies. Their goal is to have a steady supply of oil flowing out of their countries. For their oil, they expect a steady flow of money to come back into their countries.

To meet that goal, several oil-exporting countries formed the Organization of the Petroleum Exporting Countries (OPEC) in 1960. In 2009, OPEC had 12 members. Six members were Southwest Asian countries. But the organization includes six oil producers from outside the region. Algeria, Angola, Ecuador, Libya, Nigeria, and Venezuela are all OPEC members. In addition, not all Southwest Asian oil producers belong to OPEC. Bahrain, Yemen, Oman, and Syria have not joined.

OPEC wants oil prices to be steady—not too high or too low. If too much oil is offered for sale, there will be less competition among buyers to get what they need. As a result, prices will drop too low. If too little oil is offered for sale, there will be more competition between buyers. Then prices will rise too high. To keep prices steady, OPEC members agree to regulate how much oil they will sell.

However, two realities limit OPEC's ability to control oil prices. First, OPEC cannot control all of the world's oil sales. Its members export less than half of the world's crude oil. The rest comes from non-OPEC countries such as Russia and Mexico. Second, even OPEC members don't always act as a group. Sometimes some members refuse to follow OPEC decisions on how much oil to sell.

Oil-Importing Countries: Working to Protect the Flow of Oil

Other countries depend on the flow of oil from Southwest Asia to fuel their economies. The United States, Japan, and many countries in Europe are big oil importers. They have a strong interest in protecting the flow of oil around the world.

As you have read, in 1990 Saddam Hussein, the dictator of Iraq, ordered his military to invade Kuwait. This gave him control of Kuwait's oil fields. Fears grew that he would target Saudi Arabia next. If Iraq took over that country, Saddam would control much of the world's oil supply. If he decided to cut off oil sales, many oil-importing countries would suffer severe energy shortages.

The United States and many other countries formed a coalition, or alliance, to drive Iraq out of Kuwait. Some members of the coalition were oil-importing countries. They did not want their oil supplies threatened by Iraq. Others were oil-exporting countries. They feared losing control of their oil reserves to Iraq.

The coalition went to war in 1991 to drive Iraqi forces out of Kuwait. The Persian Gulf War lasted just a few weeks. In that time, Kuwait was freed from Iraqi control. The coalition victory sent the world a clear message. As long as oil is the world's main source of energy, countries that import oil will work to keep it flowing.

24.6 Beginning to Think Globally

In this chapter, you learned that crude oil forms deep in the Earth. Much of Earth's oil lies under Southwest Asia. But oil reserves are not distributed evenly among the region's countries. Nor is oil wealth distributed evenly among the citizens of oil-rich countries.

You also learned that oil is a nonrenewable resource. Eventually, the world will run out of oil. Some countries are already meeting some of their energy needs with renewable resources. One example is solar energy. This is energy from the sun that can be converted into heat or electricity. As oil runs out, other countries will have to follow their example. Think about this as you look at the map of solar energy in the next section.

Oil Fields in Flames

Oil is so valuable that countries have gone to war over it. In 1990, Iraq invaded Kuwait to get control of Kuwait's oil reserves. A coalition of countries drove Iraq's forces out of Kuwait. But they were not able to prevent Iraqi soldiers from setting more than 730 oil wells in Kuwait on fire. It took eight months to put out these raging fires.

Top Contributors to Persian Gulf War Costs

Country
United States
Saudi Arabia
Kuwait
United Arab Emirates
Japan
Germany
United Kingdom
South Korea

Sharing the Cost of War

Many countries shared the costs of the 1991 Persian Gulf War. About two thirds of the money came from oil-exporting countries. They wanted to protect their oil reserves. The rest came from oil-importing countries. They wanted to protect the flow of oil into their countries.

24.7 Global Connections

This map shows the distribution of one renewable energy resource, sunlight. The graphs show energy produced by renewable and nonrenewable resources in two different years. Renewable resources include sunlight, wind, and waterpower. They also include plants that can become fuel. Corn, for example, is used to make a fuel called *ethanol*.

What energy sources is the world using to meet most of its energy needs? What do they have in common? The world is relying mainly on nonrenewable resources to meet its energy needs. All of these energy sources will someday run out.

Why isn't the world getting more of its energy from renewable resources? In the past, generating energy from renewable resources cost more than burning oil or gas. Hydroelectric power was the only renewable resource that could compete with fossil fuels. But building hydroelectric dams on rivers is costly and can harm the environment. Recently, the cost of generating electricity from wind has dropped. As a result, many countries now use wind power to meet some of their energy needs.

How might having renewable energy resources affect a region in the future? In the future, sunlight and wind may become key resources. Regions with daily sunshine or steady winds could become major energy producers. Deserts in the U.S. Southwest are already home to solar power plants. Wind farms are sprouting up across the breezy Great Plains. On these farms, large windmills generate electricity as their blades spin in the wind.

Solar Energy Availability Around the World

One kilowatt hour is enough energy to power sixteen 60-watt lightbulbs for one hour.

World Energy Production

Source: Energy Information Association.

Solar energy power plant in California

Istanbul: A Primate City Throughout History

25.1 Introduction

Meryem lives in Istanbul, the largest city in Turkey. It is early morning. She is riding a ferryboat to get to work. The ferry carries passengers across the Bosporus Strait. This narrow waterway connects the Black Sea to the Mediterranean Sea.

Looking ahead to the west, Meryem sees the domes and spires of Istanbul's ancient mosques. The city's business district rises up among these old landmarks. Behind her, to the east, the sun is rising over the high-rise apartment building where she lives.

Every day, thousands of Turks like Meryem commute back and forth across the Bosporus Strait. In the morning, they leave their homes in Asia to travel to jobs in Europe. At night, they return to Asia. And yet they haven't left Istanbul. That's because the city spans two continents. The eastern part of Istanbul lies in Asia. The western part is in Europe.

Istanbul's unique location has helped to make its population more than twice the size of the next largest city in Turkey. Many other countries also have a dominant city that is by far the largest and most important one. Geographers have a name for such an **urban** area. They call it a **primate city**. The word *primate* means "highest ranking."

In this chapter, you will read about the traits of primate cities. You will also discover how geography, history, and culture have come together to make Istanbul a primate city.

Essential Question

Where are primate cities located, and why are they important?

This map shows where some of Turkey's cities, towns, and villages are located. The size of each dot represents the number of people living there. Istanbul is Turkey's primate city. Compare its location and size with other cities and towns. Keep this map in mind as you try to answer the Essential Question.

Graphic Organizer

- ● Primate city
- ● City
- ● Town
- · Rural village

◀ Ancient Hagia Sophia and modern buildings in Istanbul

The Site of Constantinople
This illustration, made in the 1400s, shows the site of Constantinople. The city is located on the tip of a peninsula. This location made it easy to wall off the city for protection from invasion by land. In times of danger, the city also put a chain across the Bosporus Strait. The chain helped protect against invasion by sea.

25.2 The Geographic Setting

The city now known as Istanbul was founded more than 2,500 years ago. Since then, it has had three names. The ancient Greeks who first settled there called it Byzantium. Later, the Romans changed its name to Constantinople. Later still, the Turks renamed it Istanbul. Under each name, the city has thrived as a center of trade, government, and culture. For much of that time, it was also a primate city.

Istanbul's Favorable Site and Situation The city has survived for so long because of its location. Geographers describe a place's location in two ways. First, they look at its **site**. This means the physical characteristics of a place. Second, they look at its **situation**. This is the position of a place in relation to its surrounding area.

The site of this city was well chosen. The city was built at the tip of a **peninsula** with a good natural harbor. The peninsula is protected from an overland attack by water on three sides. The peninsula is flat, fertile, and well watered.

The city's situation was equally well chosen. The city was built on the Bosporus Strait. This narrow waterway links the Black Sea to the Sea of Marmara. It is part of a waterway that flows from the Black Sea to the Mediterranean Sea. The Bosporus Strait also marks the dividing line between Europe and Asia. In ancient times, trade routes from three continents met at this point. Trade goods from as far away as China, Russia, and East Africa all flowed through this city.

The Capital of Three Empires The Greeks were the first to appreciate the city's location. But they were not the last. Over time, the city would serve as the capital of three great empires.

Byzantium became part of the Roman Empire in 196 C.E. Almost four centuries later, a Roman emperor named Constantine moved his government there. In 330 C.E., he made Byzantium the new **capital city** of the Roman Empire. A capital city is the center of government for a state, country, or empire. The new capital was renamed Constantinople after the emperor.

The western part of the Roman Empire fell in the late 400s. However, the eastern part survived and became the Byzantine Empire. That empire grew to include much of Southwest Asia and parts of Eastern Europe. It lasted for the next 1,000 years. Constantinople was its capital. During this time, the city's wealth attracted attackers. But the strong city walls kept them back.

By 1300, a group of Turks called Ottomans began to conquer Southwest Asia. In 1453, they took over Constantinople as well. They renamed the city Istanbul and made it the capital of the growing Ottoman Empire.

In 1922, the Ottoman Empire fell apart. Istanbul became part of the modern country of Turkey. But it did not become Turkey's capital city. That honor went to the much smaller city of Ankara. Even so, Istanbul remains one of the world's great primate cities.

▶ Geoterms

capital city a city that is the governmental center of a country or region. Sometimes a capital city is also a primate city.

primate city the largest and most important city in a country. A primate city has at least twice the population of the next largest city. It is a center of economic power and national culture.

site the specific place where something is located, including its physical setting

situation the way a place is positioned in relation to its wider surroundings

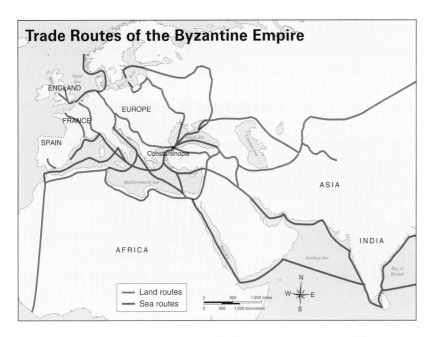

Trade Routes of the Byzantine Empire

The Situation of Constantinople

Constantinople was situated between Asia and Europe. Trade goods came from Asia by land and by sea. Other goods came from Africa and Europe. By 1000 B.C.E., trade had helped Constantinople become one of the world's largest cities.

Physical Features of Turkey

Istanbul's Site and Situation

Istanbul has outgrown its original site on a peninsula. Its situation, however, remains the same. The city has access by water to two seas. It is surrounded by fertile farmland. All of these factors have contributed to its becoming a primate city.

25.3 A Country's Largest City by Far

Mustafa moved to Istanbul to make money so that he could marry his girlfriend. He is a barber and works in the heart of the city. Before coming to Istanbul, he lived in a small town where he knew everyone. In Istanbul, he walks among crowds of strangers. His story is that of countless people living in this busy primate city.

At the Top of the Urban Hierarchy Primate cities stand at the top of the **urban hierarchy**. A hierarchy is a ranking system. An urban hierarchy ranks cities based on their size and the services they offer. A primate city is by far a country's highest-ranking city in terms of size. It has at least twice as many people as the next largest city in the country. It also ranks first in terms of just about anything else that might attract people, from schools and jobs to shopping and sports.

Istanbul is Turkey's largest city by a wide margin. In 2007, about 10 million people lived there. The capital city of Ankara, Turkey's second-largest urban area, had only 3.7 million people. Istanbul is so big that one out of every six Turks lives there.

The Urban Hierarchy

This diagram shows the ranking of urban places in terms of size and importance. Primate cities stand at the top of the urban hierarchy. A primate city has at least twice as many people as any other city in that country. People are drawn to a primate city because it has more opportunities than smaller areas.

Primate city

Cities

Towns

Rural villages

Drawing Migrants from Rural Villages Primate cities act like magnets. They attract and pull people from surrounding towns and villages. Each year, more than 400,000 people move to Istanbul. Many are like Mustafa. They leave **rural** villages and come to the big city looking for work, education, and excitement.

This rural-to-urban migration can cause problems. Some primate cities are growing too fast to meet people's needs. Many of Istanbul's new arrivals, for example, can't find housing they can afford. Instead, they build temporary shelters on open land around the city. Turks call these shantytowns *gecekondus*. This is Turkish for "built overnight." Such neighborhoods may lack such basic services as running water, electricity, and garbage collection.

Istanbul also suffers from traffic jams and air pollution. Sewage has dirtied the city's waterways. Many homes have bad plumbing. Still, people keep moving to Istanbul. For all of its problems, it remains at the top of Turkey's urban hierarchy.

25.4 A Center of Economic Power

Large ships rest in Istanbul's harbor. They hold huge containers that are filled with goods coming into or leaving Turkey. All day, big cranes lift the containers and place them on ship decks or truck beds. For centuries, Istanbul's symbols have been the domes of its many mosques. Today, the cranes are also symbols of the city.

A Hub of Business, Trade, and Travel The city is the economic center of Turkey. Almost two thirds of the country's industry is located there. Nearly half of all goods bought and sold in Turkey pass through the city. It is also Turkey's banking center.

Istanbul's busy port welcomes ships from all over the world. Ships arrive with machinery, oil, metals, medicines, plastics, and chemicals. They leave carrying textiles, clothing, steel products, foods, and minerals.

The city connects Turkey to the rest of the world. It has been a railroad center since the early days of train travel. Rail passengers took the famous Orient Express from Paris to Istanbul. From there, they boarded the Baghdad Railway to travel into Southwest Asia. Today visitors arrive by air and ship as well. Most people who travel to Turkey start or end their visit in Istanbul.

No Longer the Capital City Many primate cities are also capital cities. Government buildings and offices are housed there. Legislatures meet there to make laws.

As you read, Istanbul was once both a primate city and a capital city. However, it lost its place as a capital city in 1923, the year the Republic of Turkey was formed. The president of the new country, Kemal Ataturk, wanted Turkey to have a capital that had not been the center of ancient empires. By choosing Ankara as the capital city, he hoped to show the world that Turkey was a very modern place. Still, Istanbul remains Turkey's primate city.

Ships on the Bosporus Strait

Every year, tens of thousands of ships move through Turkey's Bosporus Strait. All of this shipping makes the Bosporus the world's most crowded waterway. Its narrow passages and tricky turns also make it one of the most dangerous.

25.5 A Center of National Life and Culture

Every day, almost half a million people shop in Istanbul's Grand Bazaar. A bazaar is a bit like an ancient shopping mall. But instead of stores, it has stalls. Instead of hired salespeople, it has traders selling their goods. The Grand Bazaar has more than 60 streets and about 5,000 shops, all under one roof. It is one of many attractions drawing people to this primate city.

The Grand Bazaar: A Reflection of Turkish Culture There are no price tags at the Grand Bazaar. Buyers bargain with sellers. As a general rule, sellers may name a price that is 10 times what the object is worth. Buyers counter with a price that may be one tenth what it's worth, and the haggling begins.

Travelers from all over Turkey and the world come to the Grand Bazaar. Here they can find pottery, jewelry, metalwork, and other items that reflect Turkey's culture. They can also find Turkey's famous carpets. Carpet weaving is an ancient and honored art in Turkey. Each village has its own traditional designs.

A Cultural and Sports Center Although Istanbul is not Turkey's capital city, it is still its cultural and sports center. The country's most important museums are found in this primate city. So are art galleries and concert halls. Musical events range from opera to jazz and rock concerts. Nightclubs offer more traditional entertainment such as Turkish songs and dances.

Istanbul has long been a sports center. Visitors can still see the ruins of the Hippodrome. That ancient sports stadium could hold 100,000 people. Romans gathered there for horse racing, chariot racing, and other athletic events. Turks still gather in Istanbul's sports stadiums. But today they come to watch soccer.

Historic Sites and Cultural Symbols The city draws tourists from all over the world. Its historic structures are cultural symbols of Turkey as well as tourist attractions.

One of the most visited historic buildings is the beautiful Hagia Sophia. Its name means "Holy Wisdom." The Byzantines built Hagia Sophia as a Christian church in the 500s. In the 1400s, the Ottomans turned it into an Islamic mosque. Today it is a museum. The Hagia Sophia reminds visitors how long Istanbul has been a major meeting place of many cultures and peoples. The city's history includes both Christian and Muslim ways of life.

The Topkapi Palace is a symbol of Turkey's Ottoman heritage. This sprawling mix of buildings and gardens was once home to the Ottoman rulers. Visitors can see great wealth on display at Topkapi. One famous object is the Topkapi dagger. Made in the 1700s, it is a sword covered with diamonds and emeralds.

The Blue Mosque is another important symbol of Turkey's Ottoman past. The mosque takes its name from the 20,000 blue tiles

Istanbul's Grand Bazaar

The Grand Bazaar reflects Turkish culture in its displays of arts and crafts. Its stalls present a colorful mix of rugs, pottery, jewelry, and clothing. There are workshops where skilled workers beat copper, brass, and silver into useful objects. This craft has been passed down from one generation to the next for hundreds of years.

that line its inside walls. Built in the 1600s, it is famous for its many domes and minarets. A minaret is a tall, slender tower attached to a mosque.

No visit would be complete without a trip to Istanbul's public baths, called *hamam*. Turks go to the baths to wash, have massages, and visit with friends. Some baths date back more than 500 years. In this ancient primate city, that is not so old.

25.6 Beginning to Think Globally

In this chapter, you learned that Istanbul is a primate city. It has more than twice the population of the next largest city in Turkey. It is also the country's business and cultural center. Its site and situation have attracted people for over 2,500 years. Today Ankara is Turkey's capital city. But Istanbul still stands out as by far the country's largest and most important city.

Some countries have primate cities, but others do not. France is one example of a country with a primate city. Its capital city, Paris, has more than twice the number of people as the next largest city. It is also France's economic and cultural center. Bangkok, the capital city of Thailand, is another primate city. It draws people and resources from the rest of the country. China and Canada are two countries that do not have a primate city. That is, they do not have one city that stands out as the center of the country's population, economic power, and culture.

Primate cities are magnets. They attract people, trade, culture, and ideas. Think about this as you look at the map of primate cities around the world in the next section.

Hagia Sophia, "Holy Wisdom"
This immense church was built in just five years. When it was completed in 537 C.E., a writer described its effect on visitors. "No one ever became weary of this spectacle, but those who are in the church delight in what they see." Today it reminds visitors that Istanbul has long been a meeting place of religions and cultures.

25.7 Global Connections

This physical features map shows primate cities around the world. Note that some countries do not have a primate city.

What role do site and situation play in the development of primate cities? As you can see on the map, many primate cities are found along a coastline. Such cities often enjoy a mild climate. Primate cities away from a coast are usually located on a river. Being next to an ocean or a river helped these cities become important trading centers.

What relationship do you see between primate cities and capital cities? Most primate cities are also capital cities. This is not surprising. Many countries choose their largest and wealthiest city as their capital. But not all capital cities have twice as many people as the next largest city. Some capital cities, including Washington, D.C., and Ottawa, Canada, just don't measure up. Others, like Ankara, Turkey, or Canberra, Australia, have been chosen as capitals because they were not their country's largest cities. This is a way of spreading power more evenly throughout a country.

What might explain why some countries do not have a primate city? Countries without primate cities usually have many large cities. But no city is by far the largest and most important in the country. This is most likely to be true of very large countries such as India or the United States. In such countries, there are often several very large cities with a lot of economic power and culture.

Primate Cities Around the World

Elevation

Feet	Meters
Over 10,000	Over 3,050
5,001–10,000	1,526–3,050
2,001–5,000	611–1,525
1,001–2,000	306–610
0–1,000	0–305
Below sea level	Below sea level

⊛ Primate and capital city
● Primate city

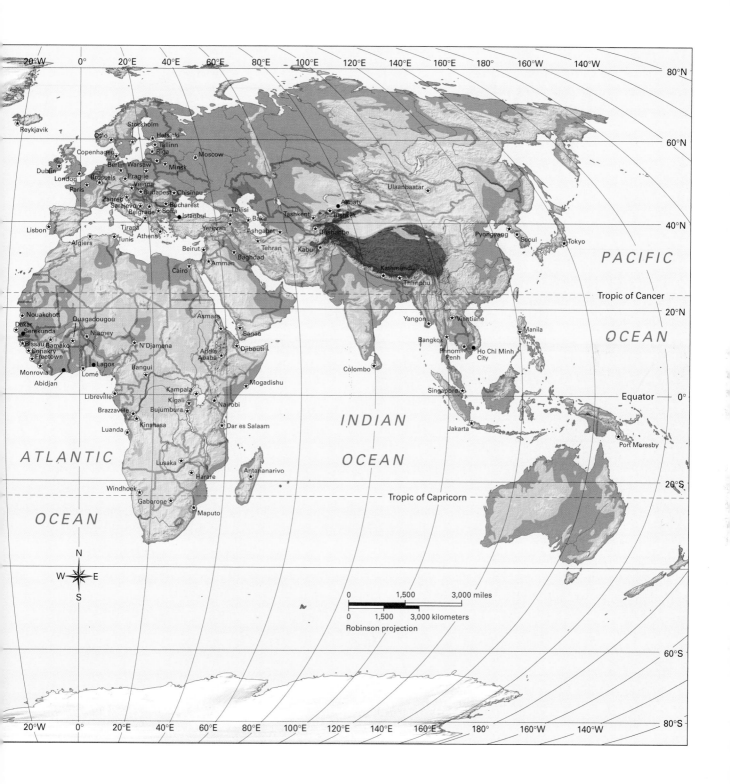

20°W　0°　20°E　40°E　60°E　80°E　100°E　120°E　140°E　160°E　180°　160°W　140°W　80°N

Reykjavik

60°N

Stockholm
Oslo　Helsinki
Copenhagen　Tallinn
Berlin Warsaw　Riga
Dublin　Brussels　Minsk
London　Prague
Paris　Vienna
Zagreb　Budapest Chisinau
Sarajevo　Bucharest
Belgrade　Sofia　Istanbul
Lisbon　Tirana
Athens

Moscow

Ulaanbaatar

Tbilisi
Baku
Tashkent
Bishkek
Ashgabat
Dushanbe

Almaty

Pyongyang
Seoul
Tokyo

40°N

PACIFIC

Algiers　Tunis
Yerevan
Tehran
Beirut
Amman
Baghdad
Cairo
Kabul

Kathmandu
Thimphu

Tropic of Cancer

OCEAN

Nouakchott
Dakar
Serekunda
Bissau　Bamako
Conakry
Freetown
Monrovia　Lomé
Abidjan

Ouagadougou
Niamey
N'Djamena
Lagos
Bangui

Asmara

Sanaa
Djibouti
Addis
Ababa

Yangon
Vientiane

Manila

20°N

Bangkok
Phnom
Penh
Ho Chi Minh
City

OCEAN

Colombo

Mogadishu

Kampala
Libreville　Kigali
Brazzaville　Bujumbura
Kinshasa
Luanda

Nairobi

INDIAN

Singapore

Dar es Salaam

OCEAN

Jakarta

Equator　0°

Port Moresby

ATLANTIC

Lusaka
Harare

Antananarivo

20°S

Windhoek
Gaborone

Tropic of Capricorn

OCEAN

Maputo

N
W　E
S

0　1,500　3,000 miles

0　1,500　3,000 kilometers
Robinson projection

60°S

20°W　0°　20°E　40°E　60°E　80°E　100°E　120°E　140°E　160°E　180°　160°W　140°W　80°S

The Aral Sea: Central Asia's Shrinking Water Source

26.1 Introduction

In 1960, Moynaq was a fishing town in the Soviet Union. It was nearly surrounded by the Aral Sea, a large lake in the Soviet republics of Uzbekistan and Kazakhstan. Visitors to Moynaq in 1960 saw fishing boats bobbing at its docks. At that time, Moynaq had a population of about 40,000 people. Its people farmed, fished, or worked in fish canneries.

All of that has changed. If you visited Moynaq today, you would find it surrounded by dust. Although a 20-foot welcome sign shows a fish and a seagull, you wouldn't see the Aral Sea anywhere. The shoreline of this **inland sea** has withdrawn, and not just a little bit. Now the water's edge is nearly 90 miles from Moynaq.

Moynaq and the surrounding area suffer from **water stress**. Water stress occurs when an area needs more water than it has. As the Aral Sea has shrunk, water stress has increased in this **region**. The area also suffers from **environmental degradation**. To *degrade* something means to damage it or wear it down. In the Aral Sea region, the environment has been degraded by misuse of what little water there is.

In this chapter, you will find out what caused the shrinking of the Aral Sea. You will learn about environmental degradation in the surrounding region. And you will see how damage to the environment has affected farming, fishing, and quality of life in this region.

Essential Question

How are humans affected by changes they make to their physical environment?

This illustration shows the Aral Sea at two different times. Note how much smaller it was in 2008 than in 1964. The arrows represent three aspects of life that have been affected by the shrinking of the sea. Keep this illustration in mind as you try to answer the Essential Question.

Graphic Organizer

◀ This captain's boat was abandoned as the Aral Sea dried up.

The Aral Sea Region

A Central Asian Sea

The Aral Sea lies in two countries, Uzbekistan and Kazakhstan. The Amu and Syr rivers feed this inland sea. It was once a large, freshwater lake. Today it is split into two parts. The larger part, in the south, is a shrunken, salty sea. The smaller part, in the north, is now growing less salty as a result of projects started in 2005 to bring fresh water back to the sea.

26.2 The Geographic Setting

The Aral Sea is located in Central Asia. It lies in two countries: Uzbekistan and Kazakhstan. Before 1991, these two countries were part of the Soviet Union. Until the 1960s, when irrigation projects began, two rivers fed the Aral Sea: the Syr Darya from the northeast and the Amu Darya from the south. (*Darya* means "river.")

From Freshwater Lake to Inland Sea The Aral Sea was first called a sea only because of its great size, not because it was salty. It was really a large lake containing fresh water.

Until the 1960s, the water in the Aral Sea was **potable,** which means that it was drinkable. Potable water can also be used to water crops. But even **freshwater** lakes and rivers have a little salt in them. This salt is washed out of the soil by the water. If the amount of salt in water is very low, we still call the water fresh. The term *salt water* refers only to water that is too salty to drink.

Although the Aral Sea's water used to be fresh, now it is **saline,** which means salty. *Salt* and *saline* both come from a Latin word, *sal,* which means salt. Today the Aral Sea is too salty to drink and too salty for watering crops.

Salinization Affects Water and Land **Salinization** refers to water or land becoming salty or saltier. It can affect a body of water, such as the Great Salt Lake in the state of Utah. Salinization can also affect **groundwater**. Groundwater lies deep underground and supplies wells and springs.

To understand salinization, start with rain. Pure rain falls from the sky as fresh water. As this water seeps into the ground or runs off into streams, it picks up some salt from the soil. Most of that salt is carried by rivers to the ocean. This is why oceans are saline.

However, not all rivers flow directly into the ocean. Some end in lakes and inland seas. If water flows both into and out of a lake, the water that flows out carries some of this salt to the ocean. If no water flows out of a lake, the salt has nowhere to go. When water evaporates from a lake, the salt is left behind. The lake grows more and more saline over time, until it becomes an inland sea.

Salinization of land happens in a different way. When farmers irrigate, they bring water from lakes and rivers to their fields. Often this fresh water contains a little salt. When the water evaporates, it leaves the salt behind on the soil's surface. There might not be enough salt to damage plants at first. But if people do not wash the salt away, the soil grows saltier as the years pass. Few plants can grow in salty soil.

Both the water and the land in the Aral Sea region have been degraded by salinization. The Aral Sea was once Earth's fourth-largest freshwater lake. Now it is about 10 percent of its original size and split into two parts. The larger part, in the south, is as salty as any ocean. The smaller part, in the north, is also still too salty to drink. But recent projects are starting to bring fresh water back into this part of the sea.

► Geoterms

environmental degradation damage to or destruction of the natural environment. When such damage occurs, habitats are destroyed, biodiversity is lost, or natural resources are used up.

groundwater water lying deep under the ground that supplies wells and springs. Over half the people in the world depend on groundwater for their drinking water.

salinization the buildup of salt in soil or water

water stress the condition that occurs when people do not have enough clean, fresh water to meet their everyday needs

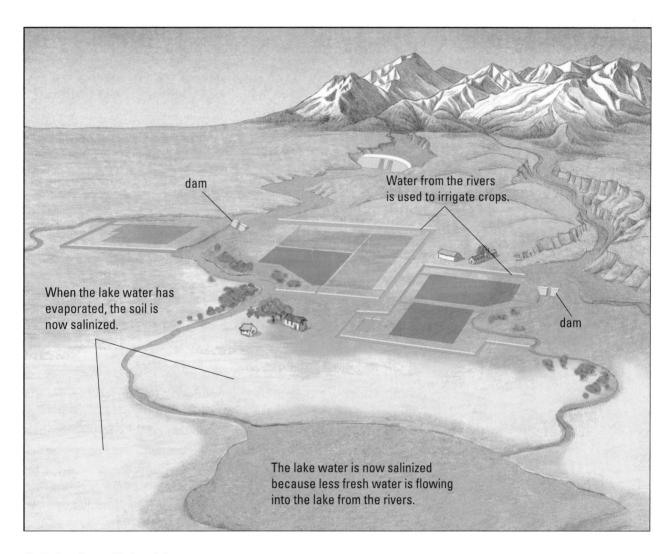

dam

Water from the rivers is used to irrigate crops.

dam

When the lake water has evaporated, the soil is now salinized.

The lake water is now salinized because less fresh water is flowing into the lake from the rivers.

Salinization of Inland Seas

A lake with no outlet to the ocean is likely to grow saltier over time. When water evaporates from a lake, any salt that was dissolved in that water is left behind. Over time, salt builds up in the lake. This process happens faster when water from the rivers that feed into a lake is used for irrigation. With less water coming in, the lake shrinks. At the same time, the concentration of salt in the lake water increases.

The Power of Cotton

Growing cotton in the desert meant more money for the people who lived there. The "white gold" crop became a central focus of life in desert communities. The city of Tashkent, Uzbekistan's capital, called its soccer team the Cotton Pickers.

26.3 The Shrinking Sea and Farming

Cotton is sometimes called "white gold." It's a **cash crop** that earns farmers a good income. But cotton needs a long, warm growing season and lots of water to thrive.

For the government of the former Soviet Union, finding a place to grow cotton posed a problem. Some areas had enough rain but were too cold. Others were warm enough but too dry. The solution was to plant cotton in a **desert** region of Central Asia. The cotton would be irrigated with water diverted, or taken, from two rivers.

From Desert to Cotton Kingdom The Soviet government provided water to cotton farms by building dams on the Amu and Syr rivers. The water stored behind the dams was used to irrigate large areas. Large amounts of chemical fertilizers and **pesticides** were used to increase production in this new cotton kingdom. At first, irrigating a desert to grow cotton seemed to work well. The new crop provided jobs for local people.

Salinization Creates a New Desert An unplanned effect of the damming of the rivers was the degradation of the Aral Sea. About 90 percent of the rivers' water was stored behind the dams. Only 10 percent reached the sea. As water evaporated from the Aral, the sea began to shrink. Large areas of dry seabed became a salty wasteland.

The shrinking of the sea changed the region's **climate**. When the sea was full, the Aral cooled the surrounding land in summer and warmed it in winter. As the sea shrank, summers became hotter and winters colder. The growing season decreased from the 200 days a year needed for cotton crops to only 170 days. As the climate cooled, some farmers turned from cotton to rice because rice has a shorter growing season. But like cotton, rice needs a lot of water.

The use of river water for irrigation also degraded the land. Year by year, salt carried by the rivers built up on farm fields. Some areas became too salty to grow crops. Many farmers were left with nothing but salty desert.

26.4 The Shrinking Sea and Fishing

A shocked visitor to Moynaq in 2001 described a spooky sight. Rusting hulks of fishing boats lay scattered across a desert. The abandoned boats were surrounded by junk. Fiberglass, metal, rusty springs, and cigarette butts littered the ground. A boat's propeller lay half-buried in the sand. The sight was so strange that the visitor almost expected to find that space aliens had left the boats there! Instead, the boats are reminders of a time when the Aral Sea was home to many fisheries. A **fishery** is a place where fish are caught, processed, and sold.

A Sea Once Rich in Fish Until about 1980, many of these boats had docked at Moynaq. Before it began to shrink, the Aral Sea was rich in fish. About 95 million pounds of fish were harvested from the lake each year. Fish canneries in Moynaq produced 20 million cans of seafood a year. This thriving industry supported about 35,000 workers.

The Collapse of the Aral Sea Fishing Industry The shrinking of the Aral Sea destroyed the fishing industry. As the sea began to withdraw, fisheries were left high and dry. Today Moynaq is more than 90 miles from the water's edge.

The small amount of water that remains in the sea is very salty. Very few organisms can live in such saline conditions. Most of the 100 species of fish that once lived in the sea are gone. Commercial fishing ended in 1982. As a result, fishing crews and cannery workers lost their jobs.

Most of these workers have not been able to find other jobs nearby. The highest level of joblessness in Kazakhstan is in the Aral Sea region. Thousands of people have left to seek work elsewhere. Often men **migrate** alone. They leave their families behind in dying towns. The women and children survive on whatever money the men send home. Of the 40,000 people who once lived in Moynaq, only about 3,000 remain.

The Aral Sea's Dying Industry

Fresh water used to cover the seabed in this photograph. As the sea has shrunk, the fish that once lived here have disappeared. Thousands of people who once worked in fisheries around the sea have lost their jobs as a result. Many have left the region to look for work.

Searching for Fresh Water

Today, water from the Aral Sea is too salty to drink. People in the region have turned to other water sources, such as rivers and groundwater. This woman relies on groundwater from her well. Unfortunately, that water may be polluted and unsafe to drink.

26.5 The Shrinking Sea and Quality of Life

Strong winds pick up sand that used to be at the bottom of the Aral Sea. People call these dust storms "black blizzards." They are a sign of the declining quality of life in the Aral Sea region.

From Plentiful Fresh Water to Water Stress Before the 1960s, the Aral Sea provided water for nearby towns. There was enough water for household use and to irrigate crops on small farms.

Today, the Aral Sea region faces severe water stress. The water in the Aral Sea is too salty to drink, so people have turned to rivers and groundwater to meet their water needs. But much of that water is unfit to drink, too. It has been polluted by salt, **sewage,** and **toxic chemicals** used on farms. These problems are caused by people, not nature.

Pollution Damages the Health of Residents Many people living around the Aral Sea have become ill from drinking polluted water. Stomach problems and liver disease are common.

Air pollution poses another threat to health. The region's "black blizzards" carry toxic chemicals along with dust. People who breathe in these chemicals develop many health problems. These problems range from throat cancer to deadly lung diseases like tuberculosis.

Widespread poverty only makes these health problems worse. Nearly all pregnant women in the Aral Sea region suffer from anemia. This is a disease caused by poor nutrition. Many babies are born sick. A significant number of them die before their first birthday.

An Uncertain Future Many scientific reports and news stories have been written about the Aral Sea region. This reporting has slowly begun to help the people there. As one Moynaq resident said, "If every scientist and journalist who visited the Aral Sea brought with them a bucket of water, the sea would be filled again."

Repairing the environmental degradation in this region will require costly changes. First, less water should be taken out of the Amu and Syr rivers for irrigation. This will allow more water to flow into the Aral Sea.

Farming practices need to change as well. With less water available for irrigation, farmers will have to plant less thirsty crops, such as grapes and fruit trees. They will also need to be more careful using fertilizers and pesticides.

Finally, governments need to improve their water management. They need to build water systems to provide safe drinking water to residents. They also need to build water treatment plants. These plants treat sewage and **wastewater** to reduce water pollution.

These changes will cost billions of dollars. This is far more than any country in the region can afford. But there is hope. In 2005, Kazakhstan and the World Bank built an $85 million dike and dam system to move water from the Syr River into the northern sea. The water level of this part of the Aral rose about 6 feet in 8 months. Saltiness was cut by about half. The sea also increased in area by 20 percent. Also, this part of Central Asia has large oil reserves. In the future, countries around the Aral Sea may be able to use money earned by selling oil to improve the quality of life in this region.

26.6 Beginning to Think Globally

In this chapter, you learned about environmental degradation in the Aral Sea region. You saw how dams on the Amu and Syr rivers reduced water flowing into the Aral Sea. The sea has shrunk as a result and split into two parts. It has also become very salty. Increased irrigation with river water has caused widespread soil salinization. Air and water pollution have increased as well. These changes have created an environmental disaster around the Aral Sea.

The Aral Sea region is not the only part of the world facing water stress. Wherever people live, they need water. But many places don't receive enough rainfall to meet people's water needs. People then turn to other water sources such as rivers or groundwater. Egypt, for example, is a desert country. For thousands of years, Egyptians have depended on the Nile River to meet all of their water needs. Without the Nile, life would be impossible in Egypt.

Water stress results when a region's need for water becomes greater than its supply. Think about this as you look at irrigation around the world in the next section.

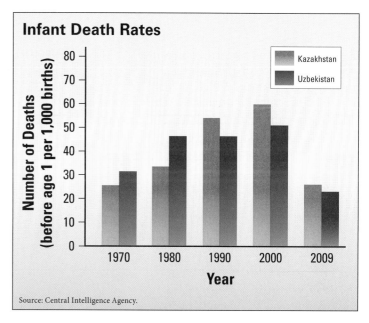

Infant Death Rates

Source: Central Intelligence Agency.

A Poor Place to Be Born
Infant mortality in the Aral Sea region rose as environmental degradation increased. Recent efforts to improve health conditions have begun to lower infant mortality rates.

Women Sick with Tuberculosis
These women in Uzbekistan are suffering from a lung disease known as tuberculosis, or TB. TB used to be one of the most common causes of death in the world. Today it is found mainly in developing countries. TB usually strikes people whose health has been weakened by bad water, dirty air, or poor nutrition.

26.7 Global Connections

This map shows regions of the world that rely on irrigation to grow crops. The colors indicate the percentage of land in each area that is irrigated. Symbols for four crops that are heavy water users are shown in the countries where the majority of the total world production of each crop is grown.

What factors might affect how much water a region uses for irrigating crops? One factor is population density. The more people in a region, the more food local farmers must grow to feed those people. Another factor is climate. Areas with a lot of year-round rainfall need little irrigation. Those with little rain depend on irrigation. A third factor is the type of crop being grown. Some crops are thirstier than others.

What areas are most likely to experience water stress? Areas with dry climates and high population densities are most likely to face water stress. Most of California, for example, is arid. Farmers there rely on irrigation to grow large amounts of cotton, fruits, and vegetables. But the urban population of California is growing. As a result, farmers have to compete with cities for limited water supplies.

What choices can people make to reduce water stress? The best way to reduce water stress is to reduce water needs. For farmers in arid regions, this means growing less thirsty crops. Switching from cotton to wheat, for example, can cut water use by more than half. For families, this means using less water for daily living. For example, fixing one dripping faucet can save 3,000 gallons of water per year.

Irrigated Lands Around the World

Percentage of irrigated land
- 0%
- 0%–0.1%
- 0.1%–1%
- 1%–5%
- 5%–10%
- 10%–20%
- 20%–35%
- 35%–50%
- 50%–75%
- 75%–100%

Four thirsty crops
- Cotton
- Rice
- Sugarcane
- Wheat

Irrigation of a rice field

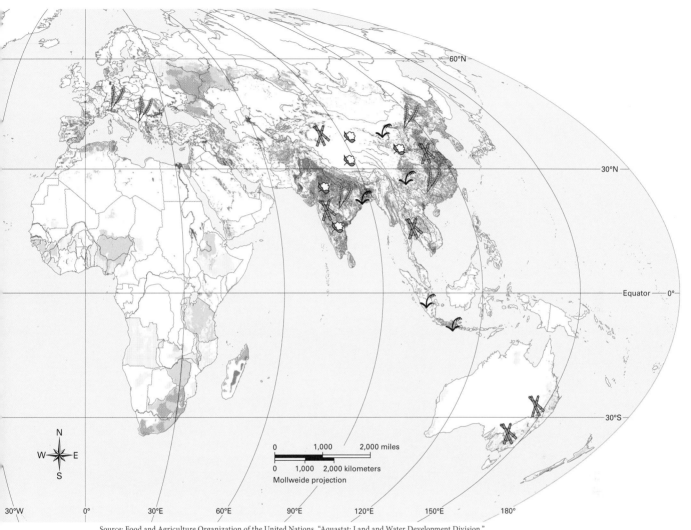

Source: Food and Agriculture Organization of the United Nations, "Aquastat: Land and Water Development Division."

Four Thirsty Crops

Crop	Symbol	Water Needed to Grow 1 Pound of Crop	Major World Producers
Cotton		840–3,500 gallons	China, India, United States
Rice		360–600 gallons	China, India, Indonesia
Sugarcane		180–360 gallons	Brazil, India, Thailand, China
Wheat		110 gallons	China, India, United States, Russia

Source: World Wildlife Fund.

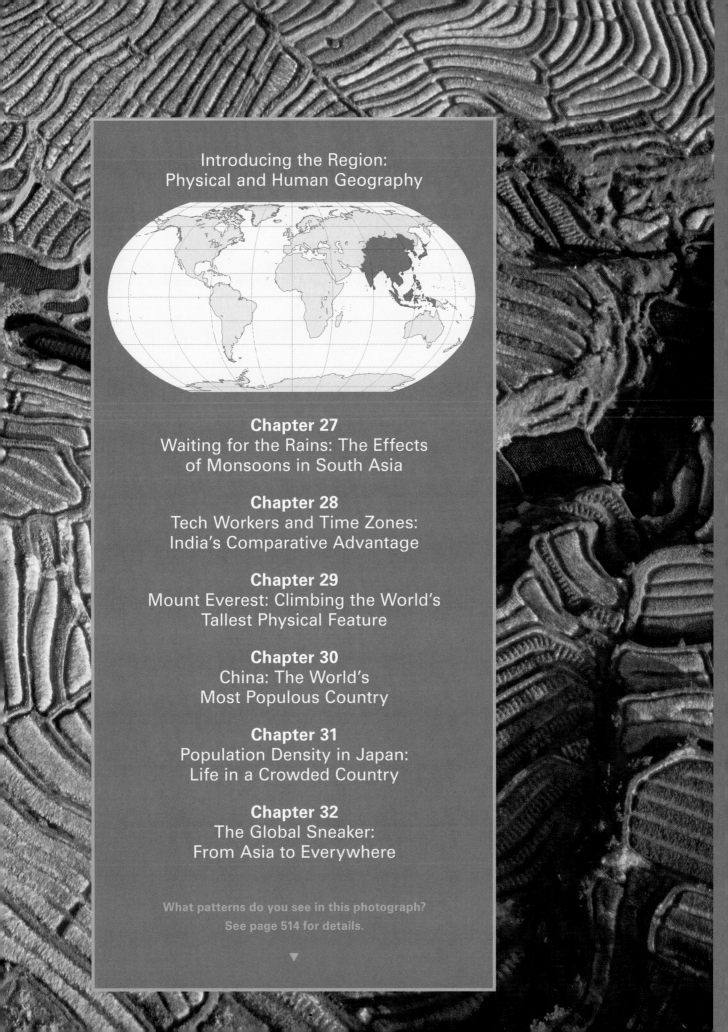

Introducing the Region:
Physical and Human Geography

What patterns do you see in this photograph?
See page 514 for details.

▼

onsoon Asia begins at the western border of India. From there, it reaches east to the Pacific Ocean. In the north, it spreads across China to the Korean Peninsula. A large **peninsula** south of China includes Vietnam, Laos, Cambodia, and Thailand. This peninsula is ringed by the South China Sea, the Gulf of Thailand, and the Bay of Bengal.

This **region** has several countries made up of many islands. They include Japan, the Philippines, and Indonesia. Sri Lanka, Brunei, and East Timor are other island **nations**.

The countries of Monsoon Asia are often grouped into three subregions. These smaller regions are South Asia, East Asia, and Southeast Asia.

Physical Features of Monsoon Asia

Elevation

Feet	Meters
Over 10,000	Over 3,050
5,001–10,000	1,526–3,050
2,001–5,000	611–1,525
1,001–2,000	306–610
0–1,000	0–305
Below sea level	Below sea level

▲ Mountain peak

0   500   1,000 miles
0   500   1,000 kilometers
Lambert Azimuthal Equal-Area projection

Physical Features

Mountains are the most commanding feature of Monsoon Asia's **landscape**. The rugged Himalayas form India's northern border. They include Mount Everest, the world's highest mountain. Like other mountain ranges, the Himalayas were formed when sections of Earth's **crust,** called *plates,* collided. The two plates that came together to create the Himalayas are still colliding. As a result, the mountains are getting higher. But mountain building is a slow process. Mount Everest grows about half an inch a year.

The Himalayas are the world's highest mountain chain.

South Asia

India makes up most of South Asia. Many people call India a *subcontinent*. Mountains and ocean separate India from the rest of Asia, so it is almost like a small continent.

Three important rivers begin in the Himalayas. They are the Indus, the Ganges, and the Brahmaputra. The Ganges and Brahmaputra meet to form one of the world's largest river **deltas**. Then, they empty into the Bay of Bengal.

The Ghats are another mountain range in India. The Eastern and Western Ghats run parallel to India's coasts. Between them lies the Deccan Plateau. The Deccan Plateau covers most of southern India's interior.

East Asia

East Asia's landscape is diverse. Mountains surround the Plateau of Tibet. The Huang He begins on this **plateau**. So does the Chang Jiang (Yangtze), the third longest river in the world. Both rivers run east across China before emptying into the Pacific.

North of the Tibetan Plateau lie the Taklamakan and Gobi **deserts**. The Gobi is one of the world's largest deserts. According to legend, an angry Mongolian chief created it. He turned the land to desert when Chinese warriors forced him to leave this area.

The hilly Korean Peninsula and the chain of islands that make up Japan are also part of East Asia. Japan's islands were formed by **volcanoes**.

Southeast Asia

Southeast Asia is not one big **landmass**. Instead, it is made up of peninsulas and islands. For example, the Malay Peninsula juts out into the South China Sea.

Thousands of islands dot the seas of Southeast Asia. Some, like Borneo, are fairly large. Others are so small that they just look like specks on a map.

Elevation Profile of Monsoon Asia

30°N Latitude

Elevation (feet) — 20,000 / 15,000 / 10,000 / 5,000 / 0 Sea Level

Elevation (meters) — 6,096 / 4,572 / 3,048 / 1,524 / 0

Himalayas — Plateau of Tibet

Ganges River

Chang Jiang (Yangtze River)

East China Sea

Climate

As the name of this region suggests, the **climate** of much of Asia is shaped by **monsoons**. Monsoons are strong winds that create the rainfall patterns in this region. In summer, monsoons blow from the ocean toward the land, bringing clouds that are heavy with rain.

In areas affected by monsoons, summers are very wet and winters fairly dry. Mumbai, India, for example, has a monsoon climate. It gets more than 70 inches of rain between June and September. But the same city gets little or no rain from December to April.

South Asia

South Asia's climate ranges from **arid** to tropical. The northwest part of the subcontinent is dry. So is part of the Deccan Plateau in central India.

The Himalayas have a **highlands** climate. In a highlands zone, the climate gets colder as elevation increases. The Himalayas are very high and very cold. Snow covers the higher peaks throughout the year. In fact, the word Himalaya means "House of Snow."

Tropical climates dominate the rest of South Asia. A **tropical wet** climate makes the west coast hot and rainy all year long. Much of interior South Asia is **tropical wet and dry**. The area has one rainy season and one dry season. Temperatures remain fairly high year-round. Finally, north central India has a **humid subtropical** climate, with hot, humid summers and mild winters.

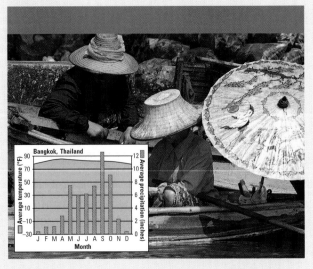

Hats and parasols protect people in Bangkok from the tropical sun. In what month are these people likely to trade their paper parasols for umbrellas?

East Asia

Like South Asia, East Asia has a variety of climates. A highlands climate is found in the Plateau of Tibet. Arid and semiarid areas border this **landform**. They include the Gobi and Taklamakan deserts.

The Korean Peninsula has a **humid continental** climate. People there endure hot, steamy summers. Then they face very cold winters. Parts of Japan and eastern China experience a humid subtropical climate. They have hot, steamy summers and mild winters. Rain falls fairly evenly throughout the year.

Southeast Asia

Southeast Asia is tropical. Most areas nearest the equator have a tropical wet climate. It is hot and rainy all year in the Philippines, Singapore, and most of Malaysia and Indonesia. Other parts of Southeast Asia have a tropical wet and dry climate. The weather is hot all year with both rainy and dry seasons in most of Thailand, Cambodia, and southern Vietnam.

The mountain regions of Japan have severe winters with heavy snow.

Vegetation

The **vegetation** in Monsoon Asia varies as much as the region's climate does. In the drier parts of the region, only **desert scrub** survives. But in the tropical zones, lush plants thrive and form thick **rainforests**.

Elevation also has a big effect on Monsoon Asia's plant life. Remember that in a highlands climate, temperature varies with elevation. Vegetation varies with elevation as well. The region's highest mountains are so cold that they are covered by ice and snow. Very little can grow in this **ice cap** vegetation zone.

South Asia

The plant life of South Asia varies with the climates and the altitude. The driest land supports only desert scrub. **Tropical grassland** covers much of central India. **Mixed forest** appears on the lower slopes of the Himalayas. In the tropical climate zones, **broadleaf evergreen forest** is common.

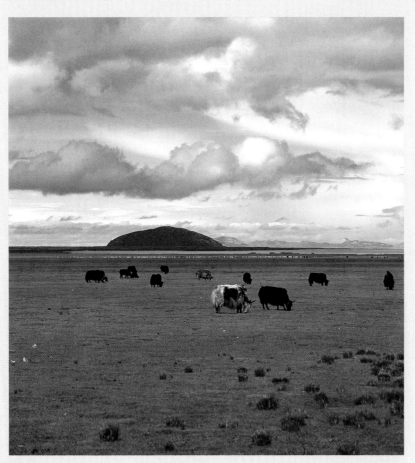

East Asia

Because East Asia has so many **climate zones,** this subregion supports many different types of plant life.

The Plateau of Tibet and mountainous parts of China support **highlands** vegetation. The large deserts are home to **desert** and desert scrub vegetation. Much of the northern part of this subregion is too dry for trees. But grasses grow well there.

The warmer and wetter areas of East Asia support forests. Northeast China, the Korean Peninsula, and Japan are covered with mixed and **deciduous forest**. Many pines grow on Japan's mountains and along its seashores.

Much of southeastern China has a humid subtropical climate. Broadleaf evergreen forests thrive where it is warm and rainy.

Southeast Asia

Just about all of Southeast Asia is warm and wet. Rainforests and tropical grassland cover most of this region. Over time, much of the rainforest has been cleared to raise crops that do well in the tropics. People grow rice, sugarcane, tea, and rubber.

Many types of bamboo grow well here. Bamboo is a grass. But unlike most grasses, it can grow to huge sizes. Some types of bamboo may reach over 100 feet high and have stems a foot in diameter. Bamboo stems are made into everything from houses to tools. Bamboo probably has more uses than any other plant in tropical areas.

Tibet is often called the "Roof of the World." Yaks graze in the highland meadows on the Plateau of Tibet, which lies more than 10,000 feet above sea level.

There are 23 countries in Monsoon Asia. Some, like China, are very old. Others, like East Timor, are quite new.

Much of Monsoon Asia is densely settled. China is the world's most populous country. It has more than 1.3 billion people. India is a close second with more than a billion people.

With so many people, it is no surprise that some of the world's largest and most crowded cities are found in Monsoon Asia. They include Kolkata and Mumbai, India; Dhaka, Bangladesh; Shanghai, China; Seoul, South Korea; Tokyo, Japan; Manila, Philippines; and Jakarta, Indonesia.

Political Boundaries of Monsoon Asia

History

Some of the world's earliest civilizations arose in Monsoon Asia. At different times, rulers united parts of the region into **empires**. Later, European countries colonized much of the region. In modern times, most Asian peoples have gained their independence.

Early Times

East Asia's first civilization took root in the Huang He valley. China was split into many kingdoms early in its history.

In 221 B.C.E., one of these kingdoms, the Qin, united China. The name China comes from the word Qin. The first ruler of this empire, the Emperor Qin, built China's first Great Wall. From the first emperor until modern times, China was ruled by a series of dynasties, or ruling families. When one family lost power, another rose to take its place.

South Asia's first civilization arose in the Indus River valley around 2500 B.C.E. One of its main cities was Mohenjo-daro. As many as 40,000 people lived there. The people of Mohenjo-daro enjoyed comforts that were very advanced for that time. Their homes had indoor bathrooms that drained into a city sewer system.

No one knows how the Indus Valley civilization ended. But by 1700 B.C.E., it had vanished. For centuries after that, South Asia was a land of small kingdoms.

In the 320s B.C.E., a powerful family called the Mauryas saw how weak these kingdoms were. The Mauryas conquered most of them and united India into one empire. The Mauryan Empire lasted for about 130 years.

Conquests and Colonies

After the Mauryan Empire fell, India once more broke apart. Then in 1526, invaders from Central Asia conquered India. The invaders, called Mughals, united India as a new empire. The Mughals ruled India into the early 1700s.

Starting in the late 1400s, Europeans colonized many parts of Monsoon Asia. The Spanish set up trading posts in the Philippines. The Dutch started colonies in Indonesia. The British began businesses in India. By the late 1700s, the British ruled most of India.

In the 1800s, France joined the race for colonies. The French took over much of Southeast Asia. They controlled the area that is now Vietnam, Laos, and Cambodia.

The Modern Era

In the last half-century, most colonies in Monsoon Asia freed themselves from European control. India gained its independence from Great Britain in 1947. The French left Southeast Asia in the 1950s.

Parts of Monsoon Asia have prospered in recent years. Japan is now one of the world's leading industrial countries. Other areas, such as South Korea, Taiwan, and Singapore, have also developed modern industrial economies.

However, Monsoon Asia has developed unevenly. Some people live very well. But in many parts of the region, most people still live in poverty.

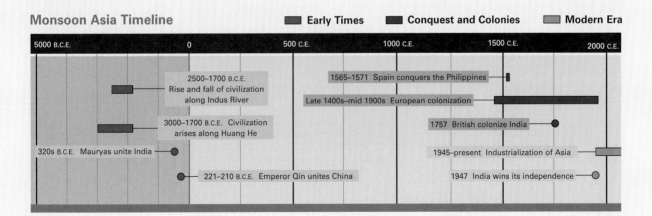

Monsoon Asia Timeline — Early Times — Conquest and Colonies — Modern Era

5000 B.C.E.	0 — 500 C.E. — 1000 C.E. — 1500 C.E. — 2000 C.E.

2500–1700 B.C.E. Rise and fall of civilization along Indus River

3000–1700 B.C.E. Civilization arises along Huang He

320s B.C.E. Mauryas unite India

221–210 B.C.E. Emperor Qin unites China

1565–1571 Spain conquers the Philippines

Late 1400s–mid 1900s European colonization

1757 British colonize India

1945–present Industrialization of Asia

1947 India wins its independence

Population

About 3.5 billion people live in Monsoon Asia. That is more than half the world's people. China, India, and Indonesia are three of the world's five most populous countries.

Monsoon Asia is mostly **rural**. However, cities are growing quickly. Every year, large numbers of people leave the countryside to look for work in cities. As a result, many cities suffer from overcrowding. The people who live there are often unemployed and poor.

Monsoon Asia is a region with many religious traditions. In India and Nepal, most people are Hindu. Islam also has many followers in Monsoon Asia. In fact, Indonesia has the world's largest Muslim population. Nine out of ten people there are Muslim.

Buddhism is the main religion in Southeast Asia. Most people in Japan practice Shinto or Buddhism. Confucianism began in China about 2,500 years ago. Its influence is still felt today. Christianity also has followers in Monsoon Asia, especially in the Philippines.

Monsoon Asia: Major Religions

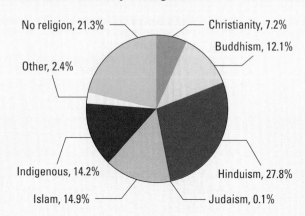

- No religion, 21.3%
- Christianity, 7.2%
- Buddhism, 12.1%
- Other, 2.4%
- Hinduism, 27.8%
- Indigenous, 14.2%
- Islam, 14.9%
- Judaism, 0.1%

Monsoon Asia: Urban and Rural Population, 2007

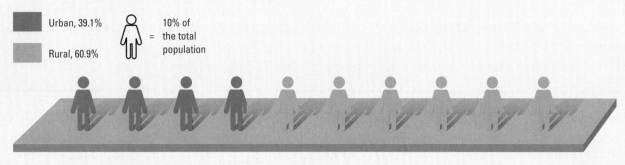

Urban, 39.1%

Rural, 60.9%

10% of = the total population

Monsoon Asia: Population Growth, 1950–2050

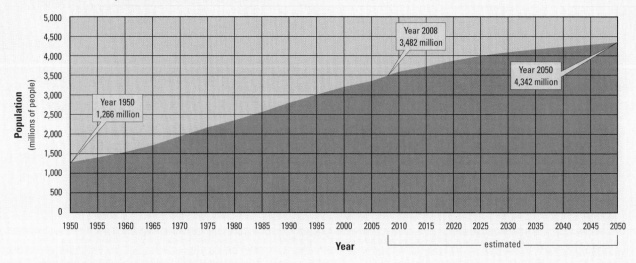

Year 2008
3,482 million

Year 2050
4,342 million

Year 1950
1,266 million

Population (millions of people)

Year

estimated

Sources: United Nations Department of Economic and Social Affairs, Population Division. Encyclopaedia Britannica.

Economic Activity

The economy of Monsoon Asia is a mix of old and new. Most people still work to feed themselves by farming and fishing. At the same time, parts of the region have become important centers for industry and finance.

The many people of Monsoon Asia who live near the seacoast have always fished for food. But fishing has also become a big business in Asia. **Commercial fishing** is different from traditional small-scale fishing. Commercial fishing boats can gather huge amounts of fish in their nets. Most of what they catch is processed, packaged, and sent all over the world.

Resources

Monsoon Asia is rich in resources. Northern China has large coal deposits. It produces more coal than any other country on Earth. Southeast Asia has much of the world's tin. Petroleum reserves lie beneath Indonesia. In addition, the region's many rivers are well suited for **hydroelectric power**.

An Indian villager watches over his fishing nets. Fishing is a major part of Monsoon Asia's economy.

Land Use

Most people in Monsoon Asia still live off the land. Some are subsistence farmers. They grow enough to feed their families. Rice is the staple for many of them. Others are commercial farmers. They grow crops for export, including tea, cotton, spices, and tobacco.

More than 90 percent of the world's rubber is produced in Southeast Asia. Rubber comes from the sap of the rubber tree. To get the sap, a rubber tapper cuts a diagonal shaving of bark from the tree. A metal spout and cup are attached to the bottom of this cut. Sap oozes from the cut and drips into the cup. Tappers collect about a teacup of sap each time they tap a tree.

China's commercial fishing industry is among the world's largest. Indonesia exports large amounts of shrimp and tuna. India, Japan, and South Korea also have large fishing industries.

Nomadic herders live in some remote parts of Monsoon Asia. Their lives are similar to their ancestors' lives. They herd cattle, goats, sheep, and yaks. Other parts of Monsoon Asia, however, have booming modern economies. International trade is strong in Taiwan, Singapore, Hong Kong, and South Korea. China is a major producer of consumer goods, as well as machinery. Japan is a world leader in the production of cars and electronics.

The Three Gorges Dam, on China's Yangtze river, was completed in 2009. It produces more hydroelectric power than any other dam in the world. This power will support the growth of industry across China.

Waiting for the Rains: The Effects of Monsoons in South Asia

27

27.1 Introduction

Every June, all of India looks to the sky. When the rains come late, people begin to worry. Indian astrologers call this time *rohini*. It is a time when hot, dry winds swirl dust across the parched plains. Women might walk for miles in 115°F heat to the nearest water source. Sometimes they collapse from heat exhaustion.

As one hot day follows another, farmers pray for help from the Hindu rain god Indra. In one region, people catch frogs to bring rain. They hope that the frogs' loud croaking will call down clouds from the sky. Even the giant crocodiles of northern India wait eagerly for the rains. Without flooded, moist riverbanks, they have nowhere to lay their eggs.

When the skies finally darken, a sense of expectation builds. The **monsoons** have arrived. These seasonal winds blow in from the ocean each summer. They are strong and violent, bringing with them clouds heavy with moisture. Almost all of the rain South Asia gets each year comes from these summer storms. All of India celebrates as sheets of rain pound the dry, thirsty land below.

In this chapter, you will find out why the monsoons blow across South Asia each year. You will explore how monsoons affect the **climate** of four cities in this region. And finally, you will discover how the people in these cities adapt to a lifetime spent waiting for the rains.

Essential Question	Graphic Organizer

How does climate influence human activity in a region?

This climagraph shows average monthly temperatures and precipitation in the city of Mumbai, India. Notice the bars. They show the average precipitation for each month. Also notice the line. It shows average monthly temperatures for this city. Keep this climagraph in mind as you try to answer the Essential Question.

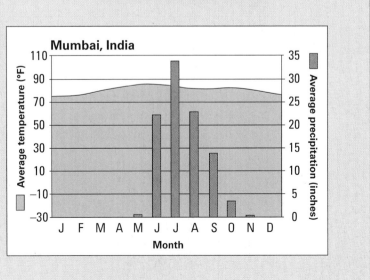

◀ A rickshaw traveling through the flooded streets of Dhaka, Bangladesh

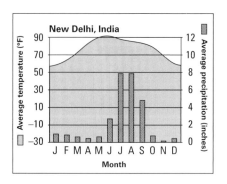

New Delhi's Monsoon Climate

Monsoon winds affect the climate of New Delhi, the capital of India. The city sits on the edge of the Thar Desert in northern India. From October to May, it stays mostly cold and dry. But during the summer monsoon months, rain can drench the city.

27.2 The Geographic Setting

South Asia juts out into the Indian Ocean like a giant triangle. This very large **peninsula** is also known as the Indian subcontinent. The Himalaya mountain range cuts the subcontinent off from the rest of Central Asia. One out of every five people on Earth lives in South Asia. Most are farmers who both look forward to and fear the coming of the monsoons.

Changes in Atmospheric Pressure Create Monsoons Have you ever heard a weather forecaster talk about an area of high or low pressure? What this means is high or low **atmospheric pressure**. This is the weight of the **atmosphere** pressing down on the surface of Earth. Falling cool air creates areas of high pressure. Rising warm air creates areas of low pressure.

In a high-pressure area, cool air from the upper atmosphere presses down toward Earth's surface. As it does so, atmospheric pressure increases. With all of this downward pressure, very little surface air can rise into the upper atmosphere to form clouds. High pressure generally means sunny days and no rain. The opposite happens in a low-pressure area. Warm surface air moves easily into the upper atmosphere. If this air is moist, it forms clouds that bring rain.

Air from high-pressure areas naturally flows into low-pressure areas. This movement of air creates wind. In the spring and summer, the air over the South Asian landmass warms up faster than the air over the Indian Ocean. As this hot air rises, it creates a low-pressure area. Cool, moist air from the Indian Ocean flows into the area of low pressure. This movement of air creates the summer monsoons.

In the fall and winter, however, the air over South Asia cools down. The cooler air sinks and forms an area of high pressure. This high pressure keeps the moist air that blew in with the summer monsoons far out to sea. Little rain falls in South Asia from October to March. During this long dry period, South Asians must deal with dusty fields and dwindling water sources.

Mountain Ranges Create Rain Shadows Mountains affect where summer storms drop their moisture. A mountain slope facing **upwind,** or against the monsoon winds, generally gets a lot of rain. A slope facing **downwind,** or in the same direction the wind is blowing, gets far less rain. Geographers call the impact that mountains have on rainfall patterns the **orographic effect**.

The orographic effect works this way. When clouds blow up against mountains, the moist air rises up the slopes. As the air rises, it cools. The cooling air cannot hold as much moisture as it did before. And so the clouds release their moisture as rain or snow.

By the time the clouds cross over the mountains, they have little moisture left. As a result, people living on the downwind side get very little rainfall. This dry area is called a **rain shadow**. People living in a rain shadow have to adapt to life with little rain.

▶ Geoterms

atmospheric pressure the weight of the atmosphere pressing down on any point of the surface of Earth. Air sinks in high-pressure areas, and few clouds form. Air rises in low-pressure areas to form clouds that produce rain.

monsoon a seasonal wind. Summer monsoon winds in South Asia usually bring rain to that region.

orographic effect the precipitation that occurs when moist air rises up the side of a mountain. As the air rises, it cools down and releases most of its moisture as rain or snow.

rain shadow a dry area on the downwind side of a mountain

South Asia's Summer Monsoons

The Orographic Effect

Monsoons and Mountains

Summer monsoon winds carry moist air from the Indian Ocean. These winds strike the Western Ghat mountain range in western India. As air rises, it cools and drops its moisture as rain. Cities on the upwind side of the mountains receive plenty of rainfall. Cities on the down-wind side, in the rain shadow, receive relatively little.

27.3 The Wet Months in Dhaka, Bangladesh

About 13 million people live in Dhaka, the **capital city** of Bangladesh. For them, July can be a difficult month. In July 1996, the homes of 3 million people were flooded. Two years later, 1,500 people died in July floods. Their deaths were blamed on everything from drowning to disease. In July 2004, rains left much of Dhaka under water.

One of the World's Wettest Capitals Most of Bangladesh lies on a river **delta** that seldom rises more than 30 feet above sea level. Rice, a crop that grows best in warm, shallow water, thrives here. In July, monsoon rains often raise rivers to dangerous levels. When the rivers flood, even rice finds it hard to survive.

Dhaka sits in the center of Bangladesh. The city has one of the wettest climates on Earth. Up to 80 inches of rain falls there each year. Most of this rain comes in the summer months. From November to April, the weather is dry.

Flooding is not Dhaka's only problem. Bangladesh is often hit by **tropical cyclones**. Tropical cyclone is another name for hurricane. Because Dhaka sits at sea level, it is often lashed by high winds and waves during these violent storms.

Life Depends on the Rains Bangladesh's economy depends on agriculture. Nearly three out of every five people farm the country's rich delta soil. They rely on monsoon rains to water their fields. When the summer rains are late, crops like rice, sugarcane, tea, and tobacco suffer. When monsoons bring too much rain too quickly, fields flood. Deep water then makes planting and harvesting impossible.

Dhaka also suffers from too much rain. When city streets flood, car and bus traffic comes to a halt. Schools and businesses close down because no one can get to work. Floodwaters pollute the city's drinking water supply. Under these conditions, disease spreads rapidly. Children growing up in Dhaka learn early that the rains that bring life to local fields can also end life in the city.

Preparing for the Rain

The people of Dhaka have come to expect flooding when the summer rains arrive. One way they have adapted is to raise their homes up on stilts. A raised home is not convenient most of the year, when everything has to be carried up and down stairs or ladders. In times of flood, however, it can be a lifesaver.

27.4 The Dry Months of Jodhpur, India

The Mehrangarh Fort rises out of the **desert** like a towering giant. The fort looks down on the "Blue City" of Jodhpur, India. In the old city, most of the houses are painted blue. Some say this is to keep away mosquitoes. In July 2002, nearly half of Jodhpur's crops could not be planted. The summer monsoons were late. The worst **drought** in more than 40 years had begun.

A City on the Edge of a Desert Jodhpur sits at the eastern edge of the Thar Desert in northern India. This region is a leading producer of cattle, spices, and grains. It has a typical **semiarid** climate. For most of the year, the weather is hot and dry.

The people living in and around Jodhpur are used to their semiarid climate. In most years, the city receives about 14 inches of rain. Average temperatures do not drop below 60°F, even in the winter. Summer monsoons bring much-needed rains from June to September.

Water Is a Critical Resource Eighty percent of the people living around Jodhpur are farmers. But farming is difficult in this dry region. The desert soil needs a great deal of water to produce crops. Farmers depend on the monsoons for that water. How much rain will come and when will it arrive are questions people here ask every year.

The rains come late in some years. Or too little rain falls. When that happens, crops fail. Drinking water vanishes. Families that run out of food sometimes survive by eating *samas*, a wild grass. As people grow weak from hunger, disease spreads more easily.

The people of Jodhpur have learned to adapt to their semiarid climate. Many raise livestock as well as crops. The animals can survive on native plants when crops fail. Some farmers have begun to use drip irrigation to conserve water. This method drips water directly on a plant's roots. Little water is wasted as **runoff** or to **evaporation**. This careful use of water makes sense in Jodhpur, where every drop counts.

The Dry Plains Near Jodhpur
Water is a luxury in the area around Jodhpur. Women must sometimes walk miles in scorching heat to fetch drinking water for their families. Wind can pick up the thin dust on the arid plains. These dust storms are common before the summer monsoons.

Life Continues Despite Floods
Monsoon rains often fill the streets of Kolkata. Buses and cars can't drive through flooded streets. But rickshaws can. A rickshaw is a small cart with two or three wheels. It is pulled by someone who walks or bicycles in front of it. Rickshaw drivers are highly valued during the summer monsoon season.

27.5 Waiting for the Rains in Kolkata, India

Kolkata is a city of contrasts. It has been called both the "City of Joy" and the "Dying City." Its modern skyscrapers tower over the muddy Hooghly River, a branch of the Ganges River. When the monsoons come in June, the river floods. After a rain shower or two, Kolkata finds itself knee-deep, or even neck-deep, in water.

Wet Summers and Dry Winters Around 15 million people call Kolkata home. About a third of them live in **slums**.

The city's winters are dry and pleasant. Moderate winds blow in from the north. From June to September, the winds shift direction. Moist monsoon air blows in from the Indian Ocean. Monsoons can dump nearly 50 inches of rain on the city in four months. Temperatures can soar to 100°F. The summer rains present a great challenge to Kolkata.

Monsoon Rains Begin and End Life Kolkata floods easily. The city's old canals overflow quickly when rain fills the streets. Buses and taxis can't drive on flooded roads. Children wade to school through waist-high water and spend the day in wet clothing. Still, the monsoon rains are welcome. Farmers need the rain to water their crops. The rains also provide relief from the sticky summer heat.

Kolkata has had to find ways to deal with summer floods. In the past, a system of canals drained floodwater out of the city. Later this system was abandoned for modern streets and sewers. But when too much rain falls, garbage clogs the old canals. Standing water in flooded streets breeds mosquitoes. Diseases spread by mosquitoes, such as malaria, spread quickly. People sicken and die.

Today, Kolkata officials are looking at rebuilding the city's old canals to help with flooding. Meanwhile, sewer lines are being repaired so that they can carry more water during storms. The city is also working to keep the river clear of debris so that more water can drain downstream during heavy rains.

27.6 Living in the Rain Shadow: Pune, India

Pune is located on the Deccan Plateau in western India. It is only 115 miles from Mumbai—a short two-hour drive. Yet Mumbai receives over 70 inches of rain during the summer monsoons. In contrast, Pune's rainfall totals only 29 inches for the entire year.

A Year-Round Dry Climate Between Mumbai and Pune lies a mountain range known as the Western Ghats. As monsoon winds rise up its slopes, the air cools and releases its moisture. By the time the winds reach the downwind side, little moisture is left.

Pune sits in a rain shadow on the opposite side of the Western Ghats from Mumbai. While the coastal city must brace for heavy rain, Pune is spared from flooding. For most of the year, the air is dry and pleasant. The monsoons bring welcome rains from June to September.

Limited Rainfall Makes Water Precious The people of Pune have learned to get by with little water. In the past, farmers here raised sugarcane, a crop that requires a lot of water. Today, they plant crops that are more drought resistant, such as sugar beets.

Pune has also tried to increase its rainfall with **cloud seeding**. This process involves scattering chemicals into clouds to bring about rain. Rain falls when the water vapor in clouds condenses into droplets. These droplets form around tiny specks of ice in the air. Under the right conditions, clouds can be seeded to help condensation to occur. Usually, this is done by spraying them from the air with tiny bits of silver iodide or dry ice. The hope is that water droplets will form around these "seeds."

It is hard to tell just how effective cloud seeding is in Pune. The reason is that no one knows how much rain might have fallen without seeding. But for people living in a rain shadow, the chance of more rain makes seeding seem worth the cost.

Living in a Rain Shadow
Pune lies in a rain shadow. Farmers in the area can grow crops like rice only if monsoon rains are plentiful.

27.7 Beginning to Think Globally

In this chapter, you learned how monsoons affect climate in South Asia. Differences in atmospheric pressure between the land and sea cause the summer monsoons. These winds bring both welcome rain and deadly floods to coastal cities. The orographic effect also shapes the climate of this region. Cities on the downwind sides of mountains often lie in a rain shadow. Unlike their coastal cousins, the people in these cities must adapt to limited rainfall.

Other regions also have monsoons. From November to April, northern Australia braces for its monsoon season. Monsoons hit the West African coast from May to July. In Arizona, monsoon rains arrive in the middle of summer, as moist air from the Gulf of Mexico blows inland.

Wherever people live, climate affects their activities. Think about this as you look at climates around the world in the next section.

27.8 Global Connections

The map shows climate zones around the world. The three climagraphs show average monthly temperatures and precipitation in three cities.

How might climate affect the type of housing people build? In hot and humid tropical climates, people build homes that let in the breeze. In dry desert climates, they make windows small to keep out the sun. In very wet climates, people build houses raised on stilts. A raised house stays dry when the land below it floods. In tundra climates, houses are also raised off the ground. This is to allow cold air to flow under the building. Otherwise, the warmth of a house could melt the **permafrost,** or permanently frozen ground, below. If this happened, the house could sink into the mud.

How might climate affect the type of clothing people wear? People who live in arid climates often wear loose-fitting, flowing clothes. They want to cover up most of their skin to avoid being too exposed to the sun. People who live in more temperate places like London have come to expect daily downpours. They keep umbrellas and raincoats handy.

How might climate affect what people do for fun? In Alaska, dog sledding and ice fishing are common cold-climate sports. Surfing is popular in Hawaii. North Africans enjoy camel racing. In Namibia, people gather at the dunes in the Namib Desert to sandboard. Much like snowboarding, sandboarding involves sliding down a slippery slope of sand on a wooden board.

Climate Zones Around the World

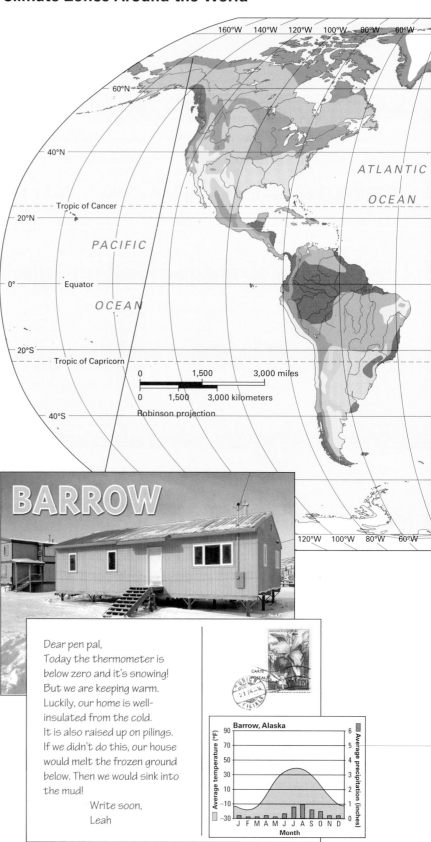

Dear pen pal,
Today the thermometer is below zero and it's snowing! But we are keeping warm. Luckily, our home is well-insulated from the cold. It is also raised up on pilings. If we didn't do this, our house would melt the frozen ground below. Then we would sink into the mud!

Write soon,
Leah

Climate

- Ice cap
- Tundra
- Subarctic
- Highlands
- Marine west coast
- Humid continental
- Humid subtropical
- Mediterranean
- Arid
- Semiarid
- Tropical wet and dry
- Tropical wet

60°N

Tropic of Cancer

PACIFIC

OCEAN

Equator   0°

INDIAN

OCEAN

ATLANTIC

OCEAN

20°S

Tropic of Capricorn

40°S

20°W   0°   20°E   40°E   60°E   80°E   100°E   120°E   140°E   160°E

N
W   E
S

TINDOUF

LONDON

73 VICTORIA STATION

23

Dear pen pal,
Today I am going to a camel
race with my family. It will be
very hot, so I'll wear a haik.
That's a loose-fitting garment
that I wrap around me to keep
me as cool as possible. Camel
racing is popular here, along with
camel dancing. The riders make
their camels move to the beat
of the music.
        Your friend,
        Ezina

Tindouf, Algeria

Average temperature (°F) / Average precipitation (inches)

J F M A M J J A S O N D
Month

Dear pen pal,
It's raining again today, but
I played soccer anyway. Luckily
for us, it doesn't get that cold
here despite all the rain. But
my mum is always reminding
me to take my umbrella and
wear my wellies, or what you
call rainboots.
        Sincerely yours,
        William

London, England

Average temperature (°F) / Average precipitation (inches)

J F M A M J J A S O N D
Month

Waiting for the Rains: The Effects of Monsoons in South Asia   **407**

Tech Workers and Time Zones: India's Comparative Advantage

28

28.1 Introduction

When people lose their credit cards or have trouble with their computers, they need help fast. Usually they phone a call center. Such centers handle large numbers of phone calls for a business. Often the callers do not realize that the call center might be halfway around the world.

Call centers have become a big business in India. They are part of a global revolution in **information technology (IT)**. IT is the use of technology to move, record, and process information. Computers, satellites, cell phones, and the Internet are all part of IT. This technology allows us to talk by phone to people almost anywhere on Earth. It also allows computers to move data around the world in an instant.

IT makes it possible for companies to **outsource** call center jobs. To outsource means to hire someone outside a company to do work that was once done inside the company. In recent years, American companies have outsourced many jobs to India. Indian workers now prepare tax returns, review medical records, and tutor students for U.S. companies.

India attracts these jobs because it has a **comparative advantage** over many other countries. This means that India can offer some services more cheaply or effectively than competing countries. As a result, companies often look to India when they want to outsource jobs. In this chapter, you will learn about some factors that give India this advantage.

Essential Question

What factors give some countries a comparative advantage in the global IT revolution?

This illustration shows a customer in the United States communicating with a worker in India. Both are part of the global IT revolution. Information technology, such as communications satellites, allows data to move quickly and cheaply around the world. This helps people in distant countries to work together. Keep this illustration in mind as you try to answer the Essential Question.

Graphic Organizer

◀ An information technology call center in Bangalore, India

An IT Worker in India

India is one of the world's poorest countries. But its economy is growing rapidly, in part thanks to the IT revolution. IT jobs like the one shown here are attractive to people because they pay more than most other work.

India's Major IT Centers

Information Technology Centers

India's IT centers attract jobs from around the globe. The main hub of IT work is the city of Bangalore. Almost 7 million people live in this bustling IT center.

28.2 The Geographic Setting

India is a large and varied country in South Asia. It has great mountains, **rainforests,** and **deserts**. It also has many large cities. India is about one third the size of the United States, but its population is more than three times as large. With over one billion people, India is the second most populous country in the world.

The World's Largest Democracy India is ruled by an elected government. This makes it the largest democracy in the world. Under India's constitution, all Indians are equal. But Indians are not always treated equally in Indian society.

For thousands of years, Indian society has been divided into many groups called *castes*. The caste system was rooted in ancient beliefs. People were born into the same caste as their parents. The system fixed what jobs each caste could do. Upper caste people were priests and warriors. They ran India. Lower caste people worked as farmers and laborers. Today the caste system is beginning to change. Members of the lower castes are improving their position. But the caste system is still a powerful force in Indian society.

India is also divided by religion. The two main faiths are Hinduism and Islam. More than three fourths of Indians are Hindus. Muslims form a large minority. The two groups disagree on many issues. At times, these religious conflicts lead to violence.

A Fast-Growing Economy Economic problems also trouble India. It is one of the world's poorest countries. More than a fourth of all Indians live in poverty. Many of the poorest people live on less than a dollar a day.

At the same time, India's economy is growing rapidly. One reason for this growth has been the global IT revolution. Indian businesses have been quick to adopt this technology. They offer IT services at low prices. As a result, they have attracted jobs from many foreign companies.

Another attraction for American companies is India's location on the other side of the world. There is a time difference of 10 or more hours between India and the United States. These differences in **time zones** mean that Indians are at work while Americans are sleeping. A time zone is an area that uses the same clock time.

American companies take advantage of these time differences by setting up night call centers in India. During the day, customers' calls may be answered by centers in the United States. At night, they are answered by call centers in India. In this way, a U.S. company can have workers answering calls around the clock without hiring a night shift in either country.

India's IT industry is spread across the country. But its main hub is the city of Bangalore in southern India. Like Silicon Valley, California's IT center, Bangalore attracts highly skilled people who are interested in new ways to get work done.

▶ Geoterms

comparative advantage the ability of one country to produce a good or provide a service at a lower cost or more effectively than another country

information technology (IT) the use of technology to move, record, and process information. IT includes computers, communication satellites, cell phones, and the Internet.

outsource to hire someone outside a company to do work that was once done inside the company. Information technology has made it possible to outsource jobs to businesses in other countries.

time zone an area that uses the same clock time. Earth is divided into 24 standard time zones. Clocks in each zone are set to the same hour and minute.

Time Zones Around the World

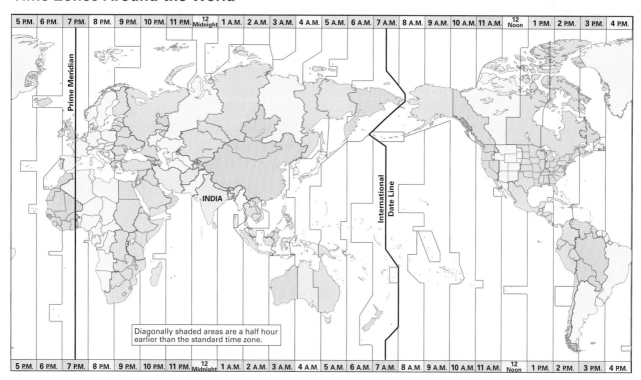

Earth's Many Time Zones

The world has been divided into 24 standard time zones. Each zone covers about 15 degrees of longitude and represents 1 hour of the 24-hour day. The United States has six standard time zones. India has a nonstandard time zone. It is a half-hour off standard time. Note the International Date Line running through the middle of the Pacific Ocean. Travelers who cross that line going west toward Asia jump ahead one day on the calendar. When they cross the line heading east to the Americas, they lose a day.

28.3 Advantage Factor One: Low Wages

In 2007, a call center worker in the United States made $45,000 a year. Sangita Ray did the same job in India. She earned only $3,500 a year. This difference in pay is one reason India attracts IT jobs. American companies that outsource work to India can save money.

A Large, Fast-Growing Workforce India has a large and rapidly growing **workforce**. In 2005, there were more people working in India than the entire population of the United States. By 2020, India is expected to have the largest workforce in the world.

Labor costs in India are among the lowest in the world. This gives India a comparative advantage in attracting IT jobs. American companies can cut their wage costs in half by shifting some of their work to India.

Several factors affect how much workers in India earn. One is the size of its workforce. With so many people looking for work, competition for jobs can be fierce. As a result, Indians often accept lower pay than workers in other countries.

Another factor is the low **cost of living** in India. Basic goods like food and clothing cost much less than in many other countries. Bangalore, in particular, is known for its low cost of living. This makes it possible for many Indians to enjoy a high **standard of living** despite pay that seems low to Americans.

Indian Workers Want IT Jobs Good pay and working conditions make IT jobs attractive to Indians. In 2007, the average Indian worker earned $950 a year. In contrast, a computer programmer might be paid $6,000 or more a year. Call center jobs may pay half that much.

Many IT company workplaces look like college campuses. They feature clean, modern buildings in parklike settings. Some have stores, swimming pools, and gyms for their workers. A pleasant work environment helps attract Indians to IT jobs. Of the thousands of Indians who apply for call center jobs, only about 5 percent are hired. Most of those who do get jobs are college graduates.

IT Worker Salaries, 2007

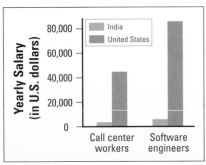

Sources: Bureau of Labor Statistics. PayScale.

Who Earns What
This graph looks at the average pay of American and Indian IT workers in 2007. Software engineers make more in both countries.

An IT Campus in Bangalore
IT companies offer workers attractive workplaces. More than 13,000 people work at this company campus in Bangalore. The company provides them with food courts, a large gym, and a small golf course.

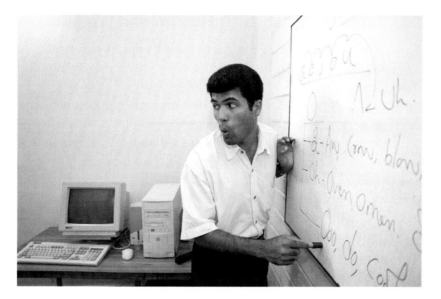

28.4 Advantage Factor Two: English Speakers

A teacher is leading a class in American English. The students are call center workers. They are learning to speak like Americans. They watch U.S. movies and TV shows to pick up American accents, expressions, and slang words. Their skill in English is a second factor that drives India's success in the IT business.

English Is Widely Spoken in India People in India speak more than 1,000 languages and **dialects**. A dialect is a version of a language that is spoken in a specific area. Hindi is India's national language. More than two fifths of Indians speak Hindi at home. But almost all educated Indians also speak English.

Traders brought English to India in the 1600s. Great Britain later took over India and made it a colony. British officials set up schools where Indians were taught in English. The schools helped train Indians to work in government jobs. The British also hoped that the use of English would help unite India's many **linguistic groups**.

India gained its independence in 1947. By that time, English was widely spoken. Today it remains the main language of business. It is also used for government business. In cities, many parents send their children to schools that teach in English. Many college classes are also taught in English.

English Skills Are a Key Advantage About a third of all Indians speak some English. This gives India a comparative advantage in attracting U.S. companies. India can provide IT services in English more effectively than countries where little English is spoken.

Because of India's colonial past, Indians tend to speak English with a British accent. That is why some companies are teaching workers how to talk with American accents. They hope the training will help workers communicate better with callers and clients in the United States.

Homegrown Technology

Indian IT companies do a lot of out-sourced work. But they also create products for use at home. In this photograph, Hirji Kantibhai Patel, chairman of Allied Computers International, displays an ACi ultra-mini laptop at its launch in Bangalore, India. Devices like this affordable computer may help bring the benefits of the global IT revolution to poor Indians.

28.5 Advantage Factor Three: Trained Workers

Rajiv Johri is 16 years old. He wants to study computer science at a top university in India, but first he must pass the college entrance exam. To prepare, Rajiv goes to a test prep class every day after school. He studies late into the night. Each morning, he gets up early to attend another test prep session before school.

Rajiv is not alone. Millions of Indians see education as their ticket to a good job. This educated workforce is a third factor in India's comparative advantage over countries with less-skilled workers. American companies send work to India because they know it will be done by well-trained workers.

India Is a Leader in Technical Education India's educated workforce is no accident. India puts a lot of money into higher education. In 2005, more than 3 million Indians graduated from college. Many of them were trained in technical fields such as math, science, and engineering. By 2010, the number of Indians with college degrees is expected to double.

India has made special efforts to promote technical education. In 1951, the Indian Institute of Technology, or IIT, was founded. Today IIT has seven campuses. It is ranked among the best technical universities in the world. Some of the world's top scientists and engineers are educated there.

Not All Indians Have Equal Access to Education Indian law says that all children up to the age of 14 must go to school. In fact, only about half of India's children attend school to that age. As a result, about a third of the population is **illiterate**. This means that roughly 350 million people in India cannot read and write.

Why don't more children go to school? One reason is poverty. Many poor children have to work to help support their families. They have no time or energy for school.

Another reason is caste. Many Indians still link education to caste. People expect children who are born into high castes to be well educated. They don't expect this for children born into low castes.

It is hard enough for many Indians to get a basic education. It is even harder to go on to college. In 2007, only about 11 percent of young people in India attended college. And only a fraction of these students will graduate with a degree in math, science, or engineering.

Technical Education in India

This graph shows the growth of engineering and IT programs in India over eight years. During this time, the number of people enrolled in these technical programs more than doubled, and the number of graduates nearly doubled.

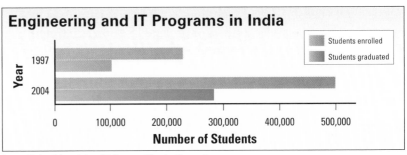

Engineering and IT Programs in India

Students enrolled
Students graduated

Year
1997
2004

Number of Students
0   100,000   200,000   300,000   400,000   500,000

Source: National Association of Software and Service Companies.

India's Brain Drain and Brain Gain In the past, many students with technical degrees could not find the jobs they wanted near home. Some left India to work in more developed countries, including the United States. The result was a serious **brain drain**.

This trend began to change when the IT industry took off in India. New opportunities for people with technical degrees opened up. Many Indians who were working out of the country returned to join the boom. These IT professionals brought with them valuable business experience as well as special skills. For the companies they joined, the brain drain turned into a brain gain.

Some Indians also returned home with money to invest in new companies. This investment has helped the Indian IT industry expand. In fact, some Indian companies have grown so fast that they now outsource jobs to IT workers in China.

28.6 Beginning to Think Globally

In this chapter, you read how India has become part of the global IT revolution. You learned about three factors that give India a comparative advantage over some other countries in attracting IT jobs from the United States. The first is low wages. The second is English speakers. The third is an educated workforce. In addition, India is located in a time zone halfway around the world from the United States. As a result, Indians work while Americans sleep. All of these factors have led U.S. companies to outsource work to India.

Outsourcing is only one way that companies do business in another country. Another way is through **foreign investment,** or investment by a person or company based in another country. Many people and businesses around the world invest money in the United States. This money is used to buy U.S. companies. It is also used to start new businesses in the United States.

In the next section, you will read more about foreign-owned companies in the United States. You will also explore this country's comparative advantages in attracting business from around the world.

Computers for Kids
These students are learning about computers at an IT exhibition in Bangalore. Not all Indian children get a good education. One project in Bangalore is helping poor children learn how to read and use computers. The project is paid for by some of the city's leading IT companies.

28.7 Global Connections

The United States loses jobs when they are outsourced to other countries. But it gains jobs when foreign companies invest here. The map shows where companies owned by foreign investors were doing business in the U.S. in 2008. The graph shows foreign investment in the U.S. between 1998 and 2008. The U.S. attracts so much foreign investment because of its many comparative advantages.

Is the number of Americans working for foreign companies rising or falling? In 1987, about 2.6 million Americans worked for foreign-owned companies. Since then, the number has more than doubled to over 5 million. The new jobs created by foreign investment help to make up for jobs lost due to outsourcing.

What kinds of jobs are created by foreign-owned companies in the U.S.? Americans working for foreign-owned companies do all kinds of jobs. They build cars, airplanes, and medical equipment. They do research and develop new technologies. In general, Americans working for foreign companies earn more than those working for U.S. businesses.

What gives the U.S. a comparative advantage in attracting foreign businesses? The U.S. is a highly developed country. It has many skilled workers. It has highly educated IT professionals, engineers, researchers, and businesspeople. Foreign companies invest here to take advantage of this talented workforce. The U.S. also has a very high per capita GDP. Many foreign companies start businesses in the U.S. to be close to its 300 million consumers.

Foreign-Company Jobs in the United States, 2008

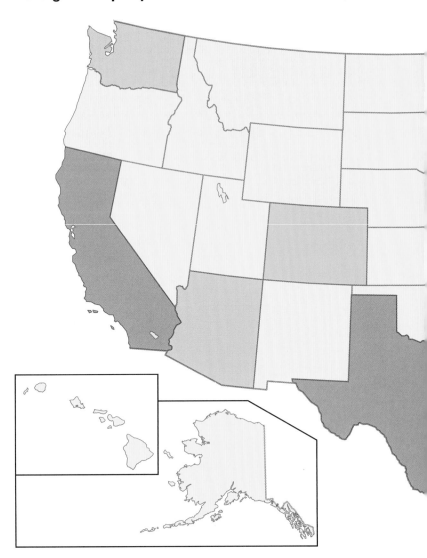

Three Foreign-Owned Companies in the U.S.

	Dassault Falcon Jet Corporation
Location of Parent Company	France
U.S. Locations	Arkansas, Delaware, New Jersey
Business Activities	• manufacturing jet airplanes • sales and service
Why Parent Company Invested in the United States	• skilled workers • talented engineers • close to customers in the Americas

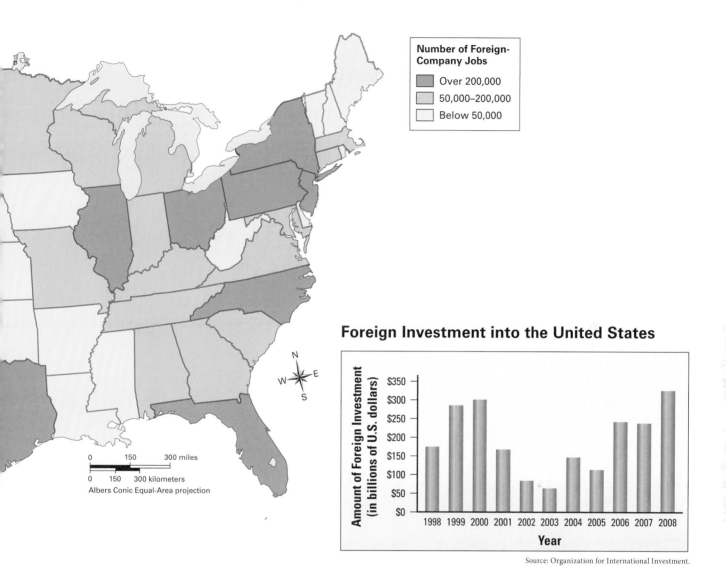

Number of Foreign-Company Jobs

- Over 200,000
- 50,000–200,000
- Below 50,000

0 150 300 miles
0 150 300 kilometers
Albers Conic Equal-Area projection

Foreign Investment into the United States

Amount of Foreign Investment (in billions of U.S. dollars)

Year	
1998	~$175
1999	~$285
2000	~$300
2001	~$165
2002	~$85
2003	~$60
2004	~$145
2005	~$110
2006	~$240
2007	~$235
2008	~$325

Source: Organization for International Investment.

Phillips Healthcare	American Honda Motor Company
Netherlands	Japan
Massachusetts	Alabama, California, Colorado, Georgia, Michigan, North Carolina, Ohio, South Carolina, Texas
• manufacturing medical equipment • research and development of new products • sales and services	• manufacturing cars, motorcycles, ATVs, boats, engines • research and development of new products • safety education • sales
• skilled workers • talented engineers and medical researchers • close to North American customers	• skilled workers • talented engineers and designers • close to North American customers

Mount Everest: Climbing the World's Tallest Physical Feature

29.1 Introduction

On the afternoon of May 10, 1996, more than a dozen climbers were near the summit, or top, of Mount Everest. Suddenly a storm blew in. It lashed the climbers with gale-force winds and driving snow. Later one of them recalled, "At times you couldn't even see your own feet." Some climbers managed to survive the blizzard and make it down the mountain. Others didn't. In the end, nine people died. Another three lost their lives on the mountain later that month. It was the deadliest climbing season ever on Mount Everest.

Mount Everest is an amazing place. At over 29,000 feet, it is the tallest mountain in the world. It lies within Nepal's Sagarmatha National Park. In 1979, this park was named a **World Heritage site**. These sites are places of great natural or cultural value to the world. **UNESCO,** a branch of the United Nations, identifies such places on its World Heritage List. UNESCO also assists countries in preserving and protecting these sites.

Climbing Mount Everest is a very difficult feat. Even so, more and more people come to Nepal each year to attempt the ascent. In this chapter, you will read about the challenges they experience on their way to the top. You will see how **tourism** to Mount Everest is affecting Nepal and its people. And you will discover what is being done to protect this very special place from overuse.

Essential Question

How can people both experience and protect the world's special places?

This diagram shows one of the main climbing routes up Mount Everest. Notice that there are several camps along the route. Each lies at a different elevation. Moving from camp to camp, climbers face tough physical challenges. Keep this diagram in mind as you try to answer the Essential Question.

Graphic Organizer

Summit (29,035 ft.)

Camp IV (26,000 ft.)

Camp III (24,500 ft.)

Camp II (21,300 ft.)

Base Camp (17,600 ft.)

Camp I (19,500 ft.)

To Lukla (9,350 ft.)

◀ The summit of Mount Everest, the world's tallest mountain

First to the Top

In 1953, Edmund Hillary and Tenzing Norgay became the first climbers to reach the top of Mount Everest.

Oxygen and Elevation

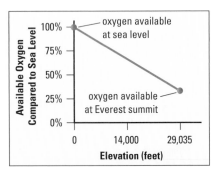

Breathing at Altitude

As altitude increases, the oxygen content in the air decreases. At the summit of Mount Everest, the air contains only about one third the amount of oxygen that it contains at sea level.

29.2 The Geographic Setting

Mount Everest is located in the Himalaya Mountains of southern Asia. It lies on the border between Nepal and the Chinese region of Tibet. In 1999, scientists measured the summit's height as 29,035 feet. In the future, this number may change as measuring methods become more accurate. Whatever its exact height, Everest is more than five miles high. The mountain was named Everest for a British official in India. In Nepal, it is known as Sagarmatha, which means "forehead in the sky." In Tibet, it is called Chomolungma, or "mother of the world."

Many Ways to the Top The first successful ascent of Mount Everest was on May 29, 1953. On that day, Edmund Hillary of New Zealand and Tenzing Norgay of Nepal reached the summit. "My first sensation was one of relief—relief that the long grind was over," Hillary later wrote. "I turned and looked at Tenzing. Even beneath his oxygen mask and the icicles hanging from his hair, I could see his infectious grin of sheer delight." Since then, a few thousand people have tried to climb the mountain. Even fewer have made it to the top.

There are many routes to the top. The two main ones are the southeast ridge from Nepal and the northwest ridge from Tibet. Most climbers take the first route. They climb in stages over a period of weeks. At each stage, they stop at camps on the side of the mountain. This allows them to **acclimatize,** or adjust to the high elevation, as they go. If climbers didn't acclimatize, they would risk getting ill from the lack of oxygen at high elevations.

Exposure is another problem for climbers. Extreme weather conditions, such as freezing temperatures and high winds, can cause injuries and even death. Most summit attempts take place in April and May, when the weather is at its best. However, the temperature drops 3.5°F for every 1,000-foot increase in elevation. So, it is no wonder that conditions can be deadly even in the spring.

Protecting the Future of Mount Everest As the popularity of climbing Everest has grown, so have the problems caused by too much use. One is trash. In the past, many climbers left their trash on the mountain. Piles of cans, bottles, and garbage could be seen at camps along the route. Most of this trash has now been picked up, but keeping the mountain clean remains a concern.

Another problem is overcrowding. During the climbing season, camps become small villages, with dozens of people. More than 30 climbers might reach the summit in a day. Sometimes lines form as climbers slowly make their way to the top.

The growing number of climbers raises questions about the mountain's **carrying capacity**. This term refers to the number of people or animals an area can support. When a population grows too large, the area is likely to be damaged. That's one reason Everest was declared a World Heritage site. By drawing attention to the region, UNESCO hopes to protect it for future generations.

▶ Geoterms

acclimatize the process of adjusting to lower oxygen levels at high elevation. Climbers adjust through exercise and rest as they gradually move higher.

carrying capacity the number of people or animals the environment of an area can support. A place's carrying capacity depends on the environment.

exposure the harmful effects of cold, wind, or other extreme weather conditions

World Heritage site a place of great natural or cultural value that has been placed on UNESCO's World Heritage List. UNESCO helps countries preserve these sites for future generations.

The Mount Everest Region

A Rugged Landscape

A topographic map uses contour lines and symbols to show physical and human features in an area. Mount Everest lies in a very rugged region of the Himalaya mountain range. Climbers hike for days just to get to Base Camp. Then they face a nearly 12,000-foot climb to reach the summit.

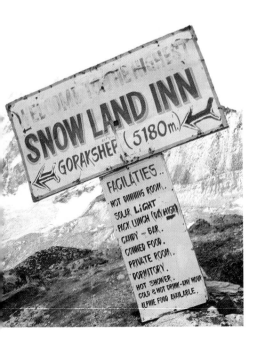

The Effects of Tourism
This sign advertises one of the many tourist hotels in Nepal. Tourism has brought lots of money to Nepal. Climbing groups have also funded schools and medical clinics. Some Nepalese have benefited from tourism, but most are still very poor.

The High Cost of Climbing
Climbing Mount Everest has become a big business. Private guide services charge as much as $70,000 per person. A typical climber may spend another $8,000 to $20,000 on personal gear and airfare.

29.3 From Lukla to Base Camp

Expeditions to Mount Everest begin with a trek to Base Camp. On the way, climbers can see Everest in the distance. "I stared at the peak for perhaps 30 minutes," recalled one climber. "The summit looked so cold, so high, so impossibly far away. I felt as though I might as well be on an expedition to the moon."

A Slow Start Helps Climbers Acclimatize For most people, the adventure begins in Kathmandu, the capital of Nepal. From there they fly to the town of Lukla at 9,350 feet above sea level. At Lukla, they begin their hike to Base Camp. This hike, which takes from six to eight days, helps hikers acclimatize to the thinning air. By the time they reach Base Camp, they are at 17,600 feet.

Base Camp is set up every climbing season at the edge of the Khumbu Glacier. It is made up of dozens or even hundreds of tents. This "tent city" includes kitchens, dining halls, and even solar-powered lights. Most climbers spend several weeks at Base Camp to get used to the thin air.

Climbers who do not acclimatize well may begin showing symptoms of altitude sickness at this point. This illness is also called Acute Mountain Sickness, or AMS. Common symptoms include nausea and headaches. In severe cases, AMS can cause fluid in the lungs, swelling of the brain, and even death.

The Impact of Tourism Nepal is a poor **developing country**. Climbing expeditions, and tourism in general, have had major effects on its people and environment. On the positive side, tourism brings in money. Tourists pay for food, lodging, and supplies. Villagers also make money as porters. They carry heavy loads of equipment and supplies for climbers. The porters often use yaks, a kind of longhaired ox, to help them move goods.

At the same time, tourism has had harmful effects. Porters, for example, are sometimes overworked and mistreated. Also, some villages have cut down trees to build hotels for the tourist trade. More trees may have been cut to provide fuel for cooking and heating for tourists. This has led to **deforestation** and soil erosion in the Everest region.

What Does It Cost to Climb Everest?

Item	Cost for a Team of Seven Climbers
Crew (includes guides, cooks, and doctor)	$98,000
Transportation and lodging en route to Base Camp	$41,000
Permits and fees	$79,000
Supplies (includes fuel, oxygen, batteries, tents, medical supplies, and climbing gear)	$49,000

29.4 From Base Camp to Camp I

Just above Base Camp lies the Khumbu Icefall. It consists of giant chunks of ice called *seracs*. "Imagine trying to hopscotch uphill through a field of ice boulders the size of houses and weighing some 30 tons, each of which could shift at any moment without warning," wrote a climber about the icefall. "It's like a jigsaw puzzle of giant blue ice puzzle pieces."

Surviving the Khumbu Icefall Climbers reach the Khumbu Icefall on the second stage of their journey. This stage takes them from Base Camp at 17,600 feet to Camp I at 19,500 feet. It usually takes one to three weeks to set up Camp I. Climbers move up and down the icefall each day, carrying supplies to the higher camp. This also helps them acclimatize.

The icefall is the most dangerous part of the climb. More climbers have died here than on any other part of the mountain. Some were crushed by shifting seracs. Others died after falling into a crevasse, or a deep crack in the ice. Still others were swept down the mountain by an **avalanche**.

Climbers try to limit the risks by starting out their hikes before dawn. Their goal is to get through the icefall before the sun melts the ice. That's when the ice starts to shift, becoming more dangerous.

Everest's Expert Climbers: The Sherpas Much of the work on Everest is done by a Himalayan people known as Sherpas. Tenzing Norgay was a Sherpa. Many of the great climbers on Everest, including a few women, have been Sherpas.

Sherpas play a critical role on Everest expeditions. They act as guides, cooks, and porters. They set up the camps and carry most of the supplies. They go through the icefall before other climbers to set up ladders and ropes for safe passage. Many Sherpas have died doing this hazardous work.

Every expedition has a head Sherpa, called a *sirdar*. The sirdar has authority over the other Sherpas. In some cases, an expedition will have two sirdars. One stays in Base Camp, while the other makes the climb to the top.

Climbing the Khumbu Icefall
The Khumbu Icefall is the riskiest section of the Everest ascent. Climbers must cross deep crevasses on shaky ladders. They have to beware of falling blocks of ice. One mountain climbing guide warns that "everything you stand or climb on can fall any minute without warning."

Sherpas Play a Key Role
Few Everest climbs would succeed without Sherpas. These natives of the Everest region work as guides and porters on most expeditions. One of the most famous Sherpa climbers was Babu Chiri Sherpa. He reached the summit 10 times and once spent 21 hours at the top. He died in an accident on Everest in 2001.

The Long Climb

Scaling Everest requires great skill and endurance. The risks of climbing are much greater at such high elevations. The lack of oxygen makes it hard to function. As people's thinking gets fuzzy, it is easy to make mistakes. And even a small mistake can prove fatal.

29.5 From Camp I to Camp IV

The third stage of the climb takes climbers from Camp I at 19,500 feet to three more camps. The highest is Camp IV at 26,000 feet. One of the most difficult parts of the climb is the Lhotse Face, a steep rock wall covered in ice. "The wind kicked up huge swirling waves of powder snow," a climber recalled of his climb up Lhotse. "Ice formed over my goggles, making it difficult to see. I began to lose feeling in my feet. My fingers turned to wood. It seemed increasingly unsafe to keep going."

Through the Valley of Silence When climbers leave Camp I, they enter a long valley called the Western Cwm (pronounced *koom*). It is also called the "Valley of Silence." Ridges on either side of the valley block the wind. The most common sounds that climbers hear are their own labored breathing and the crunch of boots on ice and snow.

The hike through the Western Cwm is a long, gentle climb. On a sunny day, the valley gets quite hot. This comes as a surprise to climbers who expect freezing conditions. "You literally pray for a puff of wind or a cloud to cover the sun," one climber said.

Crampons and Rocks: Ascending to Camp IV Camp II lies at the base of the Lhotse Face. The ice-covered wall rises up 3,700 feet. Climbers use crampons and ropes attached to the ice to make this ascent. Crampons are spikes that attach to a climber's boots. Climbers kick the crampons into the ice to get a foothold and then pull themselves up on the rope.

Camp III is perched on a narrow ledge halfway up the face. On a clear day, the view is astounding. "I sat with my feet hanging over the abyss, staring across at the clouds, looking down at the tops of 22,000-foot peaks," wrote one climber. "At long last, it seemed as though I was really nearing the roof of the world."

From Camp III, climbers ascend another 1,500 feet to the South Col. This saddle between the face and the summit is the location of Camp IV. A saddle is a low point on a ridge that connects two peaks.

At 26,000 feet, Camp IV is in the "Death Zone." At this elevation, it is difficult for humans to breathe. The lack of oxygen puts tremendous stress on the body. Climbers are at great risk of altitude sickness. With so little air getting to their brains, they are also more likely to make fatal mistakes. Most climbers breathe bottled oxygen to survive. Even then, it is hard to remain at this altitude for more than two or three days. If the weather turns bad, most climbers have to turn back.

Cleaning Up the World's Highest Junkyard Camp IV is the last camp before the summit. In the past, it was also a major dumping ground. The camp was littered with empty oxygen bottles, used climbing equipment, and human waste. Even dead bodies were left on the mountain. This led to the South Col being called "the world's highest junkyard."

Between 1953 and the mid-1990s, climbers left an estimated 50 tons of glass, plastic, and metal on Mount Everest. In recent years, groups of climbers have scaled the mountain to bring down the trash. One Japanese team came back with 2.6 tons of garbage, including old tents, fuel bottles, and plastic. As a result, the mountain is now much cleaner than it once was. One climber commented, "If you want to find garbage on Everest now, you have to go looking for it."

To keep Everest clean, the government of Nepal charges climbers a fee to use the mountain. Part of this money goes to waste cleanup. Climbing groups also have to leave a $4,000 "garbage deposit" with the government. If they don't carry their trash off the mountain, they lose their deposit.

Nepal's government is also working to reduce deforestation. Mountain climbers must now bring their own fuel with them to Everest. Cutting down trees for fires is prohibited. Tree-planting programs have been organized in many parts of Nepal. New forests have been planted and are being protected from overuse.

Empty Oxygen Cylinders

Piles of trash were once a common sight on Everest. In recent years, climbing groups have cleaned up the mountain. Here Apa Sherpa, who climbed Mt. Everest 18 times, inspects oxygen bottles collected from the mountain. Climbers use bottled oxygen to help them breathe at very high altitudes.

29.6 From Camp IV to the Summit

After resting a few hours at Camp IV, climbers set out for the summit. They are now in the Death Zone, the most grueling stage of the climb.

Climbing in the Death Zone is a real physical test. "At those altitudes you're going quite slowly. You take a step and you breathe six to eight times and then you take another step and then you breathe six or eight times," a climber recalled. "You can't look at the whole ascent. You have to break it down into small sections and into tiny little steps. That's how you eventually chew your way to the summit."

Climbing in the Death Zone It's only 3,000 vertical feet from Camp IV at 26,000 feet to the summit at 29,035 feet. But each step takes great effort. Deep snow, steep drop-offs, and exposure to harsh weather make this part of the climb even more difficult.

It takes about 12 hours to reach the summit from Camp IV. Then it takes another 4 hours to get back down. Most climbers begin the final ascent in darkness at around 11 P.M. This usually gives them enough time to reach the top and get back to camp before the end of the next day.

Climbers first set their sights on the South Summit. This is a small dome of snow and ice just below the summit. To get here, they must ascend a long, steep ridge covered in unstable snow. "It took an age to climb that ridge, hour after hour," a climber later wrote. "Each step was a monumental effort of will, requiring a kick, and another kick, to secure a footing and ensure you didn't slide with the soft snow down again to where you had started."

From the South Summit, climbers have only 300 feet to go. But they have to climb along a terrifying knife-edge ridge. One slip can mean a fall of thousands of feet and certain death.

Climbers must also get over the Hillary Step. This is a rock cliff 40 feet high that lies just below the summit. It is one of the toughest obstacles that climbers face on Everest.

On Top of the World When they reach the top, climbers are greeted by an extraordinary view. They see Tibet to the north and Nepal to the south. Surrounding them on all sides are other giant peaks of the Himalayas. They are truly on top of the world.

The summit itself is about the size of a picnic table. It is covered with flags, photos, and other offerings from previous visitors. Climbers usually don't stay at the top for long. They have to head back down before it gets dark or the weather changes.

By the time they reach the summit, climbers are exhausted. This makes the return to Camp IV extremely dangerous. Even a small mistake can cause climbers to lose their footing and plummet down the mountain. If the weather turns bad, the mistakes can multiply.

Summit Gear
Climbers who reach the top of Everest today wear special gear designed for high altitudes. Earlier climbers made the ascent with far less equipment. They wore wool sweaters, scarves, and jackets. They had heavy oxygen tanks but no radios. Note the flags left on the summit by earlier climbers.

Seeking Even Greater Challenges Over the years, climbers have sought new challenges on Everest. Some make the ascent without oxygen. Others do it very rapidly. In 2004, a Sherpa set a speed record by climbing from Base Camp to the top in just over 8 hours. In 2001, an American became the first blind person to scale Everest. And in 2003, a 70-year-old Japanese climber became the oldest person to reach the top.

Some people come down the mountain in challenging ways. A few have skied down or descended on snowboards. One man came down on a paraglider. This is a device like a large kite.

For still others, climbing Everest is part of a greater challenge called the Seven Summits. To meet that challenge, a climber must scale the tallest mountains on all seven continents. Whatever a climber's goals may be, reaching the summit of Mount Everest is an amazing feat.

29.7 Beginning to Think Globally

In this chapter, you read about the challenges that climbers experience on the world's highest mountain. You learned that climbers must acclimatize as they ascend Mount Everest. You read about exposure to extreme weather. And you discovered some of the effects of tourism on the Everest region. You saw that tourism raises questions about the carrying capacity of the mountain environment.

People come to Mount Everest because it is a very special place. But Everest is only one of the world's many wonders. Keep this in mind as you look at more World Heritage sites in the next section.

Seven Summits Challenge

Mountain (Continent)	Elevation
Denali (N. America)	20,320 ft.
Aconcagua (S. America)	22,840 ft.
Elbrus (Europe)	18,481 ft.
Kilimanjaro (Africa)	19,339 ft.
Everest (Asia)	29,035 ft.
Kosciusko* (Australia)	7,310 ft.
Vinson Massif (Antarctica)	16,067 ft.

* Some sources list Carstensz Pyramid (16,023 ft.) instead.

The Lure of Summits

The Himalayas contain 9 of the world's 10 tallest mountains. Some are visible in the photograph below, as are some climbers along the ridge. But every continent has its highest peaks. Taken together, they make up the Seven Summits Challenge. The challenge is to climb the highest mountain on each of the world's seven continents.

29.8 Global Connections

The map shows the location of many World Heritage sites. There are hundreds of these sites spread across the globe.

How does a place become a World Heritage site? Countries can nominate special places for the World Heritage List. A committee at UNESCO then votes on them. There are three types of sites: natural, cultural, and mixed. Natural sites are areas with unique physical features. The Grand Canyon in Arizona is one natural site. Cultural sites have great historic, artistic, or scientific value. They may be monuments, groups of buildings, or an old city. India's Taj Mahal is a cultural World Heritage site. Mixed sites combine natural and cultural features. The Mayan ruin of Tikal in the rainforest of Guatemala is a mixed site.

What risks do World Heritage sites face today? Many of these sites are at risk of being damaged or lost. Some are threatened by ethnic conflict or war. Others are endangered by pollution or development. Often the greatest risk is overuse. This happens when more people visit a site than its carrying capacity allows. Such a site may be in danger of being "loved to death."

Why should World Heritage sites be protected? These sites are among the greatest treasures in the world. They represent the wonders of nature or the finest expressions of human culture. People visit them to enjoy their beauty or to learn more about the history and achievements of humankind. By protecting these special places, we are preserving them not just for ourselves, but also for future generations to enjoy.

World Heritage Sites, 2008

ARCTIC OCEAN

NORTH AMERICA

ATLANTIC OCEAN

PACIFIC OCEAN

SOUTH AMERICA

World Heritage sites
● Cultural
● Natural
● Both cultural and natural

Machu Picchu, Peru

Hawaii Volcanoes National Park

ARCTIC OCEAN

ASIA

EUROPE

PACIFIC
OCEAN

AFRICA

ATLANTIC
OCEAN

INDIAN
OCEAN

AUSTRALIA

N
W   E
S

0   1,500   3,000 miles
0   1,500   3,000 kilometers
Robinson projection

ANTARCTICA

St. Oswald's Bay,
United Kingdom

Victoria Falls, Tanzania

Bandiagara, Mali

Emperor Qin's Tomb, China

Great Barrier Reef,
Australia

China: The World's Most Populous Country

30.1 Introduction

In the 1870s, there was a terrible **drought** in China. Crops failed and people began to starve. A witness to the suffering wrote,

They wait for death in their houses, stripped of everything.
The cold winds pierce through their bones. They have no rice
to cook, and the cravings of hunger are most painful.

This was not the first time the people of China had faced a terrible **famine**. There had been severe food shortages many times before. This one was made worse by a rise in China's population. By the time it was over, the famine had claimed almost 10 million lives.

This story of population growth and famine is, in some ways, the story of China. Since ancient times, China has experienced both. Despite hard times, China today is the world's most populous country. One out of every five of the world's 6 billion people lives in China.

Feeding such a huge population is a great challenge. To help meet it, China is working to achieve **zero population growth**. This happens when a country's population stops growing. The number of people who are born each year roughly equals the number who die. In this chapter, you will learn how China is dealing with the challenges created by its huge and still growing population.

Essential Question

How does a country meet the challenges created by a large and growing population?

This graph shows the population of China from 1950 to 2050. The data after 2010 are estimates. Note how fast China's population grew between 1950 and 1990. Today, China has more than 1.3 billion people. Keep this graph in mind as you try to answer the Essential Question.

Graphic Organizer

Source: United Nations Population Division.

◀ Crowds of Chinese tourists on the Great Wall of China

Natural Increase and Doubling Time

Rate of Natural Increase	Doubling Time (years)
3%	23
2%	35
1%	70
0%	no doubling time

Population Math

This table shows the relationship between the rate of natural increase and doubling time. A rate of natural increase that is greater than 2 percent a year is considered high. At that rate, a country's population will double in 35 years. The rate of natural increase varies widely around the world.

Population Growth in China

China's Doubling Time

As this bar graph shows, China's population more than doubled between 1950 and 1990. For a population to grow so rapidly, it must have a rate of natural increase above 2 percent.

30.2 The Geographic Setting

The ancient Chinese believed that China stood at the center of the world. They didn't think there were any other civilized societies on Earth. This was understandable. China was isolated from the rest of the world. To the west, **deserts** and mountains cut China off from the rest of Asia. To the east was the vast Pacific Ocean. Even today, the Chinese refer to their country as Zhong Guo, "the Middle Kingdom."

A Diverse Landscape If you picked China up and placed it on top of the United States, the two countries would match up pretty well. They are nearly equal in shape and size, although China is slightly larger. China's **landscape,** however, is very different.

Geographers sometimes describe China as a giant slope. This slope stretches from the towering mountains of Central Asia in the west to the Pacific Ocean in the east. If you stood at the top of the slope, you would look down on the mountains, **plateaus,** and **basins** that make up western China. If you took a giant step down the slope, you would be in central China. There you would find lower mountains, hills, and plateaus. You would also find the Gobi Desert.

A final giant step down would take you to eastern China. Here you would find low hills, fertile river valleys, and plains. You would see vast **floodplains** covered with rice fields. This is where most of China's 1.3 billion people live.

The First Billion-Person Country China has been the world's most populous country for hundreds of years. In the 1980s, it became the first country to reach 1 billion people.

A population grows when its **birth rate** each year is higher than its **death rate**. These rates are determined by the average number of births or deaths per 1,000 people. Birth and death rates are often shown as a percentage. To calculate the birth rate, for example, divide the number of births by 1,000. If there are 30 births for every 1,000 people in a year, the birth rate is 3 percent. Similarly, if there are 20 deaths per 1,000 people, the death rate is 2 percent.

To find out how fast a population is growing, subtract the death rate from the birth rate. In the example just given, a 3 percent birth rate minus a 2 percent death rate equals a 1 percent growth rate. This means the population is growing by 1 percent each year. This annual growth rate is also known as the **rate of natural increase**.

China's population grew a lot in the second half of the 20th century. In 1950, China had about 550 million people. Only 40 years later, in 1990, it had twice as many people. The population had doubled to about 1.1 billion. The time it takes for a population to double like this is called the **doubling time**.

The rate of natural increase and doubling time are tied to each other. The higher the rate of natural increase, the shorter the doubling time. Looking ahead from 1990, the Chinese could see that if nothing changed, their population would likely double again in just another 40 years.

▶ Geoterms

doubling time the length of time it takes for a population to double

famine a severe shortage of food that results in widespread hunger

rate of natural increase the annual rate of population growth. This percentage is calculated by subtracting the death rate from the birth rate. It does not include people moving into or out of a country.

zero population growth a condition in which the population of a country does not grow but remains stable. This condition comes about when the birth rate plus immigration equals the death rate plus emigration.

Population Distribution in China

Population Density

Per sq. mi.	Per sq. km
Over 2,000	Over 800
1,000–2,000	400–800
250–1,000	100–400
62–250	25–100
2–62	1–25
Under 2	Under 1

0   300   600 miles
0   300   600 kilometers
Conic projection

Where the Chinese Live

The purple areas on this map indicate a population density of more than 2,000 people per square mile. Notice that the majority of Chinese live in the eastern part of the country. Rivers flowing across this lowland region provide fish for food and water for irrigation. They are also used as transportation routes.

The Use of Posters in China

China uses posters to promote government policies. This poster supports the one-child policy. Traditionally, boys are favored. The government, however, is trying to change this way of thinking. This poster shows parents who are happy with their one daughter.

30.3 Plan One: Slow Population Growth

Great Teacher. Great Leader. Great Supreme Commander. Great Helmsman. These names were used to describe one of China's most important leaders, Mao Zedong. Mao led a revolution that brought a communist government to power in China in 1949. He ruled the new People's Republic of China until his death in 1976. During his long rule, Mao brought big changes to China.

The Challenge: Rapid Population Growth Mao believed that large families would make China strong. Under his rule, China's population grew rapidly. The average woman had four or five children. The natural rate of increase rose to about 3 percent.

In 1958, Mao launched a program called the Great Leap Forward. This was a plan to help China become a modern industrial country. In other countries, modernization had come with the use of new **technology,** such as machines and computers. Mao thought China could "leap forward" by getting more work out of its huge population.

One goal of the Great Leap Forward was to increase steel production. Across the country, small "backyard furnaces" were set up. People were told to melt down their metal possessions. Bicycles, cooking pans, iron bed frames, and even doorknobs were melted to make steel. Another goal was to increase food production. Small farms were lumped together to create large factory farms.

Despite people's hard work, the Great Leap Forward did not turn China into an industrial giant. Production did not increase as Mao had hoped. At the same time, there were severe droughts across China. The result was famine. More than 20 million people died of starvation between 1958 and 1962. Those deaths were a tragic reminder that China could no longer support its rapidly growing population.

The Proposed Solution: The One-Child Policy Mao died in 1976. After his death, the government took steps to control population growth. In 1979, it began a family-planning program known as the *one-child policy*. This program limited each married couple to just one child. The government rewarded those who followed the policy and punished those who did not.

The one-child policy is still in effect. There have been changes, though. The focus now is on rewards rather than punishments. Families receive benefits, including cash, for having just one child. In some **rural** areas, couples are allowed to have a second child. Punishments for having more children than allowed are less severe than in the past. Overall, though, Chinese families still must strictly limit the number of children they have.

The Benefits: Slower Population Growth China has not yet reached zero population growth. But the one-child policy is moving the country toward that goal. A majority of families today have only one child. The population is still growing, but at a much slower rate.

Slower population growth has had many benefits for China. It has reduced the strain on food and water supplies. It has also reduced the problem of having too many workers for too few jobs.

Families have benefited in other ways. Mothers and babies tend to be healthier in small families. With fewer children to support, parents have more money to spend on other things. With fewer children to care for, women have more time for a career.

The Costs: Less Choice, an Aging Population, and Natural Disasters The one-child policy has not been completely successful. Many people don't want to be told how many children they can have. This is especially true in rural areas where large families are a tradition.

The policy has also clashed with other traditions. Chinese families prefer to have sons. The family name is passed on to sons. Sons are expected to care for aging parents. There are now fewer children overall to care for older family members. This change has a major effect on the dependency ratio. As a result, China will need to find new ways to care for a larger and aging population.

Modern medicine makes it easy to determine the sex of a baby before it is born. Rather than give birth to a girl, some couples choose to end a pregnancy and try again for a boy. This is illegal. But still, in China today, about 120 boys are born for every 100 girls. In the future, this difference may lead to a shortage of wives for young men.

There is another cost as well. The loss of a child in a natural disaster is always tragic. But the one-child policy can make the loss even more terrible. For example, in 2008, an earthquake killed about 10,000 children in one Chinese province. Due to the one-child policy, many parents lost their only child in the quake. The government decided to let these parents have another child, if they could. But many are too old or otherwise unable.

China, 2008

China, 2050 (Estimated)

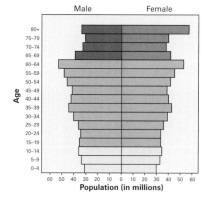

Source: United Nations Population Division.

Population Changes in China
The one-child policy has changed the population distribution in China. Compare the two population pyramids. If slow growth continues, China's population distribution will eventually look like the pyramid on the bottom.

The Three Gorges Dam

The Three Gorges Dam was built to generate clean energy. As the lake behind the dam was filled, much of the beautiful scenery in the Three Gorges area was lost.

30.4 Plan Two: Provide More Clean Energy

Huge populations require huge amounts of energy. Most of the electricity the Chinese people need is supplied by power plants that burn coal. Smoke containing **toxic chemicals** such as mercury pours out of China's power plants. High winds carry the poisonous plumes around the world. In the United States, mercury **pollution** from China has been discovered from California to New England.

The Challenge: Meeting Rising Energy Demands China has the second-largest **consumption** of energy in the world. Only the United States consumes more energy. China uses coal to meet 65 percent of its energy needs. It burns more coal than any other country.

As its population grows, China's energy needs will grow. The country has large deposits of coal. But coal is not a clean fuel. When burned, it pollutes the air. Diseases related to air pollution have become leading causes of death in China. One way to reduce air pollution is to install equipment at power plants to clean the smoke. But this equipment is very expensive.

The Proposed Solution: Generate More Hydroelectric Power To meet its growing energy needs without increasing pollution, China has looked for cleaner sources of energy. One of the cleanest sources is **hydroelectric power**. It is generated by water flowing through power plants in dams.

In 1993, China began building the world's largest dam. It spans the Yangtze River, the longest river in Asia. This river flows more than 3,700 miles through China. For thousands of years, it has been used to transport people and cargo. It has also provided water for homes and crops. The new dam, finished in 2009, provides as much as one ninth of China's electricity.

The dam across the Yangtze was built in a beautiful canyon area called the Three Gorges. The Three Gorges Dam is more than 600 feet high and more than 1.3 miles wide. The **reservoir** behind the dam stretches upstream for about 400 miles.

The Benefits: Clean Energy, Flood Control, and Shipping

Hydroelectric dams provide many benefits to the countries that build them. One is clean energy from a **renewable resource**. The power plant at the Three Gorges Dam has 26 electric generators. These generators can produce more electricity than any other hydroelectric plant in the world. And they do so without polluting the air.

Another benefit is flood control. Historically, the Yangtze River has flooded about every 10 years. These floods have caused widespread death and destruction. The dam helps reduce flooding by holding back extra water that flows downstream during heavy rains. This will improve life for people living near the river below the dam.

The dam will help river shipping, too. Before the dam was built, the Three Gorges area was difficult to navigate by boat. The lake that has formed behind the dam is much safer for river travel. Locks lift boats from the river below the dam up to the level of the lake. Now that the dam and locks are finished, shipping on the river should increase. At the same time, shipping costs should drop by about a third.

The Costs: Lost Cities and Habitat

While the Three Gorges Dam will surely benefit China, there have been costs. The Three Gorges area contains hundreds of ancient settlement **sites**. When water backed up behind the dam, these archeological sites disappeared. All that they could have revealed about China's distant past is now lost.

The reservoir covers up more than history. It has drowned 13 cities, 140 towns, and hundreds of villages. Tens of thousands of acres of farmland have been submerged as well. More than a million people were forced to move as their homes disappeared under water. The Chinese government promised to help these people start new lives elsewhere. But that hasn't made up for what they have lost.

The dam also changed the Yangtze River **ecosystem**. As the lake filled, hundreds of plant and animal species lost their **habitats**. The Chinese river dolphin and the Chinese paddlefish are two threatened species that live only in the Yangtze River. The damming of the river may be putting their survival even more at risk.

Finally, the dam sits on an earthquake **fault**. Some scientists worry that the weight of the dam and the water it holds may make a major earthquake more likely to occur. If such a quake damaged the dam, a wall of water from the reservoir could rush downstream. The result would be a disaster worse than any previous Yangtze flood.

Lost Cities and Historic Sites

The damming of the Yangtze has affected the landscape for hundreds of miles along the river. Because of this, some people call the dam "China's new Great Wall." This map shows the cities and historic sites that have been lost under the reservoir's waters. Some of these sites date back to before 2000 B.C.E.

Cities and Historic Sites of the Three Gorges Area

CHINA

Daxian
Nanchong
Wanxian
Dingfang Temple Towers
Shibaozhai
City of Ghosts
Baidicheng Temple
Zhang Fei Temple
Lichuan
Qu Yuan Memorial
Zigui
Three Gorges Dam
THREE GORGES
Yichang
Chang Jiang
Zhicheng
Jialing
Fuling
White Crane Rock
Chongqing
Chang Jiang
Changde

- • City
- ▪ Historic site
- ▨ Flooded area

0 40 80 miles
0 40 80 kilometers
Albers Conic Equal-Area projection

Special Economic Zones

China's "Open" Areas

The map shows some of China's special economic zones (SEZs) along with their capital cities. It also shows "open cities," which operate like SEZs. In these "open" zones, businesses are not as tightly controlled as in other parts of China.

From Farmland to SEZ

Before 1990, Pudong was boggy farmland on the outskirts of Shanghai. Today, the Pudong New Area is a booming special economic zone. Like other SEZs, Pudong has attracted many foreign businesses.

30.5 Plan Three: Promote Economic Growth

A water-purifying system that can filter any type of water into drinkable water. A lightbulb that lasts 10 years. A system that adjusts a building's temperature and lighting depending on the number of people indoors. These were just a few of the inventions displayed in 2008 at the China Hi-Tech Fair in the city of Shenzhen. The fair is held each year to promote Chinese technology to visitors from around the world. This is just one way China is working to promote economic growth.

The Challenge: Increasing Jobs and Wealth China was not always open to businesspeople from other countries. Under the rule of Mao Zedong, the country looked inward. Mao's goal was to make China self-sufficient. His government controlled the economy. Government officials decided what should be produced and at what price. They controlled who should do what job and for what pay.

You read about the failure of Mao's Great Leap Forward. Just as China's economy began to recover from that experiment, Mao launched a new one. In 1966, he called for a "cultural revolution." His goal was to create a new society in China. In this society, everyone would follow his ideas and work for the common good.

Like the Great Leap Forward, the Cultural Revolution was a disaster. Many people suspected of not being loyal to Mao were sent to prison. Schools were closed as students joined the revolution. Factory and farm production dropped because there weren't enough workers. The country was in chaos.

The Proposed Solution: Special Economic Zones After Mao's death, new leaders took control of China. They were more interested in economic growth than in changing society. These leaders gave up the goal of a self-sufficient China. Instead, they made plans to open China to the rest of the world. They hoped foreign companies would start businesses, create jobs, and bring modern technology to China.

There was just one problem with this new policy. Foreigners did not want to come to China if the government planned to control their businesses. They demanded far more freedom than the government was willing to give to Chinese businesses.

China solved this problem by setting up special economic zones (SEZs). These special areas have laws that are different from those in the rest of the country. In China's SEZs, businesses have the freedom to decide what to produce and at what prices. Most of the goods produced in the SEZs are for export to other countries.

The first four SEZs opened on China's south coast in 1979 and 1980. Shenzhen is the capital of one of them. Many more have been added.

The Benefits: More Jobs and Better Standard of Living

Special economic zones have brought economic growth to China. In 1980, Shenzhen was a sleepy town of perhaps 20,000 people. Today it is an international trade center with more than 7 million people. Other SEZs have seen similar growth.

China's SEZs have created millions of new jobs. These jobs are often filled by **migrant workers** from rural areas. Although wages are not high, most SEZ factory workers earn more than they could in their home villages. Many make enough to support themselves and send money back home to their families. With this extra money, their families can improve their **standard of living**.

The Costs: Income Gaps and Crime

Special economic zones have created problems as well. One is a widening income gap between rich and poor. China's booming SEZs have created a lot of wealth. But that wealth is not spread evenly over the country. Much of China remains very poor. The income gap between rich and poor may lead to unrest if it continues to widen.

Another problem has been the creation of a "floating population" of rootless migrant workers. These workers drift back and forth between their villages and SEZs. They often find only low-paying, part-time jobs. Sometimes they can't find work at all. Some turn to crime in order to survive.

30.6 Beginning to Think Globally

In this chapter, you read about the most populous country on Earth. You learned about the role of population growth and famine in China's history. You saw how a population's rate of natural increase and doubling time are related. You also looked at how China is working to achieve three goals: zero population growth, clean energy, and economic growth.

China is not the only country trying to deal with population growth. By 2050, the number of people in the world is expected to increase by over 2.5 billion. Most of that growth will happen in **developing countries**. Think about the problems these countries will face as you look at rates of natural increase in the next section.

HDI Rank by Province, 2005

HDI Rank
- Top third
- Middle third
- Bottom third

Source: United Nations Development Programme.

Varied Living Standards

The Human Development Index (HDI) measures the well-being of a people. Rankings are based on per capita GDP, education levels, life expectancy, and other variables. As this map shows, some parts of China rank higher than others on this index. The top-ranked provinces are home to most of China's special economic zones.

30.7 Global Connections

The map shows rates of natural increase in countries around the world. At these rates, the populations of the 50 poorest countries will more than double by 2050. The tables look at education for women and spending on health care in countries with various rates of growth.

How might money spent on health care affect a country's rate of natural increase? With better health care, a country's infant mortality rate drops. Life expectancy rises as well. Parents worry less that their children won't survive childhood. Because of this, they may have fewer children. Better health care also means better access to modern family-planning methods. This helps couples plan how many children they will have.

How might money spent on educating women affect a country's rate of natural increase? Women who are educated usually have more control over the number of children they have. Educated women often marry later. They may put off having children to focus on a career. When they do have children, they usually have fewer than women who lack an education.

How might a country with rapid population growth benefit by slowing its rate of natural increase? Countries that slow their rates of natural increase generally grow wealthier. With fewer children, they are better able to educate each child. They also have more money for health care. A healthy, educated population attracts trade and business. This often leads to economic growth and a rise in living standards.

Rate of Natural Increase Around the World, 2008

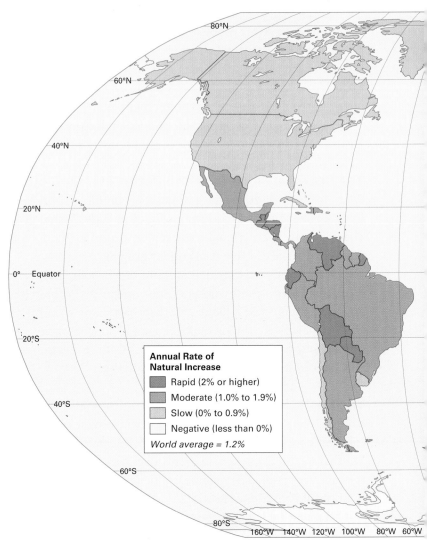

Annual Rate of Natural Increase

- Rapid (2% or higher)
- Moderate (1.0% to 1.9%)
- Slow (0% to 0.9%)
- Negative (less than 0%)

World average = 1.2%

Females Enrolled in Secondary Schools, 2004

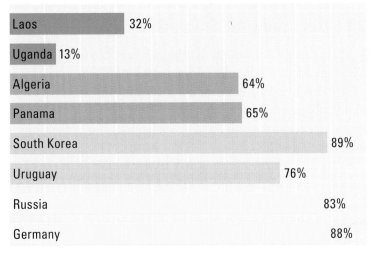

Country	Percent
Laos	32%
Uganda	13%
Algeria	64%
Panama	65%
South Korea	89%
Uruguay	76%
Russia	83%
Germany	88%

Source: United Nations Development Programme.
Note: Data are for the appropriate age group (for example, 14 to 18 years of age).

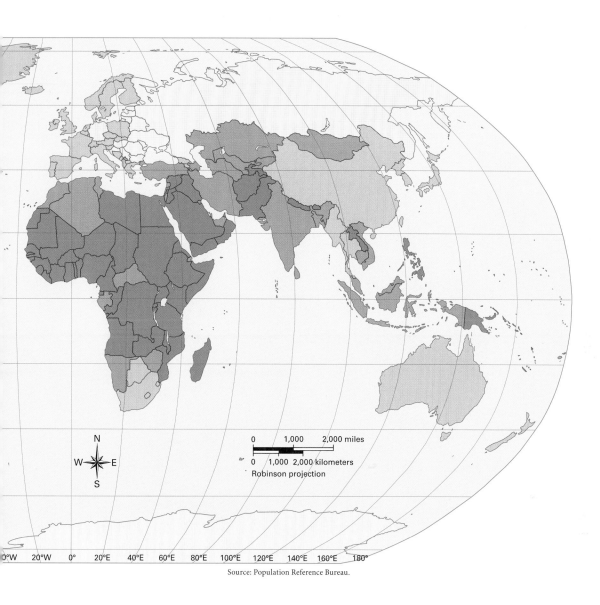

Source: Population Reference Bureau.

Health Care Spending and GDP in Eight Countries

Rate of Natural Increase	Rapid		Moderate		Slow		Negative	
Country/ Rate, 2008	Laos 2.4%	Uganda 3.1%	Algeria 1.8%	Panama 1.6%	South Korea 0.5%	Uruguay 0.5%	Russia −0.3%	Germany −0.2%
Per Person Spending on Health Care*, 2005	$18	$22	$108	$351	$973	$404	$277	$3,628
Per Capita GDP*, 2008	$2,100	$1,100	$7,100	$11,900	$26,000	$12,300	$15,800	$34,800

Sources: Population Reference Bureau. World Bank. Central Intelligence Agency.
*Amounts are in U.S. dollars.

Population Density in Japan: Life in a Crowded Country

31.1 Introduction

Imagine standing on a subway platform in Tokyo, Japan. It is rush hour. The station is crammed with people. You can barely move. The train thunders into the station and comes to a stop. The doors open. The crowd pushes you forward. Suddenly, the person behind you steps on your heel and your shoe comes off. You try to reach down and pick it up, but there are too many people. You are swept into the train without your shoe. Luckily, a station attendant will pick up your shoe and hold it for you. This is not the first time people have lost shoes during the Tokyo rush hour. And it will not be the last.

Tokyo is one of the world's most crowded cities. It is the capital of Japan, a very densely populated country. A country's **population density** is the average number of persons in a unit of area, such as a square mile. The higher that number is, the more crowded the country.

In 2009, the population density of Japan was 878 persons per square mile. In comparison, the United States had a population density of 87 persons per square mile. This means that Japan is more than 10 times as densely populated as the United States. In this chapter, you will learn how Japan's high population density affects life in that country.

Essential Question

How does population density affect the way people live?

The map in the center of this diagram shows where people live in Japan. The areas in red are the most densely populated parts of the country. Around the map are four symbols. They represent aspects of life that are affected by population density. Keep this diagram in mind as you try to answer the Essential Question.

Graphic Organizer

Transportation

Land Use

Housing

Health

◀ Swimming pool in Tokyo

Mount Fuji over Tokyo Bay

Japan's mountains limit the amount of land that is suitable for living. Many of these mountains, like Mount Fuji, are volcanoes. Mount Fuji was once thought to be a sacred place. Today this beautiful volcano attracts weekend hikers eager to escape crowded cities.

31.2 The Geographic Setting

Japan is an island nation off the coast of East Asia. It is made up of four large islands and about 3,900 smaller ones. On a map, these islands form the shape of a thin crescent moon. All together, the Japanese islands make up an area about the size of Montana. To the west, the Sea of Japan (East Sea) separates Japan from its nearest neighbors, Korea and China. To the east lies the vast Pacific Ocean.

Japan enjoys a moderate **climate**. Summers are warm. Winters are relatively mild, with heavy snowfall limited to the northern islands. Plenty of summer rainfall makes Japan an ideal place for growing rice and other crops.

A Mountainous Landscape About three quarters of Japan is made up of mountains. These mountains were formed when **tectonic plates** collided deep beneath the sea. **Volcanoes** welled up in the cracks between the plates. Over millions of years, liquid rock flowing from the volcanoes built up into mountains.

Today volcanic mountains form the backbone of Japan. Many volcanoes are still active. No one knows when they might erupt again. The highest and most famous Japanese volcano is Mount Fuji. Its snowcapped cone towers above the city of Tokyo.

The tectonic plates that built up Japan are still pushing against each other. Whenever one of them moves, the ground shakes. Small earthquakes happen almost every day in Japan. Major earthquakes occur less often, but they can cause much damage. Undersea earthquakes sometimes trigger huge sea waves called **tsunamis**. When these waves hit the coast, they can wash away whole villages.

Limited Land for Living Only about an eighth of Japan is **arable land,** or land suitable for farming. The rest is too hilly to plow and plant. It is also too mountainous for large towns and cities.

The amount of arable land affects **population distribution,** or where people live. Japan has almost 128 million people. Nearly all of them live on the four main islands of Hokkaido, Honshu, Shikoku, and Kyushu. But they are not distributed evenly on these islands. People tend to cluster where land is good for farming. In Japan, about 8 out of 10 people live on limited flat land near the ocean.

So how crowded is Japan? Geographers measure density in two ways. The first is **arithmetic population density**. This is the type of density you read about in the introduction. It compares the number of people to a country's total land area. Japan's arithmetic population density is about 878 persons per square mile.

The second measure is **physiologic population density**. It is calculated by dividing the number of people by the amount of *arable* land. Japan's physiologic population density is about 7,545 persons per square mile. By this measure, Japan is almost 17 times more crowded than the United States. As you'll see, high population density affects many aspects of life in Japan.

▶ Geoterms

arable land land suitable for growing crops

arithmetic population density the population of a country divided by its total land area

physiologic population density the population of a country divided by its arable land area

population distribution where people live in a country, whether crowded together in cities or spread out across the countryside

Earthquakes in Japan

Physical Features of Japan

When Two Plates Collide

Earth's crust below the Pacific Ocean is called the Pacific Plate. It slides under the Eurasian Plate, which is Earth's crust below the continents of Europe and Asia. When these two tectonic plates rub against each other, Japan is hit with an earthquake.

A Mountainous Landscape

About 70 percent of Japan is covered with mountains. The rivers flowing out of these mountains are too short and steep for boat travel. But they do provide hydroelectric power to Japan.

31.3 How Population Density Affects Transportation

Crowding has a big effect on transportation. What happens when millions of people in a huge city all head out for work in the morning? It takes a long time to get there! The average **commute time** in Tokyo is an hour and a half each day. This adds up to nearly 400 hours every year. That's enough time to watch 160 movies or take 40 flights from Tokyo to San Francisco. And some people's commute time is much higher than the average.

Public Transportation The Japanese have adapted to busy rush hours by creating an efficient public transportation system. Underground subways link one part of a city to another, while trains carry people from town to town. Japanese subways and trains run often. And they almost always run on time—to the minute. You can set your watch by them.

Rush hour in the Tokyo subway is an amazing sight. People wearing white gloves stand on busy platforms. The job of these *pushers* is to shove as many passengers as possible into the cars before the doors close.

The Japanese have developed some of the fastest trains in the world. Bullet trains—named for their shape and speed—called Shinkansen travel between many cities. These trains travel at speeds of up to 180 miles per hour. That's more than three times as fast as cars moving on highways when there is no traffic.

Subway Pusher in Tokyo

Tokyo's high density means that rush hours are crowded. Workers wearing white gloves push people into subway cars so that the doors will close. Some people spend two to three hours traveling to and from work each day.

Private Cars and Parking Problems Despite their excellent public transportation system, many Japanese have their own cars and love to drive them. As car ownership has increased, so have major traffic jams and parking problems.

Parking is such a problem in Tokyo that the city has strict rules about car ownership. If you live in Tokyo, you cannot own a car unless you can prove you have a place off the street to park it. Tokyo has also built high-rise garages that look like giant shoe cabinets. These garages use computer-controlled elevators to stack cars on top of one another.

31.4 How Population Density Affects Housing

Housing a dense population can present challenges. In Japan, flat land for building is scarce. As a result, Japanese houses are smaller than American homes. Many Japanese families live in apartments no bigger than a family room in an American house.

From the Country to the City The Japanese did not always crowd into small homes. Fifty years ago, Japan was largely **rural**. Most people lived in roomy one-story homes on farms. They also lived in **extended families**. Grandparents, parents, and children all lived together under one roof.

This pattern began to change in the 1950s. Many people left the countryside to go to school or work in cities. City apartments were small compared to rural homes. With space so tight, fewer people lived in extended families. Today, most Japanese live in **nuclear families**. These are families with just parents and their children.

Making the Most of Limited Space The Japanese have found clever ways to make the most of limited space. One way is to use rooms for more than one purpose. Many homes in Japan do not have separate bedrooms. At bedtime, mattresses called *futons* are taken from closets and spread on the floor of living rooms to sleep on.

The Japanese also make good use of limited space by making things smaller. Appliance makers produce small stoves and refrigerators to fit in tiny kitchens. Gardeners grow tiny trees called *bonsai* in shallow pots. A 10-year-old bonsai tree might be only a few inches tall.

Crowding even affects people after death. Most cemeteries in Japan are full. "Unless we try something new," warns a Buddhist temple leader, "all of Japan will turn into a graveyard." To save space, most Japanese have their bodies cremated, or burned, after death. A box of ashes takes up much less space than a coffin.

Capsule Hotel in Japan

Hotels that rent sleeping capsules make good use of space in crowded Japanese cities. Each capsule has a mattress, a television with headphones, and a clock. Guests can spend time in the hotel's restaurants and public areas until they are ready for bed.

Homes in the U.S. and Japan

Japanese homes are smaller than those in the United States. A typical person in Tokyo has about 170 square feet of living space. A typical person in Washington, D.C., has about 740 square feet of living space.

31.5 How Population Density Affects Land Use

Conflicts can arise when people have to share limited land. For years, homeowners blocked plans to expand Japan's Narita Airport. The government offered to move the homeowners to another area. But people resisted the plan. Neighbors even threatened to burn down the new home of anyone who agreed to move.

Conflicts over land use are common in Japan. There simply is not enough land to meet everyone's needs. The Japanese have responded in two ways. They have found better ways to use the land they have, and they have created new land.

Building Up and Down One way to make better use of land is to build taller buildings. But this is not easy in an active **earthquake zone**. Until 1965, the heights of buildings in Japan were limited for safety reasons.

Today the Japanese can build upward using **earthquake-resistant construction techniques**. These techniques allow them to construct skyscrapers that can withstand severe shaking. The Japanese have built so many tall buildings in recent years that some people call the construction crane Japan's national bird.

Terraced Rice Fields in Japan

The Japanese have claimed new land for farming by building terraces into hillsides. Working these rice fields on steep slopes is hard work.

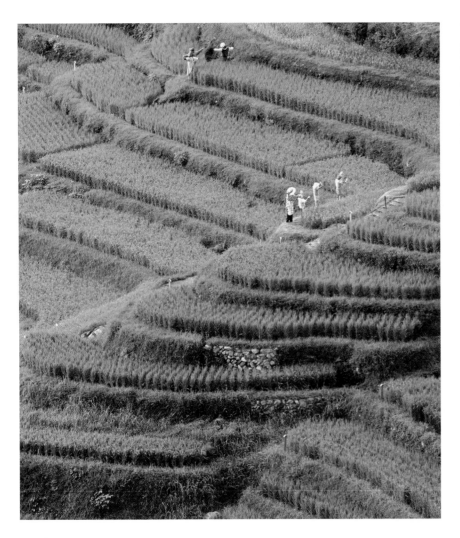

Another way to make better use of land is to build underground. Many Japanese cities have underground shopping centers. One large underground center includes a park, an art museum, a Buddhist temple, and even a zoo.

Creating New Land The Japanese have also created new land. For example, they have filled in shallow **wetlands** with dirt and rubble. Much of Tokyo is built on filled-in bays and marshes. Filling wetlands can save farmland from being used for buildings. But it also destroys valuable fish and wildlife **habitat**.

Like the Incas of South America, the Japanese create new land for farming by cutting terraces, or areas of flat land, into hillsides. **Terracing** allows farmers to grow rice—Japan's most important crop—on the islands' mountain slopes.

Land Use in a Japanese City

By building both up and down, the Japanese make efficient use of limited city land.

31.6 How Population Density Affects Health

Japanese cookies may be the best-packaged treats in the world. Each cookie is wrapped in its own cellophane packet. The packets are placed in a box. The box is wrapped in paper. When the box is sold, it may be wrapped again and then put into a bag.

All those wrappings are just one source of the 2 to 3 pounds of trash that a typical Tokyo resident creates every day. Multiply this by 12 million people, and you get piles and piles of trash that can turn into breeding grounds for rats, flies, and disease.

Pollution Problems Garbage is just one source of health problems that can build up as population density increases. Whenever people crowd into cities, **pollution** problems follow. Smoke from factories and exhaust from cars cause breathing problems. **Sewage** and **wastewater** poison rivers.

No country seems cleaner than Japan. City streets are swept every day. Yet, like most industrial countries, Japan has faced serious pollution problems. One problem is **acid rain,** rainfall that has large amounts of acid. Acid rain can pollute water and soil, harming plants and animals. Another problem is water pollution from factories and farms. In the past, **toxic chemicals** were dumped into oceans and streams. The chemicals poisoned fish and anyone who ate the fish.

One of the worst pollution problems occurred in the 1950s. Local factories dumped mercury, which is highly toxic, into Minamata Bay. People who ate fish from the bay's waters suffered slurred speech, seizures, and blurred vision. Mothers gave birth to babies with twisted limbs. Cats who ate the fish turned from pleasant pets into screeching monsters. More than a thousand people died of mercury poisoning before the bay was finally cleaned up.

Long Life Spans

The Japanese enjoy one of the world's longest life expectancies. A person born in Japan can expect to live to be more than 80 years old.

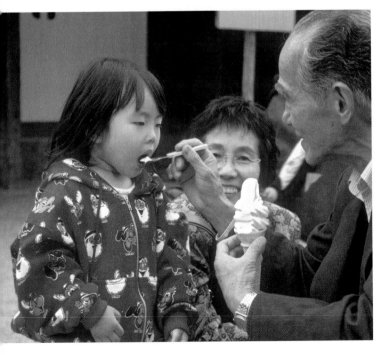

Long Lives High population density can affect health in still other ways. More car accidents happen on city streets than on country roads. Diseases spread more quickly in cities than in small towns. Even so, **life expectancy** in Japan is among the highest in the world. A person born in Japan in 2004 can expect to live 82 years. Clearly, the Japanese have found ways to overcome the health hazards of crowding.

Stand on any street corner in Tokyo and you'll see one way the Japanese try to keep crowding from causing health problems. To avoid spreading disease, people who are sick wear face masks like those used by doctors. More important, Japan has passed strict laws to clean up the air and water. As a result, the air is safer to breathe. Fish from the sea no longer poison people and their pets.

Garbage, though, remains a problem. In 1972, Tokyo opened a huge trash dump on an island in Tokyo Bay. It filled up in just eight years. Another nearby dump is filling up just as fast. "We are full up," a city official says. "We can only survive by reducing." To reduce the flow of trash, Tokyo has turned to **recycling**. Tokyo residents today recycle everything from cans and bottles to cookie wrappers.

31.7 Beginning to Think Globally

In this chapter, you have seen how population density affects aspects of life in Japan. These aspects include transportation, housing, land use, and health.

The Japanese have found many ways to deal with crowding. Japan is a wealthy country. It can afford high-rise office buildings, apartment houses, and a good public transportation system. It can also pay the costs of cleaning up its air and water. Despite crowded cities and pollution problems, the Japanese enjoy long and healthy lives.

Other densely populated countries are not so well off. India has almost the same population density as Japan. It has much more arable land per person. It is also far richer in **natural resources**. Even so, India is a much poorer country. Life expectancy there is just 70 years compared to 82 years in Japan. Think about this contrast as you look at population density around the world.

Life Expectancy in Japan and the United States, 2009

	Japan	United States
Women	86	81
Men	79	76

A Crowded Street in Tokyo
The Japanese in this street scene appear well dressed and well fed. People in other densely populated nations are not so fortunate. In many countries, crowding may add to people's misery.

31.8 Global Connections

How does population density affect the way people live around the world? The map shows how people are spread out across Earth. As you study the map, look for population patterns. One thing you may notice is that people are not evenly distributed. Nine out of 10 people live north of the equator. Most also live in mild climate zones and near coastlines. Why might this be so?

Can a place have too many people? The answer is yes and no. Consider Bangladesh and Singapore. Bangladesh is about three times as crowded as Japan. Most of its people are poor farmers with a life expectancy of only 60 years. In contrast, Singapore is just over 20 times as densely populated as Japan. Its people are well-off city dwellers with a life expectancy the same as that of the Japanese.

What other factors contribute to the well-being of crowded countries? Resources and location are both important factors. The Netherlands is a small, densely populated country in Western Europe. It has no important mineral or energy resources. But the Netherlanders have learned to make the most of their fertile soil and good harbors. They produce high-quality farm and factory goods. They trade these goods around the world for resources they lack.

How does population density affect a nation? Population density does not make a nation rich or poor. It can lead to land-use problems. It also affects how government serves the people and puts extra pressure on resources.

Population Density Around the World, 2009

Arithmetic Population Density, 2009

Country	People per Square Mile of Land
Australia	7
Bangladesh	3,018
Colombia	104
Egypt	215
Japan	878
Netherlands	1,278
Nigeria	424
Singapore	17,670
United States	87

Sources: Population Reference Bureau. Central Intelligence Agency. The World Bank.

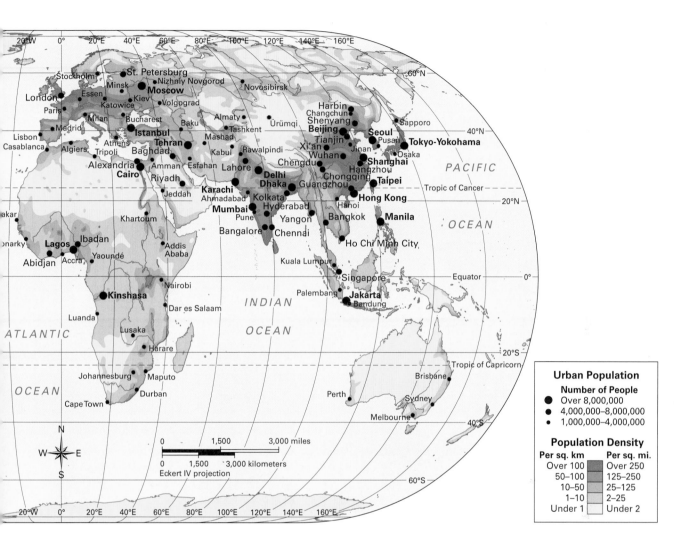

Urban Population

Number of People
- ● Over 8,000,000
- ● 4,000,000–8,000,000
- • 1,000,000–4,000,000

Population Density

Per sq. km	Per sq. mi.
Over 100	Over 250
50–100	125–250
10–50	25–125
1–10	2–25
Under 1	Under 2

Eckert IV projection

| 0 | 1,500 | 3,000 miles |
| 0 | 1,500 | 3,000 kilometers |

Life Expectancy, 2009

Country	Average Life Expectancy (years)
Australia	82
Bangladesh	60
Colombia	73
Egypt	72
Japan	82
Netherlands	79
Nigeria	47
Singapore	82
United States	78

Per Capita Income, 2007

Country	Average Income per Person*
Australia	$33,340
Bangladesh	1,230
Colombia	6,640
Egypt	5,400
Japan	34,600
Netherlands	39,310
Nigeria	1,770
Singapore	48,520
United States	45,850

*Amounts are in U.S. dollars.

The Global Sneaker: From Asia to Everywhere

32.1 Introduction

We live in a global marketplace. Many of the things we wear or use or eat every day come from other countries. Our cell phones might come from China. Our clothes might be made in Malaysia, Mexico, or Madagascar. The gas in our cars might come from oil pumped in Saudi Arabia or Venezuela. Americans drink coffee from Colombia and tea grown in Kenya. The grapes we eat in winter may have come from Chile. The shrimp in a seafood salad might have been raised in Thailand or Vietnam.

Americans buy goods from all over the world because of **globalization**. This means the development of a global, or worldwide, society. In a global society, people, money, information, and goods flow fairly freely across national borders.

It wasn't always like this. Most of the products that your grandparents used when they were growing up were probably made in their own country. But a boom in world trade has changed all of that. The globalization of the world economy has had a great impact on workers, consumers, business, and the environment.

In this chapter, you will look at one common manufactured product that has become globalized: the sneaker. Most sneakers are now made in Asia. You will read about the steps that go into the making of a sneaker. And you will also learn how the globalization of the sneaker affects people and places around the world.

Essential Question

What is globalization, and how does it affect people and places?

The sneaker is a good example of the growth and impact of globalization. The making of a pair of sneakers involves several steps and various countries. The map shows some of the places that have a role in sneaker production. Keep this map in mind as you try to answer the Essential Question.

Graphic Organizer

Stages in the Making of a Sneaker

——— Designing   ——— Manufacturing

——— Locating materials   ——— Distributing

◀ Shipping containers stacked on docks in Singapore

32.2 The Geographic Setting

Globalization affects every country in the world. But no **region** is more involved than Asia. Countries such as China, South Korea, and Japan have played a major role in the global spread of manufacturing and trade. Asian countries are key players in the global economy.

The Growth of Globalization Globalization is the result of several factors. Advances in communication and transportation have played a big part. Another major factor is the movement toward **free trade**. Free trade is the flow of goods and services across national borders with few controls by governments.

Support for free trade has grown over the past 60 years. In 1947, the United States and 22 other countries signed the General Agreement on Tariffs and Trade (GATT). They agreed to reduce **tariffs** and other barriers to trade. A tariff is a tax on goods imported from another country. This agreement led to the creation of the World Trade Organization (WTO). The WTO also works to reduce trade barriers. By 2008, the WTO had 153 member countries.

Globalization has also been helped by the rise of **multinational corporations**. These are large firms that operate in more than one country. They are key actors in the global economy. They produce and sell goods and services around the world.

Globalization has brought economic growth to many developing countries. This has meant jobs for millions of people. It has also increased **economic interdependence** among countries. Interdependent countries rely on one another for resources, technology, and trade.

Trade between China and the United States is a good example of economic interdependence. Factories in China make all kinds of goods for export to the United States. When the U.S. economy is booming, Americans have plenty of money to spend on Chinese products. When the economy is not doing so well, Americans spend less on goods. So the jobs of many factory workers in China depend on the economic health of the United States.

What's the Difference?
One of the shoes above was made in the United States. In 2001, however, the last pair of these shoes came off an assembly line in North Carolina. Now they are made in Asia. Look carefully at the labels to tell which is which.

Athletic Shoe Production: Sneaking Away from the U.S.
The history of sneaker production shows globalization at work. For years, the sneakers that Americans wore were made in the United States. Over time, however, most companies moved their production to Asia. By doing so, they were able to spend less on labor and materials. This made it possible to sell sneakers for less and still make a profit.

Look at your own shoes. The label probably says "Made in China" or another Asian country. This is true even for a famous American sneaker: the Converse Chuck Taylor All Star. This shoe's label used to read "Made in U.S.A." But now they, too, are made in Asia.

Behind every sneaker is a complex production process. This involves design, raw materials, manufacturing, and **distribution**. In this chapter, you will see what is done where and why.

▶ Geoterms

economic interdependence a condition in which countries have strong economic ties and depend on each other for resources, technology, trade, and investment

free trade the flow of goods and services across national borders, with little or no government control

globalization the development of a global, or worldwide, society in which people, money, information, and goods flow fairly freely across national borders

multinational corporation a large company that has operations in more than one country

Locations of a Multinational Corporation

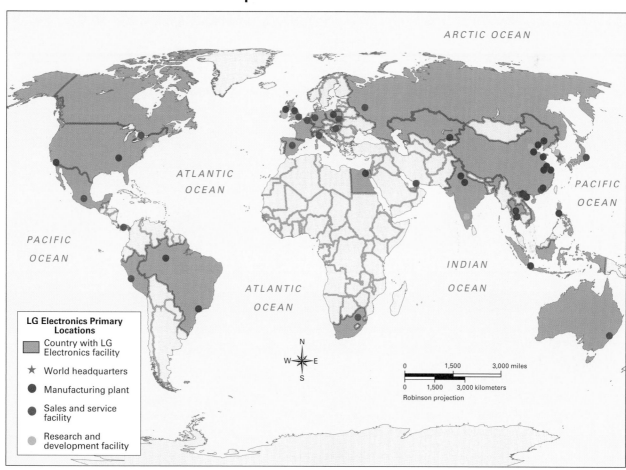

From South Korea to the World

Most multinational corporations are based in Western Europe or the United States. But Asia has its share, too. LG Electronics is a large company based in South Korea. It makes televisions, computers, and other products. It began to expand overseas in the 1970s. The countries shown in color on this map all have LG Electronics facilities today.

Shoes for All Kinds of Feet

Designing shoes for all kinds of feet and activities is a complicated process. Designers get help from scientists who study foot motion and materials. They also talk to athletes. Using their imaginations, they make drawings and models. Sample shoes are then tested in the lab and on the street. If the design works, the shoe goes into production.

New Looks Begin Here

This map shows where most sneakers are designed. Much of this work takes place in the United States. Designers often work closely with the sports stars who will wear and promote the shoes that they design.

32.3 Designing a Global Sneaker

In Britain, they're called trainers. In Australia, they're called sand shoes. Their most common name, though, is sneakers. This name came from an American who noticed how quietly people walked when they wore them. Until the late 1960s, sneakers were relatively simple shoes. Today they are far from simple.

Design Then: A Simple Sports Shoe Sneakers were first made in the mid-1800s. They were used for sports like tennis, croquet, and running. Later, they became popular for basketball.

For the next 100 years, sneaker design changed very little. The upper part of the shoe was made of cotton canvas. The sole was made of rubber. Buyers could choose from a few different brands and styles. There were high tops or low cuts, usually in black or white. Most people thought of sneakers only as athletic shoes.

In the 1950s, though, people began to change their view of sneakers. The shoes were not just for sports any more. They became casual shoes for everyday use. Men, women, and children began wearing them as fashion items.

Design Now: A Complex Fashion Statement Today's sneakers are designed for many purposes. Athletes still wear them. But so does everyone else. There are sneakers for all types of activities, from running and rock climbing to playing tennis or just walking around.

Sneaker companies have come up with new designs and materials for their shoes. These changes have improved performance and comfort. Today companies compete with each other to design the "latest and greatest" sneaker.

New designs and colors have also given sneakers more fashion appeal. To increase that appeal, athletic shoe companies often hire athletes and musicians to promote their sneakers as "cool." They know that many people will pay to wear what their favorite stars are wearing.

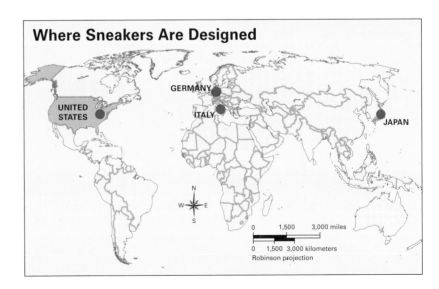

Where Sneakers Are Designed

32.4 Locating Global Sneaker Materials

Look at the soles of your sneakers. They're made of rubber. But sneakers are made of many other materials, too. Some of these materials are found in only a few places in the world. They come together at factories to create a shoe with three main parts: the upper, the midsole, and the outer sole.

The Complex Upper: Mesh Fabric, Leather, and More The upper is the top part of a sneaker. Some uppers are made of natural materials, like cotton or leather. The leather comes from cattle raised in Texas, Venezuela, and other livestock centers. The cowhides are usually sent to South Korea, where they are made ready for use.

Other uppers are made of synthetic, or human-made, materials such as nylon. Nylon fabric is light and dries easily.

The Squishy Midsole: Foam Padding and Air Bags The midsole is the part of the shoe that cushions the bottom of your foot. It is made of plastic and foam padding. These materials are made from oil found in Saudi Arabia and other oil-rich countries.

The foam used in many sneakers may be produced in South Korean factories. Chemicals are poured into molds and then baked. In the process, they form millions of tiny gas bubbles that give the foam a cushiony feel. Some midsoles also contain small "air bags" filled with pressurized gas.

The Tough Outer Sole: Synthetic and Natural Rubber Treads The tread, or sole, of a sneaker needs to be tough but flexible enough to put a spring in your step. All sneakers used to have natural rubber soles. The rubber came from the sap of rubber trees grown in tropical countries like Brazil, Indonesia, Thailand, and Malaysia.

Today most soles are synthetic rubber. This is made from coal and oil. Much of the rubber used in sneaker production comes from factories on the island of Taiwan.

Inside the Sneaker
The three main parts of a sneaker are the upper, the midsole, and the tread. Many of the materials in each part are synthetic. They are made from oil and coal.

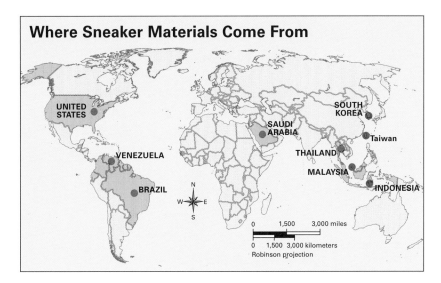

Where Sneaker Materials Come From

Global Sources
The materials used to make sneakers come from countries around the world. This map shows some of the sources of those materials. Some places supply raw materials, such as leather and oil. Others supply manufactured parts, like nylon and foam padding.

South Korean Production

In the 1980s, South Korean workers made many of the world's sneakers. They worked for low wages and were very productive. However, wages went up over time. South Korean companies moved production to countries where pay was still low. Now they "offshore" their work the same way American companies do.

32.5 Manufacturing the Global Sneaker

By now you know that sneakers are not simple shoes. A lot of work goes into creating their designs and materials. But that's not all. Manufacturing sneakers is also a big job. A single sneaker may have more than 50 pieces. It can require the labor of 120 people to put together one pair of shoes.

What Happened to "Made in U.S.A."? Most sneakers used to be made in the countries where they were sold. In the 1960s, simple canvas and rubber sneakers were still being produced in the United States, Britain, and Germany.

In the 1970s, however, sneakers became more complicated. The number of styles increased. The designs became more complex. More labor was needed to assemble these shoes. Costs began to rise. It finally became too expensive to make shoes in high-wage countries like the United States.

Production Moves to Low-Wage Countries Faced with high costs, sneaker companies began to move production offshore, or to other countries. At first, sneaker production moved mainly to South Korea. This country had a large pool of low-wage workers. It had factories that could be used to make shoes. And it had ports for shipping raw materials into the country and finished sneakers out.

Over time, wages in South Korea went up. Making shoes there became less profitable as a result. In the 1990s, production shifted again, this time to China, Indonesia, and Vietnam. All three countries offered the same advantages once found in South Korea.

In fact, many of the sneaker factories in these countries were set up and run by South Korean shoe companies. Rising labor costs at home had led the Korean companies to move their production offshore. This was just what American and European companies had done 20 years earlier—and for the same reasons.

Moving Offshore

This map shows how sneaker production has moved over time. In the 1970s, it went from the United States and Europe to South Korea, Taiwan, and Japan. By the 1990s, production shifted to China and Southeast Asia. Lower labor costs have been the reason for these moves. Sneaker production may move again, perhaps to low-wage Africa.

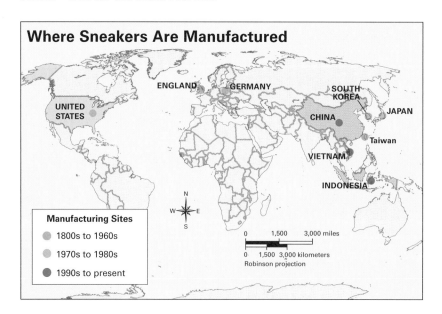

Where Sneakers Are Manufactured

Manufacturing Sites
- 1800s to 1960s
- 1970s to 1980s
- 1990s to present

32.6 Distributing the Global Sneaker

In 1990, a ship carrying sneakers from South Korea to the United States was hit by a big storm. Eighty thousand pairs of shoes spilled into the Pacific Ocean. A year later, the shoes were still washing up on American shores. Normally, though, sneakers have a smoother journey from Asia. Companies use several methods of transportation to get their shoes from the factory to the store.

Across the Globe by Ship Typically, sneakers are sent by container ship from Asia. This is the least expensive way to move goods over such long distances.

The trip to the United States takes about two weeks. The sneakers make this journey in freight containers. These are large, weatherproof steel boxes that are easy to stack on the deck of a ship. Big container ships can carry 8,000 of these boxes.

Across the Country by Train and Truck When a ship arrives on the west coast of the United States, the containers are unloaded onto trains or trucks. In some ports, train tracks run right up to the docks to make unloading easier.

Train or truck transport across the United States can take up to a week or longer. Most sneakers end up in Memphis, Tennessee. Memphis is a major distribution center where rail lines and highways meet. Sneakers are kept in warehouses here and sent by truck to stores around the country. A truck leaving Memphis in the morning can reach 75 percent of the nation's population by the next day.

From the Store to Your Home Sneakers are distributed to some 18,000 stores in the United States. You probably shop at some of them. By the time a pair of sneakers makes it from an Asian factory to your home, it may have traveled more than 7,000 miles.

In 2007, Americans bought about 425 million pairs of athletic shoes. That's nearly one and a half pairs for every man, woman, and child in the United States. Athletic shoe sales totaled more than $17 billion. And that doesn't count the rest of the world. The global sneaker is big business.

Travel Time Around the World, 1500–2000

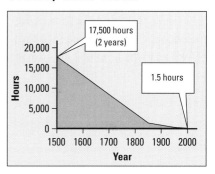

Our Shrinking World

This graph shows the time it took to travel around the world at different points in history. Around 1500, it took a sailing ship two, and sometimes three, years to circle the globe. Jet planes shrank that time to two days. A space shuttle can do it in less than two hours. As travel time has decreased, our world has seemed to shrink.

32.7 Beginning to Think Globally

In this chapter, you read about globalization and the making of the global sneaker. You learned that free trade plays a key role in the global economy. You read how shoe companies have become multinational corporations. And you have seen how the global sneaker has increased economic interdependence among several countries.

Globalization is changing the world. These changes may be either good or bad, depending on your point of view.

The Case for Globalization Globalization has benefits for both rich and poor countries. When companies in wealthy countries set up factories in poor countries, they create new jobs. The workers who fill these jobs often improve their standard of living. The money they earn also helps bring economic growth to their countries.

Companies that move production offshore do so to keep their costs low. This helps them keep their prices low as well. Low prices benefit consumers in both rich and poor countries. Many working people today can buy products that were once considered luxuries that only the rich could afford.

Globalization has other benefits. Countries that trade with one another want to maintain good relations. As a result, conflict among nations may be reduced. In this way, economic interdependence may lead to a more peaceful world.

A global society also brings the world's people together in ways never before possible. It lets us see how other people live and work in other lands. It allows us to share ideas, technology, music, and art across vast distances. As we learn more about one another, we can learn to understand and respect other ways of life.

Closed Factories, Lost Jobs
Globalization has brought new factories and jobs to developing countries. But as production has moved overseas, some U.S. factories have closed their doors. Factory closings are hard on workers who lose their jobs. Towns suffer as well from the loss of jobs and business.

THIS FACILITY IS CLOSED

The Case Against Globalization
Increased global trade can bring harm as well as good. Some developing countries lack laws to protect the environment. Factories set up in such countries often dump **toxic waste** into rivers and streams. They release deadly fumes into the air. Such polluting practices would be illegal in developed countries.

Many poor countries also lack worker protection laws. Without such laws, factories can require workers to work long hours for low wages. A sneaker factory worker in Asia might earn just $2 for a 12-hour workday. They can also hire children, who are paid even less. Factories that abuse workers are called sweatshops. Working conditions in sweatshops are often unsafe or unhealthy.

Globalization can be harmful to workers in developed countries as well. When companies send work offshore, they often close factories at home. Many Americans have lost their jobs because of factory closings. Towns and cities may also suffer when unemployed residents move to other places to find work.

Finally, globalization can upset traditional ways of life. It also can make nations too dependent on others. A country's culture may be weakened when it is flooded by foreign foods, movies, or music. Traditional arts and languages may be lost. Some countries depend on others for a major trade good, such as oil. This can make them less self-sufficient. They may get into wars in order to maintain the supply of what they need.

The Future of Globalization People often disagree about the impact of globalization. Some think its benefits outweigh its drawbacks. Others say it does more harm than good. But one thing seems certain: globalization is here to stay. And it's likely to increase.

One reason for this is that many poor countries see globalization as a path out of poverty. They have seen how countries like South Korea and Singapore have prospered from global trade. Both countries welcomed foreign companies. Both saw their economies grow rapidly as a result. Now other countries want to follow their example.

Another reason is that money now moves freely around the world. Money coming into a country from investors in another country is called **foreign investment**. Every year, billions of dollars of foreign investment move around the world. This money is used to build new factories or to invest in businesses. Think about this as you look at the map and graphs of foreign investment in the next section.

Fast Food in the Philippines
Globalization sometimes kills off local businesses. But some businesses survive by copying foreign ideas. This fast-food restaurant in the Philippines looks like an American chain. But it's owned by a local company. It now competes successfully with large fast-food chains.

32.8 Global Connections

Foreign investment is an important factor in globalization. It is the main way that multinational corporations expand offshore. The graphs show changes in foreign investment between 1914 and 2007. The map shows foreign investment flowing to the developing world in 2007.

How has foreign investment changed since 1914? Foreign investment has gone up since 1914. Most of this increase came in the years after 1960. This was a period of rapid growth in the global economy. The first circle graph shows that in 1914, more than half of the foreign investment went to Latin America and Asia. The second graph shows that by 2007, the percentages going to these regions had decreased. The total dollar amount was much greater in 2007 than in 1914.

Which developing country attracted the most investment money in 2007? How might this investment have affected life there? China received more foreign investment than any other developing country in 2007. Most of this money was used to start new businesses in urban areas. These businesses attracted workers from rural areas. As a result, China is becoming more urban year by year.

Which parts of the world attracted the least investment money? How might this affect the people living there? Most countries in Africa, Southwest Asia, and Central Asia attracted little investment. As a result, their economies have grown slowly or not at all. Most of their people still depend on agriculture to make a living. Job opportunities are often quite limited.

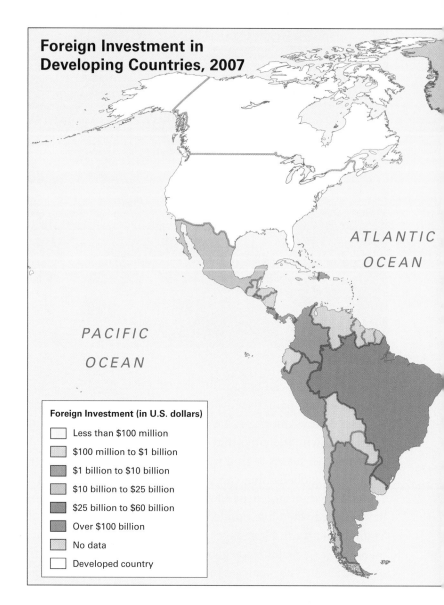

Foreign Investment in Developing Countries, 2007

Foreign Investment (in U.S. dollars)

- [ ] Less than $100 million
- [ ] $100 million to $1 billion
- [ ] $1 billion to $10 billion
- [ ] $10 billion to $25 billion
- [ ] $25 billion to $60 billion
- [ ] Over $100 billion
- [ ] No data
- [ ] Developed country

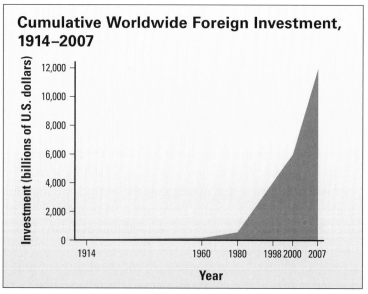

Cumulative Worldwide Foreign Investment, 1914–2007

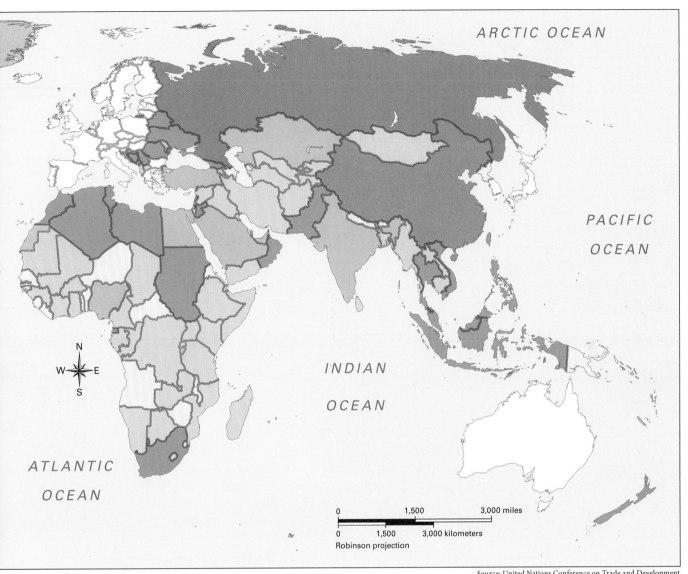

Source: United Nations Conference on Trade and Development.

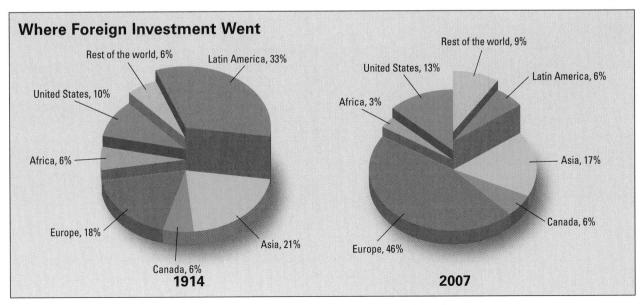

Where Foreign Investment Went

1914

- Rest of the world, 6%
- Latin America, 33%
- United States, 10%
- Africa, 6%
- Europe, 18%
- Canada, 6%
- Asia, 21%

2007

- Rest of the world, 9%
- United States, 13%
- Latin America, 6%
- Africa, 3%
- Asia, 17%
- Canada, 6%
- Europe, 46%

Oceania and Antarctica

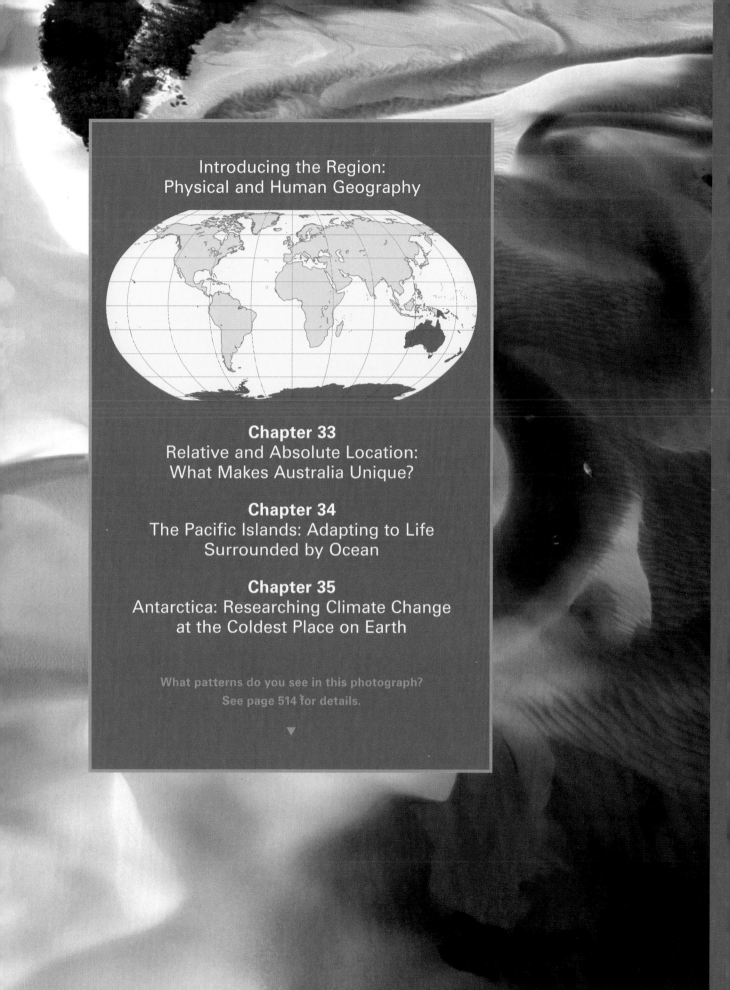

Introducing the Region:
Physical and Human Geography

What patterns do you see in this photograph?
See page 514 for details.

▼

Oceania is a vast **region** in the South Pacific Ocean. It includes the continent of Australia and the large islands of New Zealand and Papua New Guinea. There are thousands of smaller islands as well. They are scattered across hundreds of square miles of ocean. The Pacific Islands form three major groups called Melanesia, Micronesia, and Polynesia.

The continent of Antarctica lies to the south of Oceania. On some world maps, you see Antarctica as a narrow strip of land along the bottom. In fact, Antarctica is the fifth largest continent in the world. Near the center of this frozen **landmass** is the South Pole. The stormy waters of the Pacific and Indian oceans isolate Antarctica from the other lands in this region.

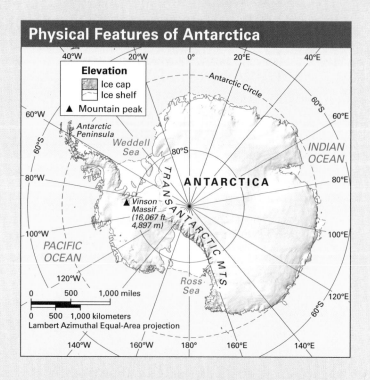

Physical Features of Antarctica

Physical Features of Oceania

Physical Features

The landmasses in this region include both continents and islands. An island is a body of land surrounded by water. But most continents are also surrounded by water. What is the difference between an island and a continent? To a geographer, the main difference is size. Islands tend to be small, and continents are large. Australia is the smallest continent. But it is still over three times as large as Greenland, the largest island on Earth.

No one knows the exact number of islands in Oceania. Geographers estimate that between 20,000 and 30,000 islands dot this region. Some of them are large, such as the North and South Islands of New Zealand. Other islands are tiny specks in the sea.

Oceania

Australia is the largest landmass in Oceania. Most of the country is low-lying and very flat. One major mountain range, Great Dividing Range, runs along the eastern edge. The interior of Australia, called the *outback*, is a series of low **plateaus** and plains. The Western Plateau covers a great part of the continent.

Three **deserts** ring the Western Plateau. The Simpson Desert is famous for its red sand dunes. Row upon row of dunes, as much as 200 miles long, ripple across the land. The Great Victoria and Great Sandy deserts also have hills of red sand.

The rest of Oceania consists entirely of islands. The cluster north and east of Australia is called Melanesia. This name means

No one lives on this Polynesian island chain, which lies off the coast of New Zealand's North Island.

"black islands." It refers to the dark skin of the people who first settled there. The islands of Melanesia lie south of the equator.

North of Melanesia are the more than 2,000 islands of Micronesia. This name means "tiny islands." Most of the islands of Micronesia are low-lying coral islands. They are scattered on both sides of the equator.

The third island area, Polynesia, is the largest of the three. This name means "many islands." Polynesia includes New Zealand, Tahiti, Samoa, and Hawaii, as well as islands too small to map. The islands of Polynesia are separated by hundreds of miles of sea.

Antarctica

Most of Antarctica is covered by ice sheets. This ice ranges from one to three miles deep. Beneath all this ice, Antarctica has mountains and valleys like other continents.

The Transantarctic Mountains wind across the continent. They divide it into East and West Antarctica. The South Pole lies in East Antarctica. The Antarctic Peninsula juts out from West Antarctica like a tail. To the east of this **peninsula** is the Weddell Sea.

Elevation Profile of Australia

Elevation (feet) — Elevation (meters)

4,000 — 1,219
3,000 — 914
2,000 — 610
1,000 — 305
Sea Level — 0

30°S Latitude

Western Plateau
Great Victoria Desert
Darling River
Great Dividing Range

INDIAN OCEAN
PACIFIC OCEAN

Climate

This geographic region covers a large part of Earth. It stretches from north of the equator all the way to the South Pole. Because there are such differences in latitude, every **climate zone** is represented.

These contrasts in **climate** result in part from the amount of sunlight each climate zone receives year round. The solar energy at the equator is the strongest. It also varies little throughout the seasons. The solar energy at the poles is the weakest. In almost all of Antarctica, the sun disappears completely in winter.

Antarctica has an **ice cap** climate zone. It is very cold all year. The snow and ice are permanent. In contrast, some places nearer the equator have a **tropical wet** climate. It is hot and rainy all year round.

Oceania

Australia has been called a "desert continent with green edges." Its center has an **arid** and **semiarid** climate.

Australia's coastal areas are not so dry. The northern coast has a **tropical wet and dry** climate. It is hot all year with rainy and dry seasons. Part of the eastern coast has a **humid subtropical** climate. Hot, rainy summers follow mild winters with some rain.

Farther south, the eastern coast has a **marine west coast** climate. Summers are warm, winters are cold, and there is rainfall year-round. Australia's southern coast has a **Mediterranean** climate. It is warm all year with dry summers and short, rainy winters.

New Zealand has a mild, marine west coast climate. Most of the other islands of Polynesia, Melanesia, and Micronesia have a tropical wet climate.

But opposite sides of some islands can have different weather. In the South Pacific, the **trade winds** near the equator blow from east to west. So when the wind hits an island's east, or **windward**, side, it stirs up rough surf near the shore.

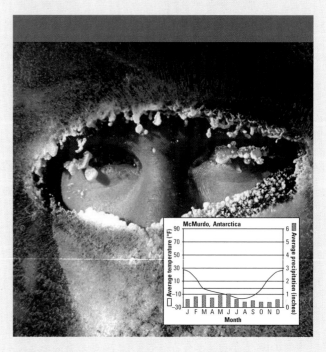

Scientists learn to live with the cold at McMurdo, a research station on Antarctica run by the United States. Which months would be the most comfortable there?

If there are **highlands** on an island, the air will rise as the wind moves up the windward slope. As air rises, it cools. The cooler air drops any moisture it might be carrying, so this side of the island gets rain.

By the time the wind reaches the **downwind**, or western, slope of the island, it has lost both moisture and strength. As a result, the downwind side of an island is usually drier than the windward side. The water on the downwind coast is calmer as well.

Antarctica

Antarctica is the coldest place on Earth. The lowest temperature ever recorded, –129°F, was at Vostok Station in Antarctica in 1983. But even this freezing ice cap climate has some variety. It is drier and colder on the inland plateau. On Antarctica's coastline, however, there are slightly warmer, wetter conditions. At McMurdo Station, summer temperatures may rise above freezing, to 40°F or even 50°F.

Vegetation

The many climate zones in this region result in a great variety of plants. Australia alone has eight different vegetation areas. One such area, **chaparral,** is found in southern Australia.

Chaparral is a major plant community in many parts of the world. It is found on the west coast of the United States and around the Mediterranean Sea.

Areas with chaparral have cool, wet winters and hot, dry summers. The most common plants are shrubs and small trees. Most have small, leathery leaves that hold in moisture. Some chaparral plants have shallow roots that spread out to catch water as rain falls. Others send roots deep into the ground to search for **groundwater.**

Because summers are so hot and dry, fires are common in chaparral zones. But chaparral plants are adapted to fire. Some plants resist fires or grow back quickly after a blaze. Fires clear the ground, making new growth possible. The seeds of some chaparral plants will sprout only after being heated in fire.

Fires are so common in the chaparral that the driest months in Australia are called "bushfire season."

Oceania

Desert and **desert scrub** cover the dry, central part of Australia. Most of northern Australia is covered in **tropical grassland**. The grasses and scattered trees are adapted to the tropical wet and dry climate. **Broadleaf evergreen forest** grows on Australia's northeastern coast. The southeastern coast is blanketed by **mixed forests**. In the mountains of southeastern Australia, a small area of **highlands** vegetation is found.

The islands of Melanesia, Micronesia, and Polynesia mostly have broadleaf evergreen forests. New Zealand is an exception. It lies farther south in a milder area. New Zealand's North Island is covered in mixed forests. The South Island has a mix of **temperate grassland,** highlands, and mixed forests.

Antarctica

Few plants can survive in Antarctica's cold climate. Some mosses grow in rocky areas of the coast. Two kinds of flowering plants grow on the Antarctic Peninsula. Lichens grow on the coast and in inland valleys.

Tropical rainforests cover many islands in the South Pacific. Ferns and other broadleaf evergreen plants surround this waterfall on the Samoa Islands.

Oceania may not look much like the rest of the world. Still, it has 14 independent countries. The smallest country is Nauru. This island of less than nine square miles has a population of more than 10,000. Australia is the largest country, in both area and population. It is home to more than 21 million people.

Antarctica has no permanent population. It is not a nation. Many countries have agreed to share this unusual continent for scientific research. The population of visitors ranges from about 4,000 in the summer to 1,000 in the winter.

The countries of Oceania are loosely linked by their location in the vast Pacific. Still, great distances separate them. For most of their history, the peoples of this region lived in isolated groups and developed their own cultures.

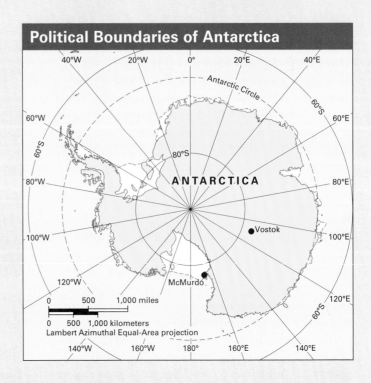

Political Boundaries of Antarctica

Political Boundaries of Oceania

History

For thousands of years, the first inhabitants of Oceania were sheltered from the rest of the world. Then European explorers came to these islands. Their arrival brought major changes to Oceania.

Early Times

Historians think that Oceania's first people came from Southeast Asia thousands of years ago. They followed land bridges from place to place when possible. They traveled by water, too, using rafts and canoes. Polynesia was the last of the island groups to be settled. The Polynesian islands are farther apart and could be reached only by long voyages.

As people settled on the islands, they built villages and a way of life that centered on the sea. Most people lived in family groups known as tribes. They ate fish, tropical fruits, and coconuts. They also grew root crops such as yams and taro.

The first people to live in Australia are called Aborigines. They were nomads who traveled in bands. They hunted and gathered their food. Aborigines lived in Australia for at least 50,000 years before Europeans came.

The Colonial Period

In the 1500s, Europeans began to explore the region. The first regular visitors to the region were whalers. People in Europe and the Americas burned whale oil in their lamps in the 1800s. Whalers came to Oceania in search of these giant sea mammals.

In time, European colonists began to settle in the region. At first, they traded with the people who lived there. Later, they established large farms and ranches. The colonists raised fruits, sugarcane, and livestock. By 1900, most South Pacific islands were colonies of European countries.

Australia has a different history from the rest of the region. In 1788, Great Britain turned Australia into a prison colony. People convicted of crimes were shipped to Australia to serve their prison terms. This practice ended by 1868. Gold was discovered in Australia in 1851. This news brought many new settlers to the colony.

The coming of Europeans was a disaster for most of the region's **indigenous peoples**. Often they lost most of their land. Many died of sickness brought by the Europeans. Some died fighting the Europeans over control of their homelands.

The Modern Era

The 1900s brought independence to much of Oceania. Australia became independent in 1901. New Zealand followed in 1907.

Since the 1960s, other South Pacific island groups have gained their freedom as well. Samoa was the first, in 1962. Fiji and Tonga followed in 1970. Palau, the newest country in the region, gained its independence in 1994.

The countries of Oceania are working to make life better for their people. In 1971, they formed the South Pacific Forum. It encourages trade and friendship among the countries of the region.

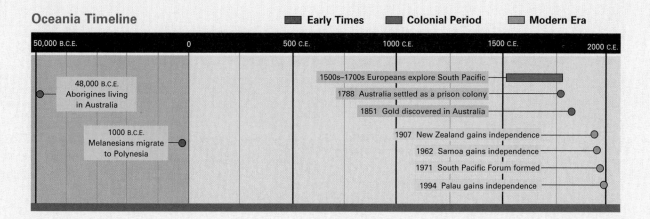

Oceania Timeline — Early Times — Colonial Period — Modern Era

50,000 B.C.E. | 0 | 500 C.E. | 1000 C.E. | 1500 C.E. | 2000 C.E.

48,000 B.C.E. Aborigines living in Australia

1000 B.C.E. Melanesians migrate to Polynesia

1500s–1700s Europeans explore South Pacific

1788 Australia settled as a prison colony

1851 Gold discovered in Australia

1907 New Zealand gains independence

1962 Samoa gains independence

1971 South Pacific Forum formed

1994 Palau gains independence

Population

Oceania and Antarctica is the most sparsely settled region in the world. It has less than one percent of the world's population. This small population is growing slowly. No one really lives in Antarctica. But more people visit every year as researchers and tourists.

Seven out of 10 people in Oceania live in **urban** areas. This number varies from place to place. In Australia and New Zealand, close to 9 out of 10 people live in cities. In Polynesia and Melanesia, fewer than half of the people live in urban areas.

Four out of five people in Oceania are Christians. Two thirds of these Christians belong to Protestant churches. One third are Roman Catholics. The next three largest religious groups are Muslims, Hindus, and Buddhists. A small part of the population still follows traditional religions of the native groups. One out of 10 people in this region practices no religion at all.

Oceania: Major Religions

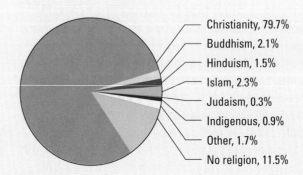

Christianity, 79.7%
Buddhism, 2.1%
Hinduism, 1.5%
Islam, 2.3%
Judaism, 0.3%
Indigenous, 0.9%
Other, 1.7%
No religion, 11.5%

Oceania: Urban and Rural Population, 2007

Urban, 70.5%

Rural, 29.5%

= 10% of the total population

Oceania: Population Growth, 1950–2050

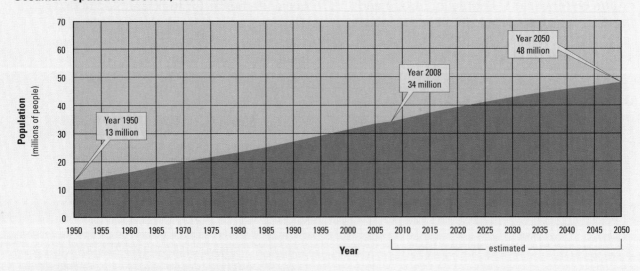

Year 1950
13 million

Year 2008
34 million

Year 2050
48 million

Population (millions of people)

Year

estimated

Sources: United Nations Department of Economic and Social Affairs, Population Division.
Encyclopaedia Britannica.

Economic Activity

Oceania is rich in minerals and energy resources. Its waters are full of fish. In areas with more land, livestock raising has become an important **economic activity**.

European settlers brought sheep and cattle with them to Oceania. These animals adapted well to conditions in Australia and New Zealand. Today there are 12 sheep for every person living in New Zealand. Wool from New Zealand sheep is used to make carpets, blankets, and fine yarn for knitting. Cattle in Australia provide beef and dairy products, much of which is sold to Asia.

Resources

Precious metals are a key resource for this region. Australia is one of the leading producers of diamonds in the world. Gold, silver, and copper are also mined there. Papua New Guinea also has gold mines.

Fossil fuels are found in many places in this region. Australia has huge resources of oil, coal, and natural gas. But these deposits are far from settlements. It is expensive to get to them. New Zealand and Papua New Guinea have **natural gas** and oil deposits. Both Australia and New Zealand use **hydro-electric power** as a source of energy.

Sheep ranches in Australia and New Zealand produce large amounts of wool. Woolen mills like this one turn that wool into yarn for cloth, sweaters, and carpets.

Land Use

Subsistence farming is common in the Pacific Islands. The biggest **cash crop** is copra, which is dried coconut meat.

Some **commercial farming** takes place on the eastern and southern coasts of Australia. But much of Australia's dry land is used for livestock raising. In New Zealand, half the land is used for farming and livestock raising. **Forestry** thrives in the islands' wooded areas.

Many people depend on **commercial fishing** across this large region. Boats from many countries fish in the waters of the South Pacific.

Trade and manufacturing are centered in the cities of this region. Factories in Australia produce a wide range of goods, including cars, medicines, and electrical appliances.

Processed foods are New Zealand's most valuable manufactured goods. Food processing plants turn milk into butter and cheese. Meat processing plants freeze lamb and beef for export around the world.

Workers shell coconuts at a copra factory in Tonga. The economy of many small South Pacific islands is dependent on copra.

Relative and Absolute Location: What Makes Australia Unique?

33.1 Introduction

Try to picture how Australia must have looked to European explorers when they first arrived there more than 200 years ago. It probably seemed a very odd place. Winter came in July. Summer heat peaked in January. Animals hopped around, carrying their young in pouches. The land was flat and very dry. Even the patterns of stars in the night sky looked strange.

As you know, the **absolute location** of a place describes its exact position on Earth. Canberra, the capital of Australia, is located at 35°S latitude and 149°E longitude. The letters S and E refer to **hemispheres**. Its latitude tells us that Canberra is in the Southern Hemisphere. This location explains why its seasons are the opposite of those in the United States. Its longitude tells us that Canberra is in the Eastern Hemisphere. This means that it is on the opposite side of the world from the United States.

In contrast, the **relative location** of a place describes where it is in relation to other places. Relative location can affect a country's history and way of life in unexpected ways. Australia's nearest neighbors are South Pacific islands. But its language and culture came from very far away: Great Britain.

In this chapter, you will learn how Australia's location has shaped life there. You will also explore how location has helped make Australia such an interesting place to live and to visit.

Essential Question

Graphic Organizer

How does a country's location shape life within its borders?

This map puts Australia at the center of the world. It is colored yellow to make it stand out. Notice where Australia is relative to the equator. Also notice how far it is from the other continents. Keep this map in mind as you try to answer the Essential Question.

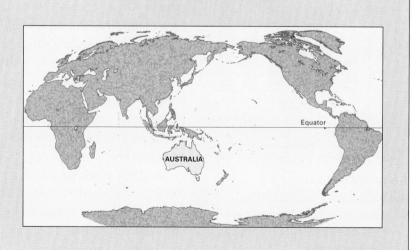

◀ The West Macdonnell Ranges in the arid center of Australia

Climate Zones of Australia

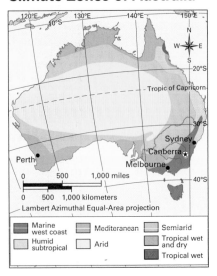

Australia's Seven Climates

Australia has a mix of climates, from tropical to arid. Rain falls mainly near the coast. Most of Australia's interior is a desert.

Rainfall on Six Continents

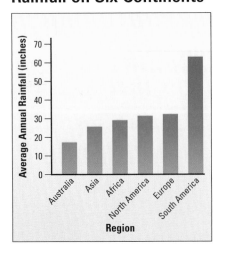

An Arid Continent

Australia is the most arid of the inhabited continents. Droughts are common. So are wildfires during the dry summer months.

33.2 The Geographic Setting

Australia is the only country in the world that is also a continent. It is set off from the rest of the world by the vast Pacific and Indian oceans. Australia gets its name from the Latin word *australis,* which means "southern." Australians also call their country "Down Under" because on maps it lies "under" the equator.

Australia is not quite as large as the United States. Much of it is **desert**. Only the continent of Antarctica is more **arid**. Australia also has one of the most diverse collections of **flora** and **fauna** in the world. Scientists trace the origins of these unusual plants and animals to Australia's formation as a continent.

How Australia Drifted "Down Under" Scientists think that Earth did not always have seven continents. About 200 million years ago, all the land was joined in one **supercontinent**. Over time, this huge **landmass** broke apart into a number of **tectonic plates**. Eventually, they formed the continents we know today. Australia reached its present location after drifting north for many millions of years.

This **continental drift theory** is based on the ideas of a German geographer named Alfred Wegener. He called his supercontinent Pangaea. This is a Greek word that means "all lands." Geographers tell us that the continents are still drifting today. The average rate of movement is less than an inch a year.

Australia's Biodiversity: From Koalas to Kookaburras One of the first Europeans to study Australia's unusual flora and fauna was a botanist named Joseph Banks. A botanist is a scientist who studies plants. Banks was surprised to find species, or types, he had never seen before. One was the small, furry koala. Another was the kookaburra, a bird with a loud laughing call.

The plants and animals that so surprised Banks are Australia's **native species**. These are species that are naturally found in an area. About 80 percent of the continent's plants and animals are found nowhere else on Earth. This is because Australia broke away from other landmasses about 50 million years ago and slowly drifted to its present location. During that time, its plants and animals developed in isolation. Until modern times, few species arrived from other places to add to Australia's **biodiversity**.

In the 1800s, Australia became a colony of Britain. The colonists brought animals and plants from their homelands to Australia. These introduced plants and animals are called **exotic species**. Many had few or no natural enemies in Australia. As a result, their populations grew quickly.

In time, exotic species of animals began to compete with native species for food and territory. The result has been a growing number of endangered and threatened species. **Endangered species** are in immediate danger of dying out. **Threatened species** may become endangered if not protected.

▶ Geoterms

continental drift theory the idea that continents are slowly drifting as the tectonic plates that they sit on move. This idea comes from Alfred Wegener, who proposed that Earth once had one giant supercontinent. This supercontinent broke apart into plates that have slowly drifted to their current locations.

endangered species animals or plants that are in danger of dying out in the immediate future

exotic species animals or plants that are brought into an area from somewhere else

native species animals or plants that occur naturally in an area

threatened species animals or plants that are likely to become endangered if not protected

Continental Drift

These maps show how Earth's continents may have moved over time. Notice the east coast of South America. It fits like a giant puzzle piece into the west coast of Africa. According to continental drift theory, both were once part of the same giant landmass. Australia was once joined to Antarctica. It drifted off on its own about 50 million years ago.

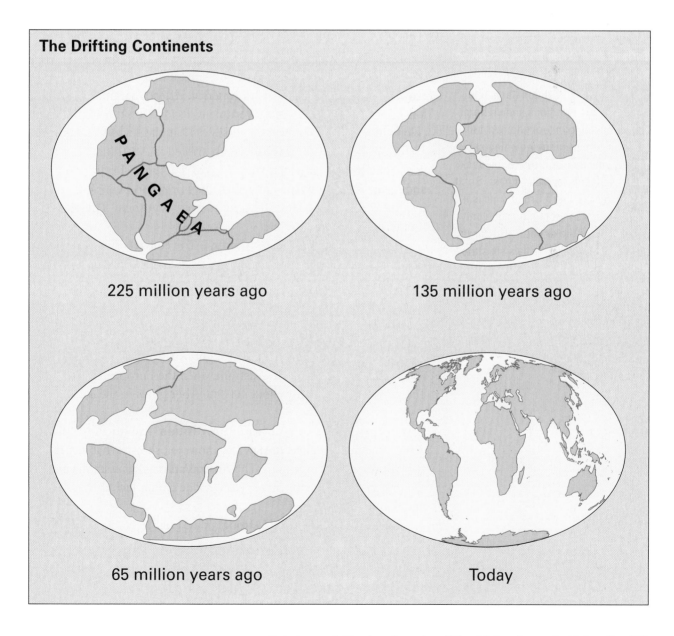

The Drifting Continents

225 million years ago

135 million years ago

65 million years ago

Today

Before and After Independence

Before independence, Australia flew the British flag, or Union Jack. It is the top of the two flags shown here. After becoming independent in 1901, Australia adopted the new flag shown below. This flag kept the Union Jack as a symbol of Australia's past. But it added the Southern Cross. This is a group of stars that can be seen only from south of the equator. The large star represents Australia's six states and its territories.

33.3 A Land Far from Great Britain

Australia's first people are known as Aborigines. The Aborigines came to Australia more than 40,000 years ago. Their way of life may be the oldest culture in the world.

The Aborigines believe in a time long ago that they call the Dreamtime. This was a time before humans when spirits roamed the Earth. These spirits formed the land and created people. They told humans how to keep the land alive. Land is sacred to Aborigines. When Europeans arrived much later, they saw the land differently. To them, land was something to be owned and used.

An Isolated Place to Send Prisoners In 1770, a British sea captain named James Cook discovered Australia while exploring the South Pacific. He claimed the land for Britain. At that time, however, Britain was having trouble with its American colonies. Nothing was done with Australia until after the Americans won their independence in 1783.

The loss of the American colonies created a problem for British prisons. Most were overflowing with convicts. Some prisoners were criminals. Others were poor people who could not pay their debts. Until the Americans rebelled, the government had reduced prison crowding by sending convicts to America. After 1783, this was no longer possible. Instead, the government decided to set up a prison colony in a place as far away as possible. That place was Australia.

In 1788, eleven ships from Britain arrived in Australia. The ships carried about 700 convicts. They also carried tools, sheep, cattle, and seeds. These convicts built Australia's first European settlement. Eventually, more than 160,000 convicts were sent there. The practice finally stopped in 1868.

The new colony grew slowly at first. The convicts supported themselves by farming. After being released from prison, many were given land of their own to farm. Over time, free settlers from Europe arrived as well. Then, in 1851, gold was discovered in the colony. Treasure hunters flooded in from all parts of the world.

As more settlers came, Aborigines were often pushed off their land. Many also died of diseases brought by the Europeans. At least 750,000 Aborigines lived in Australia when the Europeans arrived. Today there may be only about 400,000 Aborigines in the country.

British Influence in Australia Continues In 1901, Australia gained its independence. Its new flag, however, showed that its people still felt connected to Britain. The Australian flag has a small copy of the British "Union Jack" in one corner. The Union Jack is the British national flag.

Britain's influence is still strong today. English is the country's official language. Almost half of Australians claim British or Irish roots. Australians honor the British monarch. Finally, almost 10,000 Britons **immigrate** to Australia each year. They come knowing they will feel right at home "Down Under."

33.4 New Relationships with Near Neighbors

After independence, Australians adopted a "white Australia" immigration policy. The purpose of that policy was to keep people of color from entering the country. Any person who wanted to immigrate had to pass a "dictation test." An official read aloud a 50-word statement in a European language. The newcomer had to write it down word for word. Those who could not were turned away. This test limited immigration mainly to white Europeans.

Australia Opens Its Doors to the World The "white Australia" policy ended in the 1970s. The country then opened its doors to immigrants from anywhere in the world. By 2008, more than 21 million people lived in Australia. About one of every four was born in another country.

Today Australia welcomes approximately 200,000 immigrants each year. More than one half of them arrive from Asia. People migrate to Australia for both push and pull reasons. Some are **refugees** fleeing wars. Others come seeking an education or a good job.

The opening of Australia has changed the country. People of color are no longer uncommon. Old ways of life have mixed with new cultures. Sometimes this has led to tension between **ethnic groups**. But the main result has been the creation of a lively **plural society**.

New Trading Partners in the Asia-Pacific Region A century ago, more than half of Australia's exports went to Britain. Today few exports go to Europe.

The country now looks closer to home for trade. The cost of shipping goods to nearby countries is much less than shipping to Europe. By 1950, Japan was Australia's most important trade partner. In recent years, South Korea, China, and Taiwan have also increased their trade with Australia.

Australia's Export Markets, 2006

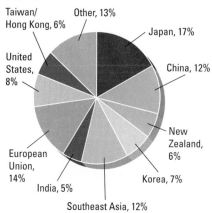

Source: Australian Department of Innovation, Industry, Science, and Research.

Shifting Trade Patterns

Australia's trade with Europe has dropped in recent years. Meanwhile, trade with nearby Asia has increased. More than half of all of Australia's exports are now sold in Asia. Japan has replaced Britain as Australia's most important trade partner.

A Plural Society in the Making

Australia once limited immigration mainly to whites. Today people from all over the world are welcome. This map shows where Australians who were born in other countries came from.

Origins of Foreign-Born Australians, 2007

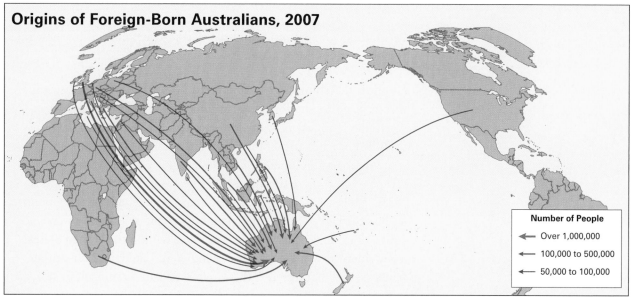

Number of People
- ← Over 1,000,000
- ← 100,000 to 500,000
- ← 50,000 to 100,000

Source: Australia Department of Immigration and Citizenship.

New Year's Eve in Sydney
Australians celebrate New Year's Eve in Sydney with fireworks over the harbor. The unusual structure on the left is the Sydney Opera House. This performing arts center is one of the world's most famous buildings.

33.5 Australia's Reversed Seasons

Australians are celebrating the New Year. Bondi Beach, near Sydney, is packed with families under beach umbrellas. The sky is a clear blue. Temperatures hover at 98°F. Surfers wait for the next big wave, while children make sandcastles on the beach. In the evening, families will picnic around Sydney Harbor while waiting for one of the world's great fireworks shows.

Sunny December in the Southern Hemisphere As you recall, Australia is in the Southern Hemisphere. Its seasons are the opposite of those in the northern half of the world. Summer there starts in December and runs through March.

In Chapter 1, you learned that seasons are caused by the tilt of Earth on its **axis**. Because of this tilt, the Southern Hemisphere receives more sunlight between December and March. These are Australia's warm summer months. Those same months are the winter season north of the equator.

Seasonal Advantages of Living "Down Under" December means bundling up for winter in much of the United States. In Australia, families get ready for summer vacation. Warm days and beautiful beaches attract tourists from north of the equator. In 2008, more than 5 million people vacationed in Australia. Many come to escape winter where they live.

The reversed seasons give Australians another advantage. Countries such as the United States and Japan import out-of-season flowers and fruit. For example, cherries are a summer fruit in the United States. They ripen "Down Under" in December and January. Many other fruits are also harvested at this time. This fruit is shipped to stores north of the equator. Stores can then offer fresh produce all year.

33.6 Australia's Amazing Wildlife

Many unusual animals live in Australia. Miniature penguins waddle ashore each night after dark. The swans you see on lakes are black, not white. Giant crocodiles are as much at home in the ocean as in **freshwater** ponds. You might even see a very odd animal that looks like a cross between a duck and a beaver. The fairy penguin, black swan, saltwater crocodile, and duck-billed platypus are just a few of the country's curious creatures.

Flora and Fauna Found Only in Australia There are more than 13 million living species of plants and animals. About one million are found in Australia. Many of these are found nowhere else on Earth.

As you read, Australia was separated from the rest of the continents a very long time ago. Its plants and animals were isolated. They developed without contact with other species elsewhere.

Within Australia, however, plants and animals adapted to a wide variety of **climates**. The northeast is hot and humid. Here you might find the cassowary, a large bird that cannot fly. The center of the country is arid. This is a perfect place for red kangaroos. Kangaroos are marsupials. These are mammals that carry their young in pouches.

Exotic Species Endanger Many Native Species Early settlers from Europe brought many plants and animals with them. One was the rabbit. Rabbits adapted easily to their new home. However, they have had a harmful effect on native species. As the rabbits multiplied, they ate grasses that native animals needed to survive.

Exotic species have disturbed the natural environment in much of the country. As a result, some native species have disappeared. Others are in danger of becoming **extinct**. A small marsupial called the *bilby* is an example. Because of competition from rabbits, it may die out.

Australia's Unique Animals

Many unique animal species are found in Australia. Three are shown here: the kangaroo, the bilby, and the platypus. The kangaroo and bilby are marsupials. They raise their babies in pouches on their bellies. The platypus is one of only two mammals that reproduces by laying eggs. The other egg-laying mammal is the echidna, a native of Australia and New Guinea.

Less Ozone, More Skin Cancer
Australia has the highest rate of skin cancer in the world. This is partly because the ozone over nearby Antarctica has been thinning. Ozone protects living things from the sun's harmful rays. Less ozone means that more of these rays reach Earth.

33.7 Living Under an Ozone Hole

Surf's up, mate! In December, Australia's beaches are usually crowded with sunbathers and surfers. It's a common sight to see young people grabbing surfboards and heading for the water. Today's surfers grab for something else as well: sunscreen. They know that because of a hole in Earth's **atmosphere,** they are at risk of getting more than sunburn at the beach.

Air Pollution Creates an Ozone Hole Scientists divide Earth's atmosphere into layers. The lowest layer contains the air we breathe. The next layer begins about six miles above Earth. It contains a gas called *ozone.* You cannot see ozone. But without it, there would be no life on Earth. Ozone keeps ultraviolet (UV) rays from the sun from reaching Earth. UV rays are harmful to living things. In humans, they cause sunburn, eye disease, and skin cancer.

In 1985, scientists discovered that the ozone over Antarctica was thinning. They called this thin patch an **ozone hole**. At times, part of this ozone hole has moved north over nearby Australia.

The loss of ozone is caused mainly by chemicals known as *chlorofluorocarbons* (CFCs). When the ozone hole was discovered, CFCs were widely used in aerosol spray cans, refrigerators, and air conditioners. When released into the air, CFCs destroy ozone. Since 1985, CFCs in the atmosphere have been reduced. As a result, the ozone hole should slowly shrink. By 2050, it may be gone completely.

"Slip, Slop, Slap" to Prevent Skin Cancer The thinning of the ozone layer has created health problems for Australians. They are used to sunbathing and enjoying outdoor activities. As a result, they are often exposed to harmful rays from the sun. In recent years, skin cancer rates have risen sharply. Two out of three Australians are now likely to develop skin cancer in their lifetime.

Australia's government is working to prevent new cases of cancer. Posters and advertisements advise Australians to "slip, slop, slap" before they go out in the sun. This means to "slip" on a shirt, "slop" on some sunscreen, and "slap" on a hat to protect their skin. There are also "no-hat, play-in-the-shade" rules at schools. Students cannot go outside to play if they are not wearing a hat.

33.8 Australia's Night Sky

Robert Evans is a retired minister. He is also an expert on Australia's night sky. Using a tiny 16-inch telescope, he has spotted 39 supernovas. A supernova is the explosion of a large star like our sun. Despite having much more powerful telescopes, many astronomers have not spotted even one exploding star. How can Evans see what so many astronomers miss? His location gives him a big advantage. The Australian night sky is clear most of the year.

A Starry Symbol: The Southern Cross The night sky at the South Pole looks very different from the view at the North Pole. There are several constellations, or groups of stars, that are visible only in the Southern Hemisphere. One of these is the Southern Cross, or Crux. Its bright stars are important to sailors. Since ancient times, they have used the Crux to find their way in the South Pacific.

33.9 Beginning to Think Globally

In this chapter, you learned how location has shaped life in Australia. You read how this continent drifted to its current location millions of years ago. It has been alone there ever since. You also met some of the unusual animals that are unique to Australia. You read how some of these native species are being threatened by exotic species introduced by colonists. As a result, some natives have become threatened species. Those most at risk are endangered species. If not protected, they are likely to disappear soon.

Australia is not the only country with threatened species. The World Conservation Union keeps a list of threatened species from around the world. These are plants and animals that are likely to disappear if they are not protected. By 2008, the number of species on that list was almost 17,000. Think about this as you look at the world map in the next section, which shows where threatened animals are located.

Antarctica's Ozone Hole
The dark blue area on this illustration shows how large the ozone hole over Antarctica has grown.

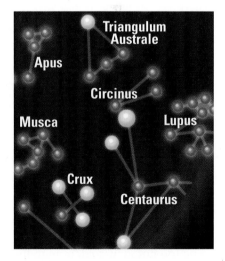

Southern Constellations
The Southern Cross, or Crux, is the smallest constellation in the sky. Four of its five stars, seen above, are so bright that sailors can use them to steer by.

33.10 Global Connections

The map shows the locations of threatened animals around the world. If nothing is done to protect them, these species could soon become endangered. This means they are in danger of rapid extinction. When a species becomes extinct, it is lost to the world forever.

What do the areas with most of the threatened species have in common? Tropical **regions** are "hot spots" for threatened species. Because of their absolute location near the equator, these areas can support great biodiversity. Thus they also have the most species to lose. Islands are also at great risk. Between 1500 and 2000, most extinctions took place on islands. Since 2000, however, about half of all extinctions occurred on continents.

What factors pose the greatest dangers to threatened species? In the past, exotic species posed the greatest risk to native plants and animals. This was especially true on islands and isolated places like Australia. Today, however, loss of habitat is the greatest danger facing most animals. More than 6 billion people live on Earth today. The human population grows by 85 million each year. As humans take over more and more land, animals are crowded out.

How does relative location affect a species' chances of survival? Animals that live far from human settlements generally have the best chances of survival. Such places tend to be too hot, dry, cold, or high for people to live in large numbers. In northern Russia, for example, there is only about one person per square mile. This leaves a lot of habitat for wolves, reindeer, and other animals.

Threatened Animal Species Around the World, 2008

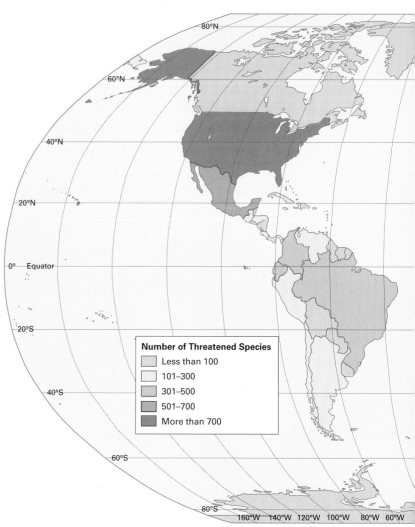

Number of Threatened Species

- Less than 100
- 101–300
- 301–500
- 501–700
- More than 700

Whooping Crane

Where threatened:
Continental United States and Canada

Estimated population:
250

Ibex

Where threatened:
European Alps

Estimated population:
less than 10,000

Black Rhinoceros

Where threatened:
Africa

Estimated population:
4,200

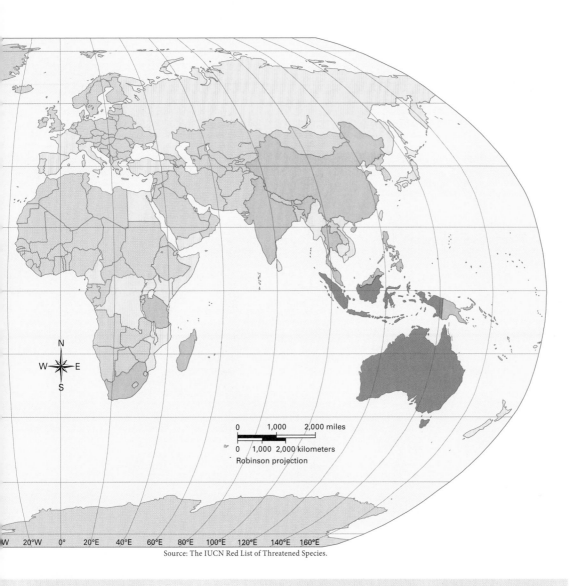

0   1,000   2,000 miles

0   1,000 2,000 kilometers
Robinson projection

Source: The IUCN Red List of Threatened Species.

Humpback Whale

Where threatened:
The world's oceans

Estimated population:
60,000

Snow Leopard

Where threatened:
Mountains of
Central Asia

Estimated population:
4,100–6,600

Long-beaked Echidna

Where threatened:
New Guinea

Estimated population:
less than 300,000

Giant Panda

Where threatened:
China

Estimated population:
less than 2,500

The Pacific Islands: Adapting to Life Surrounded by Ocean

34

34.1 Introduction

It is almost impossible to imagine how big the Pacific Ocean is. Its vast size has fascinated travelers for centuries. In 1835, a British scientist named Charles Darwin sailed across the Pacific from Tahiti to New Zealand. Darwin was shocked at the ocean's expanse. The maps he had been using, Darwin wrote, failed to give an accurate sense of the size of the Pacific Ocean. The water seemed to go on forever. As for land, there was far less of it than he had imagined.

The Pacific Ocean covers one third of Earth's surface. That is an area of about 64 million square miles. It is more than twice the size of the Atlantic Ocean. Tens of thousands of islands are scattered across its vast blue waters. These islands were formed in different ways. Volcanoes rising up from the ocean floor created **volcanic islands**. Rings of small islands called **atolls** were formed by coral reefs. **Continental islands** are chunks of land that were once part of a continent.

In this chapter, you will read about the **physical features** of all three island types. You will see how winds, water, and ocean resources shape life in this vast region. And you will read how the people who make their home on Pacific islands have adapted to a life surrounded by ocean.

Essential Question

How do people adapt to life in an island region?

This illustration shows the relative size and shape of three types of islands. All three are found in the Pacific Ocean. The largest are continental islands. The second largest are volcanic islands. Atolls are usually quite small. People adapt differently to life on each type of island. Keep this illustration in mind as you try to answer the Essential Question.

Graphic Organizer

Continental island

Atoll

Volcanic island

◀ Satellite image of the Pacific Ocean and its islands

Travel Across the Pacific

Vast distances separate the Pacific islands. And yet, in time, most islands large enough to support people were settled. The first settlers may have used rafts or oceangoing canoes like this one to go from island to island.

34.2 The Geographic Setting

Thousands of islands dot the central and southern waters of the Pacific Ocean. There may be 20,000 or even 30,000. No one knows for sure. But if you put them all together, they would add up to very little land.

As you read in the introduction to this unit, geographers divide these islands into three groups. They are called Melanesia (black islands), Micronesia (tiny islands), and Polynesia (many islands). You can see a map of the three groups at the bottom of this page. Within these island groups lie 14 countries and many territories.

A Mix of Island Types The largest islands in this expanse of ocean are continental islands. These islands were once connected to a continent by a bridge of land. Some were separated from the larger **landmass** after the last ice age. As **glaciers** melted, sea levels rose until the land bridge was covered by water. Others were cut off when ocean waves washed away the land connecting them to a continent.

The movement of **tectonic plates** formed still other continental islands. New Zealand is an example. It was once part of a huge landmass. The movement of plates broke this landmass apart to form Antarctica, Australia, and several continental islands.

Volcanic islands begin when a volcano erupts on the ocean floor. **Lava** and ash slowly build up on the seabed. When enough material builds up, the island rises above sea level. Most volcanic islands are cone shaped with steep slopes rising to a high peak. Fiji, Samoa, and the Hawaiian Islands are all examples of this type of island.

An atoll is a ring of coral islands and reefs surrounding a shallow body of water called a **lagoon**. Atolls begin as coral reefs grow around a volcanic island. Over time, the island sinks beneath the sea. Some islands sink due to the movement of tectonic plates. Others are covered by water when sea levels rise. Still others erode away. The area above the sunken volcano becomes a lagoon ringed by coral reefs. Over time, ocean waves break away parts of the reefs. The bits of broken coral pile up to form flat, sandy islands around the lagoon. The Marshall Islands and most of the Tuvalu Islands are atolls.

The Pacific Islands

▶ Geoterms

atoll a ring of coral islands and reefs surrounding a shallow body of ocean water

continental island an island that was once part of a continent

lagoon a body of shallow water partly cut off from the ocean by low-lying rock, sand, or coral reefs

volcanic island an island formed when an underwater volcano builds up enough lava and ash to rise above sea level

Atolls

An atoll, such as Tupai Island in French Polynesia, forms when a volcanic island surrounded by a coral reef sinks beneath the sea. The coral reef remains. But it surrounds a lagoon, not land. Atolls are common in the Indian and Pacific oceans.

Continental Islands

Continental islands, such as New Zealand, were once part of a continent. Some islands are separated when sea levels rise. Some are cut off from a continent by erosion. Others break away when tectonic plates move.

Volcanic Islands

Volcanic islands, such as Moorea Island in French Polynesia, form when a volcano erupts far beneath the sea. When these volcanoes rise above the ocean's surface, they form islands. Volcanic islands are steep with high peaks.

34.3 The Ocean Shapes Life in the Pacific

Visitors describe many islands in the Pacific as "paradise." Tourists travel there to relax on sunny beaches and swim in warm ocean water. But the ocean isn't always peaceful. In fact, sometimes it's dangerous.

In 2004, a very powerful earthquake shook the floor of the Indian Ocean. The quake triggered a huge wave called a **tsunami**. The tsunami flooded coastal areas from Asia to Africa. More than 200,000 people died, and many more were left homeless. For better or worse, the ocean affects every aspect of life in the Pacific.

Winds and Currents Warm the Islands Winds and ocean currents shape the **climate** of most Pacific islands. As you read in Chapter 11, winds move around Earth in circular patterns. One group of winds, called **trade winds,** blows toward the equator from both the north and south. As trade winds move toward the equator, they shift westward. This shifting is caused by the rotation of Earth.

When winds blow across the ocean, they move water on the ocean's surface. This moving surface water forms ocean currents. Like winds, ocean currents move in circular patterns. Near the equator, currents move westward with the trade winds. As these currents move along the equator, the sun warms the water.

Once these warm ocean currents hit land, they have to change direction. In the Northern Hemisphere, the currents turn to the north. In the Southern Hemisphere, they turn to the south. As these currents move away from the equator, they act as heating systems. They warm the air in coastal areas and on islands that might otherwise be cooler.

Heating and Cooling Earth

Ocean currents affect the world's climate. Warm currents can heat places far from the equator that would otherwise be cold. The warm Gulf Stream, for example, brings mild winter weather to the British Isles. Cold currents can cool places near the equator that would otherwise be hot.

Ocean Surface Currents

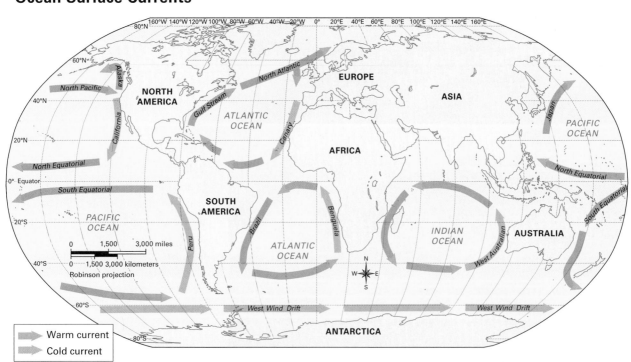

Warm current
Cold current

Warm Air and Water Bring Wet Weather As you learned in Chapter 11, warm air and warm water combine to create wet weather. Warm air can hold a lot of moisture. At the same time, warm ocean water evaporates easily to provide that moisture. As the wet, warm air rises, it forms rain clouds. Not surprisingly, Pacific islands in warm equatorial waters have **tropical wet** climates. Some get rain every day. Islands farther from the equator are both cooler and drier.

Warm ocean temperatures also cause **typhoons**. Typhoons are **tropical cyclones** that begin over the Pacific Ocean. Similar storms that begin over the Atlantic are called **hurricanes**. These huge storms have winds of at least 74 miles per hour. They drop large amounts of rain. They also cause **storm surges** that can flood coastal areas. For people on Pacific islands, typhoons, not tsunamis, are the most frequent **natural disaster**.

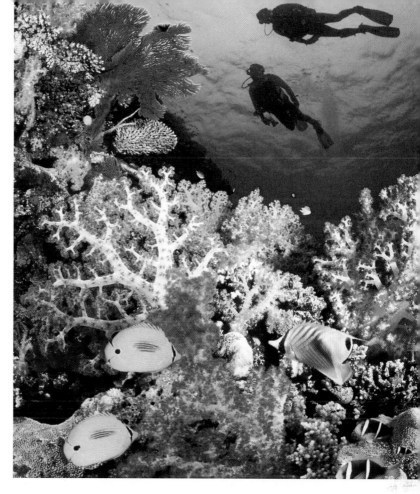

A Great Variety of Fish
Hundreds of species of fish live in the lagoons and coral reefs of the Pacific. Tourists come to Pacific islands to see this marine life. They use snorkels and scuba diving gear to get a good look at life beneath the waves.

The Ocean Is Rich in Resources Pacific islanders have always looked to the sea for much of their food—and for good reason. There is great **biodiversity** in the oceans. Many more kinds of plants and animals can be found in the sea than on land. About 13,000 species of fish live in the oceans.

For centuries, islanders have harvested some of these fish for their own use. Today they have been joined in the Pacific by commercial fishing fleets from many countries. About 60 percent of all fish eaten by humans today comes from the Pacific Ocean.

Scientists are now looking to the sea for new medicines. One drug developed from a sea sponge is already being used to treat cancer. Another developed from a marine, or sea, snail may be used to treat severe pain. William Speck, a doctor and director of the Marine Biological Laboratory in Woods Hole, Massachusetts, sees great promise in medicines from the sea. "I believe marine organisms can be used to eliminate disease and human suffering," said Speck in a 2001 newspaper interview.

Other resources are also found in the Pacific. Pearls from shellfish called *oysters* are prized for jewelry. Vast expanses of the ocean floor in the central Pacific are rich in metal **ores**. Some areas of the sea have deposits of oil and natural gas.

The jobs of Pacific islanders are often related to the ocean and its resources. Many local people work in the tourist industry. **Tourism** is now the biggest moneymaker on many islands. Others work in the fishing industry.

34.4 Life on a Continental Island: New Zealand

New Zealand is an island country in the South Pacific. It is also one of the world's most isolated countries. It is separated from its nearest neighbor, Australia, by more than 1,000 miles of ocean.

The first people to settle New Zealand knew from experience just how far it was from other places. According to legend, they were at sea for a very long time. Finally, one of them saw a long white cloud in the distance. That meant that they were near land. The settlers named their new home Aotearoa. In their language this meant "Land of the Long White Cloud."

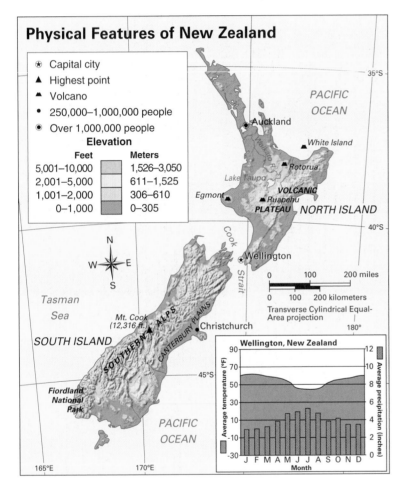

Physical Features of New Zealand

Physical Features New Zealand is made up of two large continental islands and many smaller islands. The two large islands are called the North Island and the South Island. Together they measure about 1,000 miles from north to south and 280 miles from east to west. That's roughly the size of the state of California.

Mountains dominate both large islands. Many of these mountains are volcanoes. Some of them, such as Mount Ruapehu, still erupt sometimes. The mountains of the North Island feature many rivers, lakes, hot springs, and steam-spouting **geysers**. On the South Island, the Southern Alps are high enough to be covered by snow all year. They are also steep enough to challenge mountain climbers.

The rocky west coast of the South Island is indented with fjords. A fjord is a narrow inlet between two steep cliffs. Long ago, these inlets were carved out of the coastline by glaciers.

A Varied Landscape

New Zealand boasts a great variety of physical features. The North Island is a land of volcanoes, some of which are still active. The South Island's Southern Alps are still growing at the rate of about two fifths of an inch a year.

Climate and Economy New Zealand has a **marine west coast** climate. Temperatures are moderate all year, with few extremes of hot and cold. Most days are sunny. But the islands receive regular rainfall from the warm, moist winds that blow from west to east across the Pacific Ocean.

The rain falls unevenly around New Zealand. Heavy rains drench the west side of the South Island. The western slopes of its mountains receive more than 200 inches of rain per year. By the time clouds cross the eastern side of the mountains, they have lost most of their moisture. The result is a **rain shadow** east of the mountains. This area gets only 25 inches of rain a year.

Unlike many island countries, New Zealand is blessed with large expanses of fertile land. Farming and raising livestock form the foundation of the country's economy. New Zealand farmers raise enough meat and dairy products to feed their own country and millions more people worldwide. Sheep are the most important farm animals. They are raised both for their meat and their wool. Sheep outnumber people in New Zealand by more than 12 to 1. No other country has so many farm animals compared to its population.

Because New Zealand is surrounded by water, it's not surprising that fishing is a major part of its economy. Tuna, marlin, and snapper thrive in the ocean waters. The sea life also attracts tourists. People from around the world come to see dolphins, seals, and whales.

Human Adaptations By 2008, just over 4 million people lived in New Zealand. The great majority make their home on the North Island. Most New Zealanders live in a few large cities.

Although New Zealand doesn't have extreme temperatures, it does have four distinct seasons. In the summer, New Zealanders might never need to wear more than a light jacket. In the winter, they put on warm clothing to go outdoors.

New Zealand's varied **landscape** provides many opportunities for outdoor recreation. People ski and hike on the snowcapped mountains. They surf, sail, swim, and fish along the coasts. Rivers provide opportunities for kayaking and white-water rafting. Hot springs attract people who want to relax.

New Zealand is fairly large compared with many Pacific islands. To get around, people travel by car, train, or bus. Air travel links New Zealanders to the world beyond their island home.

Living in Auckland
Auckland is New Zealand's largest city. More than 1.2 million people make their home in the city and its suburbs. This is about a third of the country's population. Homes in Auckland are similar to houses you would find in an American city.

34.5 Life on a Volcanic Island: Tahiti

Tahiti is a land of beautiful beaches and sweet-smelling flowers. Tourists from around the world travel to this island to relax. Many share the opinions of the first Europeans who arrived in Tahiti hundreds of years ago. They think Tahiti is just about perfect.

Getting to Tahiti takes a long time, even by airplane. Like other Pacific islands, Tahiti is very far from its neighbors. It is more than 3,000 miles from Australia and almost 6,000 miles from Japan. It's part of the island group called French Polynesia. Tahiti was once a French colony. Now it is a French territory with its own government.

Physical Features Tahiti is the largest island in French Polynesia, but it's only 402 square miles in area. That makes it one third the size of the tiny state of Rhode Island. From above, the island looks a bit like a hand mirror with a fat handle. The part shaped like a round mirror is called Tahiti Nui (Big Tahiti). The fat handle is Tahiti Iti (Small Tahiti). These two parts are joined together by a narrow **isthmus**.

Both Tahiti Nui and Tahiti Iti were once active volcanoes. The land in both parts of the island rises steeply from the coast. The slopes surround **craters** that once were the volcanoes' centers. The dramatic landscape also features waterfalls and cliffs. The Te Pari cliffs of Tahiti Iti are so steep that they are nearly vertical.

Climate and Economy There are two seasons in Tahiti. The wet season lasts from November to April. During that time, Tahiti gets three fourths of its annual rainfall. Temperatures range from 80 to 86 degrees Fahrenheit. The dry season, which lasts from May to October, is slightly cooler.

Much of Tahiti is too steep for farming. Only the coastal plain is flat enough to grow crops. Tahiti is known for its breadfruit. This is a large fruit that takes on the texture of bread when baked or roasted. Coconut palms, citrus fruits, and orchids also grow in Tahiti. In the past, Tahiti's farms produced enough food to support its people. But as the population has grown, much of the island's food is imported.

Tahiti's economy depends on ocean resources in many ways. Its sunny beaches, coral reefs, colorful fish, and sea turtles attract large numbers of tourists. They are a major source of income for the island.

The next most important income source is black pearls. Pearls come from oysters. When a foreign object, such as a bit of sand, gets inside an oyster's shell, the oyster coats it with a substance called *mother of pearl*. Sometimes the result is a lustrous pearl. Pearls can be white, gold, pink, or dark gray—the color of black pearls.

Steep Volcanoes

This map shows why Tahiti is sometimes called a two-part island. Tahiti Iti and Tahiti Nui are inactive volcanoes. Waterfalls tumble down steep mountain slopes. Sunlight often creates rainbows in the spray. Natives call their island "Tahiti of the many-colored waters."

Physical Features of Tahiti

To encourage oysters to make pearls, Tahitians plant a small bead inside their shells. Ideally a large, dark gray pearl will take shape around the bead over the next two years. But that doesn't happen often. In reality, only 3 oysters out of 100 make a perfect pearl.

The waters off Tahiti are full of sea life. Many Tahitian natives still fish for tuna, marlin, and shark the traditional way. They use poles and lines to catch no more than they will be able to eat.

Commercial fishing is an important part of Tahiti's economy. Fishing fleets from Japan, Korea, and the United States pay Tahiti for permission to fish in its waters. These fleets use electronic equipment to find fish and huge nets to haul their catch out of the sea.

Human Adaptations More than half the population of French Polynesia lives on Tahiti. Most live on the island's north coast. That is also the location of Papeete, French Polynesia's capital. Papeete is a crowded modern city. Other parts of Tahiti are less built up, and people live in more traditional villages.

Beginning in the 1700s, outsiders introduced new ways to Tahiti. For example, men and women traditionally wore a wrapped garment called a *pareu*. Today most wear casual clothes like jeans and T-shirts.

Housing has also changed. Traditional one-room houses were made of coconut trunks and pandanus leaves. Today houses are larger and made of more durable materials. Wealthy Tahitians live in large concrete houses. People who are less well-off live in one- or two-story wooden homes. Houses in the country may have thatched roofs.

Tahiti offers many recreation opportunities. Residents and visitors scuba dive, snorkel, and surf in the water. They hike or ride horses on the volcanic slopes. Some go hang gliding off cliffs. Local people may also participate in traditional dancing and sports.

A modern airport in Papeete brings visitors to Tahiti. Cars and buses provide local transportation. The bus service is called *le truck*. It uses trucks converted into open-air buses to take people around the island.

Bright Colors Everywhere
Traditional Tahitian clothing is made of brightly colored cloth. Both men and women wear a wraparound garment called a *pareu*.

Tahiti Attracts Artists
Artists from around the world have been coming to Tahiti ever since Europeans came to the island. Paul Gauguin was one of the most famous. He was a French painter during the 1800s. His home, shown here, is a traditional Tahitian house.

34.6 Life on an Atoll: Kwajalein Island

A String of Small Islands

Kwajalein Atoll is part of the Marshall Islands. Kwajalein is also the name of one of the islands in the atoll. Kwajalein Island is $\frac{1}{2}$ mile wide and $2\frac{1}{2}$ miles long.

Imagine living on an island that's about the size of a small town. That's what it's like for the people who live on Kwajalein Island. Kwajalein is one of the islands that make up the Kwajalein Atoll. The atoll is located just north of the equator in Micronesia. Kwajalein is part of the Republic of the Marshall Islands. It is also home to a United States Army base.

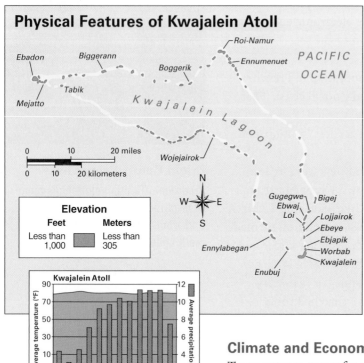

Physical Features of Kwajalein Atoll

Physical Features Kwajalein Atoll is the largest coral atoll in the world. Even so, its 97 islands have a total land area of only 6.5 square miles. The atoll surrounds a lagoon that covers more than 600 square miles. There's a lot more ocean than land in Kwajalein Atoll.

The highest points on Kwajalein Atoll are only 12 to 15 feet above sea level. Because atolls are so low, they flood easily in storms. Also, there are no rivers or springs to provide fresh water. In the past, islanders caught rainwater for drinking. Today **desalinization plants** help some islanders meet their water needs. These plants remove salt from seawater to make it suitable for human use.

Climate and Economy Kwajalein has a tropical wet climate. Temperatures range from about 80 to 88 degrees Fahrenheit no matter what the season. Rain falls daily during both the wet and the "dry" seasons. The difference is that showers don't last as long during the drier months. Tropical storms sometimes blow across Kwajalein, but typhoons are not common. Coral reefs protect the islands from storm surges. They are also home to sea turtles, sea sponges, and shellfish.

Few crops grow in the atoll's sandy soil. Islanders raise coconut palms, breadfruit, and a starchy root called *arrowroot*. Copra, or dried coconut meat, is one of Kwajalein's main products. Because farming is limited, islanders depend on fish for much of their food.

Today, however, the economy of Kwajalein is based on its importance as a U.S. military base in the Pacific. Tourism is also growing among scuba divers who like to explore old shipwrecks.

Human Adaptations People live on only 14 of Kwajalein Atoll's 97 islands. About 14,000 are citizens of the Marshall Islands. Approximately 3,000 are Americans. Only people who work for the U.S. Army, and their families, are allowed on Kwajalein Island.

Living on Kwajalein Island can be challenging. Because of the constant rain and dampness, everything made of iron rusts. Outdoor barbecues and metal furniture do not last long in this climate.

Damaged Coral Reefs
The coral reefs of Kwajalein Atoll were once used as building material by people living on the islands. In this photograph, you can still see large areas where coral has been removed.

Travel around Kwajalein can be tricky. The only cars belong to the U.S. Army. Residents use bicycles to get around. But the dampness can rust a bike in days if it isn't cared for. A person who has a bike for three years has been very careful or very lucky. Ferries and planes link the island with the rest of the atoll and the outside world.

The U.S. Army owns all housing on Kwajalein Island. People live in a mix of trailers, older concrete houses, and newer wooden houses. The most unusual houses are dome homes. They look like white plastic bowls turned upside down. The dome homes are made of materials that resist weather damage and conserve energy.

People on Kwajalein dress like most other Americans, only more casually. Many wear shorts and light shirts to beat the heat.

For those who like sports, there is a lot to do on Kwajalein. Scuba divers enjoy exploring the coral reefs with their colorful fish. Water sports such as sailing and windsurfing are popular on the lagoon. Sports fishing is popular as well. Tuna, marlin, and skipjack are popular game fish. People also enjoy team sports such as volleyball and softball. Indoor activities range from bowling to movies.

Oceans Provide Resources
Oceans are important to people around the world. Worldwide, 35 million people earn a living by catching or raising fish for food.

34.7 Beginning to Think Globally

In this chapter, you learned that the ocean affects every aspect of life in the Pacific islands. You also learned about life on three kinds of islands. Continental islands are the largest, with the most usable land. On volcanic islands, people live mostly along the coasts, where the land is flat and fertile. Atolls, in contrast, are difficult places to live. They have very little land and lack fresh water. Oceans are important to Pacific islanders. They provide food and attract tourism.

Oceans are important to the rest of the world as well. One out of every five people worldwide relies on fish for protein. As the world's population grows, the demand for fish will increase. Think about this as you look at the map of regulated fishing zones around the world in the next section.

34.8 Global Connections

This map shows regulated fishing areas around the world. Each country that borders an ocean has the power to regulate, or control, fishing off its coast. The area it can control extends 200 nautical miles (230 miles) out to sea. These regulated areas are colored dark blue. The light blue areas are unregulated waters. Anyone can fish there. The map also shows where some sea species are in danger of dying out due to **overfishing**.

What is happening to the world's fish supply and why? The supply of many species of fish is declining. Pollution and changes in climate may have contributed to the decline. But the most important cause is overfishing. So many fish are being caught that they cannot replace themselves. Overfishing is driven by a rising demand for fish. It is also the result of better technology. This technology helps fishing crews to catch more fish in less time.

What problems might overfishing cause? Overfishing damages ocean ecosystems. The food web in oceans changes when a species disappears. Overfishing also threatens a food source on which many people rely.

What can be done to prevent overfishing? Countries can try to reduce overfishing in the waters they control. One way is to outlaw fishing methods that catch too many fish. Another is to ban the catch of endangered species. But countries can only regulate limited areas. The rest of the seas are unprotected. To stop overfishing, countries must work together to protect the oceans and their resources.

Regulated Fishing Areas Around the World, 2009

Unregulated commercial fishing areas

Regulated commercial fishing areas

Overfished species (See list below.)

Salmon fishing in Ketchikan, Alaska

Some Overfished Species

	Chilean sea bass: Officially called Patagonian toothfish. A slow-growing, cold-water fish.
	Cod: Second only to herring in tons caught each year. Used mainly for food.
	Orange roughy: Sold fresh or frozen for food. Its oil is used in cosmetics.
	Salmon: These fish are often caught when they swim upstream to spawn.
	Shark: Caught for their hides, fins, and meat. The hide makes an excellent leather.
	Tuna: A popular food for people and pets. Sold canned, fresh, and frozen.

Antarctica: Researching Climage Change at the Coldest Place on Earth

CHAPTER

35

35.1 Introduction

Antarctica is the coldest continent on Earth. The average temperature at the South Pole is –74°F. At this temperature, spilled coffee can turn to ice before it hits the ground. No one lives on this cold continent. Each summer, though, Antarctica warms up a bit. During these few warmer months, researchers from around the world travel to Antarctica to work.

Researchers come to Antarctica to study many things. One of the most important, however, is **global warming**. This is a slow increase in the temperature of Earth's surface. **Climate** records for the past 25 years show a worldwide surface temperature rise of about 0.4°F. However, this warming is not uniform. Some places are warmer. Some are cooler.

Many scientists believe that this warming relates to a process called the **greenhouse effect**. This occurs when gases in the **atmosphere** prevent heat from Earth's surface from escaping into space. The trapped heat, the scientists believe, makes the Earth warmer. Studies of ice bubbles trapped in polar ice show that amounts of **greenhouse gases** in the atmosphere are increasing. Still, not all scientists think this increase explains Earth's warming. In fact, some aren't sure whether Earth is warming at all.

In this chapter, you will look at ideas about global warming and how it may be affecting Antarctica. You will also look at possible effects of global warming on the rest of the world.

Essential Question	Graphic Organizer

Essential Question

How might global warming affect the environment in the world's coldest places?

These two researchers are debating the theory of global warming. One believes that her research in Antarctica supports the theory. The other has doubts based on his research. Think about this debate as you try to answer the Essential Question.

Based on my research in Antarctica, I support the theory of global warming.

My research in Antarctica leads me to doubt the theory of global warming.

◀ Conducting research in Antarctica during the short summer season

A Polar Desert

People think that an ice-capped land must get a lot of rainfall. But Antarctica is a desert. It gets about two inches of precipitation per year. This polar desert has fewer plants and animals than most desert biomes because it is so cold as well as dry.

35.2 The Geographic Setting

The South Pole is the southernmost point on Earth. Antarctica surrounds this point. This icy continent is larger than Australia or Europe. Almost all of its land is buried under **glaciers**. A majority of Earth's fresh water is frozen here as ice.

The Coldest Place on Earth Antarctica can be unimaginably cold. On July 21, 1983, instruments in Antarctica registered a temperature of –129°F. This temperature is the coldest ever recorded on Earth.

Why does Antarctica get so cold? It is the most distant continent from the equator. As a result, it receives less sunshine than other parts of the world. On some winter days, the sun never rises above the horizon. The small amount of **solar energy** that Antarctica does receive is mostly reflected by ice back into space.

Antarctica is also the driest continent. It receives only about two inches of **precipitation** per year. Few living things can survive in such a cold, dry **biome,** or large **ecosystem**. Only two flowering plants grow here. But a variety of animals thrive in the surrounding waters. They include seals, whales, penguins, and many other kinds of birds.

Glaciers cover about 98 percent of Antarctica. Much of this ice is well over a mile thick. Moving flows of ice called **ice streams** slide across the surface of this **ice cap**. These streams carry ice from the center of the continent to the sea. Upon reaching the coast, an ice stream flows outward into the ocean. There it forms an **ice shelf,** or floating sheet of ice, that remains attached to the continent. The Ross Ice Shelf, the largest of these ice shelves, is about the size of France. In some places, it is up to 3,000 feet thick.

A Continent Reserved for International Research In 1978, a pregnant woman boarded a plane in Argentina and flew to a research station in Antarctica. While there, she gave birth to a baby boy. He was the first human to be born on the continent. Yet he could not be a citizen of Antarctica. That's because Antarctica has no country or government.

In the past, seven countries claimed parts of Antarctica. In 1959, those countries joined with others to sign the Antarctic Treaty. As part of this treaty, the seven countries agreed to set aside their claims. The treaty stated that Antarctica should be reserved for peaceful activities such as scientific investigation.

More than 4,000 people travel to Antarctica every year to take part in scientific studies. Scientists find Antarctica a good place to do research for many reasons. One reason is that it is the least populated continent on Earth. This helps researchers see how Earth has changed over time without the influence of human activity.

Also, Antarctica's glaciers serve as records of climate change. Researchers drill deep into the thick ice and pull up samples called *ice cores*. They study the cores to learn what the climate was like as far back as 420,000 years ago. Researchers use this information to help understand the warming and cooling of Earth over time.

▶ Geoterms

biome a very large ecosystem such as a desert, forest, wetland, or grassland. Each biome is home to its own community of plants and animals.

global warming the gradual increase in the temperature of Earth's surface over time. This warming may be the result of natural causes. It may also be caused by human activity.

greenhouse effect the process by which gases in the atmosphere trap heat from the sun and keep it close to Earth's surface. This trapped heat may contribute to global warming.

ice shelf a large, floating sheet of ice that is attached to the coast. Ice shelves can extend out to sea for hundreds of miles.

A Cool Place for Research

No one owns Antarctica. The Antarctic Treaty makes it a natural reserve. It can be used only for such peaceful purposes as scientific research. Many countries have research stations in Antarctica.

Research Stations in Antarctica, 2009

35.3 The Theory of Global Warming

In the past, Earth's climate has had both warm and cool periods. Changes from one period to another were caused by natural events. The last cool period ended about 12,500 years ago. Since then, Earth has been in a warm period. During the past 200 years, however, temperatures seem to have risen faster than usual. The theory of global warming tries to explain why the climate is heating up.

Three Key Ideas About Global Warming The theory of global warming is based on three key ideas. The first is that Earth's climate is getting warmer. The second is that this trend, or change over time, is mainly caused by human activity, not natural causes. The third key idea is that global warming is harmful to people and many biomes. Because of this, many people believe it should be slowed or even stopped.

The Greenhouse Effect Keeps Earth Warm Earth is kept warm by a natural process called the *greenhouse effect*. This process traps energy from the sun in our atmosphere. The atmosphere then acts like a giant greenhouse surrounding Earth. This "greenhouse" keeps Earth's average surface temperature at a warm 59°F. Without it, the temperature could drop to 0°F, or well below freezing.

The greenhouse effect works because of gases in the atmosphere. The most common greenhouse gases are carbon dioxide, methane, and water vapor. They trap heat from the sun in the atmosphere. Otherwise, this heat would escape into space.

Since around 1800, levels of greenhouse gases in the atmosphere have been rising. This increase is due mainly to people burning **fossil fuels** such as coal, oil, and natural gas. When these fuels are burned, they give off carbon dioxide. Many scientists believe that the increase in carbon dioxide and other greenhouse gases is causing Earth to warm. Others are not so sure.

Energy from the Sun

This diagram shows what happens to energy from the sun once it enters Earth's atmosphere. Some energy is absorbed by Earth's surface. Some is reflected back into space. Some is trapped in a layer of gases that surround Earth. This trapped heat may be causing global warming.

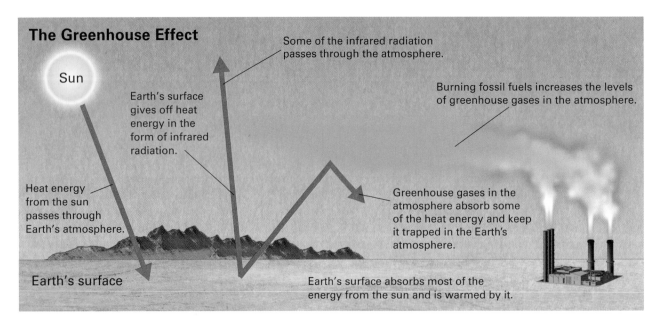

The Greenhouse Effect

Sun

Some of the infrared radiation passes through the atmosphere.

Burning fossil fuels increases the levels of greenhouse gases in the atmosphere.

Earth's surface gives off heat energy in the form of infrared radiation.

Heat energy from the sun passes through Earth's atmosphere.

Greenhouse gases in the atmosphere absorb some of the heat energy and keep it trapped in the Earth's atmosphere.

Earth's surface

Earth's surface absorbs most of the energy from the sun and is warmed by it.

35.4 Support for the Global Warming Theory

Scientists who support the theory of global warming point to three kinds of evidence. The first is climate records. These records show rising surface temperatures in many places. The second is glacier records. They show that glaciers around the world are melting as temperatures rise. The third type of evidence is rising levels of greenhouse gases in the atmosphere. Studies of air bubbles trapped in polar ice show that greenhouse gas levels are the highest they've been in 420,000 years.

Supporters of the global warming theory trace these changes back to the start of the **Industrial Revolution**. During this time, many new machines were invented. Many were powered by the burning of fossil fuels. Today we use coal, oil, and natural gas to heat our homes, run our cars, and power our factories. As a result of this activity, we add more than 4 billion tons of carbon dioxide to the air every year. This gas will stay in our atmosphere for at least the next 100 years.

The results of global warming, these scientists warn, could have terrible consequences. Some biomes may lose plants and animals that are unable to adapt to warmer conditions. Crop failures may become common, leading to widespread hunger. Ocean levels may rise as polar ice melts. Higher seas may flood low-lying islands and coastal cities. The best way to prevent these disasters, these scientists say, is to reduce activities that create greenhouse gases. This could mean difficult changes in the way many people today live.

35.5 Doubts About the Global Warming Theory

Not all scientists agree with the global warming theory. Some doubt that Earth's temperature is, in fact, rising at all.

Like supporters, the doubters support their views with evidence. They point out that temperature records of the upper atmosphere show little sign of warming. Most surface temperature records, they argue, come from urban areas. City buildings and pavement absorb more heat from the sun than green spaces. As a result, urban areas get warmer as they grow. What looks like global warming may just be city warming. The doubters also note that not all glaciers are shrinking. Some are growing.

Some doubters accept evidence that Earth is warming. But they believe this is due to natural causes. Changes in the sun's energy or in ocean currents are far more likely to cause climate change, they believe, than human activity.

Finally, some doubters question whether rising temperatures will be so disastrous. People living in cold climates, they point out, might welcome warmer winters. Areas that are now too cold for crops might become productive farmland. Also, more carbon dioxide in the air may boost plant growth. The result could be faster growing crops and forests. This might be good, not bad, for many biomes.

ASAY-reprinted by permission of the Gazette in Colorado Springs.

The Global Warming Debate
Some people believe that global warming will have disastrous effects. They argue for reduced use of fossil fuels to slow climate change. Others don't believe that global warming is a major problem. Some even suggest that warmer weather could benefit people living in cold climate zones.

35.6 Studying Temperatures in Antarctica

The impact of global warming on Antarctica could be dramatic. Warmer temperatures could cause glaciers and ice shelves to melt. If the area covered by ice shrinks, less energy from the sun would be reflected back into space. Temperatures would then rise even more.

To find out if such changes are likely, scientists gather data on air temperatures in many parts of Antarctica. They compare that data to records from recent years, noting any trends.

Researchers also collect information about Antarctica's climate from thousands of years ago. The snow that falls here each year doesn't melt. Instead, it piles up in layers. The layers are thicker in wet years and thinner in dry ones.

Researchers drill deep into glaciers to take out cores of ice. An ice core looks like a very long pole with thin cross stripes. Each stripe, or layer, represents a year's snowfall. By examining the cores, researchers can learn what the climate was like when each layer of snow fell. They can determine how much precipitation fell and what temperatures were like for that year. The deeper they drill, the farther back in time they can look.

Recording Temperatures
The coldest place on Earth is the best place to look for signs of climate change. The slightest rise in Antarctica's air temperature could begin to melt the ice. Annual temperatures are recorded to see whether they are rising.

35.7 Studying Ice Shelves in Antarctica

As you have read, ice shelves are floating sheets of ice that are still attached to the continent. Ice shelves form half of Antarctica's coastline and more than a tenth of its surface area. Every summer, the edges of Antarctic ice shelves break off to form **icebergs**. An iceberg is a large mass of ice floating around in the ocean.

Researchers in Antarctica study ice shelves to see if they are growing or melting. They also watch for large chunks of ice that break off and float away. One way they do this is by placing cameras on satellites that orbit, or circle, Earth. The cameras take pictures of ice shelves as they form and break apart.

Researchers also spend time at observation posts on or near ice shelves. From these posts, they can study how seasonal temperature changes affect the ice shelves.

The Larsen Ice Shelf
The edges of ice shelves often break off to form icebergs. If temperatures rise too much, whole ice shelves might break apart or melt. The Larsen Ice Shelf pictured here is about the size of Rhode Island. In 2002, about 1,500 square miles of this shelf broke off and floated out to sea.

Observing Penguins

Warmer temperatures could hurt Adelie penguins. These penguins eat a tiny, shrimplike animal called *krill*. Krill breed under the Antarctic ice sheets. If rising temperatures melt the ice, the krill could disappear.

35.8 Studying Penguins in Antarctica

The Adelie is the most common penguin in this polar biome. Nearly 5 million Adelies call Antarctica home. Each summer, they raise their young on the few areas of coastline that are not covered with ice.

Global warming could be bad for Adelies. Warmer air can hold more moisture. This could lead to increased snowfall in Antarctica. If snow covers the few bare spots that the penguins need for nesting, they might stop breeding.

Researchers are studying how many Adelie penguins return to their nesting grounds each year. They do this by taking a simple **census**. This means counting the number of penguins at each nesting site. Researchers also try to track the birds' movements over the year. They glue transmitters on the penguins' feathers and use satellites to track the signals given off.

35.9 Beginning to Think Globally

In this chapter, you learned that Antarctica is a very cold, remote place. Researchers visit Antarctica to study global warming. They do this by gathering information on air temperatures, ice shelves, and penguins.

Researchers don't always agree on what their studies show. For example, air temperatures are rising in some areas of Antarctica. This may be due to the greenhouse effect. But temperatures are falling in other areas. What this means is unclear.

In recent years, researchers have seen huge chunks of ice shelves break off to form icebergs. But scientists aren't sure what is causing the breakups or what effects they will have on the polar biome.

Researchers have also observed changes in penguin populations. There are far fewer Adelie penguins in some areas than in the past. But other penguin species are increasing their numbers. Neither change may be the result of global warming.

Most scientists connect global warming to rising levels of greenhouse gases in the atmosphere. They argue that this rise comes from human activity, especially the burning of fossil fuels. But countries are very unequal in their use of fossil fuels. Think about this as you look at the maps in the next section.

www.cagle.com-Mike Keefe, The Denver Post, 2002.

What If Antarctica Melts?

This cartoon looks at what could happen if global warming were to melt the ice over Antarctica. The water trapped there would flow into the ocean, and sea levels would rise. If both polar ice caps were to melt, sea levels could rise by 20 feet or more.

35.10 Global Connections

The cartogram on the opposite page shows the total amount of greenhouse gases produced by countries throughout the world in 2004. Note the size of the United States. The maps along the bottom show how global warming could affect three parts of the world. The maps show coastlines in each place as they are today. They also show how those coastlines would change were the polar ice caps to melt.

How might rising sea levels be connected to greenhouse gases? Greenhouse gases may cause surface temperatures to rise. As Earth warms, glaciers and ice shelves will melt. The result could be a dramatic rise in sea levels around the world.

Are the countries that produce the most greenhouse gases the ones that will be most affected by rising sea levels? The biggest producers of greenhouse gases are developed countries like the United States and Canada. Such countries run their factories and cars on fossil fuels. Poor countries like Bangladesh and Tuvalu have little industry. But because they are low and flat, they could be severely affected by rising sea levels.

What can people do to reduce the greenhouse gases they add to the environment? People can reduce production of greenhouse gases by using less energy from fossil fuels. One way to do this is to drive cars that get more miles per gallon of gas. Another is to use energy-saving fluorescent lights. Another is to turn off lights and televisions when not in use. Each step may seem small, but together they can add up to big greenhouse gas savings.

Flooding in Tuvalu

Tuvalu is a small island country in the South Pacific. Scientists warn that in the next 50 years, rising sea levels could swamp Tuvalu's low-lying atolls. Were that to happen, its people would have to leave their flooded homes forever.

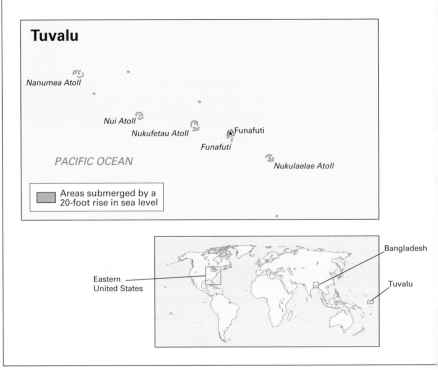

How Three World Areas May Be Affected by Global Warming and Rising Seas

Tuvalu

Nanumea Atoll

Nui Atoll
Nukufetau Atoll
Funafuti
Funafuti
PACIFIC OCEAN
Nukulaelae Atoll

Areas submerged by a 20-foot rise in sea level

Eastern United States
Bangladesh
Tuvalu

Greenhouse Gas Emissions Around the World, 2004

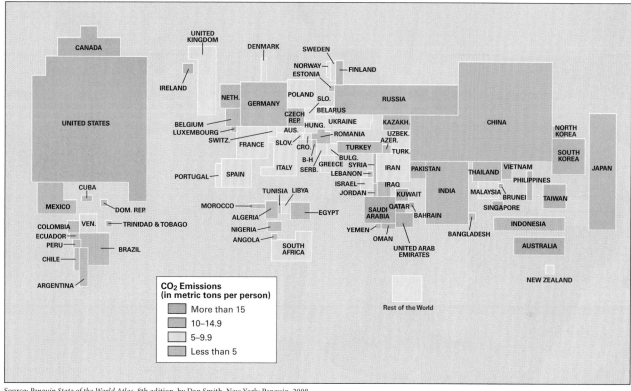

CO₂ Emissions (in metric tons per person)
- More than 15
- 10–14.9
- 5–9.9
- Less than 5

Source: *Penguin State of the World Atlas*, 8th edition, by Dan Smith, New York: Penguin, 2008.

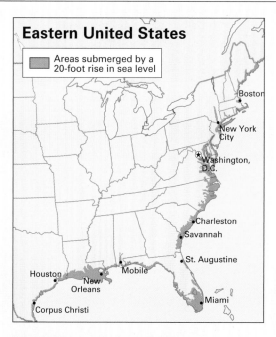

Eastern United States

Areas submerged by a 20-foot rise in sea level

Bangladesh

Areas submerged by a 20-foot rise in sea level

The Impact of Rising Seas

These maps show how the melting of the polar ice caps would affect three coastal areas. Many large U.S. cities would be under water. So would much of Bangladesh and all of Tuvalu.

Resources

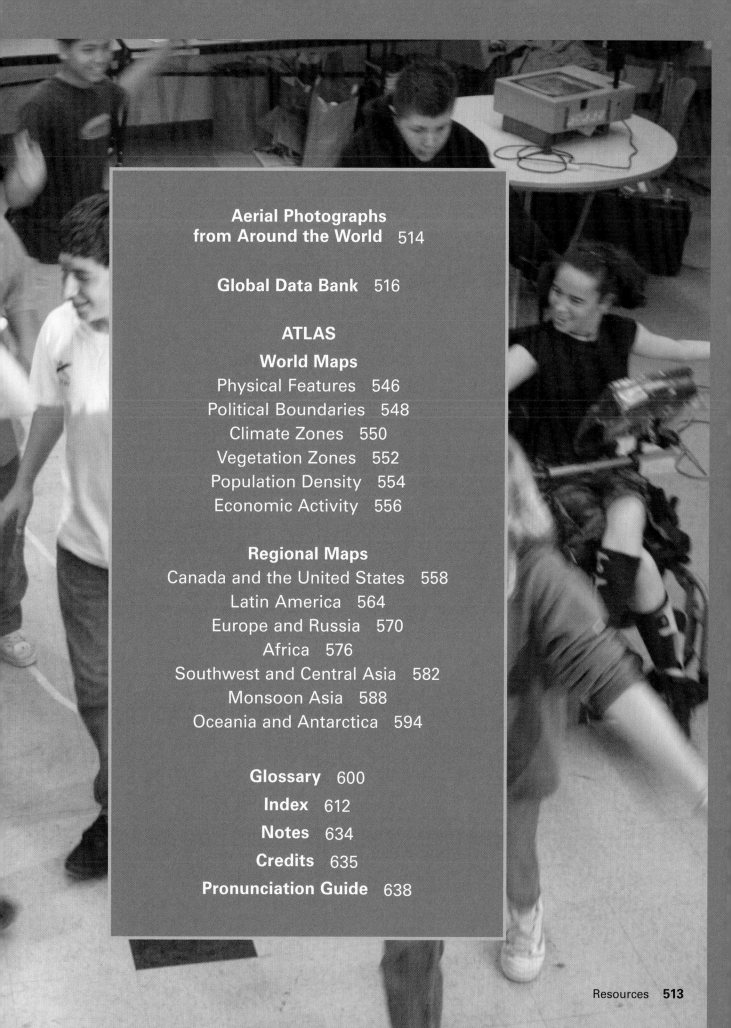

The photographs introducing each of the eight units in this book were taken around the world. They are all the work of photographer Yann Arthus-Bertrand. For more information about aerial photography, see "Aerial Photographs and Satellite Imagery" in the beginning of this book.

Unit 4: Europe and Russia

Schoolyard in Paris, France The painted symbol of this schoolyard is best seen from above. The French school system begins with three years of pre-elementary for ages 3 to 5. Students then enter elementary school, secondary school, and high school.

Unit 2: Canada and the United States

Agricultural fields near Bozeman, Montana These fields in the north central United States are an example of contour farming. Fields are plowed in strips across the natural slope. Each row acts as a mini-dam, slowing runoff when it rains and reducing soil erosion.

Unit 3: Latin America

Confluence of rivers in Bolivar, Venezuela These two rivers come together in the state of Bolivar, in southern Venezuela. The muddy brown color of the river on the right comes from soil that has been washed out by heavy rains.

Unit 5: Africa

Date palm plantation near Cairo, Egypt On a date palm plantation in northern Egypt, fresh yellow and red dates slowly turn brown as they dry in the sun. Farmers protect the drying dates from wind and water by surrounding them with soil and branches.

Unit 6: Southwest and Central Asia

Tree plantation near Irbid, Jordan
In northern Jordan, olive trees survive in rocky, sandy soil. They need little water and are rarely irrigated. This makes olives a good crop for this area. Jordan is one of the most water-poor countries on the planet.

Unit 7: Monsoon Asia

Rice fields in Bali, Indonesia On the island of Bali, farmers have built thousands of terraced fields into the hilly landscape. An elaborate system of canals brings rainwater to irrigate their rice fields.

Unit 1: The Geographer's World

Brick factory near Agra, India At this brick factory in northern India, thousands of terra cotta bricks are stacked in neat rows. These bricks are the main building material used in nearby urban centers.

Unit 8: Oceania and Antarctica

Coral sand beach on Whitsunday Island, Australia In between the northeast coast of Australia and the Great Barrier Reef lie hundreds of tiny islands. The sand on the beaches of these islands is made of coral sediment. This sediment gives the sand its brilliant white color.

Flag	Country	Capital	Total Area (square miles)	Official and Other Major Languages	Major Religions
Canada and the United States					
	Canada	Ottawa	3,849,670	**English, French**	Christian, Muslim, other
	United States	Washington, D.C.	3,717,796	**English,** Spanish	Christian, other, Jewish, Buddhist, Muslim
Latin America					
	Antigua and Barbuda	Saint John's	170	**English,** local dialects	Christian, other
	Argentina	Buenos Aires	1,073,514	**Spanish,** English, Italian, German, French	Christian, Jewish, other
	The Bahamas	Nassau	5,359	**English,** Creole	Christian, other
	Barbados	Bridgetown	166	English	Christian, other
	Belize	Belmopan	8,865	**English,** Spanish, Creole, Mayan, Garifuna, German	Christian, other
	Bolivia	La Paz	424,162	**Spanish, Quechua**	Christian

The Global Data Bank contains basic information on every country on the globe. The countries are organized by regions. Within each region, they are listed alphabetically.

On the left-hand page for each region, you will find information that is unlikely to change much over time. These data include the country's name, flag, capital, and area. Each country's major languages and religions are also listed here.

On the right-hand page for each region, you will find information that is more likely to change with time. This includes population data such as population density, life expectancy, and population growth rate. You will also find economic data here. Examples include a country's gross domestic product, televisions per 1,000 people, and Internet users.

The figures on these right-hand pages are the latest available at the time this book went to press. More recent data can be found at the Web sites of these organizations:

- CIA World Factbook
- NationMaster
- Population Reference Bureau
- UN Population Information Network

opulation	Arithmetic Population Density*	Life Expectancy	Urban Population	Annual Population Growth from Births and Deaths	Gross Domestic Product (per capita, US$)	Literacy Rate	Doctors (per 100,000 people)	Televisions (per 1,000 people)	Internet Users (per 1,000 people)
3,300,000	8	80	81%	0.3%	$40,200	97%	214	728	730
4,500,000	83	78	79%	0.6%	$48,000	95%	256	882	740
100,000	505	73	31%	1.0%	$19,100	86%	17	465	710
9,700,000	36	75	91%	1.1%	$14,500	98%	301	327	260
300,000	62	72	83%	1.1%	$29,900	96%	105	248	360
300,000	1,684	76	38%	0.6%	$20,200	97%	121	289	550
300,000	36	73	50%	2.3%	$8,500	91%	105	200	110
0,000,000	23	65	64%	2.1%	$4,700	87%	122	134	110

*People per square mile

Flag	Country	Capital	Total Area (square miles)	Official and Other Major Languages	Major Religions
Latin America (continued)					
	Brazil	Brasilia	3,300,154	**Portuguese,** Spanish, English, German	Christian, other
	Chile	Santiago	292,135	**Spanish,** Mapudungun, German, English	Christian, other
	Colombia	Bogotá	439,734	Spanish	Christian, other
	Costa Rica	San José	19,730	**Spanish,** English	Christian, other
	Cuba	Havana	42,803	Spanish	Christian, other
	Dominica	Roseau	290	**English,** French patois	Christian, other
	Dominican Republic	Santo Domingo	18,815	Spanish	Christian, other
	Ecuador	Quito	109,483	**Spanish,** Quechua, other indigenous languages	Christian, other
	El Salvador	San Salvador	8,124	Spanish, Nahua	Christian, other
	Grenada	Saint George's	131	**English,** French patois	Christian
	Guatemala	Guatemala City	42,042	Spanish, Quiche, Cakchiquel, Kekchi, Mam, Garifuna, Xinca, other indigenous languages	Christian, indigenous
	Guyana	Georgetown	83,000	English, indigenous languages, Creole, Hindi, Urdu	Christian, Hindu, Muslim, other
	Haiti	Port-au-Prince	10,714	**French, Creole**	Christian, other, indigenous
	Honduras	Tegucigalpa	43,278	Spanish, indigenous languages	Christian

opulation	Arithmetic Population Density*	Life Expectancy	Urban Population	Annual Population Growth from Births and Deaths	Gross Domestic Product (per capita, US$)	Literacy Rate	Doctors (per 100,000 people)	Televisions (per 1,000 people)	Internet Users (per 1,000 people)
95,100,000	60	72	83%	1.3%	$10,300	90%	115	358	350
6,800,000	57	78	87%	0.9%	$15,400	97%	109	321	310
4,400,000	101	72	72%	1.4%	$9,000	93%	135	299	280
4,500,000	228	78	59%	1.3%	$11,900	96%	133	239	340
1,200,000	262	77	76%	0.3%	$9,500	100%	135	267	120
100,000	194	75	73%	0.7%	$9,500	88%	50	252	370
9,900,000	526	72	67%	1.8%	$8,800	89%	188	225	170
3,800,000	127	75	62%	2.0%	$7,700	84%	148	260	130
7,200,000	888	71	60%	1.8%	$6,400	82%	124	236	110
100,000	798	68	31%	1.2%	$13,600	96%	50	383	220
3,700,000	326	69	47%	2.8%	$5,400	73%	90	158	100
800,000	10	65	28%	1.2%	$4,000	99%	12	167	260
9,100,000	849	58	43%	1.8%	$1,400	53%	25	63	100
7,300,000	168	72	46%	2.2%	$3,700	80%	57	143	60

*People per square mile

Flag	Country	Capital	Total Area (square miles)	Official and Other Major Languages	Major Religions
			Latin America (continued)		
	Jamaica	Kingston	4,243	English, English patois	Christian, other
	Mexico	Mexico City (Distrito Federal)	756,062	Spanish, Mayan, Nahuatl, other indigenous languages	Christian, other
	Nicaragua	Managua	50,193	**Spanish,** indigenous languages	Christian, other
	Panama	Panama City	29,158	**Spanish,** English	Christian
	Paraguay	Asunción	157,046	**Spanish, Guarani**	Christian, other
	Peru	Lima	496,224	**Spanish, Quechua,** Aymara, many indigenous Amazonian languages	Christian, other
	Saint Kitts and Nevis	Basseterre	139	English	Christian
	Saint Lucia	Castries	239	**English,** French patois	Christian, other
	Saint Vincent and the Grenadines	Kingstown	151	**English,** French patois	Christian, Hindu, other
	Suriname	Paramaribo	63,039	**Dutch,** English, Sranang Tongo, Hindustani, Javanese	Christian, Hindu, Muslim, indigenous
	Trinidad and Tobago	Port of Spain	1,981	**English,** Hindustani, French, Spanish, Chinese	Christian, Hindu, other, Muslim
	Uruguay	Montevideo	68,498	Spanish, Portuñol, Brazilero	Christian, other, Jewish
	Venezuela	Caracas	352,143	**Spanish,** indigenous languages	Christian, other

opulation	Arithmetic Population Density*	Life Expectancy	Urban Population	Annual Population Growth from Births and Deaths	Gross Domestic Product (per capita, US$)	Literacy Rate	Doctors (per 100,000 people)	Televisions (per 1,000 people)	Internet Users (per 1,000 people)
2,700,000	635	72	52%	1.1%	$7,700	86%	85	380	560
07,700,000	142	75	76%	1.6%	$14,400	93%	198	276	230
5,700,000	114	71	59%	2.1%	$3,000	77%	37	121	30
3,400,000	117	75	64%	1.6%	$11,900	93%	150	198	220
6,200,000	39	71	57%	2.1%	$4,300	94%	111	219	20
7,900,000	57	71	76%	1.5%	$8,500	88%	117	199	270
50,000	477	70	32%	1.0%	$19,700	98%	119	312	310
200,000	821	73	28%	0.8%	$11,300	95%	517	341	650
100,000	736	72	40%	0.9%	$9,200	88%	87	234	470
500,000	8	69	74%	1.1%	$8,900	90%	45	266	100
1,300,000	676	69	12%	0.6%	$18,600	98%	79	354	160
3,300,000	49	76	94%	0.5%	$12,300	97%	365	259	290
27,900,000	80	73	88%	2.1%	$14,000	93%	194	194	210

*People per square mile

Flag	Country	Capital	Total Area (square miles)	Official and Other Major Languages	Major Religions
Europe and Russia					
	Albania	Tiranë	11,100	**Albanian,** Greek, Vlach, Romani, Slavic dialects	Muslim, Christian
	Andorra	Andorra la Vella	174	**Catalan,** French, Castilian, Portuguese	Christian
	Austria	Vienna	32,378	**German, Slovene, Croatian, Hungarian**	Christian, Muslim, other
	Belarus	Minsk	80,154	Belarusian, Russian	Christian, other
	Belgium	Brussels	11,787	**Dutch, French, German**	Christian, other
	Bosnia and Herzegovina	Sarajevo	19,741	Bosnian, Croatian, Serbian	Christian, Muslim, other
	Bulgaria	Sofia	42,822	Bulgarian, Turkish, other ethnic languages	Christian, Muslim, other
	Croatia	Zagreb	21,830	Croatian, Serbian, other	Christian, Muslim, other,
	Czech Republic	Prague	30,448	Czech, Slovak, other	Christian, other
	Denmark	Copenhagen	16,637	Danish, Faroese, Greenlandic, German, English	Christian, Muslim
	Estonia	Tallinn	17,413	**Estonian,** Russian, other	Christian, other
	Finland	Helsinki	130,560	**Finnish, Swedish,** Sami, Russian	Christian, other
	France	Paris	212,934	**French**	Christian, Muslim, Jewish
	Germany	Berlin	137,830	**German**	Christian, other, Muslim

opulation	Arithmetic Population Density*	Life Expectancy	Urban Population	Annual Population Growth from Births and Deaths	Gross Domestic Product (per capita, US$)	Literacy Rate	Doctors (per 100,000 people)	Televisions (per 1,000 people)	Internet Users (per 1,000 people)
,200,000	293	75	45%	0.7%	$6,400	99%	131	318	150
100,000	471	84	90%	0.7%	$42,500	100%	370	462	720
,400,000	259	80	67%	0%	$39,200	98%	338	657	670
,700,000	122	70	73%	−0.3%	$12,000	100%	455	386	290
0,700,000	907	80	97%	0.2%	$38,300	98%	449	555	660
,800,000	194	74	46%	0%	$6,600	97%	134	282	280
,600,000	179	73	71%	−0.5%	$13,200	98%	356	456	310
,400,000	202	76	56%	−0.3%	$16,900	99%	244	320	450
0,400,000	342	77	74%	0.1%	$26,800	100%	351	603	480
5,500,000	329	78	72%	0.2%	$38,900	100%	293	975	810
1,300,000	78	73	69%	−0.1%	$21,900	100%	448	507	640
5,300,000	41	79	63%	0.2%	$38,400	100%	317	679	790
2,000,000	293	81	77%	0.4%	$32,700	99%	337	633	510
2,200,000	596	79	73%	−0.2%	$34,800	99%	337	675	720

*People per square mile

Flag	Country	Capital	Total Area (square miles)	Official and Other Major Languages	Major Religions
Europe and Russia (continued)					
	Greece	Athens	50,950	**Greek,** English, French	Christian, Muslim
	Hungary	Budapest	35,919	**Hungarian,** other	Christian, other
	Iceland	Reykjavik	39,768	Icelandic, English, Nordic languages, German	Christian, other
	Ireland (Republic of)	Dublin	27,135	**English,** Gaelic	Christian, other
	Italy	Rome	116,320	**Italian,** German, French, Slovene	Christian, Jewish, Muslim
	Latvia	Riga	24,942	**Latvian,** Russian, Lithuanian	Christian
	Liechtenstein	Vaduz	62	**German,** Alemannic dialect	Christian, other
	Lithuania	Vilnius	25,174	**Lithuanian,** Russian, Polish	Christian, other
	Luxembourg	Luxembourg	999	**Luxembourgish, German, French**	Christian, Jewish, Muslim
	Macedonia (Former Yugoslav Republic of)	Skopje	9,927	Macedonian, Albanian, Turkish, Roma, Serbian	Christian, Muslim, other
	Malta	Valletta	124	**Maltese, English**	Christian
	Moldova	Chisinau	13,012	**Moldovan,** Russian, Gagauz	Christian, Jewish
	Monaco	Monaco	1	**French,** English, Italian, Monégasque	Christian, other
	Montenegro	Podgorica	8,715	**Montenegrin,** Serbian, Bosnian, Albanian	Christian, Muslim
	Netherlands	Amsterdam	15,768	**Dutch, Frisian**	Christian, Muslim, other

pulation	Arithmetic Population Density*	Life Expectancy	Urban Population	Annual Population Growth from Births and Deaths	Gross Domestic Product (per capita, US$)	Literacy Rate	Doctors (per 100,000 people)	Televisions (per 1,000 people)	Internet Users (per 1,000 people)
,200,000	220	79	60%	0.1%	$32,800	97%	438	537	330
,000,000	280	73	66%	−0.4%	$20,500	99%	333	555	520
300,000	8	81	93%	0.8%	$42,600	100%	362	391	650
,500,000	166	79	60%	0.9%	$47,800	98%	279	695	560
9,900,000	515	81	68%	0%	$31,000	98%	420	494	540
,300,000	91	72	68%	−0.4%	$17,800	100%	301	859	550
40,000	583	80	15%	0.4%	$118,000	100%	data not available	532	650
,400,000	132	71	67%	−0.4%	$18,400	100%	397	518	490
500,000	490	80	83%	0.3%	$85,100	100%	266	581	760
,000,000	207	74	65%	0.2%	$9,200	96%	219	250	270
400,000	3,377	79	94%	0.2%	$24,200	88%	318	554	450
,100,000	316	69	41%	−0.1%	$2,500	99%	264	221	185
30,000	88,060	79	100%	0.9%	$30,000	99%	581	data not available	610
600,000	117	73	64%	0.3%	$10,600	96			470
6,400,000	1,026	80	66%	0.3%	$41,300	96%	315	761	840

*People per square mile

Flag	Country	Capital	Total Area (square miles)	Official and Other Major Languages	Major Religions
Europe and Russia (continued)					
	Norway	Oslo	125,050	**Bokmal Norwegian, Nynorsk Norwegian,** Sami, Finnish	Christian, other, Muslim
	Poland	Warsaw	124,807	**Polish,** other	Christian, other
	Portugal	Lisbon	35,514	**Portuguese, Mirandese**	Christian
	Romania	Bucharest	92,042	**Romanian,** Hungarian, Romany	Christian, Muslim, other
	Russia	Moscow	6,592,819	**Russian**	Christian, Muslim, other
	San Marino	San Marino	23	Italian	Christian
	Serbia	Belgrade	29,913	**Serbian, Albanian,** other	Christian, Muslim, other
	Slovakia	Bratislava	18,923	**Slovak,** Hungarian, Roma, Ukranian	Christian, other
	Slovenia	Ljubljana	7,819	Slovenian, Serbo-Croatian, other	Christian, Muslim, other
	Spain	Madrid	195,363	**Castilian Spanish, Catalan, Galician, Basque**	Christian, other
	Sweden	Stockholm	173,730	Swedish, Sami, Finnish	Christian, other
	Switzerland	Bern	15,942	**German, French, Italian, Romansch**	Christian, other
	Ukraine	Kiev	233,089	Ukrainian, Russian, Romanian, Polish, Hungarian	Christian, Jewish other
	United Kingdom	London	94,548	English, Welsh, Scottish Gaelic	Christian, Muslim, other, Hindu

Population	Arithmetic Population Density*	Life Expectancy	Urban Population	Annual Population Growth from Births and Deaths	Gross Domestic Product (per capita, US$)	Literacy Rate	Doctors (per 100,000 people)	Televisions (per 1,000 people)	Internet Users (per 1,000 people)
4,800,000	31	80	79%	0.4%	$57,500	97%	313	1,554	850
38,100,000	316	75	61%	0%	$17,800	99%	247	229	440
10,600,000	298	79	55%	0%	$22,000	95%	342	421	400
21,500,000	233	71	55%	−0.2%	$12,500	97%	191	893	240
41,900,000	21	67	73%	−0.3%	$15,800	100%	425	350	210
30,000	1,313	82	84%	0.3%	$41,900	96%	4,735	906	510
7,400,000	246	73	56%	−0.4%	$8,200	96%	206	282	200
5,400,000	285	74	56%	0%	$22,600	100%	318	424	560
2,000,000	259	78	48%	0.1%	$30,800	100%	225	366	530
46,500,000	238	80	77%	0.2%	$36,500	98%	330	549	510
9,200,000	52	81	84%	0.2%	$39,600	99%	328	965	800
7,600,000	479	82	68%	0.2%	$40,900	99%	362	578	760
46,200,000	199	68	68%	−0.6%	$6,900	99%	295	357	220
61,300,000	653	79	80%	0.3%	$37,400	99%	230	1,101	720

*People per square mile

Flag	Country	Capital	Total Area (square miles)	Official and Other Major Languages	Major Religions
Africa					
	Algeria	Algiers	919,591	**Arabic,** French, Berber dialects	Muslim, Christian, Jewish
	Angola	Luanda	481,351	**Portuguese,** Bantu, other African languages	Christian, indigenous
	Benin	Porto-Novo	43,483	**French,** Fon and Yoruba, tribal languages	Christian, Muslim, indigenous
	Botswana	Gaborone	224,606	**English,** Setswana, other African languages	Christian, indigenous
	Burkina Faso	Ouagadougou	105,792	**French,** native Sudanic African languages	Muslim, indigenous, Christian
	Burundi	Bujumbura	10,745	**Kirundi, French,** Swahili	Christian, indigenous, Muslim
	Cameroon	Yaoundé	183,568	**English, French,** 24 major African languages	Indigenous, Christian, Muslim
	Cape Verde	Praia	1,556	Portuguese, Crioulo	Christian, indigenous
	Central African Republic	Bangui	240,533	**French,** Sangho, tribal languages	Christian, indigenous, Muslim
	Chad	N'Djamena	495,753	**French, Arabic,** Sara, more than 120 other languages	Muslim, Christian, indigenous
	Comoros	Moroni	861	**Arabic, French,** Shikomoro	Muslim, Christian
	Congo	Brazzaville	132,046	**French,** Lingala, Monokutuba, Kikongo, other languages and dialects	Christian, indigenous, Muslim
	Côte d'Ivoire	Yamoussoukro	124,502	**French,** Dioula, 60 native dialects	Muslim, Christian, indigenous
	Democratic Republic of the Congo	Kinshasa	905,351	**French,** Lingala, Kingwana, Kikongo, Tshiluba	Christian, indigenous, Muslim

pulation	Arithmetic Population Density*	Life Expectancy	Urban Population	Annual Population Growth from Births and Deaths	Gross Domestic Product (per capita, US$)	Literacy Rate	Doctors (per 100,000 people)	Televisions (per 1,000 people)	Internet Users (per 1,000 people)
,700,000	39	72	63%	1.8%	$7,100	75%	113	188	100
,800,000	34	43	57%	2.7%	$9,100	67%	8	21	30
,300,000	215	56	41%	3.0%	$1,500	41%	5	107	20
,800,000	8	49	57%	0.9%	$15,800	83%	40	44	50
,200,000	145	51	16%	3.0%	$1,300	24%	6	12	10
,900,000	824	49	10%	3.0%	$400	59%	3	40	10
,500,000	101	52	57%	2.3%	$2,400	68%	19	45	0
500,000	324	71	59%	2.5%	$4,200	84%	49	105	70
,400,000	18	42	39%	1.9%	$700	49%	9	6	0
0,100,000	21	47	27%	2.7%	$1,600	32%	4	6	10
700,000	850	64	28%	2.8%	$1,100	75%	15	27	30
,800,000	28	53	60%	2.5%	$3,800	85%	20	13	20
0,700,000	166	52	48%	2.4%	$1,700	49%	12	52	340
6,500,000	73	53	33%	3.1%	$300	67%	11	4	2

*People per square mile

Flag	Country	Capital	Total Area (square miles)	Official and Other Major Languages	Major Religions
Africa (continued)					
	Djibouti	Djibouti	8,958	**French, Arabic,** Somali, Afar	Muslim, Christian
	Egypt	Cairo	386,660	**Arabic,** French, English	Muslim, Christian
	Equatorial Guinea	Malabo	10,830	**Spanish, French,** Fang, Bubi	Christian, indigenous
	Eritrea	Asmara	45,405	Afar, Arabic, Tigre, Kunama, Tigrinya, other Cushitic languages	Muslim, Christian
	Ethiopia	Addis Ababa	426,371	Amarigna, Tigrinya, Oromigna, Gauragigna, Somali, other local languages, English	Christian, Muslim, indigenous, other
	Gabon	Libreville	103,347	**French,** Fang, Myene, Nzebi, Bapounou/Eschira, Bandjabi	Christian, indigenous, Muslim
	Gambia	Banjul	4,363	**English,** Mandinka, Wolof, Fula, other indigenous	Muslim, Christian, indigenous
	Ghana	Accra	92,100	**English,** Asante, Dagomba, Ewe, Ga, other African languages	Christian, Muslim, indigenous,
	Guinea	Conakry	94,927	**French,** ethnic languages	Muslim, Christian, indigenous
	Guinea-Bissau	Bissau	13,946	**Portuguese,** Crioulo, African languages	Muslim, indigenous, Christian
	Kenya	Nairobi	224,081	**English, Kiswahili,** indigenous languages	Christian, indigenous, Muslim
	Lesotho	Maseru	11,718	**English,** Sesotho, Zulu, Xhosa	Christian, indigenous
	Liberia	Monrovia	43,000	**English,** about 20 ethnic languages	Indigenous, Christian, Muslim
	Libyan Arab Jamahiriya	Tripoli	679,359	Arabic, Italian, English	Muslim, other

pulation	Arithmetic Population Density*	Life Expectancy	Urban Population	Annual Population Growth from Births and Deaths	Gross Domestic Product (per capita, US$)	Literacy Rate	Doctors (per 100,000 people)	Televisions (per 1,000 people)	Internet Users (per 1,000 people)
800,000	96	54	87%	1.8%	$3,800	68%	18	78	10
,900,000	195	72	43%	2.0%	$5,500	66%	54	243	140
600,000	57	59	39%	2.9%	$31,400	87%	30	116	20
,000,000	111	57	21%	3.0%	$700	59%	5	68	20
9,100,000	186	49	16%	2.5%	$800	36%	3	8	2
,400,000	13	57	84%	1.5%	$14,900	86%	29	163	60
,600,000	357	58	54%	2.7%	$1,200	40%	11	15	60
3,900,000	259	59	48%	2.2%	$1,500	65%	15	52	40
0,300,000	109	54	30%	2.9%	$1,100	30%	12	18	10
,700,000	124	45	30%	3.1%	$600	42%	12	45	20
8,000,000	168	53	19%	2.8%	$1,800	74%	14	48	80
,800,000	153	36	24%	0.2%	$1,600	82%	5	44	10
,900,000	91	46	58%	3.1%	$500	90%	3	25	10
,300,000	10	73	77%	2.0%	$14,900	84%	129	149	40

*People per square mile

Flag	Country	Capital	Total Area (square miles)	Official and Other Major Languages	Major Religions
Africa (continued)					
	Madagascar	Antananarivo	226,656	**English, French, Malagasy**	Indigenous, Christian, Muslim
	Malawi	Lilongwe	45,745	**Chichewa,** other regional languages	Christian, Muslim, indigenous
	Mali	Bamako	478,838	**French,** Bambara, numerous African languages	Muslim, indigenous, Christian
	Mauritania	Nouakchott	395,954	**Arabic,** Pulaar, Soninke, Wolof, French, Hassaniya	Muslim
	Mauritius	Port Louis	788	**English,** Creole, Bhojpuri, French, other	Hindu, Christian, Muslim, other
	Morocco	Rabat	172,413	**Arabic,** Berber dialects, French	Muslim, Christian, Jewish
	Mozambique	Maputo	309,494	**Portuguese,** Makhuwa, Xichangana, Lomwe, Sena, numerous indigenous languages	Christian, Muslim, other
	Namibia	Windhoek	318,259	**English,** Afrikaans, German, Oshivambo, Herero, Nama	Christian, indigenous
	Niger	Niamey	489,189	**French,** Hausa, Djerma	Muslim, indigenous, Christian
	Nigeria	Abuja	356,668	**English,** Hausa, Yoruba, Igbo, Fulani	Muslim, Christian, indigenous
	Rwanda	Kigali	10,170	**Kinyarwanda, French, English,** Bantu, Kiswahili (Swahili)	Christian, Muslim
	São Tomé and Príncipe	São Tomé	371	**Portuguese**	Christian, other
	Senegal	Dakar	75,954	**French,** Wolof, Pulaar, Jola, Mandinka	Muslim, Christian, indigenous
	Seychelles	Victoria	174	**English,** Creole, other	Christian, Hindu, other, Muslim

opulation	Arithmetic Population Density*	Life Expectancy	Urban Population	Annual Population Growth from Births and Deaths	Gross Domestic Product (per capita, US$)	Literacy Rate	Doctors (per 100,000 people)	Televisions (per 1,000 people)	Internet Users (per 1,000 people)
3,900,000	83	58	30%	2.8%	$1,100	71%	29	18	10
3,600,000	298	46	17%	3.2%	$800	64%	2	7	10
2,700,000	26	56	31%	3.3%	$1,200	24%	8	36	10
3,200,000	8	60	40%	2.7%	$1,900	51%	11	41	10
,300,000	1,611	72	42%	0.7%	$12,400	84%	106	370	270
1,200,000	181	70	56%	1.4%	$4,000	52%	52	168	210
0,400,000	65	43	29%	2.1%	$900	44%	3	21	10
2,100,000	8	47	35%	1.0%	$5,500	85%	30	81	50
4,700,000	31	57	17%	3.1%	$700	29%	3	12	0
48,100,000	414	47	47%	2.5%	$2,200	69%	28	68	70
9,600,000	945	47	18%	2.7%	$900	65%	5	8	10
200,000	425	64	58%	2.7%	$1,400	85%	49	127	150
2,700,000	166	62	41%	3.0%	$1,800	39%	6	46	70
100,000	495	72	53%	1.0%	$18,700	92%	151	278	380

*People per square mile

Flag	Country	Capital	Total Area (square miles)	Official and Other Major Languages	Major Religions

Africa (continued)

Flag	Country	Capital	Total Area (square miles)	Official and Other Major Languages	Major Religions
	Sierra Leone	Freetown	27,699	**English,** Mende, Temne, Krio	Muslim, indigenous, Christian
	Somalia	Mogadishu	246,201	**Somali,** Arabic, Italian, English	Muslim
	South Africa	Tshwane (Pretoria)	471,444	**Afrikaans, English, Pedi, Sotho, Swazi, Tsonga, Tswana, Xhosa, Zulu**	Christian, Muslim, other
	Sudan	Khartoum	967,494	**Arabic, English,** Nubian, Sudanic languages	Muslim, indigenous, Christian
	Swaziland	Mbabane	6,703	**English, siSwati**	Indigenous, Christian, Muslim, other
	Tanzania (United Republic of)	Dar es Salaam	364,900	**Swahili, English,** Arabic, many local languages	Muslim, indigenous, Christian
	Togo	Lomé	21,927	**French,** Ewe, Mina, Kabye, Dagomba	Indigenous, Christian, Muslim
	Tunisia	Tunis	63,170	**Arabic,** French	Muslim, Christian, Jewish
	Uganda	Kampala	93,066	**English,** Ganda, Swahili, Arabic, other Niger-Congo languages, other Nilo-Saharan languages	Christian, Muslim, other
	Western Sahara*	El Aaiún	97,344	Arabic	Muslim
	Zambia	Lusaka	290,583	**English,** Bemba, Kaonda, Lozi, Lunda, Luvale, Nyanja, Tonga, about 70 other indigenous languages	Christian, Muslim, Hindu, indigenous
	Zimbabwe	Harare	150,873	**English,** Shona, Sindebele, many tribal dialects	Christian, indigenous, Muslim

*The country of Morocco considers Western Sahara under its rule.
As of 2009, this rule remains under dispute, awaiting a decision from the United Nations.

Population	Arithmetic Population Density*	Life Expectancy	Urban Population	Annual Population Growth from Births and Deaths	Gross Domestic Product (per capita, US$)	Literacy Rate	Doctors (per 100,000 people)	Televisions (per 1,000 people)	Internet Users (per 1,000 people)
5,500,000	197	48	37%	2.5%	$700	35%	3	13	2
9,000,000	36	48	37%	2.7%	$600	38%	4	26	10
48,300,000	104	50	59%	0.8%	$10,400	82%	77	195	80
39,400,000	41	58	38%	2.1%	$2,200	61%	22	387	90
1,100,000	168	33	24%	0%	$5,100	80%	16	36	40
40,200,000	111	51	25%	2.3%	$1,400	69%	2	41	10
6,800,000	308	58	40%	2.8%	$900	53%	5	30	50
0,300,000	163	74	65%	1.2%	$8,000	74%	134	218	170
29,200,000	313	48	13%	3.1%	$1,100	67%	8	19	30
500,000	5	64	81%	2.0%	data not available	data not available	data not available	data not available	data not available
2,200,000	41	38	37%	2.1%	$1,500	68%	12	64	40
13,500,000	88	40	37%	1.1%	$200	89%	16	64	100

*People per square mile

Flag	Country	Capital	Total Area (square miles)	Official and Other Major Languages	Major Religions
Southwest and Central Asia					
	Afghanistan	Kabul	251,772	**Pashtu, Afghan Persian**, Uzbek, Turkmen, Balochi, Pashai, other ethnic languages	Muslim
	Armenia	Yerevan	11,506	**Armenian**, Yezidi, other, Russian	Christian, indigenous
	Azerbaijan	Baku	33,436	**Azerbaijani**, Lezgi, Russian, Armenian, other	Muslim, Christian, other
	Bahrain	Manama	266	Arabic, English, Farsi, Urdu	Muslim, Christian, other
	Cyprus	Nicosia	3,571	Greek, Turkish, English	Christian, Muslim, other
	Georgia	Tbilisi	26,911	**Georgian**, Russian, Armenian, Azeri, other, Abkhaz	Christian, Muslim, other
	Iran (Islamic Republic of)	Tehran	630,575	Persian, Turkic, Kurdish, Luri, Balochi, Arabic, Turkish, other dialects	Muslim, Jewish, Christian, other
	Iraq	Baghdad	169,236	Arabic, Kurdish, Assyrian, Armenian	Muslim, other, Christian
	Israel	Jerusalem	8,131	**Hebrew**, Arabic, English	Jewish, Muslim, other, Christian
	Jordan	Amman	34,444	**Arabic**, English	Muslim, Christian, other
	Kazakhstan	Astana	1,049,151	**Kazakh, Russian**	Muslim, Christian, other
	Kuwait	Kuwait	6,880	**Arabic**, English	Muslim, other
	Kyrgyzstan	Bishkek	76,641	**Kyrgyz, Russian**	Muslim, Christian, other
	Lebanon	Beirut	4,015	**Arabic**, French, English, Armenian	Muslim, Christian, other

opulation	Arithmetic Population Density*	Life Expectancy	Urban Population	Annual Population Growth from Births and Deaths	Gross Domestic Product (per capita, US$)	Literacy Rate	Doctors (per 100,000 people)	Televisions (per 1,000 people)	Internet Users (per 1,000 people)
2,700,000	130	43	20%	2.6%	$800	28%	19	67	0
3,100,000	267	71	64%	0.5%	$6,600	99%	359	293	60
3,700,000	259	72	52%	1.2%	$9,500	100%	355	339	110
800,000	2,911	75	100%	1.7%	$37,200	89%	109	414	330
1,100,000	298	78	62%	1.6%	$29,200	97%	234	384	380
4,600,000	174	74	53%	0.1%	$5,000	100%	409	386	80
2,200,000	114	71	67%	1.4%	$13,100	82%	45	174	320
9,500,000	174	58	67%	2.4%	$4,000	74%	66	83	1
7,500,000	875	80	92%	1.6%	$28,900	97%	382	354	280
6,800,000	168	72	83%	2.4%	$5,000	91%	203	190	200
5,700,000	16	66	53%	1.0%	$12,000	100%	354	497	120
2,700,000	389	78	98%	1.9%	$57,400	93%	153	407	340
6,200,000	67	66	35%	1.6%	$2,200	99%	251	188	140
4,000,000	992	72	87%	1.4%	$11,100	90%	325	355	38

*People per square mile

Flag	Country	Capital	Total Area (square miles)	Official and Other Major Languages	Major Religions
	Southwest and Central Asia (continued)				
	Oman	Muscat	82,031	**Arabic,** English, Baluchi, Urdu, Indian dialects	Muslim, Hindu
	Pakistan	Islamabad	307,375	**Urdu, English,** Punjabi, Sindhi, Siraiki, Pashtu, Balochi, Hindko, Brahui	Muslim, other
	Qatar	Doha	4,247	**Arabic,** English	Muslim, Christian, other
	Saudi Arabia	Riyadh	829,996	**Arabic**	Muslim
	Syrian Arab Republic	Damascus	71,498	**Arabic,** Kurdish, Armenian, Aramaic, Circassian, French	Muslim, Christian, Jewish
	Tajikistan	Dushanbe	55,251	**Tajik,** Russian	Muslim, other
	Turkey	Ankara	299,158	**Turkish,** Kurdish, other	Muslim, other
	Turkmenistan	Ashgabat	188,456	Turkmen, Russian, Uzbek, other	Muslim, Christian
	United Arab Emirates	Abu Dhabi	32,278	**Arabic,** Persian, English, Hindi, Urdu	Muslim, other
	Uzbekistan	Tashkent	172,741	**Uzbek,** Russian, Tajik, other	Muslim, Christian, other
	Yemen	Sanaa	203,849	Arabic	Muslim, other

Population	Arithmetic Population Density*	Life Expectancy	Urban Population	Annual Population Growth from Births and Deaths	Gross Domestic Product (per capita, US$)	Literacy Rate	Doctors (per 100,000 people)	Televisions (per 1,000 people)	Internet Users (per 1,000 people)
2,700,000	23	74	71%	2.1%	$20,400	84%	132	620	130
72,800,000	562	63	35%	2.2%	$2,600	54%	74	82	110
900,000	218	75	100%	1.5%	$101,000	93%	222	423	420
8,100,000	34	76	81%	2.7%	$21,300	83%	138	275	260
9,900,000	279	73	50%	2.5%	$4,900	81%	140	193	170
7,300,000	132	67	26%	2.2%	$1,800	87%	203	375	70
4,800,000	246	72	62%	1.2%	$12,900	87%	135	538	160
5,200,000	28	62	47%	1.7%	$5,800	99%	418	183	10
4,500,000	140	78	83%	1.3%	$40,400	89%	202	197	520
7,200,000	158	67	36%	1.7%	$2,700	99%	275	226	40
2,200,000	109	61	30%	3.2%	$2,600	54%	33	337	10

*People per square mile

Flag	Country	Capital	Total Area (square miles)	Official and Other Major Languages	Major Religions
Monsoon Asia					
	Bangladesh	Dhaka	55,598	**Bangala,** English	Muslim, Hindu, other
	Bhutan	Thimphu	18,147	**Dzongkha,** Tibetan and Nepalese dialects	Buddhist, Hindu
	Brunei Darussalam	Bandar Seri Begawan	2,228	**Malay,** Chinese, English	Muslim, Buddhist, Christian indigenous, other
	Cambodia	Phnom Penh	69,900	**Khmer,** French, English	Buddhist, other
	East Timor	Dili	5,741	**Tetum, Portuguese,** Indonesian, English, Tetum, Galole, Mambae, Kemak, other indigenous languages	Christian, Muslim, Hindu
	India	New Delhi	1,269,340	**Hindi, Bengali, Telugu, Marathi, Tamil, Urdu, Gujarati, Malayalam, Kannada, Oriya, Punjabi, Assamese, Kashmiri, Sindhi, Sanskrit,** English, Hindustani	Hindu, Muslim, Christian, other
	Indonesia	Jakarta	735,355	**Bahasa Indonesia,** English, Dutch, Javanese, other local dialects	Muslim, Christian, Hindu, other
	Japan	Tokyo	145,869	**Japanese**	Buddhist, Christian, other
	Korea, North	Pyongyang	46,541	**Korean**	Government-sponsored groups, others
	Korea, South	Seoul	38,324	**Korean,** English	Christian, Buddhist, other
	Laos	Vientiane	91,429	**Lao,** French, English, many ethnic languages	Buddhist, Christian, other
	Malaysia	Kuala Lumpur	127,317	**Bahasa Melayu,** Chinese dialects, Tamil, Telugu, Malayalam, Panjabi, Thai, Iban, Kadazan, other indigenous languages	Muslim, Buddhist, Christian, Hindu, indigenous, other
	Maldives	Male	116	**Maldivian Dhivehi,** English	Muslim

Population	Arithmetic Population Density*	Life Expectancy	Urban Population	Annual Population Growth from Births and Deaths	Gross Domestic Product (per capita, US$)	Literacy Rate	Doctors (per 100,000 people)	Televisions (per 1,000 people)	Internet Users (per 1,000 people)
147,300,000	2,650	63	24%	1.7%	$1,500	53%	26	83	0
700,000	36	66	31%	2.3%	$4,800	53%	5	32	60
400,000	171	75	72%	1.6%	$53,100	95%	101	644	420
14,700,000	210	62	15%	1.8%	$2,100	76%	16	8	2
1,100,000	189	60	22%	3.2%	$2,500	50%	10	data not available	63
1,149,300,000	907	65	28%	1.6%	$2,900	66%	60	98	70
239,900,000	326	70	48%	1.5%	$3,900	92%	13	152	60
127,700,000	875	8	79%	0%	$35,300	99%	198	843	690
23,500,000	505	71	60%	0.9%	$1,800	99%	329	172	data not available
48,600,000	1,264	79	82%	0.5%	$26,000	98%	157	411	760
5,900,000	65	61	27%	2.4%	$2,100	69%	59	57	20
27,700,000	218	74	68%	1.6%	$15,700	89%	70	219	560
300,000	2,694	73	27%	1.6%	$4,500	96%	92	143	110

*People per square mile

Flag	Country	Capital	Total Area (square miles)	Official and Other Major Languages	Major Religions
Monsoon Asia (continued)					
	Mongolia	Ulaanbaatar	604,826	**Khalkha Mongol,** Turkic, Russian	Buddhist, Christian, Muslim, indigenous
	Myanmar (Burma)*	Yangon (Rangoon)	261,228	**Burmese,** other ethnic languages	Buddhist, Christian, Muslim, indigenous
	Nepal	Kathmandu	56,826	**Nepali,** other indigenous languages	Hindu, Buddhist, Muslim, indigenous
	People's Republic of China	Beijing	3,696,519	Mandarin Chinese, Yue, Wu, Minbei, Minnan, Xiang, Gan, Hakka, other minority languages	Officially atheist
	Philippines	Manila	115,830	**Filipino, English,** Tagalog, Cebuano, Ilocano, Hiligaynon, Bicol, Waray, Pampango, Pangasinan	Christian, Muslim, other
	Singapore	Singapore	239	**Chinese, Malay, Tamil, English**	Buddhist, Muslim, Christian, Hindu, other
	Sri Lanka	Colombo	25,332	**Sinhala, Tamil,** other	Buddhist, Muslim, Hindu, Christian
	Taiwan (Republic of China)†	Taipei	13,969	**Mandarin Chinese,** Taiwanese, Hakka dialects	Buddhist, Christian, other
	Thailand	Bangkok	198,116	**Thai,** English, ethnic dialects	Buddhist, Muslim, other
	Vietnam	Hanoi	128,066	**Vietnamese,** English, French, Chinese, Khmer, indigenous languages	Buddhist, indigenous, Christian, Muslim

*Military authorities in Burma adopted the name Myanmar in 1989.
As of 2009, many continue to refer to the nation as Burma.

†Taiwan considers itself an independent nation. The country of China considers Taiwan a province of their country. As of 2009, the United Nations does not officially recognize Taiwan as an independent country.

Population	Arithmetic Population Density*	Life Expectancy	Urban Population	Annual Population Growth from Births and Deaths	Gross Domestic Product (per capita, US$)	Literacy Rate	Doctors (per 100,000 people)	Televisions (per 1,000 people)	Internet Users (per 1,000 people)
,700,000	5	64	59%	1.5%	$3,300	98%	263	79	120
,200,000	189	61	31%	0.9%	$1,800	90%	36	7	0
,000,000	474	64	17%	2.1%	$1,000	57%	21	11	10
24,700,000	360	73	45%	0.5%	$6,100	93%	106	380	160
,500,000	782	69	63%	2.1%	$3,400	93%	59	192	60
,800,000	18,164	81	100%	0.6%	$52,000	93%	140	206	660
,300,000	800	71	15%	1.2%	$4,400	91%	55	125	40
,000,000	1,655	78	78%	0.3%	$31,900	96%	data not available	438	391
,100,000	334	72	36%	0.5%	$8,700	50%	37	285	580
,200,000	673	73	27%	1.2%	$2,900	90%	53	208	210

*People per square mile

Flag	Country	Capital	Total Area (square miles)	Official and Other Major Languages	Major Religions
Oceania and Antarctica					
	Australia	Canberra	2,988,888	**English,** indigenous languages, other	Christian, Buddhist, Muslim, other
	Fiji	Suva	7,054	**English, Fijian,** Hindustani	Christian, Hindu, Muslim other
	Kiribati	Tarawa	282	**English,** I-Kiribati	Christian, other
	Marshall Islands	Majuro	69	**Marshallese, English,** other	Christian, other
	Micronesia (Federated States of)	Palikir	270	**English,** Trukese, Pohnpeian, Yapese, Kosrean, Ulithian, Woleaian, Nukuoro, Kapingamarangi	Christian, other
	Nauru	Yaren District	9	**Nauruan,** English	Christian, other
	New Zealand	Wellington	104,452	**English, Maori,** sign language	Christian, other
	Palau	Koror	178	**English, Palauan, Sonsoralese, Tobi, Angaur, Japanese,** other	Christian, indigenous, other
	Papua New Guinea	Port Moresby	178,703	**English, Tok Pisin, Motu,** 860 indigenous languages	Christian, indigenous, other
	Samoa	Apia	1,097	Samoan, English	Christian, other
	Solomon Islands	Honiara	11,158	**English,** Melanesian Pidgin, 120 indigenous languages	Christian, other
	Tonga	Nuku'alofa	290	Tongan, English	Christian
	Tuvalu	Funafuti	10	Tuvaluan, English, Samoan, Kiribati	Christian, other
	Vanuatu	Port-Vila	4,707	**English, French, Bislama,** more than 100 indigenous languages	Christian, indigenous, other

Population	Arithmetic Population Density*	Life Expectancy	Urban Population	Annual Population Growth from Births and Deaths	Gross Domestic Product (per capita, US$)	Literacy Rate	Doctors (per 100,000 people)	Televisions (per 1,000 people)	Internet Users (per 1,000 people)
21,300,000	8	81	87%	0.7%	$39,300	100%	247	665	680
900,000	122	68	51%	1.5%	$3,700	94%	34	118	100
100,000	347	61	44%	1.8%	$3,200	100%	30	44	20
100,000	761	66	68%	3.2%	$2,500	94%	47	data not available	40
100,000	399	67	22%	2.0%	$2,200	89%	60	25	140
10,000	1,241	55	100%	2.1%	$5,000	95%	146	44	26
4,300,000	41	80	86%	0.8%	$28,500	99%	237	586	690
20,000	114	71	77%	0.6%	$8,100	92%	111	data not available	270
6,500,000	36	57	13%	2.1%	$2,300	58%	5	24	30
200,000	171	73	22%	2.4%	$5,000	99%	70	148	40
500,000	47	62	17%	2.6%	$1,900	77%	13	12	20
100,000	352	71	24%	2.0%	$4,400	99%	34	70	80
10,000	1,033	64	47%	1.6%	$1,600	98%	data not available	data not available	125
200,000	52	67	21%	2.5%	$4,700	78%	11	12	80

*People per square mile

80°N
160°W 140°W 120°W 100°W 80°W 60°W 40°W

Mt. McKinley
(20,320 ft.
6,194 m)

60°N

ROCKY MOUNTAINS

GREAT PLAINS

NORTH

AMERICA

Mississippi

40°N

ATLANTIC OCEAN

Tropic of Cancer

20°N

PACIFIC OCEAN

Amazon R.

AMAZON BASIN

SOUTH

BRAZILIAN HIGHLANDS

0° Equator

ANDES MOUNTAINS

AMERICA

20°S Tropic of Capricorn

Mt. Aconcagua
(22,834 ft.
6,960 m)

PAMPAS

40°S

0   1,500   3,000 miles

0   1,500   3,000 kilometers
Robinson projection

60°S

Vinson Massif
(16,067 ft.
4,897 m)

80°S
160°W 140°W 120°W 100°W 80°W 60°W 40°W

Elevation

Feet	Meters
Over 10,000	Over 3,050
5,001–10,000	1,526–3,050
2,001–5,000	611–1,525
1,001–2,000	306–610
0–1,000	0–305
Below sea level	Below sea level

▲ Mountain peak

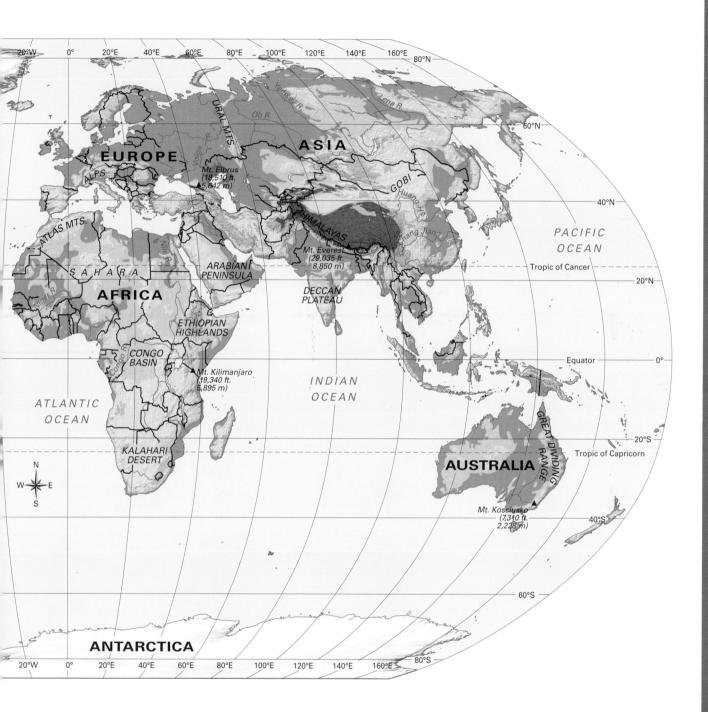

20°W 0° 20°E 40°E 60°E 80°E 100°E 120°E 140°E 160°E 80°N

60°N

EUROPE

ALPS

Mt. Elbrus
(18,510 ft.
5,642 m)

ASIA

URAL MTS.

Yenisey R.

Ob R.

Lena R.

GOBI

Huang He

40°N

PACIFIC
OCEAN

ATLAS MTS.

S A H A R A

Nile R.

Niger R.

AFRICA

ARABIAN
PENINSULA

HIMALAYAS

Mt. Everest
(29,035 ft.
8,850 m)

DECCAN
PLATEAU

Chang Jiang

Tropic of Cancer

20°N

ETHIOPIAN
HIGHLANDS

CONGO
BASIN

Congo R.

Mt. Kilimanjaro
(19,340 ft.
5,895 m)

INDIAN
OCEAN

Equator 0°

ATLANTIC
OCEAN

KALAHARI
DESERT

GREAT DIVIDING RANGE

AUSTRALIA

Tropic of Capricorn 20°S

N
W E
S

Mt. Kosciusko
(7,310 ft.
2,228 m)

40°S

60°S

ANTARCTICA

20°W 0° 20°E 40°E 60°E 80°E 100°E 120°E 140°E 160°E 80°S

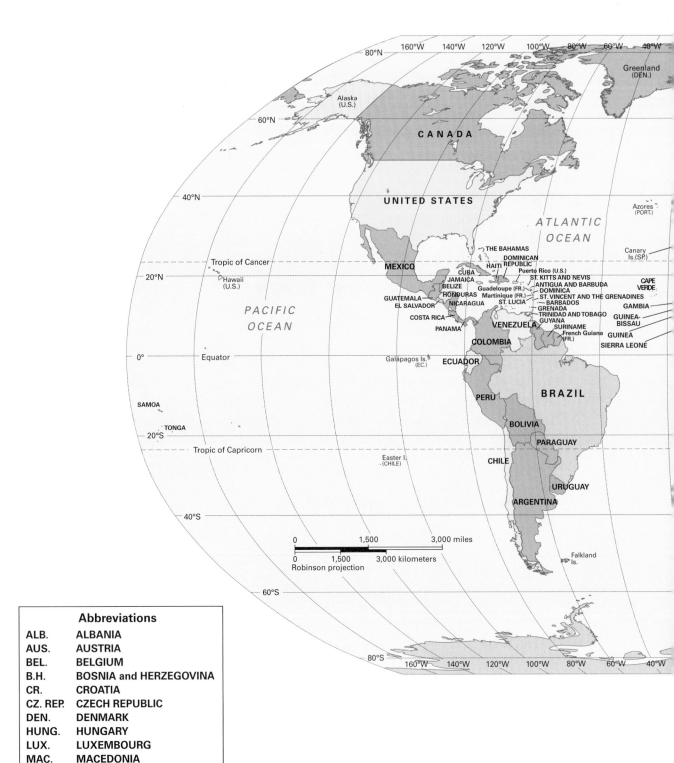

80°N 160°W 140°W 120°W 100°W 80°W 60°W 40°W

Greenland
(DEN.)

Alaska
(U.S.)

60°N

C A N A D A

40°N

UNITED STATES

ATLANTIC
OCEAN

Azores
(PORT.)

Canary
Is.(SP.)

Tropic of Cancer

THE BAHAMAS
DOMINICAN
REPUBLIC

20°N

Hawaii
(U.S.)

MEXICO

CUBA
HAITI

Puerto Rico (U.S.)
ST. KITTS AND NEVIS
ANTIGUA AND BARBUDA

CAPE
VERDE

JAMAICA
BELIZE

Guadeloupe (FR.)
DOMINICA

PACIFIC
OCEAN

GUATEMALA
EL SALVADOR

HONDURAS
NICARAGUA

Martinique (FR.)
ST. LUCIA

ST. VINCENT AND THE GRENADINES
BARBADOS

GAMBIA

GRENADA

COSTA RICA

TRINIDAD AND TOBAGO
GUYANA

GUINEA-
BISSAU

PANAMA

VENEZUELA

SURINAME
French Guiana
(FR.)

GUINEA

COLOMBIA

SIERRA LEONE

0° Equator

Galápagos Is.
(EC.)

ECUADOR

PERU

B R A Z I L

SAMOA

BOLIVIA

TONGA

20°S

PARAGUAY

Tropic of Capricorn

Easter I.
(CHILE)

CHILE

URUGUAY

40°S

ARGENTINA

0   1,500   3,000 miles

0   1,500   3,000 kilometers
Robinson projection

Falkland
Is.

60°S

80°S 160°W 140°W 120°W 100°W 80°W 60°W 40°W

Abbreviations	
ALB.	ALBANIA
AUS.	AUSTRIA
BEL.	BELGIUM
B.H.	BOSNIA and HERZEGOVINA
CR.	CROATIA
CZ. REP.	CZECH REPUBLIC
DEN.	DENMARK
HUNG.	HUNGARY
LUX.	LUXEMBOURG
MAC.	MACEDONIA
MONT.	MONTENEGRO
NETH.	NETHERLANDS
SERB.	SERBIA
SLK.	SLOVAKIA
SLO.	SLOVENIA
SWITZ.	SWITZERLAND

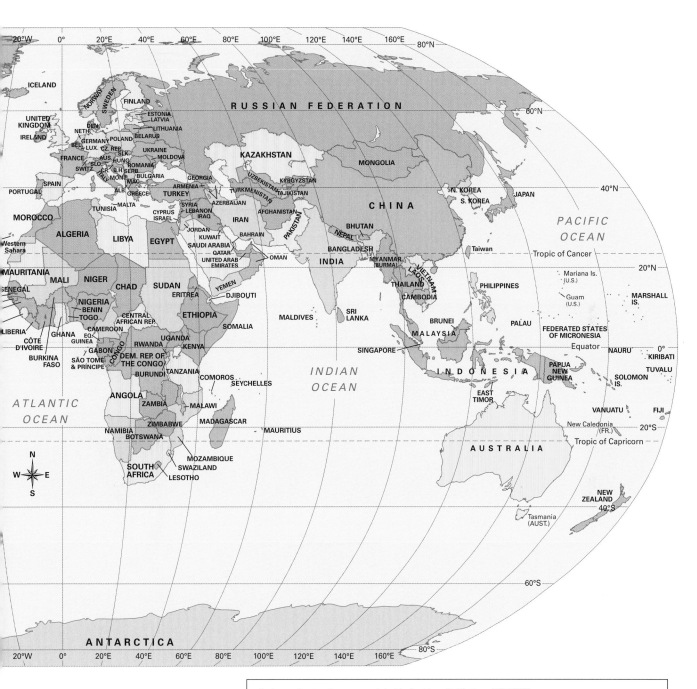

• Independent nations are printed in bold capital letters: **FRANCE**.

• Nations whose independence or governing rule is in dispute are printed in bold type: **Taiwan**.

• Territories, provinces, and the like governed by an independent nation are printed in bold type, with an abbreviation for the ruling nation: **French Guiana (FR.)**.

• Areas whose governing rule is in dispute are printed in nonbold type: Falkland Islands.

• Areas that are part of an independent nation but geographically separated from it are printed in nonbold type, with an abbreviation for the ruling nation: Hawaii (U.S.).

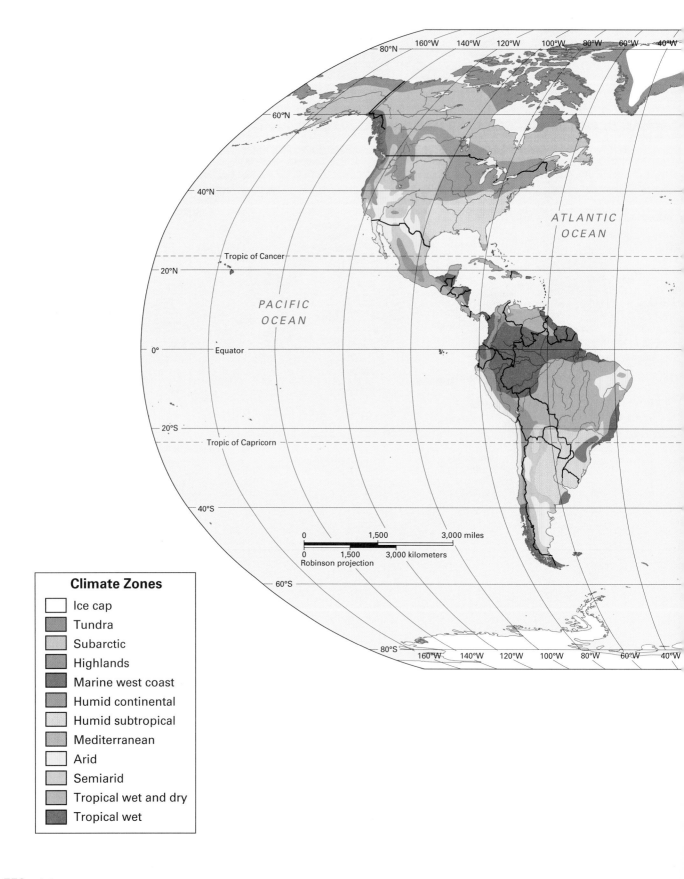

Climate Zones

- Ice cap
- Tundra
- Subarctic
- Highlands
- Marine west coast
- Humid continental
- Humid subtropical
- Mediterranean
- Arid
- Semiarid
- Tropical wet and dry
- Tropical wet

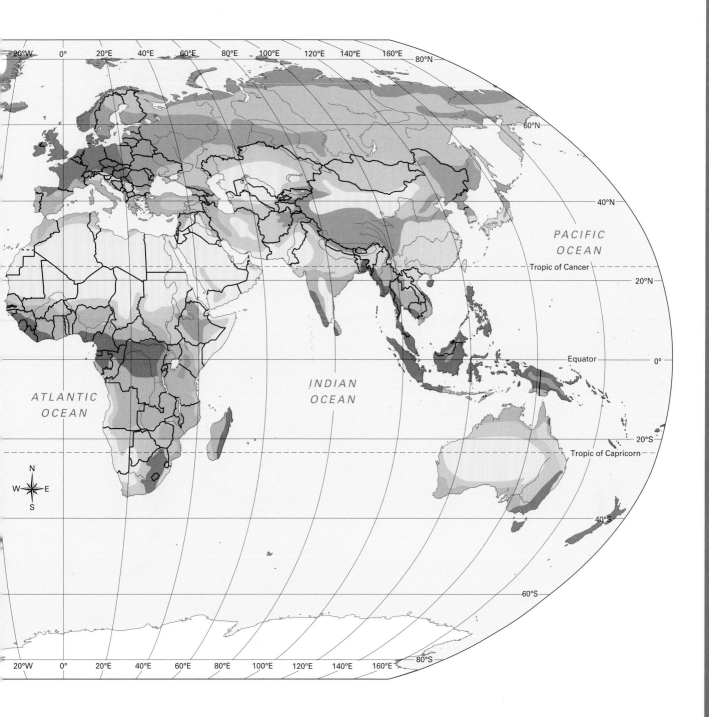

PACIFIC
OCEAN

Tropic of Cancer

ATLANTIC
OCEAN

INDIAN
OCEAN

Equator

Tropic of Capricorn

20°W 0° 20°E 40°E 60°E 80°E 100°E 120°E 140°E 160°E 80°N
60°N
40°N
20°N
0°
20°S
40°S
60°S
80°S

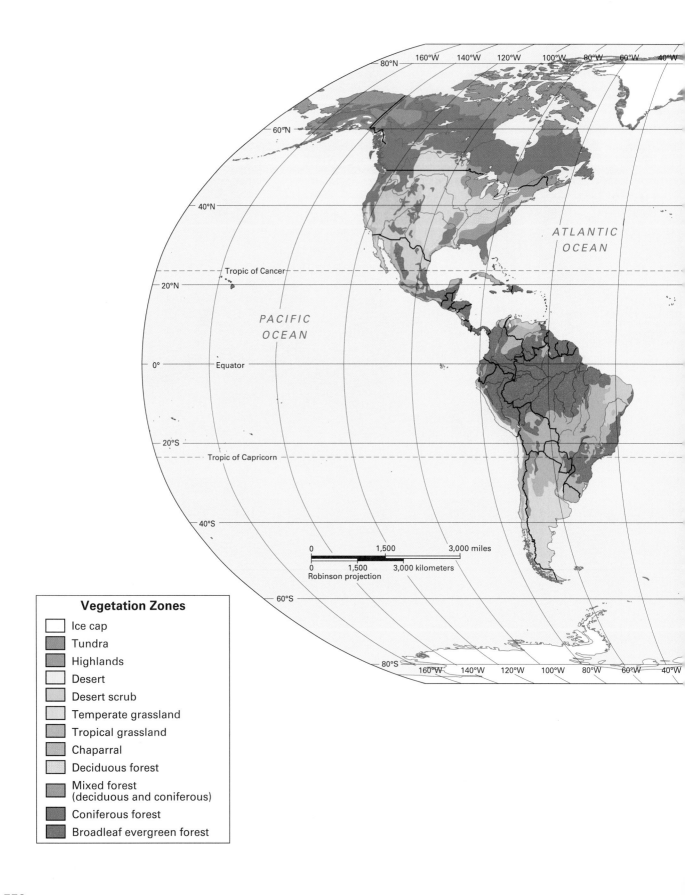

Vegetation Zones

- ☐ Ice cap
- ■ Tundra
- ■ Highlands
- ☐ Desert
- ■ Desert scrub
- ☐ Temperate grassland
- ■ Tropical grassland
- ■ Chaparral
- ☐ Deciduous forest
- ■ Mixed forest (deciduous and coniferous)
- ■ Coniferous forest
- ■ Broadleaf evergreen forest

Urban Population

Number of People
- ● Over 8,000,000
- ● 4,000,000–8,000,000
- • 1,000,000–4,000,000

Population Density

Per sq. mi.	Per sq. km
Over 250	Over 100
125–250	50–100
25–125	10–50
2–25	1–10
Under 2	Under 1

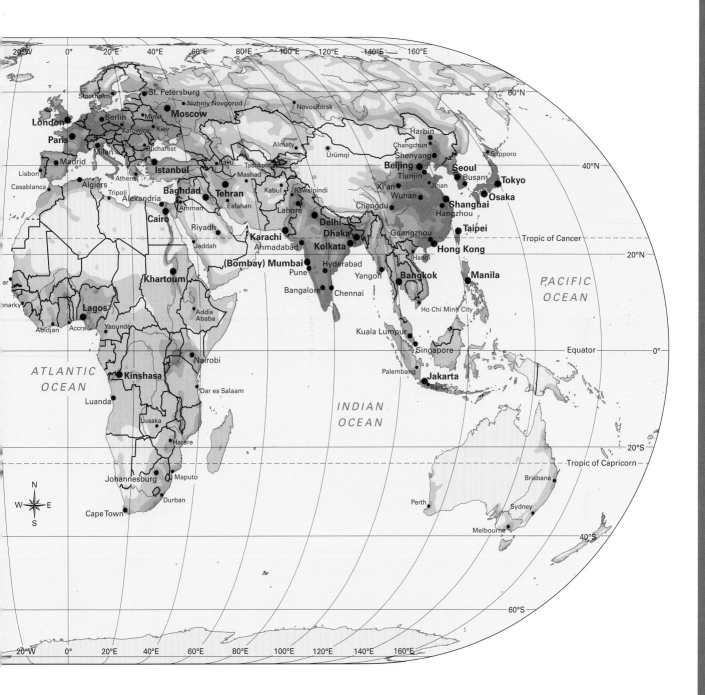

Stockholm
St. Petersburg
Nizhniy Novgorod
Moscow
London
Berlin
Minsk
Paris
Katowice
Kiev
Milan
Bucharest
Novosibirsk
Madrid
Almaty
Ürümqi
Harbin
Lisbon
Athens
Istanbul
Tashkent
Changchun
Sapporo
Casablanca
Algiers
Baku
Mashad
Beijing
Shenyang
Seoul
Tokyo
Tripoli
Alexandria
Baghdad
Tehran
Kabul
Rawalpindi
Tianjin
Busan
Amman
Esfahan
Xi'an
Jinan
Osaka
Cairo
Lahore
Wuhan
Shanghai
Riyadh
Chengdu
Hangzhou
Karachi
Delhi
Guangzhou
Taipei
Jeddah
Ahmadabad
Dhaka
Kolkata
Tropic of Cancer
(Bombay) Mumbai
Hyderabad
Hanoi
Hong Kong
Khartoum
Pune
Yangon
Bangkok
Manila
PACIFIC
OCEAN
Bangalore
Chennai
Ho Chi Minh City
Lagos
Addis
Ababa
Abidjan
Accra
Yaoundé
Kuala Lumpur
Equator
Nairobi
Singapore
ATLANTIC
OCEAN
Kinshasa
Palembang
Jakarta
Luanda
Dar es Salaam
Bandung
INDIAN
OCEAN
Lusaka
Harare
20°S
Tropic of Capricorn
Brisbane
Johannesburg
Maputo
Perth
Sydney
N
W   E
S
Durban
Cape Town
Melbourne
40°S

60°S

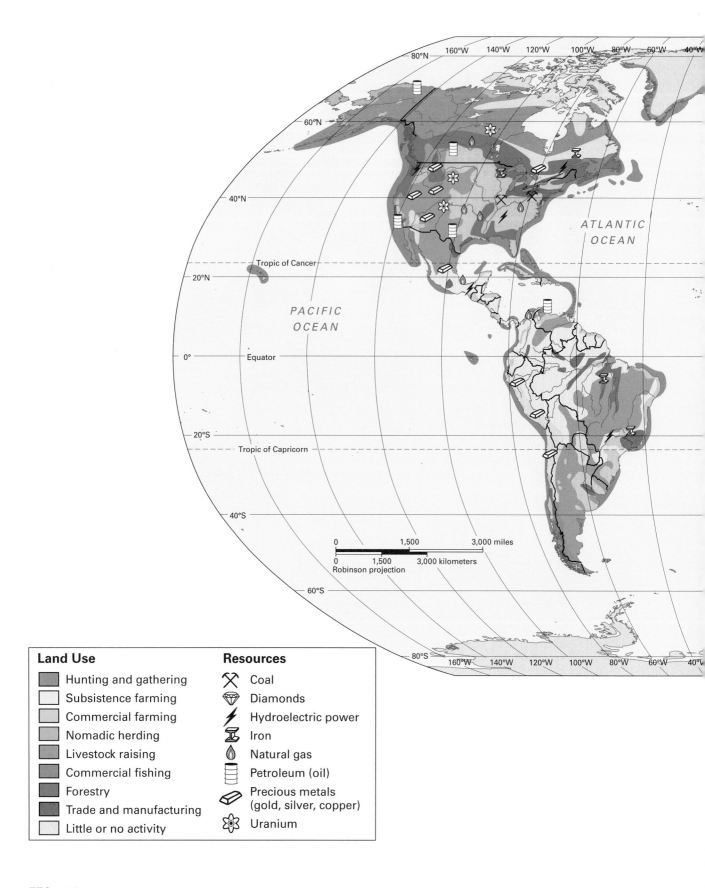

Land Use

- Hunting and gathering
- Subsistence farming
- Commercial farming
- Nomadic herding
- Livestock raising
- Commercial fishing
- Forestry
- Trade and manufacturing
- Little or no activity

Resources

- ⚒ Coal
- ◈ Diamonds
- ⚡ Hydroelectric power
- Iron
- ◌ Natural gas
- Petroleum (oil)
- Precious metals (gold, silver, copper)
- ✳ Uranium

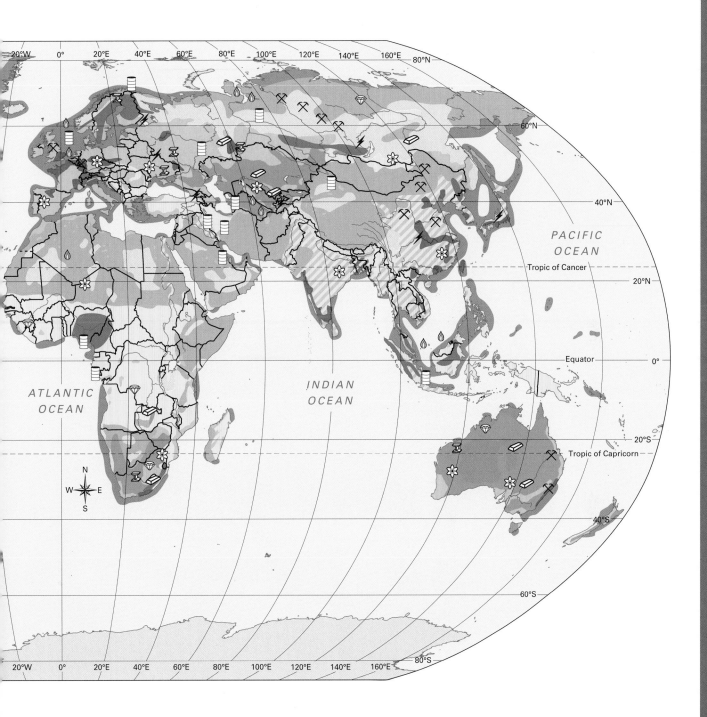

PACIFIC
OCEAN

ATLANTIC
OCEAN

INDIAN
OCEAN

Tropic of Cancer

Equator

Tropic of Capricorn

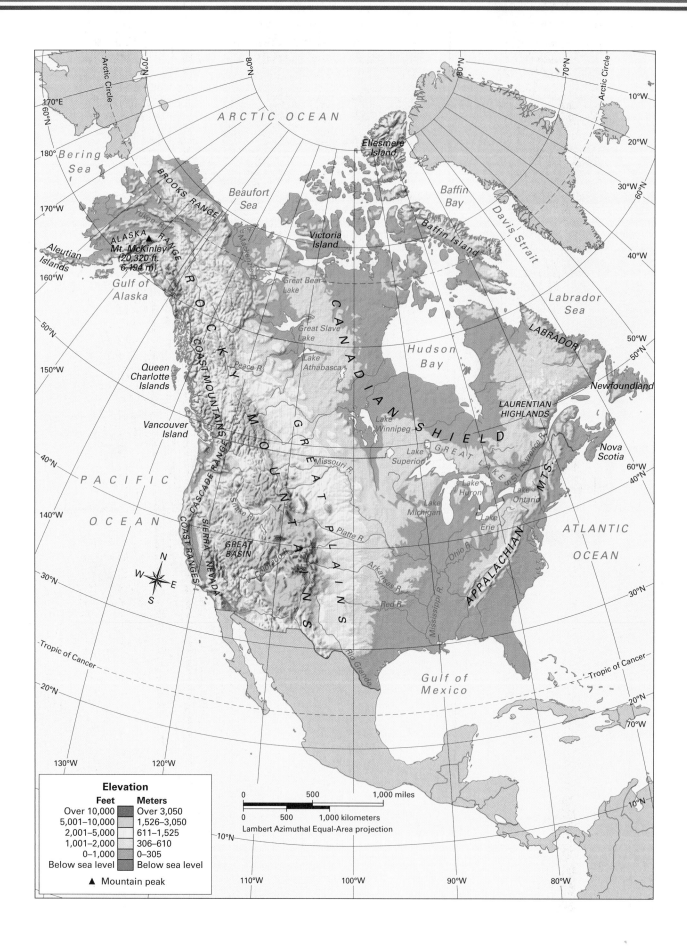

Elevation

Feet	Meters
Over 10,000	Over 3,050
5,001–10,000	1,526–3,050
2,001–5,000	611–1,525
1,001–2,000	306–610
0–1,000	0–305
Below sea level	Below sea level

▲ Mountain peak

0   500   1,000 miles
0   500   1,000 kilometers
Lambert Azimuthal Equal-Area projection

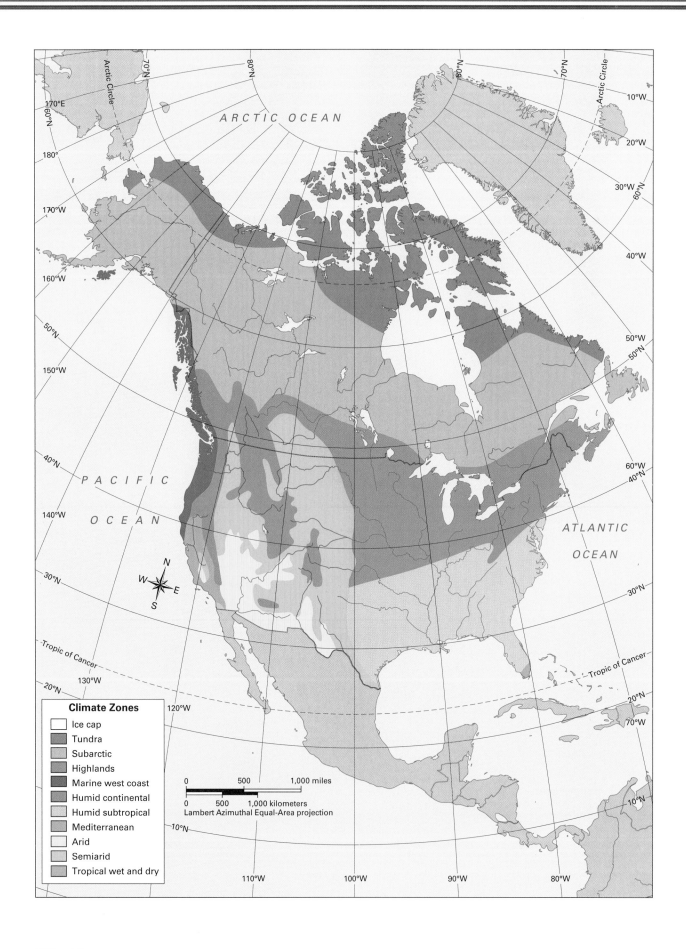

Climate Zones

- Ice cap
- Tundra
- Subarctic
- Highlands
- Marine west coast
- Humid continental
- Humid subtropical
- Mediterranean
- Arid
- Semiarid
- Tropical wet and dry

0   500   1,000 miles
0   500   1,000 kilometers
Lambert Azimuthal Equal-Area projection

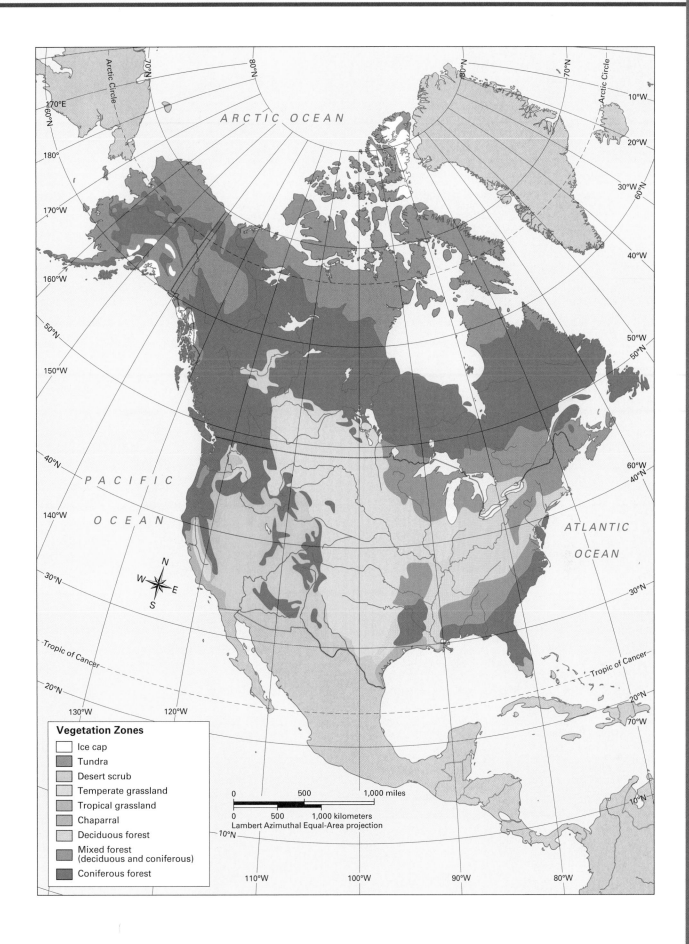

Vegetation Zones

- Ice cap
- Tundra
- Desert scrub
- Temperate grassland
- Tropical grassland
- Chaparral
- Deciduous forest
- Mixed forest (deciduous and coniferous)
- Coniferous forest

ARCTIC OCEAN

PACIFIC OCEAN

ATLANTIC OCEAN

Arctic Circle

Tropic of Cancer

0   500   1,000 miles
0   500   1,000 kilometers
Lambert Azimuthal Equal-Area projection

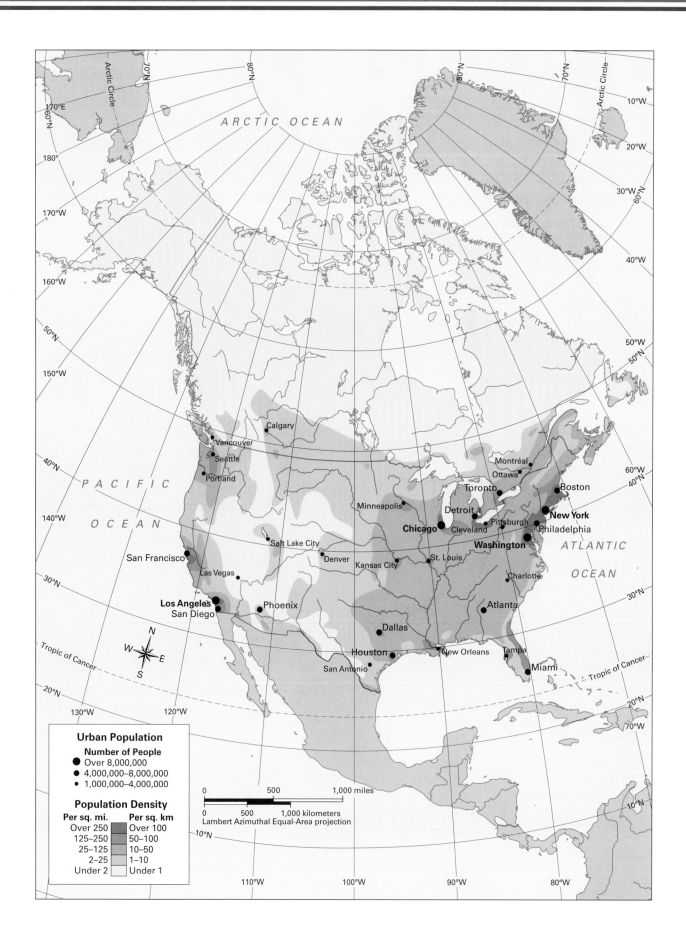

Urban Population

Number of People
- ● Over 8,000,000
- ● 4,000,000–8,000,000
- • 1,000,000–4,000,000

Population Density

Per sq. mi.	Per sq. km
Over 250	Over 100
125–250	50–100
25–125	10–50
2–25	1–10
Under 2	Under 1

0   500   1,000 miles

0   500   1,000 kilometers

Lambert Azimuthal Equal-Area projection

Land Use
- Hunting and gathering
- Commercial farming
- Nomadic herding
- Livestock raising
- Commercial fishing
- Forestry
- Trade and manufacturing
- Little or no activity

Resources
- Coal
- Hydroelectric power
- Iron
- Natural gas
- Petroleum (oil)
- Precious metals (gold, silver, copper)
- Uranium

Lambert Azimuthal Equal-Area projection

Elevation

Feet	Meters
Over 10,000	Over 3,050
5,001–10,000	1,526–3,050
2,001–5,000	611–1,525
1,001–2,000	306–610
0–1,000	0–305
Below sea level	Below sea level

▲ Mountain peak

0   500   1,000 miles
0   500   1,000 kilometers
Lambert Azimuthal Equal-Area projection

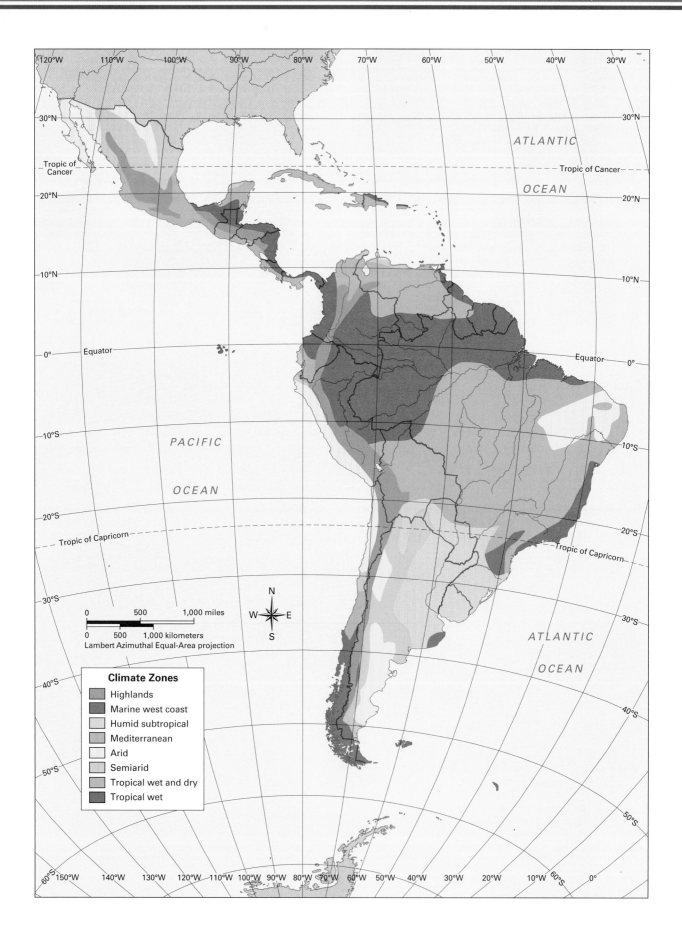

Climate Zones

- Highlands
- Marine west coast
- Humid subtropical
- Mediterranean
- Arid
- Semiarid
- Tropical wet and dry
- Tropical wet

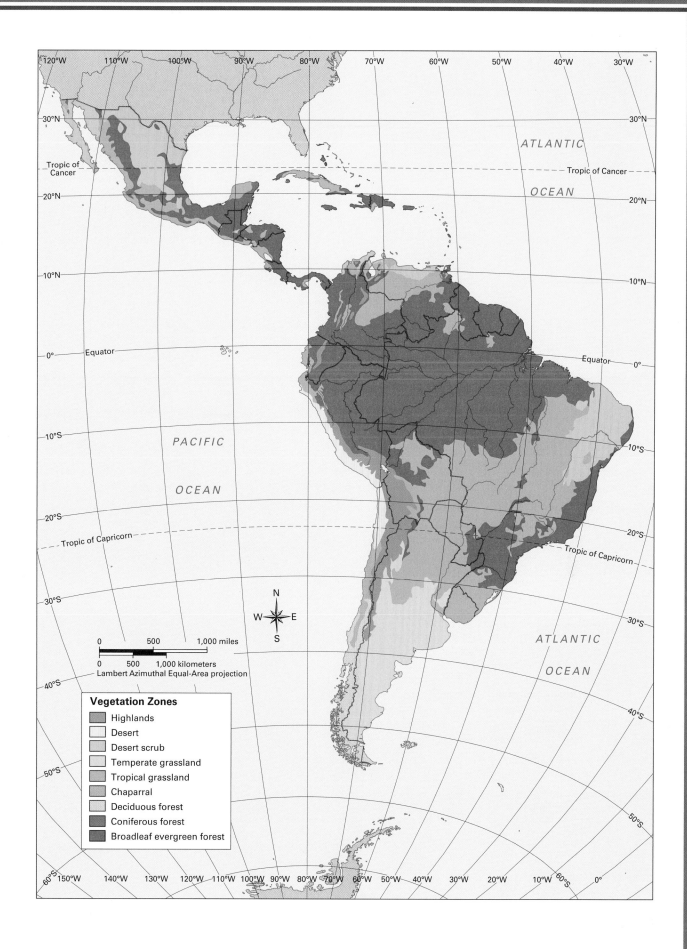

Vegetation Zones

- Highlands
- Desert
- Desert scrub
- Temperate grassland
- Tropical grassland
- Chaparral
- Deciduous forest
- Coniferous forest
- Broadleaf evergreen forest

Lambert Azimuthal Equal-Area projection

Urban Population

Number of People
- ● Over 8,000,000
- ● 4,000,000–8,000,000
- • 1,000,000–4,000,000

Population Density

Per sq. mi.	Per sq. km
Over 100	Over 250
50–100	125–250
10–50	25–125
1–10	2–25
Under 1	Under 2

Lambert Azimuthal Equal-Area projection

Land Use

- Hunting and gathering
- Subsistence farming
- Commercial farming
- Livestock raising
- Commercial fishing
- Forestry
- Trade and manufacturing
- Little or no activity

Resources

- Coal
- Diamonds
- Hydroelectric power
- Iron
- Natural gas
- Petroleum (oil)
- Precious metals (gold, silver, copper)
- Uranium

Lambert Azimuthal Equal-Area projection

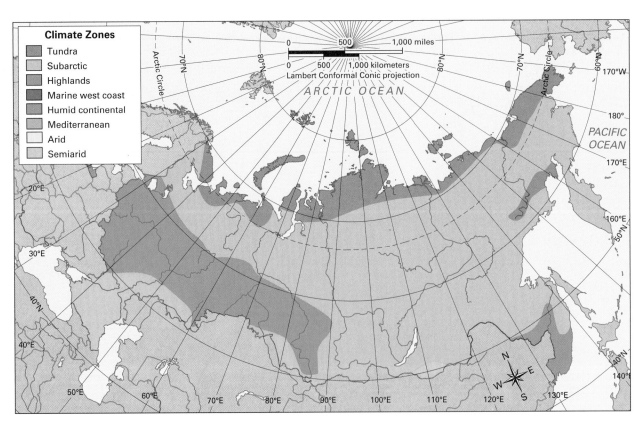

Vegetation Zones of Europe and Russia

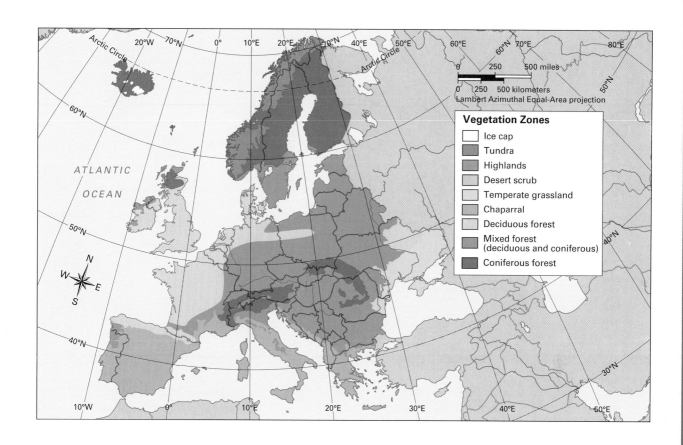

Vegetation Zones
- Ice cap
- Tundra
- Highlands
- Desert scrub
- Temperate grassland
- Chaparral
- Deciduous forest
- Mixed forest (deciduous and coniferous)
- Coniferous forest

Economic Activity of Europe and Russia

Land Use
- Hunting and gathering
- Subsistence farming
- Commercial farming
- Nomadic herding
- Livestock raising
- Commercial fishing
- Forestry
- Trade and manufacturing
- Little or no activity

Resources
- Coal
- Hydroelectric power
- Iron
- Natural gas
- Petroleum (oil)
- Precious metals (gold, silver, copper)
- Uranium

0 250 500 miles
0 250 500 kilometers
Lambert Azimuthal Equal-Area projection

Land Use
- Hunting and gathering
- Subsistence farming
- Commercial farming
- Nomadic herding
- Livestock raising
- Commercial fishing
- Forestry
- Trade and manufacturing
- Little or no activity

0 500 1,000 miles
0 500 1,000 kilometers
Lambert Conformal Conic projection

ARCTIC OCEAN

PACIFIC OCEAN

Resources
- Coal
- Hydroelectric power
- Iron
- Natural gas
- Petroleum (oil)
- Precious metals (gold, silver, copper)
- Uranium

50°W 40°W 30°W 20°W 10°W 0° 10°E 20°E 30°E 40°E 50°E 60°E 70°E 80°E

50°N 50°N

40°N 40°N

Mediterranean Sea

Strait of Gibraltar

ATLAS MOUNTAINS

Madeira
Islands

30°N 30°N

Qattara
Depression

Canary
Islands

AHAGGAR
MTS.

Tropic of Cancer Tropic of Cancer

TIBESTI
MTS.

Lake
Nasser

S A H A R A

20°N 20°N

Niger R.

Red Sea

Senegal R.

Cape Verde
Islands

Gambia R.

Lake
Chad

S A H E L

Gulf of Aden

Lake
Tana

10°N 10°N

Benue R.

Volta R.

Adamawa

ETHIOPIAN

White Nile R.

Blue Nile R.

HIGHLANDS

Uele R.

Bioko
Principe
São Tomé

C O N G O

Congo R.

Lake
Turkana

0° Equator 0° Equator

B A S I N

Mt. Kilimanjaro
(19,340 ft.
5,895 m)

Lake
Victoria

GREAT RIFT VALLEY

Pemba Is.
Zanzibar Is.

Lake
Tanganyika

Mafia Is.

10°S 10°S

A T L A N T I C

O C E A N

St. Helena

N
W   E
S

Lake
Malawi

Mozambique Channel

Madagascar

Mauritius

20°S 20°S

Zambezi R.

Reunion

Namib Desert

Tropic of Capricorn Tropic of Capricorn

Kalahari
Desert

Orange R.

30°S 30°S

I N D I A N

O C E A N

Elevation

Feet		Meters
Over 10,000		Over 3,050
5,001–10,000		1,526–3,050
2,001–5,000		611–1,525
1,001–2,000		306–610
0–1,000		0–305
Below sea level		Below sea level

▲ Mountain peak

Cape of Good Hope

40°S 40°S

0   500   1,000 miles

0   500   1,000 kilometers
Sinusoidal projection

40°W 30°W 20°W 10°W 0° 10°E 20°E 30°E 40°E 50°E 60°E 70°E

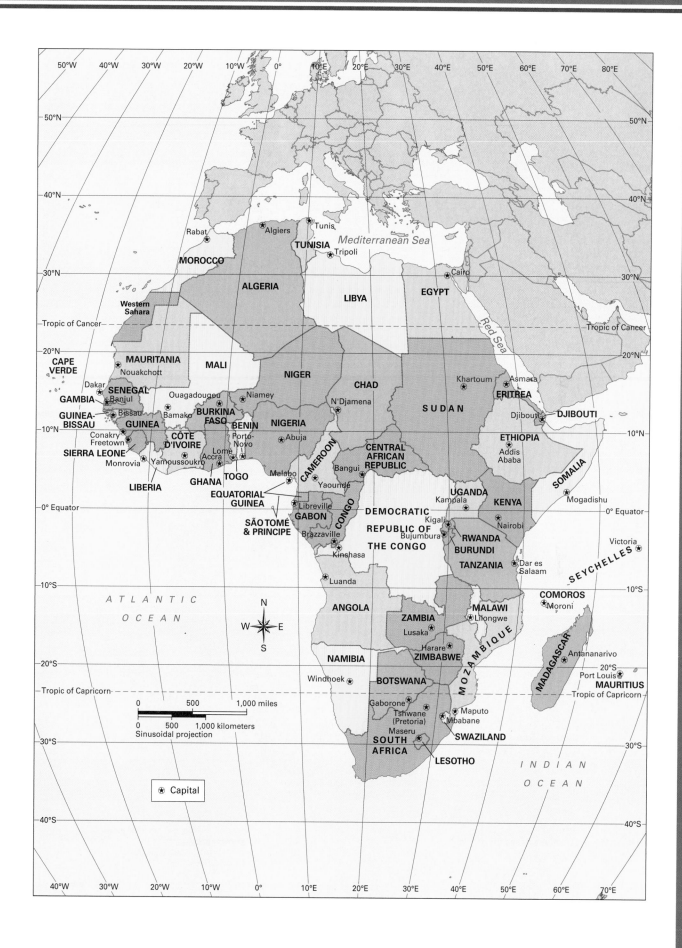

50°W　40°W　30°W　20°W　10°W　0°　10°E　20°E　30°E　40°E　50°E　60°E　70°E　80°E

50°N

40°N

Mediterranean Sea

Rabat
Algiers
Tunis ⊛
TUNISIA
Tripoli ⊛
MOROCCO
30°N

Cairo ⊛
ALGERIA
LIBYA
EGYPT

Western
Sahara
Tropic of Cancer

**CAPE
VERDE**
MAURITANIA
Nouakchott ⊛
MALI
NIGER
Khartoum ⊛
Asmara ⊛
20°N

CHAD
Dakar ⊛
SENEGAL
Ouagadougou ⊛
Niamey ⊛
ERITREA
GAMBIA
Banjul ⊛
Bamako ⊛
**BURKINA
FASO**
N'Djamena ⊛
SUDAN
Djibouti ⊛
DJIBOUTI
**GUINEA-
BISSAU**
Bissau ⊛
BENIN
NIGERIA
10°N

GUINEA
Conakry ⊛
**CÔTE
D'IVOIRE**
Porto-
Novo
Abuja ⊛
ETHIOPIA
Freetown
SIERRA LEONE
Lomé
Accra ⊛
**CENTRAL
AFRICAN
REPUBLIC**
Addis
Ababa ⊛
Yamoussoukro ⊛
Monrovia ⊛
TOGO
Malabo ⊛
Bangui ⊛
SOMALIA
LIBERIA
GHANA
CAMEROON
Yaoundé ⊛

**EQUATORIAL
GUINEA**
Libreville ⊛
UGANDA
Kampala ⊛
KENYA
0° Equator
Mogadishu ⊛

**SÃO TOMÉ
& PRINCIPE**
GABON
CONGO
**DEMOCRATIC
REPUBLIC OF
THE CONGO**
Kigali ⊛
Nairobi ⊛
Brazzaville ⊛
Bujumbura ⊛
RWANDA
Victoria ⊛
Kinshasa ⊛
BURUNDI
SEYCHELLES
TANZANIA
Dar es
Salaam ⊛
10°S

Luanda ⊛
COMOROS
Moroni ⊛

*ATLANTIC
OCEAN*
ANGOLA
MALAWI
Lilongwe ⊛
ZAMBIA
Lusaka ⊛
MADAGASCAR
Antananarivo ⊛
Harare ⊛
Port Louis ⊛
20°S
NAMIBIA
ZIMBABWE
MAURITIUS
Windhoek ⊛
Tropic of Capricorn

0　500　1,000 miles
BOTSWANA
Gaborone ⊛
0　500　1,000 kilometers
Sinusoidal projection
Tshwane
(Pretoria) ⊛
Maputo ⊛
Mbabane
Maseru ⊛
SWAZILAND
**SOUTH
AFRICA**
Lesotho ⊛
LESOTHO
*INDIAN
OCEAN*

⊛ Capital

40°S

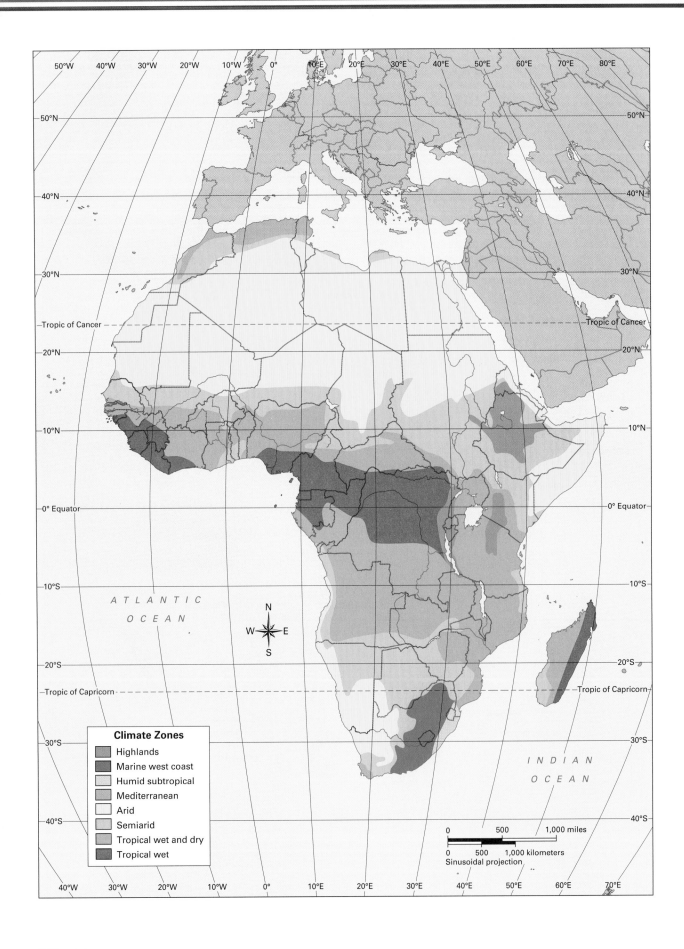

Climate Zones

- Highlands
- Marine west coast
- Humid subtropical
- Mediterranean
- Arid
- Semiarid
- Tropical wet and dry
- Tropical wet

ATLANTIC
OCEAN

INDIAN
OCEAN

Tropic of Cancer

Tropic of Capricorn

0° Equator

0   500   1,000 miles

0   500   1,000 kilometers

Sinusoidal projection

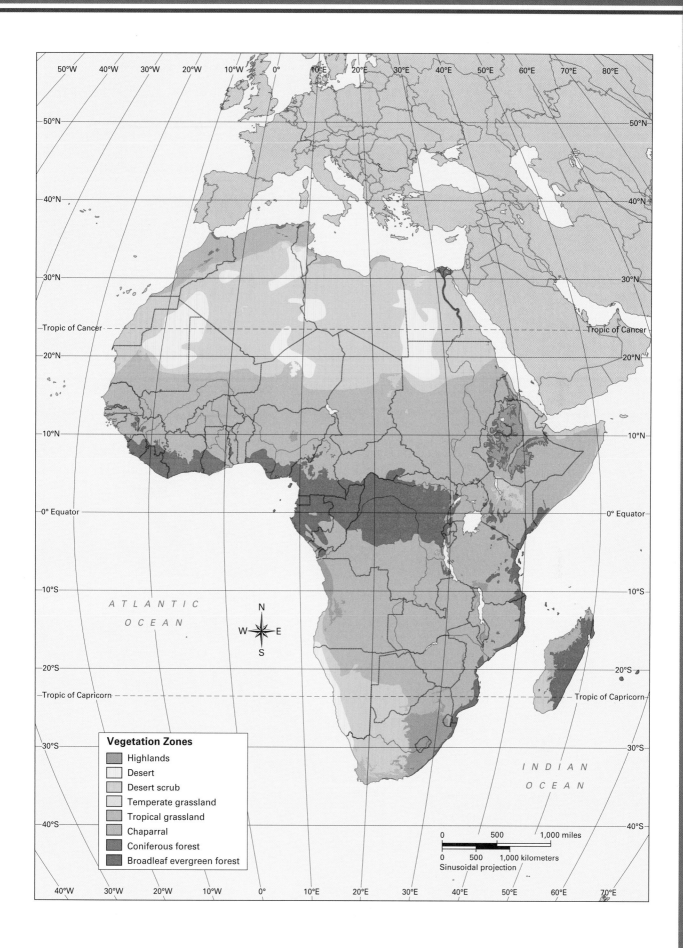

Vegetation Zones

- Highlands
- Desert
- Desert scrub
- Temperate grassland
- Tropical grassland
- Chaparral
- Coniferous forest
- Broadleaf evergreen forest

ATLANTIC OCEAN

INDIAN OCEAN

Tropic of Cancer

0° Equator

Tropic of Capricorn

0   500   1,000 miles
0   500   1,000 kilometers
Sinusoidal projection

Urban Population

Number of People
- ● Over 8,000,000
- ● 4,000,000–8,000,000
- • 1,000,000–4,000,000

Population Density

Per sq. mi.	Per sq. km
Over 250	Over 100
125–250	50–100
25–125	10–50
2–25	1–10
Under 2	Under 1

0   500   1,000 miles

0   500   1,000 kilometers

Sinusoidal projection

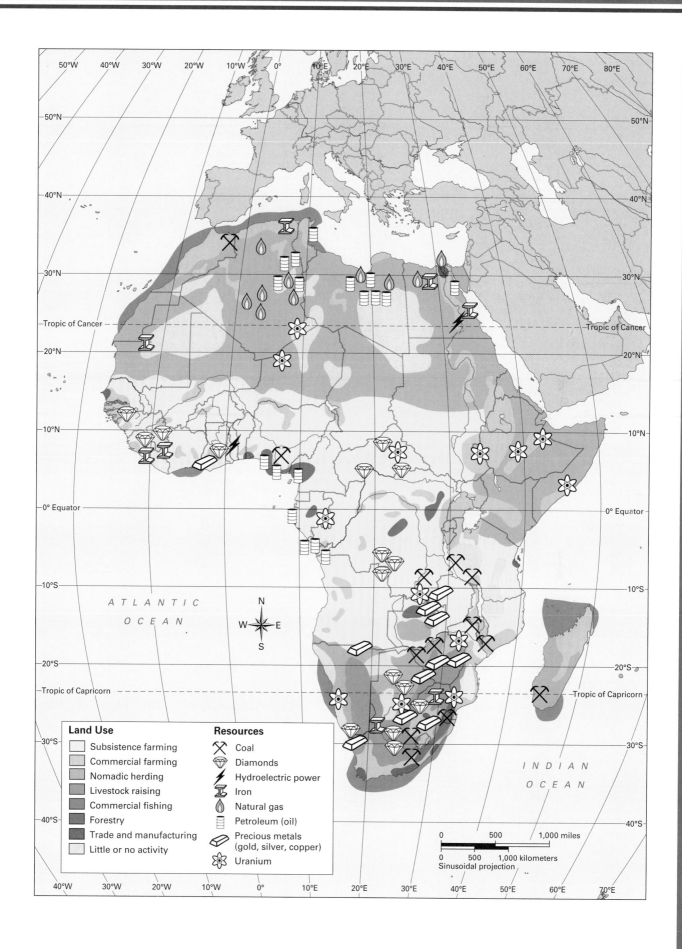

Economic Activity of Africa

Land Use
- Subsistence farming
- Commercial farming
- Nomadic herding
- Livestock raising
- Commercial fishing
- Forestry
- Trade and manufacturing
- Little or no activity

Resources
- Coal
- Diamonds
- Hydroelectric power
- Iron
- Natural gas
- Petroleum (oil)
- Precious metals (gold, silver, copper)
- Uranium

ATLANTIC OCEAN

INDIAN OCEAN

Tropic of Cancer

Equator

Tropic of Capricorn

0   500   1,000 miles
0   500   1,000 kilometers
Sinusoidal projection

Elevation

Feet	Meters
Over 10,000	Over 3,050
5,001–10,000	1,526–3,050
2,001–5,000	611–1,525
1,001–2,000	306–610
0–1,000	0–305
Below sea level	Below sea level

▲ Mountain peak

0   250   500 miles
0   250   500 kilometers
Lambert Conformal Conic projection

THE STEPPES

KAZAKH UPLAND

Caspian Depression

Lake Balkhash

Aral Sea

Syr Darya

Turan Lowland

Amu Darya

Lake Ysyk

K2 (Mt. Godwin Austen) (28,250 ft. 8,611 m)

HINDU KUSH

Black Sea

Caucasus Mts.

ANATOLIA PLATEAU

Taurus Mts.

Caspian Sea

Elburz Mts.

Lake Urmia

Mediterranean Sea

Syrian Desert

Tigris R.

Mesopotamia

Euphrates R.

ZAGROS MOUNTAINS

Dasht-e Kavir (Great Salt Desert)

Dead Sea (-1,349 ft. -411 m)

Indus R.

Persian Gulf

Strait of Hormuz

Gulf of Oman

Tropic of Cancer

ARABIAN

Red Sea

PENINSULA

Rub al Khali (Empty Quarter)

Arabian Sea

Gulf of Aden

Climate Zones

- Highlands
- Humid continental
- Humid subtropical
- Mediterranean
- Arid
- Semiarid

0   250   500 miles

0   250   500 kilometers

Lambert Conformal Conic projection

Tropic of Cancer

Vegetation Zones

- Ice cap
- Highlands
- Desert
- Desert scrub
- Temperate grassland
- Tropical grassland
- Chaparral
- Mixed forest (deciduous and coniferous)
- Coniferous forest

0 250 500 miles
0 250 500 kilometers
Lambert Conformal Conic projection

Tropic of Cancer

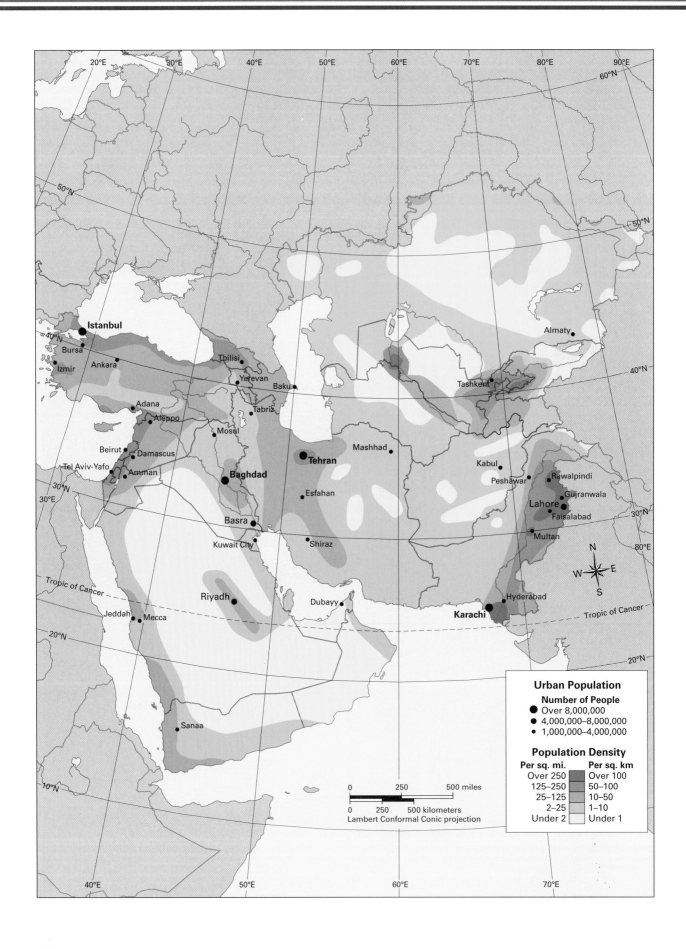

Urban Population

Number of People
- ● Over 8,000,000
- ● 4,000,000–8,000,000
- • 1,000,000–4,000,000

Population Density

Per sq. mi.	Per sq. km
Over 250	Over 100
125–250	50–100
25–125	10–50
2–25	1–10
Under 2	Under 1

0   250   500 miles

0   250   500 kilometers
Lambert Conformal Conic projection

Land Use

- Subsistence farming
- Commercial farming
- Nomadic herding
- Livestock raising
- Commercial fishing
- Trade and manufacturing
- Little or no activity

Resources

- Coal
- Hydroelectric power
- Iron
- Natural gas
- Petroleum (oil)
- Precious metals (gold, silver, copper)
- Uranium

0   250   500 miles
0   250   500 kilometers
Lambert Conformal Conic projection

Physical Features of Monsoon Asia

ALTAY MTS.
TIAN SHAN
Taklamakan Desert
KUNLUN SHAN
Gobi Desert
Amur R.
Plateau of Tibet
Indus R.
Ganges R.
HIMALAYAS
Mt. Everest
(29,035 ft.
8,850 m)
Qinghai Hu
Huang He
(Yellow R.)
Chang Jiang
Yangtze R.
Hokkaido
Sea of Japan
(East Sea)
Honshu
Shikoku
Kyushu
Yellow Sea
East China Sea
Ryukyu Islands
Taiwan
Tropic of Cancer
Deccan Plateau
Western Ghats
Eastern Ghats
Bay of Bengal
Salween R.
Annam Cordillera
Hainan
Luzon
Philippine
Islands
Mindoro
Samar
Negros
Mindanao
Palawan
Sulu Sea
Philippine Sea
PACIFIC OCEAN
South China Sea
Andaman Islands
Irrawaddy R.
Tonle Sap
Mekong R.
Gulf of Thailand
Malay Peninsula
Nicobar Islands
Maldive Islands
Celebes Sea
Halmahera
Batu Islands
Sumatra
Borneo
Celebes
Ceram
Banda Sea
Maoke Mts.
New Guinea
Mentawai Islands
Greater Sunda Islands
Java Sea
INDIAN OCEAN
Java
Sumbawa
Flores
Sumba
Timor
Arafura Sea
Timor Sea
Equator
Tropic of Capricorn

0   500   1,000 miles
0   500   1,000 kilometers
Lambert Azimuthal Equal-Area projection

N W E S

Elevation

Feet	Meters
Over 10,000	Over 3,050
5,001–10,000	1,526–3,050
2,001–5,000	611–1,525
1,001–2,000	306–610
0–1,000	0–305
Below sea level	Below sea level

▲ Mountain peak

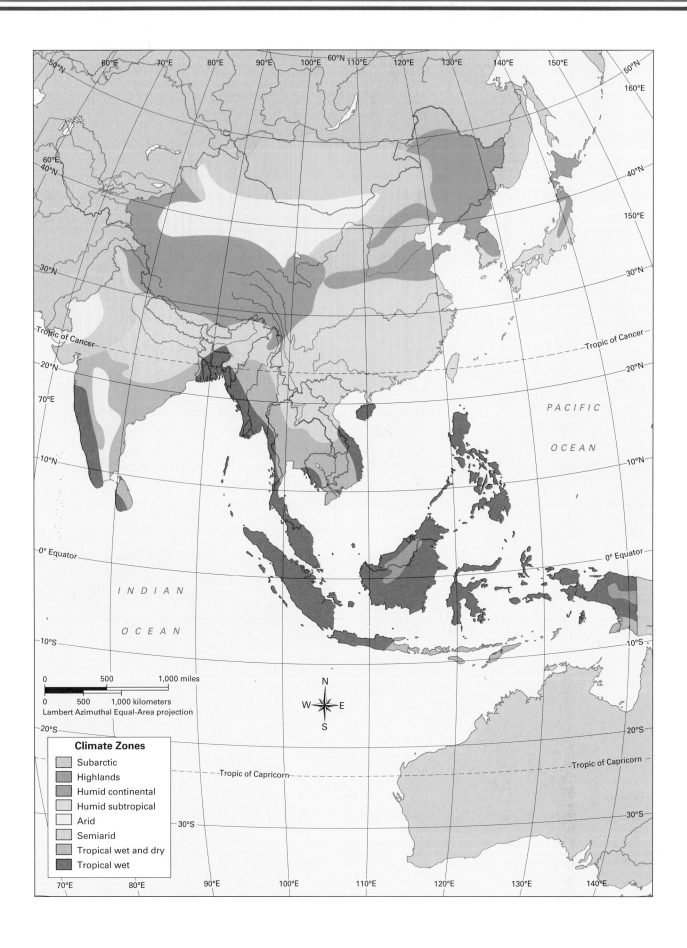

Climate Zones of Monsoon Asia

PACIFIC

OCEAN

Tropic of Cancer

Tropic of Cancer

INDIAN

OCEAN

0° Equator

0° Equator

N

W   E

S

Lambert Azimuthal Equal-Area projection

Tropic of Capricorn

Tropic of Capricorn

Climate Zones

Subarctic
Highlands
Humid continental
Humid subtropical
Arid
Semiarid
Tropical wet and dry
Tropical wet

Vegetation Zones

- Ice cap
- Highlands
- Desert
- Desert scrub
- Temperate grassland
- Tropical grassland
- Deciduous forest
- Mixed forest (deciduous and coniferous)
- Coniferous forest
- Broadleaf evergreen forest

0   500   1,000 miles

0   500   1,000 kilometers
Lambert Azimuthal Equal-Area projection

Population Density of Monsoon Asia

Urban Population

Number of People
- ● Over 8,000,000
- ● 4,000,000–8,000,000
- • 1,000,000–4,000,000

Population Density

Per sq. mi.	Per sq. km
Over 250	Over 100
125–250	50–100
25–125	10–50
2–25	1–10
Under 2	Under 1

0   500   1,000 miles
0   500   1,000 kilometers
Lambert Azimuthal Equal-Area projection

PACIFIC OCEAN

INDIAN OCEAN

Cities and places labeled: Ürümqi, Qiqihar, Harbin, Changchun, Jilin, Shenyang, Fushun, Anshan, Baotou, Beijing, Tangshan, Pyongyang, Sapporo, Tianjin, Dalian, Seoul, Yokohama, Tokyo, Taiyuan, Shijiazhuang, Daejon, Daegu, Kyoto, Nagoya, Jinan, Qingdao, Busan, Osaka, Lanzhou, Zhengzhou, Hiroshima, Fukuoka, Xi'an, Nanjing, Shanghai, Chengdu, Wuhan, Hangzhou, Chongqing, Nanchang, Ludhiana, Delhi, Jaipur, Kanpur, Lucknow, Patna, Changsha, Fuzhou, Taipei, Guiyang, Kunming, Kaohsiung, Ahmadabad, Bhopal, Nagpur, Kolkata, Dhaka, Surat, Chittagong, Guangzhou, Hong Kong, Mumbai (Bombay), Pune, Hanoi, Haiphong, Hyderabad, Yangon, Bangalore, Chennai, Madurai, Bangkok, Manila, Phnom Penh, Ho Chi Minh City, Davao, Medan, Kuala Lumpur, Singapore, Palembang, Ujungpandang, Jakarta, Bandung, Semarang, Surabaya

Land Use

- Subsistence farming
- Commercial farming
- Nomadic herding
- Livestock raising
- Commercial fishing
- Forestry
- Trade and manufacturing
- Little or no activity

Resources

- Coal
- Hydroelectric power
- Iron
- Natural gas
- Petroleum (oil)
- Precious metals (gold, silver, copper)
- Uranium

0   500   1,000 miles
0   500   1,000 kilometers
Lambert Azimuthal Equal-Area projection

INDIAN OCEAN

PACIFIC OCEAN

Tropic of Cancer

Tropic of Capricorn

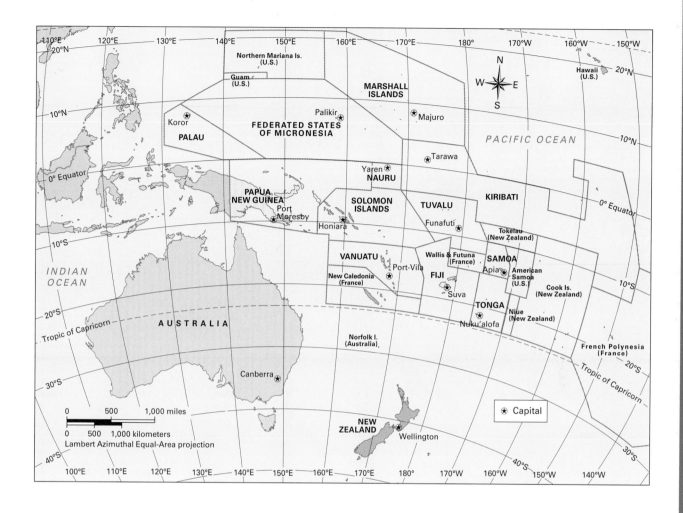

Political map of Oceania showing the following labeled features:

Latitude and longitude lines from 110°E to 150°W, and 20°N to 40°S.

- Northern Mariana Is. (U.S.)
- Guam (U.S.)
- MARSHALL ISLANDS
- Majuro (Capital)
- PACIFIC OCEAN
- Palikir (Capital)
- Koror (Capital)
- PALAU
- FEDERATED STATES OF MICRONESIA
- Hawaii (U.S.)
- Tarawa (Capital)
- Yaren (Capital), NAURU
- KIRIBATI
- PAPUA NEW GUINEA
- Port Moresby (Capital)
- SOLOMON ISLANDS
- Honiara (Capital)
- TUVALU
- Funafuti (Capital)
- Tokelau (New Zealand)
- INDIAN OCEAN
- VANUATU
- Port-Vila (Capital)
- Wallis & Futuna (France)
- SAMOA
- Apia (Capital)
- American Samoa (U.S.)
- New Caledonia (France)
- FIJI
- Suva (Capital)
- Cook Is. (New Zealand)
- TONGA
- Nuku'alofa (Capital)
- Niue (New Zealand)
- AUSTRALIA
- Tropic of Capricorn
- Norfolk I. (Australia)
- French Polynesia (France)
- Canberra (Capital)
- NEW ZEALAND
- Wellington (Capital)

⊛ Capital

0 500 1,000 miles
0 500 1,000 kilometers
Lambert Azimuthal Equal-Area projection

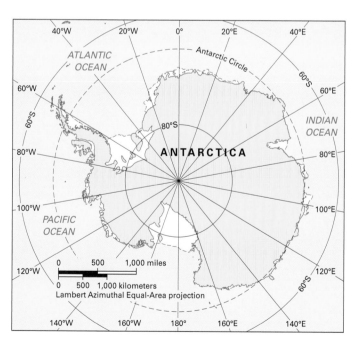

Polar map of Antarctica showing:

- ATLANTIC OCEAN
- Antarctic Circle
- INDIAN OCEAN
- ANTARCTICA
- PACIFIC OCEAN
- Latitude/longitude lines 40°W, 20°W, 0°, 20°E, 40°E, 60°E, 60°W, 80°W, 100°W, 120°W, 80°E, 100°E, 120°E, 140°W, 160°W, 180°, 160°E, 140°E; 60°S, 80°S

0 500 1,000 miles
0 500 1,000 kilometers
Lambert Azimuthal Equal-Area projection

Climate Zones of Oceania and Antarctica

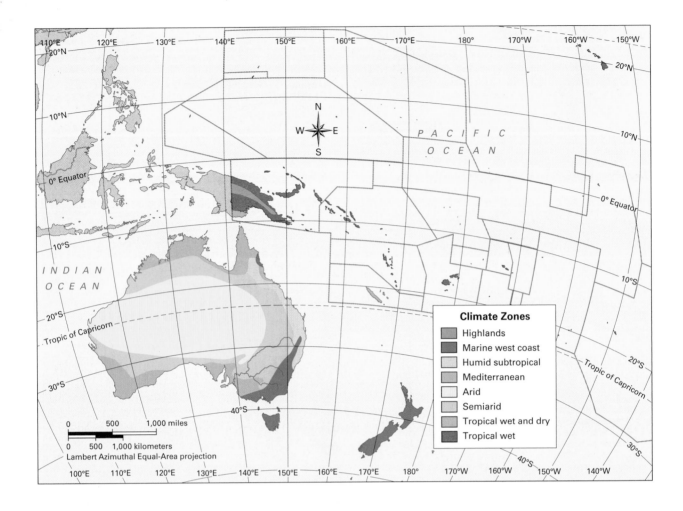

Climate Zones
- Highlands
- Marine west coast
- Humid subtropical
- Mediterranean
- Arid
- Semiarid
- Tropical wet and dry
- Tropical wet

PACIFIC OCEAN

INDIAN OCEAN

Tropic of Capricorn

0   500   1,000 miles

0   500   1,000 kilometers
Lambert Azimuthal Equal-Area projection

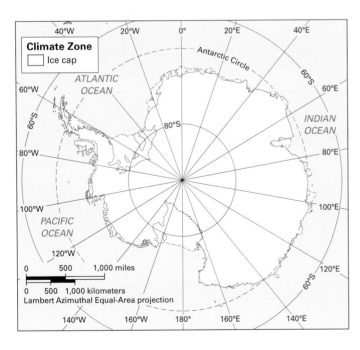

Climate Zone
- Ice cap

Antarctic Circle

ATLANTIC OCEAN

INDIAN OCEAN

PACIFIC OCEAN

0   500   1,000 miles

0   500   1,000 kilometers
Lambert Azimuthal Equal-Area projection

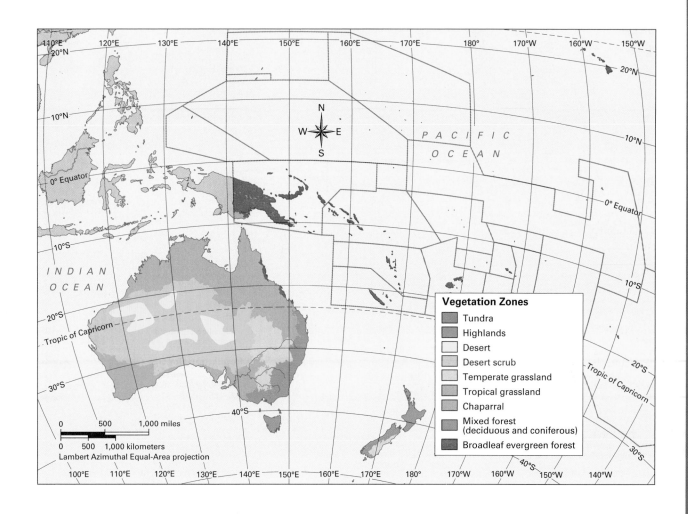

Vegetation Zones
- Tundra
- Highlands
- Desert
- Desert scrub
- Temperate grassland
- Tropical grassland
- Chaparral
- Mixed forest (deciduous and coniferous)
- Broadleaf evergreen forest

Lambert Azimuthal Equal-Area projection

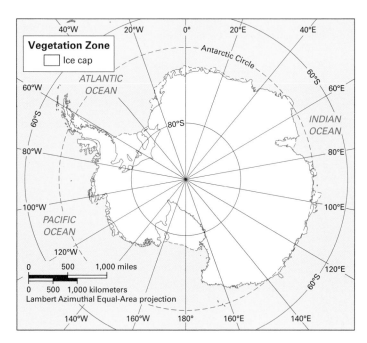

Vegetation Zone
- Ice cap

Lambert Azimuthal Equal-Area projection

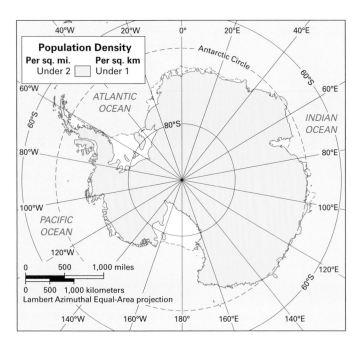

Economic Activity of Oceania and Antarctica

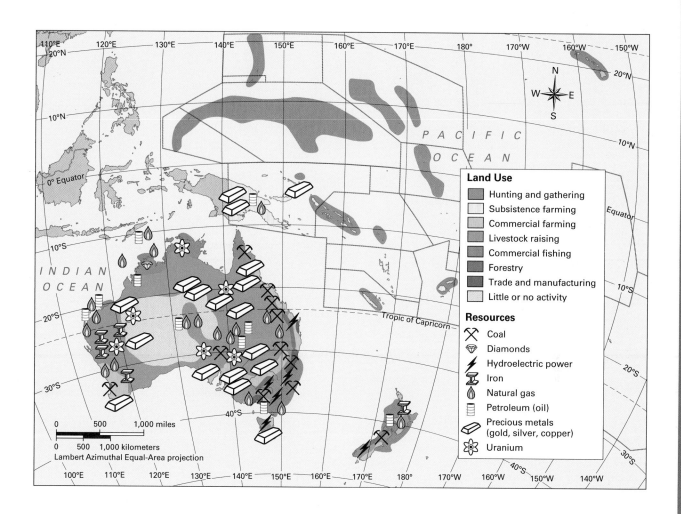

Land Use

- Hunting and gathering
- Subsistence farming
- Commercial farming
- Livestock raising
- Commercial fishing
- Forestry
- Trade and manufacturing
- Little or no activity

Resources

- ⚒ Coal
- ◆ Diamonds
- ⚡ Hydroelectric power
- ⬗ Iron
- 🜂 Natural gas
- ⬭ Petroleum (oil)
- ▱ Precious metals (gold, silver, copper)
- ✳ Uranium

0   500   1,000 miles

0   500   1,000 kilometers

Lambert Azimuthal Equal-Area projection

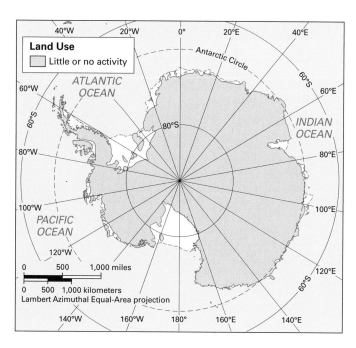

Land Use

- Little or no activity

ATLANTIC OCEAN

INDIAN OCEAN

PACIFIC OCEAN

Antarctic Circle

0   500   1,000 miles

0   500   1,000 kilometers

Lambert Azimuthal Equal-Area projection

Glossary

Geoterms are in **blue**. Vocabulary words are in **black**.

A

absolute location the precise point where a place is located on Earth

accidental pollution the release of harmful substances into the environment as the result of an accident, such as an oil tanker spilling oil into the sea

acclimatize the process of adjusting to lower oxygen levels at high **elevation**

acid rain rain that can damage the environment because it contains acid created from chemicals in factory smoke and car exhaust. Acid rain can damage plants, fish, animals, and even buildings.

adaptation a change in a way of life to suit new conditions

adobe a type of brick that is made of clay mixed with straw and dried in the sun

air quality the condition of the air based on the amount of pollution in it

alpine found in high mountains; also describes the mountain **vegetation zone** between the **tree line** and the **snow line**

alpine glacier a **glacier** formed by snowfall in a high, cold mountain valley

altitudinal zonation the division of land into zones based on **elevation**, which in turn helps determine **climate** and **vegetation**

Antarctic Circle the line of latitude at 60°30′S that marks the boundary of the southern **polar zone**

apartheid the former official South African policy of separating people according to race; it gave most of the political and economic power to whites

aqueduct a pipe or channel built to transport water from one place to another

arable land land suitable for growing crops

Arctic Circle the line of latitude at 60°30′N that marks the boundary of the northern **polar zone**

arid dry or lacking rainfall; also a **climate** or **climate zone** that is hot and dry all year with very little rain

arithmetic population density the population of a country divided by its total land area

atmosphere the layer of air that surrounds Earth

atmospheric pressure the weight of the **atmosphere** pressing down on any point of the surface of Earth

atoll a ring of coral islands and reefs surrounding a shallow body of ocean water

avalanche the sudden movement of a large mass of ice, snow, or rocks and soil down the side of a mountain

axis an imaginary line that runs from the North Pole to the South Pole through the center of Earth

B

baby boom a sudden increase in the **birth rate** of a population

barter conducting trade by exchanging goods or services instead of money

basin a bowl-shaped depression, or hollow, in Earth's surface

biodiversity the variety of plants and animals living in one area, or on Earth

biome a very large **ecosystem** such as a **desert,** forest, **wetlands,** or grassland; home to a community of plants and animals

birth rate the number of births in a year for every 1,000 people in a population

brain drain the loss of well-educated people such as doctors or engineers to another country

broadleaf evergreen forest a **vegetation** zone of mainly tall trees that remain green all year; also refers to the type of vegetation in this zone

C

calorie a measure of the amount of energy in food

canopy the thick layer of overlapping tree branches that make up the top layer of a forest

capital city a city that is the governmental center of a country or **region**

carbon-oxygen cycle the process by which carbon and oxygen cycle among plants, people and animals, and the environment

cardinal directions the four main directions on a **compass rose:** north, south, east, and west

carrying capacity the number of people or animals the environment of an area can support

cash crop a crop that is grown to be sold rather than to be consumed by the farmers and their families

cataract a series of rapids and low waterfalls on a river

census a count of a population

centrifugal forces the forces that divide people and countries

centripetal forces the forces that unite people and countries

chaparral a **vegetation zone** of mainly small trees and bushes adapted to a **Mediterranean climate;** also refers to the type of vegetation in this zone

civil war a war between groups living in the same country

clear-cut to cut down all of the trees in an area

climagraph a graph that shows the average temperature and **precipitation** in a place over a year

climate the pattern of weather over a long period of time

climate zone a large area of Earth with a particular pattern of weather

cloud forest a type of high-altitude, tropical forest that is usually covered by clouds or mist

cloud seeding the scattering of chemicals into clouds to bring about rain

colonialism a system in which one country rules another area as a colony. The ruling country controls trade with its colony for its own benefit.

commercial farming raising crops for sale, often on large farms

commercial fishing catching fish for sale, often with the use of large ships

common market a group of countries that acts as a single market, without trade barriers between member countries

communal land land that is held in common by a group of people

commute time the amount of time spent traveling to and from work

comparative advantage the ability of one country to produce a good or provide a service at a lower cost or more effectively than another country

compass rose a diagram on a map that shows directions such as north, south, east, and west

condense to lose heat and change from a vapor or gas into a liquid. Moisture, or water vapor, in the air condenses to form rain.

confluence the flowing together of two or more streams

conifer a tree with needles and cones, such as a pine tree

coniferous forest a **vegetation zone** of mainly **evergreen** trees with needles and cones; also refers to the type of vegetation in this zone

conservationist someone who works to protect the beauty and **natural resources** of the environment from destruction or **pollution**

consumption the using up of goods and services; also the purchase and use of goods and services by consumers

continent the seven largest areas of land on Earth

continental climate a type of **climate** that occurs in inland areas and other places not affected by the sea; marked by hot summers, cold winters, and relatively little **precipitation**

Continental Divide a series of mountain ridges in North America that separate the streams and rivers that flow west into the Pacific Ocean from those that flow east into the Arctic and Atlantic oceans

continental drift theory the idea that **continents** are slowly drifting as the **tectonic plates** that they sit on move. This idea comes from Alfred Wegener, who proposed that Earth once had one giant **super-continent**. This supercontinent broke apart into plates that have slowly drifted to their current locations.

continental glacier a large, thick ice sheet that covers a vast area and moves outward in many directions

continental island an island that was once part of a **continent**

convection the movement, or transfer, of heat through a gas or liquid

coordinates a set of numbers that together describe the exact location of something, such as a place on a map

core the innermost part of Earth, made of solid iron and surrounded by a layer of liquid iron

Coriolis effect the curving pattern of wind and ocean **currents** caused by Earth's rotation

cost of living the average cost of basic necessities, such as food, clothing, and shelter, in a particular place or country

crater a bowl-shaped hole in Earth's surface

crude oil petroleum as it comes out of the ground and before it has been refined or processed into useful products

crust the hard outer layer of Earth

cultural identity a feeling of belonging to a group that shares the same culture, or way of life

cultural region an area that is set apart from other places by the way of life of the people who live there

currency the bills and coins used as money in a particular country or group of countries

current the steady movement of air or water due to **convection**

D

death rate the number of deaths in a year for every 1,000 people in a population

deciduous forest a **vegetation zone** of mainly trees that shed their leaves before winter; also refers to the type of vegetation in this zone

deforestation removing or clearing away the trees from a forest. Deforestation is often done to clear land for farming or ranching.

delta the triangle-shaped deposit of sand and **sediment** that occurs where a river flows into an ocean

demographic transition model a model of how the size of a population changes as a country develops its economy

demography the study of human populations, including how they change due to births, deaths, aging, and migration

dependency ratio the number of old and young people who don't work compared with the working-age population. The higher the ratio, the more young and old people the workers have to support.

desalinization plant a facility that removes salt from seawater to make it suitable for human use

desert a geographic **region** with too little rainfall to support much plant life; also a **vegetation zone**

desertification the process by which land becomes more and more dry until it turns into **desert**; may be caused by **climate** change, human activities, or both.

desert scrub a **vegetation zone** of mainly small trees, bushes, and other plants adapted to a dry **climate**; also refers to the type of vegetation in this zone

developed country a wealthy country with an advanced economy. Developed countries have many industries and provide a comfortable way of life for most of their people.

developing country a poorer country with a less advanced economy. In general, developing countries are trying to increase their industries and improve life for their people.

dialect a version of a language spoken in a specific area

dictator a leader who governs by force, without the consent of the people

diffusion the spreading and mixing of cultures

digital divide the difference in opportunities available to people who have access to computers and the Internet and those who do not

distortion a change in shape, size, or position of a place when it is shown on a map

distribution the way people or things are spread out over an area or a space; also the way resources, power, or goods are divided among people or groups

diversity a variety or wide range of differences

doubling time the length of time it takes for a population to double

downwind in the direction that the wind is blowing

drought an unusually long period in which little or no rain falls

E

earthquake-resistant construction techniques building methods used to make structures safer during earthquakes

earthquake zone an area where earthquakes are likely, often where **tectonic plates** meet

economic activity any action that relates to the making, buying, and selling of goods and services

economic interdependence condition in which countries have strong economic ties and depend on each other for resources, **technology,** trade, and investment

ecosystem a community of all the living things in an area and the environment in which they live

ecotourism a form of **tourism** that brings people to unique **ecosystems** while trying to avoid damage to these special places

ecumene a geographic **region** that is well suited for permanent settlement by people. Areas not included in the ecumene are generally too dry, too cold, or too rugged for permanent human settlement.

elevation the height of the land above sea level

El Niño a warm ocean **current** that flows off the west coast of South America every few years. An El Niño event changes weather patterns around the world. It may also cause **extreme weather** in some regions.

emigrate to move from a country. People who leave a country are called **emigrants**.

empire a group of territories, peoples, or **nations** ruled by a single authority

endangered species animals or plants that are in danger of dying out in the immediate future

environmental degradation damage to or destruction of the natural environment. When such damage occurs, **habitats** are destroyed, **biodiversity** is lost, or **natural resources** are used up.

environmentalist a person who works to protect the natural world

equator the line of latitude that circles Earth exactly midway between the North and South Poles

erg a great sea of sand with tall sand dunes in the Sahara

erosion the gradual wearing away of Earth's surface by the action of wind, water, ice, and gravity

estate a sizable area of privately owned property with a large house

ethnic diversity a variety of people from different **ethnic groups**

ethnic group a group of people in a country who share a unique culture and identity

euro the unit of currency used in many countries of the **European Union**

European Union (EU) a **supranational organization** through which a number of European countries work together on shared issues

evaporation the process by which a liquid, such as water, turns into a vapor, or gas

exotic species animals or plants that are brought into an area from somewhere else

exposure the harmful effects of cold, wind, or other extreme weather conditions

extended family a family made up of parents, children, grandparents, and sometimes more distant relatives

extinct having completely died out. An extinct species has no living members.

extreme weather severe or unusual weather conditions, such as **hurricanes, tornadoes,** or blizzards

eye the calm area at the center of a **hurricane** or other **tropical cyclone**

eye wall the ring of thunderstorms that surrounds the **eye,** or center, of a **hurricane** or other **tropical cyclone**

F

failed state a state that no longer exists or one in which the government is so weak that it has little control over its territory

famine a severe shortage of food that results in widespread hunger

fauna all the animal life in a particular region

fault a line on Earth's surface that results from a deep crack in the **crust**

fault-block mountain a mountain created when a block of Earth's crust tilts upward as a result of **tectonic movement**

fault line a line on Earth's surface that occurs where there is a break in the **crust**

fishery place where fish are caught, processed, and sold

floodplain the flat area around a river that is covered with **sediment** as a result of frequent flooding

flora all the plant life in a particular **region**

fold mountain a mountain that is created by a folding of Earth's **crust**

food chain a series of plants and animals, each of which depends on the one below it for food. A food chain usually forms part of a much larger **food web**

food web all of the feeding relationships within an **ecosystem**. Each living thing in a food web provides food energy to other living things within that ecosystem.

foreign investment investment by a person or company based in another country

forest floor the bottom layer, or ground, of a forest

forestry the planting, growing, and harvesting of trees

fossil fuel any fuel, such as petroleum, coal, and natural gas, that is made from the remains of prehistoric plants and animals

free trade the flow of goods and services across national borders, with little or no government control

freshwater made up of water that is fresh, not salty; also describes creatures that live in fresh water, such as freshwater fish

G

GDP See **gross domestic product**.

gender-based division of labor the division of work into two categories based on sex, or gender. The result is that men and women do different kinds of work.

general pollution the release of harmful substances into the environment as a result of everyday activities, such as burning coal to make electricity

genocide the elimination of a group of people based on race, religion, or some other factor

geography the study of features on Earth's surface including landforms, water bodies, climate, plants, animals, and peoples

geothermal energy energy produced by steam or hot water from deep inside Earth

geyser a spring that throws a jet of hot water or steam into the air

glaciation the creation and movement of **glaciers**

glacier a large mass of ice found near Earth's poles (**continental glacier**) or in a high, cold mountain valley (**alpine glacier**)

global grid the system of imaginary lines (called **parallels of latitude** and **meridians of longitude**) used to divide the surface of Earth on maps and globes

global warming the gradual increase in the temperature of Earth's surface over time. This warming may be the result of natural causes. It may also be caused by human activities.

globalization the development of a global society in which people, money, information, and goods flow fairly freely across national borders

greenhouse effect the process by which gases in the **atmosphere** trap heat from the sun and keep it close to Earth's surface. This trapped heat may contribute to **global warming**.

greenhouse gas any gas, such as carbon dioxide, that helps to trap heat in Earth's **atmosphere,** contributing to the **greenhouse effect**

gross domestic product (GDP) the total value of goods and services produced in a country in a year

groundwater water lying deep under the ground that supplies wells and springs. Over half the people in the world depend on groundwater for their drinking water.

gulf a large inlet of the sea that cuts deeply into the land

H

habitat the natural environment in which a plant or animal lives

hammada a high, rock-covered flatland in the Sahara

headwaters the stream or streams that make up the beginnings of a river

hemisphere one half of a sphere. Earth can be divided into eastern and western hemispheres or into northern and southern hemispheres.

highlands a mountainous part of a country; a **climate zone** where temperature and **precipitation** vary with latitude and **elevation**; a **vegetation zone** where the mix of plants varies with latitude and **elevation**; also refers to the type of vegetation in this zone

horn a sharp mountain peak shaped like a pyramid

human geography the study of how people have spread across Earth

humid continental a **climate** or **climate zone** with warm, rainy summers and cool, snowy winters

humid subtropical a **climate** or **climate zone** with hot, rainy summers and mild winters with some rain

hurricane the name for a **tropical cyclone** that begins in the Atlantic Ocean

hydroelectric potential the electrical power that can be generated from flowing water

hydroelectric power electricity that is generated from the power of moving water

iceberg a large mass of ice floating in the ocean

ice cap a **climate** or **climate zone** that is very cold all year with permanent ice and snow; also a permanent, dome-shaped covering of ice over a large area; also a **vegetation zone** that is too cold to support plant life

ice shelf a large, floating sheet of ice that is attached to the coast. Ice shelves can extend out to sea for hundreds of miles.

ice stream a fast-moving section of a continental glacier

illiterate unable to read or write

immigrate to move to a country. People who move to another country are called **immigrants**.

impermeable rock rock that does not allow liquid or gas to flow through it

indigenous peoples natives of an area who have been conquered or dominated by others who came later

Industrial Revolution the huge social and economic change in Europe and the United States that was produced by the shift from hand tools to machines in the 18th and 19th centuries

infant mortality rate the number of infants, out of every 1,000 babies born in a particular year, who die before reaching age 1

infill the process of filling in empty or run-down parts of a city with new development

infiltration the movement of water from Earth's surface into the soil

informal economy the part of the economy in which goods and services are exchanged outside of government control. People who work in the informal economy often sell goods on the street or in a street market.

information technology (IT) the use of **technology** to move and process information. IT includes computers, communication satellites, cell phones, and the Internet

inland sea a large body of salt water with little or no connection to the ocean

intermediate directions the directions on a **compass rose,** such as southeast, that are located between the **cardinal directions**

International Date Line the **meridian of longitude** located at 180°. By international agreement, the date is one day earlier to the east of this line.

invasive species nonnative plants and animals that invade an **ecosystem**

isthmus a narrow strip of land that links two larger **landmasses**

lagoon a body of shallow water partly cut off from the ocean by low-lying rock, sand, or coral reefs

landform any natural feature of Earth's surface that has a distinct shape. Landforms include major features such as **continents**, plains, **plateaus,** and mountain ranges. They also include minor features such as hills, valleys, canyons, and dunes.

landlocked surrounded entirely by land

landmass a very large, unbroken area of land

landscape a large area with a particular kind of scenery, such as a desert landscape

land use the ways in which people use a particular area of Earth's surface; for example, for farming, development, or preservation

land use conflict disagreement over how to use a particular area of land

lava molten, or liquid, rock that flows out of a **volcano**

life expectancy the average age to which a person in a given population can expect to live. Life expectancy varies from one country to another.

linguistic group a group of people who share a common language

lithosphere the outermost part of Earth, including a layer of solid rock and Earth's **crust**

livestock raising raising animals for food, milk, wool, or other products

lower story the middle layer of a forest, consisting of shrubs and trees

lowland an area of land that is flatter or lower than nearby areas

M

magma molten, or liquid, rock that lies beneath Earth's **crust**

mantle the middle layer of Earth that lies between the **core** and the **lithosphere**

map grid a system of imaginary lines that divides up the space on a map

map key another name for **map legend**

map legend a box or other display on a map that explains the meaning of the symbols used on the map

map projection a way of representing the spherical Earth on a flat surface

map scale an element of a map that shows how a unit of distance on the map (such as an inch) relates to actual distance on the surface of Earth

marginal land land that is not well suited for growing crops

marine climate a type of **climate** that is influenced by the sea. This type of climate is marked by relatively mild winters, cool summers, and fairly regular **precipitation**.

marine west coast a **climate** or **climate zone** with warm summers, cool winters, and rainfall all year

Mediterranean a **climate** or **climate zone** with warm to hot, dry summers and mild, rainy winters

meridian of longitude an imaginary line between the North and South poles that crosses the **equator** at right angles

meteorology the scientific study of **climate** and weather patterns

metropolitan area a major population center made up of a large city and the smaller **suburbs** and towns that surround it

micro-enterprise a very small business with few or no employees

micro-entrepreneur a person who starts and runs a very small business

migrant worker a person who moves regularly in order to find work, especially in harvesting crops

migrate to move from one **region** or country to another

migration stream the constant flow of migrants from one country into another country. The largest migration stream into the United States today is from Mexico.

mixed forest a type of vegetation or **vegetation zone** that includes both coniferous and deciduous trees

mixed-use development development that combines housing and businesses in one area

monsoon a seasonal wind. Summer monsoon winds in South Asia usually bring rain to that **region**.

moraine a mass of dirt and rock that has been left by a **glacier** as it retreats

multinational corporation a large company that has operations in more than one country

multiracial made up of people from several **ethnic groups**

N

nation a large group of people who share a common history and culture. Not all nations have their own government or control a territory, but the word *nation* often means a country or **nation-state**.

nationalism feelings of loyalty and pride toward one's **nation** or **ethnic group.** Nationalism sometimes includes the belief that one's nation or group is better than all others.

national park a large area of land that a government has set aside in order to preserve it in its natural state

nation-state an independent **state,** or country, whose people mostly share a common identity

native species animals or plants that occur naturally in an area

natural disaster great destruction or loss of life caused by natural forces rather than by human actions

natural gas a gas found beneath Earth's surface that can be burned as fuel for cooking, heating homes, and other purposes

natural resource a useful material that is found in nature, such as water, wood, coal, or oil

navigable lake a lake that is large and deep enough for big ships

nomad a person who wanders from place to place

nomadic herding the raising of livestock for food by moving herds from place to place to find pasture and water

non-point-source pollution **pollution** that does not come from a single location, but rather from many sources such as runoff from farms

nonrenewable resource a resource that takes so long to form that it can't be replaced. Oil, which takes millions of years to form, is such a resource.

nuclear family a family made up of parents and their children

nuclear radiation a form of energy that comes from nuclear reactions. Radiation has no smell or taste, but it can be very harmful to living things. Materials polluted with nuclear radiation are said to be *radioactive*.

nutrient a substance that provides nourishment, such as one of the elements in soil that make it fertile

O

oasis an isolated spot in a **desert** where water is found

oil reserves oil that has been discovered but remains unused in the ground

ore a mineral from which a valuable metal can be mined

orographic effect the **precipitation** that occurs when moist air rises up the side of a mountain. As the air rises, it cools down and releases most of its moisture as rain or snow.

outsource to hire someone outside a company to do work that was once done inside the company. **Information technology** has made it possible to outsource jobs to businesses in other countries.

overfishing taking too many fish from a body of water, so that the supply of fish is used up

ozone hole an area of the upper atmosphere in which the ozone layer has become unusually thin

P

parallel of latitude an imaginary line around Earth that runs parallel to the **equator**

pastoral nomads groups of herders who move with their animals from place to place in search of pasture and water

peninsula a long, narrow stretch of land that is surrounded by water on three sides

pension a fixed amount of money paid to a retired person by a government or former employer

per capita by or for each person. A per capita figure is calculated by dividing the total amount of something by the number of people in a place.

perennial irrigation a system that allows for the year-round watering of crops

permafrost a layer of soil beneath Earth's surface that is always frozen

persecution unfair treatment of others because of who they are or what they believe

pesticide a chemical substance used to control anything seen as a pest, such as insects, weeds, or rodents

physical feature any natural characteristic of Earth's surface, such as **landforms** and bodies of water

physical geography the study of natural features on the surface of Earth

physical processes natural forces that change Earth's **physical features,** including forces that build up and wear down Earth's surface

physiologic population density the population of a country divided by its **arable land** area

plantation a large farm, especially in a hot area

plateau a raised area of land, such as a hill or mountain, with a flat top

plaza an open square or marketplace

plural society a society in which different cultural groups keep their own identity, beliefs, and traditions

point-source pollution water **pollution** from a single place, such as a discharge pipe at a plant that treats **sewage**

polar zone the area between the **Arctic Circle** and the North Pole or between the **Antarctic Circle** and the South Pole, where the **climate** is generally cold

pollutant something that pollutes, or damages, air, soil, or water

pollution damage to the natural environment caused by harmful substances; also refers to harmful substances

population density the average number of people who live in a unit of area, such as a square mile. Population density measures how crowded an area is.

population distribution where people live in a country, whether crowded together in cities or spread out across the countryside

population pyramid a graph that shows the ages and sexes in a population, with the youngest ages at the bottom. The graph is often shaped like a pyramid.

potable safe for drinking

precipitation moisture that falls from the sky as rain, snow, sleet, or hail

prevailing winds winds that usually blow in a certain direction

primate city the largest and most important city in a country. A primate city has at least twice the population of the next largest city. It is a center of economic power and national culture.

prime meridian the **meridian of longitude** labeled 0 degrees, from which all other degrees of longitude are measured. The prime meridian passes through Greenwich, England.

public transit system a network of buses, trains, and other vehicles used for moving passengers

pull factor something that encourages people to move to a new place

push factor something that encourages people to leave a place behind

R

rainband a band of dense clouds that swirls around the **eye wall** of a **hurricane**

rainforest a type of thick evergreen forest found in areas of heavy rainfall

rain shadow a dry area on the **downwind** side of a mountain

rate of natural increase the annual rate of population growth. This percentage is calculated by subtracting the **death rate** from the **birth rate**. It does not include people moving into or out of a country.

recycling the process of collecting used materials that would otherwise be thrown away and turning them into raw materials for new uses

reforestation the replanting of trees in a formerly forested area by people or by nature

refugee someone who seeks safety by going to another country

reg a gravel-covered **desert** plain

region an area defined by one or more natural or cultural characteristics that set it apart from other areas

relative location where a place is located in relation to another place

remittance a payment of money sent by an immigrant to a relative in his or her home country

renewable resource a resource that can't be used up or that can be replaced as quickly as it is used up. Sunlight is a renewable resource that cannot be used up. Wood is a renewable resource that can be replaced by planting more trees.

replacement rate the **total fertility rate** needed for a population to replace itself

reserve an area that has been set aside for a specific purpose

reservoir an artificial lake where water is stored

revolution one complete trip by Earth around the sun

ritual a set of actions performed as part of a ceremony

river basin the area drained by a river and its **tributaries**

river system a river and all the **tributaries** that flow into it

rotation the spinning motion of Earth around its **axis**

runoff water from rainfall that is not absorbed into the soil and instead flows into streams or lakes

rural found in or living in areas that are not close to cities

rural decline worsening economic conditions in the countryside, including rising **unemployment** and growing poverty

rural fringe the small towns, farms, and open spaces that lie just beyond a city's **suburbs**

S

saline containing salt

salinization the buildup of salt in soil or water

sanitation the systems that keep an area free of filth and germs that can cause disease

savanna a type of **tropical grassland**

satellite image a view, such as of Earth, created from information gathered by instruments on board a satellite

sediment bits of soil left in a place by moving water

segregation the separation of one group of people from another, such as by race. Segregation can involve laws or customs that require different groups to use different facilities and live in separate areas.

semiarid dry, with little rainfall; also a **climate** or **climate zone** with hot, dry summers and cool, dry winters

sewage solid and liquid waste from homes and other buildings that is carried away by sewers or drains

shantytown a settlement made up of crudely built shacks

shari'a traditional Islamic law

shield the large core of very old rock that lies at the base of each **continent**

shifting agriculture the practice of clearing one area for farming for a few years and then moving on to another area when the first has lost its fertility

silt sand, mud, or clay made up of fine bits of soil and found at the bottom of a river or lake

site the specific place where something is located, including its physical setting

situation the way a place is positioned in relation to its wider surroundings

slash-and-burn method a way of clearing land for farming that involves cutting down and burning trees and other plants

slum an overcrowded, dirty area of a city where the housing is usually in very poor condition

smog a haze in the air caused by **pollution,** especially the exhaust from cars and other vehicles

snow line the lowest **elevation** on mountains where snow remains year-round

solar energy energy from the sun that can be converted into heat or electricity

spatial inequality the unequal **distribution** of wealth or resources in a geographic area, so that some places are richer than others

standard of living the overall level of comfort and well-being of a group or a country

state a political unit that controls a particular territory

steppe a vast, grassy plain

storm surge a wall of water that is pushed ashore by a storm

subarctic a **climate** or **climate zone** with cold, snowy winters and cool, rainy summers

subsistence farming farming carried out mainly to provide food for farm families, with little surplus for sale to others

suburb a developed area at the edge of a city that is mainly homes. Many suburbs also have stores and businesses.

supercontinent a huge **landmass** from which the present **continents** were formed

superpower an extremely powerful country with more political, economic, or military might than most other countries

supranational cooperation a form of international cooperation in which countries give up some control of their affairs as they work together to achieve shared goals

sustainable development using resources in ways that meet the needs of people today without hurting the ability of future generations to meet their own needs. This means finding ways to use resources without using them up.

taiga a large, coniferous forest located in a far northern latitude, just south of the **tundra**

tariff a tax on goods that cross country borders

technology the creation and use of tools to meet practical needs; also refers to the tools themselves

tectonic movement the movement of plates below Earth's surface

tectonic plate a large piece of Earth's **crust** that floats on the liquid **mantle**

temperate moderate or mild, without extremes of hot or cold

temperate grassland vegetation or a **vegetation zone** of mainly grasses and scattered trees adapted to a **tropical wet and dry** climate

temperate zone the area between Earth's **tropical zones** and **polar zones,** where the **climate** is relatively mild

tenement a rundown apartment building

terracing the creation of flat areas on mountain slopes for the purpose of farming

thematic map a map that shows a particular theme, or topic

threatened species animals or plants that are likely to become endangered if not protected

time zone an area that uses the same clock time. Earth is divided into 24 standard time zones. In each zone, clocks are set to the area's own hour and minute.

topographic map a map that uses elevation, or contour, lines and symbols to show a **region's** physical and human features. These features may include hills, valleys, rivers, lakes, roads, trails, and buildings.

tornado a violent, spinning windstorm that appears as a funnel-shaped cloud

total fertility rate (TFR) the average number of children a woman in a given population will have in her lifetime. This number is different in different countries.

tourism travel for pleasure rather than business or necessity; also, the business of organizing such travel

township in South Africa, a poor urban settlement where blacks were forced to live during **apartheid**

toxic chemical a chemical that is poisonous to humans or other living things

toxic waste waste materials from industry that are poisonous to humans or other living things

trade bloc a group of countries that work together to promote trade with one another

trade winds steady winds in tropical latitudes that blow toward the **equator** from both the north and south

traditional culture customs and ways of life handed down from ancestors

transboundary pollution **pollution** that starts in one country and crosses boundaries into other countries. Generally, transboundary pollution is carried by wind or water.

tree line the highest **elevation** where trees grow on a mountain

tributary a stream or river that flows into a larger stream or river

tropical cyclone a severe storm with high winds that spiral around a calm center. Depending on where they form, tropical cyclones are called **hurricanes, typhoons,** or cyclones.

tropical depression a storm near the **equator** with winds moving in a circle at speeds of up to 38 miles per hour

tropical disturbance a cluster of thunderstorms near the **equator** that moves with the **prevailing winds**

tropical grassland vegetation or a **vegetation zone** of mainly grasses and scattered trees adapted to a **tropical wet and dry** climate

tropical rainforest a **broadleaf evergreen forest** found in wet and hot **regions** near the **equator**

tropical storm a storm near the **equator** with winds moving in a circle at speeds of 39 to 73 miles per hour

tropical wet a **climate** or **climate zone** that is hot and rainy all year

tropical wet and dry a **climate** or **climate zone** that is hot all year with rainy and dry seasons

tropical zone the area between the **equator** and the **Tropic of Cancer** and between the **equator** and the **Tropic of Capricorn,** where the **climate** is generally hot

Tropic of Cancer the northernmost line of latitude where the sun's rays ever beat straight down. This line marks the northern limit of the **tropical zone**.

Tropic of Capricorn the southernmost line of latitude where the sun's rays ever beat straight down. This line marks the southern limit of the **tropical zone**.

tsunami a huge, destructive wave caused by an earthquake or a volcanic eruption

tundra a climate zone with very cold winters, cold summers, and little rain or snow; a vast, treeless plain in the arctic **regions** between the **ice cap** and the **tree line;** also a **vegetation zone** that is a treeless plain with grasses, mosses, and scrubs adapted to a cold climate

typhoon the name for a **tropical cyclone,** or **hurricane,** that begins in the western Pacific Ocean

unemployment joblessness

UNESCO a branch of the United Nations. UNESCO stands for United Nations Educational, Scientific, and Cultural Organization.

upwind against the direction that the wind is blowing

urban found or living in a city

urban core the older part of a big city. Often the urban core serves as the downtown or central business district of a city.

urban fringe the ring of small towns and **suburbs** that surround a big city

urban growth boundary a legal border that separates an area where development is permitted from an area where development is forbidden

urban hierarchy a ranking of cities based on their size and the services they offer

urbanization the movement of people from **rural** to **urban** areas, resulting in the growth of urban areas

urban sprawl the rapid, often poorly planned spread of development from an **urban** area outward into **rural** areas

U-shaped valley a valley with a relatively flat bottom, formed by a **glacier**

V

vegetation all the plants and trees in an area

vegetation zone a large area of Earth with a certain mix of plants and trees that are adapted to similar conditions

vertical trade the trading of crops between lowland and highland areas

volcanic activity the formation and eruption of **volcanoes**

volcanic island an island formed when an underwater **volcano** builds up enough **lava** and ash to rise above sea level

volcano a break in Earth's **crust** where **magma** and other material erupts from Earth's interior

V-shaped valley a valley with a relatively narrow bottom, formed by a river

W

wadi the usually dry bed of a river or stream in a **desert** or **semiarid** area

wastewater water that has been used; for example, for washing or producing goods

water cycle the movement of water from the surface of Earth to the **atmosphere** and back again. During this cycle, water evaporates from rivers, lakes, and oceans, rises and **condenses** into clouds, and then falls back to Earth as rain, hail, sleet, or snow. This process is also known as the *hydrologic cycle.*

watershed a geographic area that includes all of the land and waterways that drain into a body of water; also called a *drainage basin.*

water stress the condition that occurs when people don't have enough clean fresh water to meet their everyday needs

water vapor water in the form of a gas, as in steam or moisture in the **atmosphere**

wetland an area where the soil is usually wet or covered with water

wildlife wild animals and birds living in their natural environment

windbreak a wall or hedge that breaks the force of the wind

windward facing the wind

workforce all the people who are available for work, for example, in a country

World Heritage Site a place of great natural or cultural value that has been placed on the **UNESCO** World Heritage List. UNESCO helps countries preserve these sites for future generations.

Z

zero population growth a condition in which the population of a country does not grow but remains stable. This condition comes about when the **birth rate** plus immigration equals the **death rate** plus emigration.

Index

Page numbers in **bold** indicate definitions.

A

absolute location, 12, **13**, 17, 477

Abuja, Nigeria, 324

acclimatize, 420, **421**
    on Mount Everest, 420, 422

acid rain, 240, **241**
    and the Black Triangle of Europe, 244–245
    impact of, 245
    worldwide, 248

adaptations, 152, **153**, 160
    deserts, life in, 303
    global ecumene, 62
    indigenous populations, 160–161
    Kwajalein Island, 498–499
    mountainous regions, 194–198
    New Zealand, 495
    oases, life in, 305
    Sahel, life in, 307
    Tahiti, 497

Africa
    economic activity, 285
    history, 283
    human geography, 282–285
    land use, 285
    natural resources, 285
    physical features, 278
    physical geography, 278–281
    political boundaries, 282
    population characteristics, 284

age distribution, in China, 435

aging populations, 232

agricultural land
    and Nile River, 294
    and urban sprawl in U.S., 82

agriculture
    in Amazon rainforest, 183
    in Aral Sea region, 382
    Dhaka, Bangladesh, 402
    Mayan Indians, 156

AIDS
    infection rates worldwide, 344–345
    in South Africa, 342–343

air pollution
    in Aral Sea region, 384
    Atlanta, GA, 87–88
    and the Black Triangle of Europe, 244–245
    causes of, 114, 241
    Mexico City, 145

North America, pollution spread from, 249
    and ozone hole, 484
    in Russia, 273
    threats to national parks, 103

Al Jazirah, Sudan, 292

Alaska, 43–45, 500

alewives, in Great Lakes, 69

alternative energy resources
    hydroelectric dams, 293, 296–297, 436–437
    hydroelectric potential, 288, 289
    solar energy, worldwide, 365–367

altitudinal zonation, 191, **193**

Amanuzsky Glacier, 261

Amazon rainforest
    biodiversity of, 185
    cattle raising in, 184
    depletion, 187
    development restrictions, 185
    ecotourism in, 186
    environmental issues, 185
    farming in, 183
    geographic setting, 178
    introduction, 177
    logging in, 182
    native Amazonians and, 180
    reducing land use conflicts, 186–187
    rubber tapping in, 181
    sustainable development in, 185–186

Amur River, 259

Andes Mountains
    geographic setting, 192
    introduction, 191
    tierra caliente (tropical lowlands), 194–195
    tierra fría (highlands), 196–197
    tierra helada (icy high elevations), 198–199
    tierra templada (uplands), 195

Ankara, Turkey, 373

Antarctic Circle, 20–21

Antarctic Treaty, 504–505

Antarctica
    climate, 470
    geographic setting, 504
    global warming, effects of, 503–509
    human geography, 472–475
    ice shelves, studying, 508
    ozone hole, 484–485
    penguins, studying, 509
    physical features, 468, 469
    physical geography, 468–471

Notes

Chapter 1

14: "The Hunting of the Snark," by Lewis Carroll, excerpted from *Project Gutenberg Online Book Catalog,* www.gutenberg.org. **19:** "Watching the World Go By," by Ed Lu, Oct. 22, 2003, at *NASA,* "Earth Observatory," eol.jsc.nasa.gov/EarthObservatory/Watchingtheworldgoby.htm.

Chapter 4

68: *Case Western Reserve University,* www.cwru.edu. **70:** *The Lorax,* by Dr. Seuss, New York: Random House, 1971.

Chapter 5

83: *Oregon Department of Land Conservation and Development,* www.oregon.gov. **86:** *Toronto,* www.toronto.ca. **87:** "Sprawling, Sprawling," by Daniel Pederson et al., *Newsweek,* July 19, 1999. **88:** Pederson et al., 1999.

Chapter 6

94: *National Park Service,* www.nps.gov. *The Yosemite,* by John Muir, New York: Century, 1912. **98:** *Anne of Green Gables,* by Lucy Maud Montgomery, Boston: L.C. Page Co., 1908.

Chapter 8

123: "Lost Boys of Sudan," by Stephanie Kriner, Aug. 14, 2001, *American Red Cross,* www.redcross.org. **124:** Kriner, 2001. **126:** Kriner, 2001. "Valdas Adamkus Biography," *Former President of Republic of Lithuania,* www.adamkus.Lt/en/biography.phtml.

Chapter 11

163: "Hurricane Ivan," *Wikipedia,* www.wikipedia.org. "Eyewitness: Hurricane Ivan," Sep. 10, 2004, *BBC News World Edition,* news.bbc.co.uk. **170:** "Hurricane Hunters," by Beth Geiger, *National Geographic Explorer,* Sep. 2004. **171:** "Reporters' Log: Hurricane Ivan," Sep. 16, 2004, *BBC News World Edition,* news.bbc.co.uk.

Chapter 12

180: *Survival International,* survival-international.org. **185:** "Brazilian Activists Log Major Victory for Amazon Forests," *International Wildlife,* Nov.-Dec. 2000, at *LookSmart Find Articles,* www.findarticles.com.

Chapter 13

198: "Sacred Peaks of the Andes," by Johan Reinhard, *National Geographic,* Mar. 1992. **199:** "Sizing Up the Earth's Glaciers," by Evelyne Yohe, June 22, 2004, at *NASA,* "Earth Observatory," eol.jsc.nasa.gov/EarthObservatory/Watchingtheworldgoby.htm.

Chapter 14

221: "EU Membership and the 'New Europe,'" by Rick Steves and Cameron Hewitt, at *Rick Steves,* www.ricksteves.com.

Chapter 15

232: "United Nations Says Elderly Will Soon Outnumber Young for First Time," by Emma Daly, *New York Times,* Apr. 9, 2002, at *Global Action on Aging,* www.globalaging.org.

Chapter 16

243: *Chernobyl,* by Don Nardo and Brian McGovern (illus.), Farmington Hills, Mich.: Thomson Gale, 1990.

Chapter 17

254: *The Virtual Museum of the City of San Francisco,* www.sfmuseum.net.

Chapter 20

302: *Sahara Unveiled,* by William Langewiesch, New York: Pantheon Books, 1996. **307:** "Niger: Coal, the New Weapon to Stop Desert Advance," UN Office for the Coordination of Humanitarian Affairs, July 1, 2004, at *UN-OCHA Integrated Regional Information Networks,* www.plusnews.org.

Chapter 21

314–315: "Makeshift 'Cuisinart' Makes a Lot Possible in Impoverished Mali," by Roger Thurow, *Wall Street Journal,* July 26, 2002. **316–317:** *Women in African Economies: From Burning Sun to Boardroom: Business Ventures and Investment Patterns of 74 Ugandan Women,* by Margaret Snyder, Kampala, Uganda: Fountain Publishers, 2000. **318–319:** "Women Street Caterers," by Earl P. Scott, *Focus Magazine,* Jan. 1, 1999.

Chapter 23

339: "United in Action: A Short History of the African National Congress (South Africa) 1912–1982," *African National Congress,* www.anc.org.za. "Historical Papers: Archival Collections: Archbishop Desmond Mpilo Tutu," *University of the Witwatersrand,* www.wits.ac.za.

Chapter 26

384: *Chasing the Sea: Lost Among the Ghosts of Empire in Central Asia,* by Tom Bissell, New York: Pantheon Books, 2003.

Chapter 29

419: *Into Thin Air: A Personal Account of the Mt. Everest Disaster,* by Jon Krakauer, New York: Anchor Books, 1998. **420:** *The Mammoth Book of Eyewitness Everest,* by Jon E. Lewis (ed.), New York: Carroll and Graf, 2003. **422:** Krakauer, 1998. **423:** "Quest Everest: Through the Icefall," *NOVA Online Adventure,* www.pbs.org/wgbh/nova/. **424:** Krakauer, 1998. "Everest: The Way to the Summit," *NOVA Online Adventure,* www.pbs.org/wgbh/nova/. **425:** Krakauer, 1998. *MSNCB,* www.msnbc.msn.com. **426:** "Alive on Everest: Into the Death Zone," *NOVA Online Adventure,* www.pbs.org/wgbh/nova/. Lewis, 2003.

Chapter 30

431: "Internal Crises I: Demographic Disasters," *Asia for Educators: Columbia University,* afe.easia.columbia.edu.

Chapter 34

492: "Scientists Seek New Medicines from the Ocean," by Sharon Kay, *The Boston Globe,* Aug. 7, 2001, at National Geographic News, news.nationalgeographic.com.

Global Data Bank

"2004 World Population Data Sheet," *Population Reference Bureau,* www.prb.org.

Global Atlas of the Health Workforce (2004), World Health Organization, www.who.int/GlobalAtlas/home.asp.

Human Development Report 2004, United Nations Development Program, hdr.undp.org/statistics/data/.

"Internet Indicators: Hosts, Users, and Number of PCs" (2004), International Telecommunications Union, *ICT Free Statistics Homepage,* www.itu.int/ITU-D/ict/statistics/.

"Population, Health and Human Well-Being Searchable Database" (2004), World Resources Institute, *EarthTrends: The Environmental Information Portal,* earthtrends.wri.org/searchable_db/index.cfm?theme=4.

The World Factbook 2005, United States Central Intelligence Agency, www.cia.gov/cia/publications/factbook/.

Photographs

Front Cover
RF/Getty Images

Unit 1 Opener
2: Yann Arthus-Bertrand/Corbis **4 c:** Frans Lemmens/Getty Images **4 l:** NASA - Earth Observatory **4 c:** Robert van de Hilst/Corbis **5 r:** Getty Images **6 r:** NOAA **6 c:** TCI **7:** James Marshall/Corbis **8:** GoodShoot/SuperStock **9 r:** Peter Essick/Aurora **9 l:** David Turnley/Corbis

Chapter 1
10: Masterfile **13 l:** TCI **16:** Getty Images

Chapter 2
26: Corbis **34 r:** Ben Mangor/SuperStock **34 l:** Corbis **35 c:** Yann Arthus-Bertrand/Corbis **35 r:** Getty Images **35 l:** Getty Images **36 cr:** Jeremy Horner/Corbis **36 cl:** Bojan Brecelj/Corbis **36 l:** Staffan Widstrand/Corbis **36 r:** Galen Rowell/Corbis **37 l:** Paul A Souders/Corbis **37 cl:** Nik Wheeler/Corbis **37 cr:** Gary Braasch/Corbis **37 r:** Gideon Mendel/Corbis

Unit 2 Opener
40: Yann Arthus-Bertrand/Corbis **43:** Muench Photography **44 t:** Earl Adams **45:** QT Luong/Terragalleria **49 t:** Troy & Mary Parlee/Index Stock Photography **49 b:** Alan Pitcairn/Grant Heilman Photography

Chapter 3
50: NASA **57:** Robert Estall/Corbis **58 b:** Richard Nowitz/Corbis **58 t:** Christopher J Morris/Corbis **59 c:** Robert Holmes/Corbis **59 t:** Andre Jenny/PictureQuest **59 ct:** Lee Snider/Corbis **59 cb:** Dave G Houser/Corbis **59 b:** Bryan & Cherry Alexander/Photo Researchers Inc **61:** Eastcott-Momatiuk/The Image Works

Chapter 4
64: SeaWiFS Project, NASA/Goddard Space Flight Center and Orbimage **68:** Cleveland State University Library, The Cleveland Press Collection **69:** Ted Spiegel/Corbis **70:** RF/TCI #26 **71 tr:** Masterfile **71 b:** Len Ebert **72 b:** USGS **72 t:** GLERL/NOAA **73:** The Great Lakes: An Environmental Atlas and Resource Book **74:** Reuters Pictures Archive

Chapter 5
78: Lester Kefkowitz/Corbis **83:** Rick Schafer/Index Stock Imagery, Inc **84:** Steve Terrill/Corbis **85:** Scott Tysick/Masterfile **86:** Toronto Urban Development Services **86:** Corbis **89:** Sebastian D'Souza/AFP/Getty Images

Chapter 6
94 t: QT Luong/Terragalleria **94 b:** QT Luong/Terragalleria **95:** Marc Muench/Muench Photography **96 t:** Lisa McKeon/USGS **96 b:** © S Cyd Read/Natural Born Hikers All Rights Reserved **96 c:** Getty Images **98 c:** Parks Canada **98 b:** Parks Canada **99 t:** Parks Canada **101 t:** Muench Photography **101 c:** Marc Muench/Muench Photography **101 b:** Marc Muench/Muench Photography **102 t:** Kennan Ward/Corbis **102 c:** NGS/Getty Images **102 b:** QT Luong/Terragalleria **103 r:** NPS/Visibility Monitoring Program/Air Resource Specialists **103 l:** NPS/Visibility Monitoring Program/Air Resource Specialists

Chapter 7
106: Randi Anglin-Syracuse Newspapers/The Image Works **110:** Getty Images **111 b:** Sarah Leen/National Geographic **112:** Getty Images **113 b:** Getty Images **115:** Getty Images

Chapter 8
118: Lee Snider/Corbis **122:** AP/Wide World Photos **123:** Janet Jarman/Corbis **124 tl:** From the film *Lost Boys of Sudan* (www.lostboysfilm.com) **125:** Peter Yates/Corbis **126:** AP/Wide World Photos **127:** Reuters Pictures Archive

Unit 3 Opener
130: Y A Bertrand/Corbis **134 b:** Getty Images **134 t:** Pablo Corral V/Corbis **135 t:** Robert Holmes/Corbis **139 b:** Collart Herve/Corbis Sygma **139 t:** Josef Pollereoss/The Image Works

Chapter 9
140: M Winkel-Zefa/Corbis **141 b:** HIRB/Index Stock Imagery **141 cr:** Stephanie Maze/Corbis **141 cl:** HIRB/Index Stock Imagery **142:** Steve Vider/SuperStock **145:** Stephanie Maze/Corbis **146:** Getty Images **147:** Kal Muller/Woodfin Camp & Associates

Chapter 10
150 background: The Lowe Art Museum, The University of Miami **150:** Jeffrey J Foxx **151:** Jeremy Horner/Corbis **153 c:** Jeffrey J Foxx **155:** SuperStock **157:** AP/Wide World Photos **158:** Jeffrey J Foxx **159:** Jeffrey J Foxx

Chapter 11
162: Getty Images **164:** RF/Corbis **170 tl:** AP/Wide World Photos **171 tr:** Henry Romero/Corbis **172:** Anna Martinez-Reuters/Corbis

Chapter 12
176 b: AP/Wide World Photos **176 t:** Dave Bartruff/Corbis **180:** Joe Cavanaugh/DDB Stock **181:** Katherine McGlynn/The Image Works **183:** Getty Images **184:** David Katzenstein/Corbis **185:** Siri Weber Feeney **186:** Carl & Ann Purcell/Corbis **187 t:** NASA **187 b:** NASA

Chapter 13
190: Pablo Corral/Corbis **192:** Herbert Stadler/Corbis **194 br:** SuperStock **195 br:** Pablo Corral Vega/Corbis **196 bl:** Craig Lovell/Corbis **197 tl:** RF/TCI #19 **198 br:** Jeffrey J Foxx **199:** NASA **201:** NASA

Unit 4 Opener
202: Yann Arthus-Bertrand/Corbis **205:** Robert Burrington/Index Stock Imagery **206 b:** Bryan & Cherry Alexander/Arctic Photo **206 t:** National Geographic Image Collection **211 t:** Getty Images

Chapter 14
212: AP/Wide World Photos **214:** US Holocaust Memorial Museum **216:** TCI **217:** Clay Bennett © 2002 The Christian Science Monitor **218:** Benoit Roland/The Image Works **219:** AFP/Getty Images **220:** Getty Images **221:** Reuters/Corbis **222:** Bob Krist/Corbis **223:** PictureQuest

Chapter 15
224: Bo Zaunders/Corbis **228:** Bridgeman Art Library **230:** Jean-Marc Charles/Corbis **232:** Jodi Hilton/Corbis **234:** Wolfgang Steche/VISUM/The Image Works **235:** Getty Images

Chapter 16
238: AP/Wide World Photos **240:** The Granger Collection **242:** AP/Wide World Photos **243:** Regis Bossu/Corbis **244:** OSF/R Pack-wood/Animals, Animals **248:** Canada National Research Council

Chapter 17
250: NASA **255:** Pat O'Hara/Corbis **257:** GoodShoot/SuperStock **259:** L Veisman/Bruce Coleman Inc **261:** John Corbett/Corbis **263:** Robert W Madden/Getty Images

Chapter 18
264 b: AP/Wide World Photos **264 t:** Time Life Pictures/Getty Images **266:** AFP/Getty Images **268:** Keren Su/Corbis **269:** Getty Images **270:** Getty Images **271:** AFP/Getty Images **272:** Charles O'Rear/Corbis **273:** Getty Images

Al Jazirah AL jeh-ZEE-ruh
Aotearoa OW-tay-uh-roe-uh
Azerbaijan ah-zer-bye-JAHN

Biafra bee-AH-frah

Canberra KAN-brah
Canyon de Chelly KAN-yun deh SHAY
Caucasus Mountains KAW-kuh-suss
Chernobyl cher-NO-bul
Chiapas chee-AH-pas
Chichicastenango chee-chee-cah-sten-
  ANG-go
Cuyahoga River kye-eh-HOE-gah
Cuzco KOOZ-KOE

Danube River DAN-yoob
Dubai dooh-BYE

Eritrea air-eh-TRAY-uh

Ganges River GAN-jeez
Giza GEE-zuh
Grenada greh-NAY-da
Guayaquil gwie-uh-KEEL

Jodhpur JAWD-purr

Kathmandu cat-man-DOO
Kazakhstan kaz-ahk-STAN
Khartoum kar-TOOM
Kiev KEE-ev
Kliuchevskoi Volcano klue-CHEV-skoy
Kobe KOE-bee
Krenitsyn Volcano kre-NEETS-un
Kwajalein Atoll KWAJ-uh-lun AH-tahl

Lake Baikal bye-KALL
Laos LAUS
Leipzig LIEP-zig

Maly Semyachik Volcano mah-LEE
  sem-EYE-uh-chik
Marseille mar-SAY
Mehrangarh Fort mare-ANG-arh
Mount Kilimanjaro KIL-uh-mun-JAR-o
Mumbai MOOM-bye

Nairobi nie-ROE-bee
Niger NIE-jair
Nunavut NOON-uh-voot

Papeete PAH-pee-AY-tay
Papua New Guinea PAH-pooh-AH noo
  GIN-ee
Pascual Abaj PAS-kwahl ah-BAH
Pune POOH-nay

Qatar KAH-ter
Quito KEE-toe

Raphstreng Tsho raf-streng TSHOW
Rio de Janeiro REE-o day jeh-NAIR-o
River Thames TEMS

Soweto so-WAY-toe
Sri Lanka SHREE LAN-kah
St. Croix SAYNT KROY
Sudety Mountains SOO-deh-tee
Syr Darya SEER DAIR-ya
Szamos River SAH-moesh

Tanzania tan-zuh-NEE-uh
Tenochtitlán tay-nowch-teet-LAN
Tisza River TIH-saw

Uzbekistan ooz-BEK-uh-STAN

Yangzte River yang-SEE
Yosemite yoe-SEM-uh-tee